ASCENT
CENTER FOR TECHNICAL KNOWLEDGE

AutoCAD® 2021
Autodesk® Certified Professional
Exam Topics Review

Certification Preparation Guide
Mixed Units - 1st Edition

AUTODESK.
Authorized Publisher

ASCENT - Center for Technical Knowledge®
AutoCAD® 2021
Autodesk® Certified Professional Exam Topics Review
Mixed Units - 1st Edition

Prepared and produced by:

ASCENT Center for Technical Knowledge
630 Peter Jefferson Parkway, Suite 175
Charlottesville, VA 22911

866-527-2368
www.ASCENTed.com

Lead Contributor: Renu Muthoo

ASCENT - Center for Technical Knowledge (a division of Rand Worldwide Inc.) is a leading developer of professional learning materials and knowledge products for engineering software applications. ASCENT specializes in designing targeted content that facilitates application-based learning with hands-on software experience. For over 25 years, ASCENT has helped users become more productive through tailored custom learning solutions.

We welcome any comments you may have regarding this guide, or any of our products. To contact us please email: feedback@ASCENTed.com.

The following are registered trademarks or trademarks of Autodesk, Inc., and/or its subsidiaries and/or affiliates in the USA and other countries: 123D, 3ds Max, ADSK, Alias, ATC, AutoCAD LT, AutoCAD, Autodesk, the Autodesk logo, Autodesk 123D, Autodesk Alias, ArtCAM, Autodesk Forge, Autodesk Fusion, Autodesk Inventor, AutoSnap, BIM 360, Buzzsaw, CADmep, CAMduct, Civil 3D, Configurator 360, Dancing Baby (image), DWF, DWG, DWG (DWG logo), DWG Extreme, DWG TrueConvert, DWG TrueView, DWGX, DXF, Eagle, , ESTmep, FBX, FeatureCAM, Flame, FormIt 360, Fusion 360, The Future of Making Things, Glue, Green Building Studio, InfraWorks, Instructables, Instructables (Instructables logo), Inventor, Inventor CAM, Inventor HSM, Inventor LT, Make Anything, Maya, Maya LT, Moldflow, MotionBuilder, Mudbox, Navisworks, Netfabb, Opticore, PartMaker, Pier 9, PowerInspect, PowerMill, PowerShape, Publisher 360, RasterDWG, RealDWG, ReCap, ReCap 360, Remake, Revit LT, Revit, Scaleform, Shotgun, Showcase, Showcase 360, SketchBook, Softimage, Tinkercad, TrustedDWG, VRED.

NASTRAN is a registered trademark of the National Aeronautics Space Administration.

All other brand names, product names, or trademarks belong to their respective holders.

General Disclaimer:

Notwithstanding any language to the contrary, nothing contained herein constitutes nor is intended to constitute an offer, inducement, promise, or contract of any kind. The data contained herein is for informational purposes only and is not represented to be error free. ASCENT, its agents and employees, expressly disclaim any liability for any damages, losses or other expenses arising in connection with the use of its materials or in connection with any failure of performance, error, omission even if ASCENT, or its representatives, are advised of the possibility of such damages, losses or other expenses. No consequential damages can be sought against ASCENT or Rand Worldwide, Inc. for the use of these materials by any third parties or for any direct or indirect result of that use.

The information contained herein is intended to be of general interest to you and is provided "as is", and it does not address the circumstances of any particular individual or entity. Nothing herein constitutes professional advice, nor does it constitute a comprehensive or complete statement of the issues discussed thereto. ASCENT does not warrant that the document or information will be error free or will meet any particular criteria of performance or quality. In particular (but without limitation) information may be rendered inaccurate by changes made to the subject of the materials (i.e. applicable software). Rand Worldwide, Inc. specifically disclaims any warranty, either expressed or implied, including the warranty of fitness for a particular purpose.

Contents

SECTION 1: Draw and Organize Objects

SECTION 2: Draw with Accuracy

SECTION 3: Advanced Editing Functions

SECTION 4: Advanced Layouts, Printing, and Alternative Outputs

SECTION 5: Annotation Techniques

SECTION 6: Reusable Content and Drawing Management

Preface

The *AutoCAD® 2021: Autodesk® Certified Professional Exam Topics Review* guide is designed for those using AutoCAD® 2021 with a Windows operating system. This guide is not designed for the AutoCAD for Mac software.

AutoCAD 2021: Autodesk Certified Professional Exam Topics Review is a comprehensive review guide to assist in preparing for the Autodesk Certified Professional: AutoCAD for Design and Drafting exam. This certification preparation guide enables experienced users to review learning content from ASCENT that is related to the exam objectives. It is divided into sections that align with the topics in the exam. The beginning of each section includes a list of the objectives that are covered in that section and the corresponding chapter where the review content is presented.

This guide is intended for experienced users of the AutoCAD software. New users of the AutoCAD 2021 software should refer to the following ASCENT learning guides:

- *AutoCAD® 2021: Fundamentals*
- *AutoCAD® 2021: Essentials*
- *AutoCAD® 2021: Beyond the Basics*
- *AutoCAD® 2021: Advanced*
- *AutoCAD® 2021: 3D Drawing and Modeling*

Autodesk Certified Professional Exam Objectives

Exam Objective	Chapter(s)
1.1 Create advanced drawing objects	
1.1.a Create and edit polylines, arcs, polygons, and splines	Ch. 1
1.1.b Work with regions	Ch. 1
1.1.c Create xlines, rays, and multilines	Ch. 1
1.1.d Create 2D isometric drawings	Ch. 1

Exam Objective	Chapter(s)
1.2 Select and organize objects	
1.2.a Use Quick Select to select objects based on shared properties	Ch. 2
1.2.b Select similar objects	Ch. 2
1.2.c Isolate or hide objects in a drawing	Ch. 2
1.2.d Control the draw order of overlapping objects	Ch. 2
1.2.e Match the properties of one object to other objects	Ch. 2
1.2.f Remove objects from a selection set	Ch. 2
1.3 Manage layers	
1.3.a Save, restore, and manage layer settings using layer states	Ch. 3
1.3.b Use layer filters to control which layers are listed in the Layer Properties Manager folder	Ch. 3 Ch. 4
1.3.c Apply and remove layer overrides per viewport	Ch. 4
1.3.d Use the Layer Walk tool to display objects on selected layers	Ch. 4
1.3.e Remove layers from a drawing	Ch. 4
1.3.f Control the properties of referenced layers	Ch. 4
2.1 Apply advanced object snaps	
2.1.a Use object snaps	Ch. 5
2.1.b Use polar tracking to restrict the cursor movement to specified angles	Ch. 5
2.2 Control the User Coordinate System (UCS)	
2.2.a Understand and define the User Coordinate System	Ch. 6
2.2.b Move the UCS origin	Ch. 6
2.2.c Rotate the UCS	Ch. 6
2.2.d Restore the UCS to the World Coordinate System (WCS)	Ch. 6
2.2.e Restore the previous UCS	Ch. 6
2.2.f Use named UCS definitions and preset orientations	Ch. 6
3.1 Control Rotate and Scale options	
3.1.a Rotate objects around a specified base point	Ch. 7
3.1.b Enlarge or reduce the size of objects	Ch. 7

Exam Objective	Chapter(s)
5.1 Apply markup tools	
5.1.a Create and modify revision clouds	Ch. 12
5.1.b Use wipeouts to mask underlying objects in specific areas of a drawing	Ch. 2
5.1.c Compare two drawings for differences	Ch. 12
5.2 Manage Hatch or Fill options	
5.2.a Specify Hatch and Fill options	Ch. 13
5.2.b Recreate the boundary around a selected Hatch or Fill pattern	Ch. 13
5.3 Format text and tables	
5.3.a Apply text and multiline text properties	Ch. 14
5.3.b Create, modify, and apply text styles	Ch. 17
5.3.c Create and adjust text columns	Ch. 14
5.3.d Insert tables and manipulate cell data	Ch. 15
5.3.e Use fields in text and tables	Ch. 15
5.3.f Insert symbols from the character map	Ch. 14
5.3.g Check the spelling of text and dimension annotation	Ch. 14
5.4 Adjust multileaders	
5.4.a Create and modify multileaders	Ch. 14
5.4.b Add and remove leaders	Ch. 14
5.4.c Align and collect leaders	Ch. 14
5.5 Create and edit annotation with advanced dimensioning techniques	
5.5.a Create and modify dimension styles	Ch. 17
5.5.b Create multiple dimensions with a single command	Ch. 16
5.5.c Set the dimension layer	Ch. 16
5.5.d Associate or re-associate dimensions to objects	Ch. 16
5.5.e Break and restore dimension and extension lines	Ch. 16
5.5.f Adjust the spacing between dimensions	Ch. 16

Exam Objective	Chapter(s)
5.6 Apply annotative properties and styles	
5.6.a Understand annotative properties and styles as they pertain to objects	Ch. 17
5.6.b Define and apply annotative object styles	Ch. 17
5.6.c Control the annotative scale of an object or viewport	Ch. 17
5.6.d Add annotative scales to an object	Ch. 17
6.1 Create blocks and apply attributes	
6.1.a Insert and modify blocks	Ch. 19
6.1.b Create and modify block definitions	Ch. 18
6.1.c Modify attribute definitions with the Block Attribute Manager	Ch. 20
6.2 Control external reference and underlay files	
6.2.a Attach external reference and underlay files	Ch. 21
6.2.b Clip and control the visibility of referenced and underlay files	Ch. 21
6.2.c Understand layer naming conventions when you bind a referenced drawing	Ch. 21
6.2.d Adjust the settings of an underlay file or image	Ch. 21
6.2.e Create a hyperlink to another file	Ch. 21
6.2.f Snap to objects in external reference and underlay files	Ch. 21
6.3 Access and apply content resources	
6.3.a Use the Blocks palette, Tool palettes, and the Design Center	Ch. 18
6.3.b Create and manage saved sets of objects using groups*	
6.3.c Transfer information between drawing files	Ch. 22
6.4 Perform file maintenance with drawing utilities	Ch. 22

*6.3.b is not covered in this learning guide. Refer to Section 6 for more information.

Prerequisites

- Access to the 2021.0 version of the software, to ensure compatibility with this guide. Future software updates that are released by Autodesk may include changes that are not reflected in this guide. The practices and files included with this guide might not be compatible with prior versions (e.g., 2020).

Note on Software Setup

This guide assumes a standard installation of the software using the default preferences during installation. Lectures and practices use the standard software templates and default options for the Content Libraries.

Students and Educators Can Access Free Autodesk Software and Resources

Autodesk challenges you to get started with free educational licenses for professional software and creativity apps used by millions of architects, engineers, designers, and hobbyists today. Bring Autodesk software into your classroom, studio, or workshop to learn, teach, and explore real-world design challenges the way professionals do.

Get started today - register at the Autodesk Education Community and download one of the many Autodesk software applications available.

Visit www.autodesk.com/education/home/

Note: Free products are subject to the terms and conditions of the end-user license and services agreement that accompanies the software. The software is for personal use for education purposes and is not intended for classroom or lab use.

Lead Contributor: Renu Muthoo

Renu uses her instructional design training to develop courseware for AutoCAD and AutoCAD vertical products, Autodesk 3ds Max, Autodesk Showcase and various other Autodesk software products. She has worked with Autodesk products for the past 20 years with a main focus on design visualization software.

Renu holds a bachelor's degree in Computer Engineering and started her career as a Instructional Designer/Author where she co-authored a number of Autodesk 3ds Max and AutoCAD books, some of which were translated into other languages for a wide audience reach. In her next role as a Technical Specialist at a 3D visualization company, Renu used 3ds Max in real-world scenarios on a daily basis. There, she developed customized 3D web planner solutions to create specialized 3D models with photorealistic texturing and lighting to produce high quality renderings.

Renu Muthoo has been a Lead Contributor for the *AutoCAD: Certified Professional Exam Topics Review* since 2015.

In This Guide

The following highlights the key features of this guide.

Feature	Description
Practice Files	The Practice Files page includes a link to the practice files and instructions on how to download and install them. The practice files are required to complete the practices in this guide.
Sections	This guide is divided into sections that align with the topics in the Autodesk Certified Professional exam. The beginning of each section includes a list of the exam objectives that are covered in that section and their corresponding chapters.
Chapters	A chapter consists of the following - Exam Objectives, Instructional Content, and Practices.
	• **Exam Objectives** lists the Autodesk certification exam objectives that are covered in the chapter.
	• **Instructional Content**, which begins right after Exam Objectives, refers to the descriptive and procedural information related to various topics. Each main topic introduces a product feature, discusses various aspects of that feature, and provides step-by-step procedures on how to use that feature. Where relevant, examples, figures, helpful hints, and notes are provided.
	• **Practice** for a topic follows the instructional content. Practices enable you to use the software to perform a hands-on review of a topic. It is required that you download the practice files (using the link found on the Practice Files page) prior to starting the first practice.

Practice Files

To download the practice files for this guide, use the following steps:

1. Type the URL **exactly as shown below** into the address bar of your Internet browser, to access the Course File Download page.

   Note: If you are using the ebook, you do not have to type the URL. Instead, you can access the page simply by clicking the URL below.

   ## https://www.ascented.com/getfile/id/loxozonus

New Tab	×	+	◄ address bar of a browser	—	□	×
← → C	**TYPE URL HERE**			☆	☻	⋮

2. On the Course File Download page, click the **DOWNLOAD NOW** button, as shown below, to download the .ZIP file that contains the practice files.

   DOWNLOAD NOW ▶

3. Once the download is complete, unzip the file and extract its contents.

   The recommended practice files folder location is:
   C:\AutoCAD 2021 ACP Exam Topics Review Practice Files

   Note: It is recommended that you do not change the location of the practice files folder. Doing so may cause errors when completing the practices.

   Stay Informed!
   To receive information about upcoming events, promotional offers, and complimentary webcasts, visit:
   www.ASCENTed.com/updates

SECTION
1

Draw and Organize Objects

Exam Objective	Chapter(s)
1.3 Manage layers	
1.3.a Save, restore, and manage layer settings using layer states	Ch. 3
1.3.b Use layer filters to control which layers are listed in the Layer Properties Manager folder	Ch. 3 Ch. 4
1.3.c Apply and remove layer overrides per viewport	Ch. 4
1.3.d Use the Layer Walk tool to display objects on selected layers	Ch. 4
1.3.e Remove layers from a drawing	Ch. 4
1.3.f Control the properties of referenced layers	Ch. 4

Advanced Drawing Objects

Exam Objectives Covered in This Chapter

- 1.1.a Create and edit polylines, arcs, polygons, and splines
- 1.1.b Work with regions
- 1.1.c Create xlines, rays, and multilines*
- 1.1.d Create 2D isometric drawings

*Note: Multilines are not covered in this learning guide. Refer to the AutoCAD Help documentation for "multilines" to review that part of objective 1.1.c.

1.1 Drawing Arcs

The **Arc** command is used to add curved segments to a drawing, as shown in Figure 1–1. The information or geometry you have originally determines the option you use.

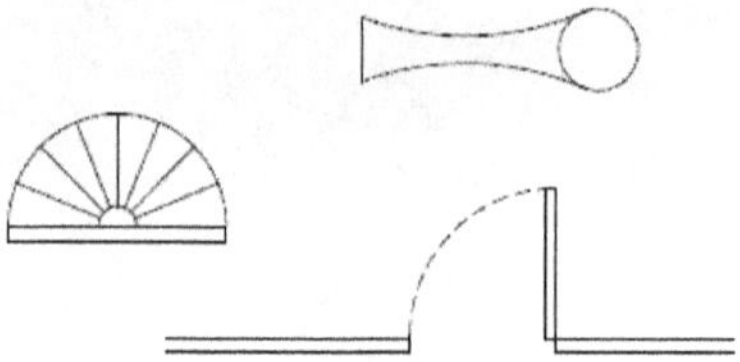

Figure 1–1

Arc Command Options

The **Arc** command has many options that enable you to create arcs. In the *Home* tab>Draw panel, expand (Arc flyout) to access the different arc construction options available in the software, as shown on the left in Figure 1–2. The geometric definitions used for drawing arcs is shown on the right in Figure 1–2.

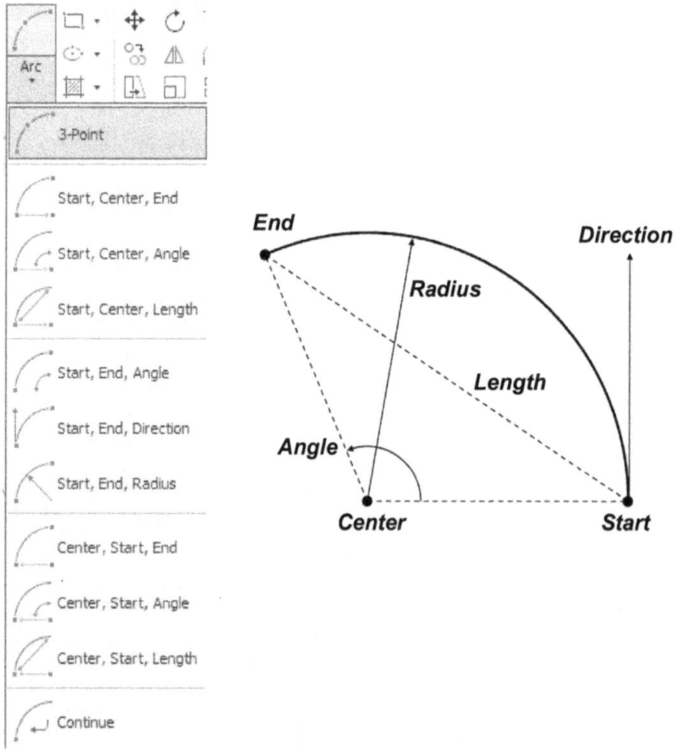

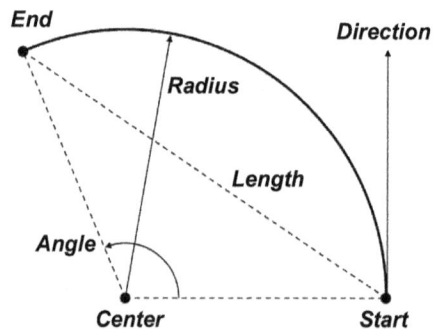

Figure 1–2

Start	Starting point of an arc.
Center	Center (or focal) point of an arc.
End	Ending point of an arc.
Radius	Radius of an arc.
Angle	Included angle turned by an arc.
Direction	Starting direction of an arc.
Chord (Length)	Chord length of an arc. (Distance between arc start and end points.)

Notes on Arcs

- Most arcs in the AutoCAD software are drawn in a counter-clockwise direction from the starting point. You can hold <Ctrl> to reverse the direction when constructing an Arc.

- Pressing <Enter> at the *Specify start point:* prompt starts drawing the arc from the end point of the last line or arc segment drawn. (This feature is only available when the *Specify start point:* prompt is the first prompt for the type of arc being created.)

- You can also type, use the shortcut menu, or use the <Down Arrow> menu to access the arc options.

Practice 1a | Drawing an Arc

Practice Objective

- Draw arcs using various options.

In this practice, you will draw door swings in a floorplan using the various options of the **Arc** command, as shown in Figure 1–3.

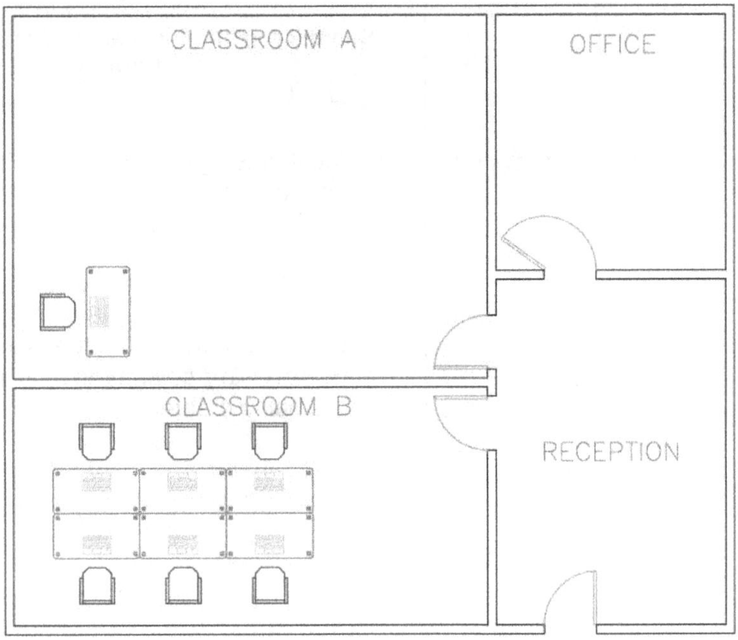

Figure 1–3

1. Open **Class-A.dwg** from your practice files folder.

2. In the Layer Control, set the current layer to **Doors**.

3. Verify that the **Endpoint** Object Snap is on.

4. Zoom in on the office door.

5. In the *Home* tab>Draw panel, expand  (Arc flyout) and click  (Start, Center, End).

6. At the *Specify start point of arc:* prompt, select the upper right corner of the doorway wall, as shown in Figure 1–4.

7. At the *Specify center point of arc:* prompt, select the point where the door and wall meet, as shown in Figure 1–4.

8. At the *Specify end point of arc:* prompt, select the upper left corner of the door, as shown in Figure 1–4. The arc that represents the door swing is created, as shown in Figure 1–4.

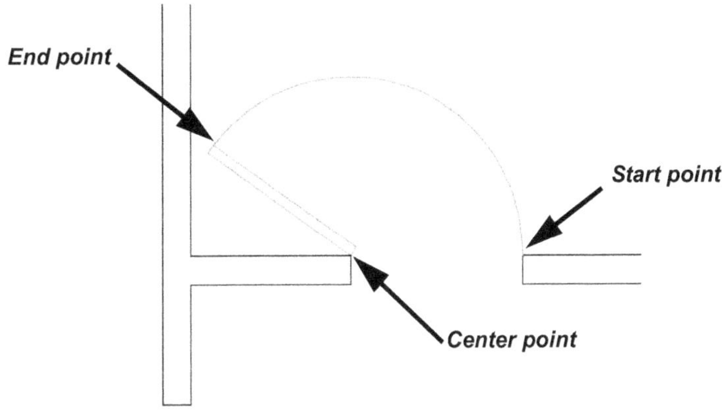

Figure 1–4

9. Pan and Zoom over to Classroom A's door.

10. In the *Home* tab>Draw panel, expand the Arc flyout and click

    (Start, Center, Angle).

11. At the *Specify start point of arc:* prompt, select the upper left corner of Classroom A's doorway wall.

12. At the *Specify center point of arc:* prompt, select the point where the door and wall meet.

13. For the angle, enter **90** and press <Enter>.

14. Pan and Zoom over to Classroom B's door.

15. In the *Home* tab>Draw panel, expand the Arc flyout and click

    (Start, Center, Angle).

16. For the start point, select the lower left corner of Classroom B's doorway wall. For the center point, select the point where the door and wall meet, and for the angle, enter -**90**. Press <Enter> to create the door swing and complete the command.

17. Pan over to the last door of the Reception room. Add the arc for the door swing using a **Start, Center, End**. **Tip:** To create the door arc in clockwise direction, press and hold <Ctrl> before selecting the end point of the arc.

18. Save and close the drawing.

1.2 Drawing Polylines

Polylines are complex objects consisting of lines and arcs. Each segment in a polyline sequence is considered to be part of a single object. In addition, polylines can be assigned a width that can vary for each segment.

Polylines are ideal for drawing complex single objects, such as walls, transmission lines, ductwork, and schematic traces or area outlines, as shown in Figure 1–5.

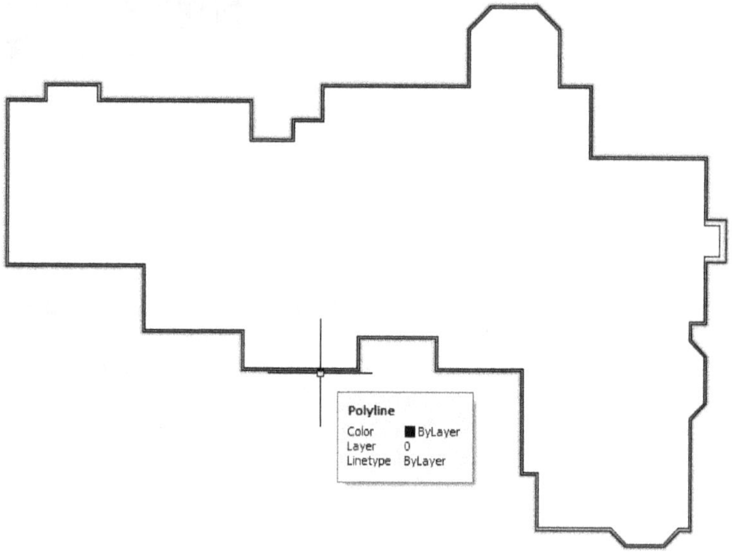

Figure 1–5

- Polylines can be used anywhere a regular line or arc can be used.

- When creating one continuous object, you cannot exit and restart the **Polyline** command.

- A polyline can be either open or closed. An open polyline has one start point and one end point.

How To: Draw a Polyline with Width and Arcs

1. In the *Home* tab>Draw panel, click ⌐◦ (Polyline).
2. Select a start point. A cross displays, indicating that it is the start point. This is useful when creating complex polylines. The cross disappears when the polyline creation is completed.

3. (Optional) Select the **Width** option in the <Down Arrow> menu (as shown on the left in Figure 1–6), or type **W** and press <Enter>.
4. Enter a starting width or select two points to define the width.
5. Enter an ending width. If you want it to be the same as the starting width, you can press <Enter> to accept the default.
6. Select the next point(s).
7. (Optional) When you want to create an arc segment, do not end the **Polyline** command. Instead, select the **Arc** option in the <Down Arrow> menu or type **A** and press <Enter>.
8. Follow the prompts to create the required type of arc. The prompts are similar to those in the **Arc** command. When drawing an arc, you can press <Ctrl> to draw in the opposite direction.
9. To switch back to line segments, type **L** and press <Enter> or select the **Line** option from the <Down Arrow> menu, or the shortcut menu, as shown on the right in Figure 1–6.

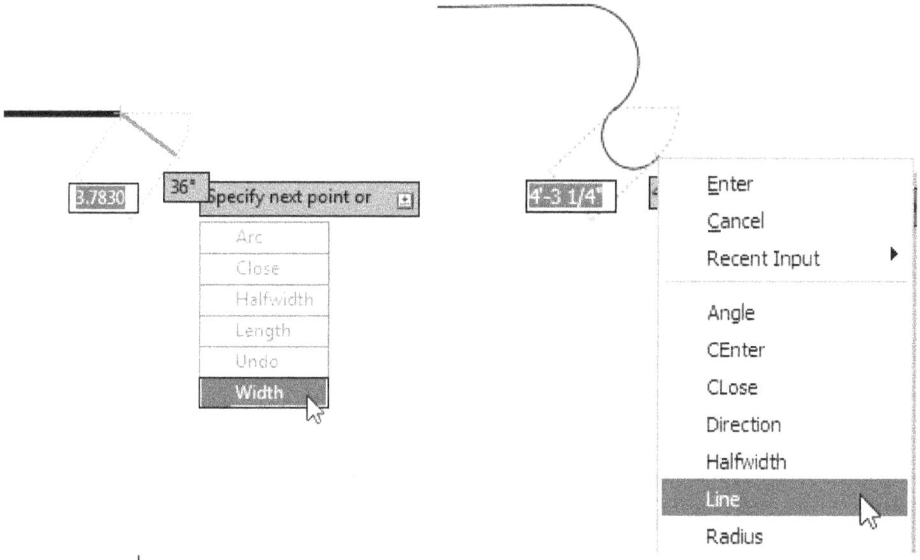

In the Polyline arc, use <Down Arrow> to display the Arc options.

Figure 1–6

10. If you want to create a closed polyline, use the **Close** option (CL). It attaches the last segment back to the start point.

- You can use the **Undo** option to remove the last segment drawn without ending the command.

- Other options include **Halfwidth**, which specifies the distance from the center of a wide polyline to one of its edges, and **Length**, which draws a segment of the specified length at the same angle as the previous segment.

1.3 Editing Polylines

You can edit polylines by moving a vertex, changing its width, joining polylines or lines and arcs together, and converting polylines into individual segments. You can also add and remove vertices from existing polylines and convert arcs to lines and vice-versa.

How To: Change the Width of an Existing Polyline

1. In the *Home* tab>expanded Modify panel, click ✐ (Edit Polyline).
2. At the *Select polyline:* prompt, select the polyline. An options menu displays, as shown in Figure 1–7.

You can also double-click on a polyline to display the options menu.

Enter an option
Close
Join
Width
Edit vertex
Fit
Spline
Decurve
Ltype gen
Reverse
Undo

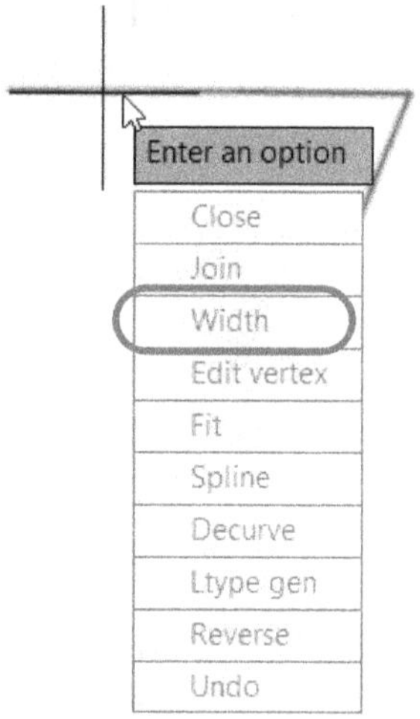

Figure 1–7

3. Select the **Width** option.
4. At the *Specify new width for all segments:* prompt, enter the new width and press <Enter>.
5. Press <Enter> to end the command.

How To: Modify Vertices in Polylines using Edit Polyline

1. In the *Home* tab>expanded Modify panel, click ✐ (Edit Polyline).
2. Select the polyline that you want to edit. You can also double-click on a polyline to display the options menu.
3. Select the **Edit vertex** option.

4. An icon displays on the polyline, indicating the vertex that is currently being edited. To select a different vertex, select the **Next** option until the one you want to edit displays.
5. Select one of the following options to modify the current vertex:

Break	Breaks the polyline at the selected vertex, separating it from the rest of the polyline. If you break a polyline in more than one place, the separated objects remain polylines.
Insert	Inserts a new vertex at the selected point on the polyline. You can place the new vertex anywhere on the polyline.
Move	Moves a vertex to a new position on the polyline. You can move the current vertex to a new location, anywhere on the polyline.
Straighten	Deletes segments and vertices between two selected vertices, and replaces them with a single straight line segment.
Tangent	Attaches a tangent direction to the selected vertex to be used for curve fitting later.
Width	Modifies the width of the selected line or arc between two adjacent vertices.

6. Use the **Next** and **Previous** options to continue modifying vertices. Select **eXit** to return to the **Edit Polyline** command options, or press <Esc> to end the command.

Modifying Polyline Vertices Using Grips

If you select a polyline when you are not in a command, the vertex grips and midpoint grips display. You can modify them by adding or deleting vertices, stretching them, and converting them from a line to an arc and vice-versa. You can access these options by hovering the cursor over a multifunctional vertex grip and selecting an option in the list, as shown in Figure 1–8.

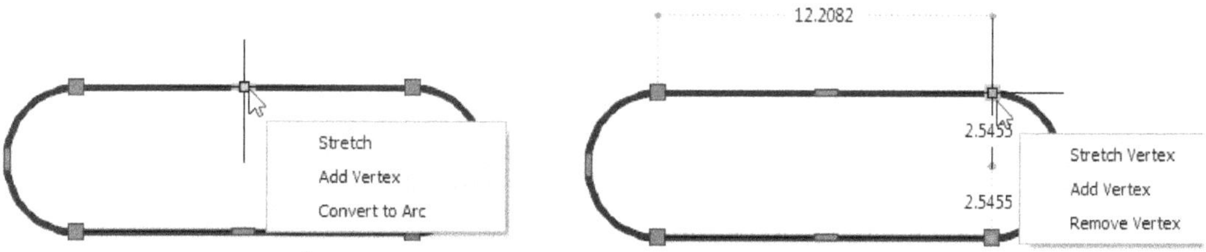

Figure 1–8

Converting Lines and Arcs to Polylines

How To: Use Vertices to Convert a Line to an Arc

1. When not in a command, select a polyline to display its vertices.
2. On the object, hover on a vertex that you want to change. For example, if you want to change a line into an arc, hover on the midpoint vertex on the line.
3. Select **Convert to Arc**.
4. Drag the arc to the required size or enter the required dimension.
5. Continue selecting vertices and modifying them or press <Esc> to end the command.

In some cases, creating lines and arcs and then turning them into a polyline is easier than using the **Polyline** command from the start. While separate lines and arcs work in most cases, having them work together as a polyline can be useful. For instance, selecting one object to move is easier than selecting all of the pieces from which it has been created, as shown in Figure 1–9.

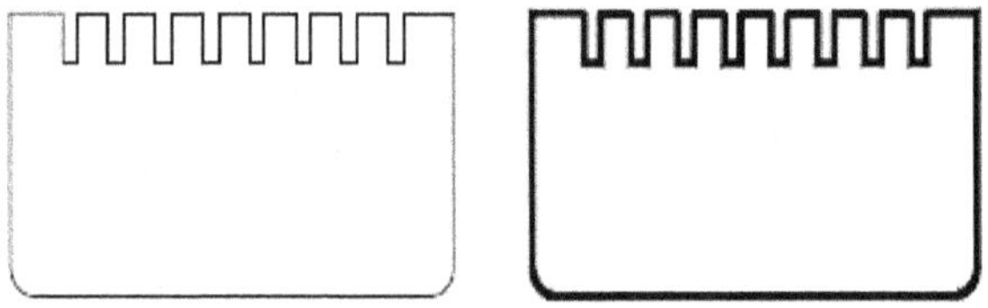

Figure 1–9

How To: Convert Lines and Arcs into a Single Polyline

1. In the *Home* tab>expanded Modify panel, click ⟲ (Edit Polyline).
2. At the *Select polyline or:* prompt, select a line or arc.
3. At the *Do you want to turn it into one?:* prompt, press <Enter> to select the **Y** option.
4. Select **Join** in the options menu that displays.
5. Select the other objects that you want to join to the polyline, which get highlighted.
6. Press <Enter> once to end the *Select objects:* prompt.
7. Press <Enter> again to end the command.

- The **Multiple** option (at the *Select Polyline:* prompt) enables you to edit several polylines at once, or to convert multiple line segments into polylines at the same time.

- To be joined, each line segment or arc must be attached to the end point of the next.

- For open polylines, **Edit Polyline** displays the **Close** option; for closed polylines, it displays the **Open** option.

Turning Polylines into Lines and Arcs

When a polyline has been created, you might want to break it into all of its separate component parts, so that you can remove individual segments or make other changes.

- In the *Home* tab>Modify panel, click ☐ (Explode) to convert a polyline into individual arcs and lines.

- Exploding a wide polyline causes it to lose its width information.

- The **Explode** command works on other object types that are made from polylines, such as rectangles or polygons. It also works on blocks.

Practice 1b

Drawing and Editing Polylines

Practice Objectives

- Draw polylines and convert a polyline into separate lines and arcs.
- Convert lines and arcs into a polyline.
- Change the width of a polyline.

In this practice, you will draw polylines. You will edit several polylines and change their width so that they will be used as symbols in a flowchart.

Task 1 - Draw polylines for a flowchart.

In this task, you will create several polylines as symbols to be used in a flowchart, as shown in Figure 1–10. The dimensions are for your reference only.

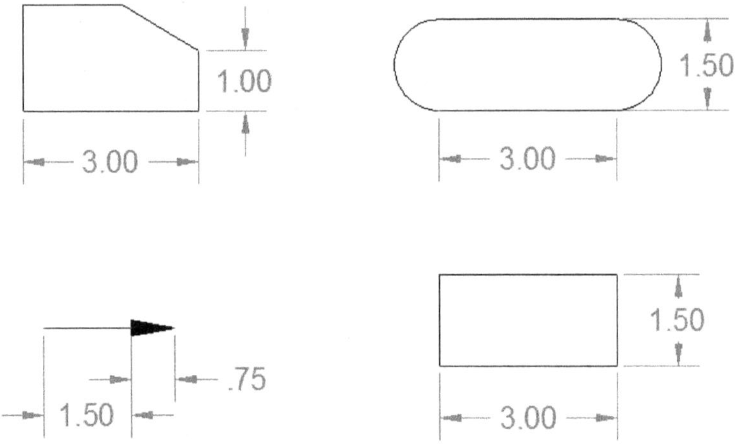

Figure 1–10

1. Start a new drawing based on **Mech-Inches.dwt**, which is located in your practice files folder, and save it as **Flowchart.dwg**.

2. Ensure that ⬜ (Object Snap) and ∠ (Object Snap Tracking) are both toggled on. The Object Snaps should be set to **Endpoint, Midpoint**, and **Extension**.

3. Expand ⟳ ▼ (Polar Tracking) and select **30,60,90,120....** Ensure that it is toggled on.

4. In the *Home* tab> Draw panel, click ⌐⌐ (Polyline) and draw the top left symbol, as shown in Figure 1–11.
   - Specify the start point anywhere.
   - Move the cursor right, enter **3**, and press <Enter>.
   - Move the cursor straight up, enter **1**, and press <Enter>.
   - Move the cursor at an angle of **150** degrees, enter **1.5**, and press <Enter>.
   - Make the next point straight to the left, but track it to make it directly above (even with) the start point.
   - Type **C** and press <Enter> to close the figure and finish the command.

5. Start the **Polyline** command again and draw the top right symbol, as shown in Figure 1–11.
   - To specify the start point, track it from the lower right corner of the object drawn in Step 4.
   - Move the cursor right, enter **3**, and press <Enter>.
   - Type **A** and press <Enter> to switch to the **Arc** option.
   - Move the cursor straight up, enter **1.5**, and press <Enter>.
   - Type **L** and press <Enter> to switch to the **Line** option.
   - Move the cursor left, enter **3**, and press <Enter>.
   - Switch to the **Arc** option and type **CL** to close the figure and finish the command.

6. Start the **Polyline** command and draw the arrow below the symbol drawn in Step 4, as shown in Figure 1–11.
   - Specify the start point anywhere.
   - Move the cursor right, enter **1.5**, and press <Enter>.
   - Type **W** and press <Enter> to switch to the **Width** option.
   - For the starting width, enter **0.25** and press <Enter>.
   - For the ending width, enter **0** and press <Enter>.
   - Move the cursor straight to the right, enter **0.75**, and press <Enter>.
   - Press <Enter> to finish the command.

A rectangle is also a polyline.

7. The bottom right symbol shown in Figure 1–11 can be drawn using the **Rectangle** command or **Polyline** command.

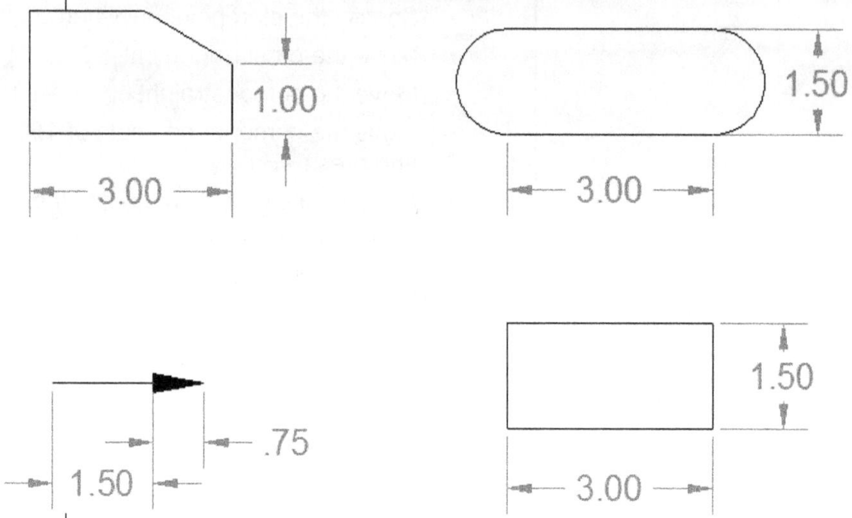

Figure 1–11

8. Arrange the objects to create the simple flowchart shown in Figure 1–12. Move, copy, and rotate the objects as required.

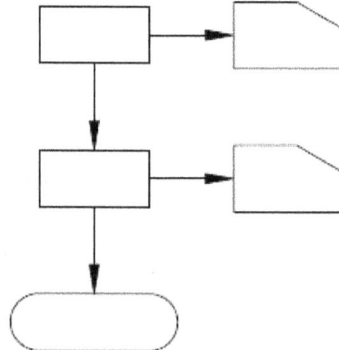

Figure 1–12

9. Save the drawing.

Task 2 - Edit polylines.

In this task, you will explode a polyline, and then use the **Edit Polyline** command to join arcs and lines into a polyline and change the width, as shown in Figure 1–13.

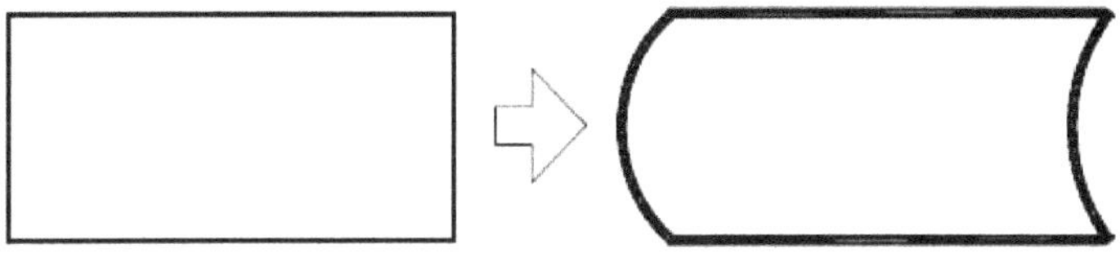

Figure 1–13

1. Make a copy of the rectangle.

2. Select the copied rectangle and explode it (in the *Home* tab>Modify panel, click ⬚ (Explode)). Erase the two vertical lines. You can select the lines individually because the object is no longer a polyline.

3. Draw a 3-point arc at each end of the two horizontal lines that are left from the rectangle that you exploded in Step 2. Use the **Endpoint** object snap to connect the arcs to the lines. (**Tip:** Draw it at one end and then copy it to the other end).

4. In the *Home* tab>expanded Modify panel, click ⬭ (Edit Polyline) and select any one of the lines. At the *Do you want to turn it into one?:* prompt, press <Enter> to select the **Y** (yes) option.

5. In the options menu, select **Join**.

6. At the *Select objects:* prompt, select the other line and the arcs and press <Enter>.

7. Select the **Width** option. Set the *width* to **0.05** and press <Enter>. Press <Enter> again to exit the command.

8. Use the **Move** command to move the shape. It is now all one object.

9. Verify that you are not in a command and select the polyline.

10. Hover the cursor over one of the midpoint grip vertices on one of the arcs and select **Convert to Line**.

11. Repeat the previous step for the other arc. The shape is now a rectangle.

12. Save and close the drawing.

1.4 Drawing Polygons

The **Polygon** command generates closed geometric figures with three or more equal sides, such as triangles, hexagons, and diamonds, as shown in Figure 1–14.

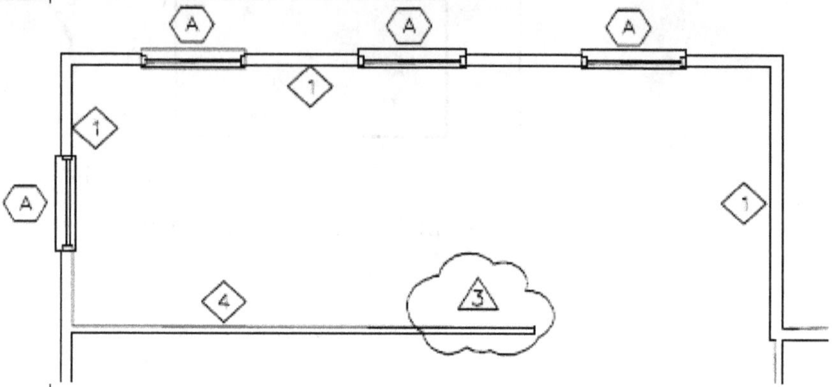

Figure 1–14

- The AutoCAD software builds these objects from polylines. Therefore, all of the sides form one unified object.

- Since polygons are made from polylines, you can use the **Edit Polyline** command to assign a width, explode them to create separate segments, or edit the vertices.

How To: Draw an Inscribed or Circumscribed Polygon

1. In the *Home* tab>Draw panel, expand the Rectangle flyout and click (Polygon).
2. Enter the number of sides for the polygon, and press <Enter>.
3. Locate the center point anywhere in the drawing window.

4. Select **Inscribed in circle** or **Circumscribed about circle**, as shown in Figure 1–15.

   - An *inscribed* polygon is defined by the distance from the specified center to one of its vertices (inscribed in the imaginary circle).

   - A *circumscribed* polygon is defined by the distance from the specified center to one of the edges (circumscribed about the imaginary circle).

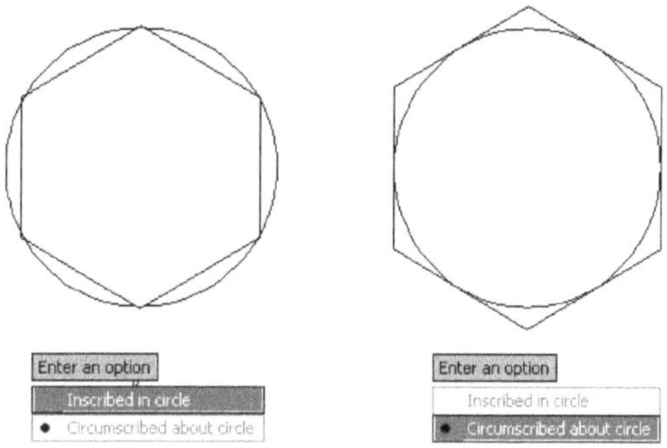

Enter an option		Enter an option
Inscribed in circle		Inscribed in circle
• Circumscribed about circle		• Circumscribed about circle

Figure 1–15

5. Enter the radius of the circle.

How To: Draw a Polygon by Edge

1. In the *Home* tab>Draw panel, expand the Rectangle flyout and click (Polygon).
2. Enter the number of sides for the polygon, and press <Enter>.
3. At the *Specify center of polygon:*, type **E** for the **Edge** option.
4. At the *Specify first endpoint of edge:*, select a point to locate an endpoint of one of the sides of the polygon.
5. At the *Specify second endpoint of edge:* prompt, select a point to locate the other endpoint of the side of the polygon. This input defines the length of all of the sides (edges) and the angle at which the polygon is rotated, as shown in Figure 1–16.

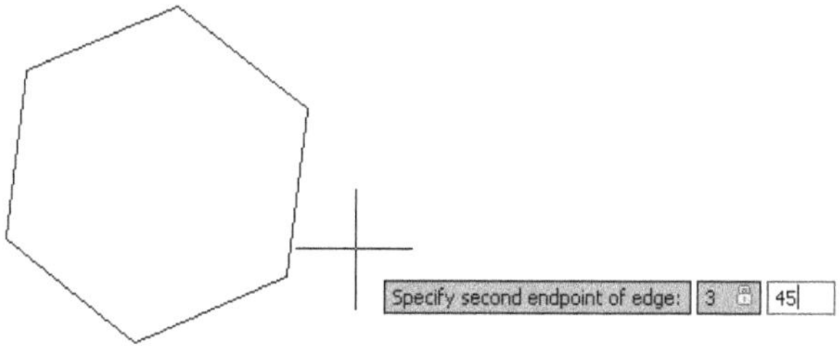

Specify second endpoint of edge: 3 45

Figure 1–16

Practice 1c

Drawing Polygons

Practice Objective

- Create polygons.

In this practice, you will create symbols using the **Polygon** and **Rectangle** commands, as shown in Figure 1–17.

R0.2500

Window Tag

0.2500

0.7500

Room Number

0.5000

Revision Triangle

Figure 1–17

1. Start a new drawing based on **AEC-Imperial.dwt** which is located in your practice files folder. Save it as **Symbols.dwg**.

Draw only the objects. The text and dimensions are for reference only.

2. Draw the symbols shown in Figure 1–17. For the Window Tag object, start the **Polygon** command (In the *Home* tab>Draw panel, expand the Rectangle flyout and click  (Polygon)). For the number of sides, enter **6** and press <Enter>. Select anywhere in the drawing window as its center. Select **Circumscribed about circle** and enter **0.25** as the radius. Press <Enter> to complete the command. To see the polygon, zoom in closely using **Zoom Extents**.

3. Draw the Room Number using the **Rectangle** command.
   - Zoom out to make space for other objects.
   - Start the **Rectangle** command and click near the right side of the hexagon to set the first corner.
   - At the *Specify other corner point.* prompt, enter **0.75,0.25**.
   - Press <Enter> to complete the command.

4. Draw the Revision Triangle using the **3-sided Polygon** command.

- Start the (Polygon) command. For the number of sides, enter **3** and press <Enter>.
- Press <Down Arrow> and select the **Edge** option. Click anywhere to set the first endpoint of the edge.
- For the second endpoint, enter **0.50**, press <Tab>, and enter **0** as the angle.
- Press <Enter> to complete the command.

5. Save and close the drawing.

1.5 Splines

Splines

A spline consists of smooth curve segments that are blended together to form a flowing shape. Splines are important in special drawing applications that use curves extensively (such as contour maps) or that require exact control of complex curves (such as the shape of a hull in shipbuilding or the aerodynamic surfaces of airplanes and cars). You can use 〜 (Spline Fit) or 〜 (Spline CV) in the *Home* tab>expanded Draw panel for creating true spline curves.

How To: Draw a Spline

1. In the *Home* tab>expanded Draw panel, click 〜 (Spline Fit).
2. Click to specify the start point of the spline.
3. Click to specify the next point of the spline. Move your cursor to display the shape of the curve, as shown in Figure 1–18.

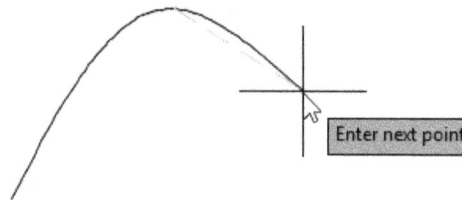

Enter next point

Figure 1–18

4. Continue clicking and specifying the points for the curves.
5. Press <Enter> to complete the creation of the spline, as shown in Figure 1–19.

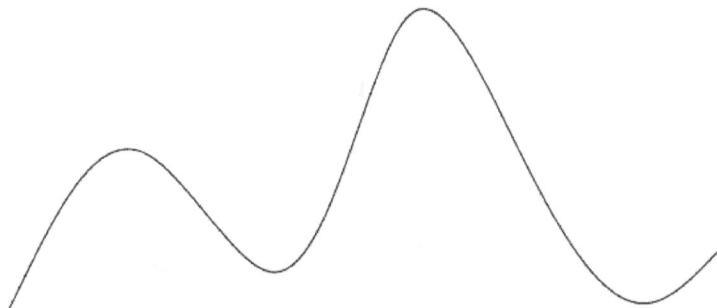

Figure 1–19

- The ⌒ (Edit Polyline) command has a **Spline** option that converts a polyline into an approximation of a smooth curve, called a *spline curve*, as shown in Figure 1–20. (The **Fit** option is similar but the curve is not as smooth.)

Figure 1–20

- ⁀ (Spline Fit) and ⁀ (Spline CV) create true spline curves. These are mathematically more exact and easier to control than splined polylines.

- After a spline has been created, its shape can be further refined using ⁀ (Edit Spline) in the *Home* tab>expanded Modify panel.

Blend Command

The **Blend** command combines two selected lines or curves by creating a spline in the gap between them. The ⁀ (Blend Curves) command is available in the *Home* tab>Modify panel, in the Fillet flyout. Start the command and select the first line or curve as shown in Figure 1–21.

Select first object or ⊞

Figure 1–21

Select the second line or curve to create a new spline in the gap between the two curves, as shown in Figure 1–22.

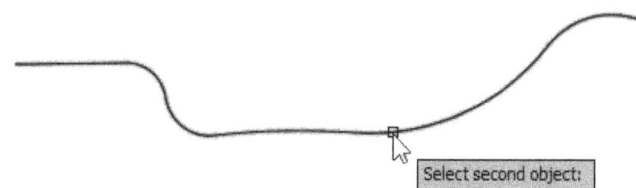

Select second object:

Figure 1–22

- Although a spline is added in the gap, the objects are three separate objects. Use ━┼┼━ (Join) to convert them into a single spline.

- You can use 〰 (Edit Spline)>Convert to Polyline to convert the spline into a polyline.

Joining Objects

In the *Home* tab>expanded Modify panel, ━┼┼━ (Join) joins broken polylines, lines, arcs, elliptical arcs, and splines, as shown in Figure 1–23. If you select two lines, they need to be touching each other end to end.

Figure 1–23

You can join objects of different types (e.g., lines, polylines, and splines). The final joined object becomes the most complex of the selected objects. Therefore, if you select a line and a polyline, the final joined object is a polyline.

- With arcs, the **Close** option can be used to close arcs (e.g., to form circles).

- The source object determines the properties (e.g., layer, color, etc.) of the new object.

1.6 Creating Boundaries and Regions

Creating Boundaries

Sometimes you need to create a complex polyline from several existing objects using the **Boundary** command, as shown in Figure 1–24.

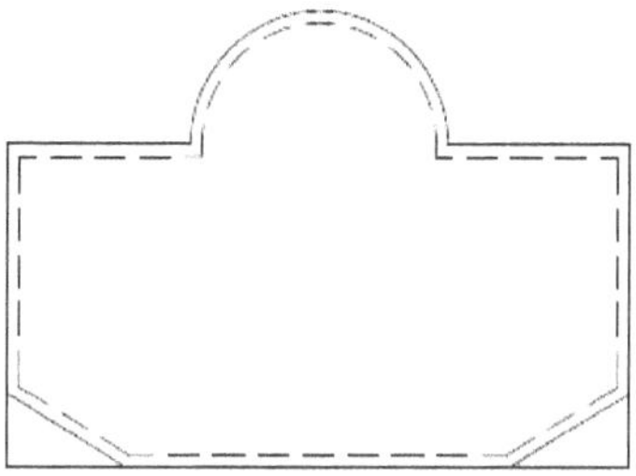

Figure 1–24

- The **Boundary** command can also create regions.

How To: Create Boundaries

1. In the *Home* tab>Draw panel, in the **Hatch** flyout, click ⊟ (Boundary).
2. In the Boundary Creation dialog box, select the required options.
3. Click ⊠ (Pick Points) or click **OK**.
4. Select a point inside a closed area, as shown in Figure 1–25. You can select points in multiple closed areas.

The AutoCAD software creates a closed polyline or region that is defined by the edges of the first objects it detects.

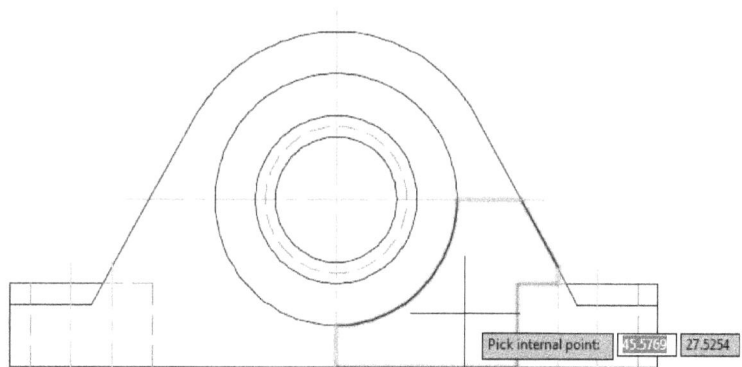

Pick internal point: 45.5769 27.5254

Figure 1–25

5. Press <Enter> to create the boundary.

Boundary Options

When you create boundaries, you can specify what is included in the boundary area with the options shown in Figure 1–26.

The new polyline is placed directly on top of the existing boundary lines. It is recommended that you create the boundary on a separate layer from the other objects.

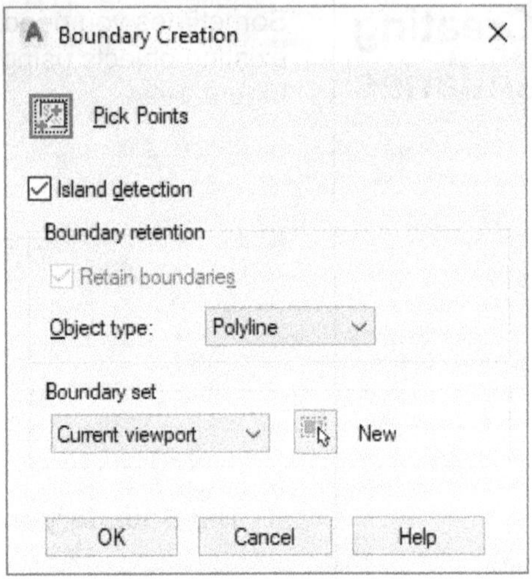

Figure 1–26

Island detection	Select this option if you want the **Boundary** command to find any interior objects (*islands*) and create polylines around them, in addition to finding the exterior boundary.
Object type	You can create a polyline or a region. If a boundary set includes ellipses, elliptical arcs, or splines, the **Boundary** command automatically creates a region.
Boundary set	The default option, **Current viewport**, calculates the boundary based on all of the objects that are visible in the current viewport.
	To select the objects that should be considered when calculating the boundary, click (New - Select new boundary set). This enables you to exclude objects from the boundary calculation and it can make the boundary calculation faster in a complex drawing.

Working with Regions

A polyline is a continuous object. It can be closed, but cannot contain holes. Regions are used to create single objects that contain an outline and holes, as shown in Figure 1–27.

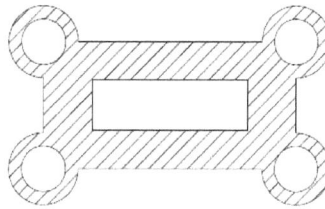

Figure 1–27

- A *region* is a 2D solid object or infinitely thin surface. The edges cannot be separated from the shape. Therefore, if you move an edge, the entire surface moves. Typical uses for regions include a plate with holes or a wall with windows.

- You can create objects with holes that are part of the object.

- Regions can be used in many cases to quickly create complex geometry using the **Union**, **Subtract**, and **Intersect** commands.

- The area of a region, even one with holes, can easily be found using the **Area** command with the **Object** option.

How To: Create a Region

1. Draw the closed shape for the region using lines, polylines, etc. The lines must connect precisely end point to end point.
2. In the *Home* tab>expanded Draw panel, click ⬚ (Region).
3. Select the objects. You can select several closed shapes and convert them all into regions at the same time. In the Command Line, the AutoCAD software reports the number of regions it has created.
   - Regions can be created out of existing closed shapes made of lines, arcs, polylines, circles, etc.
   - If the closed shape consists of separate segments, the segments must connect end point to end point to make a region.
4. The original objects are consumed when you use them to create a region.

- You can **Explode** a region to convert it into lines, arcs, splines, or circles, depending on the shapes involved.

Combining Regions

Regions are useful construction tools because of the ways in which they can be combined. For example, you can create a hole or cutout in a region by subtracting one region from another. You can also add regions and find the intersection of regions as shown in Figure 1–28. The addition (union), subtraction, and intersection actions are called *Boolean Operations*.

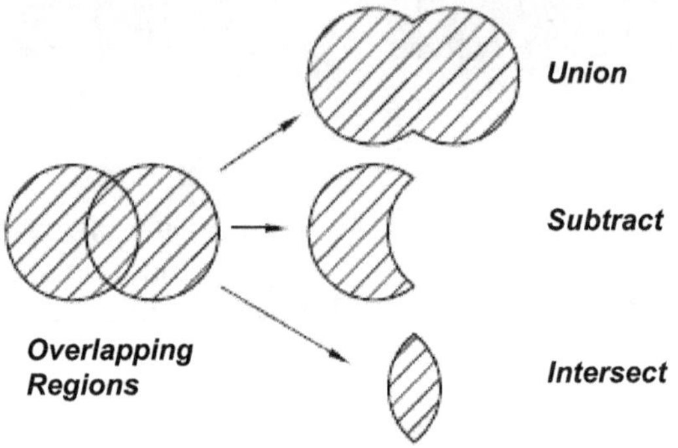

Figure 1–28

- You can union, subtract, or intersect two or more regions at a time.

- The regions on which the Boolean Operations are performed do not need to intersect. However, the intersection of two objects that do not overlap erases the regions.

You are required to be in the 3D Modeling workspace for the 3D ribbon to display.

- Regions are considered solid objects and the tools for editing them are located in the *Home* tab>Solid Editing panel (as shown in Figure 1–29) when the 3D Modeling workspace is active.

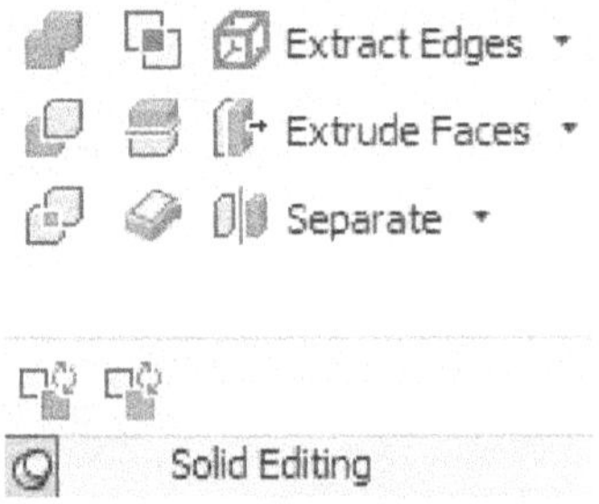

Figure 1–29

- You can type the name of the command if you do not want to switch workspaces.

Union

(Union) combines two or more regions into a single region as shown in Figure 1–30.

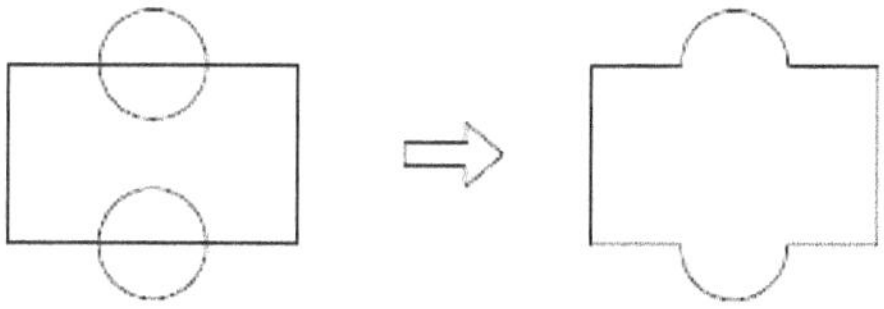

Figure 1–30

Subtract

(Subtract) removes the area of one region from another where they overlap as shown in Figure 1–31. You can also use **Subtract** to create regions containing holes. By subtracting the holes, you can also find out the area of the closed shape.

Figure 1–31

- Select the region(s) to *subtract from* first. Then select the regions that you want to subtract.

Intersect

(Intersect) finds the common area of two or more regions as shown in Figure 1–32. Only the area that is shared by the selected regions remains in the new region.

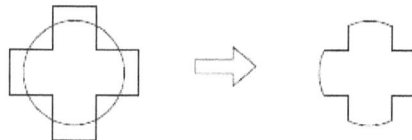

Figure 1–32

1.7 Construction Lines

Use temporary construction lines as guidelines for creating the more permanent parts of your design, as shown in Figure 1–33. Regular lines can serve as construction lines, but do not always provide the required length. Construction Lines and Rays are infinite lines that can be used to help construct your drawing.

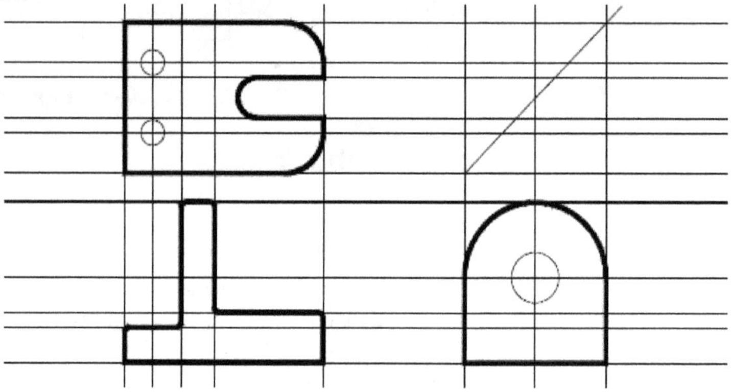

Figure 1–33

Construction Lines

The **Construction Line** command creates a line that is infinite in both directions.

How To: Draw a Construction Line

1. In the *Home* tab>expanded Draw panel, click

   ✎ (Construction Line).

2. Select two points on the screen for the line to go through or select an option in the menu. If you select two points, you can create additional construction lines by continuing to select points at different angles around the first point.

3. Select the **Hor**, **Ver**, or **Ang** options before selecting the first point if you want to make a series of horizontal, vertical, or angled construction lines.

4. If you want to create construction lines offset by a specific distance, select the **Offset** option.

5. The **Bisect** option creates a construction line that bisects a selected angle. It is determined by three points: angle vertex point, angle start point, and angle endpoint.

The command options provide several methods of specifying the location and angle of the line.

• Construction lines are not affected by zooming.

• Construction lines should be placed on a separate layer that can be toggled off or made non-plotable.

Rays

A ray extends infinitely in one direction from a specified point and you can input more than one ray from the same point.

How To: Draw a Ray

*Ray does not have the same options as **Construction Line**.*

1. In the *Home* tab>expanded Draw panel, click ✎⟋ (Ray).
2. Select the start point for the ray. This becomes the end point of the ray.
3. Select a through point for the ray.
4. Continue to select other through points to create additional rays at different angles, but with the same end point.
5. Press <Enter> to end the command.

• Use object snaps to place construction lines and rays precisely on existing objects.

Practice 1d | Construction Lines

Practice Objective

- Create guidelines that are used to add geometry.

In this practice, you will draw circles and then add more circles to the plate using construction lines for precise placement, as shown in Figure 1–34.

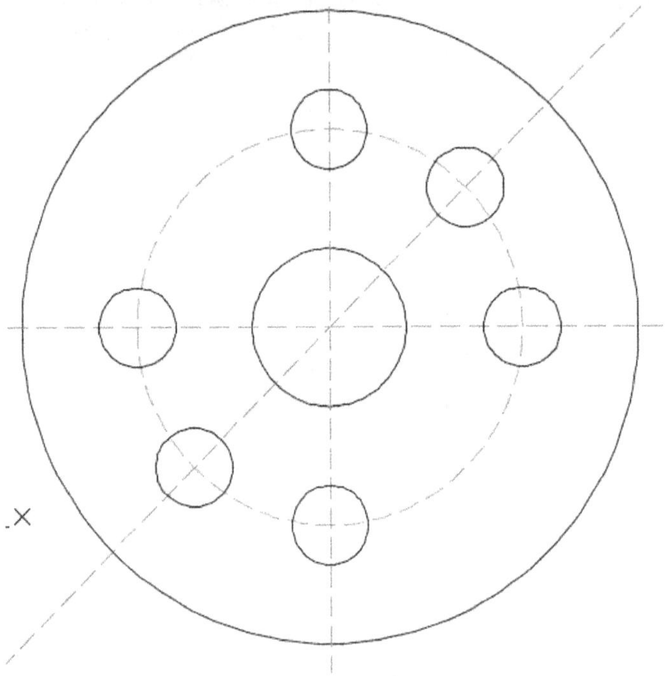

Figure 1–34

1. Create a new drawing based on **Mech-Inches.dwt**, which is located in your practice files folder. Save it as **Round Plate.dwg**.

2. Draw two circles (**R=2** and **R=8**) around the *center point* **10,5**. Use the **Zoom Extents** command to display the entire drawing.

3. Toggle on the **Center** object snap.

4. Set the current layer to **Constructions**.

5. Draw a third circle (**R=5**) around the same center point.

6. In the *Home* tab>expanded Draw panel, click

   ↗ (Construction Line). Place the following three
   construction lines through the center point of the circles:
   - Horizontal
   - Vertical
   - Angular at 45 degrees

   Select the **Hor**, **Ver**, or **Ang** options in the <Down Arrow>
   menu before selecting the first point, as shown in
   Figure 1–35.

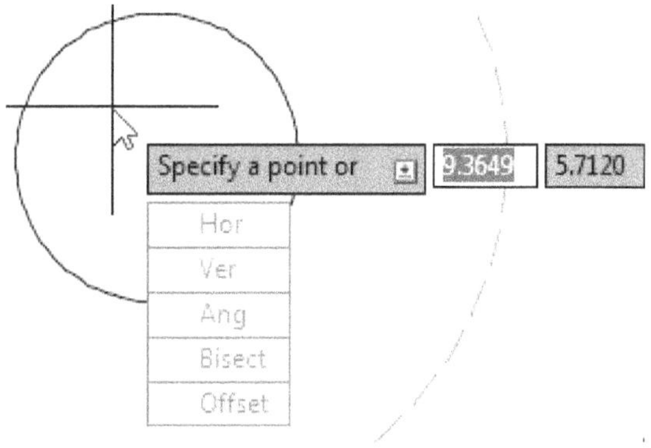

Figure 1–35

7. Set the current layer to **Object**.

8. Draw six circles with **R=1.0** at the intersection (**Intersection**
   object snap) of the construction lines and the middle circle.

9. Toggle off the layer **Constructions**.

10. Save and close the drawing.

1.8 Isometric Drawing Environment

In the Drafting Settings dialog box (*Snap and Grid* tab), when the *Snap type* is set to **Isometric snap** (as shown in Figure 1–36), or in the Status Bar, when you toggle the ⟍⁺ (Isometric Drafting) on, the grid and cursor become angled.

Figure 1–36

This enables you to draw 2D isometric parts quickly and efficiently, as shown in Figure 1–37.

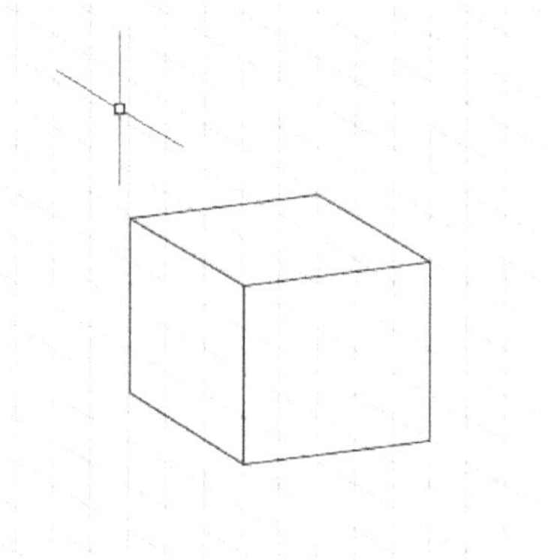

Figure 1–37

The rotation of the grid and the cursor can be controlled using the **Isometric Drafting** tool in the Status Bar.

When the Isometric Drafting is toggled on, the crosshairs display in red and green.

- Expand ↖ ▾ (Isometric Drafting) and click on one of the following options to set the required isometric drawing environment.

  - ↖ (Isoplane Left)
  - ✕ (Isoplane Top)
  - ✗ (Isoplane Right)

  The cursor (crosshairs) and grid display is oriented to suit the selected option, as shown for **Isoplane Top** in Figure 1–38.

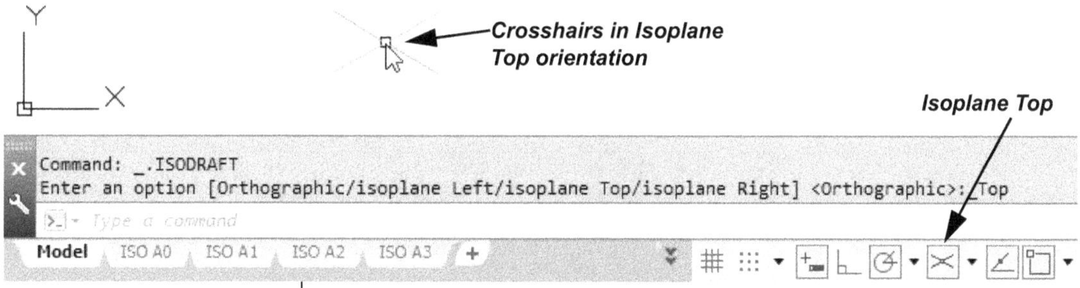

Crosshairs in Isoplane Top orientation

Isoplane Top

```
Command: _.ISODRAFT
Enter an option [Orthographic/isoplane Left/isoplane Top/isoplane Right] <Orthographic>: Top
```

Model ISO A0 ISO A1 ISO A2 ISO A3 +

Figure 1–38

Selecting Objects

Exam Objectives Covered in This Chapter

- 1.2.a Use Quick Select to select objects based on shared properties
- 1.2.b Select similar objects
- 1.2.c Isolate or hide objects in a drawing
- 1.2.d Control the draw order of overlapping objects
- 1.2.e Match the properties of one object to other objects
- 1.2.f Remove objects from a selection set
- 5.1.b Use wipeouts to mask underlying objects in specific areas of a drawing

2.1 Working with Object Properties

Every object in the AutoCAD® software has properties, such as layer, color, and linetype, and geometric information such as vertex points, length, etc. Many properties can be changed using Quick Properties, the Properties palette, or **Match Properties**. You can also use properties to help you select objects when using **Quick Select**.

- Hover the cursor over an object to display a tooltip containing basic information about the object, as shown in Figure 2–1.

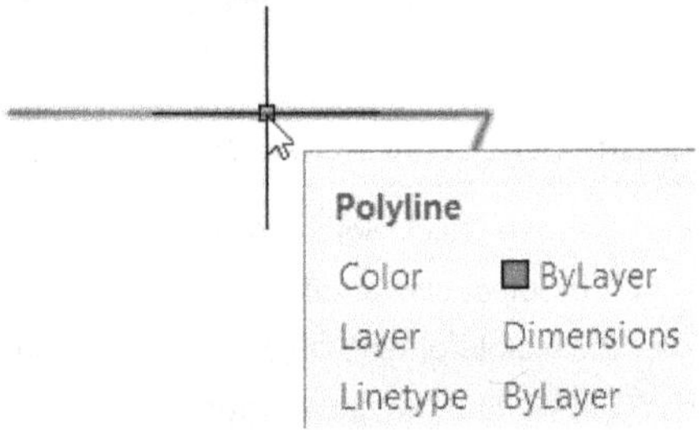

Figure 2–1

Quick Properties

If you select an object, when not in a command, and display its grips, the basic information about that object displays in the Quick Properties panel, as shown in Figure 2–2. These vary depending on the type of object selected.

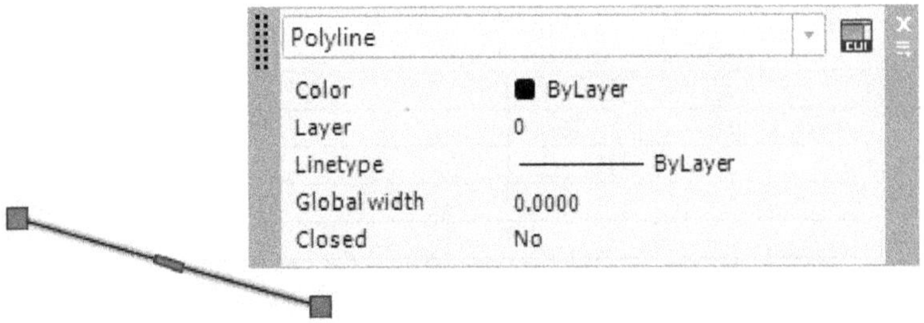

Press <Esc> to clear a selected object.

Figure 2–2

*To display ▤ (Quick Properties) in the Status Bar, expand ☰ (Customization) and select **Quick Properties**.*

- The Quick Properties panel displays along with the selected object (in grip mode) when ▤ (Quick Properties) is toggled **On** in the Status Bar.

- When ▤ (Quick Properties) is toggled **Off**, you can display the Quick Properties for individual objects by selecting them (in grip mode), right-clicking, and selecting **Quick Properties** in the shortcut menu.

- In addition to viewing the information about the selected object, you can also change some properties in the Quick Properties panel. Click on a property and select a different option from the drop-down list, as shown in Figure 2–3.

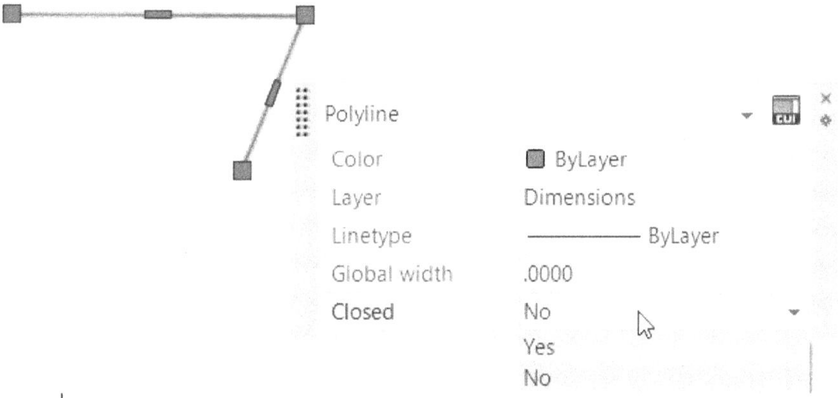

Polyline		
Color	◻ ByLayer	
Layer	Dimensions	
Linetype	———— ByLayer	
Global width	.0000	
Closed	No	
	Yes	
	No	

Figure 2–3

- You can also display a list of the basic properties for an object using ▤ (List) in the *Home tab*>expanded Properties panel. The AutoCAD Text window opens, displaying some of the properties of the selected object. You cannot change any properties using the **List** command. The List command can quickly provide the length of lines, and the area and perimeter of closed polylines.

Properties Palette

The primary way to get detailed information about the objects in your drawing is to use the Properties palette, as shown in Figure 2–4. It reports all of the properties of the object and enables you to change many of them.

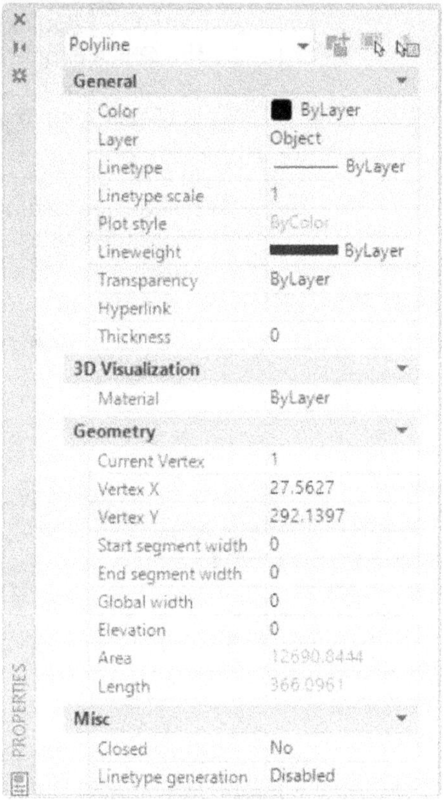

Figure 2–4

- You can toggle the Properties palette on or off using any of the following methods:
  - In the *View* tab>Palettes panel, click [icon] (Properties).
  - Press <Ctrl>+<1>.
  - In the *Home* tab>Properties panel, click [icon].
  - In grip mode, right-click on an object and select **Properties** in the shortcut menu.

- You can have the Properties palette open even when an object is not selected. Once you select any object, its properties display in the open Properties palette.

- As with other palettes, you can dock the Properties palette to any side of the screen. Click, hold, and drag using its title bar and move it to either side of the screen. Once it shows the docking outline, leave the cursor as it automatically docks it in place. You can also hide the palette by clicking the

  ⊮ (Auto-hide) icon located in the Properties title bar, as shown in Figure 2–5. Once hidden, it displays as a bar along the docked side and you can temporarily unhide it by hovering the cursor over the bar. You can also unhide it

  permanently by clicking ⊯ in the title bar. Use **X** to close the palette.

Figure 2–5

How To: Modify Objects Using Properties

1. Open the Properties palette if it is not already open and select an object. The properties of the object display in the palette, as shown in Figure 2–6.

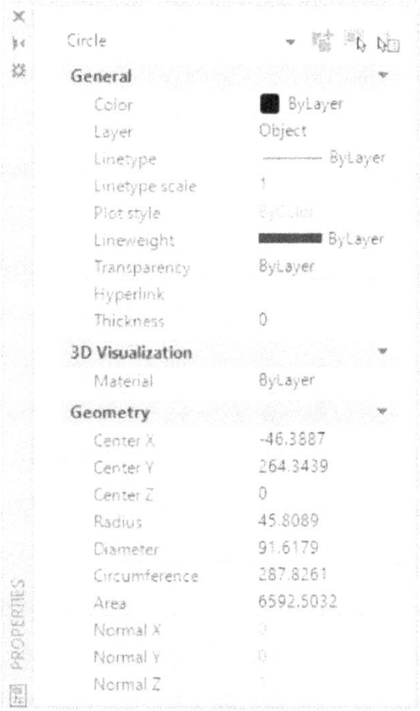

Figure 2–6

2. Change the properties as required by clicking in the value field of the property you want to change and then typing or selecting a new value.

  - As you move the cursor over the options in the drop-down lists, the object in the Drawing window changes to provide a preview of the highlighted option.

3. To clear the object, move the cursor into the drawing window and press <Esc>.

- Some properties display a list of options, such as the *Layer* property shown on the left in Figure 2–7.

- Some properties are numerical, as shown on the right in Figure 2–7. Once you click in the value field, you can enter a number, click 🔲 to open the QuickCalc calculator dialog box, or click ⌖ to modify the location of a point on the screen.

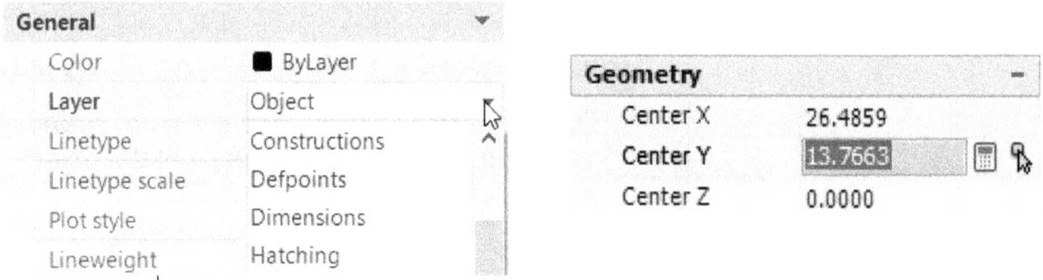

General	▼
Color	■ ByLayer
Layer	Object
Linetype	Constructions
Linetype scale	Defpoints
Plot style	Dimensions
Lineweight	Hatching

Geometry	—
Center X	26.4859
Center Y	13.7663
Center Z	0.0000

Figure 2–7

- Information in grayed-out cells cannot be changed.

Properties of Multiple Objects

- If you select more than one object of the same type (e.g., two circles), the AutoCAD software lists the types of properties that they have in common. If their values are different they are listed as ***VARIES***, as shown in Figure 2–8. You can change these properties for all of the selected objects at the same time (e.g., select several circles and change their radius to 2.25).

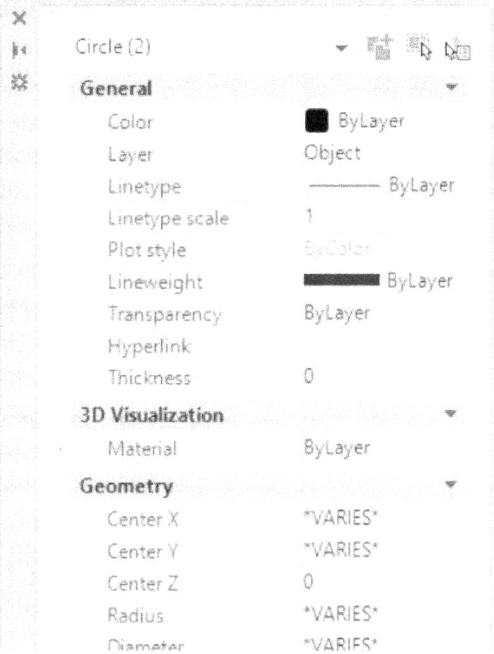

Figure 2–8

- If you select different types of objects (e.g., a circle and a line), the AutoCAD software displays the only types of properties that they have in common. If their values are different, they are listed as ***VARIES***. You can change the common properties of all of the selected objects at the same time. You can also switch between different types of objects using the drop-down list, as shown in Figure 2–9.

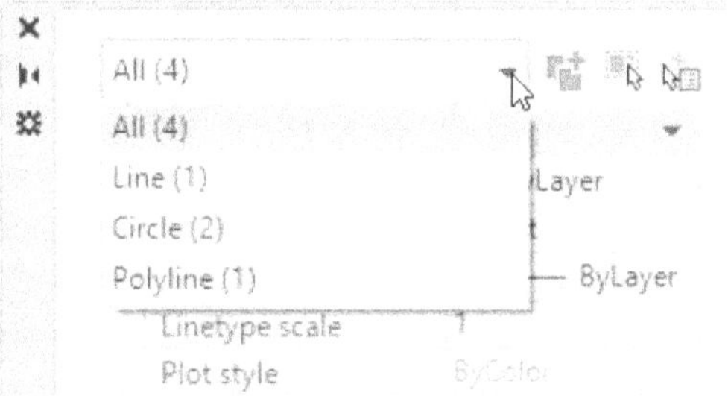

Figure 2–9

Matching Properties

To make objects in your drawing have the same properties as another object, use the **Match Properties** command. It enables you to select one object as a *model* and then copy its properties to any other object you select.

How To: Copy an Object's Properties

1. In the *Home* tab>Properties panel, click ⬚ (Match Properties).
2. At the *Select source object:* prompt, select the object you want to use as a model. The cursor changes into a small square box with a paint brush.
3. As you move the cursor over the object that you are going to select, the object changes and displays a preview of the new properties. Select the objects to which you want the properties to be copied.
4. Press <Enter> to end the command.

- **Match Properties** works across drawings. Specify the source object in one drawing, and in the drawing tab bar click on another drawing to switch to it and select the destination objects. If the layer does not exist in the destination drawing, it is created. When you hover over the object in the second drawing, the object highlights but does not display a preview of the new properties.

- **Match Properties** enables you to match all or some of an object's properties. To control which properties are matched, use the **Settings** option (available in the shortcut menu or Command Line) when you have started the command and selected the source object. By default, all of the properties are selected, as shown in Figure 2–10.

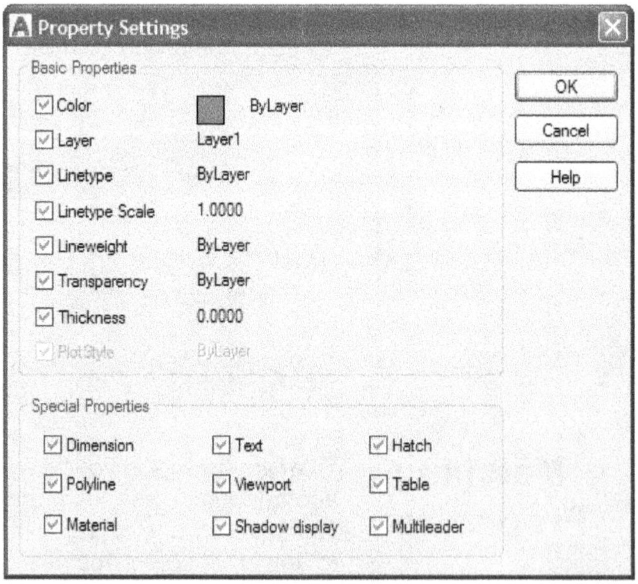

Figure 2–10

Quick Select

Quick Select can be used to select objects using their properties. It opens a dialog box in which you can specify a selection set by object type and/or properties (such as all of the circles with a radius of 0.25), as shown in Figure 2–11.

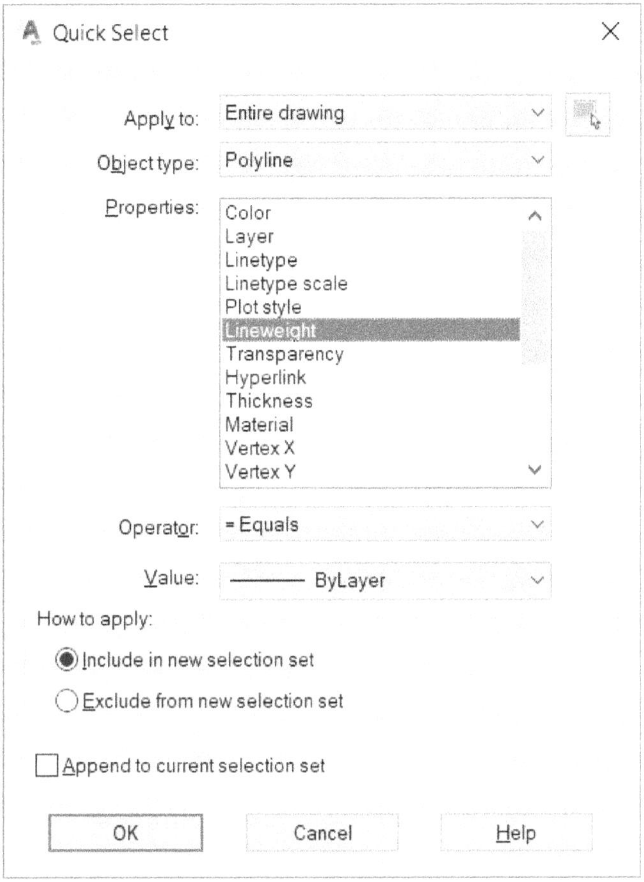

Figure 2–11

How To: Select Objects Using Quick Select

1. In the *Home* tab>Utilities panel or in the Properties palette, click ⬛ (Quick Select).

2. In the Quick Select dialog box, in *Apply to*, use **Entire drawing** or click ⬛ (Select objects) to create a selection set.

3. Select the required *Object type*. **Multiple** selects all of the object types. Only object types that are currently in the selection set display in the drop-down list.

To select all of the objects in your drawing, in the Home tab>Utilities panel, click ⬛ (Select All).

4. In *Properties:*, select the property that you want to filter. This varies according to the selected object type.
5. Select an *Operator*, as shown in Figure 2–12. The available operators vary depending on the selected property type.

Operator:	= Equals
Value:	= Equals
	<> Not Equal
apply:	> Greater than
	< Less than
lude in new	Select All

Figure 2–12

6. Specify the value that you want to find for the selected property. The available values vary depending on the selected property type. For example, values for the property **Layer** include all of the layers defined in the drawing. For the Radius value (of a circle), you need to enter a number.
7. Select an option for how the filter is going to be applied:
   - **Include in new selection set:** Places all of the objects that meet the criteria in a new selection set.
   - **Exclude from new selection set:** Places all of the objects that DO NOT meet the criteria in a new selection set.
8. If you want to build a selection set from several filters, select the **Append to current selection set** option, which adds the results to the current selection, rather than creating a new selection set.
9. Click **OK** to close the Quick Select dialog box. Objects that match the criteria are selected.
10. Use an editing command on the selected objects (such as **Erase** or **Properties**) to modify them.

*To select all of the objects of a specific type, regardless of their properties, use **Select All** for the Operator. For example, you can use this method to find all of the circle objects.*

Practice 2a

Working with Object Properties (Mechanical)

Practice Objective

- Obtain information about objects.

In this practice, you will get information about some objects (as shown in Figure 2–13) and then make changes to them, using the Quick Properties panel and the Properties palette.

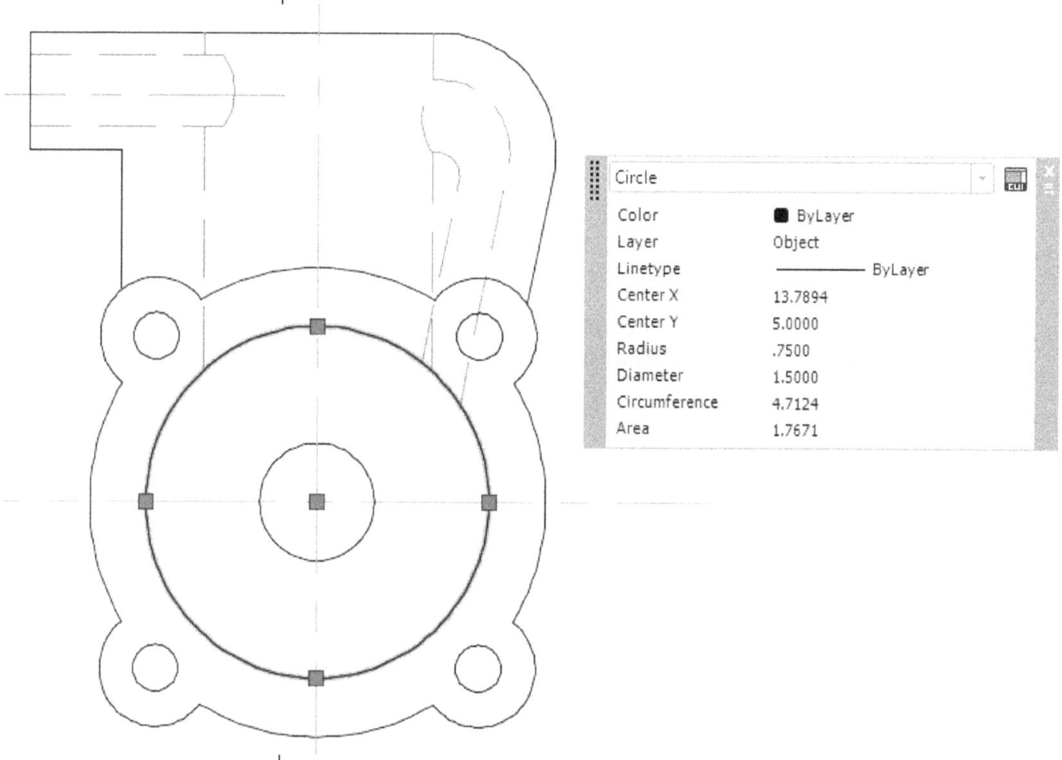

Circle	
Color	ByLayer
Layer	Object
Linetype	ByLayer
Center X	13.7894
Center Y	5.0000
Radius	.7500
Diameter	1.5000
Circumference	4.7124
Area	1.7671

Figure 2–13

1. Open **Crank-I.dwg** from your practice files folder.

2. In the Status Bar, toggle on 🖾 (Quick Properties).

3. Select the large full circle to display the Quick Properties panel, as shown in Figure 2–13. Press <Esc> to clear the selection.

4. Select the gray horizontal center line near the top left of the object. In its Quick Properties, note that it is drawn on the *Layer* **CONSTRUCTION**. Click anywhere in the *CONSTRUCTION* row to open its edit box. Expand the Layer drop-down list. Hover the cursor over the **Center** layer and note how the gray line previews as orange, as shown in Figure 2–14. Select **Center** to change the layer.

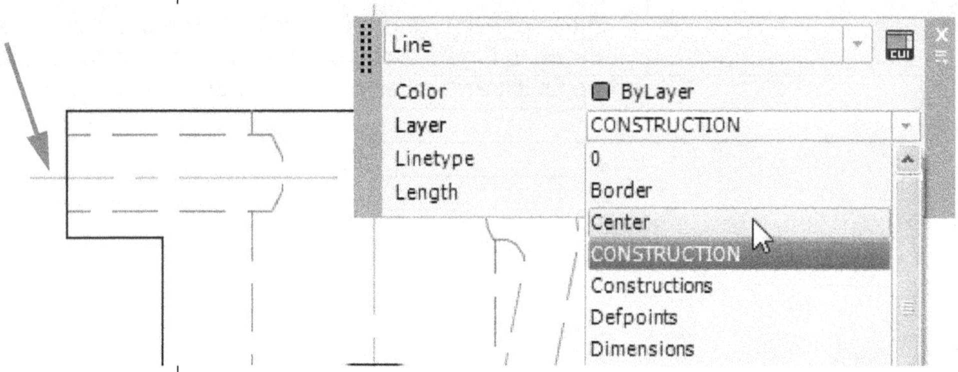

Figure 2–14

5. Clear your selection by pressing <Esc> and toggle ▦ (Quick Properties) off in the Status bar.

6. In the *Home* tab>Utilities panel, click ▦ (Quick Select).

7. In the Quick Select dialog box, verify that *Apply to* is set to **Entire drawing**. Set the *Object type* to **Circle**, *Properties* to **Diameter**, and *Operator* to **= Equals**. In the *Value* edit box, enter **0.2** and click **OK**. The objects with the above properties (four small circles with the diameter 0.2) are selected and highlighted in the drawing.

You can also click

▦ *(Properties) in the View tab>Palettes panel, to open the Properties palette.*

8. *Click* ▦ *in the Home* tab> *Properties panel to open the Properties palette.* To dock the palette to one side of the screen, click, hold, and drag using its title bar and move it to either side of the screen. Once it shows the docking outline, leave the cursor as it automatically docks it in place.

9. In the *Geometry* area, click in the Diameter value field and enter **0.2750**, as shown in Figure 2–15. As soon as you press <Enter>, note that the selected circles become bigger.

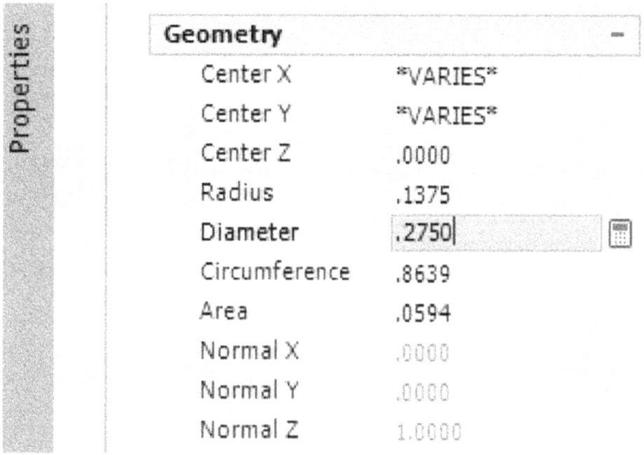

Geometry		−
Center X	*VARIES*	
Center Y	*VARIES*	
Center Z	.0000	
Radius	.1375	
Diameter	.2750	
Circumference	.8639	
Area	.0594	
Normal X	.0000	
Normal Y	.0000	
Normal Z	1.0000	

Figure 2–15

10. Clear the selection.

11. Hover the cursor on the Properties title bar and click **X** to close the Properties palette.

12. Save and close the drawing.

Practice 2b

Working with Object Properties (Architectural)

Practice Objective

*   Locate objects based on their properties and change their values.

In this practice, you will use the Properties palette and Quick Select to find objects based on their layer, and then move them to the correct layer. You will also find text based on its height and change it to the correct height, as shown in Figure 2–16.

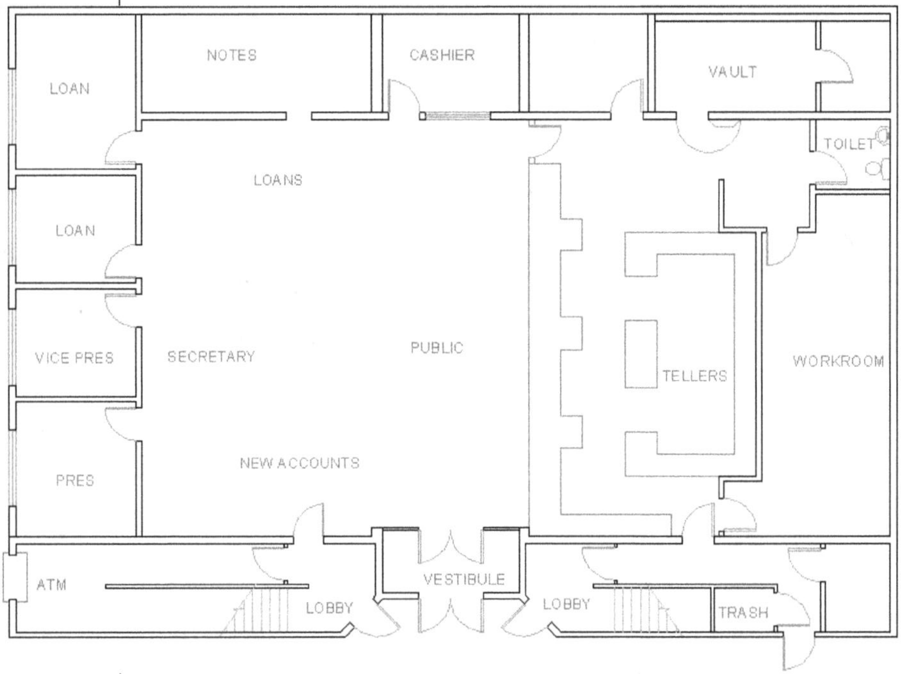

Figure 2–16

1. Open **Bank-Building-A.dwg** from your practice files folder.

2. In the *Home* tab>Layers panel, expand the Layer Control and scroll through the names. The Layer Control contains the layers **WALL** and **Walls**. You need to place all of the walls on the layer **Walls**.

Click ⬚ in the Home tab>Properties panel or use <Ctrl>+<1> to open the Properties palette.

3. Open the Properties palette, if it is not already open. Dock it to one side and hide it by clicking the ◄ icon located in the Properties title bar.

4. In the *Home* tab>Utilities panel, click ▨▦ (Quick Select). To select everything on the layer **WALL**, in the Quick Select dialog box, set the *Object type* to **Multiple**. Select **Layer** in the *Properties* list, set *Operator* to **= Equals**, and *Value* to **WALL**, as shown in Figure 2–17. Click **OK**. All the objects on layer **WALL** are highlighted in the drawing.

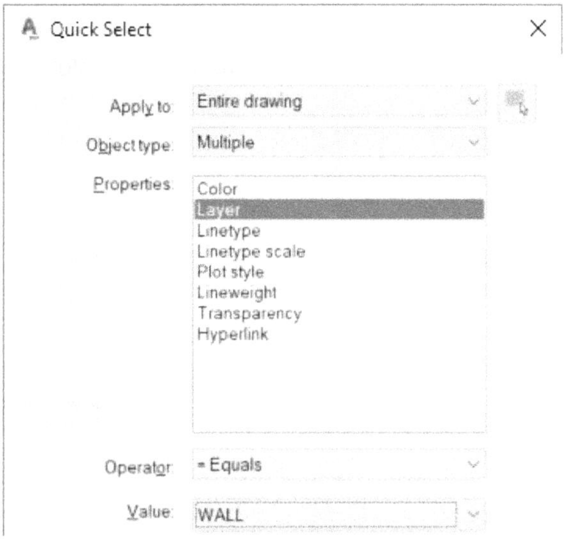

Figure 2–17

5. Hover the cursor over the title bar of the Properties palette to unhide it. In the *General* area, in the *Layer edit box,* change the *WALL* to **Walls** and press <Esc> to clear the object selection.

6. In the *Home* tab>Utilities panel, click ▨▦ (Quick Select), and in the dialog box, set the *Object type* to **Text** and the *Operator* to **Select All**. Click **OK**. All of the text in the drawing is highlighted. What layer is the text on? In the Properties palette, change the layer of the text objects to layer **Text** and press <Esc> to clear the object selection. All the text objects turn blue.

7. Use ▨▦ (Quick Select) and the Properties palette to select all of the text that is less than **11"** in height and change its *Height* to **1'-0"**.

8. Close the Properties palette.

9. Save and close the drawing.

Practice 2c | Working in Multiple Drawings

Practice Objectives

- Match the properties of objects between drawings.
- Copy and paste objects between drawings.

In this practice, you will switch between multiple drawings using *File* tabs and Open Documents. You will display drawings side by side using the Tile Vertical command. You will then copy and paste objects between the drawings, as shown in Figure 2–18.

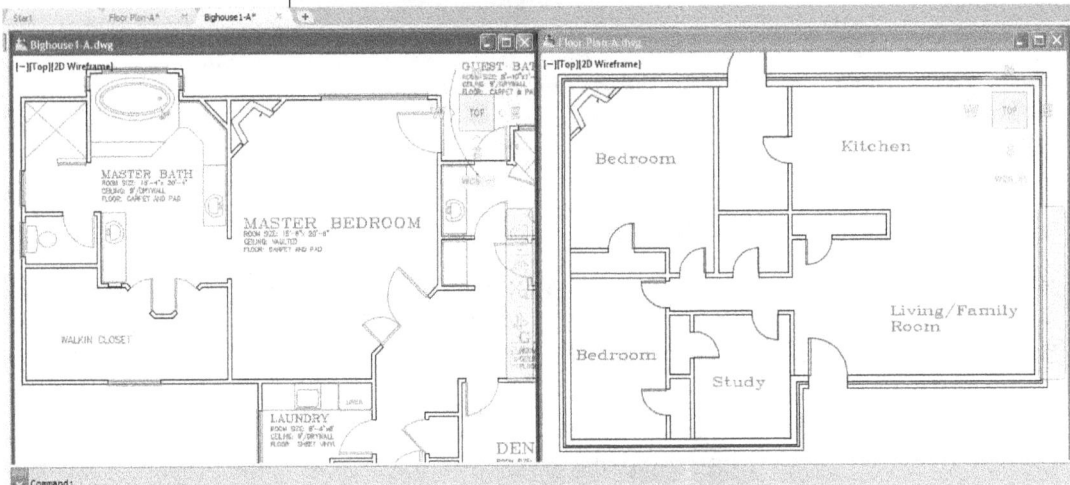

Figure 2–18

*Use <Ctrl> to select both files in the Select File dialog box and click **Open**.*

1. Open **Floor Plan-A.dwg** and **Bighouse1-A.dwg** from your practice files folder. Close any other open drawings.

2. If not already active, in the *Files* tab bar, select the **Bighouse1-A.dwg** tab. Then, hover the cursor over the **Floor Plan-A.dwg** tab to display the preview images of the drawing and its layouts, as shown in Figure 2–19. Select the **Model** preview to switch to **Floor Plan-A.dwg** with its *Model* tab active.

Depending on the selection of the filenames in the Select File dialog box, your drawing tabs might be reversed.

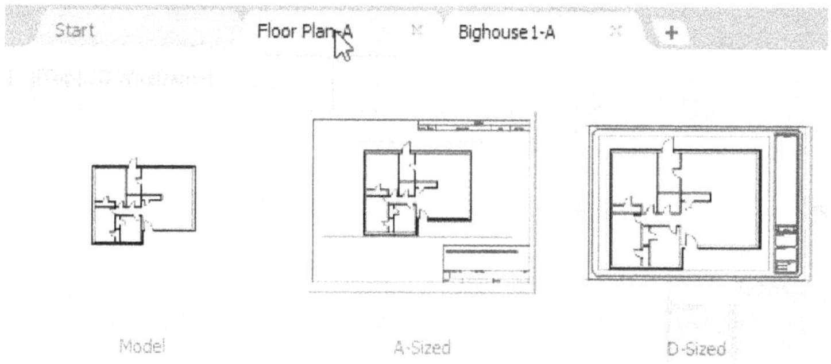

Figure 2–19

3. Thaw the layer **Text**.

4. In the Application Menu, click ◻ (Open Documents) and display the thumbnails of the two drawings by hovering the cursor over them, as shown in Figure 2–20. Select **Bighouse1-A.dwg** to make that drawing current.

Figure 2–20

5. In the *View* tab>Interface panel, click ◻◻ (Tile Vertically) to display the drawings side-by-side. Minimize the *Start* window display and click ◻◻ (Tile Vertically) again so that only the two drawings fill the drawing window.

6. In **Bighouse1-A.dwg**, zoom into the Master Bedroom (upper left corner of floorplan) and start the ▦ (Match Properties) command (*Home* tab>Properties panel). Select the text **MASTER BEDROOM** as the source object. Note that the cursor changes into a brush with a little square.

Your drawing might be in a reverse position than that shown in Figure 2–21.

7. Click inside **Floor Plan-A.dwg** once to activate it (the brush cursor is now available in **Floor Plan-A.dwg**). Select each of the text labels in **Floor Plan-A.dwg** as the destination object, as shown in Figure 2–21. Press <Enter> to exit the command. The text properties are matched in both drawings.

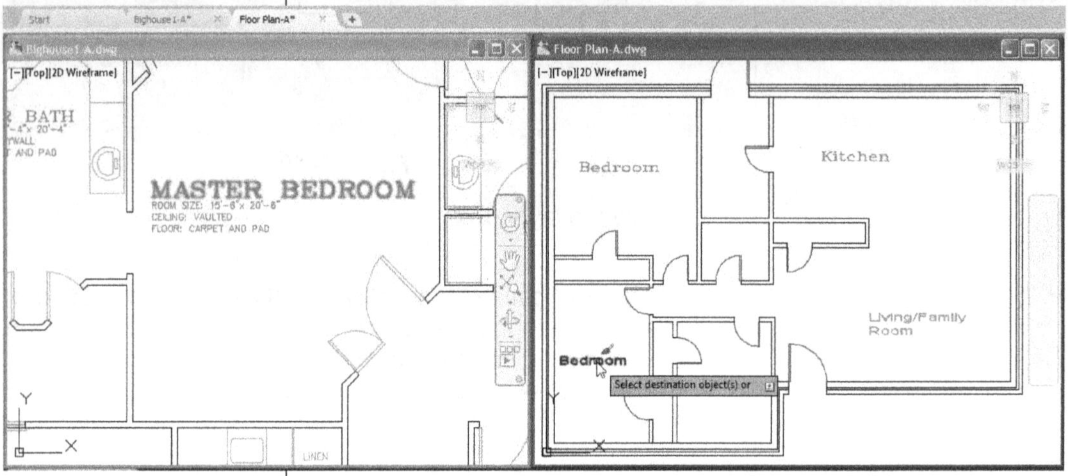

Figure 2–21

8. Make **Bighouse1-A.dwg** the active window by clicking in it. Right-click and select **Clipboard>Copy with Base Point**. For the basepoint, select the corner of the walls behind the fireplace (in the master bedroom). Select the fireplace (they might be separate objects) and the short diagonal walls that frame it, as shown in Figure 2–22. Press <Enter>.

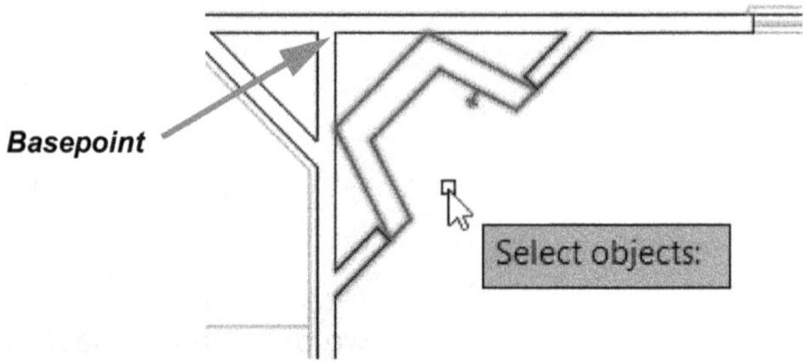

Figure 2–22

9. In the *File Tabs* bar, select the *Floor Plan-A* tab to switch to it and make it active. Right-click and select **Clipboard>Paste**. For the insertion point, select the top left corner of the larger bedroom to paste the fireplace there.

10. Close both drawings. Do not save changes.

11. Maximize the Start window.

2.2 Object Creation, Selection, and Visibility

Object Creation

You can use **Add Selected** to create new objects of the same type and properties as the selected object. Select an object, right-click, and select **Add Selected** as shown in Figure 2–23. The AutoCAD software launches the command that was used to create the selected object and sets some of the properties (such as the layer or color) to be the same as the original object.

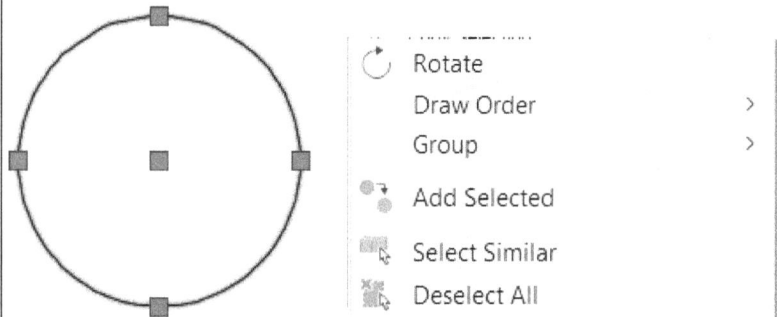

Figure 2–23

Selecting Similar Objects

You can use **Select Similar** (as shown in Figure 2–23) to select an object and automatically select other objects of the same type and properties at the same time. For example, if you select a red rectangle on the layer **Walls**, all of the other red rectangles on the layer **Walls** are also selected.

How To: Select Similar Objects

1. Select an object.
2. Right-click and select **Select Similar**. All of the other objects that match the settings are selected.

- If you select more than one object and then use **Select Similar**, all of the objects that match the properties of all of the selected objects are selected.

How To: Modify Select Similar Settings

1. Without any object selected, at the Command Line, type or dynamically input **selectsimilar**.
2. At the Select objects prompt, press <Down arrow> and select **Settings**.

3. In the Select Similar Settings dialog box (shown in Figure 2–24), select the property types by which you want to filter the selection set.

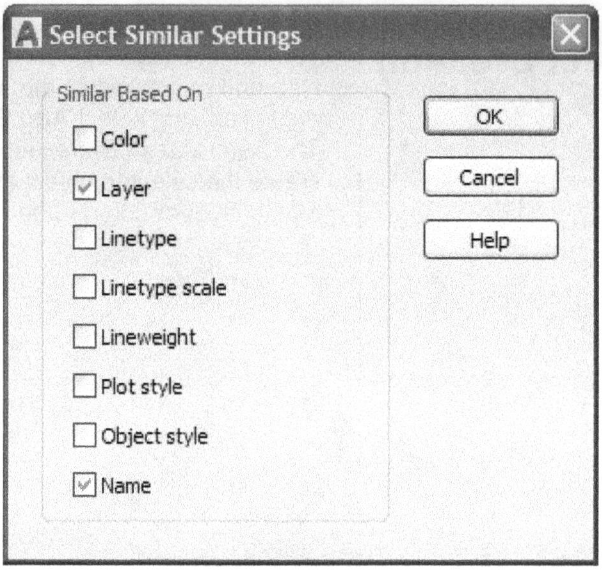

Figure 2–24

- The properties that are set in the dialog box are used to filter the selection process. The objects that are selected have the same properties.

- If you clear the **Name** option in the dialog box, the command looks for all of the objects that match the properties no matter what type they are.

Object Selection Cycling

If you need to select an object in a location in which many objects overlap, you can use **Object Selection Cycling**. When it is toggled on, and you hover the cursor over an area where some objects are overlapping, ⊡ displays, indicating that more than one object can be selected. Clicking on the object displays the Selection dialog box where you can select an object from the list, as shown in Figure 2–25.

In the Status Bar,

(Selection Cycling) must be toggled on for this to work.

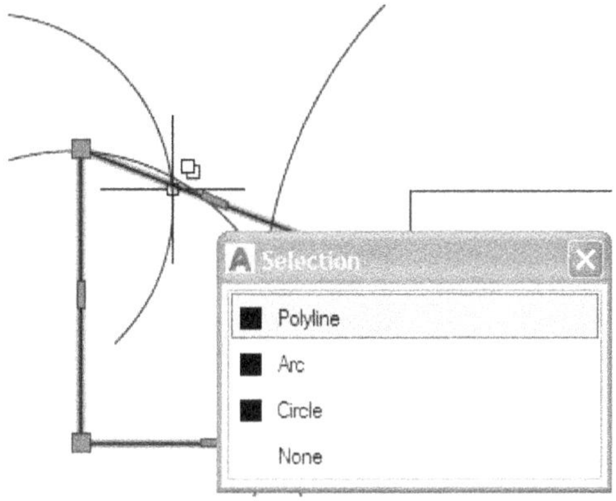

Figure 2–25

How To: Use Object Selection Cycling

1. In the Status Bar, toggle on (Selection Cycling).
2. Hover the cursor over some overlapping objects close to where the objects intersect. ⊡ displays, indicating that there are overlapping objects.
3. Click to open the Selection dialog box.
4. Select the object that you want to use.

Object Visibility

You can control whether objects are displayed or hidden in the drawing. The **Isolate Objects**, **Hide Objects**, and **End Object Isolation** commands control this display.

Isolate Objects	Select the objects that you want to isolate, right-click, and select **Isolate>Isolate Objects**. The selected objects display and all other objects are hidden.
Hide Objects	Select the objects that you want to hide, right-click, and select **Isolate>Hide Objects**. The selected objects are hidden.
End Object Isolation	Right-click anywhere in the drawing window and select **Isolate>End Object Isolation**. All hidden objects display.

- If a drawing contains hidden or isolated objects, (Unisolate Objects) (highlighted) displays in the Status Bar.

- If a drawing does not contain hidden objects, (Isolate Objects) displays in the Status Bar.

You can also use

🔲○ (Isolate/Hide/
Unisolate) in the Status
Bar.

How To: Isolate or Hide Objects

1. Right-click and select **Isolate>Isolate Objects** or **Hide Objects**, as shown in Figure 2–26.

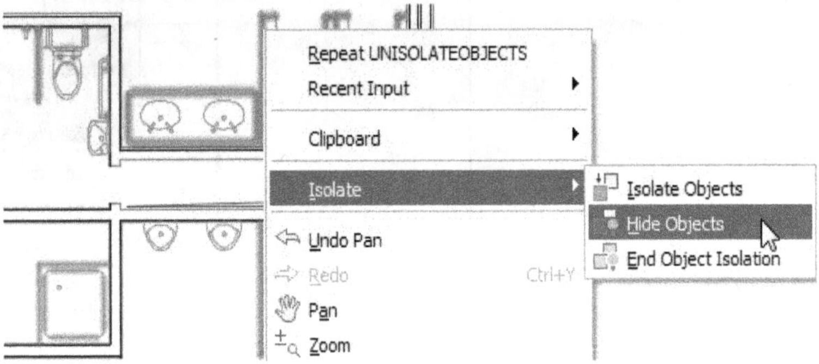

Figure 2–26

2. If you selected objects before starting the command, the objects are hidden or isolated. If you did not select objects, you are prompted to select them.

3. To display the isolated or hidden objects, right-click and select **Isolate>End Object Isolation** or click on

   🔲○ (Unisolate Objects) in the Status bar, and select **End Object Isolation**.

• If objects are already hidden or isolated, you can add additional objects to the isolated selection set by clicking on

   the 🔲○ (Unisolate Objects) in the Status bar, and selecting **Isolate Additional Objects**, as shown in Figure 2–27.

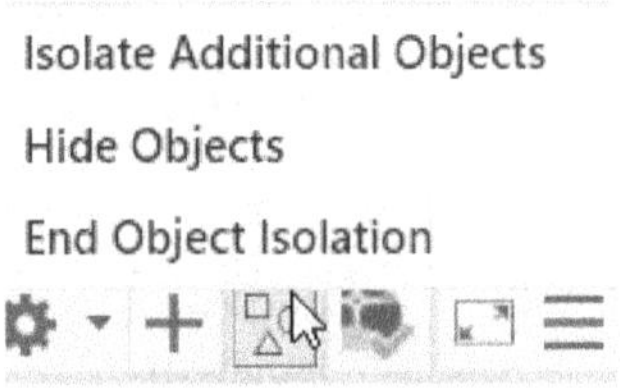

Figure 2–27

Setting Transparency

Transparency can be applied to objects similar to applying other properties (such as Layer, Color, or Linetype). It can be set individually, ByLayer, or ByBlock. It is very useful when displaying hatches, as shown in Figure 2–28.

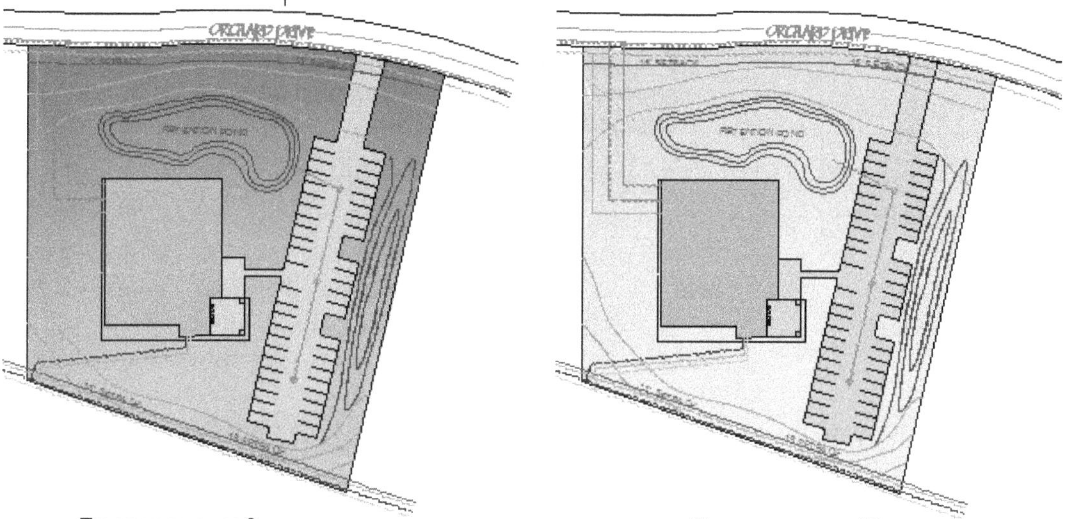

Transparency = 0 *Transparency = 50*

Figure 2–28

- Transparency values vary from **0** (least transparent) to **90** (most transparent).

- When you are creating or editing objects, you can set the transparency in the *Home* tab>expanded Properties panel. You can also expand the Transparency drop-down list and select one of the options shown in Figure 2–29.

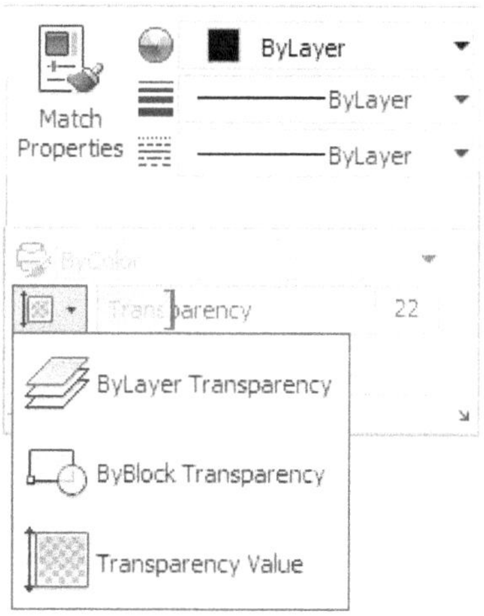

Figure 2–29

- Transparency is also available in the Properties palette when objects have been selected.

- You can toggle ▦ (Transparency) on and off in the Status Bar.

- Transparency can be set in the Layer Properties Manager, as shown in Figure 2–30. It can also be modified by layer in a viewport.

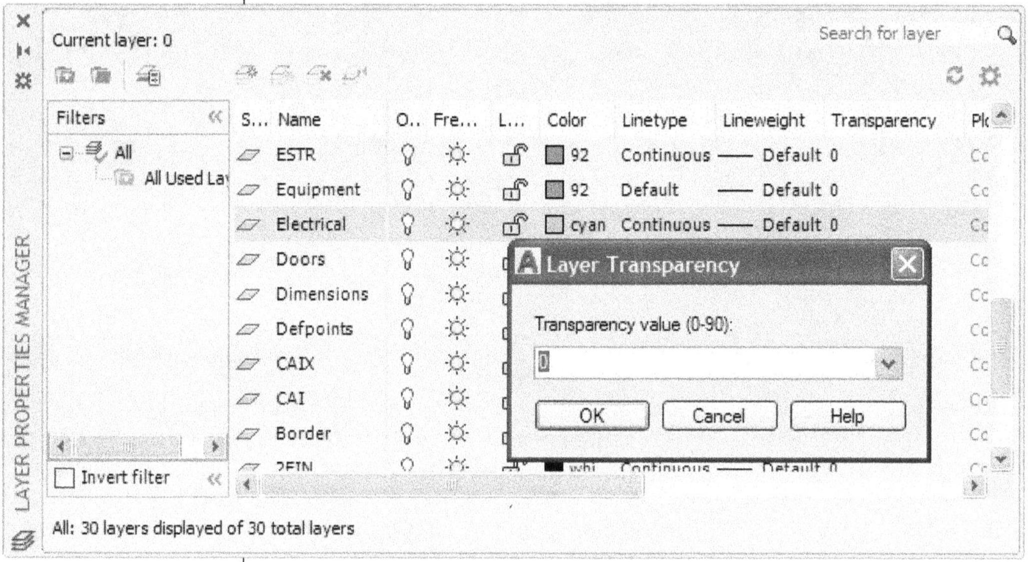

Figure 2–30

- Transparency can be set for **Match Properties**, as shown in Figure 2–31, and for **Quick Select** and **Filter**.

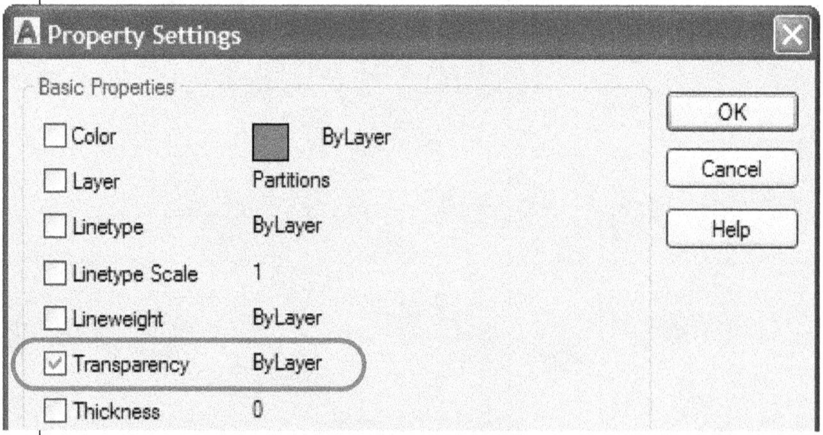

Figure 2–31

- To plot transparent objects, select the **Plot transparency** option shown in Figure 2–32, in either the Plot dialog box or Page Setup. This is toggled off by default because the file must be converted into raster for the transparency to plot.

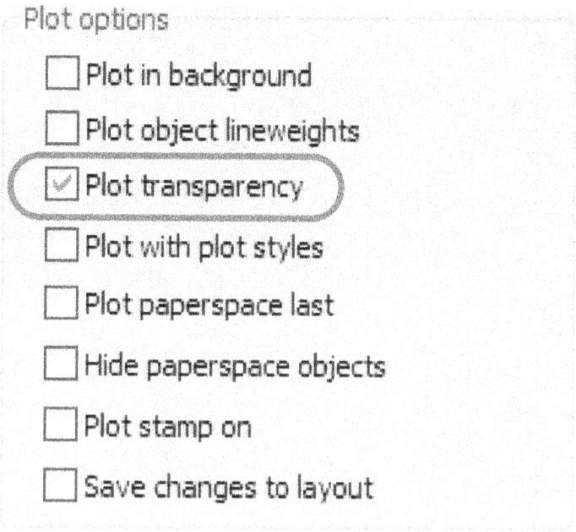

Plot options

- [ ] Plot in background
- [ ] Plot object lineweights
- [x] Plot transparency
- [ ] Plot with plot styles
- [ ] Plot paperspace last
- [ ] Hide paperspace objects
- [ ] Plot stamp on
- [ ] Save changes to layout

Figure 2–32

Practice 2d

Object Creation, Selection, and Visibility

Practice Objective

- Modify the display of objects using various commands and options.

In this practice, you will modify the way objects display in a drawing using **Select Similar**, **Hide Objects**, and **Isolate Objects**. You will also modify the display of objects using the **Transparency** option.

Task 1 - Use selection and visibility tools.

1. Open **Office-Plan1-A.dwg** from your practice files folder.

2. In the Status bar, ensure that ⬚ (Isolate Objects) is displayed. If not, select it from the ≡ (Customization) list.

3. Select one of the double sided corner desks on the layer Cubicles (blue color).

4. Right-click and select **Select Similar**. All of the double sided corner desks are selected, as shown in Figure 2–33. Press <Esc> to exit the command.

*Some of the objects you will be selecting throughout this task might not be blocks, but instead consist of lines, circles, etc. Therefore, you might need to perform the **Select Similar** command several times.*

Figure 2–33

There are different types of red desks in the drawing.

5. Select one of the red desks and one of the red chairs and use **Select Similar**. All of the chairs are selected along with a few desks (which are similar to the original one you selected).

6. Right-click and select **Isolate>Hide Objects**. Note how the ⬚○△ (Unisolate Objects) is highlighted in the Status bar.

You can also click on ⬚○△ *(Unisolate Objects) and select **Hide Objects**.*

7. Use **Select Similar** to select the rest of the furniture (red colored objects). Hide them as well.

8. How would you make it easier to select all of the furniture in the drawing?

You can also click on ⬚○△ *(Unisolate Objects) and select **End Object Isolation**.*

9. Right-click and select **Isolate>End Object Isolation** to unhide the objects.

Task 2 - Modify object transparency.

1. Toggle on the layer **Hatching**.

2. In the Status bar, toggle on 🎟 (Transparency).

3. Select one of the hatches.

4. In the *Hatch Editor* contextual tab>Properties panel, for the Hatch **Transparency** option, use the slider bar to increase it and note that it lightens the selected hatch.

5. Open the Layer Properties Manager.

6. In the *Hatching* row, set the *Transparency* value to **50**, as shown in Figure 2–34.

S...	Name	O..	Fre...	L...	Color	Linetype	Lineweight	Transpar...	Plot St...
⬭	0	♀	☼	🔓	whi...	Continuous	— Default	0	Color_7
⬭	Border	♀	☼	🔓	blue	Continuous	— Default	0	Color_5
⬭	Cubicles	♀	☼	🔓	132	Continuous	— Default	0	Color_1
⬭	Defpoints	♀	☼	🔓	whi...	Continuous	— Default	0	Color_7
⬭	Dimensions	♀	☼	🔓	red	Continuous	— Default	0	Color_1
⬭	Doors	♀	☼	🔓	40	Continuous	— Default	0	Color_40
⬭	Electrical	♀	☼	🔓	132	Continuous	— Default	0	Color_1
⬭	Furniture	♀	☼	🔓	red	Continuous	— Default	0	Color_1
⬭	Hatching	♀	☼	🔓	red	Continuous	— Defau	50	Color_1
⬭	Headers	♀	☼	🔓	whi...	Continuous	— Default	0	Color_7
⬭	HVAC	♀	☼	🔓	40	Continuous	— Default	0	Color_40

Figure 2–34

7. All of the other hatches (except the one selected in Step 3) are lightened because they are all on the same layer, and each of their *Transparency* options is set to **ByLayer**.

8. Save and close the drawing.

2.3 Controlling the Draw Order

As you are annotating a drawing, you might need to adjust the order of the overlapping objects. For example, you might have hatching on top of text but actually need to have the text on top of the hatching, as shown in Figure 2–35. You might also need to have a boundary around the text so that it stands out more prominently.

This Obj   This Object on Top

Figure 2–35

You can use several tools to make these adjustments, three of which include the following:

Draw Order

You can also select a draw order by right-clicking on an object and selecting Draw Order.

When you create new objects, they are created on top of existing objects in the drawing by default. Some objects, such as a wide polyline or hatch, can cover objects that were drawn earlier.

- You can select the **Draw Order** tool in the *Home* tab> expanded Modify panel.

- The various Draw Order options are listed as shown in Figure 2–36. You can change the objects to a different draw order by selecting the required option in the drop-down list.

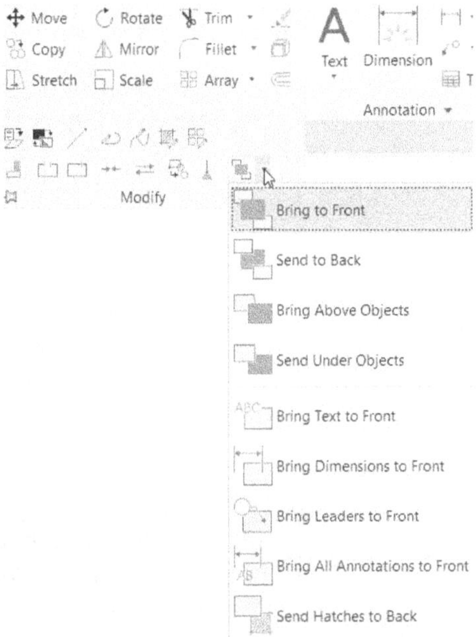

Figure 2–36

A few of the most commonly used options include:

Icon	Description
(Bring to Front)	Puts the object at the top of the drawing order (in front of all of the other objects).
Send to Back)	Puts the object at the bottom of the drawing order (behind all of the other objects).
(Bring All Annotations to Front)	Puts all of the text, leader, and dimension objects at the top of the drawing order (in front of all of the other objects).
(Send Hatches to Back)	Puts hatches at the bottom of the drawing order (behind all of the other objects).

• When you assign a Draw Order to an object it maintains its position even after editing.

• A copied object inherits the Draw Order status of the original object.

Draw Order of Hatching

You can set the draw order of hatches while creating them by selecting an option in the *Hatch Creation* contextual tab> expanded Options panel. The **Send Behind Boundary** option makes it easier to select the hatch boundary after the hatching has been applied. The other options are shown in Figure 2–37.

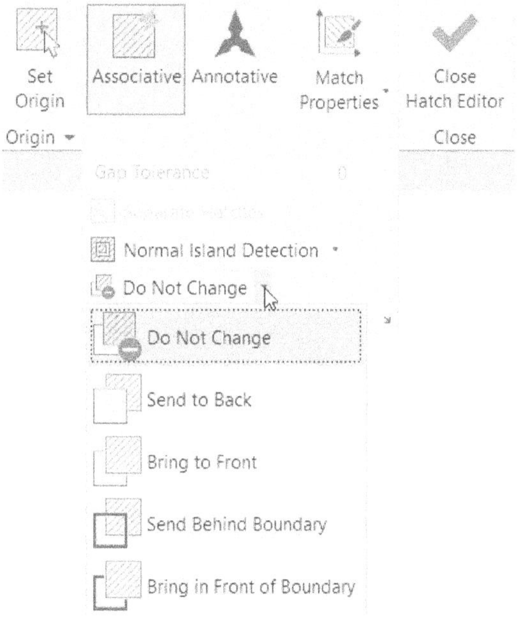

Figure 2–37

Masking Annotation Objects

You can mask objects behind text and dimension text. This is useful when you need to place text in front of other objects but do not want to trim the objects where they overlap, as shown in Figure 2–38.

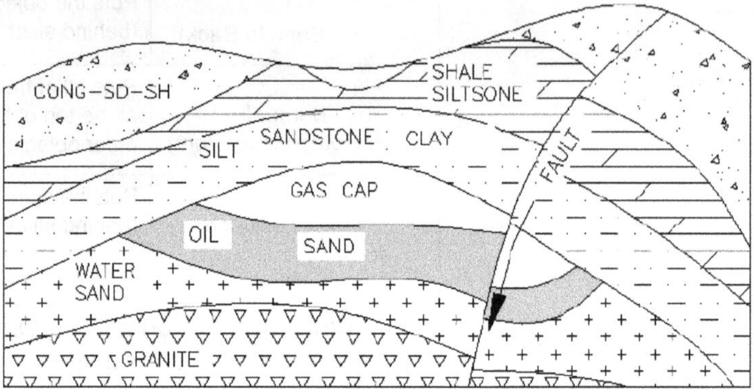

Figure 2–38

- You can select A (Background Mask) in the *Text Editor* contextual tab>Style panel.

- In the *Multiline Text* field, right-click in the Edit window and select **Background Mask**. The Background Mask dialog box opens, as shown in Figure 2–39.

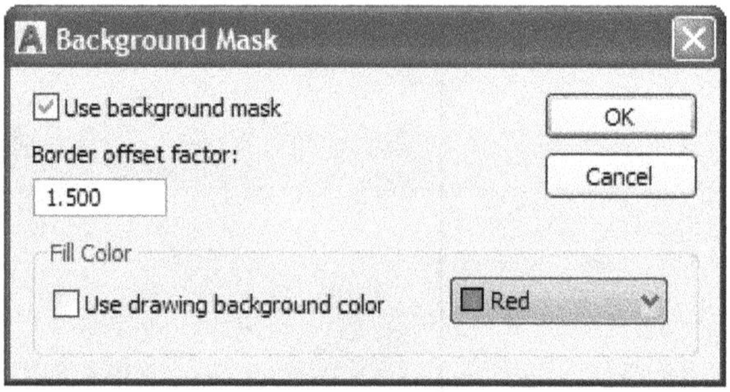

Figure 2–39

- You can select **Use background mask** and then set the **Border offset factor** (the space around the text) and the **Fill color**. You can use the background of the drawing or any other color as the fill color.

- The *Border offset factor* also sets the location of the text frame which can be toggled on using the Properties palette, as shown in Figure 2–40.

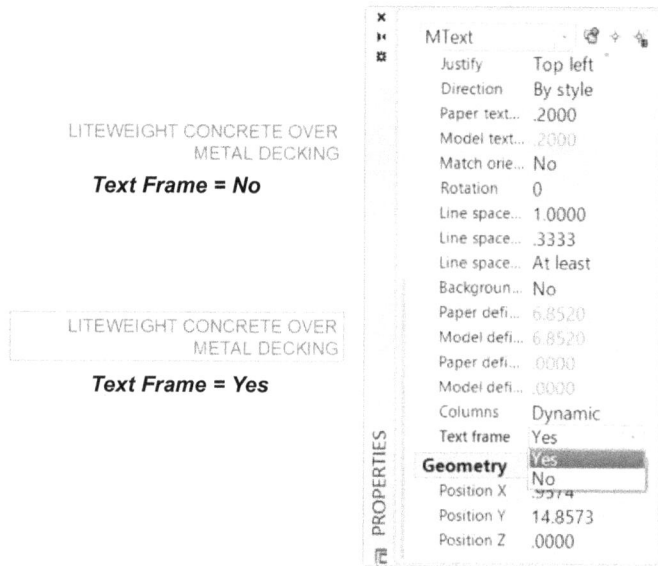

LITEWEIGHT CONCRETE OVER
METAL DECKING

Text Frame = No

LITEWEIGHT CONCRETE OVER
METAL DECKING

Text Frame = Yes

MText	
Justify	Top left
Direction	By style
Paper text...	.2000
Model text...	.2000
Match orie...	No
Rotation	0
Line space...	1.0000
Line space...	.3333
Line space...	At least
Backgroun...	No
Paper defi...	6.8520
Model defi...	6.8520
Paper defi...	.0000
Model defi...	.0000
Columns	Dynamic
Text frame	Yes
Geometry	Yes / No
Position X	.9574
Position Y	14.8573
Position Z	.0000

Figure 2–40

- You can add a mask to existing text or modify an existing mask. Open the text in the Text Editor again and right-click to open the Background Mask dialog box.

- Dimension text can be assigned a background mask in the dimension style. Set the *Fill color* in the *Text* tab in the Dimension Style dialog box to use the required mask, as shown in Figure 2–41.

Modify Dimension Style: Standard

Lines | Symbols and Arrows | Text | Fit | Primary Ur

Text appearance

Text style: Standard

Text color: ByBlock

Fill color: Background

Figure 2–41

In the Home tab> expanded Modify panel, in the Draw Order drop-down list, you can use ᴬᴮᶜ⌷ (Bring Text to Front) and ⌷ (Bring Dimensions to Front).

- Text and dimension text objects need to be in front in the Draw Order for the text mask to be visible. You can move all of the text and dimensions to the front by typing **texttofront** in the Command Line. You can bring **Text**, **Dimensions**, **Leaders**, or **All**, to the front, as shown in Figure 2–42.

Figure 2–42

Adding a Wipeout

Another useful tool for overlapping objects, hatches, or other images is **Wipeout**. A wipeout puts a blank image on top of objects in an area that you want to mask or hide. For example, you could use a wipeout to mask objects behind text (as shown in Figure 2–43) or to break a dimension line where another one passes over it.

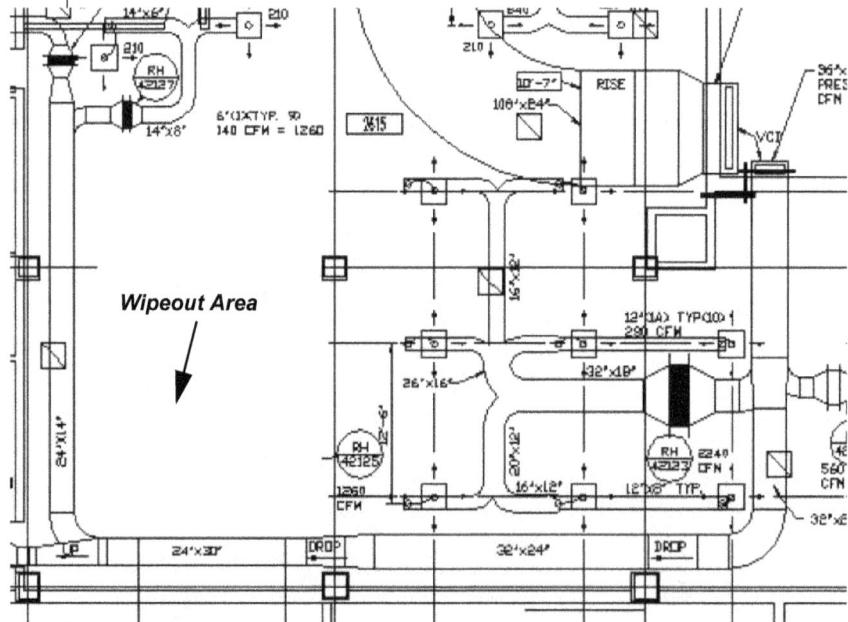

Wipeout Area

Figure 2–43

- A wipeout can be defined in two ways: using a polyline as the outline for the wipeout or picking points.

How To: Create a Wipeout

1. In the ribbon, *Home* tab>expanded Draw panel, or in the

    Annotate tab>Markup panel, click (Wipeout).
2. Pick points to define the boundary of the wipeout or press <Enter> to select a polyline.
3. If you select a polyline, you are prompted to erase it.
4. Press <Enter> to finish selecting points and create the wipeout.
5. Use the **Draw Order** command to move objects above or below the wipeout.
6. In the **Wipeout** command, use the **Frames** option to toggle off the frames around the wipeouts when you are finished, as shown in Figure 2–44.

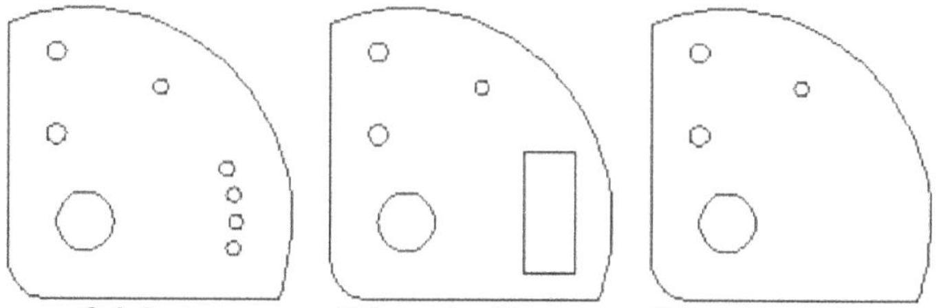

Original   Wipeout w/Frames   Wipeout w/o Frames

Figure 2–44

Options

First Point	Enables you to pick points to define the area to mask.
Polyline	Enables you to use an existing polyline to mask the area. The polyline must be closed, must be made of straight line segments, and cannot have a width. Only keep the polyline if you need to use it for plotting purposes.
Frames	Toggles the frames around all of the wipeouts in the drawing on, off, or to be displayed in the drawing window without being printed on the drawing sheets. If you need to select wipeout objects, toggle the frames **On** or **Visible**.

Practice 2e

Controlling the Draw Order

Practice Objective

- Control the display of objects by changing their overlapping order, adding a background mask to text, and covering part of the drawing with a Wipeout object.

In this practice, you will use the **Draw Order** command to control the display of an object, add a background mask to text, and add a Wipeout to cover part of a drawing, as shown in Figure 2–45.

Figure 2–45

1. Open **Subdivision-F.dwg** from the practice files folder.

2. Note a solid yellow hatch in the right side of the plan. In the *Home* tab>expanded Modify panel, expand the Draw Order flyout and click (Send Hatches to Back). The buildings and roads that were hidden behind the hatch are now displayed, because the hatch is now behind them.

3. In the *Home* tab>expanded Modify panel, expand the Draw Order flyout and click (Send to Back) and select various buildings in Zone 3B (the yellow hatched area). Press <Enter> to exit the command. The selected buildings disappear as they are now hidden behind the hatch.

4. Zoom in on the text **ZONE 3B** text in the upper part of the yellow hatch area. The lines of the buildings make the text difficult to read.

*Alternatively, right-click inside the Text Editor and select **Background Mask**.*

5. Double-click on the text to open the Text Editor. In the *Text Editor* contextual tab>Style panel, select A (Background Mask).

6. In the Background Mask dialog box, select **Use background mask** and **Use drawing background color** for the *Fill Color*. Click **OK** to apply the settings. Close the *Text Editor* contextual tab. Note a background rectangular mask for the text.

7. Draw a closed polyline around one of the blocks of buildings and some portion of the street in Zone 3B, as shown in Figure 2–46.

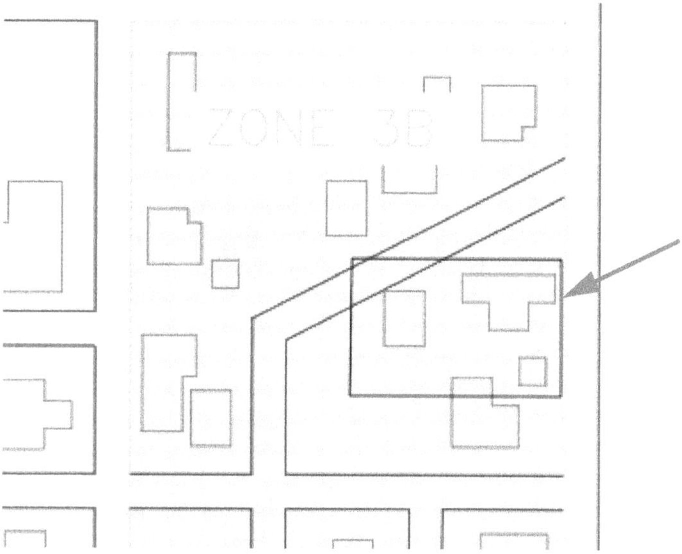

Figure 2–46

8. In the *Home* tab>expanded Draw panel, click (Wipeout).

9. Press <Enter> for the **Polyline** option and select the polyline that you just drew. Select **Yes** at the prompt to erase the polyline. The wipeout masks all of the objects enclosed in the polyline because it is drawn on top of them.

10. Start the **Wipeout** command again. Type **F** and press <Enter> to use the **Frames** option. Select **OFF** to toggle off the frame.

11. In the *Home* tab>expanded Modify panel, expand the Draw Order drop-down list and click (Bring to Front). Select anywhere on the street that is covered by the wipeout. Press <Enter>. Note that the street becomes visible over the wipeout.

12. Save and close the drawing.

2.4 Selecting and Removing Objects

When you start most editing commands, the crosshairs display as a small selection box along with the Select objects prompt, as shown in Figure 2–47.

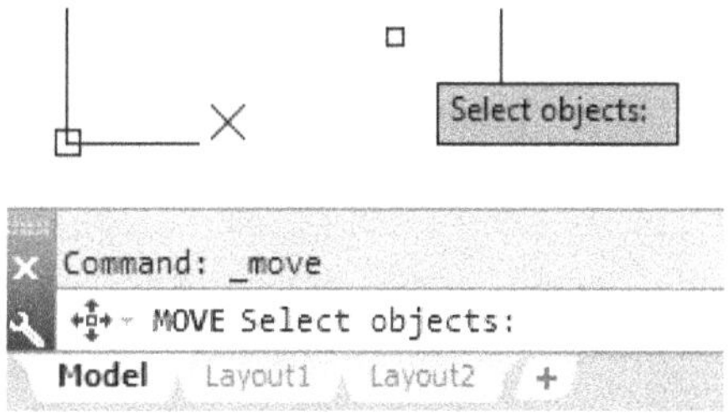

Figure 2–47

How To: Select Objects

1. After starting an editing command (such as **Move**, **Copy**, **Scale** etc), you are required to select the objects and the cursor crosshairs change to a selection box. Hover the small selection box over an object. The object is highlighted in a thicker line weight.
2. Click to select the object, which then highlights in blue, as shown in Figure 2–48.

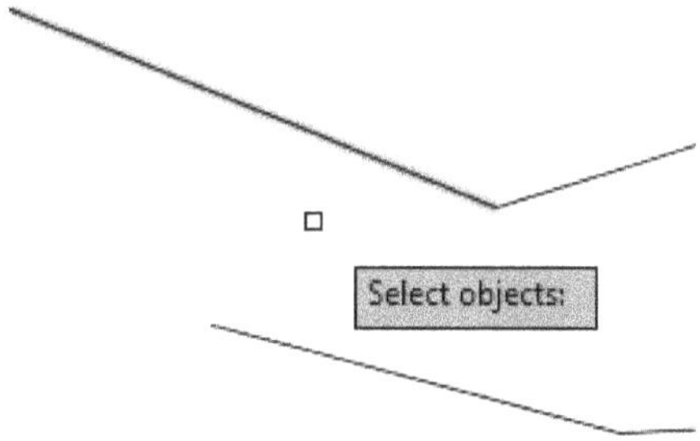

Figure 2–48

3. The cursor continues to display as the small selection box. You can click on another object to add to the selection.
4. Continue selecting objects if you want to add more objects to the selection.

   • If you need to remove an object from a set of selected objects, press <Shift> and click on the required object. With <Shift>+click, only a single object is removed while keeping the rest of the objects selected.

5. When all of the objects have been selected, press <Enter> or right-click to exit the *Select objects:* prompt and continue with the command.

Implied Selection

You can select individual objects or draw a box, line, or lasso around multiple objects to select them together. When using any of the selection methods, the objects to be selected are highlighted in a thicker line weight before the selection is completed. Once the objects have been selected, they are highlighted in blue and a thicker line weight.

*You can also start a Window or Crossing selection by typing **W** or **C** at the Select objects: prompt. With this method, it does not matter how you select the points to define the selection box.*

• **Window selection:** If you click to select the first point and then move the cursor to the right, a blue area with a solid border displays, as shown on the left in Figure 2–49. Any objects that are completely inside the boundary are selected.

• **Crossing selection:** If you click to select the first point and then move the cursor to the left, a green area with a dashed border displays, as shown on the right in Figure 2–49. Any objects inside or crossing the boundary are selected.

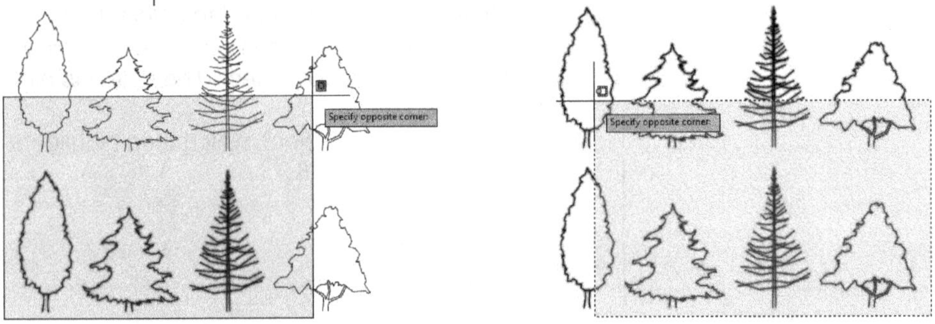

Window (blue)   *Crossing (green)*

Figure 2–49

• **Lasso selection:** If you click and hold the mouse button to select the first point and then drag the cursor to the left or right, a lasso shape displays. If you drag to the right, the selection area displays in blue with a solid outline, as shown on the left in Figure 2–50. Objects are selected as they would be when using a Window selection. If you drag to the left, the selection area displays in green with a dashed border, as shown on the right in Figure 2–50. Objects are selected as they would be when using the Crossing selection. You can use the Lasso selection to create non-rectangular shapes. You can also press <Spacebar> to toggle between the Window, Crossing, and Fence selection modes when using the Lasso selection.

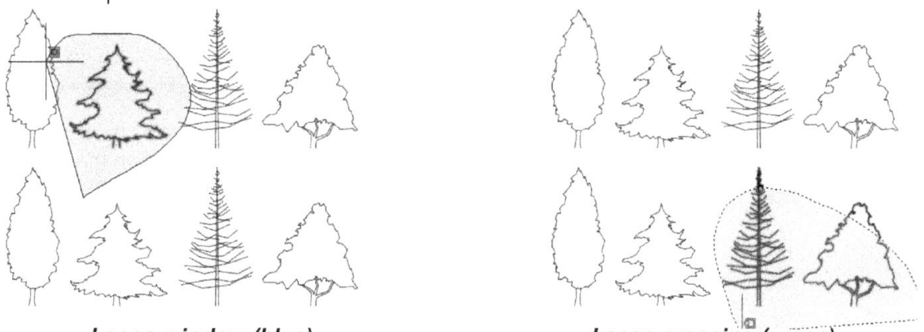

Lasso window (blue)   *Lasso crossing (green)*

Figure 2–50

- **Fence selection:** You can also type **F** at the *Select objects:* prompt to start a Fence style object selection in which you pick a first point, and then continue to select additional points as if creating line segments. When you have finished creating the fence, press <Enter> to make the selection. Any object that the fence crosses is also selected.

- You can also start a Window or Crossing Polygon selection by typing **WP** or **CP** at the *Select objects:* prompt. With this method, you pick a first point, and then various other points to define an irregularly shaped area.

- You can clear a selected object from a group of objects by pressing <Shift> and selecting the object. This enables you to select a group of objects quickly with a Window, Crossing, or Lasso, and then clear any object that you do not want to include in the selection set.

- You can also type **R** at the *Select objects:* prompt and use any selection method to clear objects from the selection set. Then type **A** at the *Select objects:* prompt to return to adding objects to the selection set.

- A variety of selection methods can be combined in a single command to build the selection set.

Practice 2f | Selecting Objects

Practice Objective

• Select objects using the various selection methods.

In this practice, you will use the Crossing, Window, and Lasso methods to select objects shown in Figure 2–51, for use with an editing command.

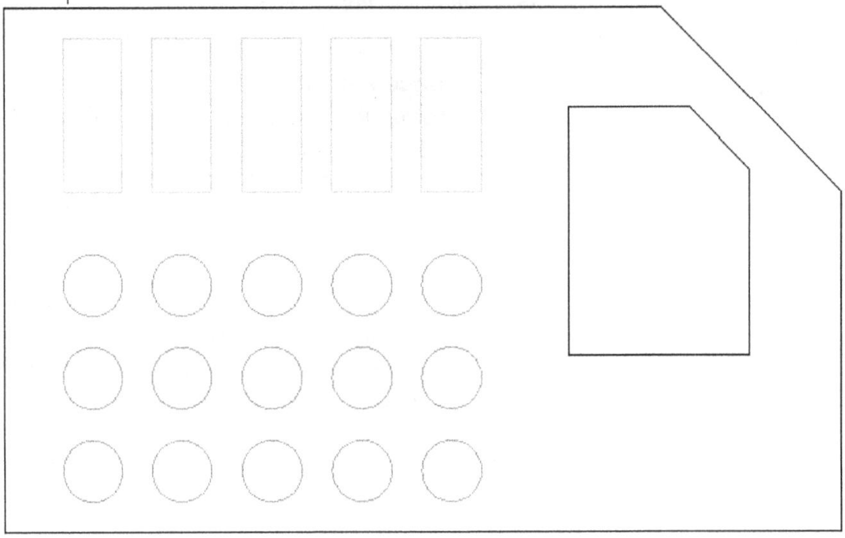

Figure 2–51

1. Open **Select.dwg** from your practice files folder.

2. Start an editing command, such as **Move,** by clicking

   ✛ (Move) in *Home* tab>Modify panel.

3. At the *Select objects:* prompt, click in an empty area near the right side of the top row of circles and then move the cursor left and down to create a crossing window (green), as shown on the left in Figure 2–52. Note that the objects that touch the crossing boundary are highlighted.

4. Click to complete the selection. Note that the selected objects display in blue with a thicker line weight, as shown on the right in Figure 2–52.

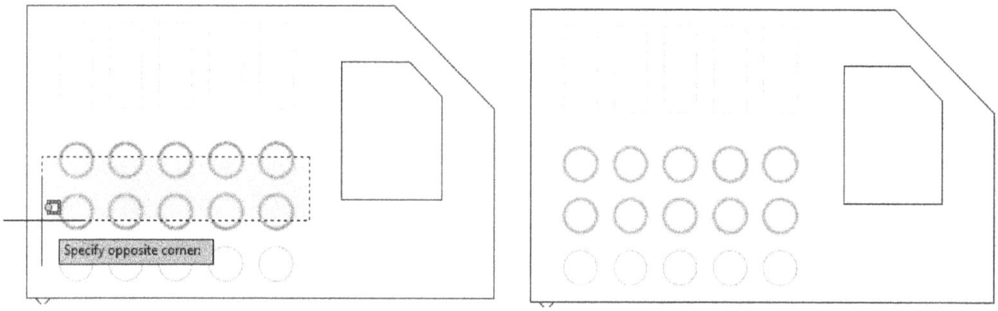

Crossing (green)   *Selected objects*

Figure 2–52

5. Press <Esc> to abort the command and leave the circles intact.

6. Start the ⁺ᵗ⁺ (Move) command again. At the *Select objects:* prompt, click in an empty area near the left side of the top edge of the shape and then move the cursor diagonally right to create a selection window (blue), as shown in Figure 2–53. Note that the objects that touch the window boundary are not highlighted and only the objects completely inside the window boundary are selected, as shown in Figure 2–53.

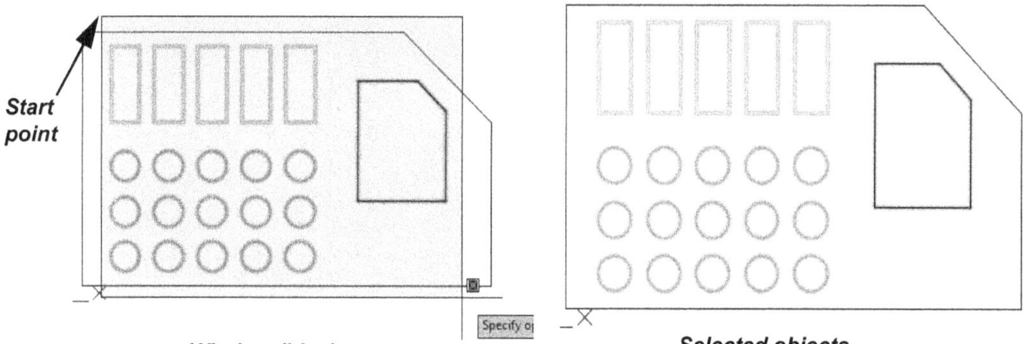

Window (blue)   *Selected objects*

Figure 2–53

7. Hold <Shift> and create a window around the top row of rectangles to remove them from the selection.

8. Click on the middle rectangle to add it to the selection set.

9. Press <Esc> to abort the command and leave the geometry intact.

10. Close the drawing. Do not save changes.

Chapter 3

Managing Layers

Exam Objectives Covered in This Chapter

- 1.3.a Save, restore, and manage layer settings using layer states
- 1.3.b Use layer filters to control which layers are listed in the Layer Properties Manager folder

3.1 What Are Layers?

The AutoCAD software enables you to create an infinite number of layers in a drawing to organize the objects. Similar to overlays or transparencies, layers assist with editing, presentation, and system performance.

Layers organize a drawing into logical categories. For example, in mechanical drafting, views, hidden lines, sections, symbols, notes, and dimensions might be placed on separate layers. In an architectural drawing, there would be layers for walls, furniture, plumbing features, etc., as shown in Figure 3–1.

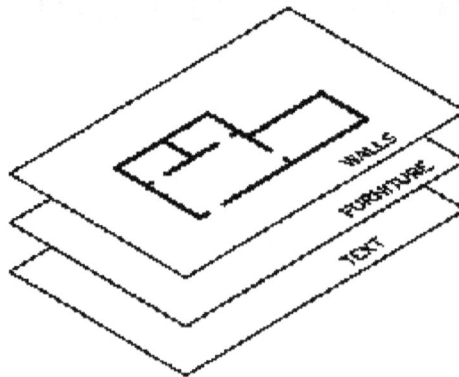

Figure 3–1

- The *current layer* is the layer on which newly drawn objects, such as lines, circles, and text, are placed.

- A color, linetype, and lineweight are assigned to each layer. When a layer is made current, you are automatically drawing in its assigned color, linetype, and lineweight.

- By toggling layers *on* or *off*, you can control which part of the drawing is displayed or is plotted.

- The layer **0** is present in every drawing and cannot be removed or renamed. It is normally not used like the other layers and has special properties for blocks.

Setting the Current Layer

The current layer displays in the Layer Control in the *Home* tab>Layers panel, as shown on the left in Figure 3–2. Selecting the current layer name displays the drop-down list containing all of the existing layers in the current drawing, as shown on the right in Figure 3–2.

Current layer

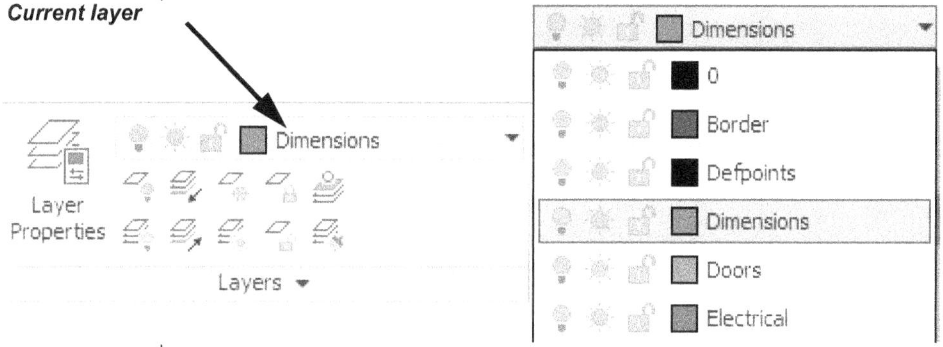

Figure 3–2

- To make a layer active, select its name in the Layer Control drop-down list.

Using ⬚ (Make Current) indicates the active layer name in the Command Line as well.

- Another way to make a layer active is to select an object in the drawing and then in the *Home* tab>Layers panel, click ⬚ (Make Current). This makes the selected objects' layer active. You can also click ⬚ (Make Current) first and then select an object.

- For easy access to various Layer tools, you can display the Layer Control bar in the Quick Access Toolbar, as shown in Figure 3–3. By default, the Layer Control does not display in the Quick Access Toolbar, but you can display it by selecting **Layer** in the ⬚ (Quick Access drop-down menu).

Figure 3–3

Hint: Properties Panel

You can change the layer and *color*, *linetype*, *lineweight*, *plot style*, and *transparency* of individual objects. In the *Home* tab, the Properties panel enables you to set these characteristics for objects (as shown in Figure 3–4), just as the Layer Control enables you to set the layer.

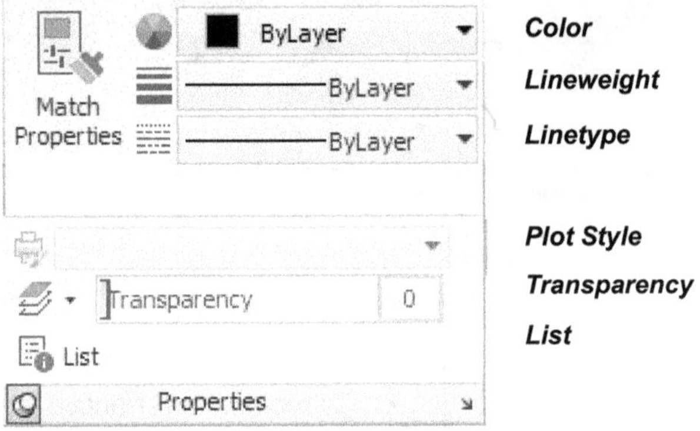

Figure 3–4

Normally, these properties are set to **ByLayer**, indicating that the objects do not have a specific color, linetype, lineweight, plot style, and transparency of their own. Instead, the layer that the objects are drawn on defines their properties.

Although you can assign colors, linetypes, lineweights, plot style, and transparency to individual objects, it is usually best to let the object take its properties from its layer. This method ensures consistency and control over properties. You can easily change the color, lineweight, linetype, plot style, and transparency of all of the objects on a specific layer by changing the properties of the layer.

3.2 Layer States

The state of the layer determines how the objects on it are displayed and selected.

- The following three aspects of a layer's state can be changed in the Layer Control by selecting the appropriate symbol, as shown on the left in Figure 3–5.

- You can also use an object in the drawing to change its layer state by using the appropriate icon in the Layers panel, as shown on the right in Figure 3–5.

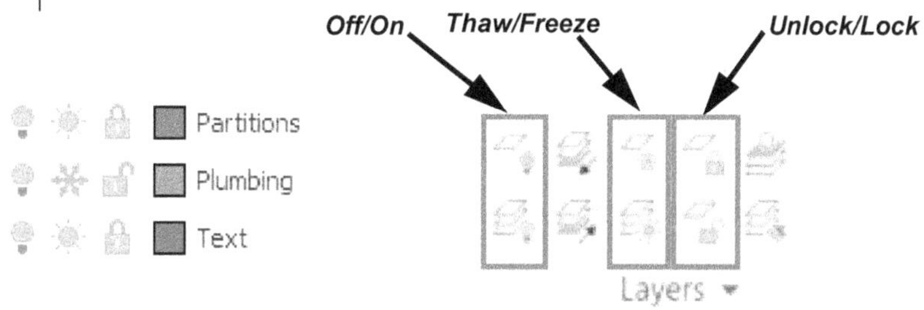

Figure 3–5

On/Off

A layer can be toggled on (displayed) or toggled off (hidden). Toggling a layer off is like temporarily removing it from the drawing. Layers that are toggled off are not displayed and are not plotted.

- The current layer can be toggled off, but the software warns you with an alert that provides you with options of either turning the current layer off or keeping it on. If the current layer is toggled off, you can draw but cannot see what you are drawing.

Thaw/ Freeze

Layers that are not needed or displayed for a long time should be frozen. Freezing a layer is similar to toggling it off, except that the layer does not require calculation time when regeneration occurs.

- You cannot freeze the current layer and a frozen layer cannot be made current.

- The objects on the frozen layers are not displayed in the drawing and those objects are not regenerated as well.

- Once you thaw a layer, you might need to perform a regeneration operation to display the layer.

Lock/ Unlock

Objects on layers that are locked can be viewed but not edited. When you hover the cursor over them, a small lock icon displays. By default, locked layers are also slightly grayed out.

- Locking a layer is useful when you do not want to accidentally edit the objects in the layer.

Returning a Layer to Its Previous State

You sometimes need to change the state of layers to edit a drawing and then change them back to their previous state. After you have changed the current layer or state of layers, in the

Home tab>expanded Layers panel, use (Layer Previous) to return to the previous layer settings.

Practice 3a

Working with Layers and Layer States

Practice Objectives

- Draw objects on specific layers.
- Change the state of a layer using Layer Control.

In this practice, you will draw objects on specific layers and then change the state of the layers.

Task 1 - Draw on and change layers.

In this task, you will draw an object on specific layers, as shown in Figure 3–6.

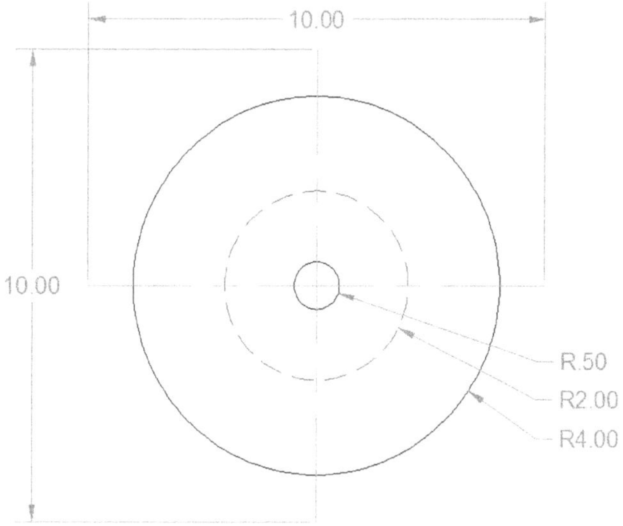

Figure 3–6

1. In the Application Menu, click **New**. Start a new drawing based on **Mech-Inches.dwt**, which is located in your practice files folder.

2. In the *Home* tab>Layers panel, expand the Layer Control and select **Center** to set it as the current layer.

3. Draw a horizontal line, **10 units** long near the center of the screen. Note that the line has a centerline style (dashed).

For easy access to the Layer tools, display the Layer Controls in the Quick Access Toolbar

*(select **Layer** in the ▼ drop-down menu).*

4. Draw a vertical line, **10 units** long separate from the line you just drew. Move it so that its midpoint is on the midpoint of the other line.

5. Change the current layer to **Object** by selecting it in the Layer Control.

6. Draw a circle with a radius of **4** with its center point at the intersection of the two centerlines that you drew. The circle should be white on a black background (or black if the background is white).

7. Change the current layer to **Hidden**.

8. Draw another circle with a radius of **2** at the same center point as the first circle. It should be blue/green with a hidden line style.

9. In the *Home* tab>Layers panel, click 🖾 (Make Current) and select the largest circle. The current layer changes to **Object**.

10. Draw another circle with a **0.5** radius at the same center point. It should be white (or black) and continuous linetype of the **Object** layer.

11. Save the drawing as **Wheel.dwg**.

Task 2 - Change the layer state.

In this task, you will change the state of layers.

1. Make layer **0** the current layer.

2. Use the Layer Control to toggle off the layer **Center**, as shown in Figure 3–7. The two center lines disappear in the drawing.

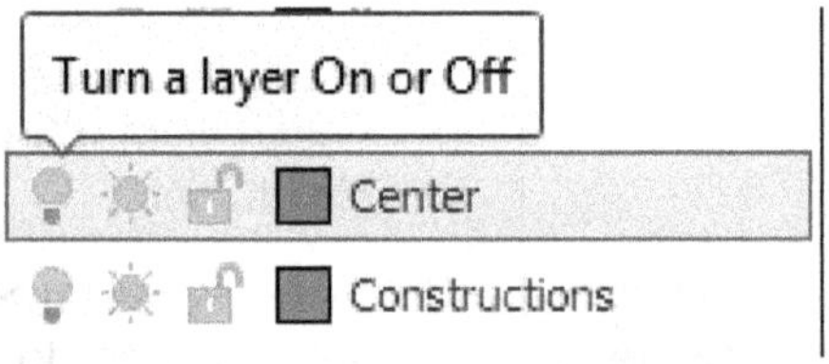

Figure 3–7

3. Use the Layer Control to freeze the layer **Hidden**, as shown in Figure 3–8. The blue/green circle disappears.

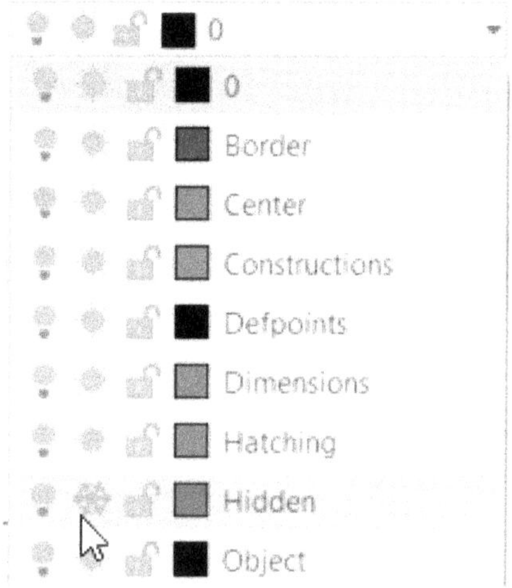

Figure 3–8

4. Use the Layer Control to lock the layer **Object**. The circles on that layer stay displayed, but are slightly grayed out.

5. Try to erase the largest circle and then try to move it. You cannot edit the circle because it is on the locked layer **Object**.

6. Use the Layer Control to unlock the layer **Object**.

7. Erase the largest circle. Use **Undo** to bring it back.

8. Save and close the drawing.

3.3 Changing an Object's Layer

You can move objects from one layer to another so that they show differently in the drawing, as shown in Figure 3–9.

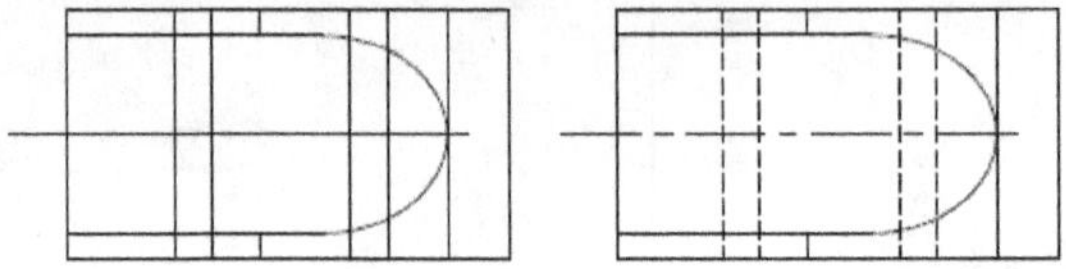

Figure 3–9

Change with Layer Control

You can change the layer of a selected object(s) using the Layer Control.

How To: Change Object Layers with the Layer Control

1. Select an object before you start a command.The Layer Control displays the layer of the object.
2. Expand the Layer Control, and hover the cursor on another layer. Note that the selected object previews with the new layer, as shown in Figure 3–10.

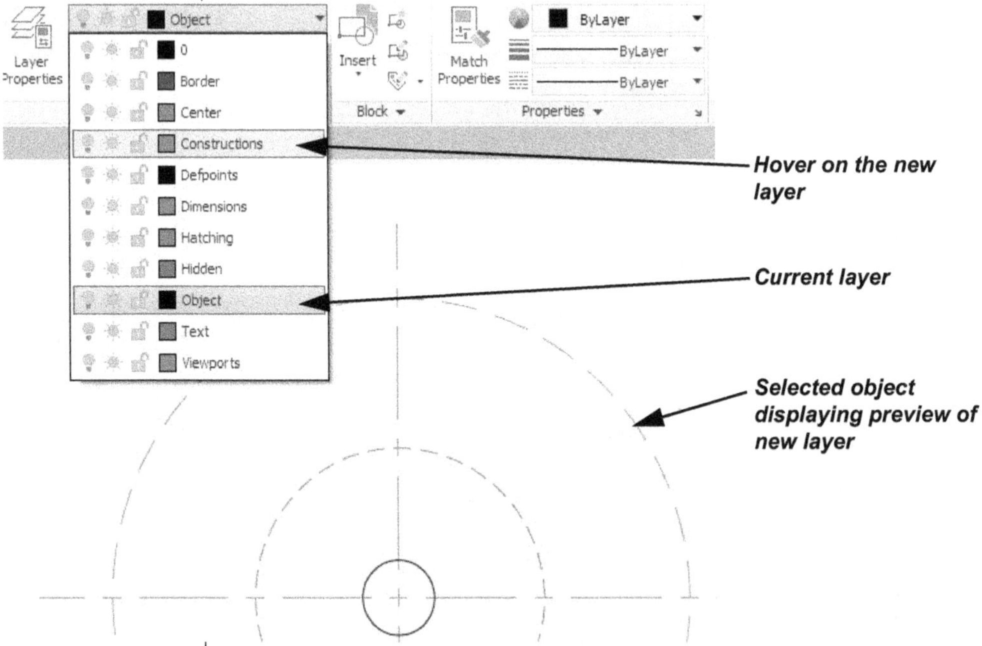

Hover on the new layer

Current layer

Selected object displaying preview of new layer

Figure 3–10

3. Select the layer to change it.

4. Press <Esc> to clear the selected object.

• You can select multiple objects to change their layers. If the selected objects are on different layers, a layer name does not display in the Layer Control. You can still hover to preview and then select a layer to move all of the objects to that layer.

Match Layer

Another way to change the layer of an object is to use the **Match Layer** command. This command can be used when you have other objects on that layer in your drawing.

How To: Match Layers

1. In the *Home* tab>Layers panel, click ☒ (Match Layer).
2. Select the objects that you want to change.
3. Press <Enter> to finish the selection set.
4. Select an object on the destination layer.

   or

   • Instead of selecting an object on the destination layer, you can press the <Down Arrow> which lists the **Name** option. Selecting **Name** opens the Change to Layer dialog box, in which you can select a layer name from a list, as shown in Figure 3–11.

Use this option if you do not know which object layer to select. Otherwise, it is faster to select the objects and then select the layer in the Layer Control.

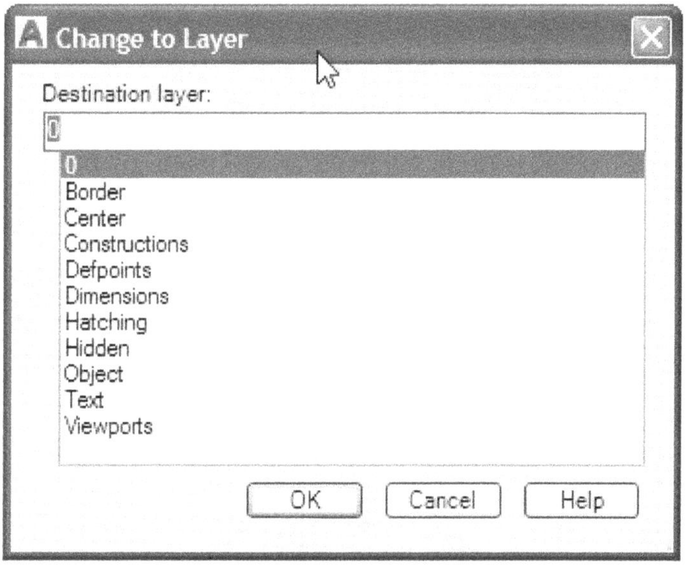

Change to Layer

Destination layer:

0

0
Border
Center
Constructions
Defpoints
Dimensions
Hatching
Hidden
Object
Text
Viewports

OK   Cancel   Help

Figure 3–11

Practice 3b | Changing an Object's Layer

Practice Objective

- Move objects to different layers.

In this practice, you will use the Layer Control and the **Match Layer** command to move objects to different layers, as shown in Figure 3–12.

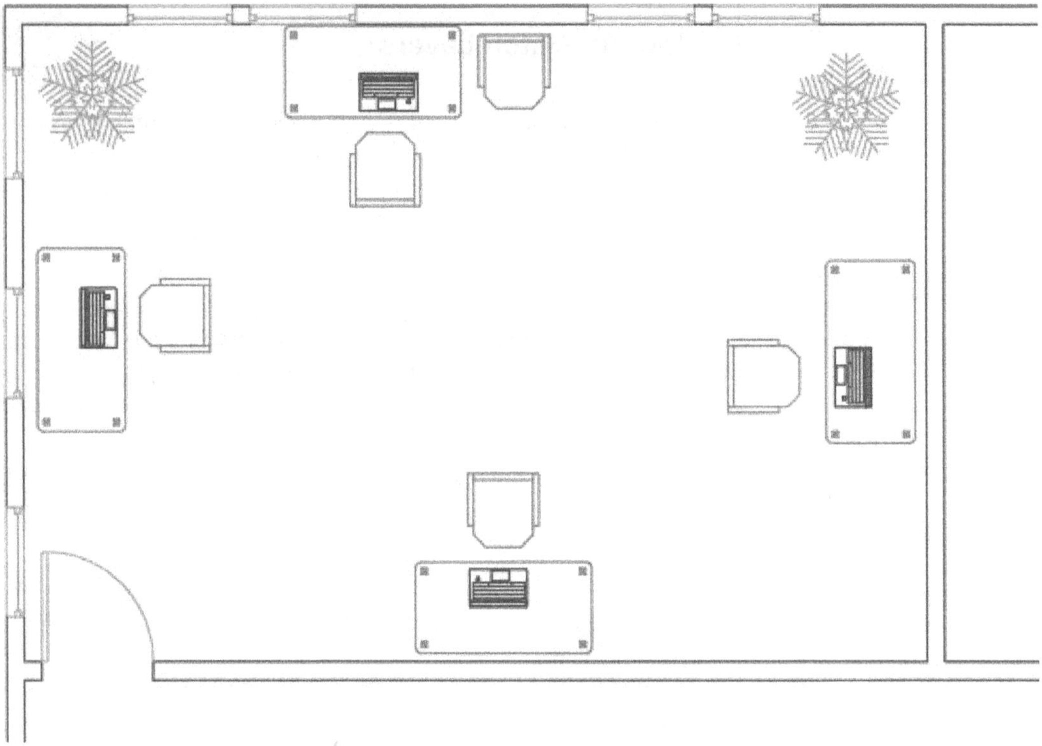

Figure 3–12

1. Open **Suite-A.dwg** from your practice files folder. Currently, all of the objects are on layer **0**.

2. With no command active, select any one line of the wall (blue grips display on the line and it highlights in blue with a thicker lineweight). The layer of that line (layer **0**) displays in the Layer Control.

3. Expand the Layer Control and hover the cursor over the layer **Walls**. The selected wall changes to blue color, which is the color of the layer **Walls**. Click to change the layer to **Walls**. Press <Esc> to clear the selection of line.

4. Select one of the desks and repeat Step 3 to change its layer to the layer **Furniture** (it turns red).

5. In the *Home* tab>Layers panel, click (Match Layer). Select the other desks in the room as the objects to be changed, and then press <Enter> or right-click. Select the desk that you changed in Step 4 as the object on the destination layer. All of the desks change layers to match the destination desk.

6. Use (Match Layer) to change the remaining walls to the layer **Walls** using the changed wall as the destination layer.

7. With no command active, select the two plants. Use the Layer Control to change their layer to **Misc**.

8. Change the remaining objects (chairs, laptops, door, and windows) to the appropriate layers. Use layer **Furniture** for chairs and layer **Electrical** for laptops.

9. Save and close the drawing.

3.4 Working in the Layer Properties Manager

The Layer Properties Manager (shown in Figure 3–13) can be used to create new layers and to work with layer property overrides in viewports.

- The Layer Properties Manager contains other tools that can be use to manage layers, including controlling the properties columns and the layer settings.

You can resize the Layer Properties Manager by dragging its edges.

- The Layer Properties Manager can be opened by clicking

  (Layer Properties Manager) in the *Home* tab>Layers panel or *View* tab>Palettes panel.

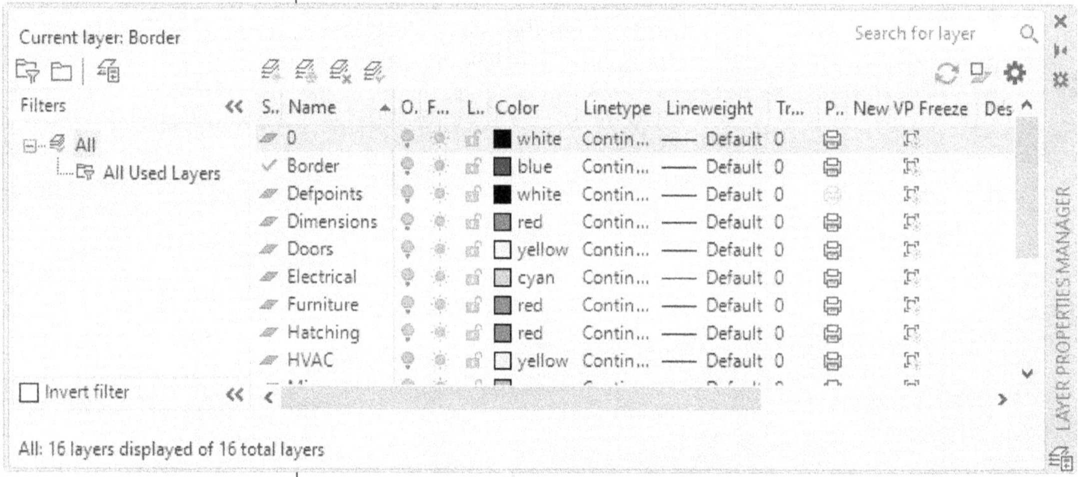

Figure 3–13

Displaying Columns in the Layer Properties Manager

The Layer Properties Manager column display order can be rearranged to suit your needs. Select a column header and drag it to a new location, as shown in Figure 3–14. The AutoCAD® software retains the new location of the column.

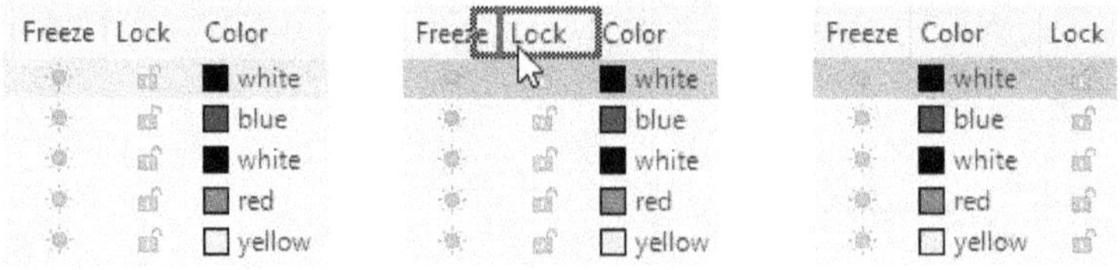

Figure 3–14

Note that if the name is grayed out, it cannot be removed.

Columns that you do not want to display can also be removed. Right-click on a column header and select a column name to clear the check and remove it from the display, as shown in Figure 3–15.

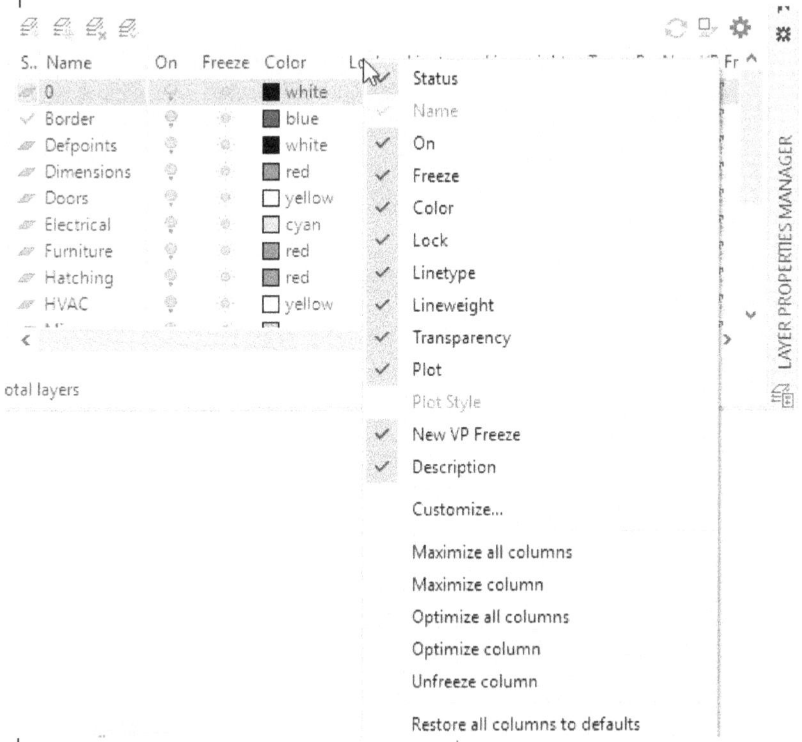

Figure 3–15

- Additional column names display if you are in a layout. These provide access to the viewport layer property overrides.

- Other selections in the shortcut menu include:
    - **Maximize column** and **Maximize all columns:** The maximize options change the column width so that the full header name displays.
    - **Optimize all column** and **Optimize column:** The optimize options change the column width based on the length of the column content
    - **Freeze/Unfreeze column:** The *Freeze* column acts like freeze panes do in Excel. It causes the selected column and columns to the left of it to constantly display. When scrolling to the right to show other columns, the frozen column remains visible.
    - **Restore all columns to defaults:** Sets the column display back to the default options.

- **Customize...:** Enables you to modify more than one column at a time.
- Selecting **Customize...** opens the Customize Layer Columns dialog box (shown in Figure 3–16), in which you can clear the checkmark from any columns that you do not want to display. Use **Move Up** and Mo**ve Down** to change a selected column's position in the display.

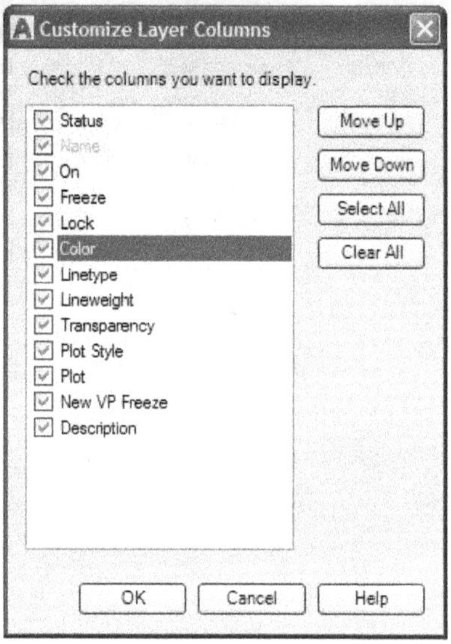

Figure 3–16

- Freezing keeps the column visible even if you scroll to the end of the options. For example, you might want to freeze the *Name* column (shown in Figure 3–17), so that it displays when you make changes to the plot columns.

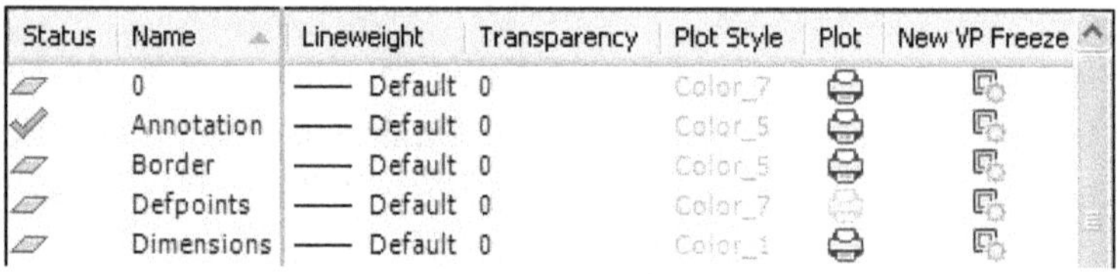

Figure 3–17

- The tooltips for the column headers display the column name and a description of the information displayed in the column, as shown in Figure 3–18.

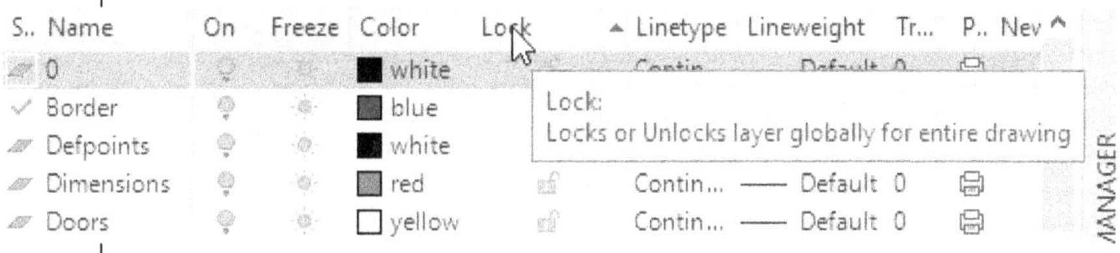

Figure 3–18

Layer Settings

Click ⚙ (Settings) to open the Layer Settings dialog box, as shown in Figure 3–19. These options are helpful when you use reference files that have different layer property overrides or might impact the created Layer States.

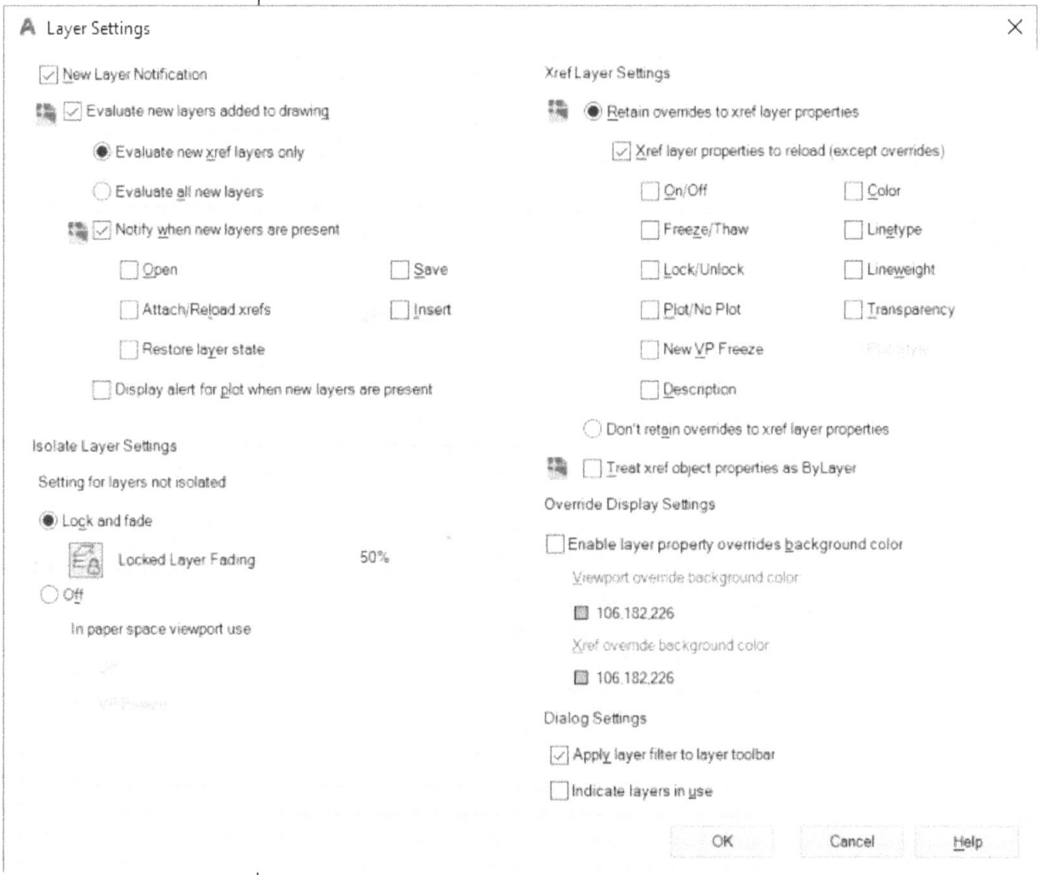

Figure 3–19

Layer Settings Options

Evaluate new layers added to drawing	If selected, evaluates and detects whether new XREF layers or new layers have been added to the drawing based on the setting.
Notify when new layers are present	Notifies you that new layers (or XREF layers) have been added to the drawing and enables you to customize the actions that trigger the display of the notification. Options include **Open**, **Attach/Reload xrefs**, **Restore layer state**, **Save**, and **Insert**.
Display alert for plot when new layers are present	Layer Notification Warning box opens when you use **Plot** in a drawing containing new layers.
Settings for layers not isolated	Controls the behavior of layers that are not selected when using **Layer Isolate**.
Xref Layer Settings	Control the layer properties that you want to reload. These properties are stored in the **VISRETAINMODE** system variable.
Override Display Settings	Sets color of background highlight indicating that viewport settings override overall layer settings.
Apply layer filter to layer toolbar	Layer filter set in Layer Properties Manager is also applied to Layer Control.
Indicate layers in use	Displays icon in list view to indicate layers that contain objects.

Reconciling New Layers

When there are unreconciled layers in a drawing, a new layer filter is automatically created in the Layer Properties Manager. Click on **Unreconciled New Layers t**o display only the layers that are unreconciled, as shown in Figure 3–20.

- To reconcile layers, select the ones you want to accept into your main list of layers, right-click and select **Reconcile Layer**.

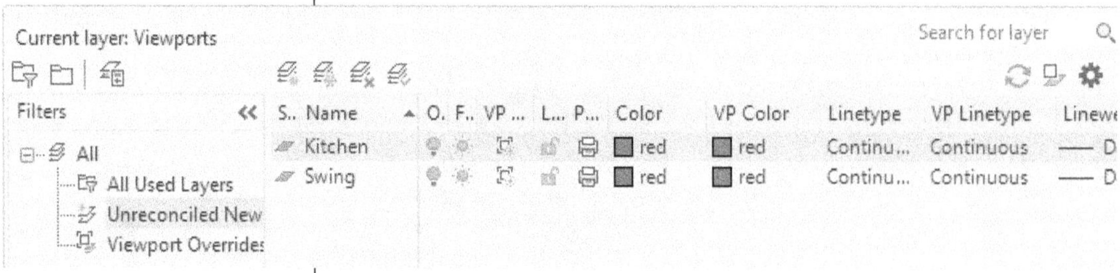

Figure 3–20

Freezing Layers in New Viewports

The *New VP Freeze* column displays whether or not the layer is frozen in new viewports, as shown in Figure 3–21. For example, you might want to create a layer that is only displayed in one viewport. Select **New VP Freeze** so that layer is not displayed in any additional viewports that you create.

New VP Freeze

Figure 3–21

Freezing Layers in All Viewports Except Current

You can freeze selected layers in all viewports except the current viewport. Activate the viewport in which you want to keep the layer(s) visible. In the Layer Properties Manager, select the layer(s), right-click and select **VP Freeze Layer>In All Viewports Except Current**, as shown in Figure 3–22. Select **VP Thaw Layer in All Viewports** to return the layer back to normal.

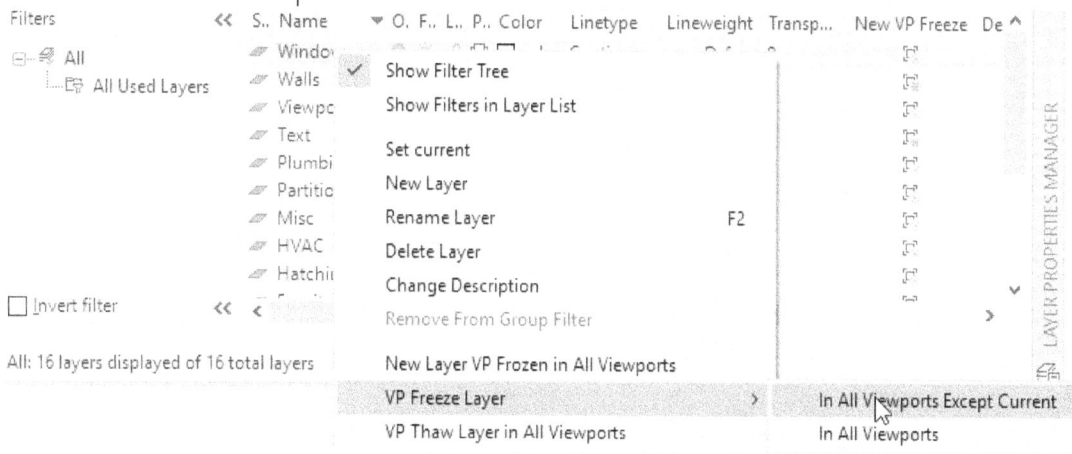

Figure 3–22

Overriding Layer Properties in Viewports

You can change layer properties (such as color, linetype, lineweight, and plot style) in a viewport without that change being made in other viewports. The changes only affect the current viewport and not the model or other viewports.

- The viewport-specific options include:
  - New VP Freeze
  - VP Freeze
  - VP Color
  - VP Linetype
  - VP Lineweight
  - VP Transparency
  - VP Plot Style
- To create these changes, you must be in a layout tab (Status Bar) and working through a viewport.

How To: Modify Layer Properties in a Viewport

1. In a layout tab, double-click in a viewport to activate Model Space.
2. Open the Layer Properties Manager and modify the viewport properties as required. They are highlighted as they are modified.

- The ⌨ (Toggle Override Highlight) option must be toggled on for the highlight to display

- When you select a viewport with Layer property overrides, ⌨ (Viewport has Layer property overrides) displays in the Status Bar. If a viewport does not have layer overrides, it does not display.

- The **Viewport Overrides** layer filter is automatically created when you have viewport overrides and you maximize a specific viewport, as shown in Figure 3–23.

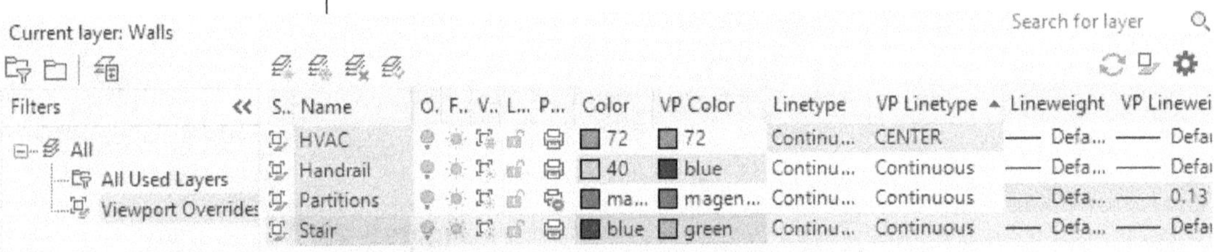

Filters		S..	Name	O.	F..	V..	L..	P...	Color	VP Color	Linetype	VP Linetype ▲	Lineweight	VP Linewei
⊟ ⌨ All		⌨	HVAC	☼	☀	⌨	⌨	⊟	■ 72	■ 72	Continu...	CENTER	── Defa...	── Defa
├ ⌨ All Used Layers		⌨	Handrail	☼	☀	⌨	⌨	⊟	□ 40	■ blue	Continu...	Continuous	── Defa...	── Defa
└ ⌨ Viewport Overrides		⌨	Partitions	☼	☀	⌨	⌨	⊟	■ ma...	■ magen...	Continu...	Continuous	── Defa...	── 0.13
		⌨	Stair	☼	☀	⌨	⌨	⊟	■ blue	□ green	Continu...	Continuous	── Defa...	── Defa

Current layer: Walls

Search for layer

Figure 3–23

- The layer name and any viewport-specific modifications are highlighted in the Layer Properties Manager.

Practice 3c

Working in the Layer Properties Manager

Practice Objective

- Modify the layer settings and the way in which columns display in the Layer Properties Manager.

In this practice, you will change the way the columns display in the Layer Properties Manager, modify the Layer Settings, and reconcile new layers in a drawing. The Layer Properties Manager is shown in Figure 3–24.

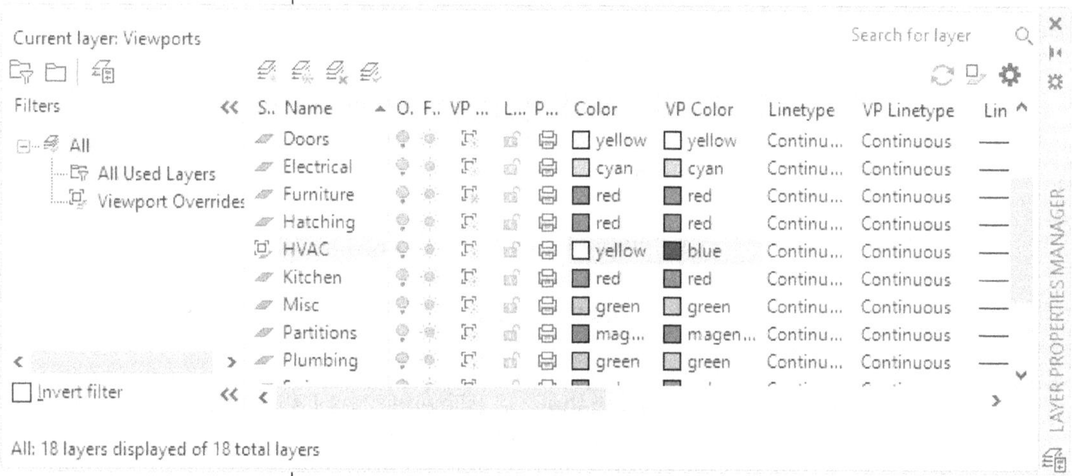

Figure 3–24

1. Open **Small House-A.dwg** from the practice files folder.

2. In the *Home* tab>Layers panel, click ⛁ (Layer Properties). In the Layer Properties Manager, the layers and their properties are listed in the columns.

This option maximizes to either the column's heading or its contents, whichever is larger.

3. Right-click on any of the column titles and select **Maximize all columns**. The columns shift so that the information listed in each column is completely displayed.

4. For the layers **Electrical** and **Furniture**, click 🔲 (New VP Freeze) to freeze them.

5. Auto-hide the Layer Properties Manager.

6. Switch to the **Proposal** layout. The existing viewport displays all of the layers as thawed.

7. In the Layer Properties Manager, right-click on the **Viewports** layer and select **Set current**.

*The **Electrical** and **Furniture** layers are frozen in this viewport, but not in the already existing viewport.*

8. Create a new viewport in the right half of layout. Note that the objects on the **Furniture** (red colored) and **Electrical** (cyan colored) layers are not displayed.

9. Make the new viewport active and display the Layer Properties Manager.

10. More properties are now available for Layer Property Overrides. Override the layer **HVAC** by making the *VP Color* **blue**.

   • Verify that the 🔲 (Toggle Override Highlight) is toggled on for the highlight to display.
   • Note that the change is highlighted in blue, as shown in Figure 3–25.
   • Note that 🔲 (Viewport has Layer property overrides) displays in the Status Bar.

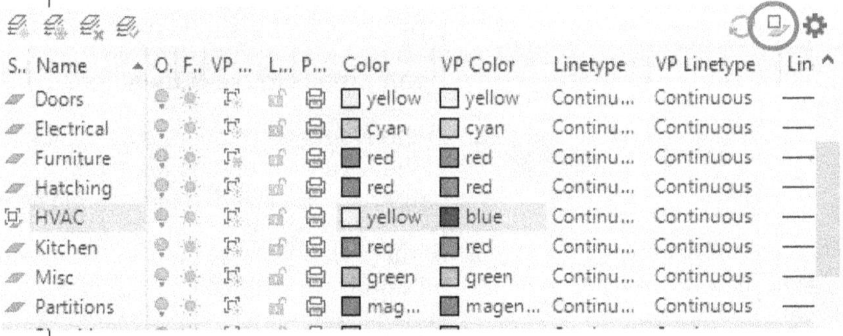

S..	Name	▲	O.	F..	VP ...	L...	P...	Color	VP Color	Linetype	VP Linetype	Lin ^
◢	Doors		⚪	⚫	🔲	🔓	🖨	☐ yellow	☐ yellow	Continu...	Continuous	—
◢	Electrical		⚪	⚫	🔲	🔓	🖨	☐ cyan	☐ cyan	Continu...	Continuous	—
◢	Furniture		⚪	⚫	🔲	🔓	🖨	■ red	■ red	Continu...	Continuous	—
◢	Hatching		⚪	⚫	🔲	🔓	🖨	■ red	■ red	Continu...	Continuous	—
🔲	HVAC		⚪	⚫	🔲	🔓	🖨	☐ yellow	■ blue	Continu...	Continuous	—
◢	Kitchen		⚪	⚫	🔲	🔓	🖨	■ red	■ red	Continu...	Continuous	—
◢	Misc		⚪	⚫	🔲	🔓	🖨	☐ green	☐ green	Continu...	Continuous	—
◢	Partitions		⚪	⚫	🔲	🔓	🖨	■ mag...	■ magen...	Continu...	Continuous	—

Figure 3–25

11. Click ⚙ (Settings) to open the Layer Settings dialog box.

12. Select **Evaluate all new layers**, **Notify when new layers are present**, and **Save**, as shown in Figure 3–26.

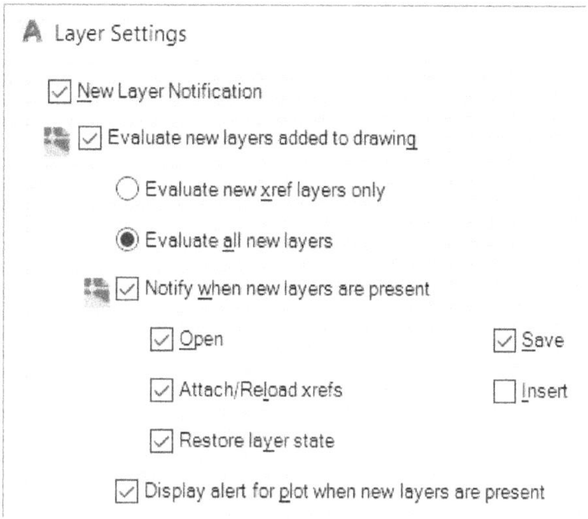

Figure 3–26

13. In the *Override Display Settings* area, select **Enable layer property overrides background color** and change the *Viewport override background color* to **green**, as shown in Figure 3–27.

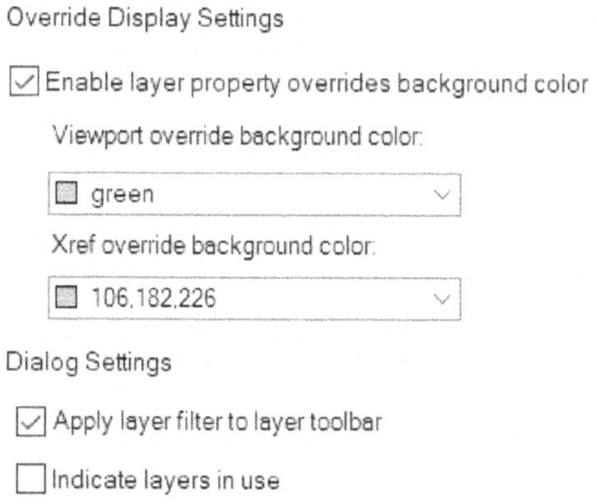

Figure 3–27

14. Click **OK** to return to the Layer Properties Manager and note that the override changes are highlighted in green.

15. Create three new layers using the default layer settings.

16. Save the drawing.

17. The Layer Properties Manager displays with the *Unreconciled New Layers* filter active. Select the **Unreconciled New Layers** filter to display only the layers that are unreconciled, as shown in Figure 3–28.

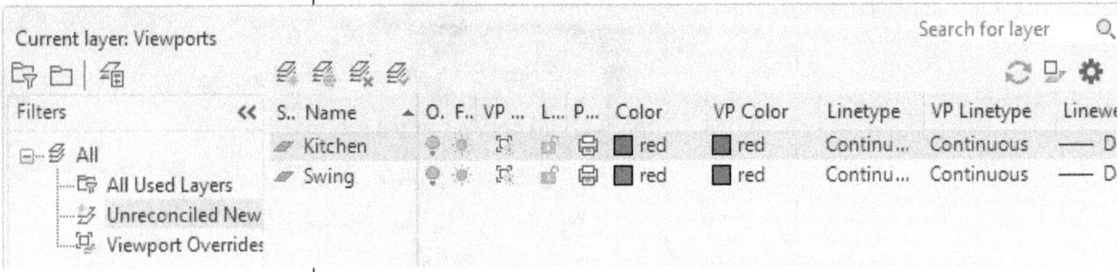

Figure 3–28

18. Select the layers, right-click and select **Reconcile Layer**. The layers are reconciled. Note that the **Unreconciled New Layers** filter is removed.

19. Save and close the drawing.

3.5 Creating Layer Filters

As you set up your layer standards, several additional tools in the Layer Properties Manager can help coordinate multi-layer systems.

*   *Property filters* provide a way to define lists of layers based on specified properties.

*   *Group filters* enable you to group any layers you specify so that you can manipulate them as a group.

Using the Filter Tree

In drawings with large numbers of layers, finding the ones that you want to manipulate in the list can be time-consuming. Layer Filters enable you to control which layers display in the layer list in the Layer Properties Manager, as shown in Figure 3–29. The Filter tree (the pane to the left of the layer list) displays the Property and Group Filters.

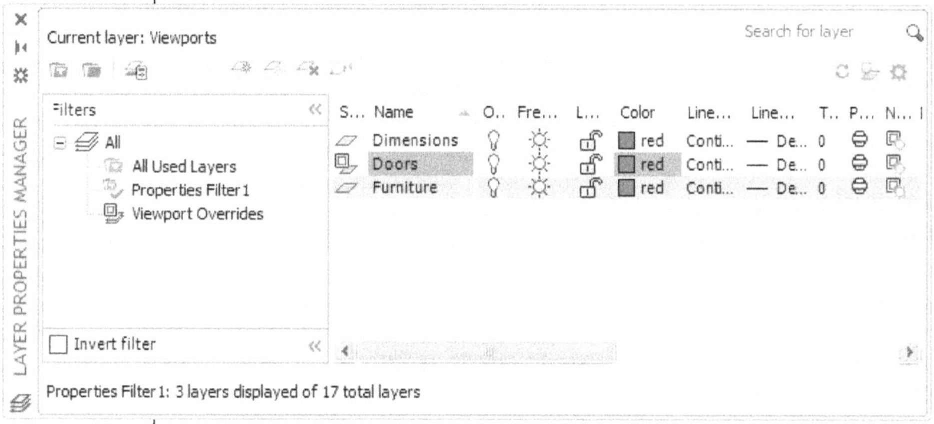

Figure 3–29

*   Select a filter name to only display the layers in that filter.

*   There are predefined filters for *All* and *All Used Layers* as well as a filter for each XREF in a drawing and if applicable, *Unreconciled New Layers*.

- Right-click on a filter to change its **Visibility**, **Lock**, **Viewport** (**Freeze/Thaw**), or **Isolate Group** (freeze all layers not in the filter) options, as shown in Figure 3–30. This enables you to use filters to control the display of layers in the drawing.

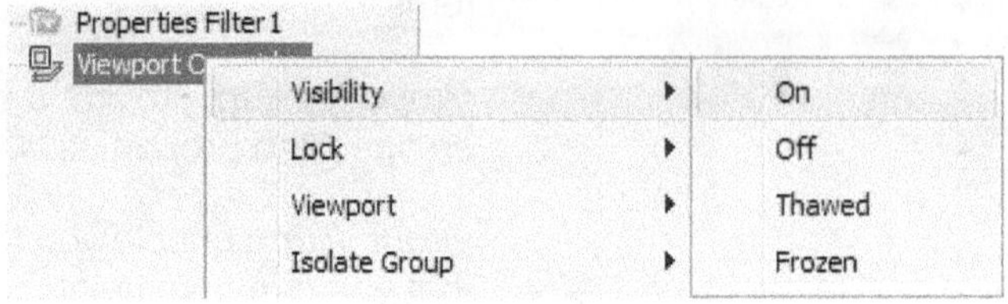

Figure 3–30

- You can create a temporary filter using ~~Search for layer~~ 🔍 in the top right corner of the Layer Properties Manager. When you click in the field, the cursor is placed in front of an asterisk (*) wildcard character. You can type a letter or group of letters and have the software look for layers that have those letter(s) at the beginning of their names.

- The Filters pane can be collapsed if you do not want to use it by clicking **«** (Collapses Layer filter tree), as shown in Figure 3–31.

*Click **»** (Expands Layer filter tree) to restore it.*

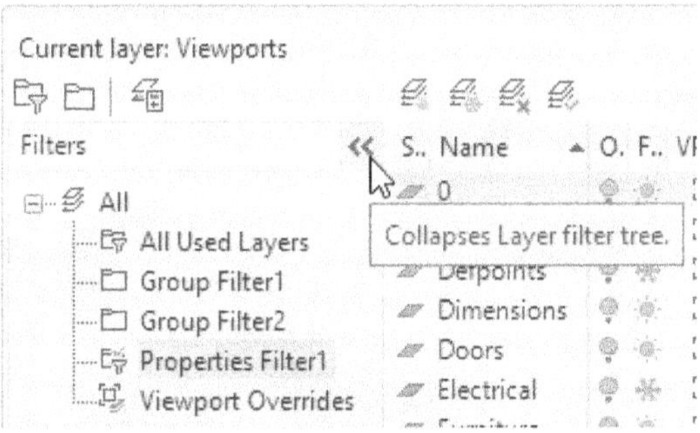

Figure 3–31

- When the Filters pane is collapsed, you can still specify a filter by expanding 🗁▾ (Expands or collapses the Layer filter tree) in the lower left corner of the Layer Properties Manager, as shown in Figure 3–32.

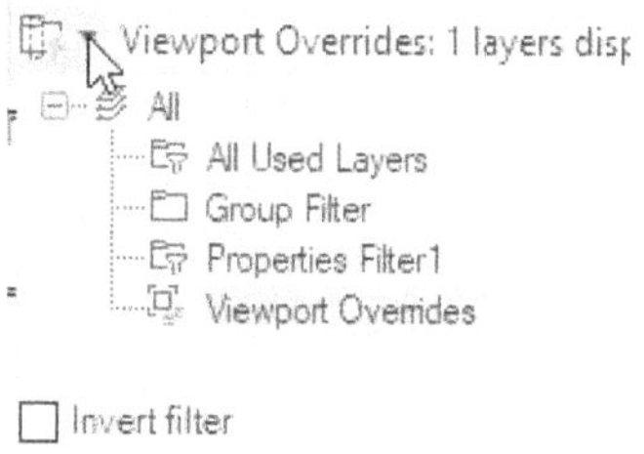

Figure 3–32

- The **Invert Filter** option below the filter list enables you to reverse the currently applied filter. For example, selecting **Invert Filter** with the filter *All Used Layers*, lists all of the unused layers.

Property Filters

Property filters include any layers that match a specified property. For example, you can define property filters for all of the layers that are frozen (as shown in Figure 3–33), all of the layers of a specific color, or all of the layers whose names begin with a specific prefix.

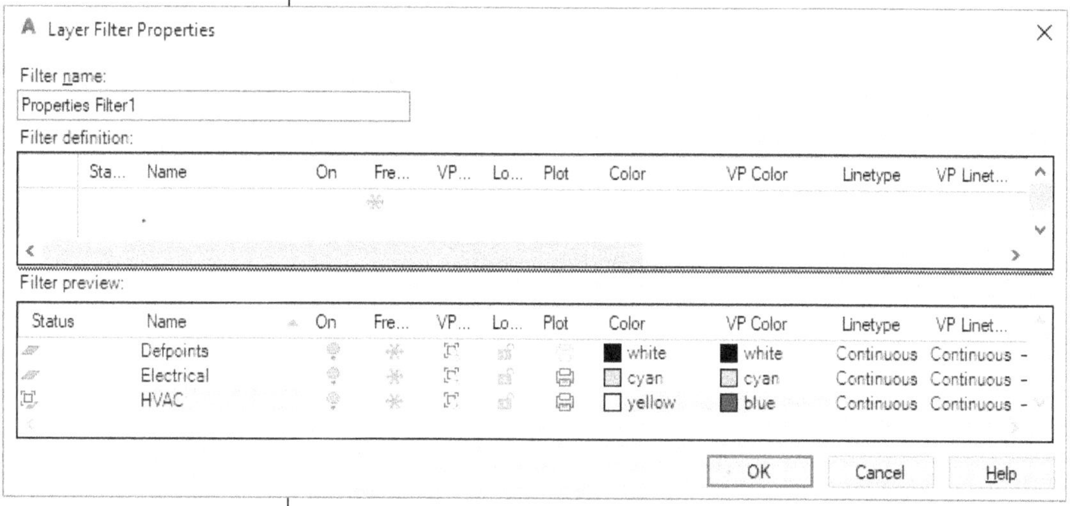

Figure 3–33

How To: Create a Property Filter

1. In the Layer Properties Manager, click ⬚ (New Property Filter). The Layer Filter Properties dialog box opens.
2. Type a name for the filter.

3. Add the Filter definition information. You can expand the drop-down lists and select an option. For example, if you click the field under the *Freeze* column, you can select an empty space (no property), a ❄ (Freeze), or a ☀ (Thaw), as shown in Figure 3–34.

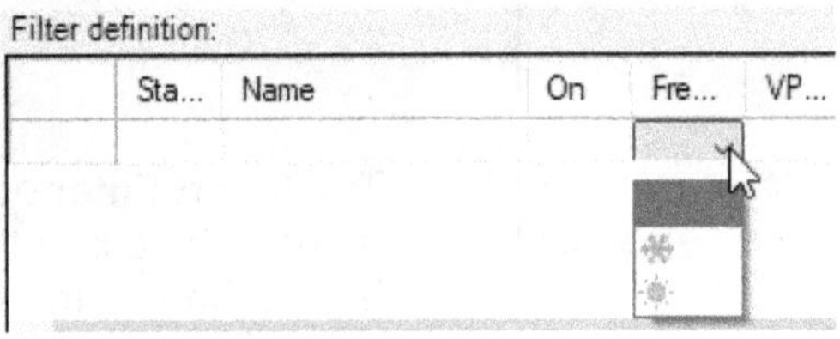

Figure 3–34

- If you are typing a name, you can use standard wildcards, such as * (asterisk), for everything. For example, **D*** would list all of the layer names that start with D, as shown in Figure 3–35. The bottom pane displays a preview of the Filter.

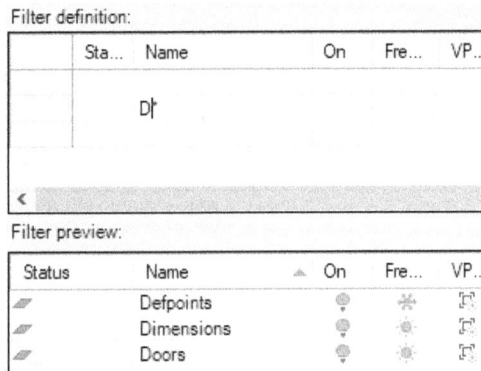

Figure 3–35

4. Click **OK** to continue.

- Double-click on a property filter to modify it or right-click on its name and select **Properties...**.

- If you add several filter properties in one row (such as **A*** and **Freeze**), the filter works as an **AND** operation (the layer must start with A and be frozen).

- If you add filter properties on separate rows (such as **A*** on one row and **Freeze** on another) the filter works as an **OR** operation (the layers must either start with A or be frozen).

Group Filters

A group filter can include a number of specified layers, as shown in Figure 3–36. The layers do not have to have a name or state in common, as is required for Property filters. You can add layers to a group filter by dragging-and-dropping the layer name from the list or by selecting objects in a layer in the drawing.

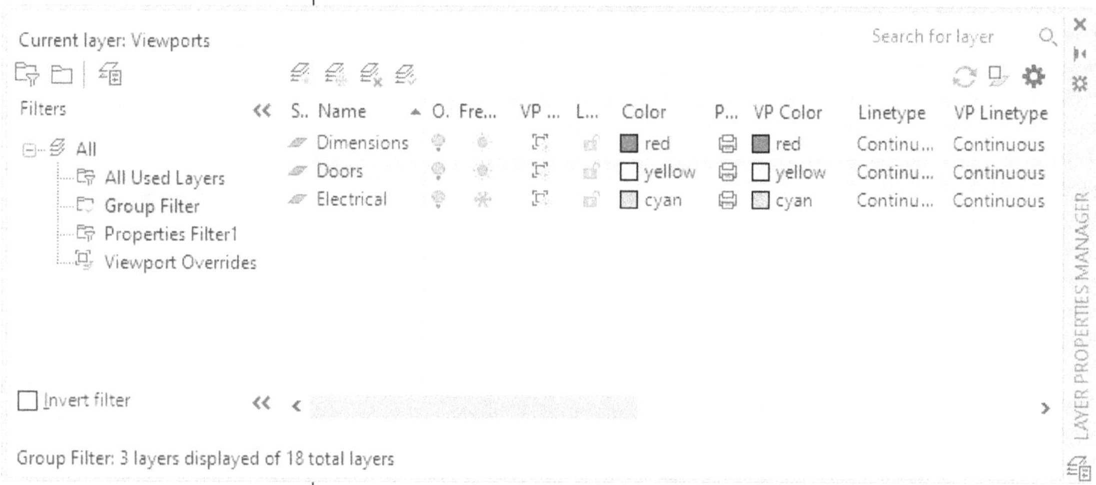

Figure 3–36

How To: Create a Group Filter

1. Open the Layer Properties Manager.
2. Click ☐ (New Group Filter) and give the filter a name.
3. Apply the *All* filter to display the complete layer list.
4. Drag and drop layers from the layer list into the group. You can also right-click on the filter name and select **Select Layers>Add** (or **Replace**).
   - The AutoCAD software switches to the drawing window in which you can select objects on the required layers. Press <Enter> when you complete the selection set. You return to the Layer Properties Manager in which the layers in the group display in the layer list.
5. You can then use the group to quickly modify the state or properties of all of the layers it contains.

   - You can remove a layer from a group filter by right-clicking on it in the group filter list in the Layer Properties Manager and selecting **Remove from Group Filter**.

   - Layers that are added to an existing group filter do not automatically use the visibility settings or other settings that you have already applied to the filter. You need to reapply these settings using the shortcut menu in the filter.

- Group filters can be nested under other group filters. You can also nest property filters under group filters.

- You can convert a property filter to a group filter by right-clicking on the filter and selecting **Convert to Group Filter.**

3.6 Setting Layer States

Layer States enable you to save a specific configuration of layers (their status of on/off, thawed/frozen, etc.) and later restore it. Layer States can be created, edited, saved, and renamed in the Layer States Manager, as shown in Figure 3–37. You can also import and export layer states to use in other drawings.

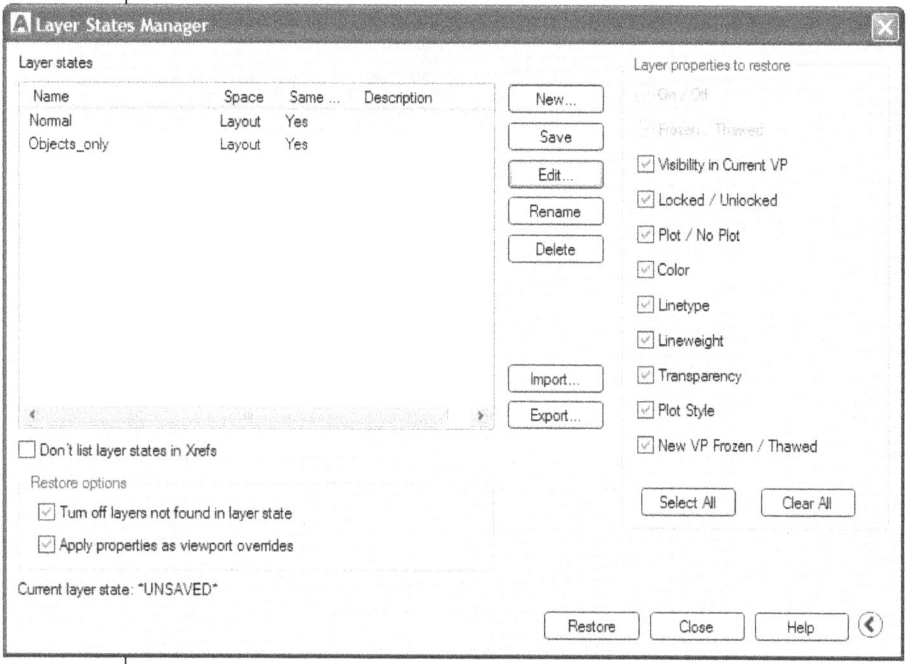

Figure 3–37

For example, in a floor plan drawing you could set up a layer state to display the appropriate layers for the Reflected Ceiling Plan, another state with the appropriate layers displayed for dimensions, etc. Restoring the saved state is easier than adjusting the individual layers each time you need to view or print the drawing in different ways.

How To: Create a New Layer State

1. Set the status of the layers in the drawing (on or off, thawed or frozen, etc.) as required.
2. In the *Home* tab>expanded Layers panel>Layer State drop-down list, select **Manage Layer States**.
3. In the Layer States Manager, click **New**.

The layer state also saves which layer is active.

You can also open the Layer States Manager by clicking ▤ (Layer States Manager) in the Layer Properties Manager.

4. Type a name and description for the Layer State and click **OK**.
5. You can create additional states and click **Edit** to modify them.
6. When you are finished, select the layer state that you want to use and click **Restore**. If you do not want to restore a layer state at this time, click **Close**.

- Layer States can be saved and restored in the model or in a layout view.

- By default, all of the layer settings, such as on/off, color, and lineweight, are included in the layer state.

Click ◉ (Less Restore Options) to hide it again.

- You can modify the *Layer properties to restore* area in the Layer States Manager by expanding ◉ (More Restore Options).

- The **Don't list layer states in Xrefs** option, filters the list of layer states to only display those in the current drawing.

- If you expect other layers to be added after you create a layer state and you do not want the new layers to be included in the layer state, select **Turn off layers not found in layer state**. When you restore the state, the new layers are toggled off.

- By default, the **Apply properties as viewport overrides** option is selected. After selecting a viewport, you can select this option and save a layer state that overrides the viewport's layer properties.

- To rename a Layer State, select it and click **Rename**. The layer state's name highlights in blue and you can type a new name.

- The *Same as Dwg* column displays **Yes** or **No** depending on whether the Layer State settings match those in the drawing.

Restoring a Layer State

Layer States can be restored from the Layer States Manager. Double-click on the Layer State name or select the name and click **Restore**.

You can also restore a layer state using the Layer State drop-down list in the *Home* tab>Layers panel, as shown in Figure 3–38.

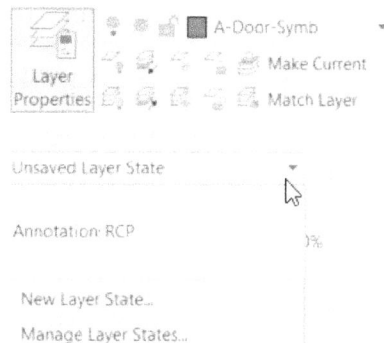

Figure 3–38

How To: Edit a Layer State

You can modify the information saved by a layer state including the current layer, layer status, layer properties, etc. For example, you might want the layer **Walls** in an electrical plan to be gray so that the walls fade into the background while the electrical layers have a heavier lineweight.

1. Open the Layer States Manager.
2. Select the Layer State that you want to modify and click **Edit**. The Edit Layer State dialog box opens, as shown in Figure 3–39.

Figure 3–39

3. Modify the layers, as required.

4. If you want to add a layer that is not included in the state, click [icon] (Add layer to layer state). The Select Layers to Add to Layer State dialog box opens, in which you can select the layers that you want to add.

5. To delete a layer from the layer state, select the layer(s) and click [icon] (Remove layer from layer state).

6. When you are finished, click **Save** to save the changes and close the Edit Layer State dialog box. You can also click **Cancel** to exit without saving changes.

How To: Import a Layer State

Layer states can be imported from other drawing files, drawing template files, and drawing standards files, as well as from layer states files, as shown in Figure 3–40.

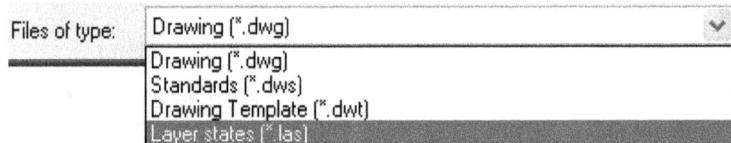

Figure 3–40

1. Open the Layers States Manager and click **Import**.
2. The Import Layer State dialog box opens. In the Files of Type drop-down list, select **Drawing (.dwg)**, **Standards (.dws)**, **Drawing Template (.dwt)**, or **Layer states (.las)**.
3. Browse to the location of the file that you want to import, select it, and click **Open**. The Select Layer States dialog box opens.
4. Select the Layer States that you want to import, as shown in Figure 3–41.

Figure 3–41

5. Click **OK**.

6. If a Layer State of the same name exists in the drawing, a warning box opens. Click **Replace** to replace the existing Layer State and **Cancel** to cancel importing the new Layer State.

• You can click **Export** to export a Layer State to an .LAS file. It can then be imported into other drawings. If the layers are not defined in a drawing, they are automatically created when the Layer State is imported.

> **Hint: Layer Previous**
>
> If you make a quick, temporary change to the status of your layers and want to return to the previous status, use **Layer Previous**, as shown in Figure 3–42. Similar to **Zoom Previous**, this tool can step back repeatedly through a series of layer changes. The only layer changes that it does not affect are the renaming of layers and creating new ones.

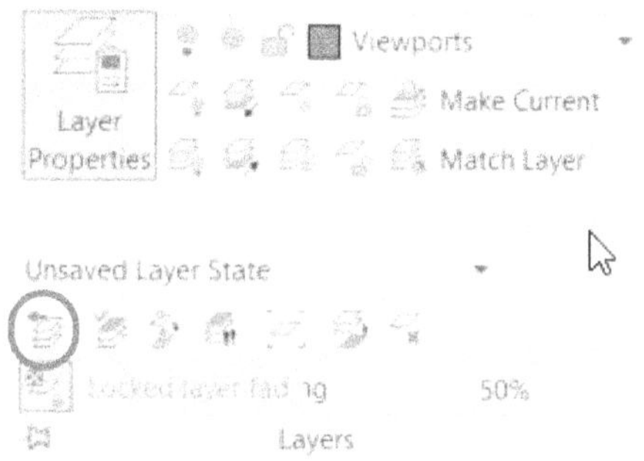

Figure 3–42

Practice 3d

Layer Filters and Layer States

Practice Objectives

- Create layer property and layer group filters.
- Create and restore layer states.

In this practice, you will create layer property and layer group filters and create and restore several layer states.

Task 1 - Create layer filters.

In this task, you will create layer property and layer group filters, as shown in Figure 3–43.

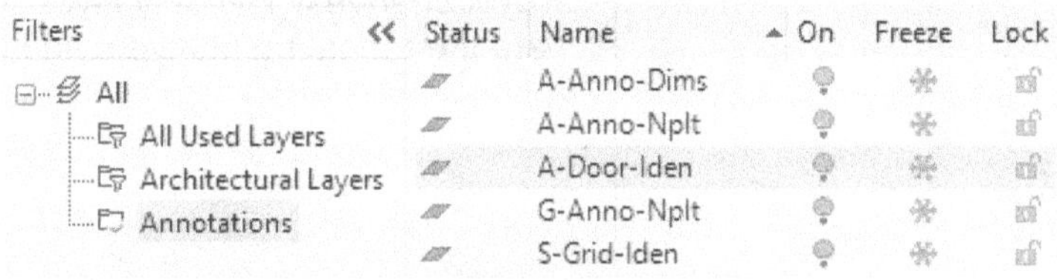

Figure 3–43

1. Open **Layer Plan-A.dwg** from the practice files folder.

2. Open the Layer Properties Manager (if it is not already open). All of the layers are on and thawed except for **A-Door-Head** and **A-Glaz-Head**.

3. Click ⬚ (New Property Filter). Name the filter **Architectural Layers**. In the *Filter definition* area, in the *Name* field, type **A-***. The layers that match the filter should be displayed in the preview. Click **OK** to set the filter.

4. Click ⬚ (New Group Filter) and name the new filter **Annotations**.

5. Click on **All** in the *Filters* list to display all of the layers. Drag and drop the layers **A-Anno-Dims** and **A-Door-Iden** from the layer list into the **Annotations** group.

6. Click on **Annotations** in the *Filters* list and verify that only those two layers are displayed.

7. In the drawing window, select any of the red grid bubbles along the right side of the drawing, the blue center line, and the blue section callout at the bottom left of the drawing.

8. In the Layer Properties Manager, select the *Annotations* filter.

9. Right-click on the **Annotations** filter, expand Select Layers and select **Add**. Five layers are listed in the **Annotations** filter.

*The layers that are part of the **Annotations** filter are frozen.*

10. In the Layer Properties Manager, right-click on the **Annotations** filter again, expand **Visibility** and select **Frozen**. Note that the objects on these layers are not displayed in the drawing anymore.

11. Save the drawing.

Task 2 - Set up layer states (Architectural).

In this task, you will create and restore several layer states. The final layer state is shown in Figure 3–44.

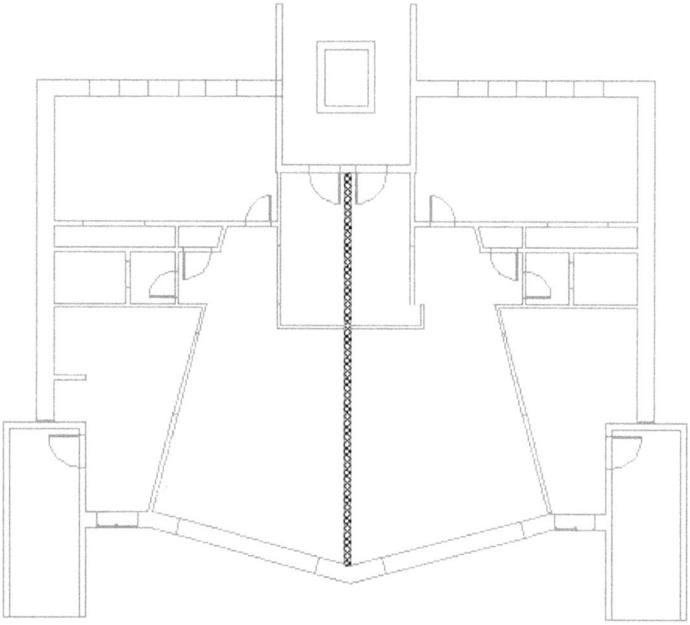

Figure 3–44

1. Use the **Annotations** layer filter to verify that all of the annotations are frozen.

2. Click (Layer States Manager) and create a new layer state called **Annotations Off**.

3. Create another new layer state and name it **RCP** with the description **Reflected Ceiling Plan**.

*You might need to **Regen** to refresh the screen after switching layer states.*

4. Select the new layer state **RCP** and click **Edit**.

5. In the Edit Layer State dialog box, freeze all of the layers except the current layer (**A-Door-Symb**), **A-Wall**, **A-Door-Head**, **A-Glaz-Head**, and **E-lite-Eqpm**. Change the *color* of these layers to **gray** and click **Save**.

6. Close the Layer States Manager.

7. In the *Home* tab>Layers panel, use the Layer State drop-down list to try the two new layer states in your drawing.

8. Save and close the drawing.

Additional Layer Tools

Exam Objectives Covered in This Chapter

- 1.3.b Use layer filters to control which layers are listed in the Layer Properties Manager folder
- 1.3.c Apply and remove layer overrides per viewport
- 1.3.d Use the Layer Walk tool to display objects on selected layers
- 1.3.e Remove layers from a drawing
- 1.3.f Control the properties of referenced layers

4.1 Additional Layer Tools

The additional layer commands in the *Home* tab>Layers panel, can help you to work quickly with layers. They include commands that enable you to select layers rather than their names, and to change their layer state or current status.

Changing Object Layer States

The commands to freeze, toggle off, lock, and unlock layers are the most basic of the additional layer commands. They can be accessed in the *Home* tab>Layers panel, as shown in Figure 4–1.

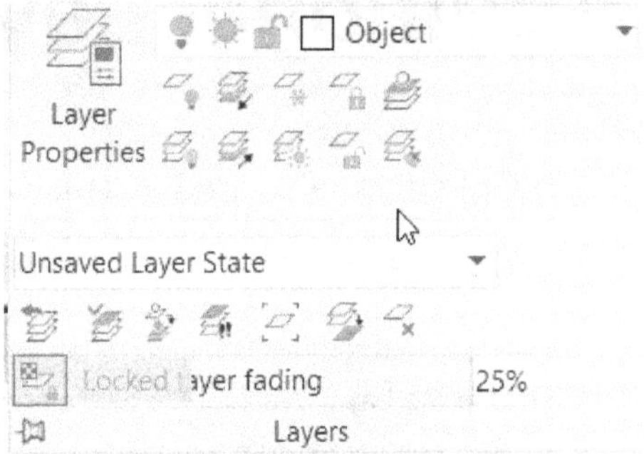

Figure 4–1

How To: Freeze or Turn Layers Off

1. Start (Layer Freeze) or (Layer Off).
2. Select an object on the layer that you want to change. It changes automatically.
3. You can continue selecting objects on other layers as required.
4. Press <Enter> to finish the command.

   Two other commands are helpful with layer states:

   - (Turn All Layers On)

   - (Thaw All Layers)

In the Home tab>extended Layers panel, use ⬚ (VP Freeze in All Viewports except Current) to freeze a selected layer in all other viewports except the active one.

Settings

Layer Freeze and **Layer Off** have settings for how blocks, Xrefs, and Viewports respond to the commands. These settings remain in effect until you change them.

Block selection	Sets the nesting level of a block or Xref:
	Block (default): Freezes or turns off the layer on which the block was inserted. If it is part of an Xref, it freezes the layer of the object.
	Entity: Only freezes or turns off the layer in the block or Xref that you actually select.
	None: Freezes or turns off the layer on which the block or Xref was inserted.
Viewports	Sets the way the command responds when you are working in a Paper Space viewport.
	VPFreeze (default): Only freezes or turns off the layer in the current viewport.
	Freeze/Off: Freezes or turns off the layer across the entire drawing.

How To: Lock or Unlock Layers

1. Click ⬚ (Layer Lock) or ⬚ (Layer Unlock).
2. Select an object on the layer that you want to change. It changes automatically.

- A small padlock icon displays when you hover the cursor over a locked layer, as shown in Figure 4–2.

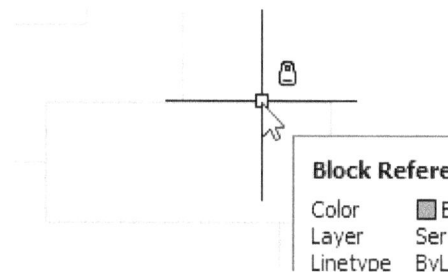

Figure 4–2

- Locked layers fade but are still displayed in the drawing. Use the **Locked layer fading** slider in the extended Layers panel to control how much the layers fade, as shown in Figure 4–3.

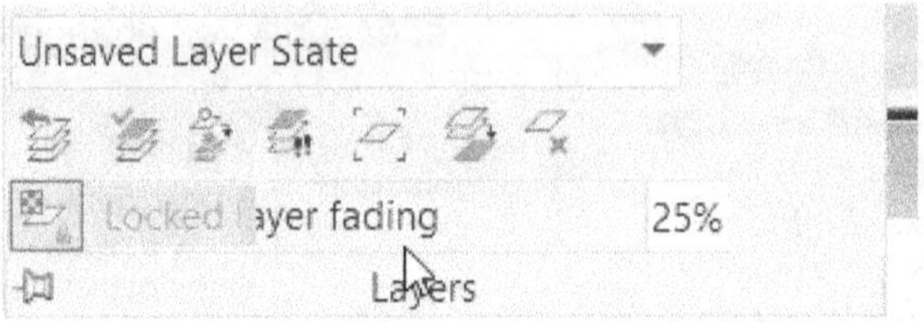

Figure 4–3

Isolating Layers

(Layer Isolate) is similar to changing the layer state, but it locks and fades (or turns off) all of the objects in a drawing EXCEPT those that are on the layers that you selected to isolate, as shown in Figure 4–4. When you have finished working with the isolated layers, you can return them to their original layer state.

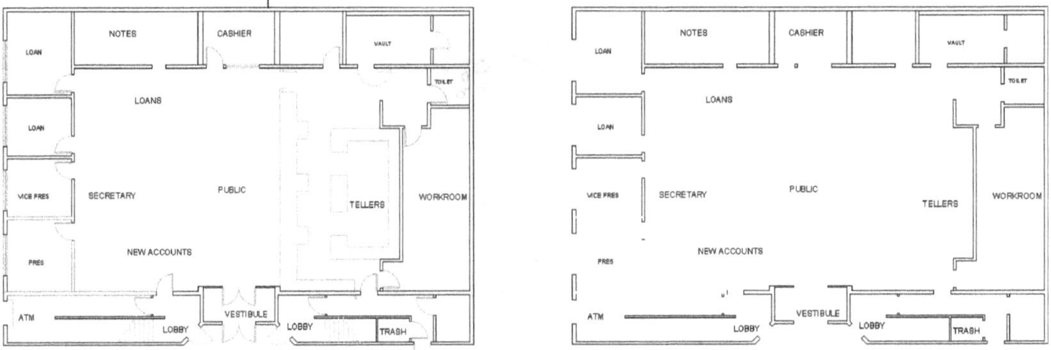

Figure 4–4

How To: Isolate Layers

1. Click (Layer Isolate).
2. Select objects on the layer(s) in which you want to work.
3. Press <Enter>. All of the other layers are locked and faded.

- If you only select one layer to isolate and it is not the current layer, it becomes current.

- The layers that are not selected to be isolated are either locked and faded or toggled off. To change this, start the **Layer Isolate** command, select **Settings**, and select the required option, as shown in Figure 4–5.

Enter setting for layers not isolated
• Off
Lock and fade

Figure 4–5

- When you select **Off** you are prompted to set the way it works in Paper Space viewports. The **Vpfreeze** option freezes the unisolated layers in the active viewport, and the **Off** option turns the unisolated layers off in all of the viewports.

How To: Unisolate Layers

1. Click (Layer Unisolate).
2. All of the isolated layers are restored.

- (Layer Previous) also restores layers that have been isolated and changes the current layer back to the original if **Layer Isolate** was last used to change it.

Changing an Object's Layer

There are other ways of changing the layers of objects in a drawing including: (Change to Current Layer) and (Copy Objects to New Layer). These commands change an object's layer by selecting other objects.

How To: Change to the Current Layer

1. Click (Change to Current Layer).
2. Select the objects that you want to place on the current layer.
3. Press <Enter> to complete the command and note that the objects are moved to the current layer.

How To: Copy an Object to a New Layer

This command creates new copies of selected objects and places them on a new layer. You can then move the copies to a new location while you are still in the command or leave them on top of existing objects.

1. Click ⬚ (Copy Objects to New Layer).
2. Select the objects that you want to copy and press <Enter> to complete the selection set.
3. Select an object on the destination layer or use the **Name** option to open the Copy to Layer dialog box, in which you can select a layer name, as shown in Figure 4–6.

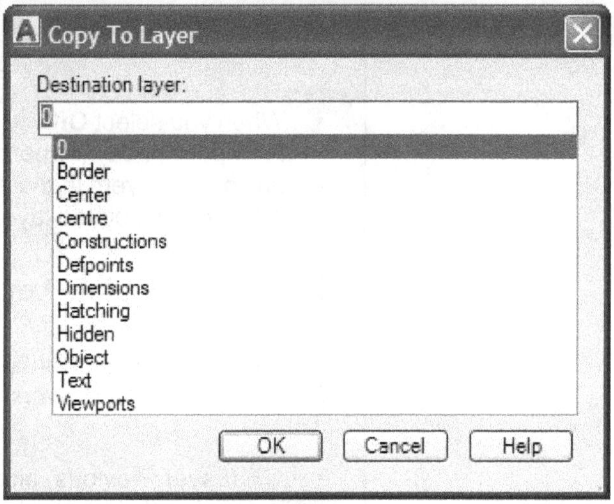

Figure 4–6

4. Select a base point from which to copy. If you want the new copies to be on top of the originals, you can press <Enter> to exit without moving the objects.
5. Select a second point to place the new objects on the selected layer.

• The new layer to which objects are going to be copied must exist for this command to be used.

Modifying Layers

In the *Home* tab>extended Layers panel use ⬚ (Layer Merge) to move all of the objects on selected layers to a target layer and then delete the selected layers. ⬚ (Layer Delete) removes a layer and any objects associated with that layer.

• The default response to the final prompt of *Do you wish to continue*? for each of these commands is **No**. You must specify **Yes** to complete the process.

How To: Merge Layers

1. Click ✏️ (Layer Merge).
2. Select an object on the layer that you want to merge. You can select several layers before pressing <Enter> to continue.
3. Select an object on the target layer.
4. A warning box opens, listing the layers that you are going to merge into the target layer. If you type **Y** for **Yes**, the objects are moved to the target layer and the other layers are deleted from the drawing.

How To: Delete Layers

1. Click ✏️ (Layer Delete).
2. Select an object on the layer that you want to delete. You can select several layers before pressing <Enter> to continue. If you select multiple layers, the objects disappear from the drawing as you click them.
3. A warning box opens, listing the layers that you are going to delete. If you type **Y** for **Yes**, the objects and layers are deleted from the drawing.

- If blocks are associated with the layer, they are redefined with objects from the deleted layer.

Layer Walk

✏️ (Layer Walk) provides an interface in which you can quickly display objects on specified layers and then modify them in a dialog box, as shown in Figure 4–7.

Use this command to find out which layers the objects display on and then use other commands to move them to the correct layer.

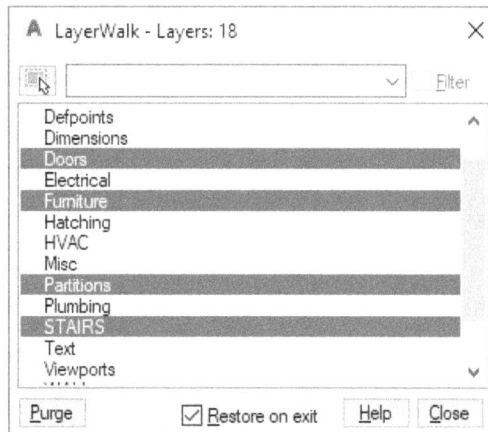

Figure 4–7

- You can either select from the list of layer names in the LayerWalk dialog box or use ![icon] (Select Objects) to select objects in the drawing window.

- Use <Ctrl> and <Shift> or drag to select multiple layers.

- Double-click on the name if you always want a layer to be displayed. An asterisk displays next to the name. You can also right-click and select **Hold Selection**. You can release the hold layers individually or as a group by right-clicking and selecting **Release Selection** and **Release All**.

- If a layer does not contain any objects, you can click **Purge** to remove it from the drawing.

- When you have finished working in the dialog box, you can display the layer setup in your drawing if you clear the **Restore on exit** option. If it is selected, the modifications you made in the dialog box are not displayed in the drawing window.

Filtering Layers

You can use filters to select layers more quickly. Type information including a wildcard character (such as *) and press <Enter> to only display the layer names that match the filter, as shown in Figure 4–8.

*All of the layers display if you clear the **Filter** option.*

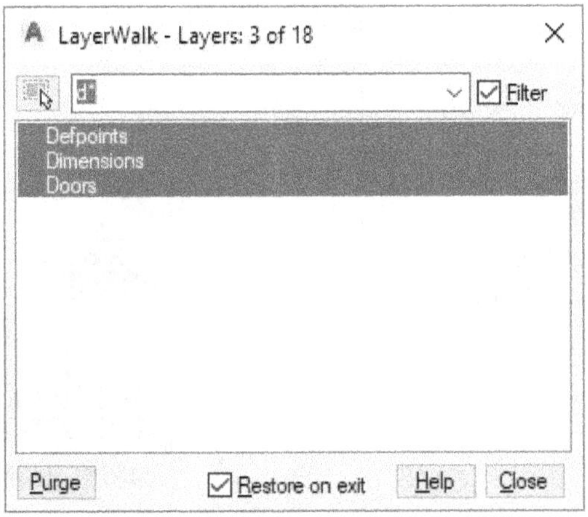

Figure 4–8

- To save a filter, right-click in the Layer list and select **Save Current Filter**. The filter is added to the drop-down list.

- In the LayerWalk dialog box, right-click and select **Save Layer State** to save the current selection of layers to be used later in the Layer State Manager.

- In the LayerWalk dialog box, right-click and select **Inspect...** to display the number of layers in the drawing, number of layers selected, and number of objects on the selected layers, as shown in Figure 4–9.

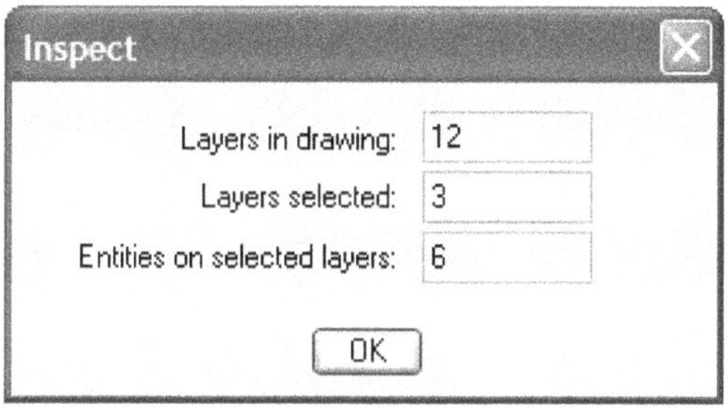

Figure 4–9

Practice 4a | Layer Tools

Practice Objective

- Modify the layers using the additional layer commands.

In this practice, you will freeze and toggle off layers, as shown in Figure 4–10, and then restore the layer states. You will isolate and unisolate layers. You will use the **Layer Walk** and **Layer Merge** commands to determine whether any layers are incorrect in the drawing and then fix them as required.

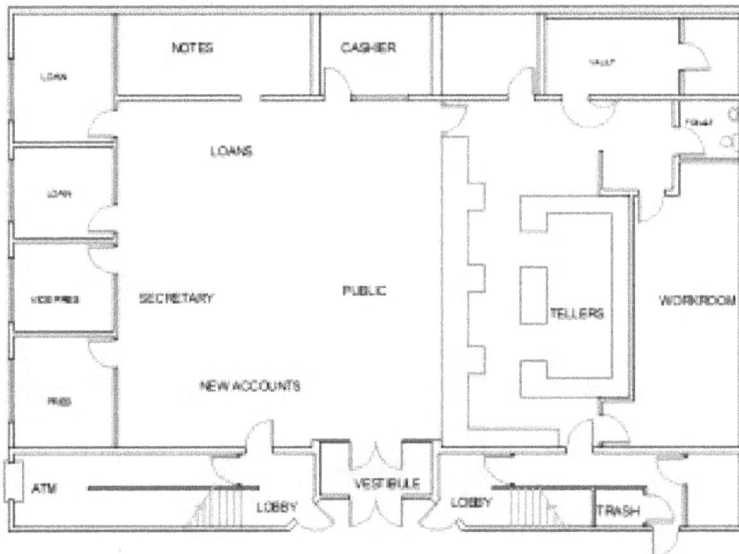

Figure 4–10

1. Open **Bank-A.dwg** from your practice files folder.

2. In the *Home* tab, expand and pin the Layers panel.

3. Practice freezing and toggling off layers using (Layer Freeze) and (Layer Off).

4. Restore the layer states using ⌖ (Turn all Layers On) and ⌖ (Thaw All Layers).

5. You can also try isolating layers using ⌖ (Layer Isolate) and ⌖ (Layer Unisolate).

6. Set the current layer to **Electrical**.

7. Click ⌖ (Layer Freeze). At the *Select an object* prompt, press <Down Arrow> and select **Settings>Block selection>Block** from the down arrow menus. Select a door to freeze and note what happens. All the doors disappear from the drawing.

8. Click ⌖ (Thaw All Layers).

9. Hover your cursor on one of the text in the drawing. Note that the text is on layer **Walls**.

10. Set the current layer to **Text**.

11. Click ⌖ (Change to Current Layer). Select the text and note how the color changes to blue, which is the color of the layer **Text**. Select the rest of the text objects. Press <Enter> to complete the command.

12. Click ⌖ (Layer Walk). In the LayerWalk dialog box, select **Doors**. All the objects on layer **Doors** are displayed with everything else disappearing. Similarly, select **Furniture** and **STAIRS** to display the objects on each layer. Select the layer **Walls** first and then select the layer **WALL**. Note that the walls in the drawing are on two different layers. Close the Layer Walk dialog box.

13. Set layer **0** to be active. Click ⌖ (Layer Merge) and select an object on the layer **Walls** (top most horizontal wall of the layout). Press <Enter>.

14. Select an object on the layer **WALL** (a wall between the rooms **VICE PRES** and **PRES**). Click **Yes**.

15. Expand the Layer Control in the Layers panel to verify that the one of the wall layers is deleted and all the walls are on a single layer.

16. Save and close the drawing.

4.2 Layer Overrides in Viewports

When you are working in viewports, you might want to modify the layers that display in the various viewports, as shown in Figure 4–11. You can modify layers per viewport and change their color, linetype, lineweight, and plot style using the Layer Properties Manager. To create the viewport specific changes, you need to be working in a *Layout* tab.

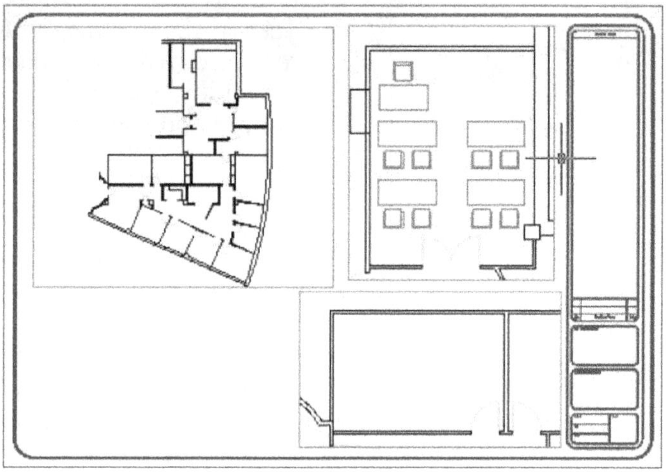

Figure 4–11

Overriding Layer Properties in Viewports

You can use the Layer Properties Manager to change layer properties (such as color, linetype, and lineweight) in a single viewport without the change being made in other viewports. The changes only affect the current viewport and not the model or other viewports, as shown in Figure 4–12.

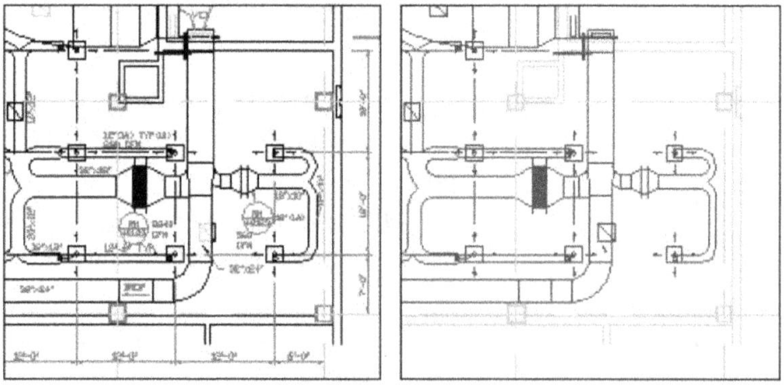

Figure 4–12

- Viewport specific settings include: **New VP Freeze**, **VP Freeze**, **VP Color**, **VP Linetype**, **VP Lineweight**, **VP Transparency**, and **VP Plot Style**. As the name specifies, the **VP Freeze** can be used to freeze/thaw a layer in only one viewport. Similarly, **VP Color** enables you to change the color of a layer in a single (current) viewport. The **New VP Freeze** tool can be used to freeze/thaw a layer in any subsequent viewport that you might create and does not affect the current viewport.

- To create these changes, you must be in a Layout tab and working through a viewport.

How To: Modify Layer Properties in a Viewport

1. In a *Layout* tab, double-click in a viewport to enter Model Space.
2. Open Layer Properties Manager and modify the viewport properties as required. Their icon changes to 🖫 and the changes are highlighted as they are modified, making it easy to see the changes (the 🖉 (Toggle Override Highlight) should be toggled on), as shown in Figure 4–13.

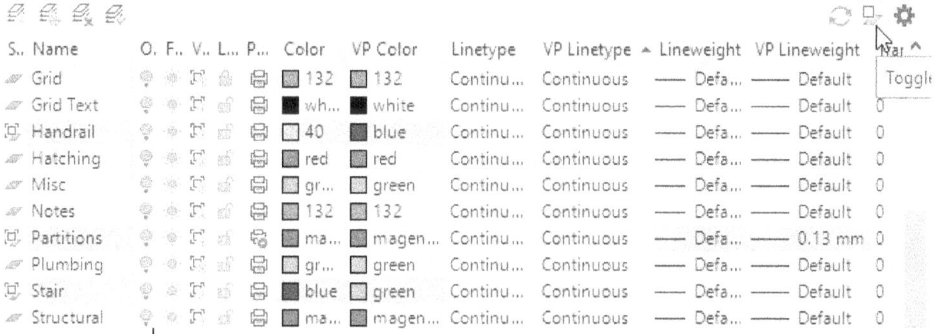

You might need to extend the Layer Properties Manager to display all the columns.

S...	Name	O.	F..	V..	L...	P...	Color	VP Color	Linetype	VP Linetype ▲	Lineweight	VP Lineweight	Var ▲
	Grid	♀	☀	🖫	🔒	🖨	132	132	Continu...	Continuous	—— Defa...	—— Default	Toggle
	Grid Text	♀	☀	🖫	🔒	🖨	wh...	white	Continu...	Continuous	—— Defa...	—— Default	0
	Handrail	♀	☀	🖫	🔒	🖨	40	blue	Continu...	Continuous	—— Defa...	—— Default	0
	Hatching	♀	☀	🖫	🔒	🖨	red	red	Continu...	Continuous	—— Defa...	—— Default	0
	Misc	♀	☀	🖫	🔒	🖨	gr...	green	Continu...	Continuous	—— Defa...	—— Default	0
	Notes	♀	☀	🖫	🔒	🖨	132	132	Continu...	Continuous	—— Defa...	—— Default	0
	Partitions	♀	☀	🖫	🔒	🖨	ma...	magen...	Continu...	Continuous	—— Defa...	—— 0.13 mm	0
	Plumbing	♀	☀	🖫	🔒	🖨	gr...	green	Continu...	Continuous	—— Defa...	—— Default	0
	Stair	♀	☀	🖫	🔒	🖨	blue	green	Continu...	Continuous	—— Defa...	—— Default	0
	Structural	♀	☀	🖫	🔒	🖨	ma...	magen...	Continu...	Continuous	—— Defa...	—— Default	0

Figure 4–13

3. These changes are immediately and automatically reflected in the viewport.

- The layers also highlight in the Layer Control in the Layers panel as shown in Figure 4–14.

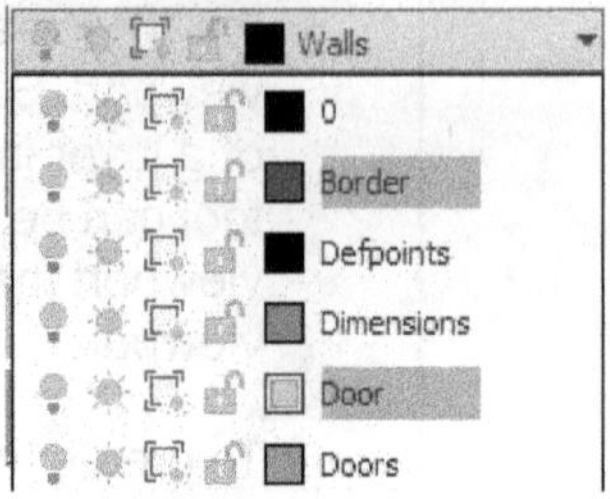

Figure 4–14

- The Viewport Overrides layer filter is automatically created when you use viewport overrides. Selecting **Viewport Overrides** displays only those layers that contain viewport overrides, as shown in Figure 4–15.

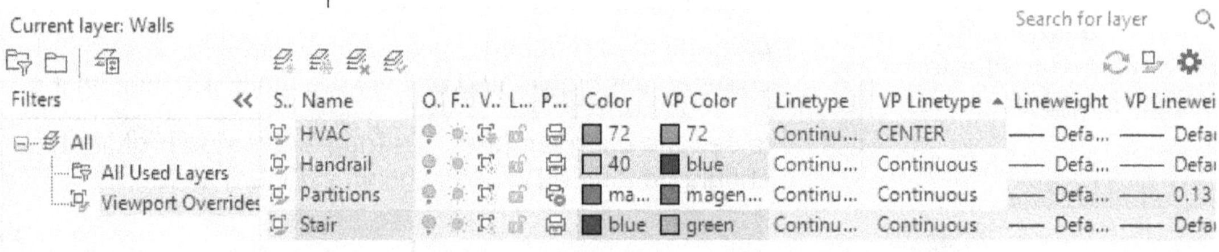

Figure 4–15

Freezing Layers in Viewports

If you freeze a layer or toggle it off using the standard tools, it becomes hidden in all of the viewports.

The **VP Freeze** tool is also available in the Layer Control for easily freezing a layer in a viewport. In the Layer Control, use

(Freeze or Thaw in current viewport) to freeze/thaw a layer in only one viewport.

How To: Freeze a Layer in a Viewport

1. Make the viewport active in which you want to freeze the layer.
2. In the Layer Control, click (Freeze or thaw in current viewport) so that it displays for the required layer.
3. Repeat for any other layers that you want to freeze in the current viewport.If you use this tool when you are in a layout but not in a viewport, it freezes a layer in the layout without affecting other layouts. It does not affect the layer display in any viewports when used this way.

4.3 Xref Layers

When you attach or overlay a drawing reference file, it brings the drawing objects and its named objects, such as layers and blocks, into the host drawing.

- In the Layer Properties Manager, you can quickly display all of the layers in a specific drawing reference file by selecting the **Xref** filter, as shown in Figure 4–16. The **Xref** filter is automatically created when you attach a drawing reference file.

- A special prefix is added to any named objects from the referenced drawing when the names display in the host drawing, as shown in Figure 4–16. It consists of the name of the referenced drawing and a vertical bar ("|"). For example, a layer named **1F** in a reference file named **Factory Floorplan-M** would display as **Factory Floorplan-M|1F**.

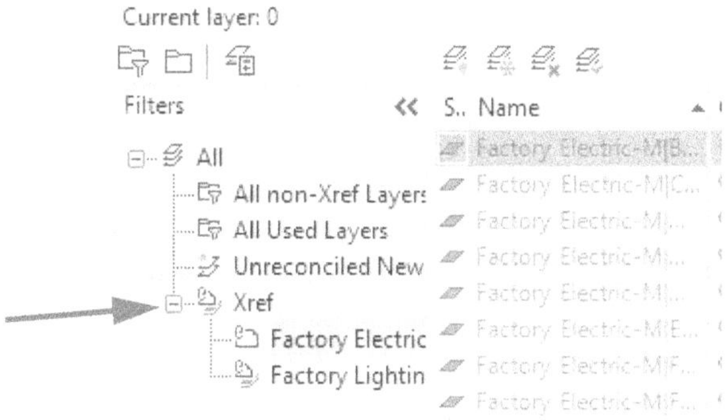

Figure 4–16

- In order to clearly distinguish which layers come from referenced drawings and which layer reside in the active drawing, xref layers are shown in gray text in the Layer Properties Manager and the Layer Control drop-down list, as shown in Figure 4–17. Additionally, you can change the visibility of xref layers in the layer panel drop-down.

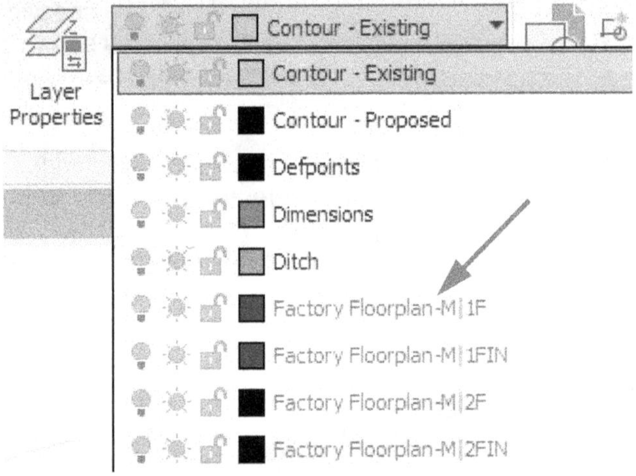

Figure 4–17

- You can change the Xref layers state or properties (**Freeze/Thaw**, **Color**, etc.) in the current drawing. However, you cannot make an Xref layer current in the host drawing.

- The layer on which the drawing reference file is inserted controls the visibility of the drawing reference file. The drawing reference file is hidden when that layer is frozen. To specify a default layer on which you want the reference files inserted, use the **XREFLAYER** system variable.

- Renaming or deleting an Xref layer in the Xref drawing, automatically renames and deletes the layer when the xref is reloaded in the host drawing.

- If you change the properties of an Xref layer, the change does not affect the referenced drawing. However, the change is retained in the host drawing by default. The default is controlled by the **VISTRETAIN** system variable. You can also control it in the Layer Settings dialog box, in the *Xref Layer Settings* area, by using the **Retain overrides to Xref layers properties** option.

The Layer Settings dialog box can be opened in the Layer Properties Manager by clicking ⚙ *(Settings).*

- In the Layer Settings dialog box, you can specify the various Xref layer properties that you want to reload, as shown in Figure 4–18. These Xref layer properties are stored in the **VISRETAINMODE** system variable.

Xref Layer Settings

    (•) Retain overrides to xref layer properties

         ☑ Xref layer properties to reload (except overrides)

☐ On/Off	☑ Color
☐ Freeze/Thaw	☐ Linetype
☑ Lock/Unlock	☐ Lineweight
☐ Plot/No Plot	☐ Transparency
☐ New VP Freeze	☐ Plot Style
☐ Description	

    ( ) Don't retain overrides to xref layer properties

    ☐ Treat xref object properties as ByLayer

Figure 4–18

- In the Layer Properties Manager, a 🖳 icon is displayed beside xref layers that contain overrides. Hovering the cursor over this icon displays a tooltip that lists the override information, as shown in Figure 4–19. In the top right corner of the Layer Properties Manager, the 🖳 icon (shown in Figure 4–19) can be used to toggle the shading background of the layers with overrides.

Layer Settings dialog box

Shading background on/off

S..	Name	O.	Fre...	Lo...	Color	Linetype	Lineweight	
	Factory Electric-M|B...				blue	Continuous	Default	
	Factory Electric-M|C...				white	Continuous	0.35 mm	
	Factory Electric-M|...				blue	Continuous	0.25 mm	
	Factory Electric-M|...				red	Continuous	Default	
	Factory Electric-M|...				yellow	Continuous	Default	
	Factory Electric-M|E...				magenta	Continuous	Default	
	Factory Electric-M|F...				white	Continuous	Default	
	Factory Electric-M|F...				magenta	Divide	Default	
	Factory Electric-M|F...				blue	Continuous	Default	
					red	Hidden	Default	
					red	Continuous	Default	
	Factory Electric-M|...				yellow	Continuous	Default	

Filters

⊟ 🖾 All
    All non-Xref Layers
    All Used Layers
    Unreconciled New
⊟ Xref
    Factory Electric
    Factory Lightin
    Xref Overrides

Layer: Factory Electric-M\|FRAME 050
Xref Linetype override: Divide

Figure 4–19

- In the Layer Properties Manager, an **Xref Overrides** filter is automatically created when some xref layers have overrides applied to them.
  - Clicking **Xref Overrides** displays only the list of xref layers with overrides.
  - To reset any or all of the layer properties to their original state, right-click on **Xref Overrides** and select **Reset Xref Layer Properties** to access the options, as shown in Figure 4–20.

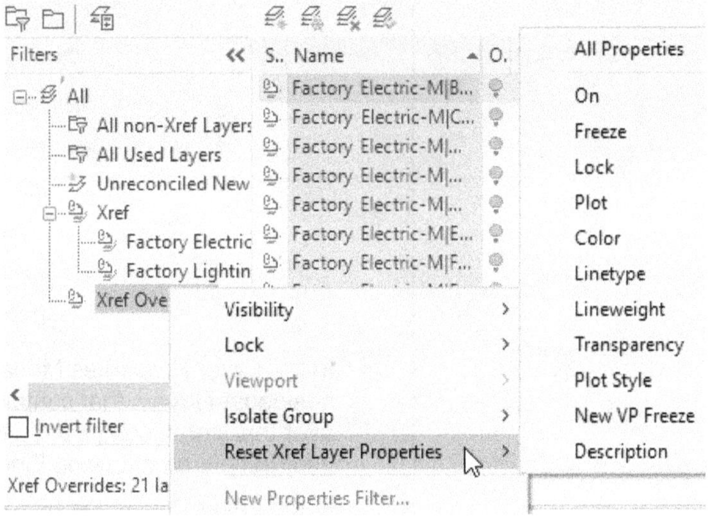

Figure 4–20

- You can control the display of layers for objects in an xref drawing that were not set to "ByLayer" for the layer property updates in the original xref. The **XREFOVERRIDE** variable enables you to force objects to be set to ByLayer in the host file.
  - Setting the **XREFOVERRIDE** to **1** enables the original file to set the properties and enables xref objects to be forced to use ByLayer in the host file.
  - Setting the **XREFOVERRIDE** to **0** enables the drawing in which it is referenced to control the properties and only enables xref objects that are already set to ByLayer to be changed in the host file.
  - This can also be controlled in the Layer Settings dialog box>*Xref Layer Settings* area, using the **Treat Xref object properties as ByLayer** option.

Draw with Accuracy

Object Snaps and Polar Tracking

Exam Objectives Covered in This Chapter

- 2.1.a Use object snaps
- 2.1.b Use polar tracking to restrict the cursor movement to specified angles

5.1 Using Running Object Snaps

When the AutoCAD® software saves information in a drawing file, it saves geometrical descriptions of the objects you have created. For example, a line is saved as two end points and a circle by its center point and radius. Object snaps enable you to take advantage of this geometrical precision by snapping to exact points on objects while you are in a command, as shown in Figure 5–1. You need some object snaps to be on most of the time, which can be set up as *running* object snaps.

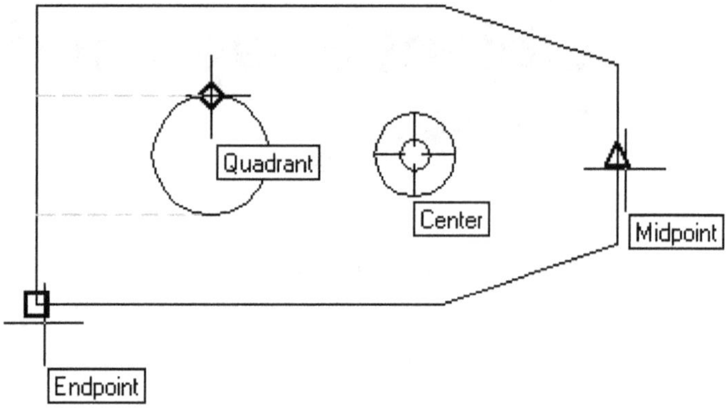

Figure 5–1

How To: Use Running Object Snaps

You can also use <F3> to toggle object snaps on and off.

1. In the Status Bar, toggle on ⬚ (Object Snap).
2. Start a command, such as **Line** or **Circle**.
3. Hover the cursor over an object. When the cursor is near a snap location, an icon displays that is specific to the object snap option that the cursor finds.
4. Click to select the object snap point.
5. Continue selecting other points, as required.

- When using an Object Snap on an object that might have more than one such point (e.g., **Endpoint** or **Midpoint**), select a point on the object that is close to the required point.

Object Snap Settings

To display the Object Snap drop-down list, either click on the arrow symbol next to the icon, or right-click on the icon.

Clicking ⬚ ▾ (Object Snap) toggles Object Snaps on or off.

You can set the various running object snap options that are available for use while picking a point. To use them, toggle on the Object Snap in the Status Bar. You can set the running object snaps at the following locations:

- In the Status Bar, in the ⬚ ▾ (Object Snap) drop-down list, as shown on the left in Figure 5–2.

- In the Drafting Settings dialog box, in the *Object Snap* tab, as shown on the right in Figure 5–2. To open the dialog box, expand ⬚ ▾ (Object Snap) in the Status Bar and select **Object Snap Settings....**

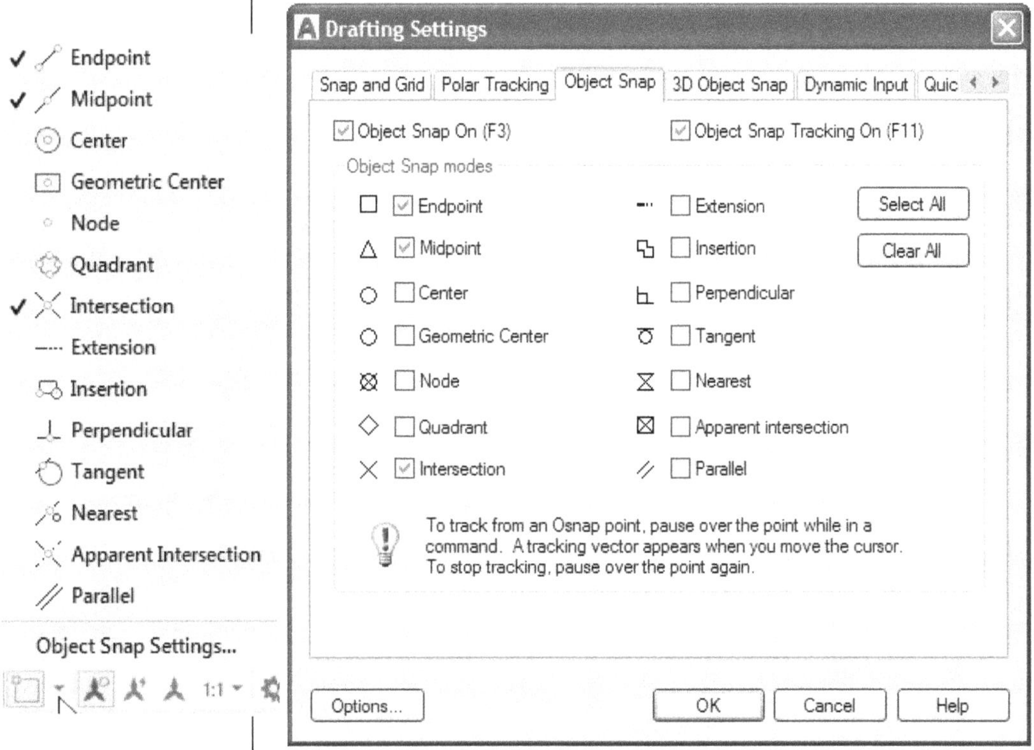

✓ ⟋ Endpoint
✓ ⟋ Midpoint
◎ Center
▣ Geometric Center
◦ Node
◌ Quadrant
✓ ✕ Intersection
┄ Extension
⟋◿ Insertion
⏄ Perpendicular
◓ Tangent
⟋◦ Nearest
⟋◦ Apparent Intersection
⫽ Parallel

Object Snap Settings...

⬚ ▾ 🖈 🖈 🖈 1:1 ▾ ⚙

Figure 5–2

- Running object snaps are indicated by a checkmark.

- You can add or remove the Object snap options when you are in the middle of a command.

- The symbol for each Object snap mode displays in the drawing window when you hover the cursor over the snap location. After a short delay, a small tooltip also displays the name of the snap.

- Object snap settings are saved in the system (not in individual drawings) and remain set until changed.

- When you toggle ⬚ (Object Snap) on or off in the Status Bar, it does not change the settings.

*You can also open the Options dialog box by right-clicking in the drawing window and selecting **Options**. Click on the Drafting tab to open it.*

- Clicking **Options** in the Drafting Settings dialog box opens the Options dialog box in the *Drafting* tab. Here, you can change the color of the Autosnap marker and modify other settings, as shown in Figure 5–3.

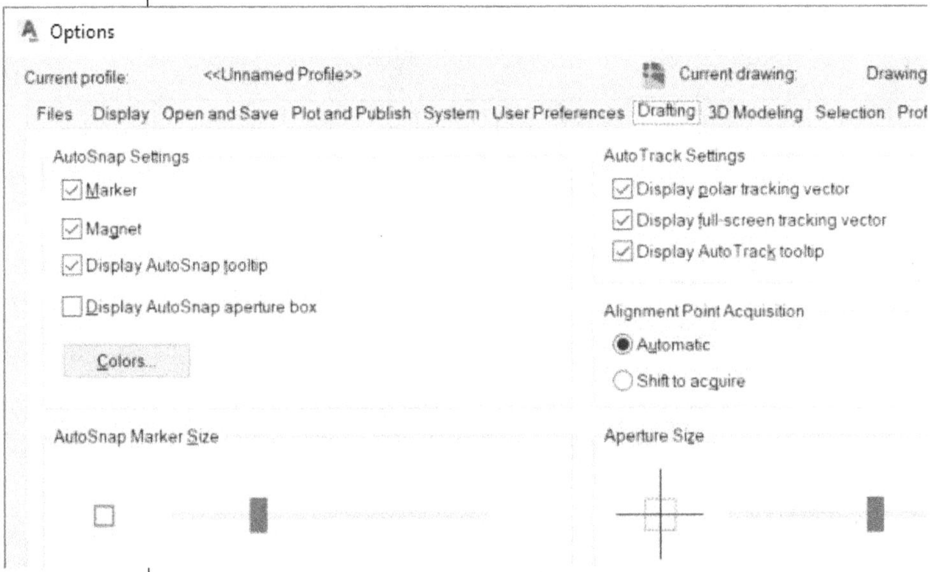

Figure 5–3

Primary Object Snaps

The most frequently used Object Snaps are **Endpoint**, **Center**, **Intersection**, and **Extension** where as **Quadrant**, **Midpoint**, and **Node** are also helpful in certain situations.

☐ ☑ Endpoint	Snaps to the end point of a line or arc.
△ ☑ Midpoint	Snaps to the midpoint of a line or arc.
○ ☑ Center	Snaps to the center point of a circle or arc. You can hover the cursor over the edge of the circle or arc to get the center point, if **Quadrant** is not toggled on.
⊠ ☐ Node	Snaps to a permanent reference point.
◇ ☐ Quadrant	Snaps to the quadrant point of a circle or arc (often described as clock positions (i.e., 12, 3, 6, and 9 o'clock).
✕ ☑ Intersection	Snaps to the intersection of two objects. **Intersection** can be used in two ways: click directly on the intersection, or select the first object for the intersection and then the second. Intersections that do not actually exist, but would if the two lines were extended, can be selected in this manner.
⋯ ☑ Extension	Snaps to a point on the continuation of an object.

How To: Use the Extension Object Snap

The **Extension** Object Snap works differently than the rest of the primary Object Snaps. Instead of selecting a point, it enables you to specify a start point at a distance from another point. In the example shown in Figure 5–4, the **Extension** Object Snap is used to start a new wall at a distance from another wall.

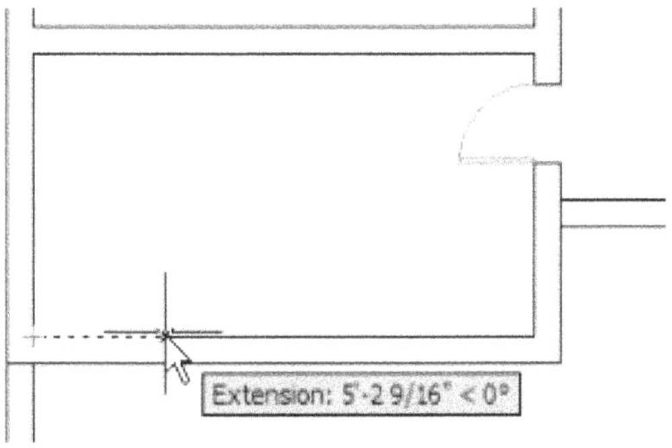

Extension: 5'-2 9/16" < 0°

Figure 5–4

1. In the Status Bar, toggle on ⬜ (Object Snap) and verify that the **Extension** object snap is selected.
2. Start a command, such as **Line** or **Circle**.
3. Hover the cursor over an object in the drawing. One of the standard Object Snap icons displays. Instead of selecting a point, move the cursor away. A small plus symbol (glyph) displays at the snap location.
4. When the cursor reaches a point along the line of the object, a dashed line displays from the end of the object to the crosshairs. In addition, a snap tip displays indicating the distance from the object and its angle. Enter the distance that you want to be from the original point.

Geometric Center Object Snap

The **Geometric Center** object snap tool finds the geometric center (centroid) of a closed polyline, as shown in Figure 5–5. It finds the geometric center of any closed irregular shape.

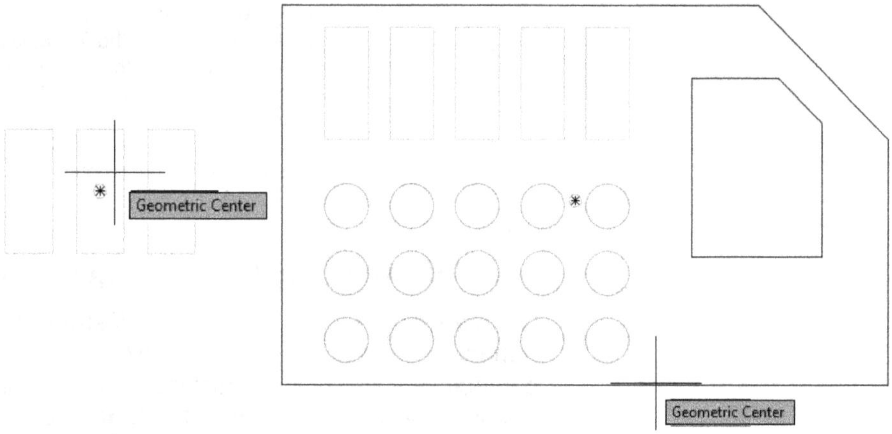

Figure 5–5

Practice 5a

Using Object Snaps

Practice Objective

- Draw a fence and rooflines using Object Snaps.

In this practice, you will set Object Snaps and use them to draw a fence line and rooflines, as shown in Figure 5–6.

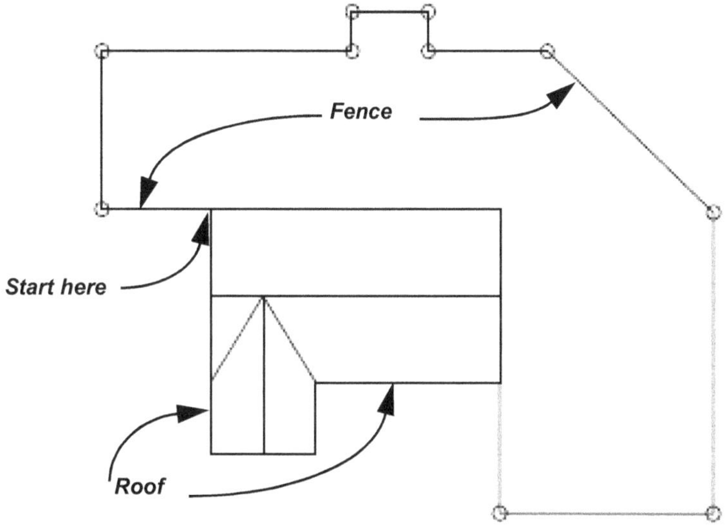

Figure 5–6

Task 1 - Draw the fence.

1. Open **Fence-A.dwg** from your practice files folder.

2. In the Status Bar, click on the ⬚ ▾ (Object Snap) arrow to display the object snaps list. Set the Object Snap modes to **Endpoint**, **Midpoint**, **Center**, and **Extension**. Toggle Object Snap on.

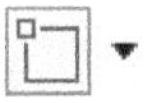

3. Start the **Line** command to draw a fence as shown in Figure 5–6. Start by snapping and clicking to the endpoint of the upper left corner of the house. Moving clockwise, snap and click to the center of each of the fence posts (i.e., the small circles provided in the drawing). End the fence by snapping and clicking to the endpoint of the bottom right corner of the house.

Task 2 - Draw the roof lines.

1. In the Status Bar, click on the ⬛ ▾ (Object Snap) arrow and select **Intersection**.

2. In the Status Bar, toggle on ⟲ (Polar Tracking), if required.

3. Start the **Line** command again and draw line (1) from the midpoint on the right side of the house straight left to the point where it intersects the left side, as shown in Figure 5–7. This indicates the main roof ridge.

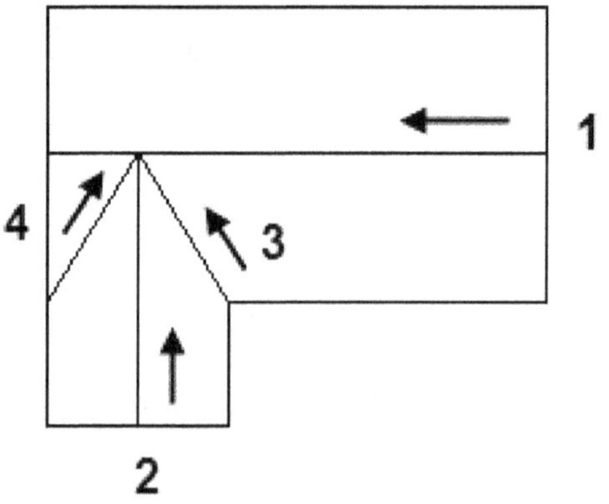

Figure 5–7

4. Draw line (2) from the midpoint of the front wing of the house straight up to the intersection of the ridge you just drew. This creates the ridge of the wing.

5. Draw line (3) from the top right corner endpoint of the wing to the intersection of the two ridge lines.

6. For line (4), after starting the **Line** command, hover the cursor over the bottom left corner of the house and then pull it up without selecting the point. A dotted line and the **Extension** Object snap tooltip displays near the cursor indicating that it is enabled. Enter a distance of **10'-0"**. Press <Enter>. The line starts at this point. End it at the intersection of the two ridge lines.

7. Save and close the drawing.

5.2 Using Object Snap Overrides

You can use ⬚ (Object Snap) for the points to which you normally snap. Other snaps, such as **Tangent** or **Perpendicular**, are required less often. Instead of selecting and then clearing

those Object snaps using the ⬚ (Object Snap) list, you can apply them as one-time *object snap overrides*. Object Snaps applied as overrides are only active for the next point you select. You can access overrides through the shortcut menu when you are in a command, as shown in Figure 5–8.

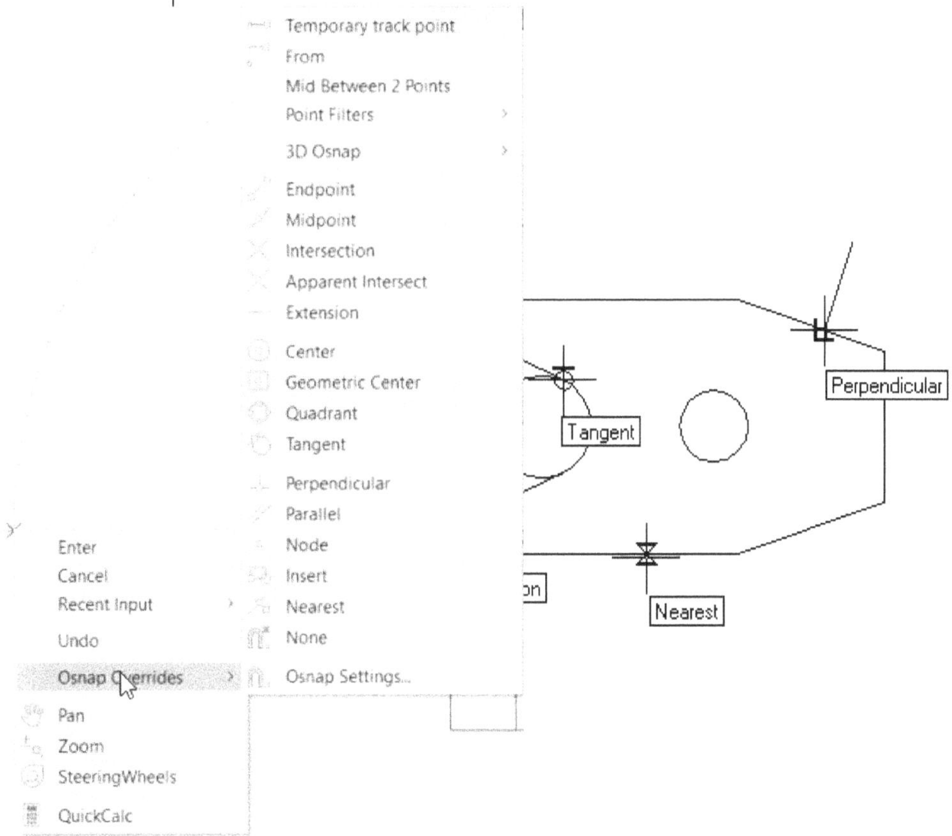

Figure 5–8

- You must start a command before using an Object Snap override. You can then set the Object Snap override in the shortcut menu by selecting **Osnap Overrides**, or by holding <Shift> while right-clicking.

How To: Use an Object Snap Override

1. Start a command where point input is required, such as **Line** or **Circle**.
2. Before selecting the point, select an Object Snap override.
3. Move the crosshairs near the location of the object to which you want to snap. An icon for the running object snap displays at the snap location.
4. Click to select the point.

- If you select the wrong Object Snap, do not press <Esc> or use the **Undo** command (doing so would cancel the command). Instead, select the correct Object Snap override twice. The first time cancels the previous snap and the second sets the new snap.

Typical Object Snap Overrides

Tangent	Snaps to a point on a circle or arc that forms a line tangent to the object.
Perpendicular	Snaps to a point that creates a perpendicular line from one object to another.
Parallel	Snaps to a point that creates a line parallel to the selected object.
Insert	Snaps to the insertion point of text, a block, or an external reference.
Nearest	Snaps to the point on an object that is visually closest to the crosshairs.
None	Toggles off object snaps for the next point selected.

How To: Use the Parallel Object Snap

Parallel can only be used to draw linear objects. At least one point must be selected before **Parallel** can be used. The new line is drawn parallel to the selected object, as shown in Figure 5–9.

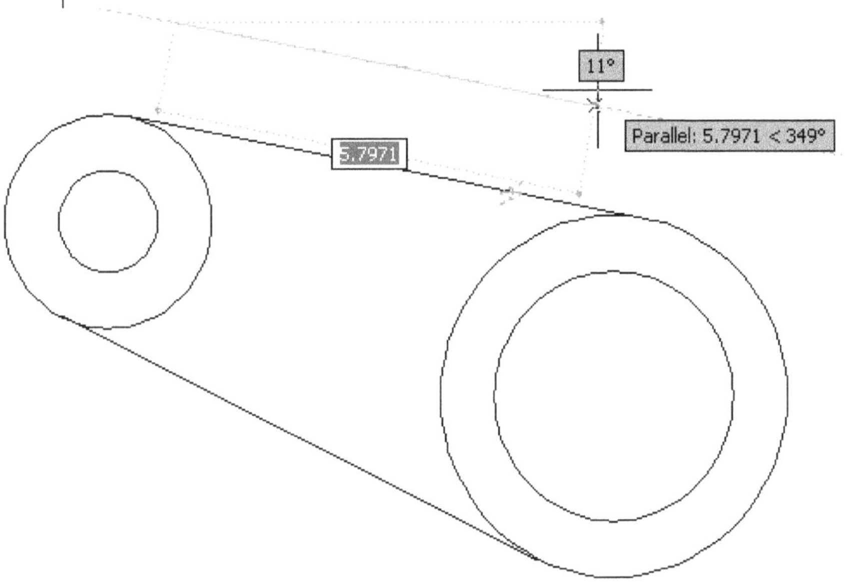

Figure 5–9

1. Start the **Line** command.
2. Select a starting point in the drawing.
3. Select the Parallel Object Snap override.
4. Hover the cursor over the object to which the new line should be parallel. First, the **Parallel** icon displays and when you move the cursor away a small plus symbol displays on the object.
5. Move the crosshairs away from the object. When you reach a point that makes the new line parallel to the selected object, a dashed line displays indicating the parallel direction. In addition, a parallel marker and snap tip display. Enter the distance or select the point that you want to use.

Practice 5b

Object Snap Overrides

Practice Objective

- Draw objects at precise locations with respect to already present objects in a drawing.

In this practice, you will use a variety of running object snaps and overrides in conjunction with the **Line** and **Circle** commands to complete a drawing, as shown in Figure 5–10.

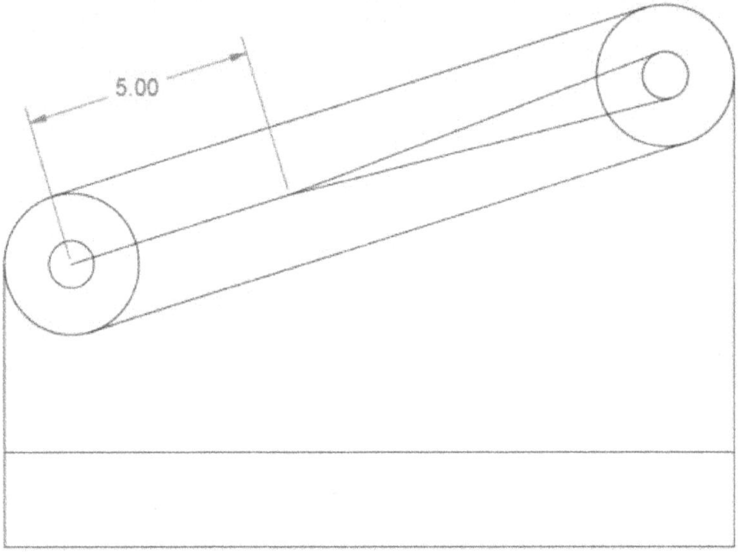

Figure 5–10

1. Open **Arm.dwg** from your practice files folder.

2. Set the object snaps to **Endpoint**, **Midpoint**, and **Center** and toggle ⬚ (Object Snap) on, if required.

3. With Circle> ◯ (Center Radius), draw circles with a radius of **0.5** at the center of the two existing circles.

The object snap override must be selected each time you want to use it.

4. Draw lines connecting the large circles tangent to each circle. Start the **Line** command and at *Specify first point*, hold <Shift> and right-click to open the shortcut menu. Select **Tangent** override. Click anywhere along the upper edge of the bigger lower left large circle, as shown in Figure 5–11.

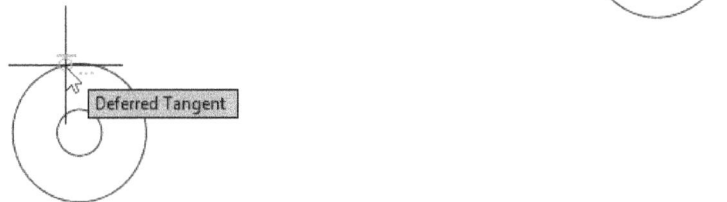

Figure 5–11

5. Use <Shift>+ right-click again and select the **Tangent** override again. Click along the upper edge of the bigger upper right large circle. Press <Enter> to exit the **Line** command. A line is drawn along the top tangent points of the two large circles.

6. Similarly, draw another line along the bottom tangent points of the two large circles.

7. Start the **Line** command and hold <Shift> and right-click to select the **Quadrant** override. Click along the 9 o'clock quadrant of the lower large circle, as shown in Figure 5–12. Click along the upper left end point of the rectangle to draw the line. (The **Endpoint** object snap is already selected.)

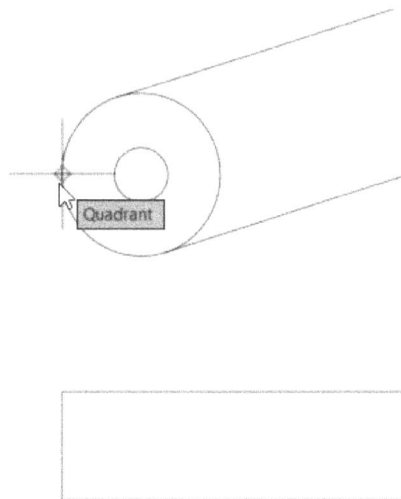

Figure 5–12

8. Draw a line from the 3 o'clock quadrant of the lower large circle perpendicular to the top of the rectangle.

9. Draw a line that starts at the center of the small circle on the left, parallel (use the **Parallel** override) to one of the diagonal lines and **5 units** long (shown in Figure 5–13).

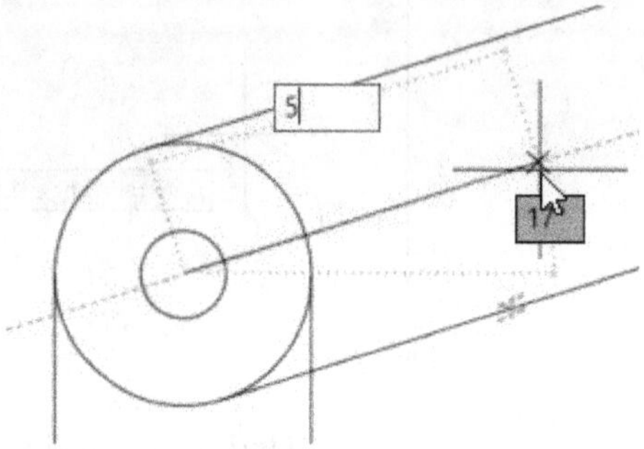

Figure 5–13

10. From the endpoint of the 5 units parallel line, draw a line tangent along the top of the small circle on the right.

11. Draw one more line from the end point of the parallel line that is tangent along the bottom of the small circle on the right.

12. Save and close the drawing.

5.3 Drawing Vertical and Horizontal Lines

Ortho Mode

Ortho Mode restricts the movement of the cursor to horizontal and vertical directions by forcing lines to use only 0°, 90°, and 180° angles.

To toggle Ortho Mode on or off, in the Status Bar, click ⌐ (Ortho Mode), as shown in Figure 5–14. The keyboard shortcut for this command is <F8>.

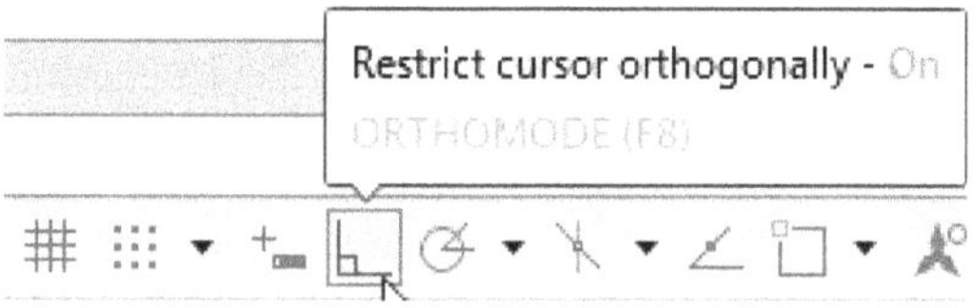

Restrict cursor orthogonally - On
ORTHOMODE (F8)

Figure 5–14

How To: Use Ortho Mode to Draw Vertical and Horizontal Lines

The tool has a blue background when it is toggled on.

1. In the Status Bar, click ⌐ (Ortho Mode) to toggle it on.
2. In the Status Bar, click ⊞ (Dynamic Input) to toggle it on.
3. In the *Home* tab>Draw panel, click ╱ (Line) to start the **Line** command.
4. At the *Specify first point:* prompt, select a starting point for the line.
5. At the *Specify next point:* prompt, move the crosshairs in the direction that you want the line to extend. Note that the line is restricted to either the horizontal or vertical direction, as shown in Figure 5–15.

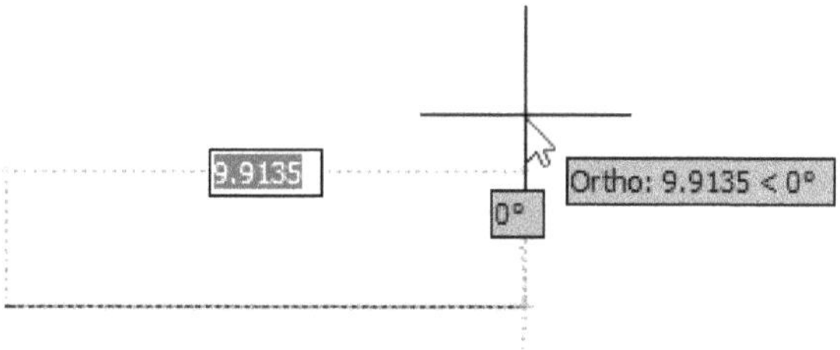

9.9135   0°   Ortho: 9.9135 < 0°

Figure 5–15

6. When the line displays in the required direction, enter a distance.

7. Press <Enter>. The line is drawn to the set length in the direction you selected.
8. Repeat Steps 4 to 7 for additional line segments, or press <Enter> to end the **Line** command.

Polar Tracking

Another way to draw horizontal and vertical straight lines is to use the Polar Tracking command. This command restricts the movement of the cursor to specified (preset) angles. Although, you can set the polar angles as required, but this section of the guide uses the standard 90° increments to draw horizontal and vertical lines.

• Polar Tracking makes it easy to work with preset angles as you draw. Rather than typing the angle, you move the cursor to find the tracking line (dotted line) and enter the distance.

• To toggle Polar Tracking on and off, click ⟳ (Polar Tracking) in the Status Bar, as shown in Figure 5–16. The keyboard shortcut for this command is <F10>.

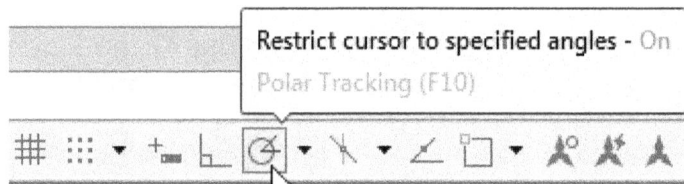

Restrict cursor to specified angles - On
Polar Tracking (F10)

Figure 5–16

• Between Polar Tracking and Ortho Mode, Polar Tracking is versatile, as it permits the use of other angles in addition to the 90° angles.

• Ortho Mode and Polar Tracking cannot be toggled on at the same time.

How To: Use Polar Tracking to Draw Vertical and Horizontal Lines

1. In the Status Bar, click the arrow in ⟳ ▼ (Polar Tracking) to display the angles list. Select **90,180,270,360**, as shown in Figure 5–17.

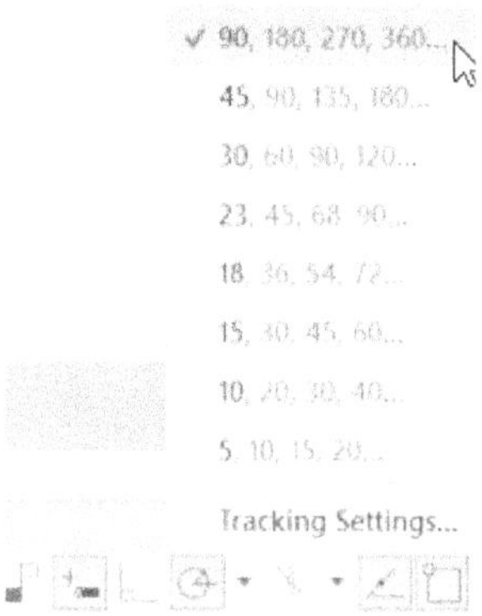

✓ 90, 180, 270, 360...

45, 90, 135, 180...

30, 60, 90, 120...

23, 45, 68, 90...

18, 36, 54, 72...

15, 30, 45, 60...

10, 20, 30, 40...

5, 10, 15, 20...

Tracking Settings...

Figure 5–17

The tool has a blue background when it is toggled on.

2. Click ⟳ (Polar Tracking) or press <F10> to toggle it on, if required.
3. In the *Home* tab>Draw panel, click ✐ (Line) to start the **Line** command.
4. At the *Specify first point:* prompt, select a starting point for the line.
5. At the *Specify next point:* prompt, move the crosshairs in the direction in which you want the line to extend.
6. When the correct Polar Tracking line displays, enter a distance.
7. Press <Enter>. The line is drawn that length in the direction in which you pick.
8. Repeat for another line segment or press <Enter> to end the **Line** command.

• When the cursor approaches one of the polar angles, the dotted tracking line displays with a tooltip specifying *Polar:*, followed by the distance and angle from the last point (distance<angle), as shown in Figure 5–18.

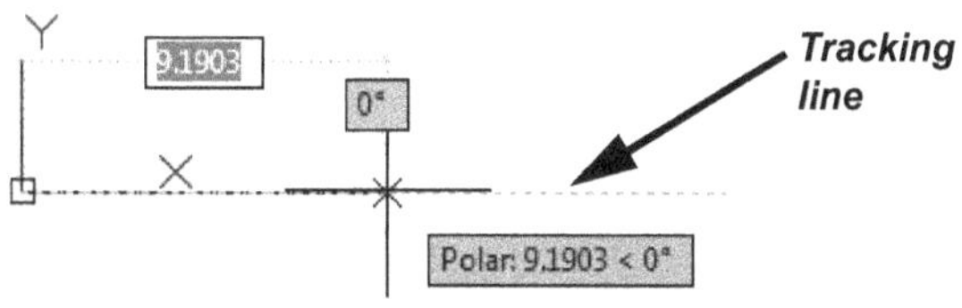

9.1903

0°

Tracking line

Polar: 9.1903 < 0°

Figure 5–18

• You can use Polar Tracking with or without Dynamic Input.

5.4 Polar Tracking at Angles

You can use Polar Tracking to draw horizontal lines, vertical lines, and lines at specific increment angles. ⟳ (Polar Tracking) can be toggled on or off in the Status Bar. Right-click on ⟳ ▾ (Polar Tracking) to select from the list of standard angles (as shown in Figure 5–19) to set the increment angles. You can also set the increment angle while working in a command.

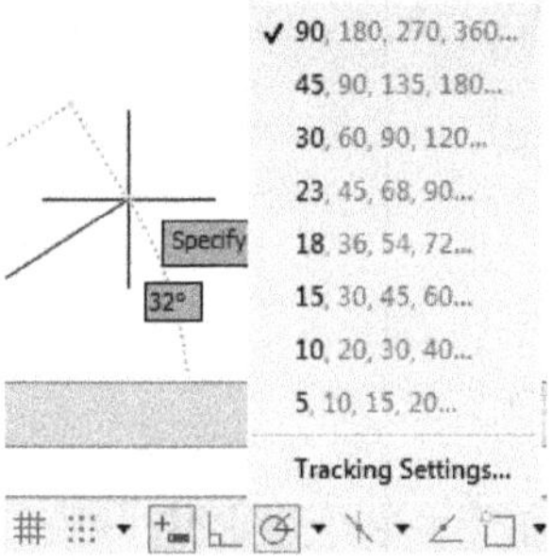

✓ 90, 180, 270, 360...
45, 90, 135, 180...
30, 60, 90, 120...
23, 45, 68, 90...
18, 36, 54, 72...
15, 30, 45, 60...
10, 20, 30, 40...
5, 10, 15, 20...

Tracking Settings...

Figure 5–19

Polar Tracking Settings

*You can also click on the arrow beside ⟳ ▾ (Polar Tracking) and select **Tracking Settings....***

For more Polar Tracking options, expand ⟳ ▾ (Polar Tracking) (by right-clicking) and select **Tracking Settings...** to open the Drafting Settings dialog box, as shown in Figure 5–20. In this dialog box you can specify additional angles and modify other settings.

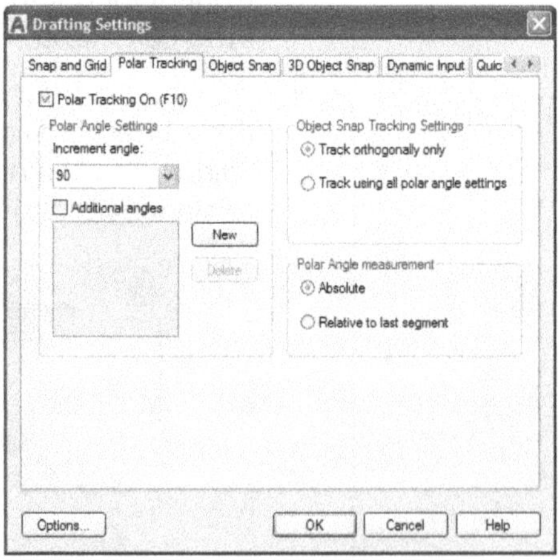

Figure 5–20

Increment angle: 30	Select an angle in the Increment angle list. All these angles are listed in the Polar Tracking list, which is available in the Status Bar.
☑ Additional angles 35	Select this option to use angles other than the one specified in the Increment angle list. You can only snap to this angle (not to its multiples) and to multiples from the Increment angle list. The angle gets added to the Polar Tracking list.
New	Click to add an additional angle. You can add up to ten additional polar tracking alignment angles.
Delete	Deletes selected additional angles.

- When the **Absolute** option is selected, Polar Tracking is relative to the current X- and Y-axes. For example, if the *Increment Angle* is set to **90** and you draw a diagonal line at 40 degrees for the first segment, the subsequent line is still drawn in increments of 90 degrees relative to the X- and Y-axes (to the right, left, up, or down), as shown on the left in Figure 5–21.

- When the **Relative to last segment** option is selected, Polar Tracking is relative to the last segment drawn or to a segment to which you snap using OSNAP. This means that you can draw the subsequent line in 90 degree increments from the diagonal line drawn, as shown on the right in Figure 5–21.

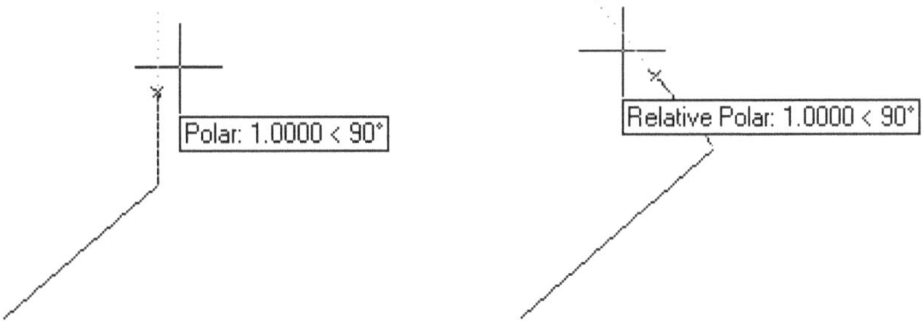

Figure 5–21

- In the Polar Tracking settings, you can select **Track orthogonally only** (i.e., horizontally and vertically) or **Track using all polar angle settings**.

Practice 5c

Polar Tracking

Practice Objective

- Draw an outline of a part using Polar Tracking and by setting the Polar Tracking options.

In this practice, you will adjust the Polar Tracking settings and then use **Polar Tracking** to draw the outline of the part, as shown in Figure 5–22.

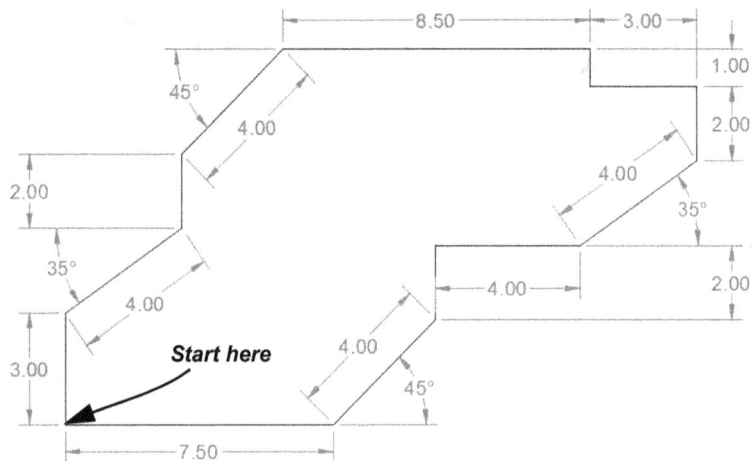

Figure 5–22

1. Open **Pattern.dwg** from your practice files folder. It is an empty drawing file.

2. In the Status Bar, expand ◔ ▾ (Polar Tracking) and select **Tracking Settings...**.

3. In the Drafting Settings dialog box (in the *Polar Tracking* tab), select **Additional angles** and click **New.** In the edit box that is highlighted, enter **35** to add an additional angle. Click **OK**.

4. In the Status Bar, expand ◔ ▾ (Polar Tracking) and select **45,90,135,180...**. Ensure that **Polar Tracking** is toggled **On**.

5. Start the **Line** command and select any point in the lower left corner of the screen (shown as "Start here" in Figure 5–22). Move the cursor straight to the right so that the tracking line at 0 degrees displays. Enter **7.5** and press <Enter>.

The opposite (or complementary) angle for 45 degrees is 135 degrees.

6. Move the cursor up and to the right until the 45 degree tracking line displays. Enter **4** and press <Enter>.

7. Continue to draw the outline (as shown in Figure 5–22) finding the appropriate tracking angle and typing the distance for each segment. Note that you can snap to 35 degree angle as well.

8. For the last angled segment, the 35 degree tracking does not work (because the opposite or complementary angle for 35 degree is 145 degrees, which was not set). Enter a distance of **4** (do not press <Enter>) and then press <Tab>. Note that the angle edit box is highlighted. Enter the angle as **145** and press <Enter>.

9. Draw the last vertical line of **3** units to complete the drawing.

10. Save and close the drawing.

5.5 Object Snap Tracking

Object Snap Tracking enables you to locate new points in relation to one or two existing points, as shown in Figure 5–23. Using Object Snaps and Object Snap Tracking together can speed up your work.

Object Snaps must be toggled on to use Object Snap Tracking.

Midpoint: < 270°, Endpoint: < 180°

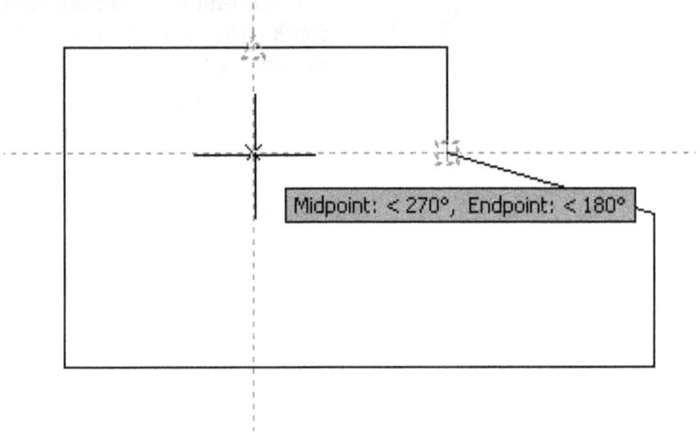

Figure 5–23

- Tracking builds a new point based on coordinates taken from two other points. The new X-coordinate is from one point and the new Y-coordinate is from another point.

- When a point is selected for Object Snap Tracking, a small plus displays at the point. The point is said to be *acquired*. A dotted line displays from that point to indicate tracking.

- To clear an acquired point, move the cursor over the point again. Ensure that the small plus disappears.

- You can use Object Snap Tracking with Polar Tracking toggled on or off. However, in some cases Polar Tracking can interfere with the effects of Object Snap Tracking.

How To: Use Object Snap Tracking With One Point

You can also use <F11> to toggle object snap tracking on and off.

1. In the Status Bar, toggle on both ⬜ (Object Snap) and ◿ (Object Snap Tracking) and set the Object Snap options that you want to use.
2. Start a command, such as **Line**.

3. Hover the cursor over the point from which you want to track (do not click on it). A small plus marks the point, as shown in Figure 5–24.

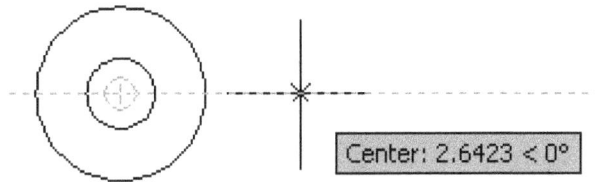

Center: 2.6423 < 0°

Figure 5–24

4. Move the cursor away from the point. A dotted line and tooltip display when the cursor locks into a tracking angle.
5. Enter the distance that you want to use and press <Enter>.

How To: Use Object Snap Tracking With Two Points

1. In the Status Bar, toggle on both ⬚ (Object Snap) and

   ⬚ (Object Snap Tracking) and set the Object Snap options that you want to use.
2. Start a command, such as **Line**.
3. Hover the cursor over the points from which you want to track (do not click on them). Small plus signs mark each point.
4. Two dotted lines display, each passing through an acquired point. Move the cursor to the point at which the lines intersect. A description of each dotted line displays in the tooltip, as shown in Figure 5–25.

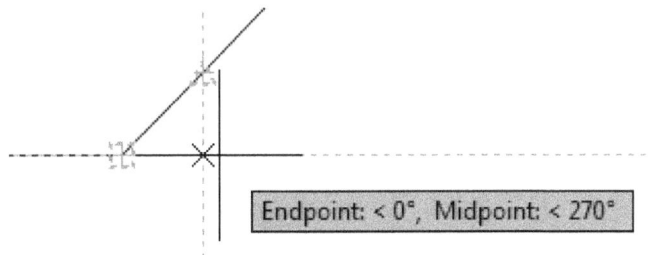

Endpoint: < 0°, Midpoint: < 270°

Figure 5–25

5. Select the point at the intersection of the tracking lines.

Practice 5d

Object Snap Tracking

Practice Objective

- Create a top view of a part by using Object Snap Tracking.

In this practice, you will create a top view of a part by tracking the locations from the existing front and side views, as shown in Figure 5–26. Construction lines have been provided from the side view, and the other construction lines do not need to be drawn.

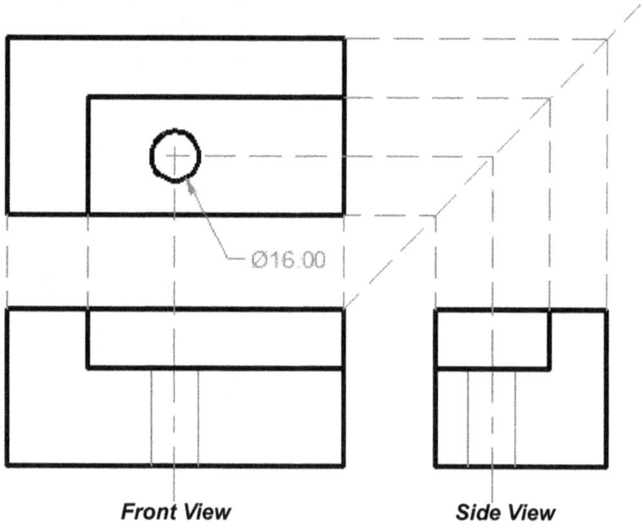

Front View　　　　　　　　**Side View**

Figure 5–26

1. Open **Missing View.dwg** from your practice files folder.

2. Set the current Object Snaps as **Endpoint**, **Midpoint**, **Center**, **Quadrant**, and **Intersection**.

3. Toggle on ▭ (Object Snap) and ◩ (Object Snap Tracking), if required.

4. Start the **Line** command. At the *Specify first point:* prompt, hover the cursor over the top left corner of the front view, which displays the **Endpoint** object snap icon. Then, without clicking, move the cursor. Note that a small green plus mark displays at the top left corner of the front view. Hover the cursor over the top end point of the shortest construction line coming from the side view.

5. Move the cursor to where the two tracking lines intersect at a point, as shown in Figure 5–27. Select that point as the first point for the line.

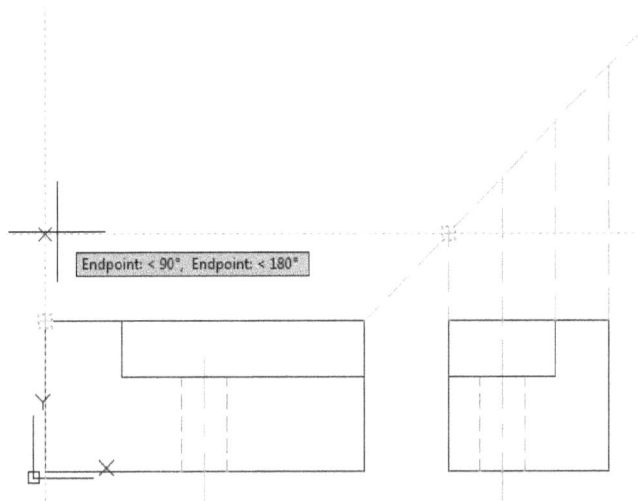

Figure 5–27

6. Continue to draw the rectangular outline of the top view, tracking from the appropriate points.

7. Draw the two interior lines on the top view (as shown in Figure 5–26) using tracking points.

8. Draw a circle (diameter=**16**) whose center point is established by tracking points, as shown in Figure 5–28.

Figure 5–28

9. Save and close the drawing.

5.6 Locating Points with Tracking

Object Snap Tracking Review

You can track from two points to find the intersection point of their tracking lines.

You can use the technique of Object Snap Tracking to locate a new point based on existing object snap points. For example, you can find the precise center of an object in your drawing by tracking from the midpoints of two sides, as shown in Figure 5–29.

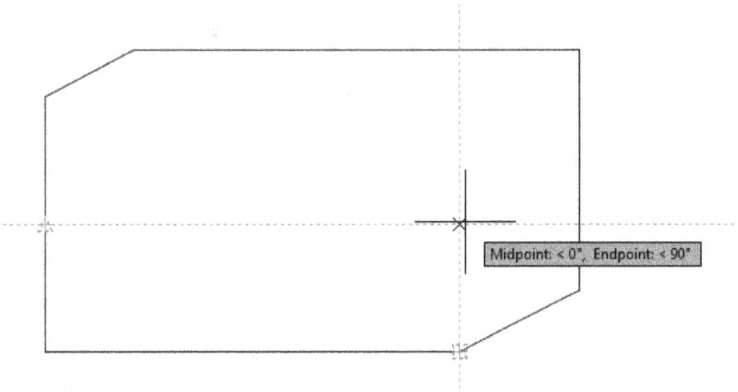

Figure 5–29

- (Object Snap) and  (Object Snap Tracking) must both be toggled on to use Object Snap Tracking.

- Hover the cursor over the object snap point and then move it away vertically or horizontally to display the tracking line.

- You can select one point and type a distance to move in one direction along a tracking line from that point.

Temporary Track Point

(Temporary Track Point) can create additional tracking points, which can be useful when you are using Object Snap Tracking and need to have more than two tracking points. It enables you to find a location based on two distances from another point. For example, if you need to position a circle with its center five units to the left and three units up from an endpoint, you need to use Temporary Track Point to add the additional point.

-  (Object Snap) and  (Object Snap Tracking) must both be toggled on to use Temporary Track Point.

- You can start a Temporary Track Point by right-clicking and selecting **Osnap Overrides>Temporary track point** in the shortcut menu or by typing **TT** in the Command Line, after invoking a draw command.

How To: Use a Temporary Track Point

1. In the Status Bar, toggle on 📋 (Object Snap) and ◿ (Object Snap Tracking).
2. Start a command, such as **Line** or **Circle**.
3. When prompted for a point, start ▭—○ (Temporary Track Point) by typing **tt**.
4. Hover the cursor over an existing point, which is then marked with a small plus mark.
5. Move the cursor to lock the required tracking angle from the temporary point, and then type a distance to move in relation to the temporary point, as shown in Figure 5–30.

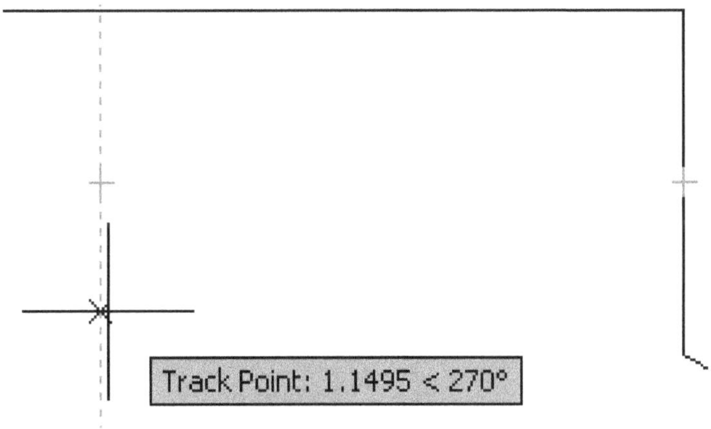

Track Point: 1.1495 < 270°

Figure 5–30

- Tracking lines display when you have locked a tracking angle from the temporary point.

- **IMPORTANT:** Do not move the cursor directly over the cross that marks the temporary point. Doing so clears the point.

Practice 5e

Locating Points with Tracking (Mechanical)

Practice Objective

- Place holes at certain locations.

In this practice, you will use Object Snap Tracking and Temporary Track Point to place holes on a machine part, as shown in Figure 5–31.

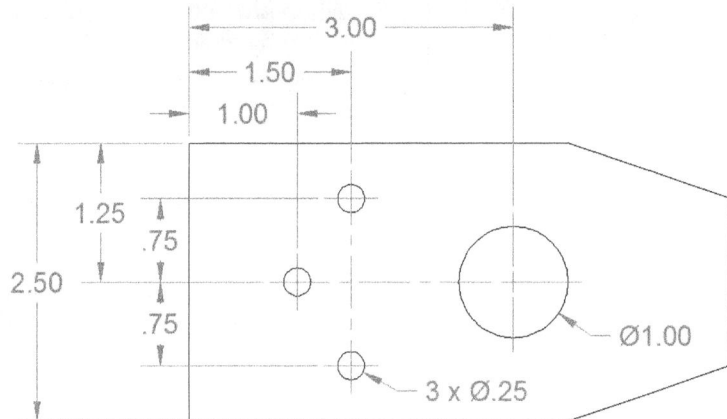

Figure 5–31

1. Open **Track-I.dwg** from your practice files folder.

2. Set the Object Snap Settings to **Midpoint**, and verify that ⬚ (Object Snap) and ∠ (Object Snap Tracking) are toggled on.

3. To draw a circle using the **Circle** command, hover the cursor over the midpoint of the left line as a tracking point, and then pull the cursor to the right. Type **3,** press <Enter>, and set the *diameter* (using the <Down arrow>) to **1**.

4. Repeat this process to place the **0.25 diameter** circle, **1 unit** from the midpoint of the left vertical line, as shown in Figure 5–31.

5. Start the **Circle** command again and start the **Temporary Track Point** override, by right-clicking anywhere and selecting **Osnap Overrides>Temporary track point**.

6. Hover the cursor over the midpoint of the left vertical line, and pull the cursor to the right. Type **1.5** (as shown on the left in Figure 5–32) and press <Enter>. A small plus mark displays at the temporary track point. Move the cursor directly below the plus mark. A vertical tracking line displays. Type **0.75** (as shown on the right in Figure 5–32) and press <Enter> to select another point 0.75 units down from the temporary point.

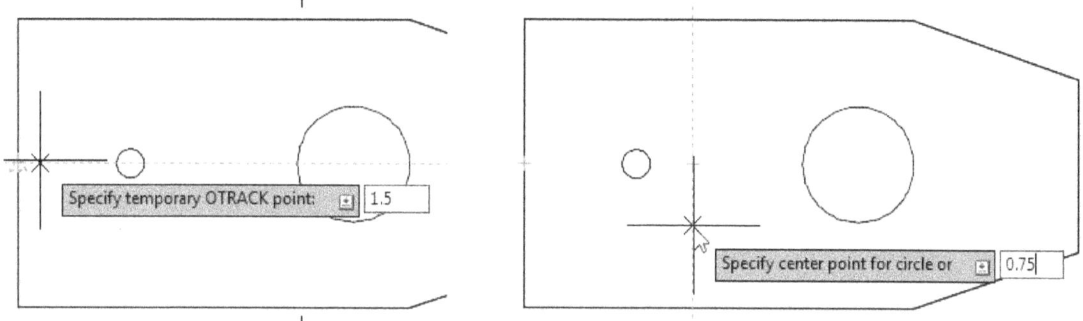

Figure 5–32

7. The cursor snaps to the point. Place a **0.25 diameter** circle at this temporary track point location.

8. Repeat this process to place the last circle (**0.25 diameter**), but move the cursor directly above the cross as shown in Figure 5–31.

9. Save and close the drawing.

Practice 5f

Locating Points with Tracking (Architectural)

Practice Objectives

- Draw the walls of a building.
- Position additional wall lines using tracking methods.

In this practice, you will create walls for a simple building outline using the Polyline command and then use Object Snap Tracking and Temporary Track Point methods to help position interior partitions, as shown in Figure 5–33.

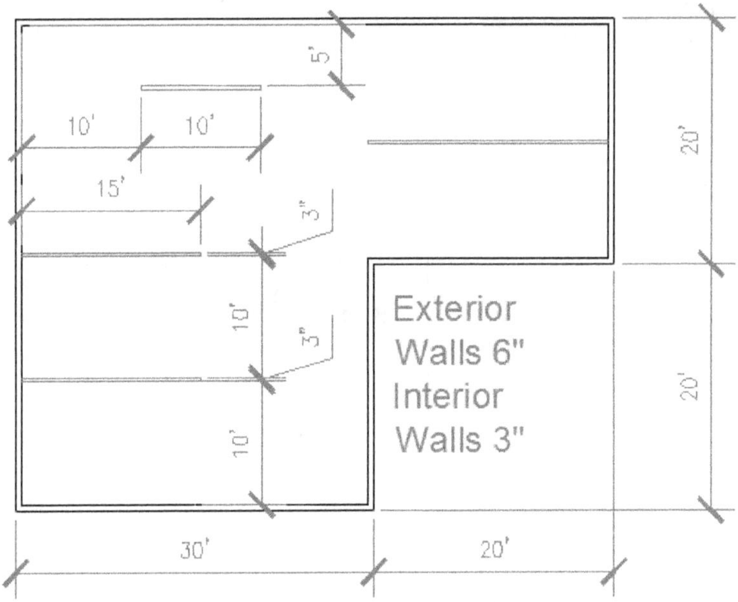

Figure 5–33

1. Start a new drawing based on **AEC-Imperial.dwt,** which is found in your practice files folder.

2. Make the layer **Walls** current. Using the **Polyline** command, verify that the **Width** option is set to **0**, and then draw the outside of the building as shown in Figure 5–33. Start from the lower left corner and draw counter-clockwise.

   - ✐ (Object Snap Tracking) can help to position the point for the top left corner.

Note: Ignore the undimensioned partition wall.

3. Offset the exterior walls **6"** to the inside.

4. Make the layer **Partitions** current and draw the interior partitions.

5. Use (Object Snap) and (Object Snap Tracking) to help position the bottom partition line and then make it **3"** wide.

6. From this wall, use the (Object Snap) and (Object Snap Tracking) to draw the middle partition wall.

7. For the top-most floating wall, start the **Pline** command. Hover the cursor over the top left inner corner (Endpoint) of the wall. Enter **tt** (for **Temporary Track Point**) and press <Enter>.

8. Drag the cursor down, enter **5'** and press <Enter>. A plus mark is established. Drag the cursor right, enter **10'** and press <Enter>. The first point of the polyline is established. Draw the floating wall starting from this point.

9. Save the drawing as **Open Office.dwg** and close the drawing.

Chapter 6

User Coordinate System

Exam Objectives Covered in This Chapter

- 2.2.a Understand and define the User Coordinate System
- 2.2.b Move the UCS origin
- 2.2.c Rotate the UCS
- 2.2.d Restore the UCS to the World Coordinate System (WCS)
- 2.2.e Restore the previous UCS
- 2.2.f Use named UCS definitions and preset orientations

6.1 Introduction to the User Coordinate System (UCS)

In the AutoCAD software, 2D objects are created on a single flat plane, which is usually the XY plane. In 3D, you can work on the XY plane or change to another plane, as shown in Figure 6–1.

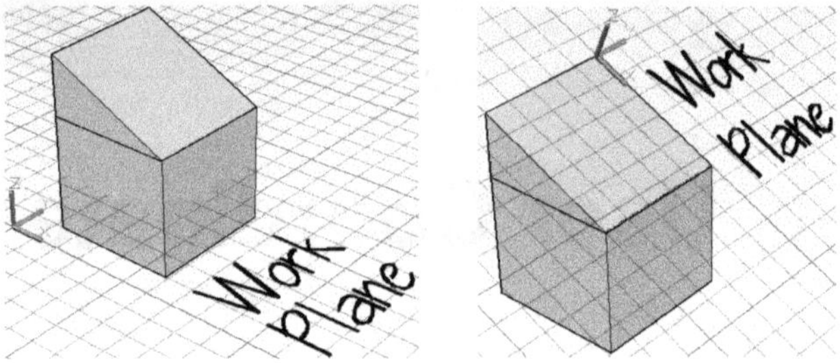

Figure 6–1

There are three axes: the X-axis, Y-axis, and Z-axis. Three planes are also automatically created by the intersections of these axes. They are the XY plane, the YZ plane, and the XZ plane. Together these three axes and their planes make up a user coordinate system, or UCS. The UCS is a user-defined working plane with X,Y coordinates that can be positioned at any location or orientation in space.

When you draw on the UCS, you can use the same commands and methods regardless of the angle or location to which the XY plane has changed. Drawing in 3D is very similar to drawing in 2D. The only difference is that you add information for the Z-direction as well for the thickness, elevation, or height. Many 2D commands can be used to start or add to 3D drawings.

• Do not confuse the UCS position with the viewing direction. The position from which you view your drawing, known as the viewpoint, determines how you see your drawing. The UCS determines where you are drawing. It sets the position of the working plane.

• Each viewport can have its own UCS.

How To: Start the UCS Command

1. You will be required to work in the 3D Modeling workspace. In the Status Bar, select **3D Modeling** from Workspace Switching, as shown in Figure 6–2.

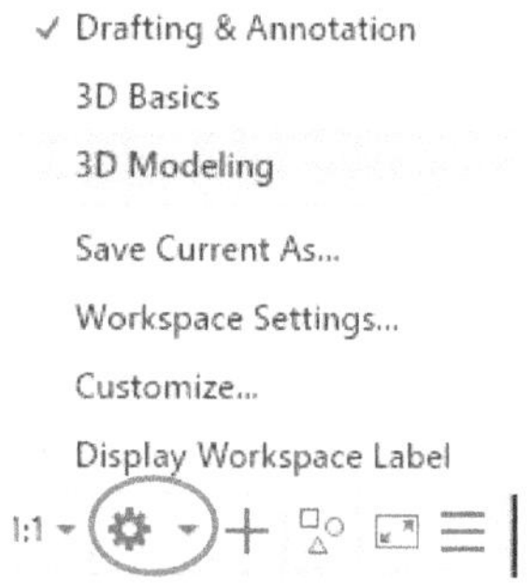

✓ Drafting & Annotation

3D Basics

3D Modeling

Save Current As...

Workspace Settings...

Customize...

Display Workspace Label

Figure 6–2

2. In the *Home* tab>Coordinates panel, click ⤤ (UCS).

   • Alternatively, you can access the command in the *View* tab>Viewport Tools panel or type **UCS** at the command line.

• You should always be able to return to the UCS home position. The fastest way to do so is to restore the ⤤ (World UCS). You can also type the command name: type **UCS**, press <Enter>, type **W**, and press <Enter>.

• To return to the last UCS used, click ⤤ (UCS, Previous). The AutoCAD® software retains up to 10 previous UCSs.

• If you have multiple viewports in Model Space, each viewport can have a different UCS.

UCS Icon

In 2D drawings, you rarely need to use any other coordinate system than the World UCS. The UCS icon can be toggled off. However, in 3D models the UCS icon can be very helpful for indicating where the UCS is located and how it is oriented. You can toggle the UCS icon on and off, and have it display at the actual UCS origin point or always at the lower left corner of the screen.

• The UCS Icon is on by default in the **acad3D.dwt** template. It also is set to move to any new UCS origin.

You need to be in the 3D Modeling workspace.

- If you want to change the status of the UCS icon, on the *Home* tab>Coordinates panel, expand

  (Show UCS Icon at Origin) and select an option, as shown in Figure 6–3.

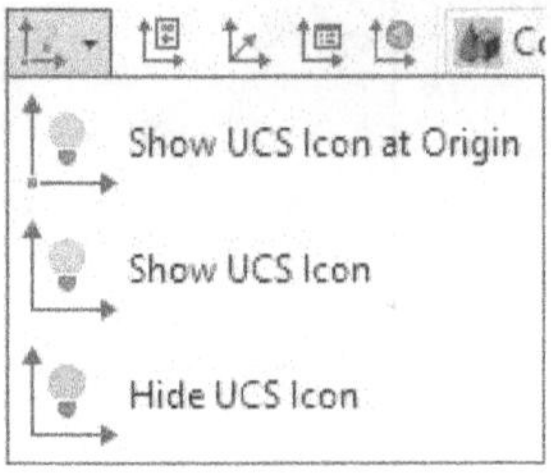

Figure 6–3

- The visual properties of the UCS icon can be modified in the UCS Icon dialog box. On the *Home* tab>Coordinates panel,

  click (UCS Icon, Properties) to open the dialog box. You can modify the icon's style, size, and color, as shown in Figure 6–4.

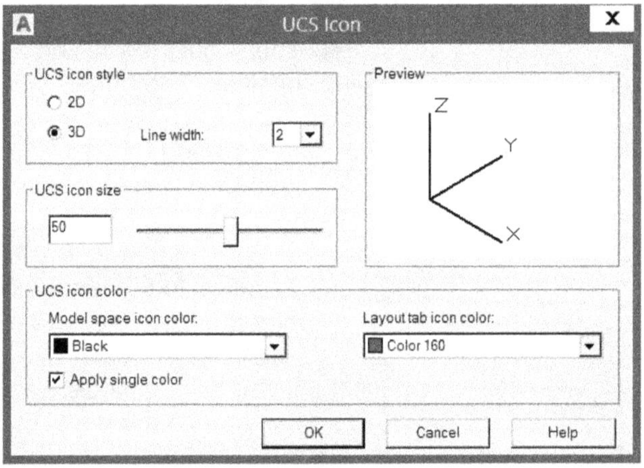

Figure 6–4

UCS and UCS Icon Settings

To modify the settings for the UCS and the UCS icon, click (UCS, UCS Settings) in the *Home* tab>Coordinates panel. The UCS dialog box opens to the *Settings* tab, as shown in Figure 6–5.

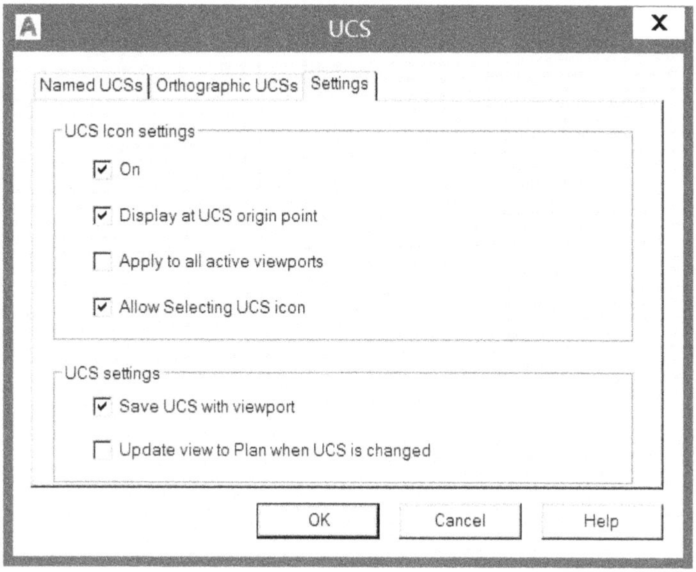

Figure 6–5

The UCS icon display and behavior settings for the current viewport enable you to:

- Toggle the display of the UCS icon.

- Display the UCS icon at its origin or (if the origin is hidden) in the lower left corner.

- Apply the settings to all active viewports.

- Enable the selection of the UCS icon.

- Save the UCS settings with the current viewport.

- Restore the view to Plan view when the UCS is changed.

If the UCS icon is set to be selectable, relevant options display in the Properties palette when the UCS icon is selected, as shown in Figure 6–6.

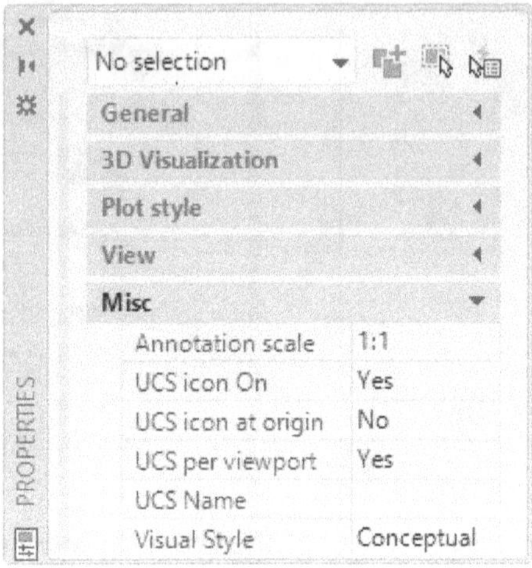

Figure 6–6

- Many UCS controls are also available in the shortcut menu by right-clicking on the UCS icon.

Moving the UCS Origin

The first UCS technique to learn is how to change the UCS origin, or 0,0,0 point. Moving the origin to a new location enables you to work at different elevations (by moving the UCS in the Z-direction) and different locations in your 3D model, as shown in Figure 6–7.

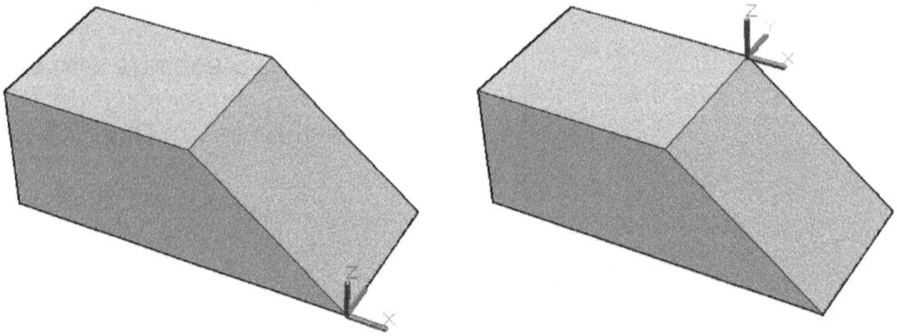

Figure 6–7

- If [icon] (Dynamic UCS) is toggled on in the Status Bar, you can hover the cursor over a face or point cloud to highlight it before selecting the new origin point. Doing so moves the UCS origin and changes the orientation to the face.

How To: Move the UCS Origin

1. In the *Home* tab>Coordinates panel, click ⬆️ (UCS, Origin).
2. Using object snaps, select a point on the object at which you want to locate the new origin or type the new coordinates.

- If ⊞ (Grid Display) is toggled on in the Status Bar, the grid moves to the new origin/workplane.

Moving the UCS to a Face

When you are working with solids, you can place the UCS on a specific face. This option is useful when working with faces whose points are not easy to select.

How To: Move the UCS to a Solid Face

1. In the *Home* tab>Coordinates panel, expand the UCS, View flyout and click ⬆️ (UCS, Face).
2. Select a face to use as the UCS. Hold <Ctrl> to highlight specific faces.
3. In the menu:
   - Select **Next** to switch to a face nearby.
   - If you need to adjust the direction of the X- or Y-axis, you can use the **Xflip** and **Yflip** options to rotate the UCS.
4. When the UCS is located correctly, select **Accept** or press <Enter>.

Moving the UCS Using 3 Points

The **UCS, 3 Point** command enables you to specify a new working plane by selecting three points in 3D space, most typically on an object, as shown in Figure 6–8.

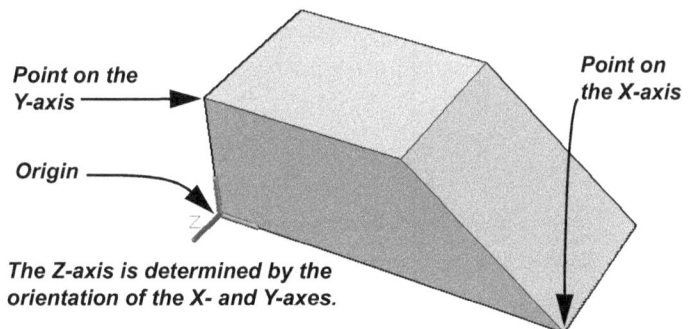

Point on the Y-axis

Point on the X-axis

Origin

The Z-axis is determined by the orientation of the X- and Y-axes.

Figure 6–8

How To: Select 3 Points to Establish a UCS

1. In the *Home* tab>Coordinates panel, click ⬆️₃ (UCS, 3 Point).
2. Select a point for the new UCS origin.
3. Select a second point on the new X-axis.
4. Select a third point on the new Y-axis.

- Use object snaps when selecting points on objects.

- ⬆️ (UCS, World) sets the current UCS to align with the WCS (World Coordinate System), a fixed Cartesian coordinate system.

Hint: The UCS View Option

⬆️ (UCS, View) uses the current screen orientation to create a new UCS. The location of the origin does not change, but the X-, Y-, and Z-directions do. This option is useful when adding text labels to the Isometric views of an object, as shown in Figure 6–9, and for creating the top, front, and side views of a drawing if you are not using a layout.

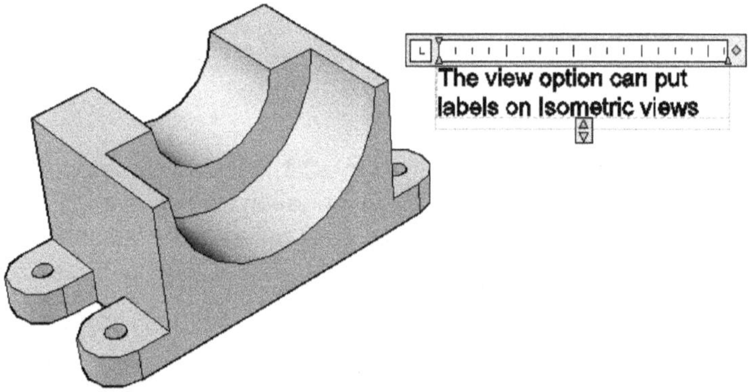

The view option can put labels on Isometric views

Figure 6–9

- ⬆️ (UCS, View) sets the UCS to be parallel to the screen.

Practice 6a

Using the UCS

Practice Objectives

* Change the current UCS to different locations and create similar objects at those locations.
* Align the current UCS with the WCS.

In this practice, you will change the current UCS to various locations using the **UCS, Origin**, and **UCS, Face** commands, as shown in Figure 6–10. You will create objects at the different UCS locations and align the current UCS with the WCS.

Figure 6–10

You are required to be in the 3D Modeling workspace for this practice.

1. Open **Bracket-UCS.dwg**.

2. Open the Properties palette.

3. Select the **UCS icon**, which should be in the lower left corner of the drawing window.

4. In the Properties palette, set *UCS icon at origin* to **Yes**. The UCS icon should move to the corner of the bracket model, as shown in Figure 6–11.

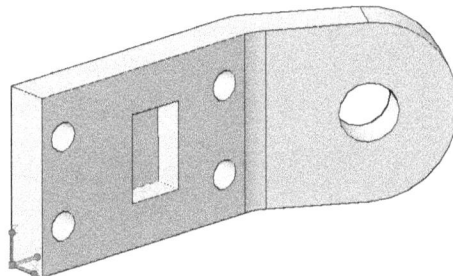

Figure 6–11

5. In the Status Bar, toggle on ⊞ (Grid) display the grid under the bracket model, as shown in Figure 6–12.

Figure 6–12

6. On the *Home* tab>Modeling panel, click ⬜ (Box) to create a box. Specify the first corner at **0,0,0** and the other corner at **2,2,0**. Move your cursor above the base and then set the height to **2**. Note that it is placed at the origin lying on the grid, but is overlapping the bracket model, as shown in Figure 6–13.

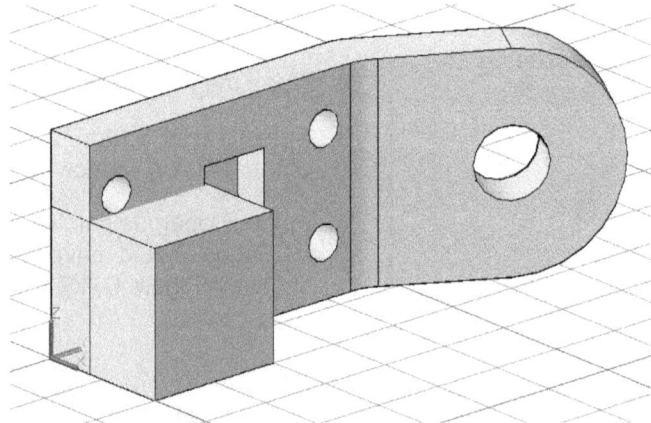

Figure 6–13

7. Delete the box that you just created.

8. On the *Home* tab>Coordinates panel, click ⬆⬈ (UCS, Origin).The UCS icon attaches itself to the cursor. At the *Specify new origin point* prompt, select the top left corner of the bracket model. Both the UCS icon and the grid move to the new location, as shown in Figure 6–14.

9. Recreate the same box with its starting point at **0,0,0**, other point at **2,2,0**, and a height of **2**. Note that it still is created at the origin, but is no longer overlapping the bracket model. Instead, it is above the bracket model, as shown in Figure 6–15.

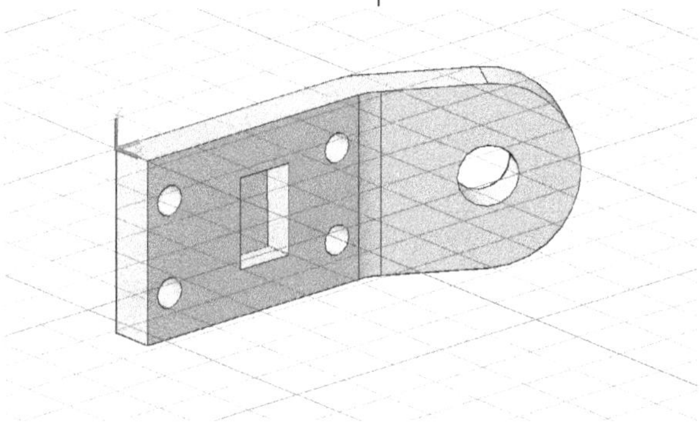

Figure 6–14

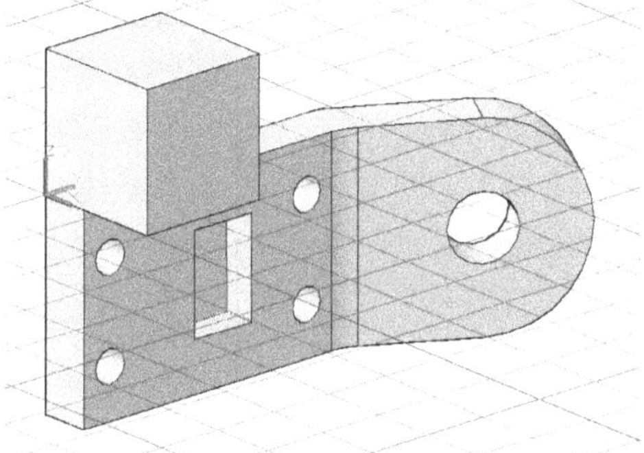

Figure 6–15

10. Delete the box that you just created.

11. On the *Home* tab>Coordinates panel, click ⬆◱ (UCS, Face). At the *Select face of solid, surface, or mesh* prompt, select any face of the bracket model and press <Enter> to accept the defaults. Note the change in location of the UCS icon and the grid display.

12. On the *Home* tab>Coordinates panel, click ⬆◉ (UCS, World). The UCS icon and grid display move to align with WCS.

13. Save and close the file.

6.2 UCS X, Y, and Z Commands

Most 3D objects are made of several planes. If you know the relationship between the planes, you can move the UCS from one plane to another by rotating the UCS about an axis. The **UCS X**, **Y**, and **Z** commands enable the User Coordinate System to be rotated around the required axis by a specified number of degrees. You can use these tools to set the UCS before drawing objects such that you can draw on a different plane. For example, you might need to create a 3D model from a 3-view mechanical drawing and need to start on the front view, rather than the top view. To do this, you rotate the UCS 90 degrees around the X-axis, as shown in Figure 6–16.

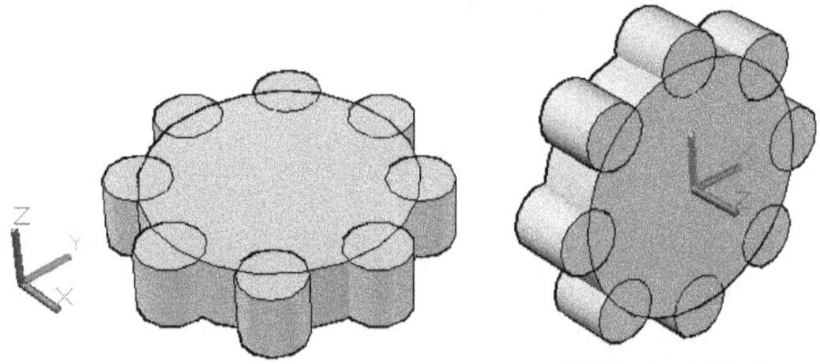

Model drawn at World UCS

UCS rotated before model is drawn

Figure 6–16

How To: Use the UCS X, Y, or Z Commands

1. In the *Home* tab>Coordinates panel>UCS, View flyout, click

    ⌐Cˣ X, ⌐Cʸ Y, or ⌐Cᶻ Z.
2. Specify the rotation around the axis. You can type a value for the angle or select two points on the screen to establish the angle.
3. The UCS rotates.

Right-hand Rule

Use the right-hand rule to help you to determine which way to rotate the UCS. By placing your right thumb in the direction of a particular axis, the curl of your fingers point in the direction of a positive angle, as shown in Figure 6–17. This is important when you define a UCS, or when you rotate or array objects.

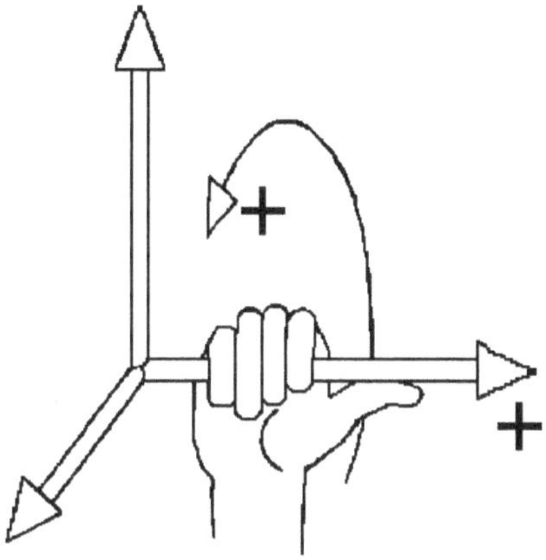

Figure 6–17

Hint: Z-axis Vector

(Z-Axis Vector) uses two points to define a new Z-axis rather than rotating about the Z-axis. The first point you select is the new origin and the second point is the direction of the positive Z-axis. It rotates the XY plane and is very useful when defining the direction of an extrusion.

Moving the UCS to a 2D Object

With (UCS, Object), the AutoCAD software enables the User Coordinate Systems to match the alignment of existing 2D objects in the drawing. The new working plane is perpendicular to the extrusion direction (positive Z-axis) of the object.

With this command, the point you select on the object generally determines the orientation of the new UCS. For example, if a circle is selected, the center of the circle is the new origin, and the positive X-axis passes through the point where the circle was selected. For a line or rectangle, the end point or corner closest to the selected point becomes the new origin.

Practice 6b

X, Y, and Z Commands

Practice Objective

- Draw a mechanical part using the **UCS Origin**, **X**, **Y**, and **Z** commands to modify the location of the UCS.

In this practice, you will draw the part shown in Figure 6–18 using the **UCS X**, **Y**, and **Z** commands.

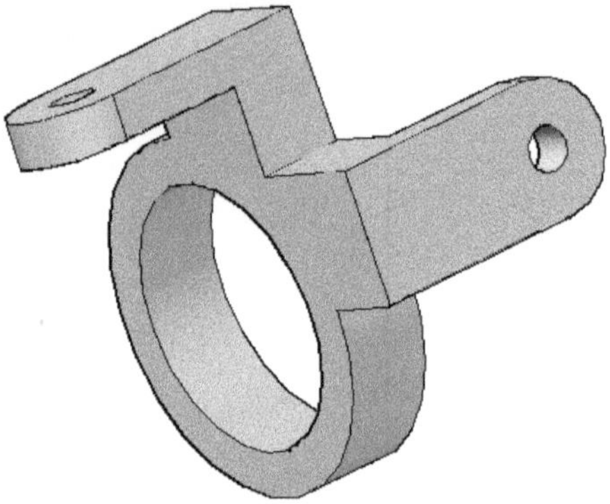

Figure 6–18

*You are required to be in the **3D Modeling** workspace for this practice.*

1. Start a new drawing based on **acad3D.dwt** and save it in your practice files folder as **Angle.dwg**.

2. In the Status Bar, toggle off ⬚ (Dynamic UCS). Right-click on the ViewCube and set the projection mode to **Parallel**.

3. In the **View Controls** list of the drawing window or in the *Home* tab>View panel, switch to the **Front** view (this also changes the UCS to the front).

4. Set the *Visual Style* to **2D Wireframe**.

Change the color of the layer 0 to a darker shade of gray if your drawing window background color is white.

5. Draw a cylinder with a *radius* of **3** and a *height* of **2**. Draw another cylinder on the same center with a *radius* of **4** and a *height* of **2**.

6. On the *Home* tab>Coordinates panel, click ⬚ (UCS, Origin) and place the origin at the center of the cylinders.

7. On the *Home* tab>Coordinates panel, click ⬚ (UCS, Z) and rotate the UCS **30 degrees** around the Z-axis.

8. Verify that ⬚ (Polar Tracking) is toggled on.

9. On the *Home* tab>Draw panel, click ⟳ (Polyline) and draw the object shown in Figure 6–19.

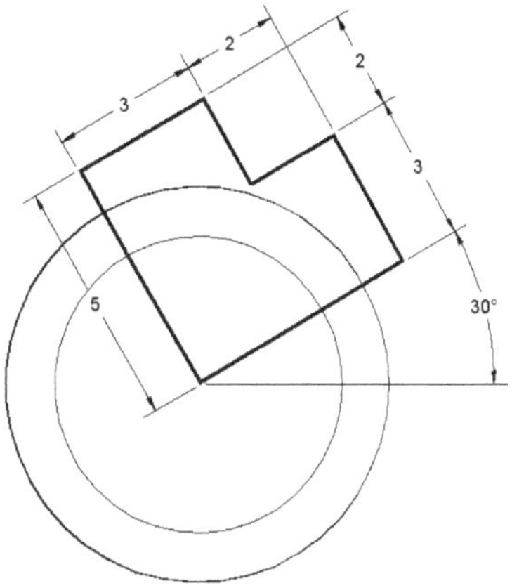

Figure 6–19

10. Set the *Visual Style* to **Shades of Gray**.

11. Use **Orbit** to orbit around such that the height of the cylinders is visible. If required, use ✛ (Move) to move the cylinders such that they overlap each other.

12. On the *Home* tab>Modeling panel, click (Extrude). Select the polyline and extrude it **2** units in the direction of the cylinders.

13. Switch to the **SE Isometric** view (**View Controls** list of the drawing window).

14. Union the outside cylinder and the extruded object. Subtract the inside cylinder, as shown in Figure 6–20.

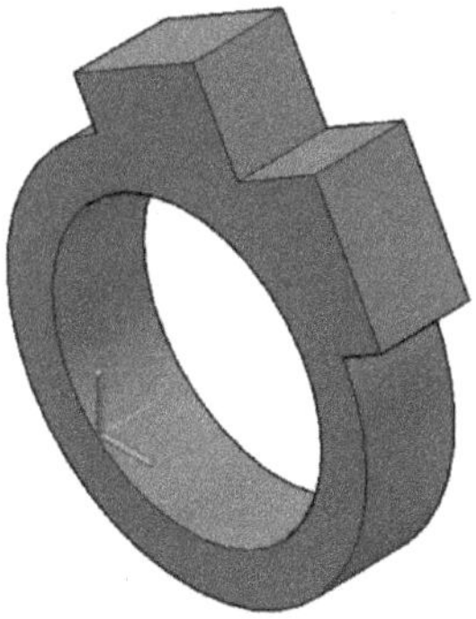

Figure 6–20

15. On the *Home* tab>Coordinates panel, click (UCS, Face). At the *Select face of solid, surface, or mesh* prompt, move the cursor over the bottom edge of the face of the extruded polyline that is facing towards you. Verify that the X axis is parallel to the bottom edge of the face, as shown in Figure 6–21. Click to place the UCS on the face.

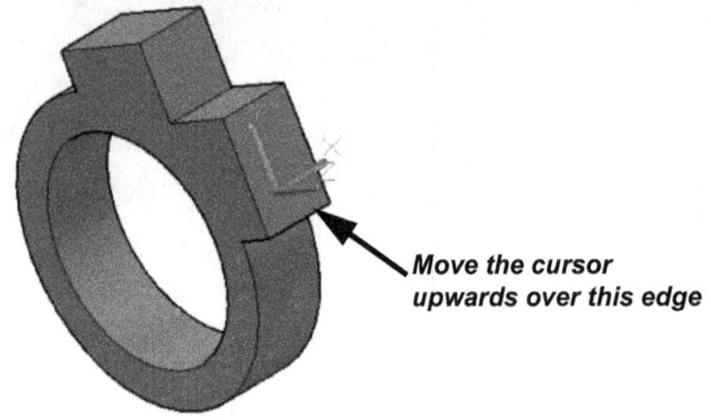

Move the cursor upwards over this edge

Figure 6–21

16. Draw the closed polyline and circle shown in Figure 6–22, with the lower left corner of the polyline touching the lower left corner of the object's face. Hint: To draw the arc, use the **Arc** option of **Pline** command with a diameter of **3.0** (as shown on left of Figure 6–22). Select the **Line** option of the **Pline** command to draw the rest of the lines.

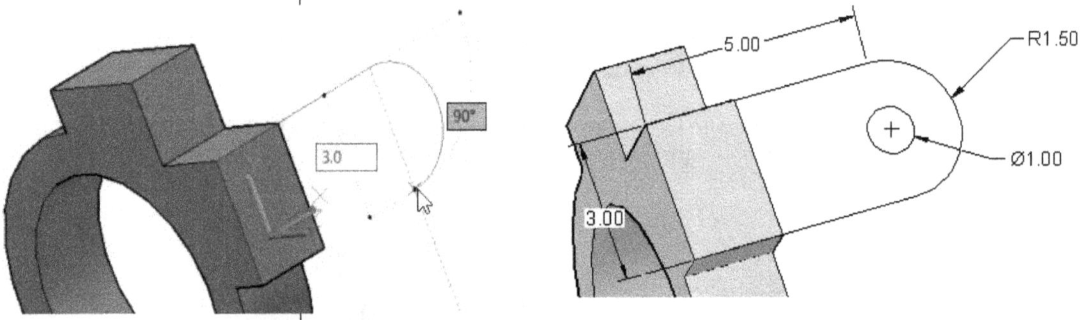

Figure 6–22

17. Extrude the polyline and circle **1** units away from the solid. Union the extruded polyline solid with the rest of the solid and subtract the cylindrical hole.

18. On the *Home* tab>Coordinates panel, click (UCS, Face) and place the UCS as required to view the other angled face. Draw the same polyline and circle in the opposite direction to the one shown in Step 16.

19. Extrude and union the polyline and circle. The model displays as shown in Figure 6–23.

Figure 6–23

20. Save and close the drawing.

6.3 Saving a UCS by Name

You often need to reuse a UCS in your drawing. The AutoCAD software enables any defined UCS to be saved and recalled by name, as shown in Figure 6–24. You can also access the Named and Orthographic UCSs in the UCS dialog box.

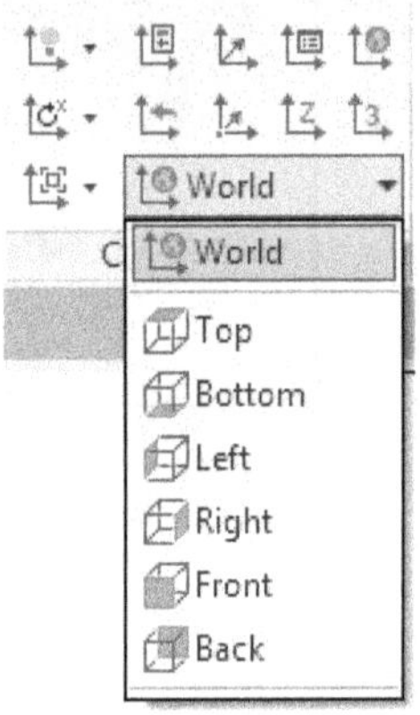

You can save an unlimited number of UCSs with each drawing.

Figure 6–24

- The Named UCSs are located in the Named UCS Combo Control in the *Home* tab>Coordinates panel.

How To: Name and Save a UCS

1. Set up the UCS as required.

2. In the *Home* tab>Coordinates panel>, click (Named UCS).

3. In the UCS dialog box, select the *Named UCSs* tab.

4. In the list, right-click on Unnamed and select **Rename**, as shown in Figure 6–25.

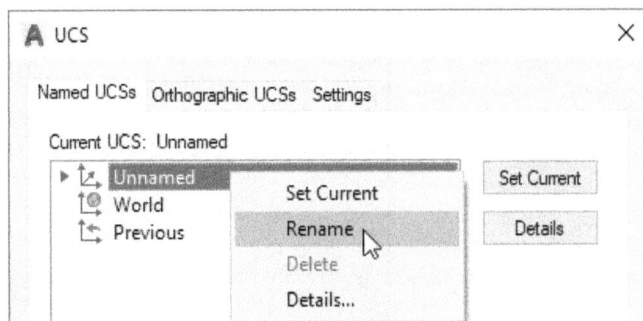

Figure 6–25

5. Type a new name for the UCS.

6. Click **OK**.

- To delete a named UCS, right-click on its name and select **Delete**.

- To make a UCS current, select its name and click **Set Current**, or double-click on the name. The current UCS displays an arrow to the left of its name.

How To: Set a UCS Relative to a Named UCS

Once you have named a UCS, you might want to define another UCS relative to it. For example, if you place the UCS on the top of a part, you might want to change the UCS quickly to the bottom or side of the part.

1. Start the **Named UCS** command.
2. In the UCS dialog box, select the *Orthographic UCSs* tab.
3. Select the Orthographic UCS that you want to use.
4. In the Relative to: drop-down list, select the named UCS you want to move relative to, as shown in Figure 6–26.

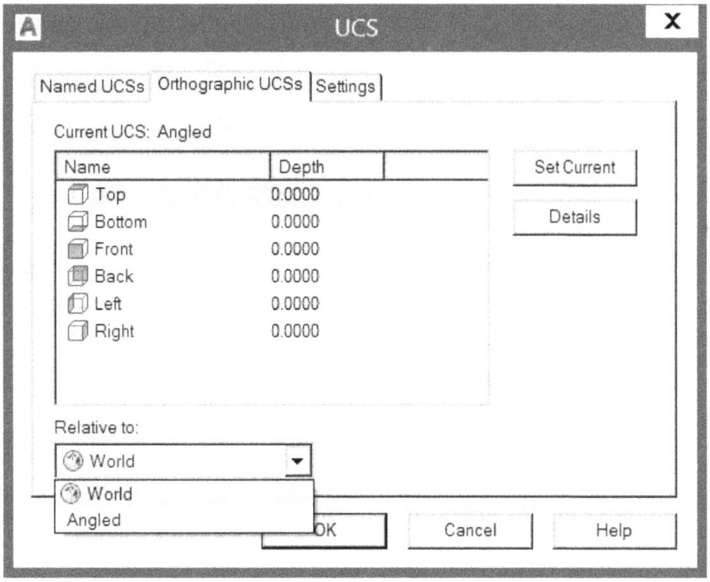

Figure 6–26

5. Click **OK**.

- The origin of these UCSs is the same as the origin of the *Relative to:* UCS.

Hint: Aligning the View to the UCS Manually

When you have defined a new UCS, you might want to view it head-on to make drawing easier. You can do this by changing the Plan View to the **Current UCS**, **World UCS**, or a **Named UCS**. Use the **Plan** command at the Command Prompt and select the appropriate options to change the Plan View.

Aligning the View to the UCS Automatically

To automatically update the view to the current UCS, open the UCS dialog box, switch to the *Settings* tab, and select **Update view to Plan when UCS is changed**, as shown in Figure 6–27. It is off by default.

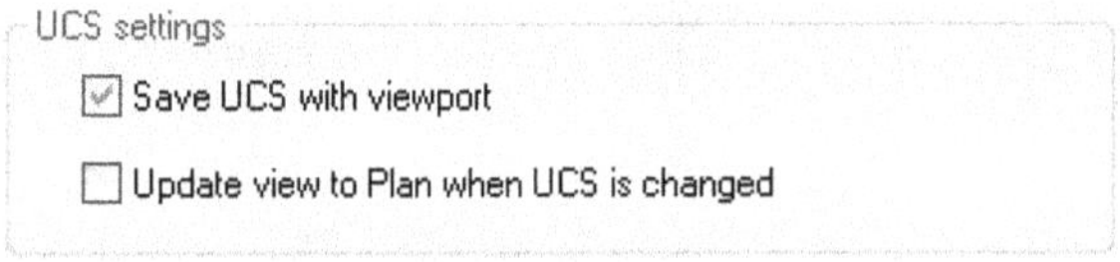

UCS settings

☑ Save UCS with viewport

☐ Update view to Plan when UCS is changed

Figure 6–27

- This setting can be helpful when using multiple viewports. One viewport can be set to change with the UCS so that it always displays a head-on view of the current UCS. Other viewports would have views that would not be affected by UCS changes.

- The **Save UCS with viewport** option is on by default. It controls whether a viewport has its own UCS (option selected) or if it automatically matches the UCS of the active viewport (option not selected). If you are using the **Update view to plan when UCS is changed** option, you should toggle this setting off.

Practice 6c

Working with Named UCSs

Practice Objective

- Define, save, and restore UCSs in a model.

In this practice, you will save and restore the UCSs that you define on the ratchet drawing shown in Figure 6–28.

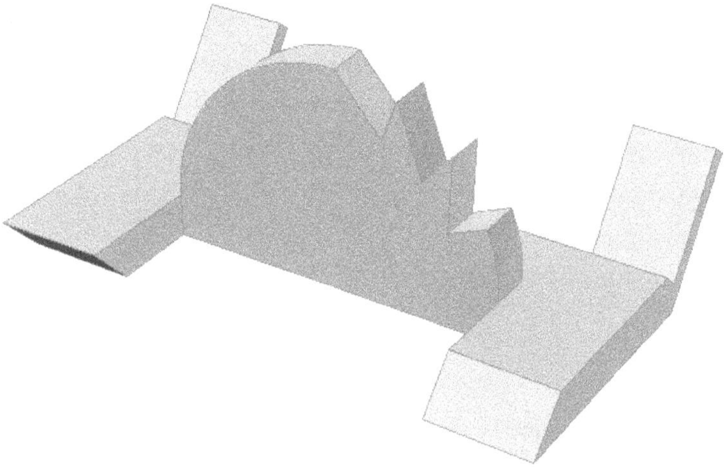

Figure 6–28

*You are required to be in the **3D Modeling** workspace for this practice.*

1. Open **Ratchet.dwg**.

2. On the *Home* tab>Coordinates panel, click ⌐₃ (UCS, 3 Point) and set up a UCS on any face of the object.

3. On the *Home* tab>Coordinates panel, click ⌐ (UCS, Named). In the UCS dialog box, right-click on the Unnamed UCS and select **Rename**. Type **RatchetUCS** and click **OK**. Click OK again to exit the dialog box.

4. Use different UCS commands and the UCS multi-functional grips to create 2 more UCSs on different faces of the object.

   Save them using Fro ⌐ (UCS, Named).

*You will be required to revert back to the Drafting & Annotation Workspace to work with the rest of the certification objectives. In the Status Bar, select **Drafting & Annotation** from Workspace Switching.*

5. After you have saved the UCSs, restore and test each one by drawing circles on the object.

6. Save and close the drawing.

SECTION
3

Advanced Editing Functions

Exam Objective	Chapter(s)
3.6 Apply Fillet and Chamfer options	
3.6.a Create a fillet between two parallel objects	Ch. 7
3.6.b Create a corner between two non-parallel objects using the <Shift> key	Ch. 7
3.6.c Use the Multiple and Polyline options	Ch. 7
3.6.d Understand the effects of Trim mode	Ch. 7

Making Changes in Your Drawing

Exam Objectives Covered in This Chapter

- 3.1.a Rotate objects around a specified base point
- 3.1.b Enlarge or reduce the size of objects
- 3.2.a Work with arrays
- 3.3.a Use the advanced options of the Trim, Extend and Lengthen commands
- 3.4.a Use the advanced options of the Offset command
- 3.6.a Create a fillet between two parallel objects
- 3.6.b Create a corner between two non-parallel objects using the <Shift> key
- 3.6.c Use the Multiple and Polyline options
- 3.6.d Understand the effects of Trim mode

7.1 Moving Objects

The **Move** command enables you to relocate a selected object or group of objects from one place in the drawing to another.

How To: Move an Object

1. In *Home* tab>Modify panel, click ⊹ (Move).
2. Select the objects that you want to move.
3. Press <Enter> or right-click to end the object selection.
4. Specify the base point, which is the *handle* by which you hold the objects.

5. Move the cursor. ◈ displays at the cursor and the selected objects get attached to the cursor. A temporary rubber-band (dashed) line extends from the original location to the new location of the objects, as shown in Figure 7–1. A paler (light gray) version of the selected object(s) displays at its original location.

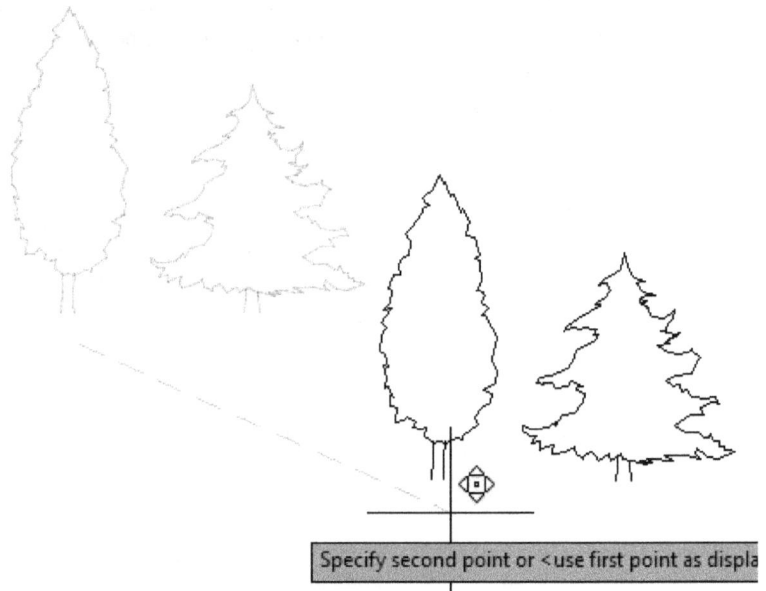

Specify second point or <use first point as displa

Figure 7–1

6. Specify a second point at which to place the objects. The original objects are moved to the new location.

- You can select the objects first and then start the **Move** command.

- You can also select the objects first (highlighted in blue with a thicker line weight and contains *grips)* and then click and drag them to a new location. Ensure that you do not select one of the grips. This method does not permit you to move precisely.

- You can also select the objects first, press and hold <Ctrl>, and use the appropriate arrow key to **Nudge** the selected objects a few pixels in the specified direction.

Hint: Drawing Aids for Moving Objects

Several drawing aids can help you to move objects precisely including Object Snaps, Coordinate Entry, and Object Snap Tracking.

- **Object Snaps:** Start the **Move** command and select an object to move. Use Object Snaps to select a base point on the object, such as an end point. Then use Object Snaps to select the new location for the object, such as the center of a circle.

- **Coordinate Entry:** Start the **Move** command and select an object to move. Enter coordinates for the base point and press <Enter> when prompted for the second point. The coordinates determine the distances and directions in which the object is moved. For example, entering **2,5** for the base point moves the object 2 units in the X-direction and 5 units in the Y-direction.

- **Object Snap Tracking:** Start the **Move** command and select an object to move. With Osnap Tracking toggled on, hover the cursor over objects where the selected object is going to be placed and select two tracking points. Place the selected object at the intersection of the tracking points.

You can also combine these methods to move an object. For example, you can use Object Snaps to select the base point and then enter coordinates for the second point.

7.2 Copying Objects

The **Copy** command is used to make additional copies of selected objects. The prompts for this command are similar to those used for **Move**.

How To: Copy an Object

1. In the *Home* tab>Modify panel, click (Copy).
2. Select the objects that you want to copy.
3. Press <Enter> or right-click to end the object selection.
4. Select the base point.
5. Move the cursor to copy the objects to a new location.

   displays at the cursor and the selected object(s) get attached to it. A temporary rubber-band (dashed) line extends from the original location to the new location of the objects, as shown in Figure 7–2. A highlighted version of the selected object(s) displays at the original location.

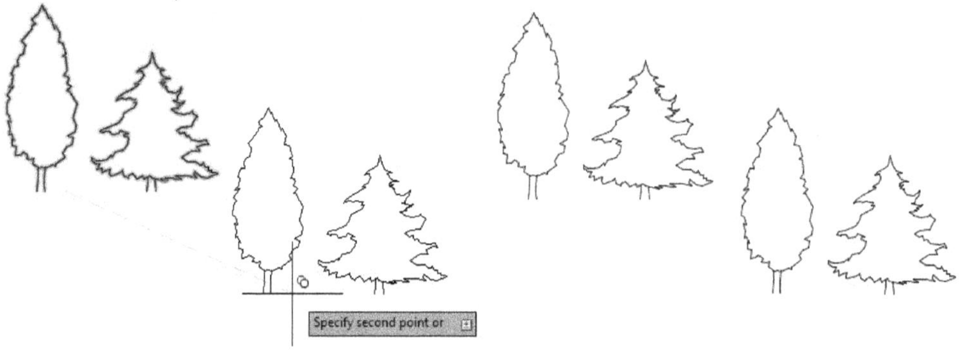

Specify second point or

Select second point   *Original and copied objects*

Figure 7–2

6. Continue selecting points to create more copies, or press <Enter> or <Esc> to finish.

- Copied objects have the same color, linetype, and layer properties as the original. This rule also applies to other commands that make duplicates of objects.

- The **Undo** option enables you to undo the placing of a copy while remaining in the command.

- You can select the objects first and then start the **Copy** command.

- Similar to the **Move** command, you can use Object Snaps, Coordinate Entry, and Object Snap Tracking to select points for the **Copy** command.

- You can also select the objects first, select a point on an object that does not touch a grip, drag the objects to a new location, and press <Ctrl> to make a copy. Do not press <Ctrl> until after you have started dragging, as it has a different purpose when you are selecting objects in 3D.

Hint: Editing Commands in the Shortcut Menu

If you select objects when a command is not active and then right-click, the shortcut menu displays some basic editing commands, as shown in Figure 7–3. This is another way of starting these commands.

Clipboard	>	Cut	Ctrl+X
Isolate	>	Copy	Ctrl+C
Erase		Copy with Base Point	Ctrl+Shift+C
Move		Paste	Ctrl+V
Copy Selection		Paste as Block	Ctrl+Shift+V
Scale		Paste to Original Coordinates	
Rotate			
Draw Order	>		
Group	>		
Add Selected			
Select Similar			
Deselect All			
Subobject Selection Filter	>		
Quick Select...			
QuickCalc			
Find...			
Properties			
Quick Properties			

Figure 7–3

You can also **Cut**, **Copy**, and **Paste** to the Clipboard from the shortcut menu by expanding the **Clipboard** option. The objects you select can then be pasted into other AutoCAD drawings and programs, such as spreadsheets and documents.

The **Clipboard>Copy** command in the shortcut menu is actually **Copy to Clipboard**. The **Copy Selection** command is the same as the standard AutoCAD **Copy** command.

Hint: Rubber-band line color

By default, the rubber-band line that you get after selecting and moving the cursor in the **Move** and **Copy** commands, is a light orange color. You can control its color in the *Interface element* list in the Drawing Window Colors dialog box, which can be opened from Options dialog box>*Display* tab>**Colors**.

7.3 Rotating Objects

Design changes sometimes require modifying the placement angle of an object. The **Rotate** command rotates selected objects around a defined pivot point.

How To: Rotate an Object

1. In the *Home* tab>Modify panel, click ↻ (Rotate).
2. Select the objects to rotate.
3. Press <Enter> to end the object selection.
4. Select the base point around which the objects are going to rotate.
5. Move the cursor to rotate the objects. A dashed line indicates the location of the base point. ⟳ displays at the cursor, indicating that the **Rotate** command is active, as shown in Figure 7–4. It also indicates the direction in which typed values are going to be rotated, in this case, counter-clockwise (default). The original objects fade to gray while the new objects maintain their original properties.

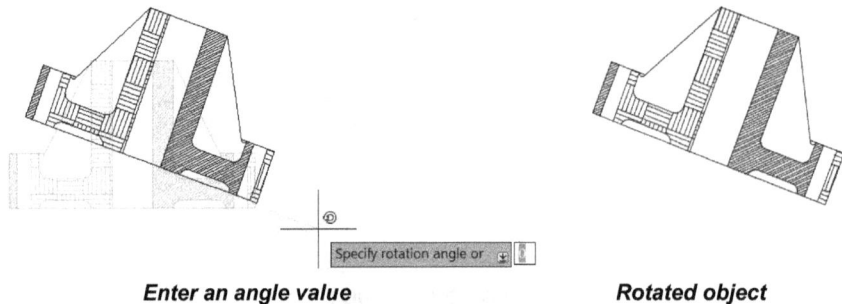

Specify rotation angle or

Enter an angle value   *Rotated object*

Figure 7–4

6. Enter a *Rotation Angle* or select a point to specify the rotation.

- A negative rotation angle enables you to turn the object clockwise.

- Polar Tracking can be used to constrain the rotation to a precise angle.

- At Specify rotation angle prompt, you can access the **Copy** option, which leaves the original object in place and rotates a copy of it.

- You can select the objects first and then start the **Rotate** command.

- You can change the default rotation direction used by the **Rotate** command by selecting or clearing the **Clockwise** option in the Drawing Units dialog box, as shown in Figure 7–5 (Application Menu> **Drawing Utilities>Units**).

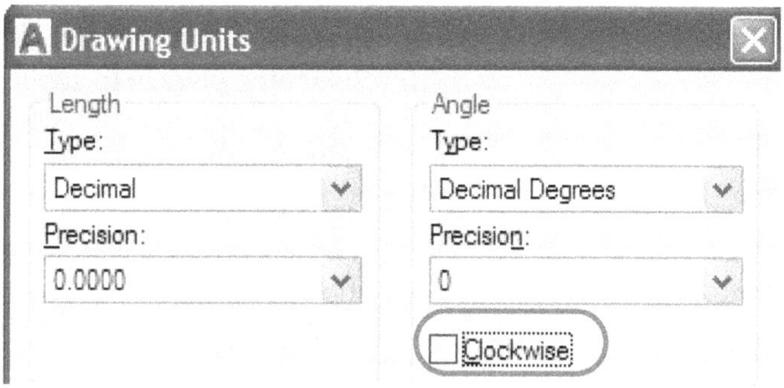

Figure 7–5

7.4 Scaling Objects

The **Scale** command enlarges or reduces the size of selected objects around a defined reference point.

How To: Scale an Object

1. In *Home* tab>Modify panel, click ⬜ (Scale).
2. Select the objects to scale.
3. Press <Enter> or right-click to end the object selection.
4. Select the base point to be used for scaling.

5. Move the cursor to scale the objects. ⬜ displays at the cursor, indicating that the **Scale** command is active, as shown in Figure 7–6. The original objects fade to gray while the new objects maintain their original properties.

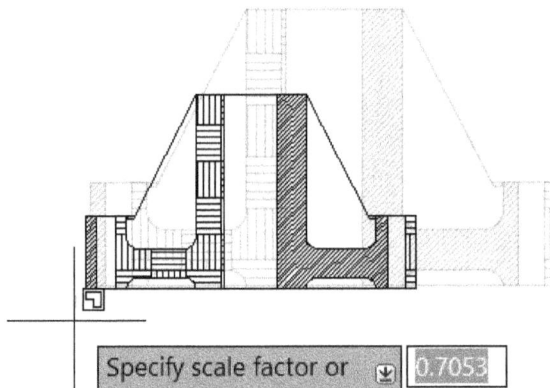

Specify scale factor or ⊻ 0.7053

Figure 7–6

6. Enter a value for the scale factor.

* The **scale factor** enables you to set the required level of enlargement or reduction in size. Scale factors smaller than 1 decrease the size and scale factors larger than 1 increase the size.

* The **Copy** option in the **Scale** command leaves the original object unscaled and creates a scaled copy.

Practice 7a

Modifying Objects

Practice Objective

- Modify the location, quantity, and size of objects.

In this practice, you will use the **Move**, **Copy**, **Rotate**, **Scale**, and **Mirror** commands to place furniture in a floorplan, as shown in Figure 7–7. Some of the objects in the drawing are locked in place so that you do not move them by mistake.

Figure 7–7

Task 1 - Move an object.

In this task, you will use the **Move** command to place furniture in a floorplan, as shown in Figure 7–8.

Figure 7–8

1. Open **Arrange-A.dwg** from your practice files folder.

2. In the Status Bar, toggle off ⟳ ▾ (Polar Tracking) and
    ∠ (Object Snap Tracking). Toggle on ⬚ (Object Snap)
    and verify that **Endpoint** object snap is selected.

3. In the *Home* tab>Modify panel, click ✛ (Move).

4. Select the desk and press <Enter> to end the object
    selection.

5. For the base point, snap to the end point at the back corner
    (upper right) of the desk.

6. Hover the cursor and snap it (without clicking) to the inside
    corner of the top right cubicle, as shown in Figure 7–9. The
    original objects fade to gray while the new objects maintain
    their original properties.

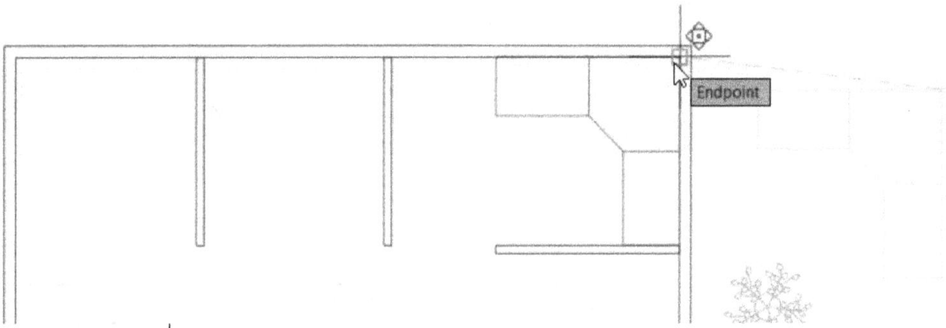

Figure 7–9

7. Click at that point to confirm the move.

You can toggle off

⬚ *(Object Snap), if it snaps to some point.*

8. Move the chair to place it in front of the desk (use
    approximate location) and move the laptop onto the desk, as
    shown in Figure 7–8. Do not rotate them now.

9. Move the plant to the open space next to the desk, as shown
    in Figure 7–8.

Task 2 - Copy an object.

In this task, you will use the **Copy** command to copy several chairs and plants in the floorplan, as shown in Figure 7–10.

Figure 7–10

1. In the *Home* tab>Modify panel, click (Copy).

2. Select the plant and press <Enter> to end the object selection.

3. For the base point, click near the center of the plant.

4. Move the cursor near the bottom of the left most inner wall, as shown in Figure 7–11. Note that a copy of the plant is attached with the cursor. A dashed line connects with the cursor indicating the new location with the original object highlighted, as shown in Figure 7–11. Once you locate the required location for the copy (bottom of the leftmost inner wall), click to place the plant.

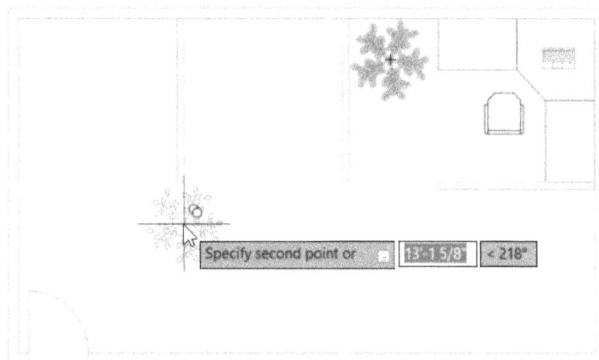

Figure 7–11

5. With the plant and the dashed line still attached to the cursor, move the cursor again and click to place another copy along the bottom wall. Press <Enter> to exit the command.

6. Copy the chair to the locations shown in Figure 7–10. (**Tip:** To position the chairs flush along the wall, use the **Midpoint** or **Endpoint** object snap to select the base point at the back of the chair. Then, select the **Nearest** object snap override (<Shift>+ right-click) to select points along the wall.)

Task 3 - Rotate an object.

In this task, you will rotate the chair and laptop and then copy the entire set of furniture to other locations, as shown in Figure 7–12.

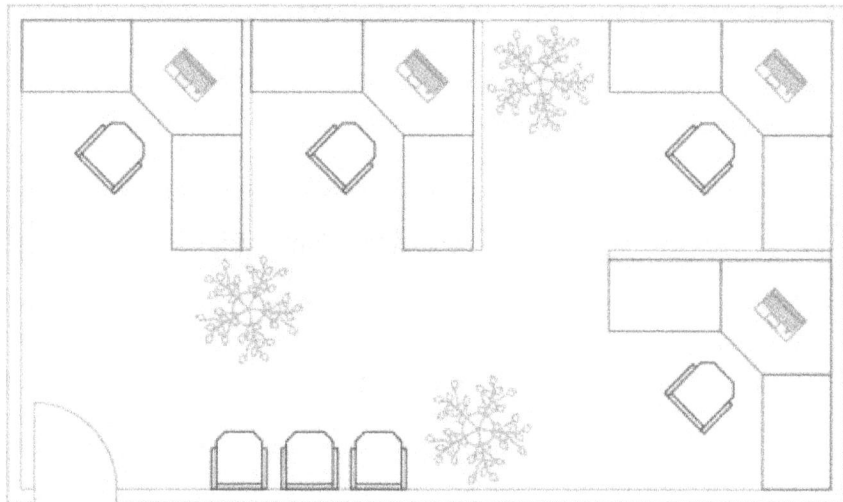

Figure 7–12

1. In the Status Bar, expand ↺ ▼ (Polar Tracking) and select **45,90,135,180...**, if required. Toggle on ↺ (Polar Tracking) and toggle off ▭ (Object Snap).

2. In the *Home* tab>Modify panel, click ⟳ (Rotate) and select the chair near the desk. Press <Enter> and select the base point near the center of the chair's seat. Pull the cursor away from the chair until you see the 315 degree angle (multiple of 45) and the seat is facing the desk, as shown in Figure 7–13. Note that the original object fades to gray while the new object maintains the original properties. Click to accept the angle.

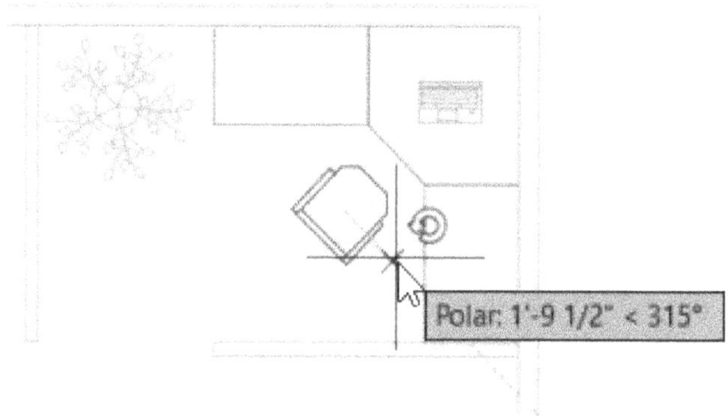

Figure 7–13

3. Repeat the process to rotate the laptop using 315 degree angle so that the screen is facing the chair, as shown in Figure 7–12.

4. Move the chair as required, to place it correctly in front of the desk. Do the same for the laptop to center it on the desk.

Select the object, hold <Ctrl>, and then use the required arrow key to nudge the objects in place.

5. Toggle on ▢ (Object Snap) and verify that it is set to **Endpoint**.

6. Start the **Copy** command. Select the chair, desk, and laptop, and then press <Enter>. For the base point, select the back corner (top right) of the desk. Copy the objects to the other three cubicles, as shown in Figure 7–12.

7. Save the drawing.

Task 4 - Scale an object.

In this task, you will copy and scale some of the plants, as shown in Figure 7–14.

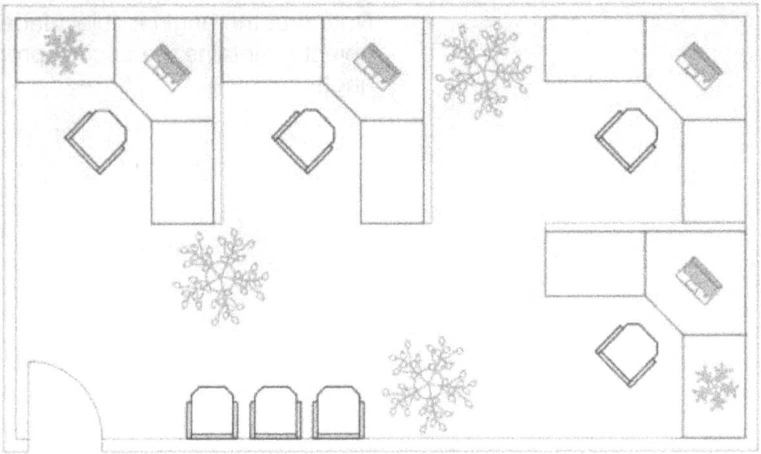

Figure 7–14

1. Copy one of the plants to the desk in the upper left cubicle.

2. In the *Home* tab>Modify panel, click (Scale). Select the plant, press <Enter>, and select the center of the plant as the base point. Enter **0.5** for the scale factor and press <Enter> to make it half of the original plant, as shown in Figure 7–14.

3. Copy the scaled plant to the desk in the lower right cubicle, as shown in Figure 7–14.

Task 5 - Mirror objects.

In this task, you will use the **Mirror** command to mirror the contents of a cubicle, as shown in Figure 7–15.

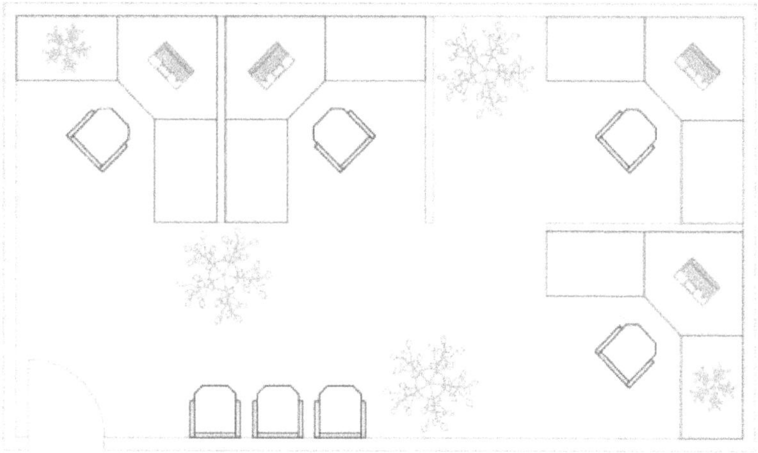

Figure 7–15

1. In the *Home* tab>Modify panel, click ⚠ (Mirror).

2. At the *Select objects:* prompt, select the desk, laptop, and chair in the middle cubicle, and press <Enter>.

3. At the *Specify first point of mirror line:* prompt, select the end point of the line that separates the corner desk section from the straight desk section at the top of the cubicle, as shown on the left in Figure 7–16.

4. At the *Specify second point of mirror line:* prompt, select a bottom end point, as shown on the right in Figure 7–16. At the *Erase source objects?* select **Yes** from the drop-down list. The contents of the middle cubicle are mirrored and the original objects are deleted.

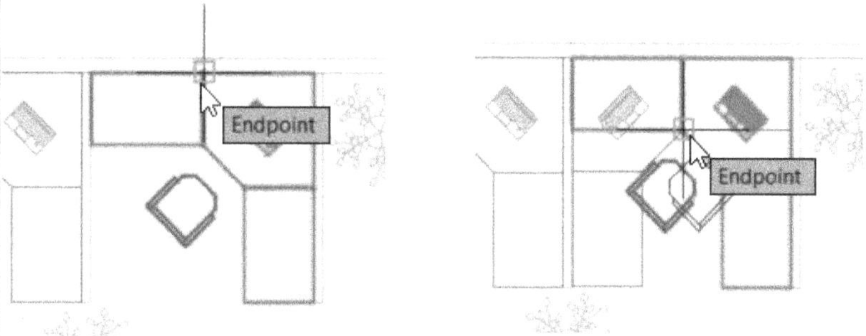

Figure 7–16

5. Save and close the drawing.

7.5 Trimming and Extending Objects

Trim and **Extend** commands can be used to modify already existing objects to ensure that they have the correct size and length, as shown in Figure 7–17.

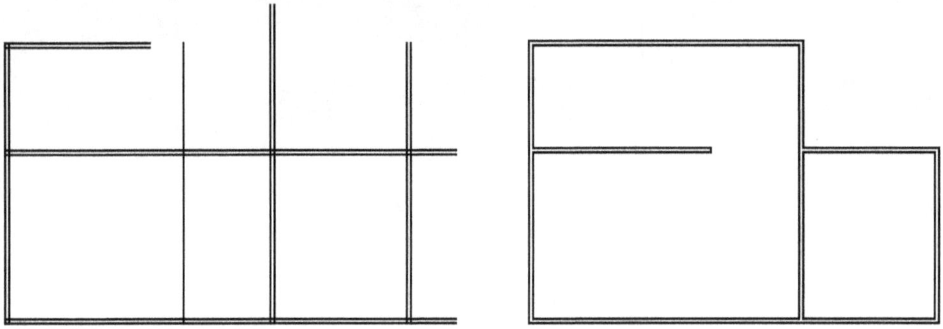

Figure 7–17

The commands are located in the *Home* tab>Modify panel, in the Trim/Extend flyout, as shown in Figure 7–18.

Figure 7–18

Trimming Objects

The **Trim** command erases any part of an object that extends past a cutting edge. It simplifies many drawing tasks. For example, an easy way to create an arc is to draw a circle and then trim it.

How To: Trim Objects

1. In the *Home* tab>Modify panel, click ✂ (Trim).
2. Hover the cursor over the part of the object that you want to trim. The software determines all the potential cutting edges by default and displays the trimming portion as faded in a light gray line weight. This provides a preview of the part that is going to be removed, as shown in Figure 7–19.

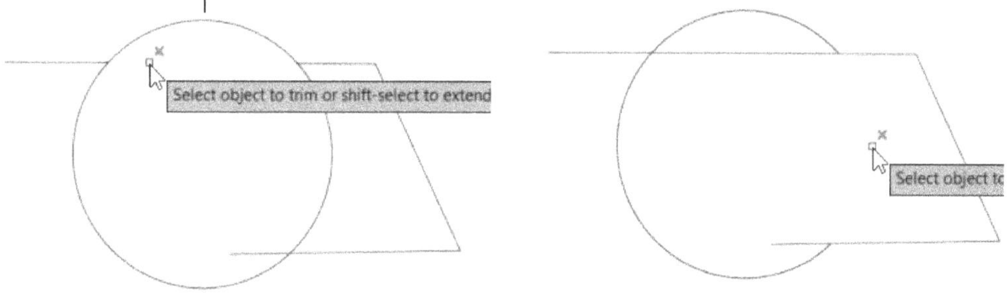

You can also use the **Trim** *command to extend an object. At the Select object to trim or Shift-select to extend prompt, you can hold <Shift> and select to extend an object.*

Select object to trim or shift-select to extend

Select object to

Figure 7–19

3. Select the part to be removed.
4. Press <Enter> to complete the command.

Extending Objects

Using the **Extend** command, any object that does not reach a boundary edge is lengthened until it meets the boundary, as shown in Figure 7–20.

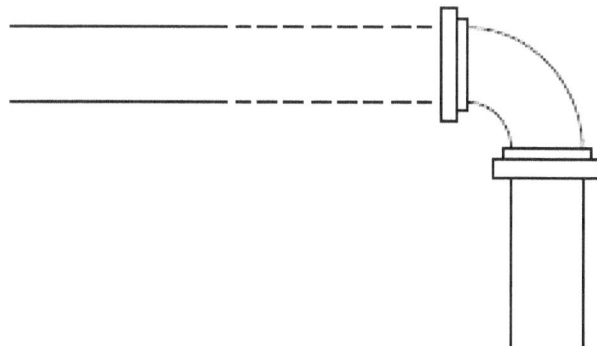

You can also use the **Extend** *command to trim an object. At the Select object to extend or Shift-select to trim prompt, you can hold <Shift> and select to trim an object.*

Figure 7–20

How To: Extend Objects

1. In the *Home* tab>Modify panel, click ➝| (Extend).
2. Hover the cursor over the object that you want to extend (closer to the boundary edge), and a preview of the part that is going to be added displays. The extended part is highlighted in blue with a thicker line weight.
3. Select to extend the object.
4. Press <Enter> to complete the command.

Selecting Objects to Trim and Extend

By default, objects to be trimmed or extended can be selected using the following methods:

- **Individual selection**: The objects can be selected individually by picking.

- **Freehand Selection**: For the Freehand selection, hold down the left-mouse button and then drag the cursor over one or more objects for trimming/extending, as shown in Figure 7–21.

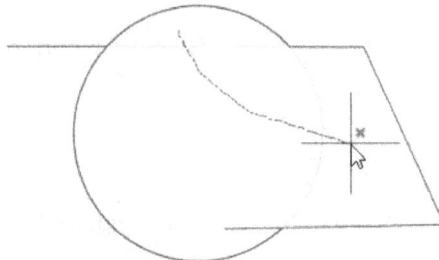

Figure 7–21

- **Two-Point Fence selection:** Use this selection by clicking two points to create a segment that passes through the objects that need to be trimmed or extended, as shown in Figure 7–22.

Figure 7–22

If you select something by mistake, you can use the **Undo** option in the command (<Down Arrow> menu) to restore the last object trimmed. You can also click 🔄 (Undo) in the Quick Access Toolbar for the **Trim** and **Extend** commands, however this loses all of the trimming you have done to that point.

Hint: Trim or Extend Options

When you start the **Trim** or **Extend** command, you are provided with various options (Down arrow menu or Command Line selection) before you select objects for trimming/extending. They are the **cuTting edges/Boundary edges** and the **Crossing** selection option.

The Crossing option for selecting objects is not a default option and needs to be explicitly selected from the menu. When you select the **Crossing** option, you are prompted to select two opposite corners, as shown in Figure 7–23. Everything touching or in the box is previewed (faded light gray) and is then trimmed or extended when you select the second corner. You remain in the command so that you can select more objects as required.

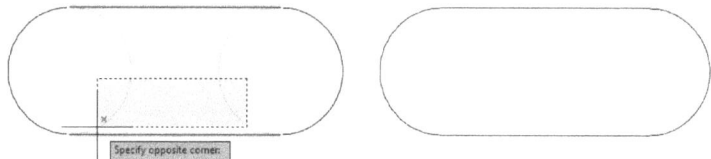

Figure 7–23

When you select the **cuTting edges/Boundary edges** option, you are prompted to select the required edges first. The selected cutting or boundary edges are highlighted in blue with a thicker line weight, as shown in Figure 7–24. Select the objects that need to be trimmed or extended.

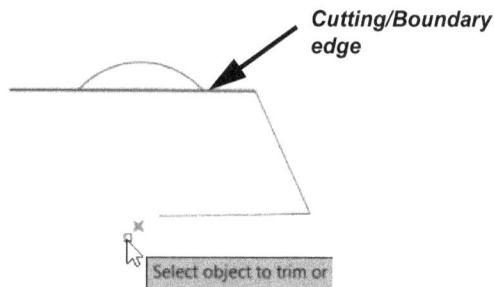

Figure 7–24

Hint: Breaking Objects

The **Break** command can be used to cut an object without any overlapping edges. Two different options of the command are available in the *Home* tab>expanded Modify panel:

- (Break): Removes a portion of an object between two user-defined points, leaving a gap. This has the same effect as trimming between two cutting edges.

- (Break at Point): Breaks an object at one point so that it becomes two pieces, but does not have a gap. This option is useful if you need to change a portion of a line into a different linetype. This command can be repeated by pressing <Enter>.

7.6 Modifying Length

You can use the **Lengthen** command to change the length of an object or the included angle of an arc as shown in Figure 7–25. However, you cannot change the length of a closed object.

Shorter   *Original*   *Longer*

Figure 7–25

How To: Lengthen an Object

1. In the *Home* tab>expanded Modify panel, click

   (Lengthen).
2. Select the object. Its current length displays in the Command Line.
3. Select an option to modify the object's length:
   - **Delta:** Specify the increments by which the object's length is to be modified. To extend the object, enter a positive value. To shorten it, enter a negative value. The length is always measured from the closest end point to the selection point. Use the same method to change the angle of an arc.
   - **Percent:** Modify the object by a percentage of its length.
   - **Total:** Modify the object's length by a specific amount from a fixed end point. Specify the total required angle to modify the included angle of an arc.
   - **Dynamic:** Toggle on Dynamic Dragging mode. Pick an object's end point and drag it to the required length. The other end point does not change.
4. Hover over the object to preview the changes depending on the selected option and the specified values. Select the object to change it.
5. Press <Enter> to end the command.

Practice 7b | Extending and Trimming Objects

Practice Objective

- Remove and extend objects.

In this practice, you will extend and trim lines to complete a drawing, as shown in Figure 7–26.

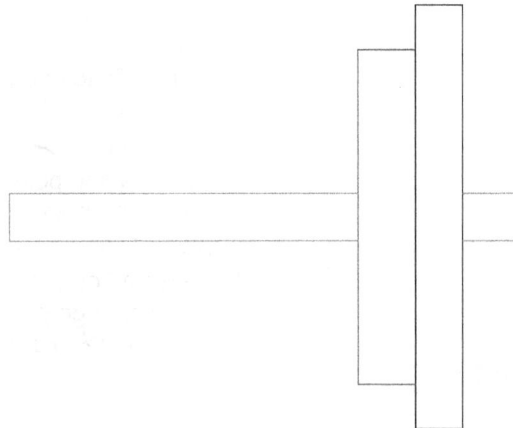

Before

After

Figure 7–26

1. Open **Shaft-M.dwg** from your practice files folder.

2. In the *Home* tab>Modify panel, click ⇥ (Extend).

3. Click above and then below the two short horizontal red lines, closer to their right endpoints, such that they extend until the red vertical line (last line) located on the right hand side, as shown in Figure 7–27.

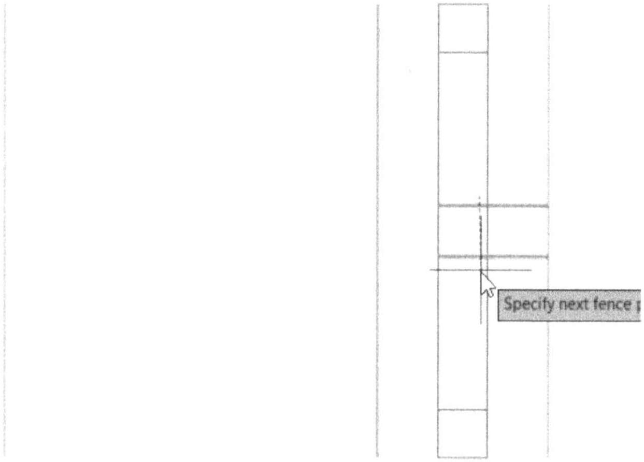

Specify next fence

Figure 7–27

If you exited the command, select it again in the ribbon.

4. While remaining in the **Extend** command, open the down arrow menu at the Command prompt, and select **Boundary edges**.

5. Select the vertical red line on the left hand side as the boundary edges, and press <Enter>. Note that they are highlighted in blue and a thicker line weight.

6. Select the pair of short horizontal red lines closer to their left endpoints, to extend them to the selected red line. Press <Enter> to complete the command.

7. Start the **Extend** command again and individually select the pair of short horizontal blue lines along their left endpoints, to extend them to the vertical blue line. Press <Enter> to complete the command.

8. In the *Home* tab>Modify panel, click ✂ (Trim). Select the top and bottom portions of both vertical red lines to trim their top and bottom portions.

9. While remaining in the **Trim** command, select the top and bottom portions of the vertical blue line to trim its top and bottom portion.

10. Inside the black rectangular area, select two fence selection points, above and below the blue horizontal lines, (as shown in Figure 7–28) to trim the inner four lines.

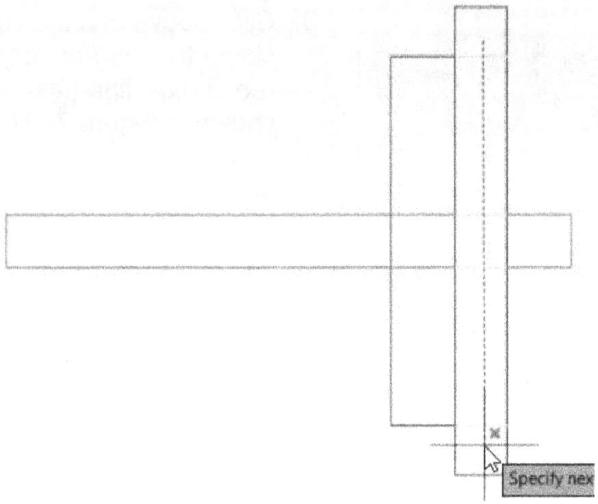

Figure 7–28

11. Similarly, trim the two red horizontal lines within the blue rectangular area.

12. Save and close the drawing.

Practice 7c

Trimming Objects on a Drawing

Practice Objective

- Remove parts of objects.

In this practice, you will use the **Trim** command to remove parts of lines and to trim circles to create slots, as shown in Figure 7–29.

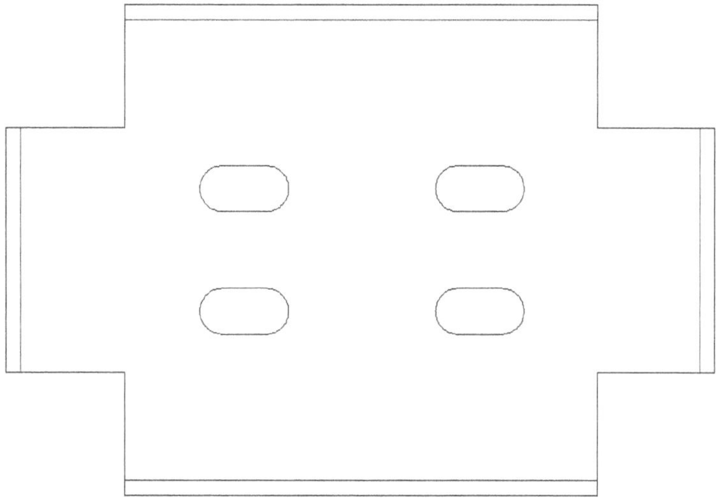

Figure 7–29

1. Open **Bracket-l.dwg** from your practice files folder.

2. Start the **Trim** command.

3. Click and hold the left mouse button and then drag it to create a freehand line over the four inner lines that creates the inner rectangle, as shown in Figure 7–30. Let go of the left mouse button to trim all the four lines in one go.

Figure 7–30

4. While remaining in the **Trim** command, open the down arrow menu at the Command prompt, and select **Crossing**.

5. Create a crossing window inside the slot to trim the inner portions of the circles, as shown in Figure 7–31. Individually select the small portion left behind to clean the slot.

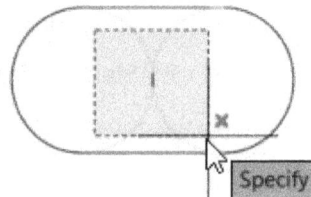

Figure 7–31

6. Similarly, clean up the other three slots.

7. Press <Enter> to exit the command.

8. Save and close the drawing.

7.7 Creating Fillets and Chamfers

Fillets and chamfers are used to create rounded corners and beveled edges respectively, as shown in Figure 7–32.

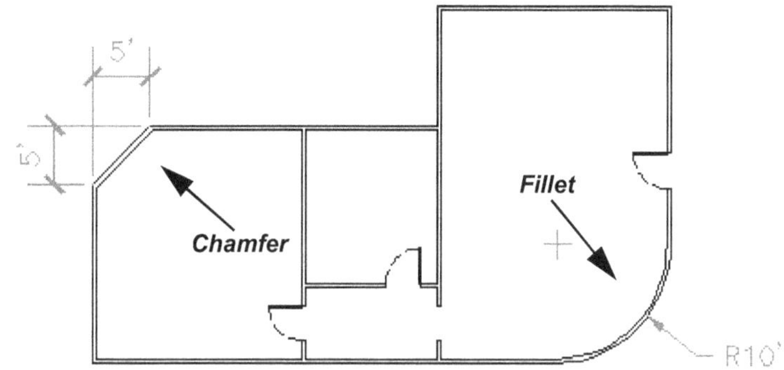

Figure 7–32

Filleting Objects

*The **Radius** option enables you to specify the fillet radius. This value should be selected and set before you pick the objects to fillet.*

The **Fillet** command modifies the intersection of two objects and can be used to create inside and outside rounded corners, as shown in Figure 7–33. It can also be helpful in cleaning up a drawing by forcing lines to meet at an exact intersection.

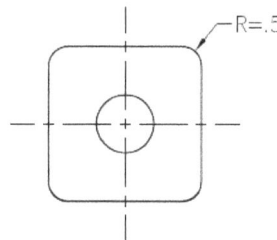

Figure 7–33

How To: Fillet Objects

1. In the *Home* tab>Modify panel, click (**Fillet**).
2. Select the **Radius** option (<Down Arrow> menu), enter the new radius, and press <Enter>.
3. If you are filleting several sets of objects, select the **Multiple** option (<Down Arrow> menu).
4. Select the first line that you want to fillet.

5. Hover the cursor over the second line that you want to fillet. A preview displays the fillet being highlighted in blue and the original object faded in light gray, as shown in Figure 7–34.

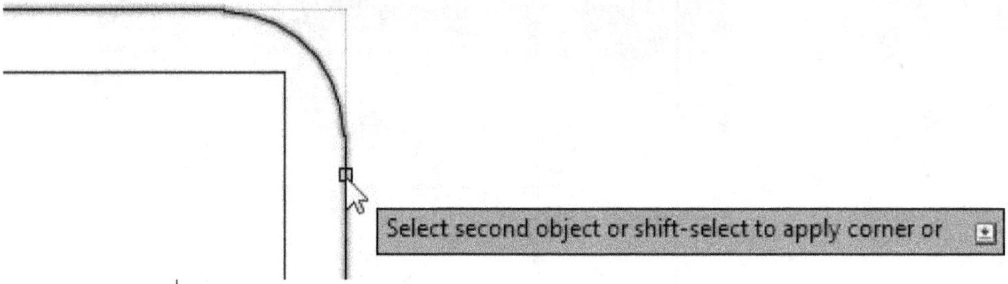

Select second object or shift-select to apply corner or ▣

Figure 7–34

6. Select the second line to confirm the fillet.
7. If you have selected the **Multiple** option, you can continue selecting two lines to fillet until you press <Enter> to complete the command.

- A fillet with the **Radius** option set to **0** can be used to make lines meet at a square corner. You can also hold <Shift> as you select the two lines without having to change the radius.

- You can fillet two parallel lines. In this case, the radius is automatically calculated so that the arc is tangent to both lines.

- The **Undo** option undoes the last fillet without exiting the command.

- The **Polyline** option fillets all of the vertices of a selected polyline. You can still fillet one vertex by selecting segments to fillet.

- The **Trim/NoTrim** option determines whether selected lines are trimmed after the arc is added.

- You can fillet both lines and arcs in a polyline.

Chamfering Objects

The **Chamfer** command angles or bevels the intersection of two lines to create an angled corner, as shown in Figure 7–35.

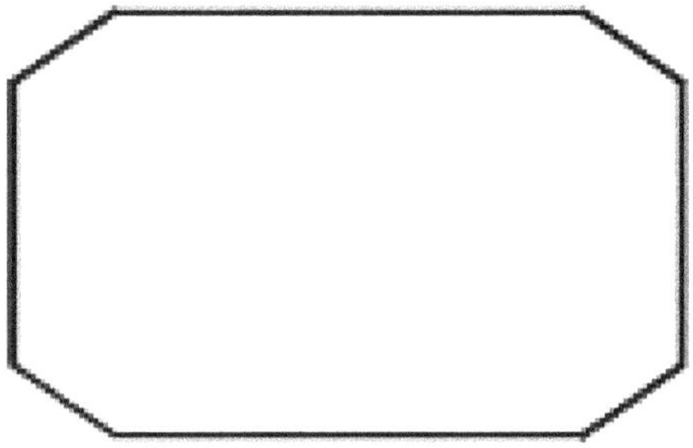

Figure 7–35

How To: Chamfer Objects

1. In the *Home* tab>Modify panel, click (Chamfer).
2. Select the **Distance** option and enter two distances.
3. If you are chamfering several sets of objects, select the **Multiple** option.
4. Select the first line that you want to chamfer, which is highlighted in blue.
5. Hover the cursor over the second line that you want to chamfer. A preview displays the chamfer being highlighted in blue and the chamfered portion being faded in light gray, as shown in Figure 7–36.

The first chamfer distance is used on the first line that you select and the second chamfer distance is used on the second line that you select. Distances are measured from the intersection of the two lines.

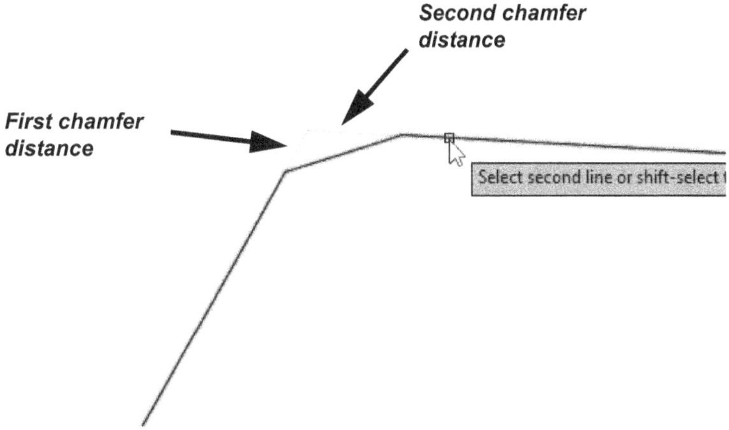

Second chamfer distance

First chamfer distance

Select second line or shift-select

Figure 7–36

6. Select the second line.
7. If you selected the **Multiple** option, you can continue selecting two lines to chamfer until you press <Enter> to complete the command.

- Another way to specify the chamfer is to set the **Angle** option, which sets the chamfer length of the first line you select and then the angle between the original line and the chamfered edge.

- The distance and angle information are stored separately. Therefore, you can use the **Method** option to change between the two options in the same command. The last method you selected is used when a new command is started.

- The **Undo**, **Trim/NoTrim**, and **Polyline** options work the same way as when using the **Fillet** command.

Practice 7d | Filleting Objects

Practice Objective

- Create rounded corners and fillet parallel lines.

In this practice, you will use the **Fillet** command to round the outer corners of a part with two different radius sizes, as shown in Figure 7–37. You will also fillet parallel lines to create slots.

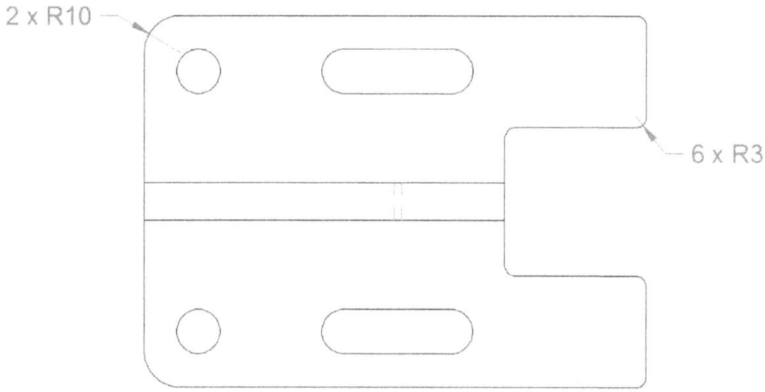

2 x R10

6 x R3

Figure 7–37

1. Open **Visebase-M.dwg** from your practice files folder.

2. In the *Home* tab>Modify panel, click ⌐ (Fillet). Set the **Radius** option (select in the <Down Arrow> menu or type **R**). Set *Radius* to **10**.

3. Select the upper horizontal line and then hover your cursor on the left vertical line, as shown in Figure 7–38. Note the fillet preview.

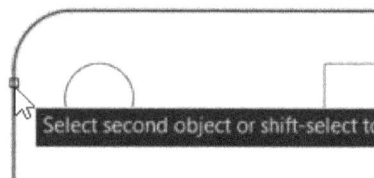

Select second object or shift-select to

Figure 7–38

4. Select the left vertical line to fillet the upper left corner.

5. Repeat the command to fillet the lower left corner with the same radius. Select the lines without entering the **Radius** option.

You are not required to re-enter the radius. It has been set in Step 2.

6. Start the **Fillet** command again. Select the **Radius** option and enter the radius as **3**. Select the **Multiple** option to repeat the prompts. Fillet the six corners on the right side of the object. Press <Enter> to exit the **Multiple** option.

The fillet radius is automatically calculated between the two parallel lines of the rectangle.

7. Continue in the **Fillet** command and select the top horizontal line of the rectangle that is located in the upper area of the part. Select the bottom horizontal line of the rectangle closer to the left corner to create a fillet, as shown in Figure 7–39. Repeat for the right end of the lines.

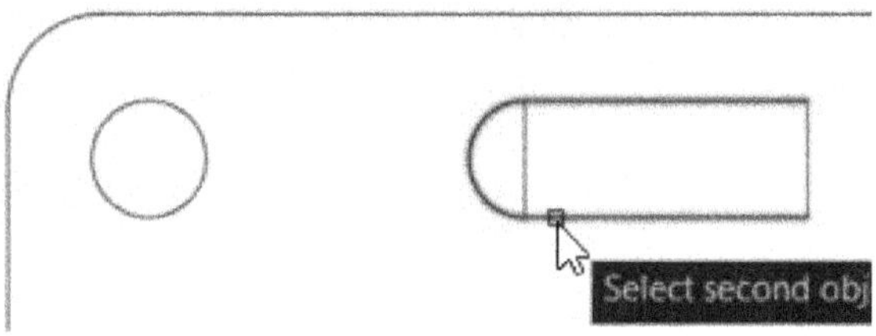

Figure 7–39

8. Repeat Step 7 for the bottom rectangle.

9. Erase the short vertical lines to clear out both the slots.

10. Save and close the drawing.

Practice 7e | Chamfering Objects

Practice Objective

- Create different sizes of angled edges.

In this practice, you will use the **Chamfer** command with several different distances to create the angled edges on a part, as shown in Figure 7–40.

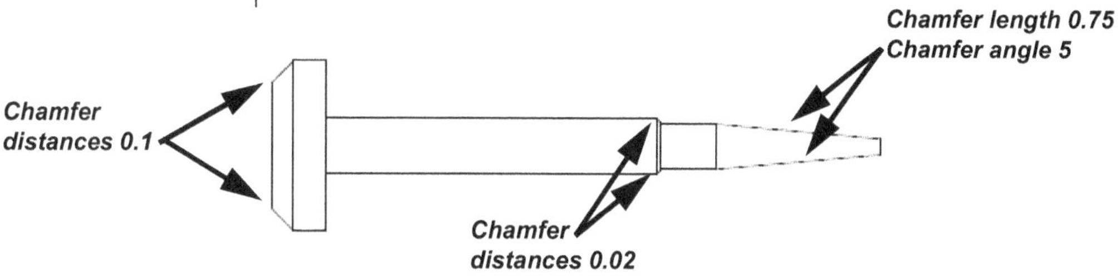

Figure 7–40

1. Open **Punch-I.dwg** from your practice files folder.

*Select **Distance** in the <Down Arrow> menu or type **D**.*

2. In the *Home* tab>Modify panel, click ⌐ (Chamfer). Select the **Distance** option. Set both *Chamfer distances* to **0.1**.

3. Select the two lines in the top left corner of the part to apply the chamfer.

4. Repeat the command to chamfer the bottom left corner using the same distances.

5. Start the **Chamfer** command and select the **Distance** option. Set both *Chamfer distances* to **0.02**. Select the **Multiple** option to repeat the prompts. Chamfer both corners where the shaft changes size.

*Select **Angle** in the <Down Arrow> menu or type **A**.*

6. While remaining in the **Chamfer** command, select the **Angle** option. Set the *Chamfer length* on first line to **0.75**. Set the *chamfer angle* to **5**. Apply the chamfer to the right end of the part, selecting the top horizontal line first, and then the short vertical line. Repeat for the bottom corner of the right end.

7. Add vertical lines to indicate the edges of the three chamfers, as shown in Figure 7–40.

8. Save and close the drawing.

7.8 Offsetting Objects

The AutoCAD software enables you to create parallel shapes with a single editing command called **Offset,** as shown in Figure 7–41.

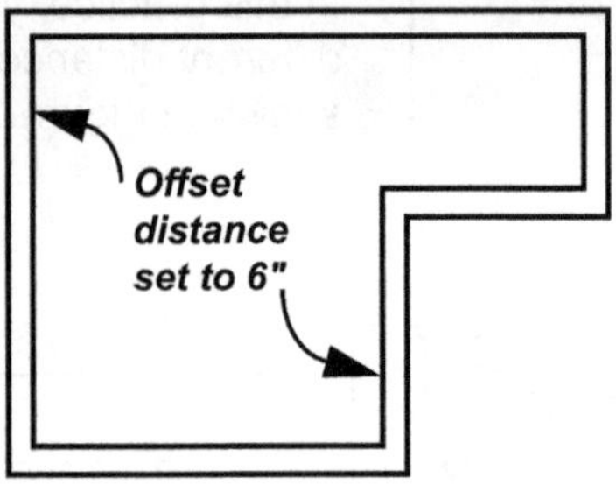

Offset distance set to 6"

Figure 7–41

- The **Offset** command works with lines, circles, arcs, and polylines.

- You can specify a distance between the original object and the offset copy, or select a point through which the copy is going to pass.

How To: Offset Objects Using a Distance

1. In the *Home* tab>Modify panel, click ⊆ (Offset).
2. Enter the offset distance and press <Enter>.
3. Select the object to offset.
4. Hover the cursor on either side of the object to display a preview of the offset copy.

- You can change the offset distance before selecting the side to place the offset copy.

5. Select a point on either side of the object to place the offset copy on that side.
6. Select another object to offset by the same distance, or press <Enter> to complete the command.

- If you want to offset one object multiple times, select the **Multiple** option before you select the side you want to offset. The new objects are placed at the same distance from the last object that was offset.

- The **Through** option enables you to select a point through which the offset object must pass. You can drag the cursor on either side of the object to display a preview of the offset copy before placing the offset.

- The **Erase** and **Layer** options are settings that remain active until you change them. By default, objects from which you offset are not erased, and the layer of the new object matches the layer of the source object rather than the current layer.

- If you offset a polyline, all of the sides are offset equally, as shown in Figure 7–42. To only offset one side of a polyline, you need to explode it first.

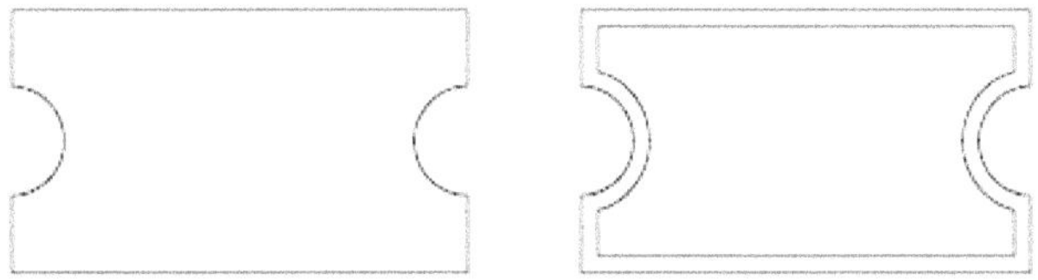

Figure 7–42

Practice 7f

Offsetting Objects

Practice Objective

- Offset polylines, lines, and arcs.

In this practice, you will use the **Offset** command on polylines, lines, and arcs to create walls and steps, as shown in Figure 7–43.

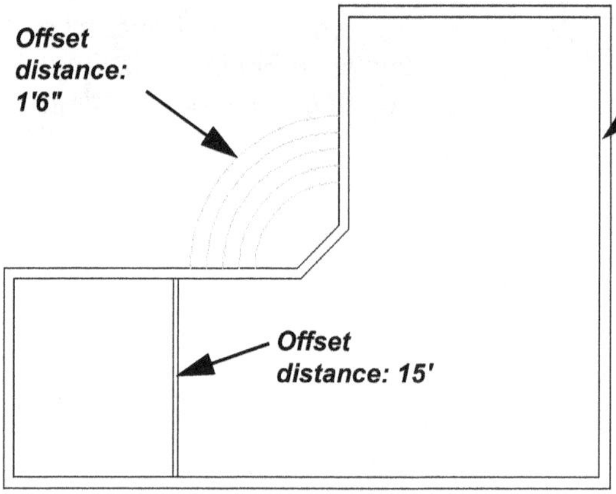

Offset distance: 1'6"

Offset distance: 1'

Offset distance: 15'

Figure 7–43

1. Open **Offset-A.dwg** from your practice files folder. Distances in the drawing are in feet and inches.

2. In the *Home* tab>Modify panel, click ⊆ (Offset). Enter the *offset distance* as **1'** and press <Enter>. Select the large polyline as the object to offset. Move the cursor inside the polyline to display the preview of the offset copy towards inside.

3. Select a point inside the polyline to create the offset copy on the inside. Press <Enter> to complete the command.

4. Start the **Offset** command. Enter the *offset distance* as **1'6"** and press <Enter>. Select the yellow arc as the object to offset. Drag the cursor outside (above) the arc to display the preview and select a point outside (above) the arc to create the offset copy.

5. Note that you are still in the **Offset** command and at the *Select object to offset:* prompt, select the arc you just created. At the *Specify point on side to offset:* prompt, press <Down Arrow> and select the **Multiple** option to make the command repeating. Select three points above the arcs to have a total of five arcs. Press <Enter> twice to complete the command.

6. In the *Home* tab>Modify panel, click ☐ (Explode) and select the inner black polyline, that you created in Step 3. Press <Enter>. The polyline is turned into multiple single line objects.

7. Start the **Offset** command again, and set the *offset distance* to **15'**. Select the inside vertical line on the left bottom as the object to offset. Move the cursor to right of the line to preview the offset line (as shown on the left in Figure 7–44). Select a point to place the offset line.

Since you had previously selected the **Multiple** *option, the setting remains active.*

8. Note that you are still in the **Offset** command. At the *Select object to offset:* prompt, select the line you just created. Note that an offset line is previewed at 15'. In the offset distance edit box, enter **6"**, (as shown on the right in Figure 7–44) to change the offset distance. Press <Enter> to place the offset line to make an interior wall. Press <Enter> again to exit the command.

Figure 7–44

9. Save and close the drawing.

7.9 Creating Arrays of Objects

The **Array** commands generate copies of selected objects at fixed intervals of rows and columns, around a center point, or along a path, as shown in Figure 7–45. For example, a rectangular array can be used to create light fixtures in a ceiling grid. Holes around a circular gasket or radial wings of a building are examples of a polar array. A path array can be used for lights along a walkway or the edge of an irregular shaped pool.

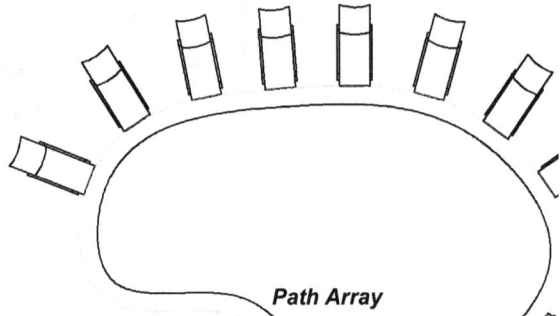

Rectangular Array   *Polar Array*   *Path Array*

Figure 7–45

- The different methods of Array can be accessed in the *Home* tab>Modify panel>Array flyout, as shown in Figure 7–46.

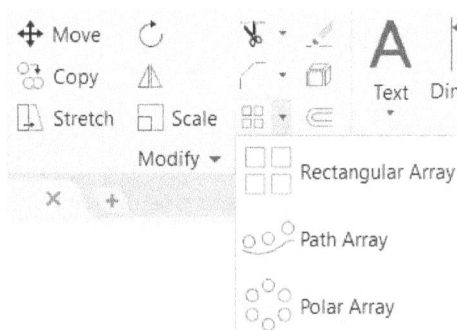

Figure 7–46

- You can create arrays using two methods: using grips, or using the *Array Creation* contextual tab. Once the required objects have been selected to be arrayed in any array style, the grips display on the array and the *Array Creation* contextual tab displays in the ribbon. You can use either method to set the number of items, rows, columns, levels, or other properties. The *Array Creation* contextual tab for creating a Rectangular array is shown in Figure 7–47.

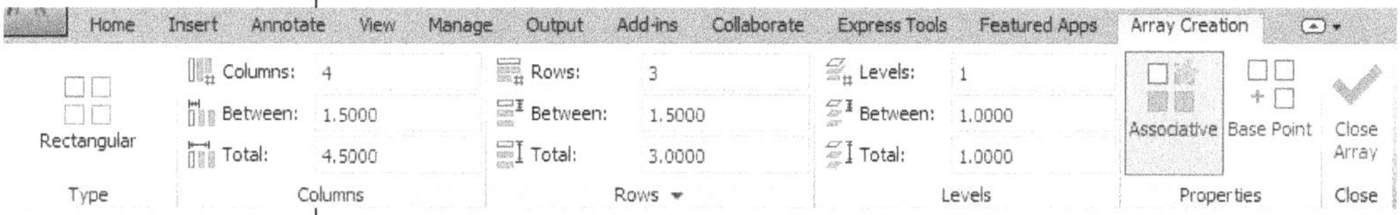

Figure 7–47

Rectangular Array

A rectangular array consists of a pattern of objects that are divided into rows and columns.

How To: Create a Rectangular Array Using Grips

1. In the *Home* tab>Modify panel, expand the Array flyout and click ▦ (Rectangular Array).

You can use windows or crossing selection to select objects.

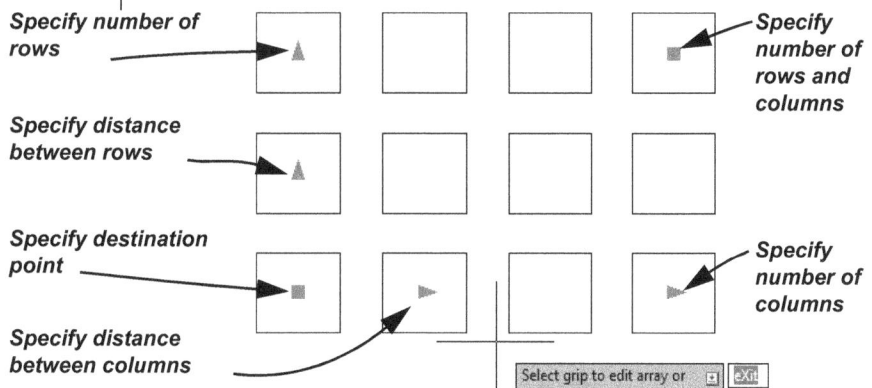

2. At the *Select objects:* prompt, select the object(s) that you want to array and press <Enter>.
3. A preview of the array displays a default number of objects in rows and columns, as shown in Figure 7–48. It also displays grips that enable you to modify the array.

Figure 7–48

4. To specify the number of items to be in the array, use one of the following methods:

- Use the *Specify number of rows*, *Specify number of columns*, and *Specify number of rows and columns* grips to change the number of columns and rows.

- At the *Select grip to edit array or:* prompt, type **COU** and press <Enter> to use the **Count** option. Enter a value for the number of columns, and then for the number of rows. Press <Enter> after each value.

5. Specify the spacing between the arrayed items, using one of the following methods:

- Use the *row* spacing and *column spacing* grips to change the number of columns and rows.

- At the *Select grip to edit array or:* prompt, type **S** and press <Enter> to use the **Spacing** option. Enter a value for the distance between the columns and then for between the rows. Press <Enter> after each value.

6. If required, you can modify the location of the array by selecting the *Specify destination point* grip and then picking a destination point in the drawing window.

7. Press <Enter> to complete the command.

Polar Array

A polar array consists of a pattern of objects that are copied about a central radius.

How To: Create a Polar Array Using Array Creation Contextual Tab

1. In the *Home* tab>Modify panel, expand the Array flyout and click (Polar Array).

2. At the *Select objects:* prompt, select the object(s) that you want to array. Press <Enter> to end the selection of objects.

3. At the *Specify center point of array:* prompt, select a point on the screen to be the center of the polar array.

4. A preview of the array displays a default number of objects in a radial pattern, as shown in Figure 7–49. Additionally, it displays grips and an *Array Creation* contextual tab in the ribbon that enable you to modify the array.

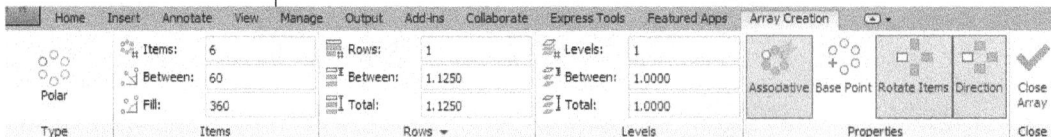

Home	Insert	Annotate	View	Manage	Output	Add-ins	Collaborate	Express Tools	Featured Apps	Array Creation

Polar	Items:	6	Rows:	1	Levels:	1			Close Array
	Between:	60	Between:	1.1250	Between:	1.0000	Associative Base Point Rotate Items Direction		
	Fill:	360	Total:	1.1250	Total:	1.0000			
Type		Items		Rows ▾		Levels		Properties	Close

Figure 7–49

5. Specify the number of items in the Items panel.
6. Depending on the number of items and the *Fill* angle, the *Between* angle value changes to fit the specified number.
   - Using the **Fill** option, enter the angle that you want the arrayed items to fill.
7. If required, you can modify the rotation of the items and the direction of the array using the **Rotate Items** and **Direction** buttons in the contextual tab.
8. Press <Enter> to complete the command.

   - When creating polar arrays, you can use the **ROWs** option to add additional offset rows around the center point and the **Rotate Items** option to change the orientation of the arrayed items, as they are being placed around the center point.

Path Array

A path array consists of a pattern of objects that are copied along a straight, curved, or irregular linear path.

How To: Create a Path Array

1. In the *Home* tab>Modify panel, expand the Array flyout and click (Path Array).
2. At the *Select objects:* prompt, select the object(s) that you want to array. Press <Enter> to end the selection of objects.
3. At the *Select path curve:* prompt, select the object that you want to use as the path.
4. A preview of the array displays a default number of objects copied along a path, as shown in Figure 7–50. It also displays grips that enable you to modify the array.

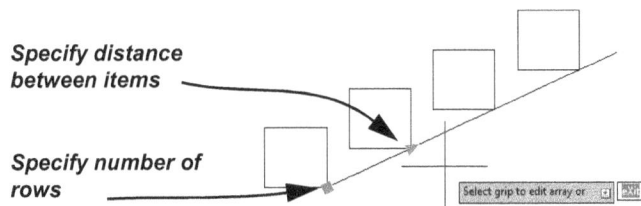

Specify distance between items

Specify number of rows

Select grip to edit array or

Figure 7–50

5. Specify the number of items in the array by selecting the square grip (as shown in Figure 7–50), typing a value, and pressing <Enter>.
6. Specify the distance between the items along the path by selecting the arrow grip (as shown in Figure 7–50), typing a value, and pressing <Enter>. You can also select the grip and drag the cursor to change the value.

7. Press <Enter> to complete the command.

- When using the path array, you might want to place the arrayed object in its final orientation and position. You need to place it near the start point of the path. Otherwise, you need to use the **Orientation** option to indicate how the object is to be oriented and positioned along the path.
- You can use the **Method** option, with its **Divide** option to evenly space the objects along the path.

Hint: Associative Arrays

By default, arrays are created as associative arrays where all the objects of the array maintain a relationship with each other. This is useful if you want to adjust the array patterns, spacing, and the location. This way you can easily modify all the objects in the array together and with respect to each other.

Practice 7g | Rectangular Array

Practice Objective

• Make copies of objects at fixed intervals of rows and columns.

In this practice, you will use a **Rectangular Array** to make copies of a workstation in a classroom, as shown in Figure 7–51.

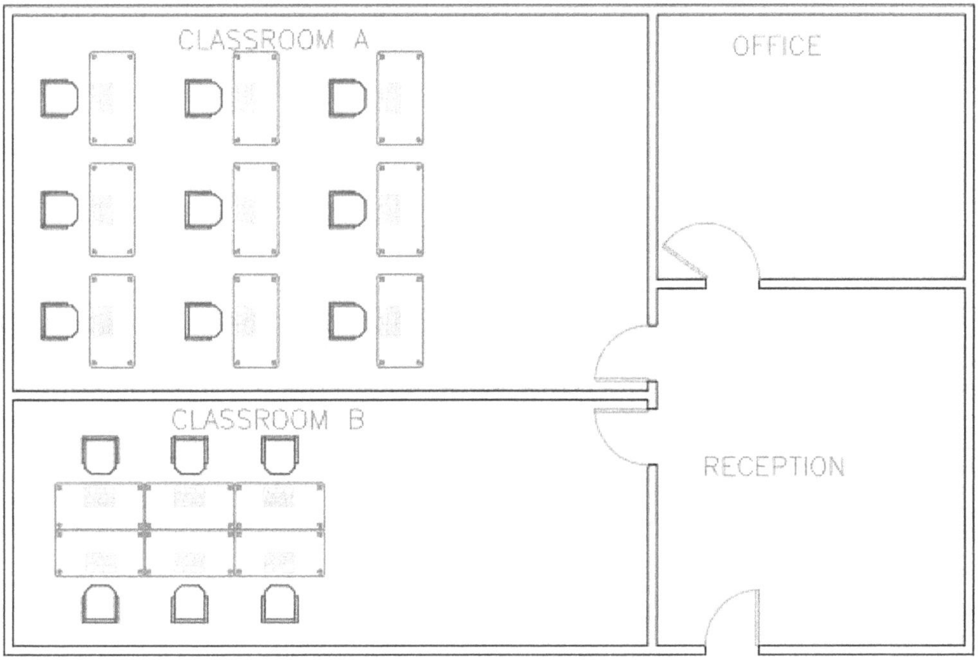

Figure 7–51

1. Open **Class3-A.dwg** from your practice files folder.

2. In the *Home* tab>Modify panel, expand the Array flyout and select ___ (Rectangular Array).

You can use the window or crossing selection to select the three objects.

3. At the *Select objects:* prompt, select the desk, chair, and laptop in Classroom A and press <Enter>.

The top right square grip specifies the number of rows and columns.
You can use the Array Creation contextual tab to enter all the values.

4. At the *Select grip to edit array*, select the top-right corner grip (square grip) and enter **3**, as shown in Figure 7–52. Press <Enter>.

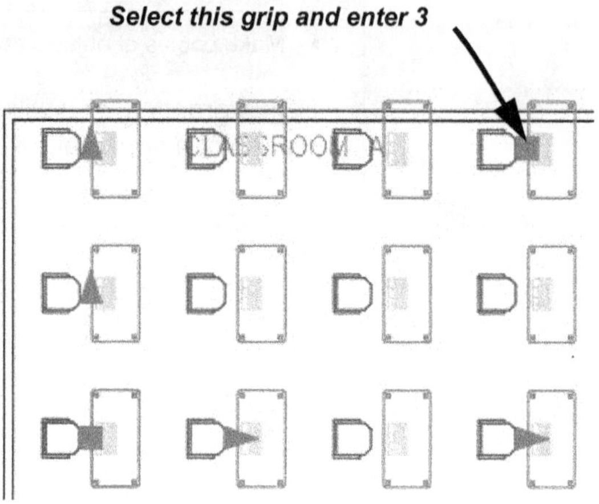
Select this grip and enter 3
CLASSROOM A

Figure 7–52

The middle left arrow grip specifies the row spacing.

5. Select the middle grip along the left side (upward facing arrow grip) and verify that **ROW SPACING** displays at the cursor prompt. Enter **6'**, as shown on the left in Figure 7–53. Press <Enter>.

The middle bottom arrow grip specifies the column spacing.

6. Select the middle grip along the bottom (right facing arrow grip) and verify that **COLUMN SPACING** displays at the cursor prompt. Enter **8'**, as shown on the right in Figure 7–53. Press <Enter>.

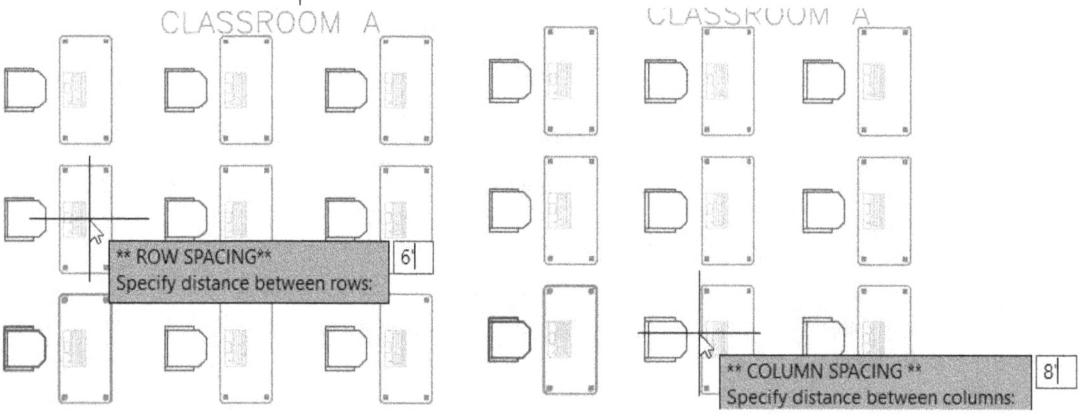
CLASSROOM A
** ROW SPACING**
Specify distance between rows:
6'
CLASSROOM A
** COLUMN SPACING **
Specify distance between columns:
8'

Figure 7–53

7. Press <Enter> to exit the command.

8. Save and close the file.

Practice 7h

Polar Array

Practice Objective

- Make copies of an object around a center point.

In this practice, you will use **Polar Array** to make copies of the nut around the flange, as shown in Figure 7–54.

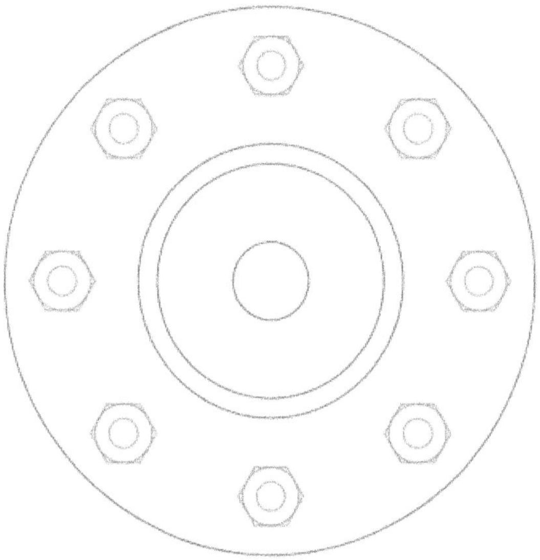

Figure 7–54

1. Open **Flange-I.dwg** from your practice files folder.

2. Select the **Center** object snap option and verify that **Object Snap** is toggled on in the Status Bar.

3. In the *Home* tab>Modify panel>Array flyout, click   (Polar Array).

4. At the *Select objects:* prompt, select the nut. Press <Enter> to finish selecting objects.

5. At the *Specify center point of array:* prompt, select the center of any circle.

6. Note that the *Array Creation* contextual tab displays in the ribbon. In the Items panel, for *Items*, enter **8** and press \<Enter\>. Note that the *Between* angle value changes to 45 so that it accommodates the specified number of items, as shown in Figure 7–55. Note how the nuts are rotated around the center of the circles.

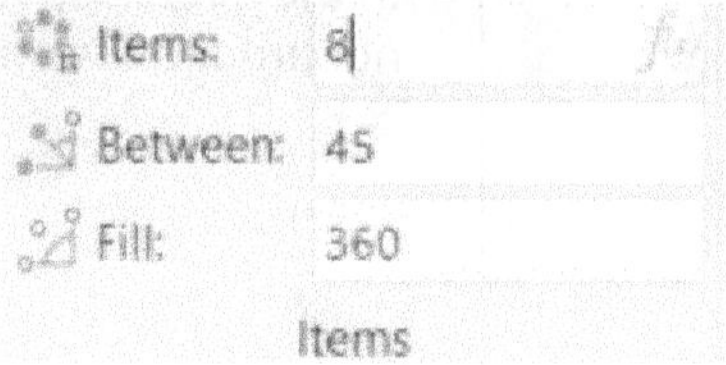

Items:	8	
Between:	45	
Fill:	360	

Items

Figure 7–55

7. In the preview of the array, note that the nuts are rotated in different directions and are not oriented correctly. In the *Array Creation* tab>Properties panel, click (Rotate Items) to clear it. Note that the nuts are correctly oriented around the flange.

8. Press \<Enter\> or click (Close Array) to complete the command.

9. Save and close the file.

Practice 7i

Path Array

Practice Objective

- Make copies of an object along a selected path.

In this practice, you will use a **Path Array** to make copies of a deck chair around the edge of a pool, as shown in Figure 7–56.

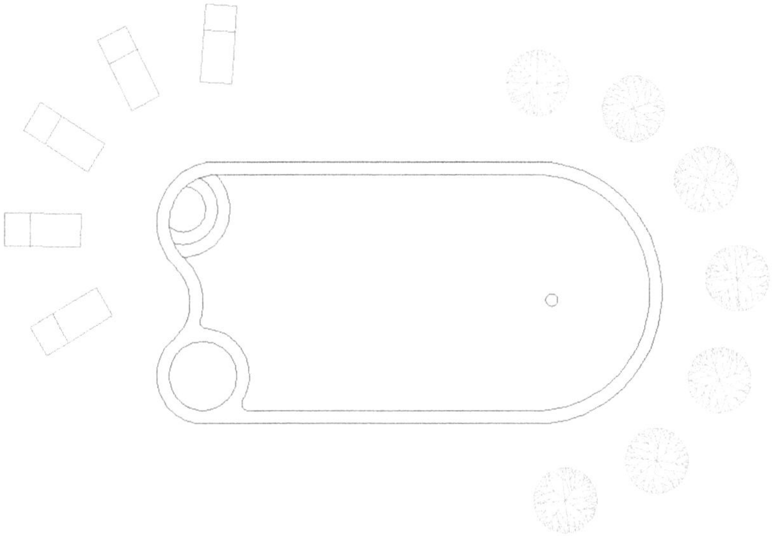

Figure 7–56

1. Open **Deckchair-I.dwg** from your practice files folder.

2. In the *Home* tab>Modify panel>Array flyout, click ⌃ (Path Array).

3. At the *Select objects:* prompt, select the tree near the top right of the pool. Press <Enter> to finish selecting objects.

4. At the *Select path curve:* prompt, select the magenta arc that starts at the tree.

5. Note that the trees do not cover the arc fully. In the *Array Creation* contextual, in the Items panel, for *Between* enter **8'** and press <Enter>, as shown in Figure 7–57. Note how the trees spread out to cover the arc completely.

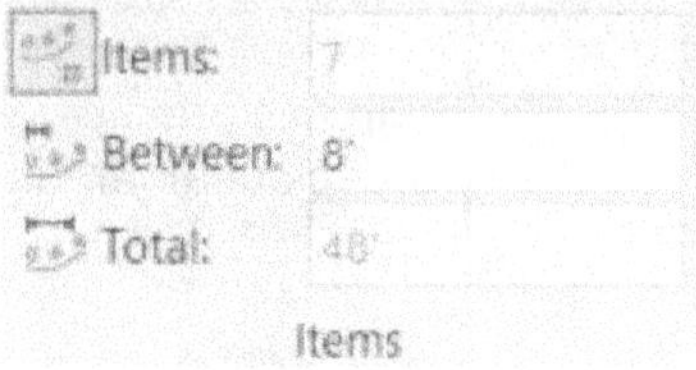

Items:	7	
Between:	8'	
Total:	48'	

Items

Figure 7–57

6. Press <Enter> again to exit the command.

7. Start the **Path Array** command again.

Select both the rectangle and the line that makes up the chair.

8. At the *Select objects:* prompt, select the chair to the left of the pool. Press <Enter> to finish selecting objects.

9. At the *Select path curve:* prompt, select the magenta arc that starts at the chair.

10. In the *Array Creation* contextual tab, in the Properties panel, expand the Measure drop-down list and click ⋔ (Divide). The chairs are now evenly spaced along the path.

11. In the *Array Creation* contextual tab>Items panel, in the *Items* field, enter **5** (as shown in Figure 7–58), and then press <Enter>. Note that the 5 chairs are placed along the path at an equal distance from each other.

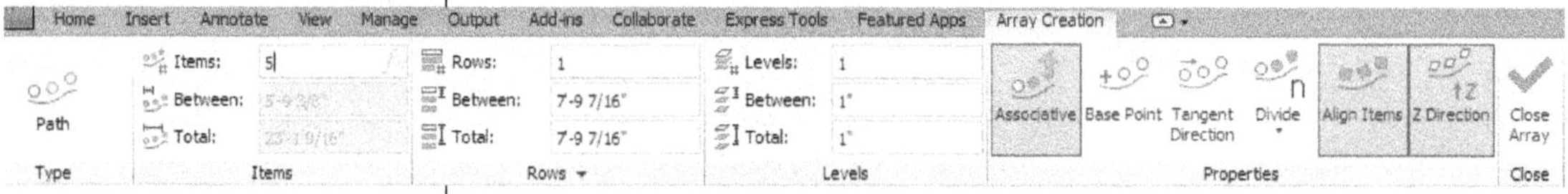

Home	Insert	Annotate	View	Manage	Output	Add-ins	Collaborate	Express Tools	Featured Apps	Array Creation

Items:	5	Rows:	1	Levels:	1			
Between:	3-4 3/8"	Between:	7-9 7/16"	Between:	1"	Associative	Base Point	Tangent Direction	Divide	Align Items	Z Direction	Close Array
Total:	23-1 9/16"	Total:	7-9 7/16"	Total:	1"			
Path								
Type		Items		Rows ▾		Levels		Properties	Close

Figure 7–58

12. Press <Enter> to end the command.

13. Toggle off the layer **Path** to hide the paths that were used to create the arrays.

14. Save and close the file.

Multi-Functional Grip Editing

Exam Objectives Covered in This Chapter

- 3.5.a Copy objects using grips
- 3.5.b Add, stretch, or remove vertices from an object
- 3.5.c Convert an object segment to an arc or line
- 3.5.d Lengthen an arc
- 3.5.e Use the multi-functional grips of selected objects

8.1 Editing with Grips

You can modify objects by using their grips without using an editing command. The AutoCAD software stores information about objects as geometric formulas. Therefore, lines are defined by their end points, circles by their center and radius, etc. The software can easily compute additional points, such as the midpoint of a line or quadrants of a circle, and enable you to modify them, as shown in Figure 8–1.

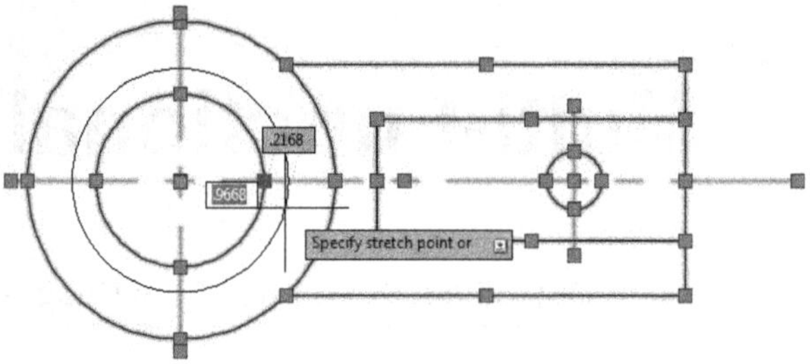

Figure 8–1

- By default, grips display as blue boxes on an object when it is selected without starting a command.

- If you hover the cursor over a grip but do not select it, the color changes to pink.

Working with Hot Grips

When you click directly on a grip, it changes to a selected or *hot grip* (red by default), as shown in Figure 8–2.

- Depending on the grip you make hot, the default mode is automatically enabled. For example, the quadrant grip of a circle stretches it, but the center grip moves the circle, as shown in Figure 8–2.

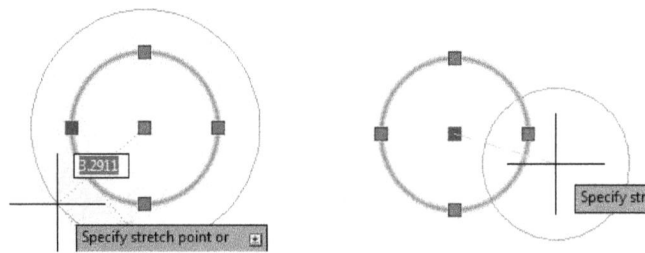

Hot grip selected on quadrant and used as Stretch

Hot grip selected in center and used as Move

Figure 8–2

- If you hover the cursor over certain multi-functional grips, additional options display, as shown in Figure 8–3. The options for the endpoint grips of line segments and arcs include **Stretch** and **Lengthen**, and for the middle grip of arcs include **Stretch** and **Radius**.

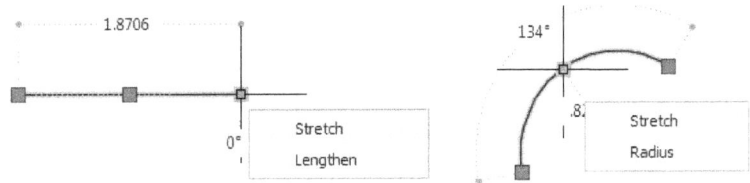

Figure 8–3

- To select a different option after you make a grip hot, you can right-click to display the various editing commands in the shortcut menu, as shown in Figure 8–4.

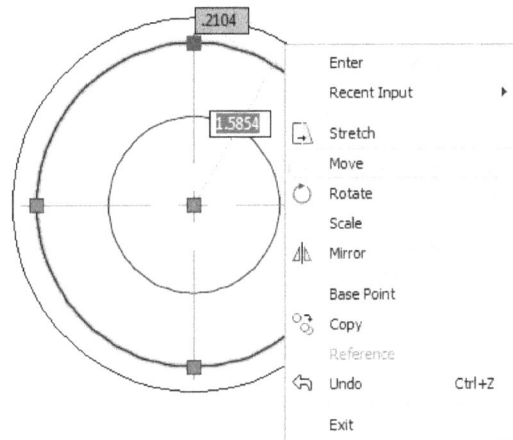

Figure 8–4

You can also press <Spacebar> to cycle through the available commands.

- Once a grip and an editing command have been selected, various advanced options (for the selected command) display by pressing <Down Arrow>, as shown in Figure 8–5.

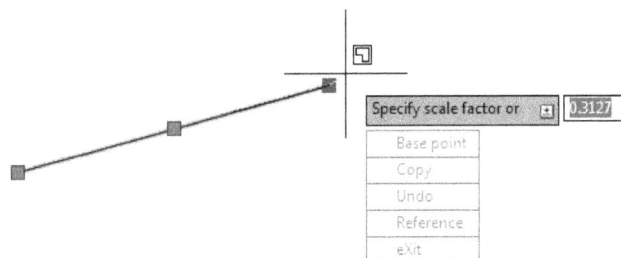

Figure 8–5

- To clear objects and their grips, press <Esc>.

- When using grips, their default mode and multi-functional mode only apply to the object with the hot grip. However, **Move**, **Mirror**, **Scale**, and **Rotate** affect all of the selected objects.

- You can hold <Shift> to activate multiple modes of grips.

- When using grips on a block, **Stretch** has the same effect as **Move**. This is because you cannot stretch a standard block object.

- You can change the display of grips (size and color) and other settings in the *Selection* tab in the Options dialog box (Application Menu>**Options**).

Grips with Dynamic Dimensions

Grips enable you to quickly check the dimensions of an object. For example, when you hover the cursor over the end point grip of a line, dynamic dimensions display the line's length and angle and the quadrant grip on a circle displays the circle's radius, as shown in Figure 8–6.

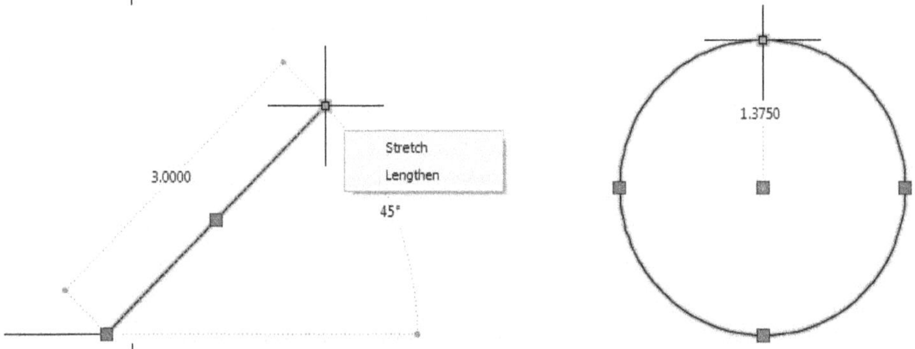

Figure 8–6

- ⊹▭ (Dynamic Input) must be toggled on for the dimensions to be displayed.

- When you select the stretch grip of an object, you can edit the dimension instead of dragging the hot grip.

How To: Stretch a Line by 5 Units Using Grips

1. Select the line to display the grips.
2. Select the endpoint grip of the line, as shown in Figure 8–7.

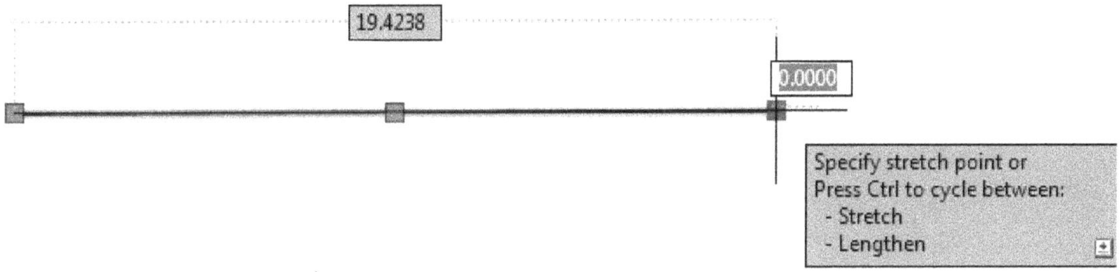

19.4238

0.0000

Specify stretch point or
Press Ctrl to cycle between:
- Stretch
- Lengthen

Figure 8–7

3. Two dimensions display for the length: one with the current overall length and one with the change in length (which is 0 unless you move the cursor). The change in length can be edited.

4. Enter **5** (as shown in Figure 8–8), and press <Enter> to change the length. The line length increases by 5 units and the angle does not change.

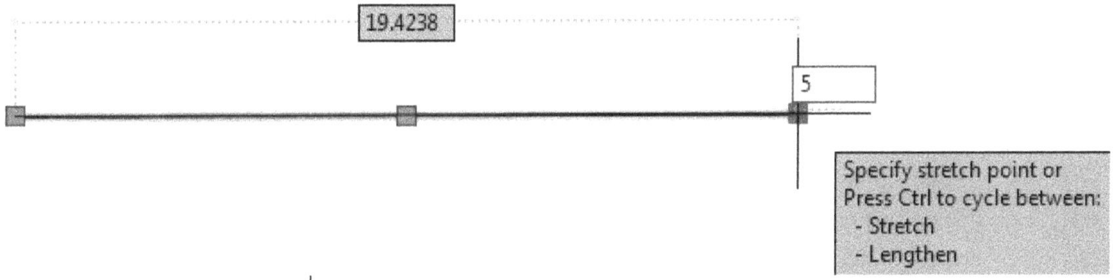

19.4238

5

Specify stretch point or
Press Ctrl to cycle between:
- Stretch
- Lengthen

Figure 8–8

• Press <Tab> to change the angle. You might have to enter <Tab> twice to get the angle edit box (shown in Figure 8–9).

Specify stret
Press Ctrl to
- Stretch
- Lengthen

Figure 8–9

| Practice 8a | # Editing with Grips I |

Editing with Grips I

Practice Objective

- Modify objects using grips.

In this practice, you will use grips to move, copy, rotate, mirror, and scale objects on the façade of a building. You will also use <Shift> to copy and specify a new base point, as shown in Figure 8–10.

Figure 8–10

1. Open **Facade-A.dwg** from your practice files folder.

2. Set the object snaps to **Endpoint**, **Midpoint**, and **Intersection**, and toggle 🔲 (Object Snap) on. Toggle 🔄 ▼ (Polar Tracking) off. Toggle on ⊞ (Dynamic Input), if it is not already on.

3. With no command active, select the double door. Select the grip to make it hot (red by default). Move the door to the midpoint of the bottom line on the building. Press <Esc> to clear the object.

4. Repeat Step 3 with the arched window and place the grip at the midpoint of the top of the door.

5. Select the square window and select the grip. Right-click and select **Copy**. Select the intersections of the blue center lines (except the one inside the door) to place windows at each intersection (9 in total). Press <Esc> twice to finish.

6. Erase the blue center lines.

7. Select the four angled lines of the roof. Select the grip at the right end of one of the lines. Right-click and select **Mirror**, then right-click again and select **Copy** to keep the original objects. Select the midpoint of the roofline as the second point for the mirror line. Press <Esc> twice to finish.

8. Select the center square window above the door and select the grip. Right-click and select **Base Point**. For the base point, select the intersection (or midpoint) of the mullions at the center of the window.

9. Right-click again and select **Rotate**. For the rotation angle, enter **45** and press <Enter>.

10. Select the window grip again. Right-click and select **Base Point** and select the intersection (or midpoint) of the mullions. Right-click and select **Scale**. For the scale factor, enter **0.7** and press <Enter>. Press <Esc> to finish.

11. Select the arched window above the door and select the grip. Right-click and select **Scale**. For the scale factor, enter **0.65** and press <Enter>. Press <Esc> to finish.

12. Select the bottom line along the base of the building. Hover the cursor over the grip at either end point to display the dimension. What is the length of the line?

13. Select the top roofline on the left side of the building, and hover the cursor over the end point at the top. What is the length and angle of the line?

14. Save and close the drawing.

Practice 8b | Editing with Grips II

Practice Objective

- Modify objects using grips.

In this practice, you will use grips to move, copy, rotate, and scale objects as shown in Figure 8–11.

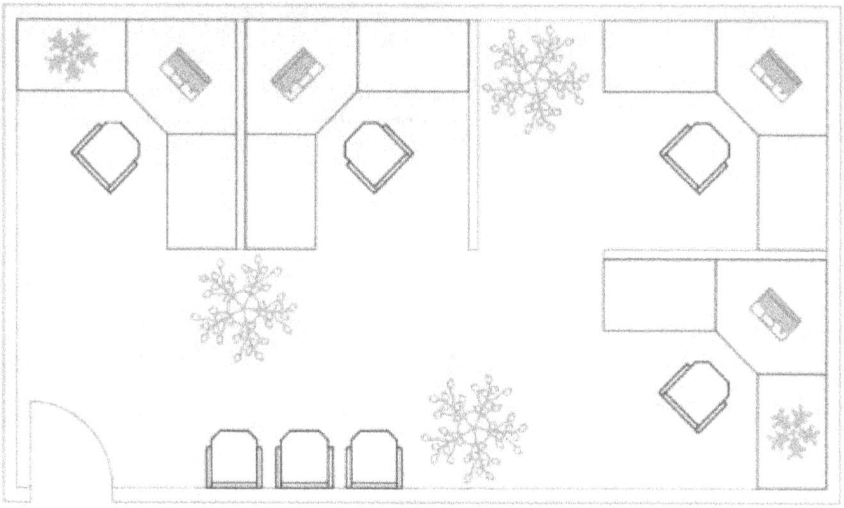

Figure 8–11

1. Open **Arrange-Grips-A.dwg** from your practice files folder.

2. Use grips to move, copy, rotate, and scale objects (as shown in Figure 8–12) so that they are placed as shown in Figure 8–11.

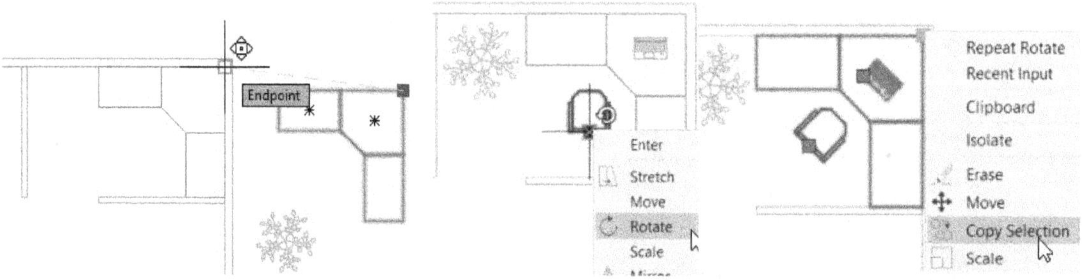

Hot grip used as Move

Using Rotate in the hot grip Shortcut menu

Using Copy Selection in the hover grip Shortcut menu

Figure 8–12

8.2 Using Grips Effectively

Grips are a very powerful tool and using them helps you to quickly and easily modify drawings. You can increase the effectiveness of using grips by changing the base point, copying with grips, using the reference option, stretching multiple objects (as shown in Figure 8–13), and modifying grip settings.

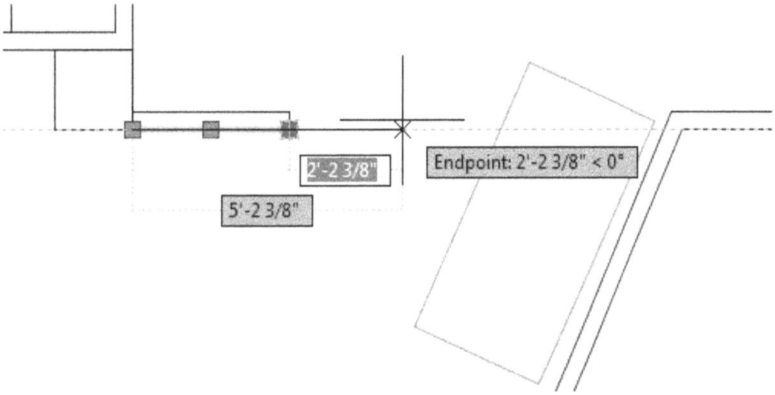

Figure 8–13

- If ![icon] (Dynamic Input) is on, dynamic dimensions (and if it is a multifunctional grip, a dynamic list of options) display when you hover the cursor over a grip. Select one of the optional commands, such as **Stretch**, **Lengthen**, or **Add Vertex**.

- When you select a grip you can edit the dimensions to stretch the object. Use <Tab> to highlight the dimension that you want to change.

- Depending on which grip is selected, the Stretch mode either stretches or moves the object. Centers of circles and midpoints of lines move the objects. Standard blocks move because they cannot be stretched. Dynamic blocks have special grips.

- Pressing <Enter> while a grip is hot, sequentially toggles through **Move**, **Rotate**, **Scale**, **Mirror**, and then back to **Stretch**.

- To clear grips from objects, press <Esc> or right-click and select **Exit**.

Changing the Base Point

The hot grip becomes the default base point for moving, rotating, etc. To use a different base point, right-click and select **Base Point** as shown in Figure 8–14 (or type **B** in the Command Line). Select the new base point and continue with the command.

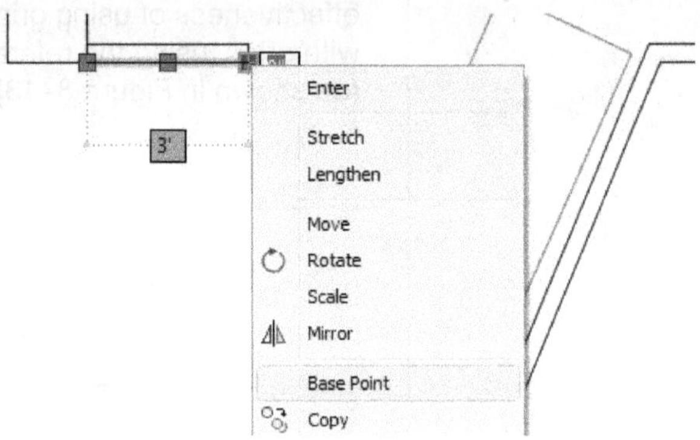

Figure 8–14

Copying with Grips

Use the **Copy** option with any of the grip editing modes to create multiple copies while you move, rotate, etc.

How To: Copy with Grips

1. Select the objects and make one grip hot.
2. Right-click and select the editing mode (**Stretch**, **Move**, **Rotate**, etc.).
3. Select the **Copy** option in the shortcut menu or Command Line.
4. Select (or type) the second point, rotation angle, mirror line, or scale factor.

• If you hold <Ctrl> while selecting the location for additional copies, the new objects snap to the same spacing as the first copy, as shown in Figure 8–15.

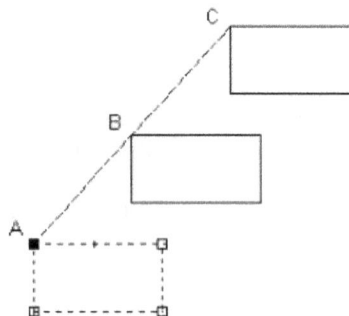

Holding <Ctrl> while selecting the point for stretching, moving, rotating, etc., also starts the multiple copy mode.

Figure 8–15

Rotate and Scale with the Reference Option

The **Reference** option enables you to select reference points in your drawing to describe the rotation angle or scale factor.

How To: Rotate and Scale with Grips and Reference

1. Select the objects that you want to rotate or scale.
2. Select the grip to be the base point for rotating or scaling.
3. Right-click and select **Rotate** or **Scale**.
4. Right-click and select **Reference**.

   - **For Rotate:** Specify the reference angle by typing the angle or selecting two points. Specify the new angle by typing the angle or selecting a second point. The first point of the new angle is the base point.

   - **For Scale:** Specify the reference length by typing the length or selecting two points. Specify the new length by typing the length or selecting a second point. The first point of the new length is the base point.

For example, you might want to straighten a rectangle that is rotated at an unknown angle, as shown in Figure 8–16. Select the rectangle and then select the grip at point 1 as the base point for rotation. Right-click and select **Rotate** and **Reference**. For the *Reference angle*, select the end points at **1** and **2** (this is the current angle of the object). For the *New angle*, type **0**.

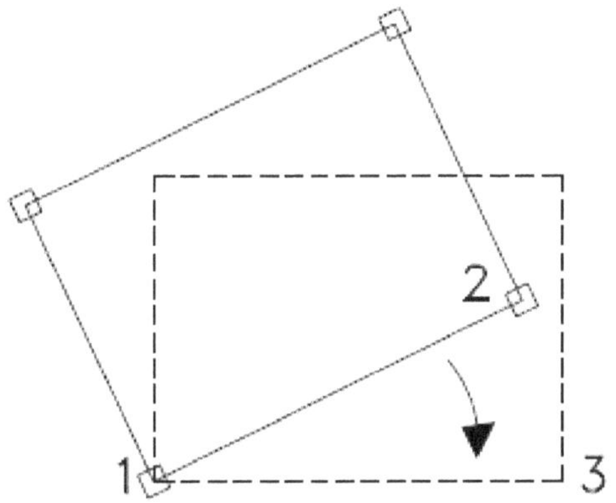

Figure 8–16

- The **Reference** option is also available with the regular **Rotate** and **Scale** commands.

Stretching Multiple Objects

In the Stretch mode, only hot grips or objects that contain hot grips are stretched. You can make multiple grips hot by holding <Shift> when selecting each grip, as shown in Figure 8–17.

Figure 8–17

How To: Stretch with Grips

1. Select the objects that you want to stretch.
2. Hold <Shift> and select all of the grips that you want to move using **Stretch**.
3. Release <Shift>.
4. Select the grip that you want to use as a base point.
5. Select the point that you want to use as the second point of displacement.

Converting to Arcs or Lines

The multi-functional grips of certain objects enable you to convert an object segment into an arc or an arc segment into a line.

How To: Convert an Object Segment into an Arc or Line Segment

1. Select the object to display its multi-functional grips, as shown for a rectangular object in Figure 8–18.

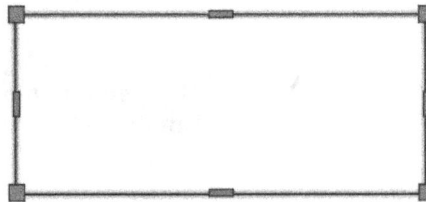

Figure 8–18

2. Hover your cursor over the top middle bar grip, as shown in Figure 8–19. You can stretch, add a vertex, and convert to an arc using the grip options.

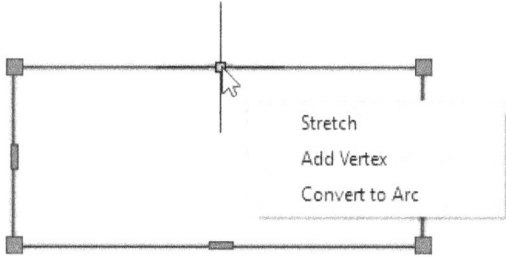

Figure 8–19

3. Click **Add Vertex** and move that point to add a vertex and manipulate the shape of the object, as shown in Figure 8–20.

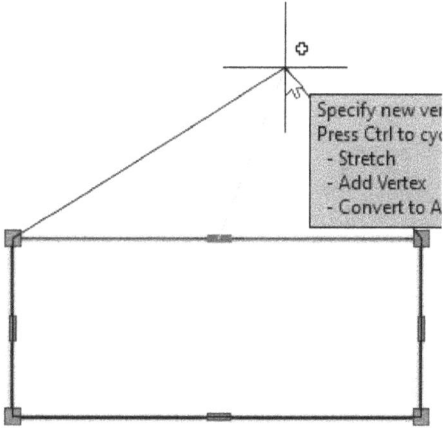

Figure 8–20

4. Hover your cursor over one of the bar grips and select **Convert to Arc**. Move the cursor to define the position and radius of the arc, as shown in Figure 8–21.

Figure 8–21

Grip Settings

In the Options dialog box (expand the Application Menu and click **Options**), in the *Selection* tab, there are several settings related to grips, as shown in Figure 8–22.

Figure 8–22

- *Grip size* enables you to control the size of the grip as it displays in the drawing window.

- You can also change the grip colors by clicking **Grip Colors...** and adjusting the values in the Grip Colors dialog box, as shown in Figure 8–23.

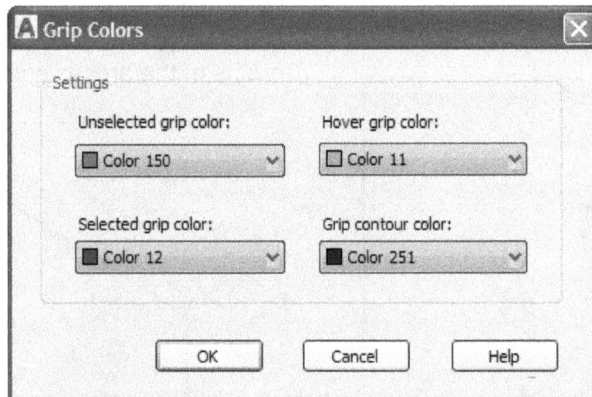

Figure 8–23

In addition to grip size and color, you can set the following:

Show grips	Turns grips on or off globally.
Show grips in blocks	Controls whether grips only display on a block's insertion point (off) or on all nested objects in the block (on). Normally it is easier to work with this option off. This only applies to standard blocks. Dynamic blocks still display grips.
Show grip tips	Grip tips are not available in the basic AutoCAD software, but can display for objects from software such as the AutoCAD® Architecture software.
Show dynamic grip menu	Controls whether a menu displays next to a dynamic grip.
Allow Ctrl+cycling behavior	Controls whether you can use <Ctrl> to cycle through the grip's options.
Show single grip on groups	Displays a single grip for an object group.
Show bounding box on groups	Displays a bounding box around the extents of grouped objects.
Object selection limit for display of grips	If you select more objects than the number set here, grips do not display on them.

Practice 8c | Using Grips Effectively

Practice Objective

- Modify a drawing using grips.

In this practice, you will use grips to edit the schematic drawing, as shown in Figure 8–24.

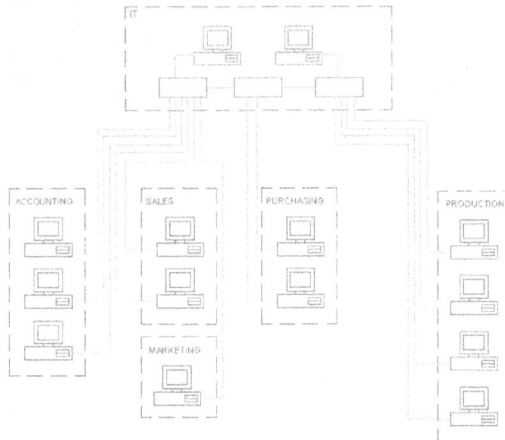

Figure 8–24

1. Open **Computer-I.dwg** from your practice files folder.

2. Use grips to add three, evenly spaced computers to **PRODUCTION**. Use <Ctrl> when selecting the locations for the copies, to place them at even intervals.

3. Use grips to stretch the red rectangle to include the new computers. Use <Shift> to select more than one hot grip.

4. Select the three, yellow polylines connecting the **ACCOUNTING** computers to the hubs. **Mirror** and **Copy** the three polylines to the **PRODUCTION** computers using grips and a base point at the midpoint of the middle hub.

   - Hint: After selecting the three middle grips using <Shift>, use the shortcut menu to select **Mirror** and hold <Ctrl> to make mirrored copies. Select the three middle grips of the mirrored copies, right-click and select **Move** to move those to the **PRODUCTION** computers.

5. Use grips to manipulate the new lines so they match up with the new computers.

6. Save and close the drawing.

SECTION

4

Advanced Layouts, Printing, and Alternative Outputs

Chapter

9

Working with Layouts

Exam Objectives Covered in This Chapter

- 4.1.a Use the Page Setup Managers
- 4.1.b Define and apply custom scales (scale list)
- 4.1.c Customize the size and shape of viewport boundaries
- 4.1.d Assign a named view to a viewport

9.1 Adding Standard Layouts to Templates

You can simplify your day-to-day work by creating layouts in your template files that match the printers and paper sizes that you normally use, as shown in Figure 9–1. These layouts are then ready to use in new drawings based on the templates.

*To create a new Layout tab from an existing layout, right-click on the one that you want to use and select **Move or Copy**. In the dialog box, select **Create a copy** and select a layout before which the copy is going to be placed.*

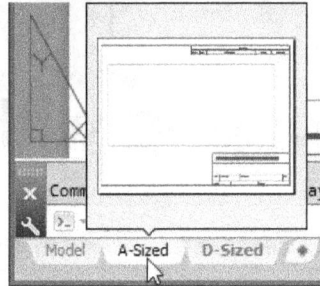

Figure 9–1

Working in the Page Setup Manager

When you set up template files for your office, you need to be able to specify the layouts that use your office printers and title blocks. To do so, create page setups in the Page Setup Manager (as shown in Figure 9–2), and then associate standard page setups with the Layout tabs.

In the Page Setup Manager, you can assign an existing page setup to the current Layout tab, create new page setups, modify existing page setups, and import page setups from another file.

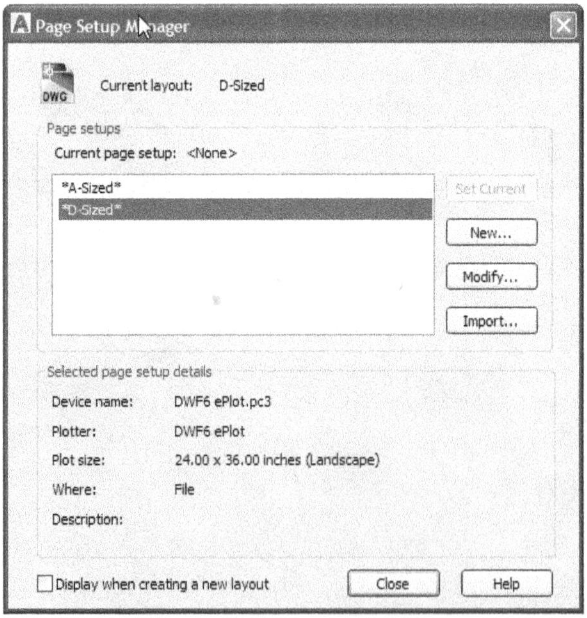

Figure 9–2

How To: Create a Page Setup

1. In the *Output* tab>Plot panel, click (Page Setup Manager). Alternatively, in the Application Menu, select **Print>Page Setup**.
2. In the Page Setup Manager dialog box, click **New**.
3. In the New Page Setup dialog box shown in Figure 9–3, type a name for the setup. Select an existing setup in the *Start with* area if the new setup is similar to an existing one.

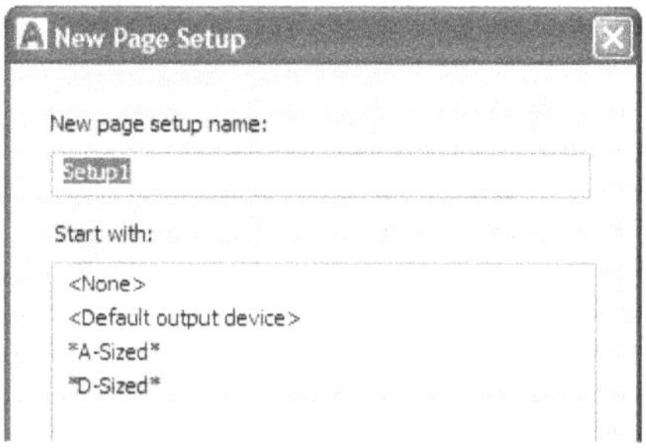

Figure 9–3

4. Click **OK**.

5. In the Page Setup dialog box (shown in Figure 9–4), select the printer or plotter that you want to use. This determines the paper sizes from which you can select.

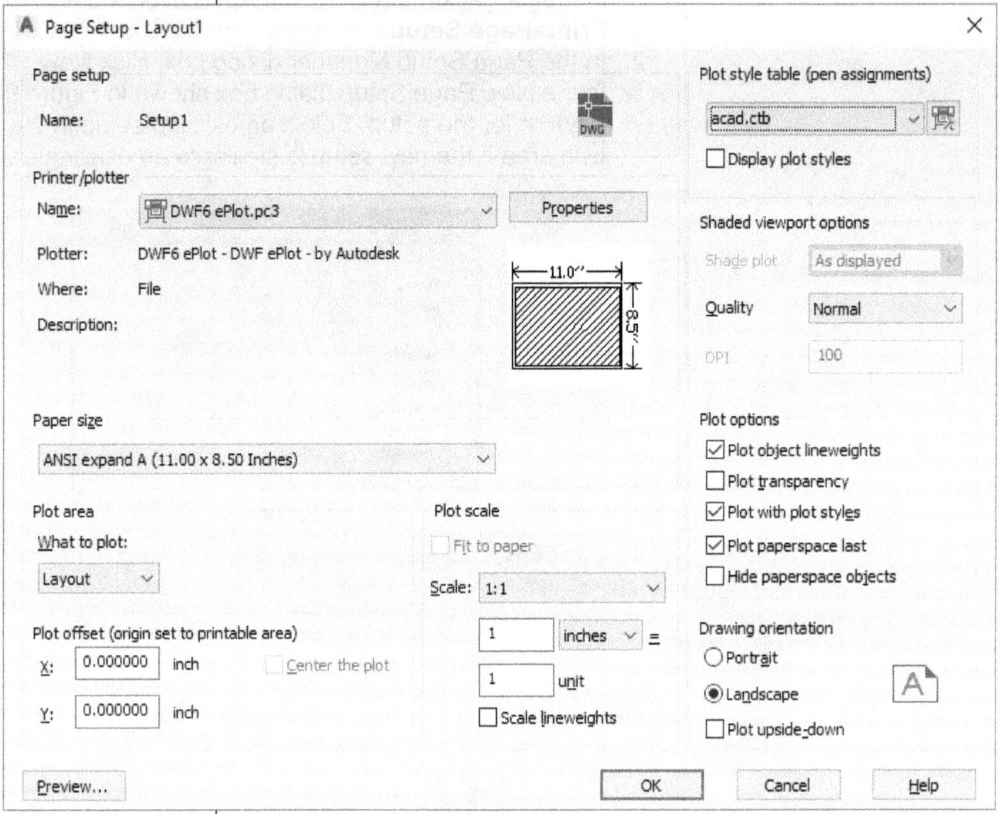

Figure 9–4

6. Specify the *Paper size*, *Plot area*, *Plot offset*, *Plot scale*, *Plot style table*, *Shaded viewport options*, *Plot options*, and *Drawing orientation*.
7. Click **Preview...** to display a preview of how the setup is going to print on the sheet.
8. Right-click in the preview and select **Exit**.
9. When the page setup is finished, click **OK** to return to the Page Setup Manager. The new page setup can now be applied to a layout.

Page Setup Options

Printer/ plotter	Enables you to select from the list of available printing devices. Check with your CAD manager if the printer/plotter you want to use is not in the list. The AutoCAD software includes several predefined plotter configurations, such as DWF6 e-plot.

Printer/plotter

Name: DWF6.ePlot.pc3   ∨   Properties

Plotter: DWF6 ePlot - DWF ePlot - by Autodesk |← 24.0" →|

Where: File

Description:

Paper size	Enables you to set the size of the layout. The available sizes depend on the selected plotter.

Paper size

ARCH D (24.00 x 36.00 Inches)   ∨

Plot area	Sets the printable area. Normally, you use the **Layout** option to plot the entire layout to the extents of the printable area. You can also print the Extents of the drawing, the Display in the drawing area, a Window that you select, or a View that has been defined in the drawing.

Plot area

What to plot:

Layout   ∨

Plot offset	Controls where the drawing starts to plot on the paper. Depending on your plotter, you might need to set this so that the drawing fits correctly on the paper. The **Center the plot** option is not available when the *Plot area* is set to **Layout**.

Plot offset (origin set to printable area)

X: 0.000000   inch   Center the plot

Y: 0.000000   inch

Plot scale	Sets the scale when you are printing from a layout. The default scale is 1:1. However, you can set a different scale if you are creating a check plot on a smaller piece of paper. **IMPORTANT**: The *Plot scale* for a layout is almost always 1:1 because the layout is created at the actual size required to fit on the piece of paper. The scaling of the model is done using the Viewport Scale.
Plot style table	Coordinates the layer color to pen weight, or sets up other special effects for plotted output. Consult your CAD manager about which one you should use.
Shaded viewport options	For 3D models, this enables you to set viewports to be hidden or rendered and to control the image quality.
Plot options	Enables you to plot using lineweights or plot styles and to specify how to treat Paper Space objects.

Drawing orientation	Sets the paper orientation to **Portrait** (the short edge of the paper is at the top of the page) or **Landscape** (the long edge of the paper is at the top of the page). 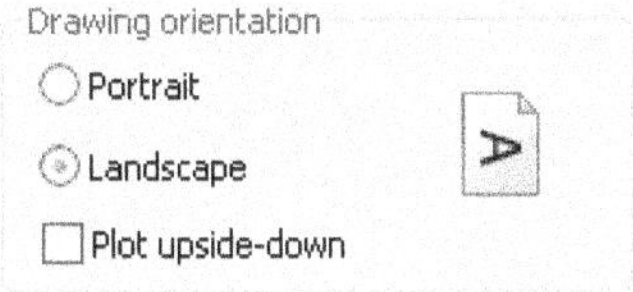

Layout Size: Printable Area

The AutoCAD software displays the *printable* area of the layout as a dashed boundary, as shown in Figure 9–5. Because printers or plotters cannot print to the edges of the sheet, the printable area is smaller than the actual paper size. The size of the margins varies from one printer model to another, and even from one sheet size to another. Ensure that the objects you place on the layout fit in the printable area.

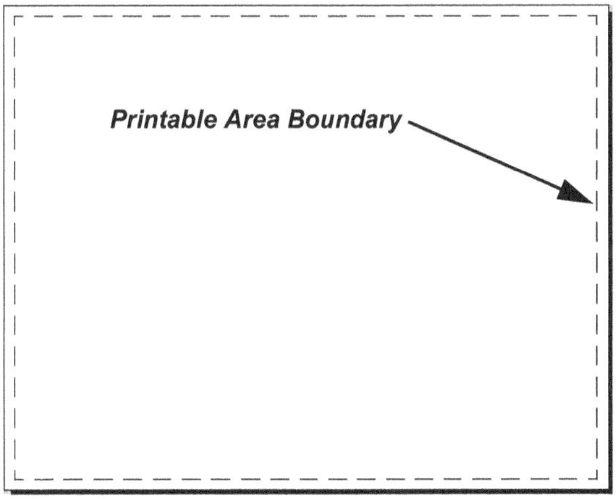

Printable Area Boundary

Figure 9–5

How To: Apply a Page Setup to a Layout

1. Right-click on the layout that you want to set and select **Page Setup Manager...**
2. In the Page Setup Manager, select a page setup with the required plotter and paper size.
3. Click **Set Current** to apply it to the layout.
4. Click **Close** to close the Page Setup Manager.

How To: Import a Page Setup from Another File

1. Open the Page Setup Manager.
2. Click **Import...**.
3. In the Select Page Setup From File dialog box, select the file that contains the page setup you want to use and click **Open**.
4. In the Import Page Setups dialog box, select the setup that you want to import, as shown in Figure 9–6.

If names are not displayed in the list, the drawing might have layouts but they have not been saved as page setups.

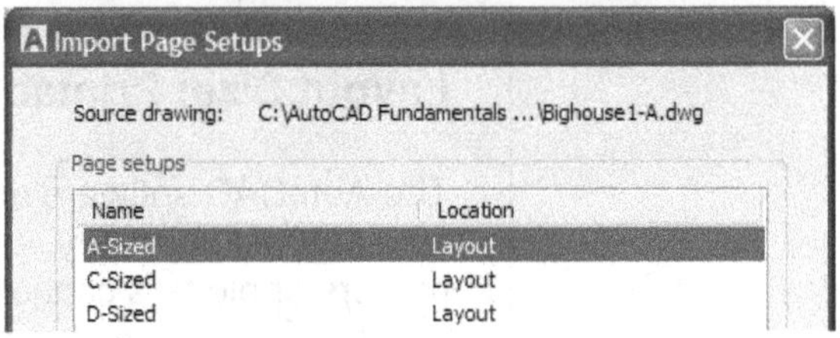

Figure 9–6

5. Click **OK** to complete the process. The imported page setup can now be used in your current drawing.

Setting Up Layouts to Use in a Template

To prepare layouts to be used in a template, specify generic names for the *Layout* tabs, add title blocks, and set up at least one viewport on each Layout.

- Rename new layouts using a generic name. For example, it might be one that reflects the printer and paper size, such as **Printer-ANSI C**. When it is used in a project, you can change the label to match the sheet number and/or sheet name.

- Your company title block should be designed to fit on the paper size specified in the page setup.

- Verify that the viewport is on the layer **Viewport**.

- Repeat the steps for each plotter and paper size required.

9.2 Creating Layout Viewports

You can create the required viewports in a layout using one of several viewport commands, or the Viewports dialog box. You can insert a single viewport, a standard configuration of multiple viewports, a polygonal viewport, or convert an object to a viewport. Each viewport in a layout can contain a different view of the model, displayed at any scale.

- Viewports should be placed on a layer that is used specifically for storing viewports. Toggling the layer off (or making it a non-plotting layer) hides the viewport border, but not the model objects inside the viewport.

- You can create multiple viewports in various shapes and sizes in a layout.

- You can create multiple viewports that overlap, but you should not place one completely inside another's boundaries.

- The various viewport commands can be accessed through the *Layout* tab in the ribbon (as shown in Figure 9–7) which is displayed when you are in a layout and in Paper Space.

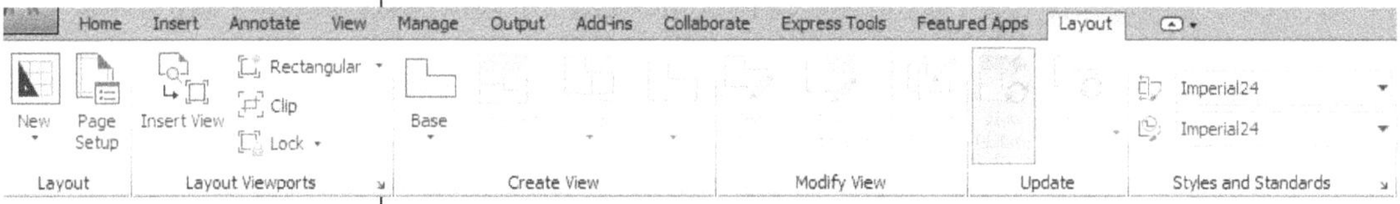

Figure 9–7

Rectangular Viewports

How To: Create a New Rectangular Viewport

1. Verify that you are in a layout and in Paper Space.
2. Set the layer to which you want to add the viewports to be current.
3. In the *Layout* tab>Layout Viewports panel, expand the Viewports drop-down list and click ⬜ (Rectangular).
4. Select the first corner of the viewport.
5. Select the opposite diagonal corner of the viewport.

- After starting the **Viewports, Rectangular** command, you can use the options at the Command Prompt to switch to the **Polygonal** or **Object** viewport creation by typing **P** for **Polygonal** or **O** for **Object**.

- Other options available at the start of the **Viewports, Rectangular** command are as follows:

ON/OFF	Toggle an existing viewport on or off.
Fit	Fits an entire rectangular viewport in the printable area of the layout sheet.
Shadeplot	Sets how viewports are plotted. Select from the **As Displayed**, **Wireframe**, **Hidden**, **Visual Styles**, and **Render Presets** options.
Lock	Locks or unlocks a viewport's view and scale.
Restore	Restores the settings of a saved viewport.
Layer	Removes any layer overrides in the selected viewport and resets them to the global layer properties
2/3/4	Creates multiple preconfigured viewports.

Polygonal Viewports

How To: Create a New Polygonal Viewport

1. Verify that you are in a layout and in Paper Space.
2. Set the layer to which you want to add the viewports to be current.
3. In the *Layout* tab>Layout Viewports panel, expand the Viewports drop-down list and click ⬚ (Polygonal).
4. Select a start point for the viewport.
5. Select the next point(s).
6. If you want to create an arc segment, select the **Arc** option in the <Down Arrow> menu or press <A>, and follow the prompts to create the arc. To switch back to straight line segments, select the **Line** option or press <L>.
7. Complete the command, using the **Close** option or by pressing <Enter>.

Object Viewports

How To: Convert an Object to a Viewport

1. Verify that you are in a layout and in Paper Space.
2. Set the layer to which you want to add the viewports to be current.
3. In the *Layout* tab>Layout Viewports panel, expand the Viewports drop-down list and click ⬚ (Object).
4. Select a closed object to convert to a viewport.

Viewports Dialog Box

How To: Create a Viewport Using the Viewports Dialog Box

1. Verify that you are in a layout and in Paper Space.
2. Set the layer to which you want to add the viewports to be current.
3. In the *Layout* tab>Layout Viewports panel, click ⊿ on the right corner of the panel title. The Viewports dialog box opens.
4. Verify that you are in the *New Viewports* tab, as shown in Figure 9–8.

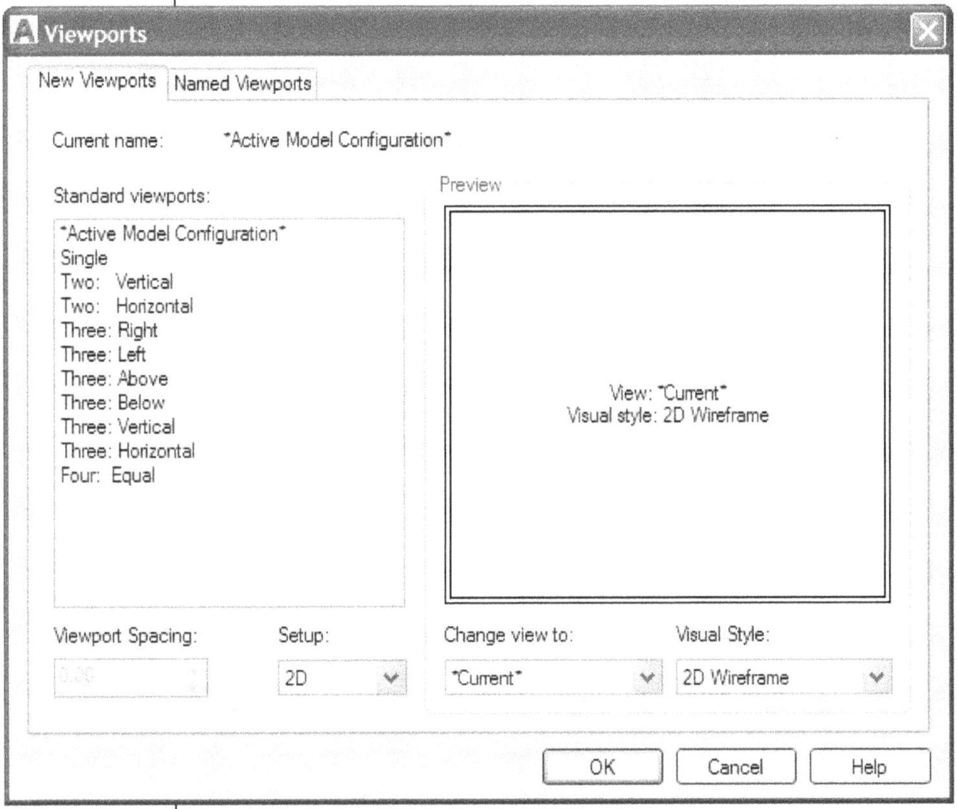

Figure 9–8

5. In the *Standard viewports* area, select the configuration you want to use. A preview of the arrangement displays in the *Preview* pane on the right, as shown in Figure 9–9.

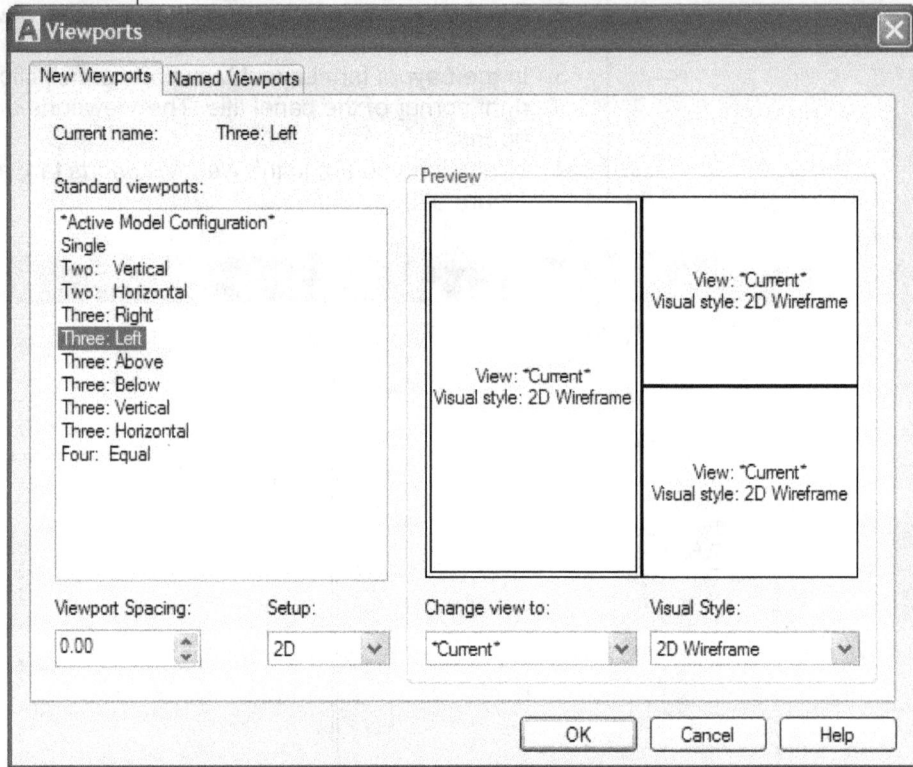

Figure 9–9

6. If you are creating multiple viewports, set the *Viewport Spacing*, which is the space or gap between viewports. The other options are primarily used in 3D drawings.
7. Click **OK**.
8. Select two corners to define the size and location of the viewport(s) in the layout.

Modifying Viewports with Grips

Once you have created and placed viewports in the layout, you can move, resize, and scale them using grips. To modify a viewport, you must be in Paper Space. When you select the edge of a layout viewport, three types of grips display. If the **Quick Properties** option is toggled on, the layout viewport property palette also displays, as shown in Figure 9–10.

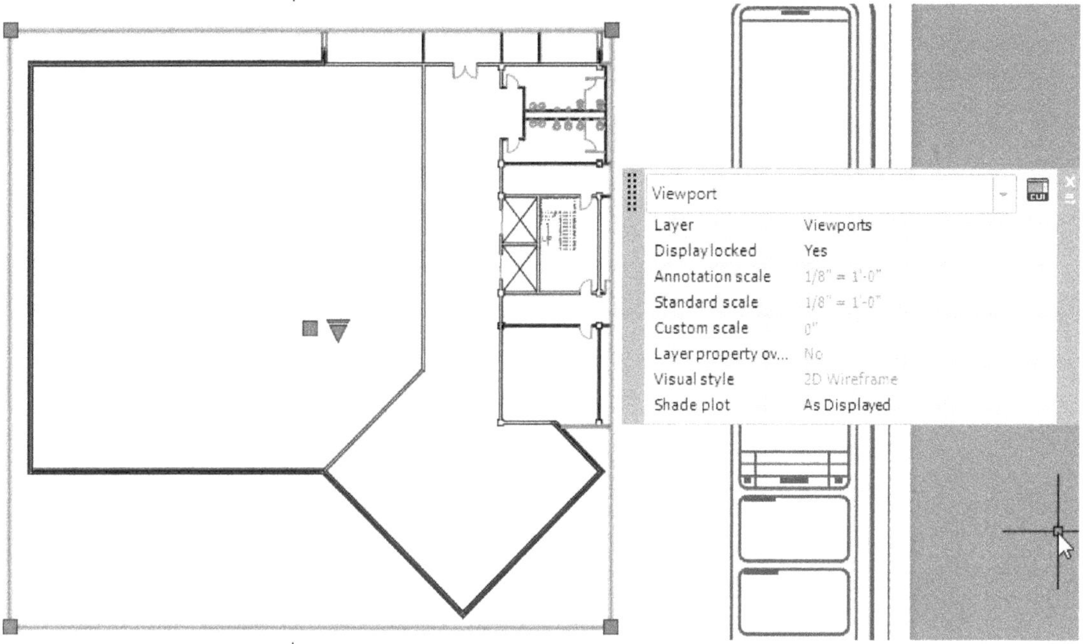

Figure 9–10

The available viewport grips are:

- **Corner square grip** ■: The corner grips are used to resize the viewport, as shown in Figure 9–11.

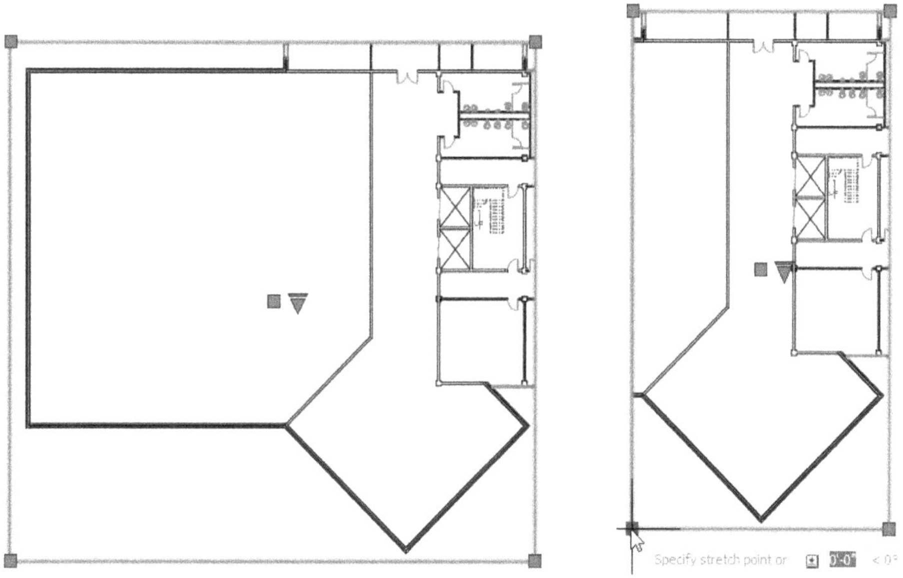

Original viewport   *Resized viewport*

Figure 9–11

- **Middle square grip** ■: The middle square grip is used to move and place the viewport at a new location in the layout, as shown in Figure 9–12.

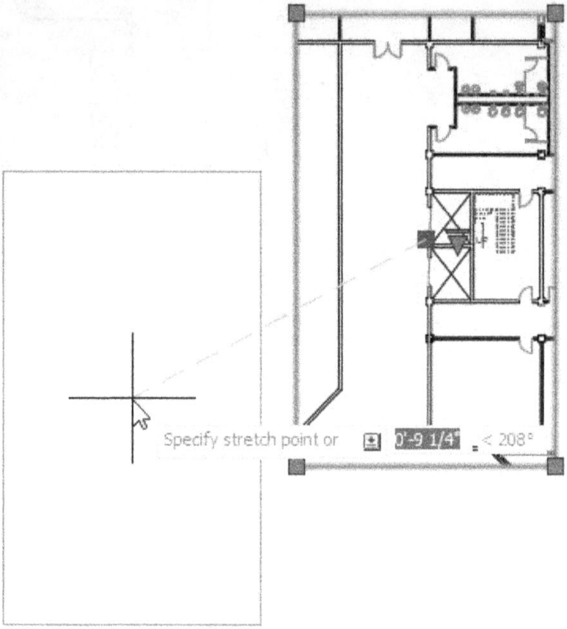

Figure 9–12

- **Middle arrow grip** ▽ : The middle arrow grip is a list grip which lists the various scales that you can use to set the viewport scale, as shown in Figure 9–13.

  - You can scale the objects in a viewport to print at a specific scale factor relative to the paper. The scale sets the size of the drawing relative to the paper space and sets the Annotation scale to match. This becomes critical when you need to dimension and annotate the drawing.

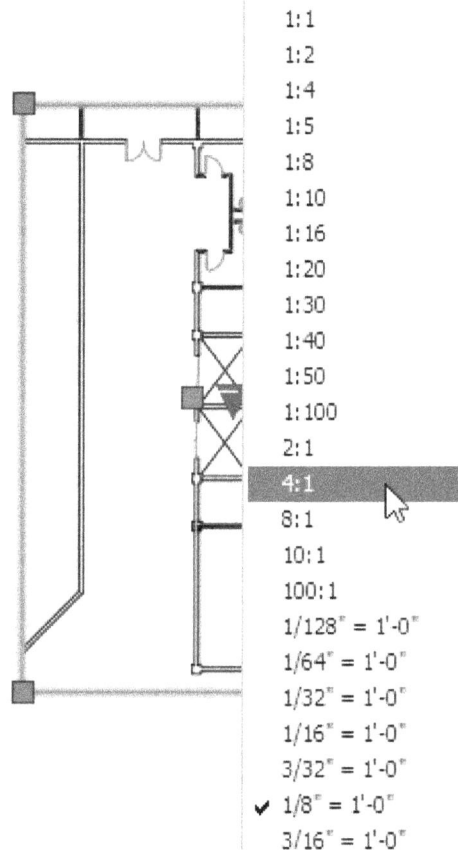

1:1
1:2
1:4
1:5
1:8
1:10
1:16
1:20
1:30
1:40
1:50
1:100
2:1
4:1
8:1
10:1
100:1
1/128" = 1'-0"
1/64" = 1'-0"
1/32" = 1'-0"
1/16" = 1'-0"
3/32" = 1'-0"
✔ 1/8" = 1'-0"
3/16" = 1'-0"

Figure 9–13

- **Status Bar**: You can also set the scale factor of the layout view using the Status Bar. Select the edge of the viewport or make the viewport active to display the viewport tools in the Status Bar, as shown on the left in Figure 9–14. Expand

1/8" = 1'-0" ▾ (Scale of the selected viewport) and select a scale, as shown on the right in Figure 9–14.

Use the scroll bar in the list to display the required scale.

1/64" = 1'-0"
1/32" = 1'-0"
1/16" = 1'-0"
3/32" = 1'-0"
✔ 1/8" = 1'-0"
3/16" = 1'-0"

Figure 9–14

*You can use **Regen** or **Regenall** to regenerate the views.*

- It is useful to activate the viewport and zoom in on the part of the drawing you want to display before setting the scale.

- Once you have set the scale, you can pan in the viewport without changing the scale. However, using the **Zoom** command modifies the scale.

- If the scale you want to use is not in the list, you can add a custom scale factor (e.g., **1:200** or **1"=6"**) by selecting **Custom...** in the Scale of the selected viewport list. In the Edit Drawing Scales dialog box, click **Add**, type a name for the scale, and enter the values for the *Paper units* and *Drawing units*. Click **OK** to add the custom scale to the list.

Locking the Viewport

When the viewport is displaying the correct view and scale, you should lock the display so that it is not changed by accident. When you try to **Zoom** or **Pan** in a locked viewport, the entire layout zooms or pans instead.

- To lock a viewport, select it and click 🔓 (Lock/Unlock Viewport) in the Status Bar. To unlock a viewport, click 🔒 (Lock/Unlock Viewport).

- You can also use the shortcut menu to lock and unlock viewports. In Paper Space, select the viewport border, right-click, and select **Display Locked>Yes or No**, as shown in Figure 9–15.

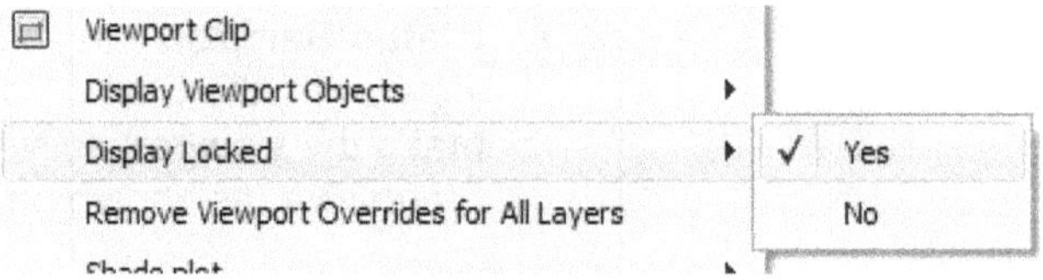

Viewport Clip	
Display Viewport Objects	▶
Display Locked	▶ ✓ Yes
Remove Viewport Overrides for All Layers	No
Shade plot	▶

Figure 9–15

9.3 Named Views

If you are working on a complex drawing, you might want to break it into views so that you can access the Model Space and Paper Space viewports. Named views are areas of the drawing that are saved under specific names. For example, you can use named views to define a view of each quadrant in a map, or an area in a large mechanical assembly or architectural plan. Once saved, you can switch to these views for quick reference. Although these named views are created in the model space, you can also insert the views as viewports into a layout. The

 (New View) command can be used to create named views of the drawing currently displayed on the screen. You can either save the entire drawing or a specific area of the drawing, by creating a window around that area. This command is available in the *View* tab>Named Views panel, as shown in Figure 9–16.

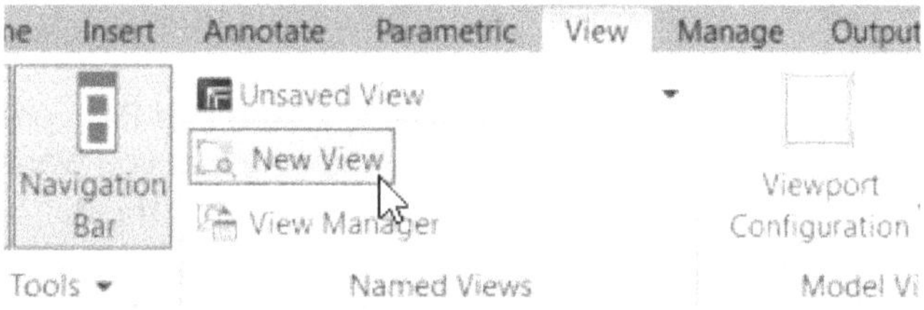

Figure 9–16

How To: Create a Named View

1. In the *View* tab>Named Views panel, click (New View).
2. In the New View/Shot Properties dialog box that opens, in the *View name* field, enter the name for the view.

3. In the *Boundary* area, select **Define window**, as shown in Figure 9–17. This option enables you to create a window around the area of the model that you want to work on or make a viewport of in the layout.

- The **Current display** option enables you to save the current screen view.

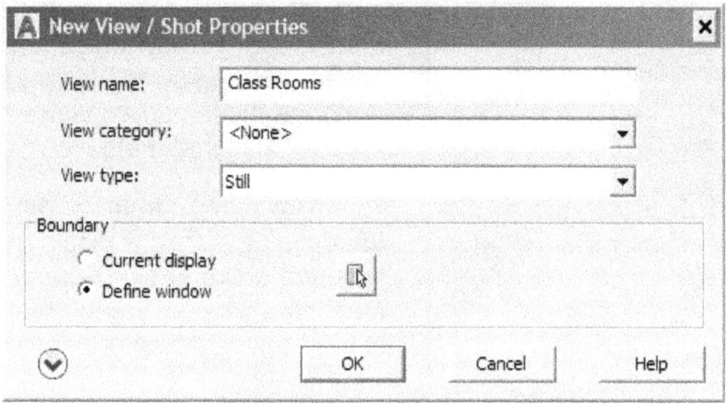

Figure 9–17

4. Using **Zoom** and **Pan**, create a window around the portion of the drawing that you want to save as a named view, as shown in Figure 9–18.

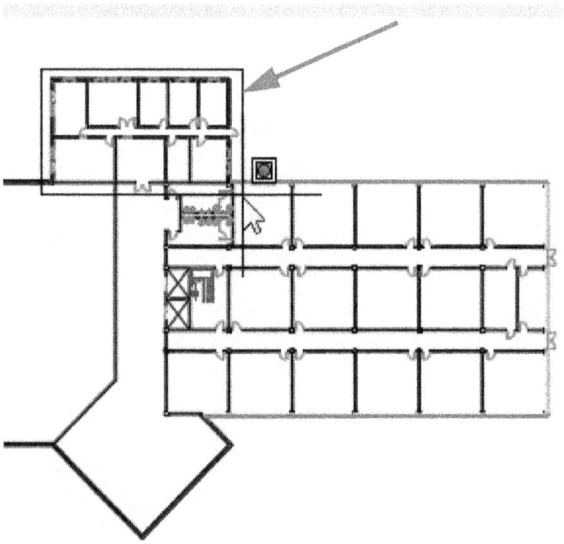

Figure 9–18

5. Press <Enter>.
6. In the New View/Shot Properties dialog box, click **OK**.

7. In the *View* tab>Named Views panel, expand the Views drop-down list to display the named views that you created, as shown in Figure 9–19.

User- created named views

- Unsaved View
- Class Rooms
- Elevators and Stairs
- Toilets
- Top
- Bottom
- Left

Figure 9–19

8. Click on any named view to restore it and zoom into the area that you have saved as that view. This is useful when you are working in big drawings, as it becomes easier to locate and work on specific areas.

Insert Views

When inserting a view of the model on paper, you can set the scale at which the model should be printed. The ⌧ (Insert View) command enables you to create viewports of the named views. This command also enables you to create a new view directly from a layout, if a named view of the desired area has not been created.

The advantage of using the ⌧ (Insert View) command is that it enables you to set the scale before placing the view. This can help you understand how the view fits on the sheet. When using the Viewport commands to create views, you set the scale after you place the view on the sheet.

To access the Layout Panel, you must be in a layout, and in Paper Space.

The ⌧ (Insert View) command is located in the *Layout* tab>Layout Viewports panel, as shown in Figure 9–20.

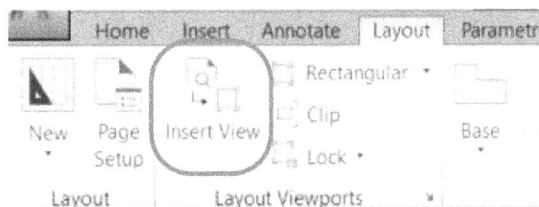

Figure 9–20

How To: Insert a Named View into a Layout

1. Ensure that you are in a layout and in Paper Space.

2. In the *Layout* tab>Layout Viewports panel, expand the

   (Insert View) drop-down list. The user-created named views are displayed in the gallery, as shown in Figure 9–21.

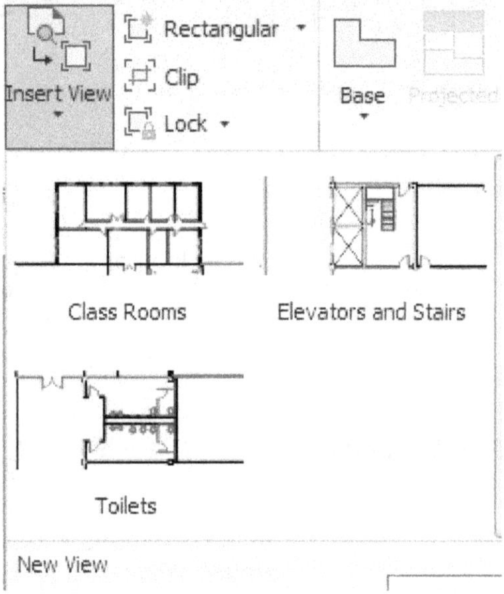

Figure 9–21

3. In the gallery, select the view that you want to insert. The view window attaches to the cursor, as shown in Figure 9–22. Click to place the view inside the paper space.

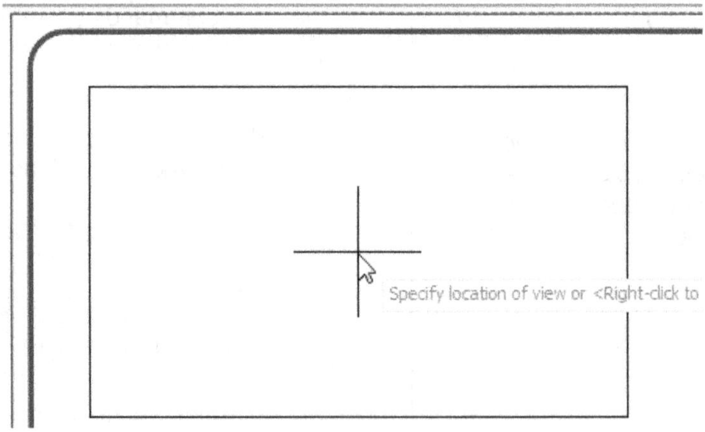

Figure 9–22

4. Depending on the preview window, you can change the size of the view so that it fits on the layout as required. To set the scale of the view, right-click on the view and select the scale, as shown in Figure 9–23.

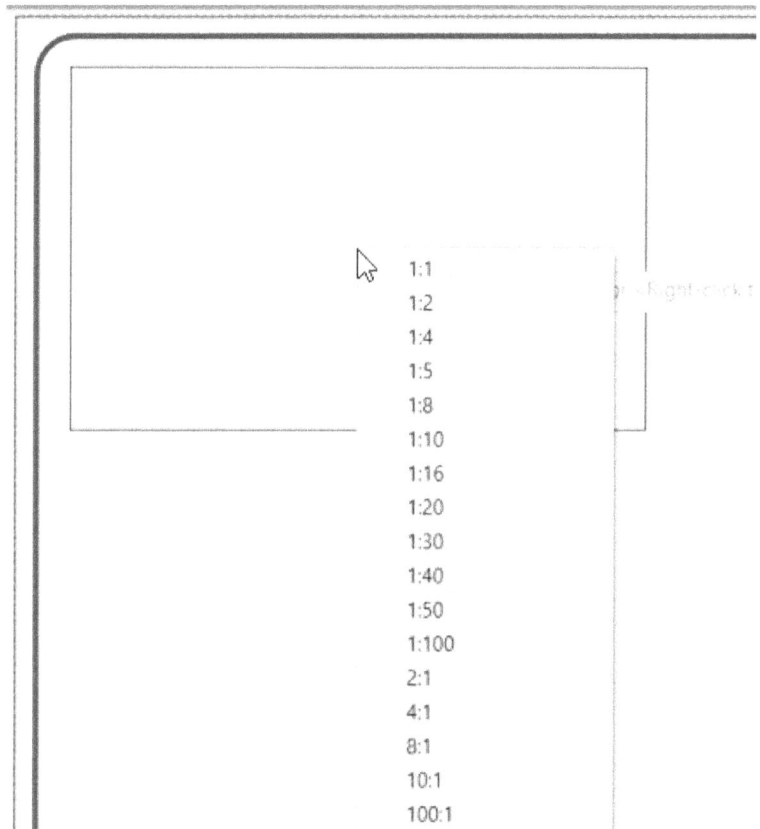

1:1
1:2
1:4
1:5
1:8
1:10
1:16
1:20
1:30
1:40
1:50
1:100
2:1
4:1
8:1
10:1
100:1

Figure 9–23

5. Click to place the viewport of the defined view in the layout.

6. Press <Enter>.

How To: Insert a View when the desired Named View does not exist

1. Ensure that you are in a layout and in Paper Space.
2. Determine the layer on which you want to add the viewports. Set that layer to be the current layer.
3. In the *Layout* tab>Layout Viewports panel, expand the

   (Insert View) drop-down list.
4. If the required view was not created as a named view, then it is not located in the gallery. Create a new view by selecting **New View**, as shown in Figure 9–24.

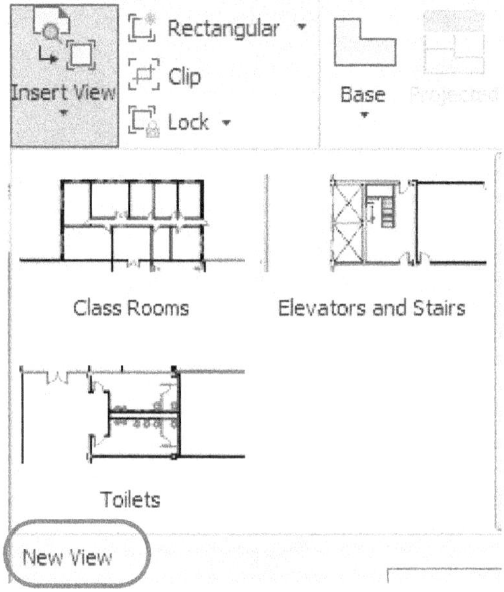

Figure 9–24

5. Note that you are now in the Model space. You are prompted to specify how much of the model you want to display in Paper space. Create a window around the portion of the drawing that you want to define as a view, as shown in Figure 9–25.

If you plan to create dimensions in the model space, ensure that you leave enough space to fit them.

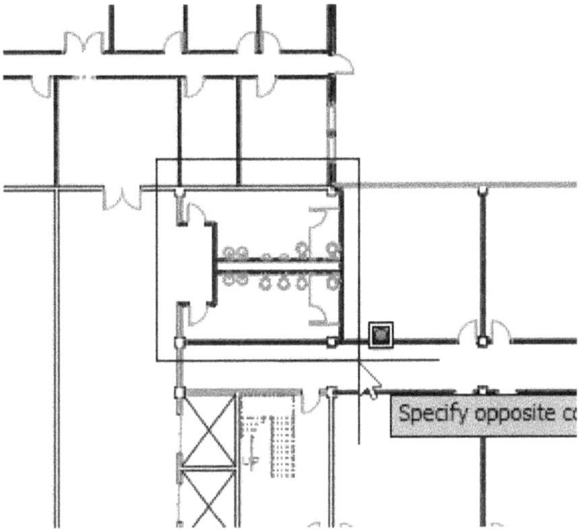

Figure 9–25

6. Press <Enter>. You are switched back to Paper space, and the view window is attached to the cursor.

7. Depending on the preview window, you can change its size so that it fits on the layout as required. Right-click to select the view scale.

8. Click to place the viewport of the defined view in the layout.

• Note that this view is not saved in the gallery as a named view. To ensure that the view can be reused, you must save it as a named view.

How To: Create a Named View Using View Manager

1. In the *View* tab>Named Views panel, click ⬚ (View Manager) to open the View Manager dialog box, and then click **New**.
2. In the New View / Shot Properties dialog box, type a name in the *View name:* field, as shown in Figure 9–26.
3. The *View type* should be set to **Still**, as this option is typical for 2D views. The other *View type* options relate to 3D features.

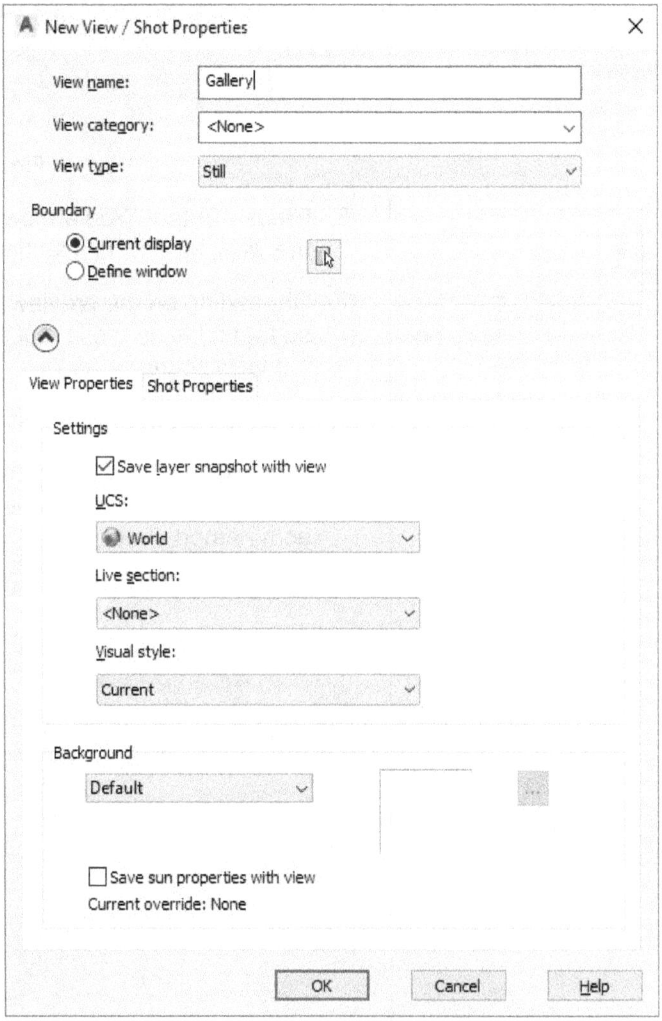

Figure 9–26

4. In the *Boundary* area, select the **Current display** option to save the current screen view, or select the **Define window** option to define a different view by clicking ⬚ (Define view window).
5. In the *Settings* area, select whether to save the layer snapshot with the view.
6. Click **OK** to create the view.

*   The view can be defined to store the current layer settings (On/Off, Freeze/Thaw, etc.), so that these layers are automatically displayed when the view is restored.

Additional View Manager options

In the View Manager dialog box, there are additional options available for you to control and modify named views.

*   After a view has been defined, you can modify its boundaries by selecting it in the *Views* area, under the **Model Views** node and clicking **Edit Boundaries**, as shown in Figure 9–27. The current view area is then highlighted. Select two points on screen to define a new area and press <Enter>.

*   Views that store layer settings are marked **Yes** in the *Layer snapshot* under General properties. You can select a view in the *Views* area and click **Update Layers** (as shown in Figure 9–27) to save the current layer settings with the view.

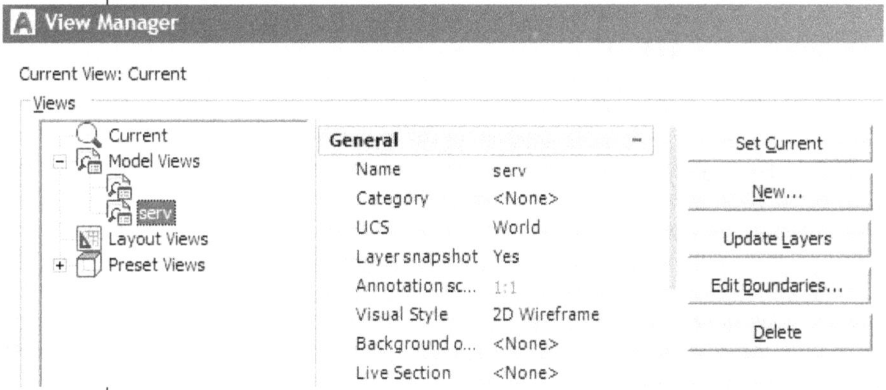

Figure 9–27

9.4 Advanced Viewport Options

To be more efficient in the creation of layouts, you can use previously created Named Views of your model as the basis for Viewports in a layout. You can also modify the shape of existing viewports, as shown in Figure 9–28.

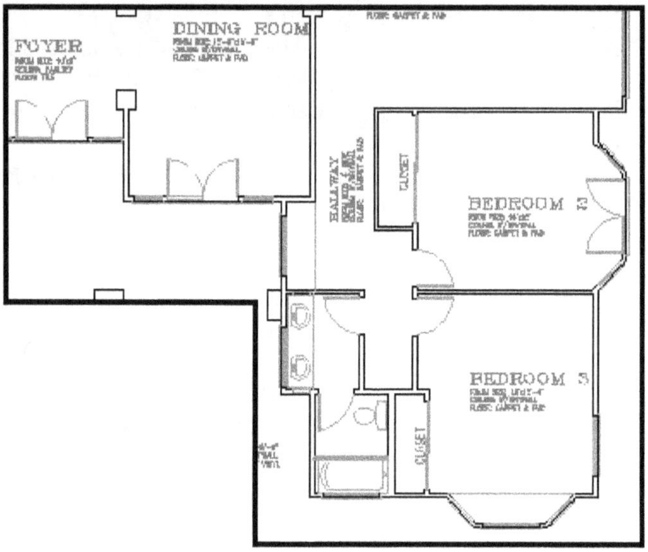

Figure 9–28

Creating Viewports from Named Views

In this section, you create viewports using the Viewports dialog box.

For the Layout tab to display in the ribbon, you must be in one of the layouts.

Once a named view has been created, you can insert it as a viewport in a layout. You can create viewports from named views using the *Layout* tab>Layout Viewports panel:

- The ⌹ (Insert View) drop-down menu displays all of the named views that you have created in a gallery. Once you insert a view, use the various grip options to size, move and scale the view and the layout viewport.

- The Viewports dialog box enables you to select named views to create single or multiple named view viewports at the same time.

How To: Create Viewports Using the Viewports Dialog Box

1. Verify that you are in an active layout.
2. Set the layer to which you want to add the viewports to be current.
3. In the *Layout* tab>Layout Viewports panel, click 🔽 (arrow).
4. In the Viewports dialog box, select the *New Viewports* tab.
5. In the *Standard viewports* area, select the standard viewport configuration that you want to use. If required, set the **Viewport Spacing**.
6. In the *Preview* area, select one of the Views as shown in Figure 9–29. The Preview View is highlighted.

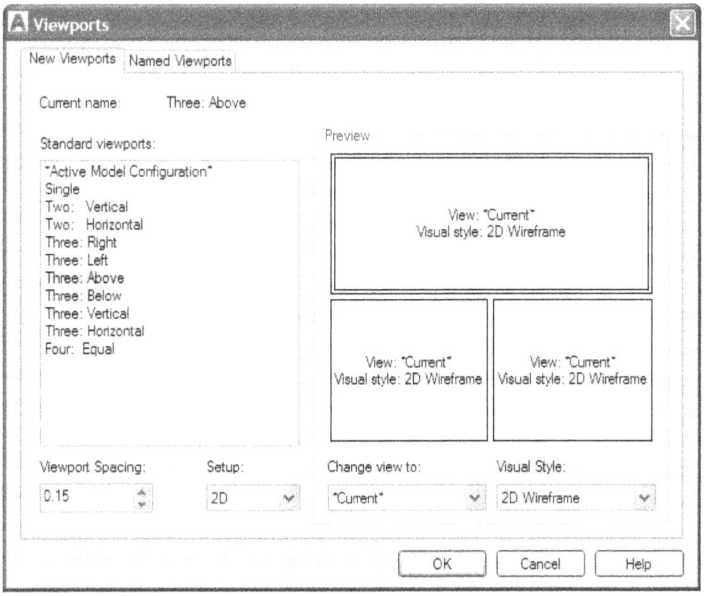

Figure 9–29

*By default, **2D** puts the current view in all of the viewports. **3D** puts standard 3D views (Top, Front, and SE Isometric) in the new viewports.*

7. In the Change view to drop-down list, select a Named View (if any have been saved), as shown in Figure 9–30, to display in that Viewport location.

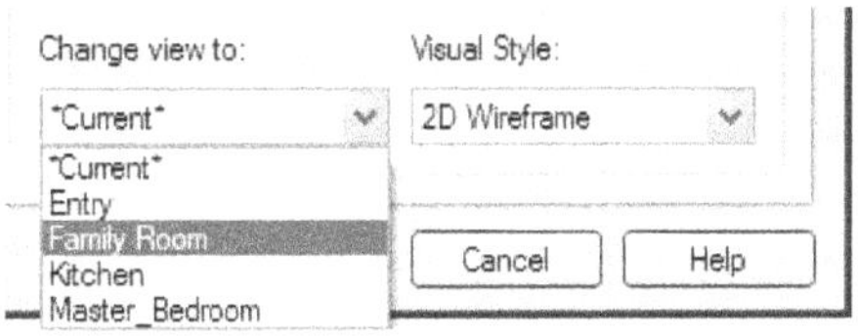

Figure 9–30

8. The view name displays in the *Preview* area, as shown in Figure 9–31.

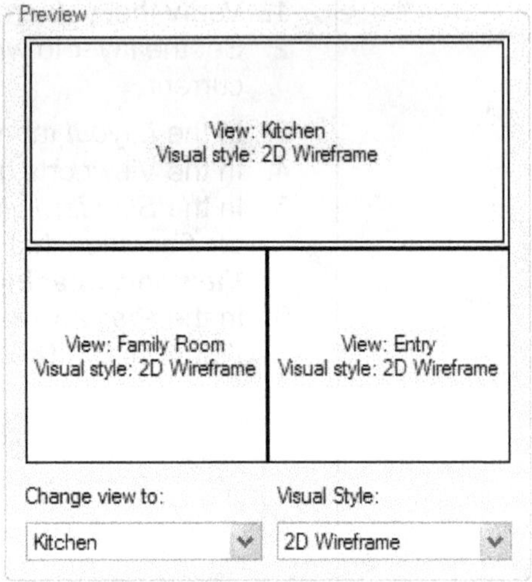

Figure 9–31

9. The Visual Style can be preselected if you are working in 3D.
10. Click **OK** to continue.
11. If you are working in a layout, you are prompted to select two corners or to use fit to place all of the viewports on the sheet.

• The *Named Viewports* tab enables you to restore the saved configurations of Model Space viewports. However, the configuration of viewports in a layout cannot be saved.

• The Viewports dialog box works in both Model Space (for *tiled* viewports) and Paper Space or Layout mode (for *floating* viewports).

Hint: Model Space Viewports

Model Space can also be divided into viewports, but only for viewing. For example, if you have a very complex drawing you might need to display multiple close-up views at the same time as shown in Figure 9–32. The viewport that is currently active is highlighted with a blue border. You can drag the edges of the viewports to resize them.

Figure 9–32

In Model Space, you can use **Named** in the *View* tab>Model Viewports panel to create a new viewport configuration.

However, it is easier to expand ⬛ (Viewport Configuration) in the *View* tab>Model Viewports panel and select the required arrangement, as shown in Figure 9–33.

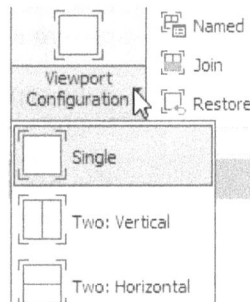

Figure 9–33

Clipping Viewports

You can remove any portions of a viewport that are not required, or make its shape fit better in the available layout space. This is most effective if you have already created the viewport with the correct scale and view of the drawing.

How To: Clip a Viewport

1. In the *Layout* tab>Layout Viewports panel, click ⊡ (Clip).
2. Select the viewport that you want to clip.
3. Select a clipping object (which has already been created) or press <Enter> to draw a polygonal object, as shown in Figure 9–34.

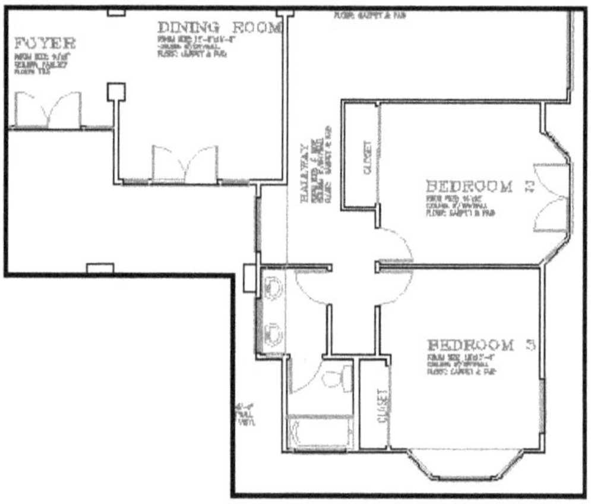

Figure 9–34

- Use the **Delete** option to remove the clipping boundary and restore the original viewport.

- If the clipping boundary extends outside the current viewport boundary, the viewport is extended in that direction.

- You can reclip a viewport without needing to delete the old clip boundary first.

- You can also change the shape of a polygonal viewport (without clipping) by using grips to stretch the vertices to new locations.

Practice 9a

Working with Layouts

Practice Objectives

- View Model Space and Paper Space in layouts.
- Create, update, modify, and delete viewports in a layout.

In this practice, you will note the differences between Model Space and Paper Space and switch between Model Space and Paper Space in a viewport in a layout. You will create, scale, and lock viewports in a layout. You will then create copies of the layout, rename the new layouts, and update them with different viewport information, such as the **Auditorium Wing** layout shown in Figure 9–35. You will also delete unused layouts.

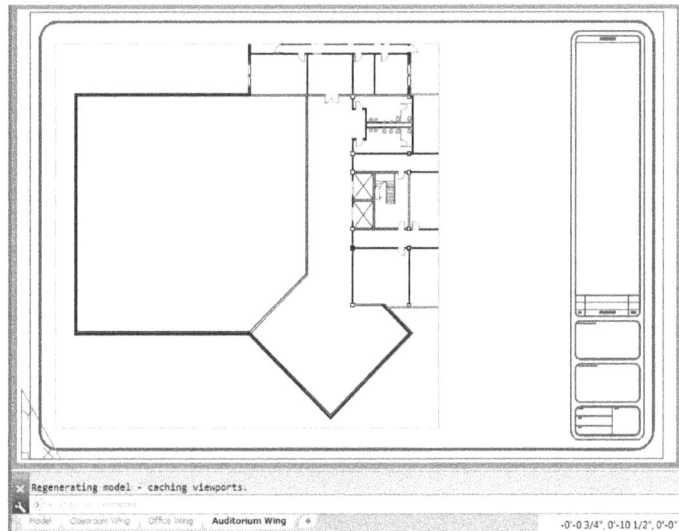

Figure 9–35

Task 1 - View Model Space and Paper Space in layouts.

In this task, you will note the differences between Model Space and Paper Space, and switch between Model Space and Paper Space in a viewport on a *Layout* tab.

1. Open **College Building-A.dwg** from your practice files folder. Note that the *Model* tab is active and that you are in Model Space as shown in Figure 9–36.

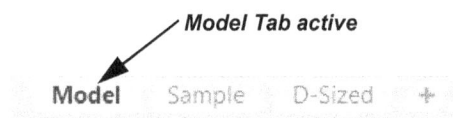

Figure 9–36

2. Zoom in on one of the single doors. Use the **Measure>Quick** command to measure its opening. Note that it displays as **3'** which is the *real-world* distance in Model Space.

3. Select the *Sample* layout tab. Note that the viewport boundary around the model is thick, indicating that you are working on the model through the viewport and you are still in model space. This is also indicated by the MODEL display in the Status bar.

4. Ensure that ⬚ (Object Snap) is toggled on and is set to **Endpoint** osnap.

5. Zoom in on one of the open single doors and using the **Measure>Distance** command, check the distance of the door. It displays the actual size of the door (**3'**).

6. Double-click outside the viewport boundary and note that now you are in Paper space. Note that the viewport boundary is faded. The paper space icon displays along the bottom left corner, and PAPER displays in the Status bar.

7. Using the **Measure>Distance** command, check the distance of the door again. It displays a size other than **3'** as this is the length of its printed size on the paper.

8. Zoom out and measure the length of the border. It is drawn at the actual size required to fit on an A-sized sheet of paper.

9. Double-click inside the viewport (faded rectangle) to make it active. Note that you are now in the Model space.

10. In the Status Bar, note that the 🔒 (Lock/Unlock Viewport) is toggled off. Note the viewport scale.

11. **Zoom** and **Pan** so that only the Office Wing, near the top of the building displays, as shown in Figure 9–37. In the Status Bar, note the viewport scale. The scale factor of the viewport is changed.

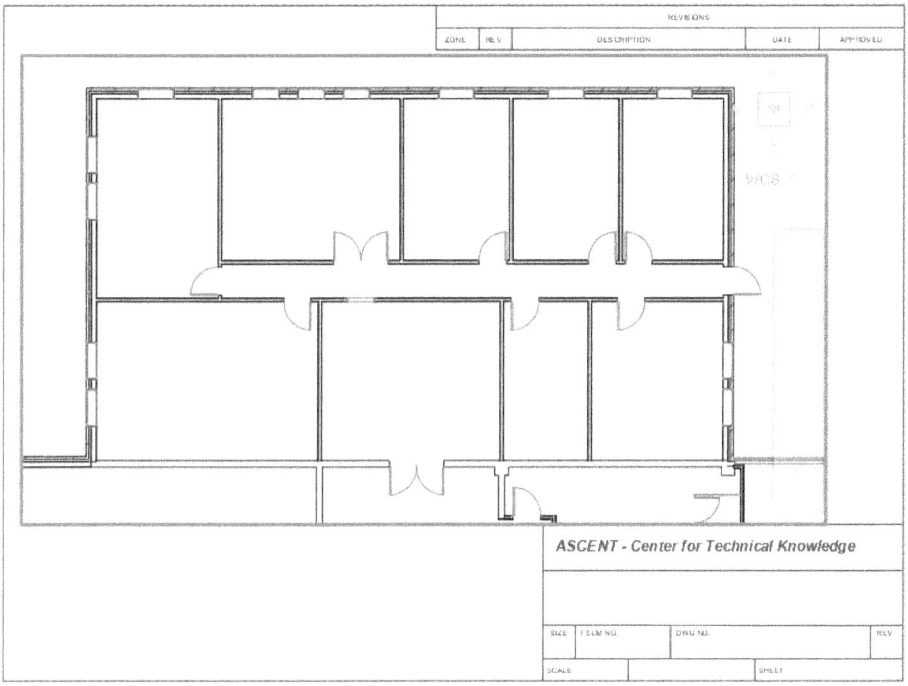

Figure 9–37

12. Save the drawing.

Task 2 - Create Named Views.

In this task, you will create named viewports in the Model space.

1. Enter Model space by clicking on the *Model* tab. Zoom to the extents of the drawing.

2. In the *View* tab>Named Views panel, expand the Unsaved View drop-down list, as shown in Figure 9–38. Note that there are no user-created named views.

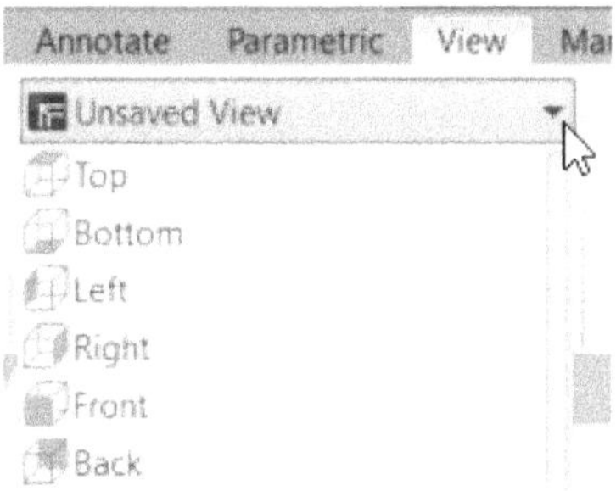

Figure 9–38

3. In the *View* tab>Named Views panel, click (New View).

4. In the New View/Shot Properties dialog box, in the *View name* field, type **Class Rooms**. In the *Boundary* area, select **Define window**, as shown in Figure 9–39.

5. Create a window around the classrooms near the top of the drawing, as shown as shown in Figure 9–40. Press <Enter>.

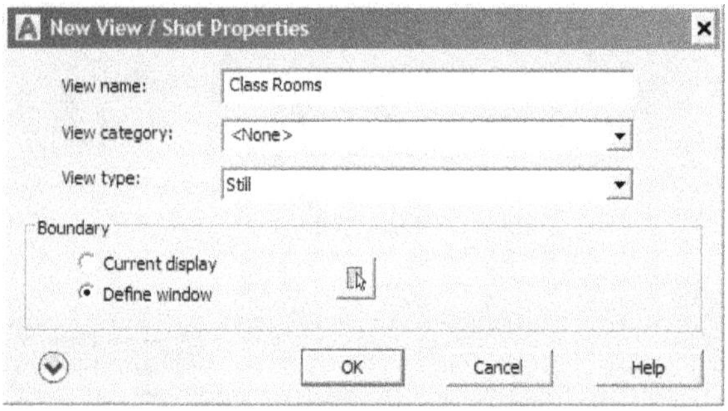

Figure 9–39

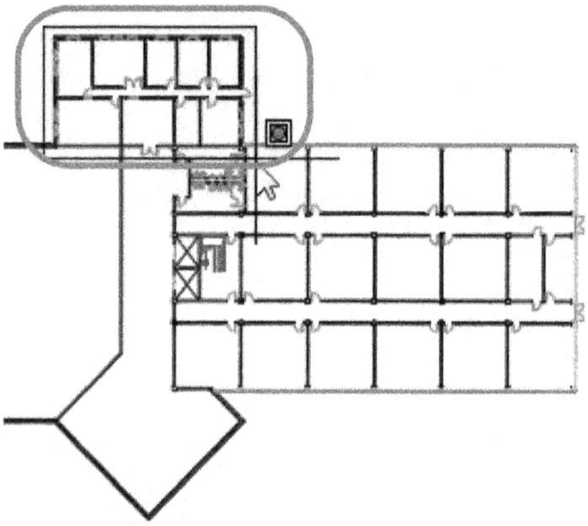

Figure 9–40

6. In the New View/Shot Properties dialog box, click **OK**.

7. Repeat Steps 3 to 6 to create the two additional views shown in Figure 9–41:
   - For the first view, name it **Toilets**, and then, using **Define window** create a window around the toilets area.
   - For the second view, name it **Elevators and Stairs** and using **Define window** create a window around the area containing elevators.

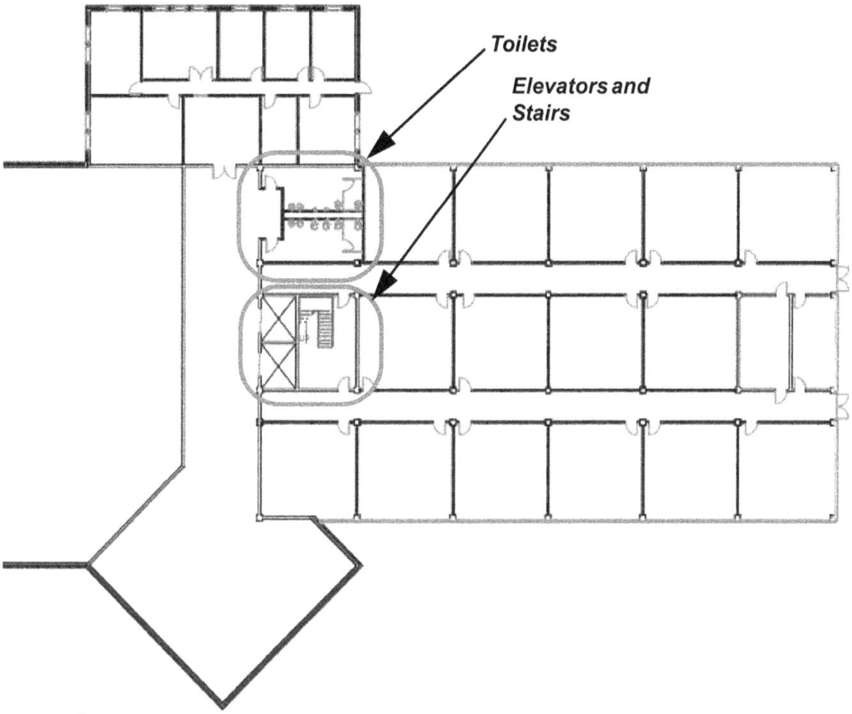

Toilets

Elevators and Stairs

Figure 9–41

8. Expand the Unsaved View drop-down list. Note that the three named views have been added as shown in Figure 9–42.

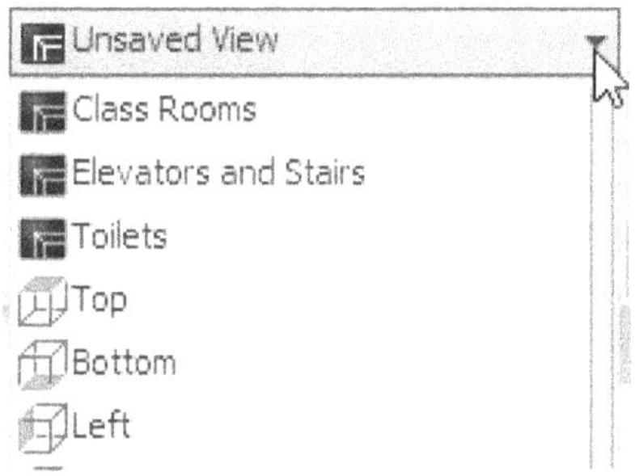

Unsaved View
Class Rooms
Elevators and Stairs
Toilets
Top
Bottom
Left

Figure 9–42

9. Zoom to the extents of the drawing.

10. In the Unsaved View drop-down list, select **Elevators and Stairs** and note how the drawing zooms into the Elevators and Stairs area that you have selected for the named view.

11. Similarly, select **Toilets** and note the area you are zoomed into.

12. Save the drawing.

Task 3 - Insert views in a layout.

In this task, you will insert named views in a layout.

1. Switch to the **D-Sized** layout tab.

2. Delete the existing viewport in this layout by selecting the gray rectangle and pressing <Delete>. Only the titleblock is left in the Paper space.

3. In the *Layout* tab>Layout Viewports panel, expand the
   (Insert View) drop-down menu. The three named views are displayed in the gallery, as shown in Figure 9–43.

Figure 9–43

4. Select the **Class Rooms** view and note how it attaches to the cursor, as shown in Figure 9–44.

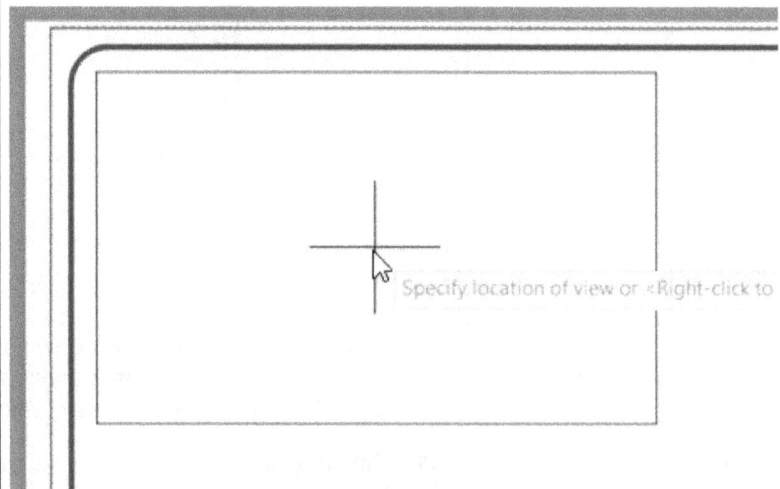

Figure 9–44

5. Right-click and select **1/4"=1'-0"**. Place the view near the upper left corner inside the title block border.

In the Properties palette, note that both ***Annotation Scale*** *and* ***Standard Scale*** *are grayed out.*

6. Click on the **Class Rooms** border (gray border) to display its grips. Click on the Middle arrow grip (▽): to display the scale list, and then select **1/8"=1'-0"**, as shown in Figure 9–45.

- In the Status Bar, note that 🔒 (Lock/Unlock Viewport) is highlighted, indicating that the selected viewport is locked.

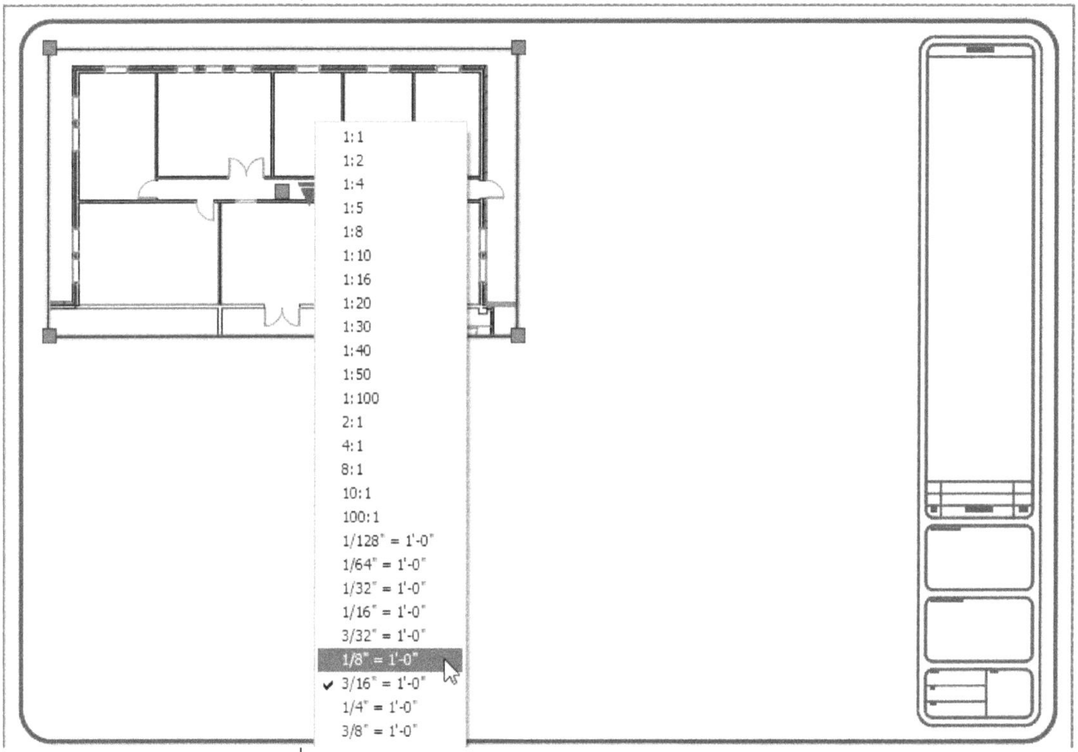

1:1
1:2
1:4
1:5
1:8
1:10
1:16
1:20
1:30
1:40
1:50
1:100
2:1
4:1
8:1
10:1
100:1
1/128" = 1'-0"
1/64" = 1'-0"
1/32" = 1'-0"
1/16" = 1'-0"
3/32" = 1'-0"
1/8" = 1'-0"
✓ 3/16" = 1'-0"
1/4" = 1'-0"
3/8" = 1'-0"

Figure 9–45

7. Using the square grip in the middle, move the viewport closer to the upper left corner of the title block border, as shown in Figure 9–46.

Figure 9–46

8. Press <Esc> to clear the viewport selection.

9. Using the (Insert View) drop-down menu, insert the other two views (**Toilets** and **Elevators and Stairs**).

10. Right-click and set the viewport scales to **1/4"=1'-0"** for each of the views and arrange the viewports inside the border similar to that shown in Figure 9–47.

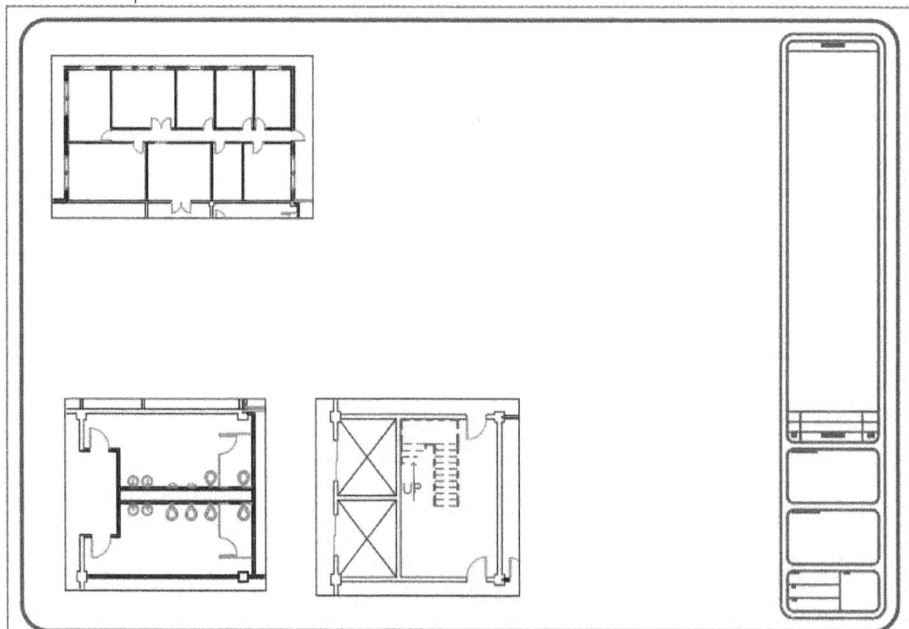

Figure 9–47

Task 4 - Create a view from the layout.

In this task, you will create and insert a view from the layout.

1. Make the **Viewports** layer current.

2. In the *Layout* tab>Layout Viewports panel, expand the  (Insert View) gallery and select **New View**.

3. Note that you are now switched to the Model space. You are prompted to specify how much of the model you want to display in Paper space. Create a window around the foyer portion of the drawing as shown in Figure 9–48.

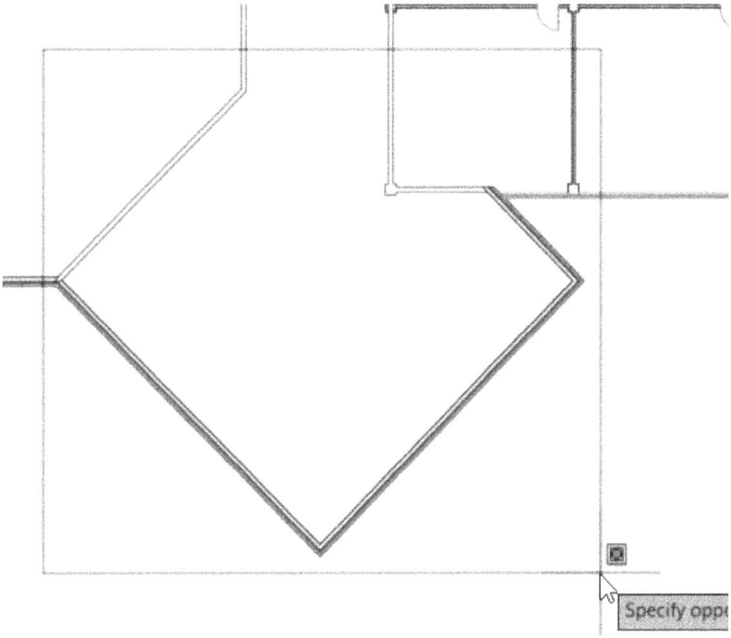

Figure 9–48

4. Press <Enter>. You return to Paper space, and the preview window is attached to the cursor.

5. Click to place the viewport in the top right corner of the layout, as shown in Figure 9–49.

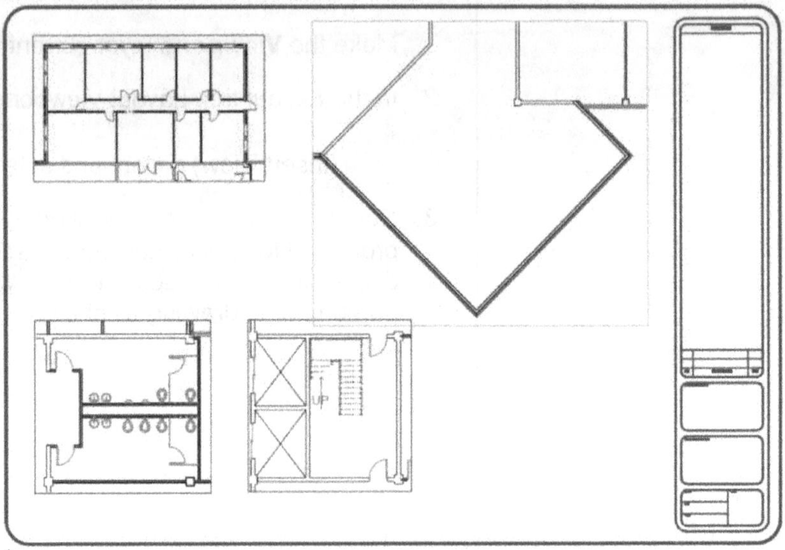

Figure 9–49

6. Expand the ⬚ (Insert View) gallery and note that the view you just created is not available in the gallery. The view is not a saved view.

7. If the foyer viewport overlaps the **Elevators and Stairs viewport**, use the grips to move the **Toilets** and **Elevators and Stairs** viewports a little lower.

8. Save the drawing.

Task 5 - Work in a layout.

In this task, you will create, scale, and lock viewports in a layout.

The active viewport has a thicker boundary edge.

1. Double-click inside the Foyer viewport that you inserted in Task 4. It becomes active.

2. Try to Pan inside the window. The whole Paper Space is panned as the viewport scale is locked at **3/16" = 1'-0"**, as shown in the Figure 9–50.

Figure 9–50

3. In the Status Bar, toggle off the Viewport Lock.

4. Now **Zoom** and **Pan** the view inside the viewport. Note how the viewport scale changes.

5. With the viewport activated, **Zoom** and **Pan** until the auditorium (i.e., the large, empty room) and the foyer display. Note that some other areas might also display.

6. In the Status Bar, use the Viewport Scale Control list and select several different scales. Finish with a scale of **1/16"=1'-0"**, as shown in Figure 9–51.

Figure 9–51

If you Pan and Zoom before locking the viewport, the scale changes.

7. Switch to Paper Space by double-clicking in an empty area outside any viewport. Select the edge of the viewport and use the corner grips to adjust the viewport size, so that only the auditorium and the foyer are inside the viewport, as shown in Figure 9–52. Make sure not to pan or zoom.

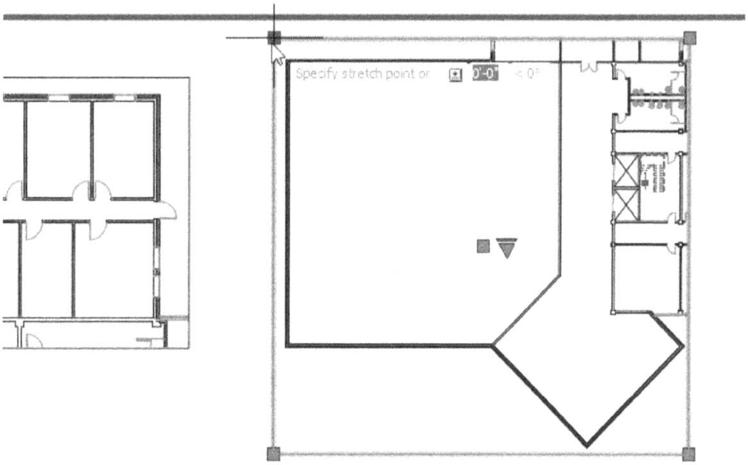

Figure 9–52

8. Use the middle square grip to move the top of the viewport in line with the classrooms viewport.

9. When you are satisfied with the way the viewport looks, select its edge and then, in the Status Bar, click (Lock/Unlock Viewport) to lock the viewport.

10. Press <Esc> to clear the viewport selection.

11. Save the drawing.

Task 6 - Copy and modify layouts.

In this task, you will create copies of the layout, rename the new layouts, update them with different viewport information, and delete unused layouts.

1. Make a copy of the **D-sized** layout by right-clicking on its tab name in the Status bar and selecting **Move or Copy....** In the dialog box, select **(move to end)** and **Create a copy, as shown in** Figure 9–53. Click **OK** to add a copy of the tab, named **D-Sized (2)** to the end of the row. Repeat the process to create one more (**D-Sized (3))** layout.

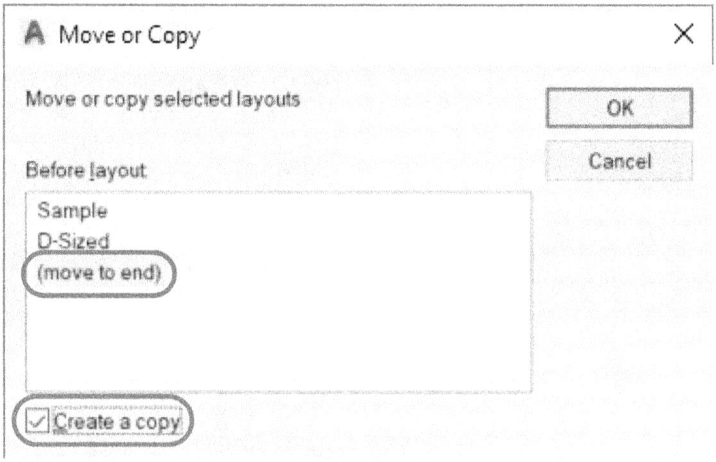

Figure 9–53

2. Double-click on **D-Sized** tab name so that it highlights in blue. Type the name **Classroom Wing** to change it. Rename the other two layouts based on the **D-sized** layout as **Office Wing** and **Auditorium Wing**, as shown in Figure 9–54.

Figure 9–54

3. Select each of the new layouts and note that they contain the same information.

4. Open the **Office Wing** layout and delete the right side and bottom two viewports by selecting the boundary of each viewport and then pressing <Delete>.

Even though the *(Lock/Unlock Viewport) is locked in the Status Bar, you can easily use the middle arrow grip to change the scale factor.*

5. Click the boundary of the remaining viewport to display its grips. In the Status Bar, note that the (Lock/Unlock Viewport) is locked and the Scale factor is grayed out. Using the middle arrow grip, set the scale to **1/4"=1'-0".**

6. Use the middle square grip to place the viewport in the center of the layout. Press <Esc> to clear the selection.

7. Open the **Auditorium Wing** layout and delete the left and the bottom two viewports.

8. Select the auditorium viewport edge to display the grips and using the middle arrow grip, set the scale to **1/8"=1'-0"**. Using the middle square grip, place the viewport in the center of the layout. Press <Esc> to clear the selection.

9. Delete the **Sample** layout by right-clicking on the layout tab in the Status Bar, selecting **Delete**, and then clicking **OK** in the confirmation dialog box.

10. Save the drawing.

Practice 9b   Viewports and Named Views

Practice Objectives

- Create and use named views.
- Modify an existing viewport and remove a viewport clip.
- Apply viewport overrides.

In this practice, you will create and use named views using the Viewport Manager and the **Viewports** command. You will set up multiple viewports based on Named Views. You will remove a viewport clip using the **Clip** command. You will also freeze layers in individual viewports and apply layer overrides to the color settings for layers in a viewport.

Task 1 - Create and use named views.

In this task, you will create and restore views in a drawing.

1. Open **Office-M.dwg** from your practice files folder.

2. Zoom in on the stairway in the upper right corner, as shown in Figure 9–55.

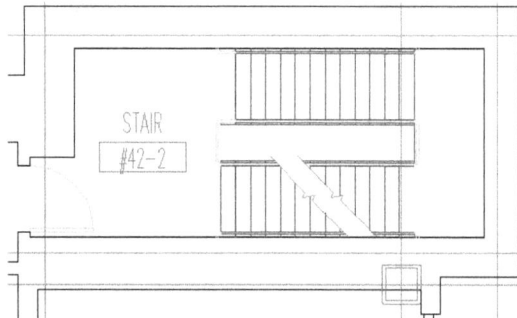

Figure 9–55

3. In the *View* tab>Named Views panel, click (View Manager). The View Manager dialog box opens.

4. Click **New...** to open the New View / Shot Properties dialog box.

5. In the *View name* field, type **Stairs** and verify that the **Save layer snapshot with view** option is selected.

You might have to expand the details portion of the dialog box.

6. Accept the other default settings and click **OK**. Click **OK** to close the View Manager dialog box.

7. Zoom out to display the entire drawing, and toggle off the layer **HVAC**.

8. In the *View* tab>Named Views panel, click ⌞🔍 (New View)

9. In the New View / Shot Properties dialog box, type **Elevators** for the view name.

10. Verify that the **Save layer snapshot with view** option is selected.

11. In the *Boundary* area, click 🔲 (Define window). The drawing area displays.

12. Use **Zoom** and **Pan** to display the two elevators in your drawing window. Select two corner points of a window to define the view, as shown in Figure 9–56, and press <Enter> to return to the dialog box.

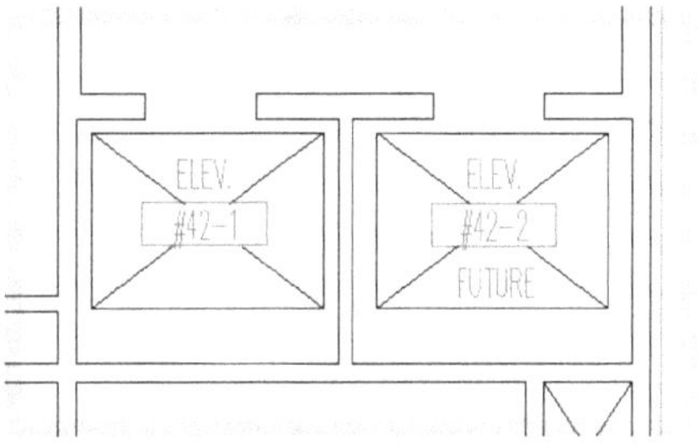

Figure 9–56

13. Click **OK** to complete the view creation. Click **OK** again to close the View Manager dialog box.

14. In the *View* tab>Named Views panel, use the Unsaved View list to select the view **Stairs,** as shown in Figure 9–57. The stairs area displays in the drawing window. Zoom out and note that the **HVAC** layer is toggled on (green HVAC components display).

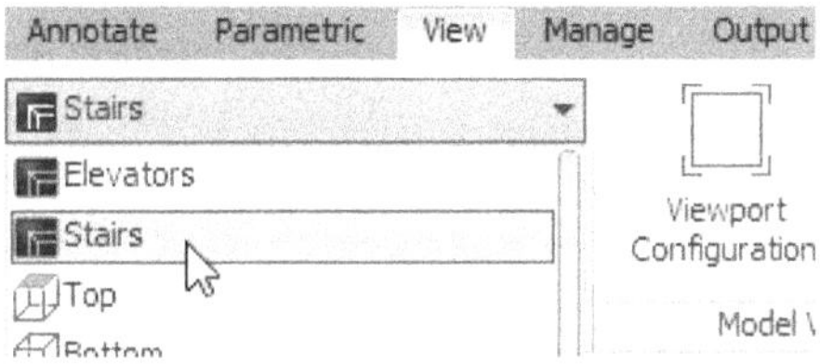

Figure 9–57

15. In the Unsaved View list, select the view **Elevators**. Zoom out and note that the layer **HVAC** is toggled off.

Task 2 - Create multiple viewports from Named Views.

In this task, you will create multiple viewports based on Named Views using the Viewports dialog box, as shown in Figure 9–58.

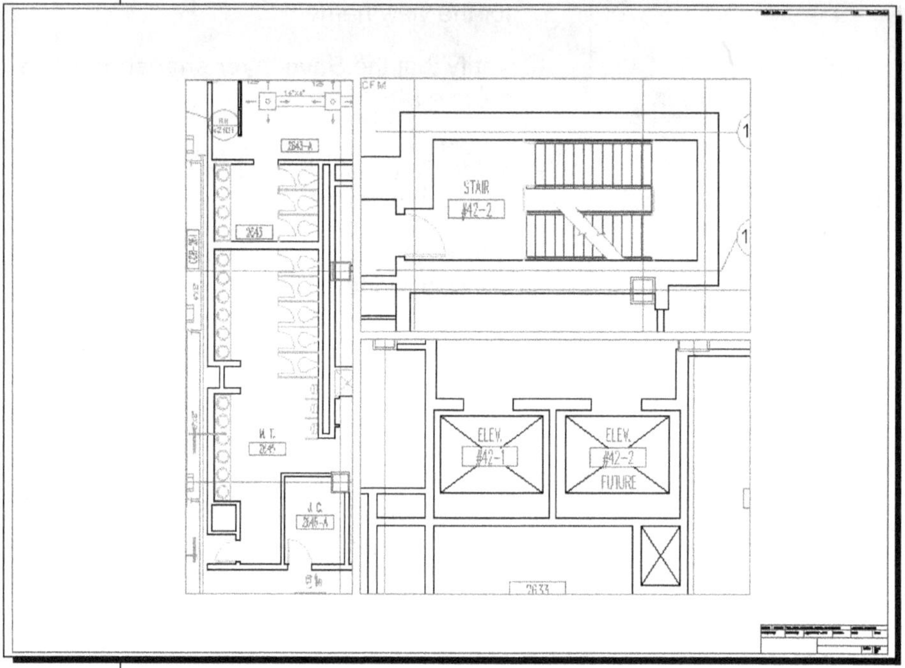

Figure 9–58

1. Switch to the **A-401 Detail Plans** layout and set the current layer to **Viewports**.

2. In the *Layout* tab>Layout Viewports panel, click ⬆ (arrow). In the Viewports dialog box, select the *New Viewports* tab. In the *Standard viewports* area, select **Three: Left**, and set the *Viewport Spacing* to **10** (distances in this drawing are in millimeters).

3. In the *Preview* area, click in the top right viewport. In the Change view to drop-down list, select **Stairs**. Click in the bottom right viewport and change the view to **Elevators**. Click **OK** to close the Viewports dialog box.

4. Select two corners to place the three viewports in the layout, as shown above in Figure 9–58.

5. Activate the top right viewport, and pan to display the stairs. In the Status Bar, change the scale to **1:20**.

6. Activate the viewport on the left and pan inside it to display the restrooms located near the center left of the drawing. Change the scale to **1:30**, and then use grips to make the viewport narrower to only display the restrooms, as shown in Figure 9–58.

7. Use grips to make the other 2 viewports wider. Move the three viewports as required to center them better in the layout.

Task 3 - Clip a viewport.

In this task, you will clip an existing viewport using the **Polygonal** option.

1. Copy the existing layout by right-clicking on the tab and selecting **Move or Copy**. In the dialog box select **A-401 Detail Plans** and select the checkbox for **Create a copy**. Click **OK**. The new layout is placed before **A-401 Detail Plans.** Rename the new layout as **A-201 1st Floor Plan**.

2. If required, switch to the **A-201 1st Floor Plan** layout. Delete the two viewports on the right side.

3. Use grips to resize the narrow remaining viewport so that it fills most of the sheet. Display the floor plan at a *scale* of **1:50**. Pan to center the drawing in the viewport.

4. In the *Layout* tab>Layout Viewports panel, click 🔲 (Clip).

5. Select the viewport, press <Enter> to select the **Polygonal** option. Starting from the lower left corner of the viewport, select points to define a clipping boundary that cuts out the bottom right portion of the view, as shown in Figure 9–59. Select the **Close** option to complete the polygon.

6. In Paper Space, in the cleared area that was created by clipping the original rectangular viewport (i.e., the bottom-right corner area), draw a circle with a *radius* of **150**.

7. In the *Layout* tab>Layout Viewports panel, expand

   ⌐┐ (Viewports flyout) and click ⬚ (Viewports, Object) and select the circle. Activate the circular viewport and set its viewport scale to 1:30 and pan in it to display any one room of the plan, as shown in Figure 9–59.

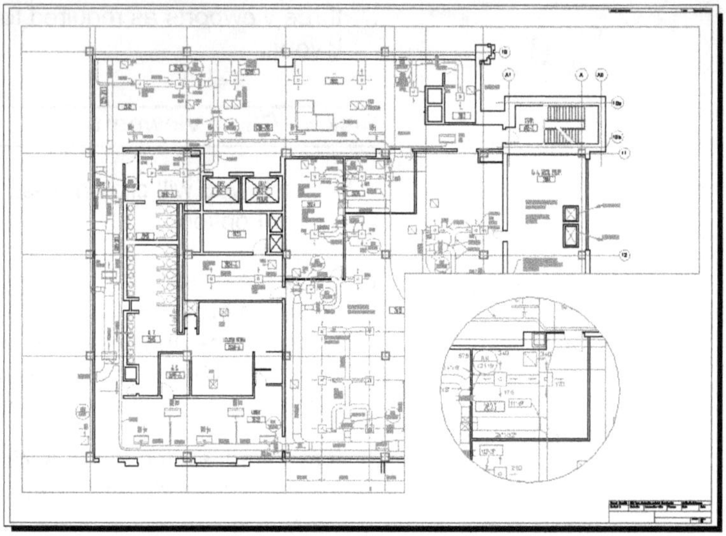

Figure 9–59

Task 4 - Remove viewport clip and apply viewport overrides.

In this task, you will remove a viewport clip, freeze layers in individual viewports, and apply layer overrides to the color settings for layers in a viewport, as shown in Figure 9–60.

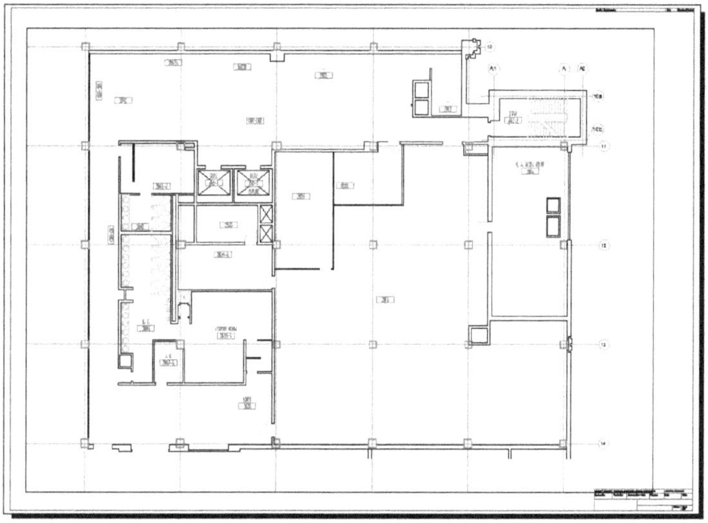

Figure 9–60

1. Copy the **A-201 1st Floor Plan** layout and rename it as **H-201 1st HVAC Floor Plan**.

2. Switch to the **H-201 1st HVAC Floor Plan** layout, if required.

3. Delete the circular viewport.

4. Select the large clipped viewport. In the *Layout* tab>Layout Viewports panel, click ⊡ (Clip).

5. At the *Select clipping object* prompt, press <Down arrow> and select the **Delete** option (as shown in Figure 9–61) to remove the clipping boundary. Note that it becomes a rectangular area again.

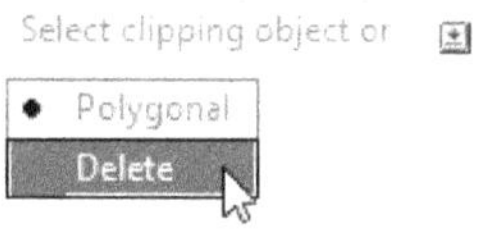

Figure 9–61

6. Activate the large viewport. for layer **HVAC, t**oggle to freeze option, 🔲 (Freeze or thaw in current viewport, so that the HVAC components do not display in this viewport only.

7. Open the Layer Properties Manager and change the *VP Color* for the layer **Stair** to **Green** (as shown in Figure 9–62) so that the stairs are green in this viewport only. Note that their regular color is still blue.

S.. Name	O. F.. V.. L.. P..	Color	VP Color	Linetype	VP Linet...	Lineweight	VP Linew...
Grid Text	♀ ☀ 🔅 🔓 🖨	■ wh...	■ white	Continu...	Continu...	—— Defa...	—— Defa..
Gridline	♀ ☀ 🔅 🔓 🖨	■ 132	■ 132	CENTER	CENTER	—— Defa...	—— Defa..
Handrail	♀ ☀ 🔅 🔓 🖨	☐ 40	☐ 40	Continu...	Continu...	—— Defa...	—— Defa..
Hatching	♀ ☀ 🔅 🔓 🖨	■ red	■ red	Continu...	Continu...	—— Defa...	—— Defa..
HVAC	♀ ☀ 🔅 🔓 🖨	■ 72	■ 72	Continu...	Continu...	—— Defa...	—— Defa..
Misc	♀ ☀ 🔅 🔓 🖨	☐ gr...	☐ green	Continu...	Continu...	—— Defa...	—— Defa..
Notes	♀ ☀ 🔅 🔓 🖨	■ 132	■ 132	Continu...	Continu...	—— Defa...	—— Defa..
Partition	♀ ☀ 🔅 🔓 🖨	☐ gr...	☐ green	Continu...	Continu...	—— Defa...	—— Defa..
Partitions	♀ ☀ 🔅 🔓 🖨	■ ma...	■ magen...	Continu...	Continu...	—— Defa...	—— Defa..
Plumbing	♀ ☀ 🔅 🔓 🖨	☐ gr...	☐ green	Continu...	Continu...	—— Defa...	—— Defa..
Stair	♀ ☀ 🔅 🔓 🖨	■ blue	☐ green	Continu...	Continu...	—— Defa...	—— Defa..
Structural	♀ ☀ 🔅 🔓 🖨	■ ma...	■ magen...	Continu...	Continu...	—— Defa...	—— Defa..

Figure 9–62

8. Switch to the **A-201 1st Floor Plan** layout. It should display differently from the **H-201 1st HVAC Floor Plan** layout. The **HVAC** layer should be visible and the stairs should be blue.

9. Save and close the drawing.

Chapter
10

Output and Publishing

Exam Objectives Covered in This Chapter

- 4.2.a Publish one or more drawings to a plotter, printer, DWF, or PDF file
- 4.2.d Save or export the objects in a drawing to a different file format

10.1 Printing Concepts

As you work on a drawing, it sometimes needs to be printed. For example, you can print a check plot while the drawing is in progress, and when the drawing is finished, you can print a full set of working drawings with dimensioning, text, and titleblocks, as shown in Figure 10–1. Depending on the size of your project, you can do all of these things from one or several drawing files.

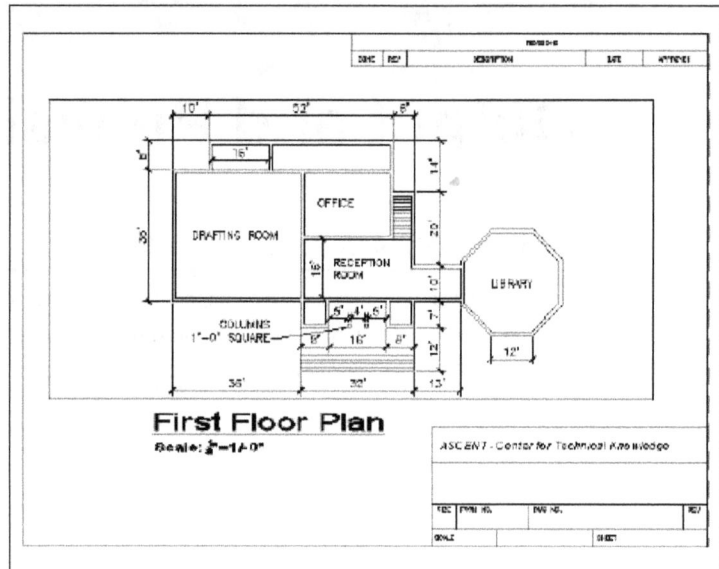

Figure 10–1

There are two methods of printing in the AutoCAD software:

- From *Model Space*.

- From *Paper Space Layouts*.

Hint: Printing vs. Plotting

Both of these terms are used to describe the process of getting an AutoCAD drawing onto a piece of paper. Most of what you do now is technically printing, but many people refer to large format printing as plotting because of the old plotters that were used before laser technology. Printing and plotting mean essentially the same thing today.

Model Space Printing

Everything you have done so far has been in AutoCAD *Model Space*. In Model Space, you draw the model full-size in its real-world units. You can print directly from Model Space for a quick *check plot* of all or part of the drawing, as shown in Figure 10–2.

- When you print from Model Space, you set a scale in the **Plot** command. DO NOT scale the objects in the drawing.

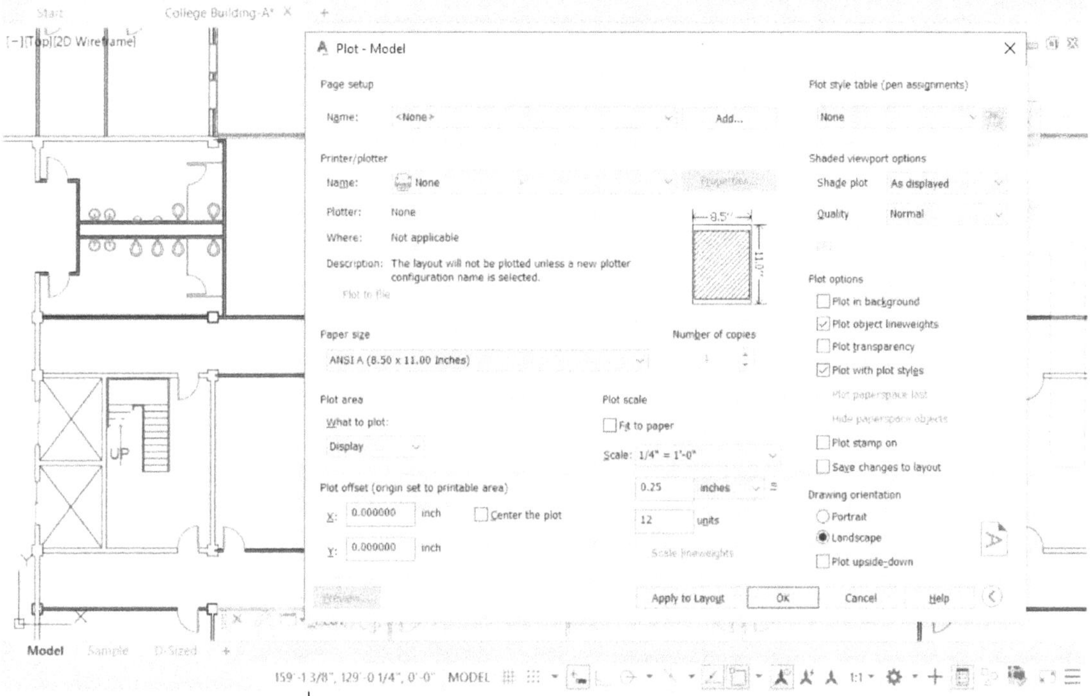

Figure 10–2

- You can set the scale in the **Plot** command to print the model at a precise scale factor, such as **1/4"=1'-0"**.

- If you need a border, titleblock, dimensions or other annotations to be printed at a specific size, these non-representational objects need to be scaled up to the scale of the drawing. This ensures that when the drawing is shrunk down to fit on the sheet of paper during the **Plot** command, their sizes are printed correctly.

- With Model Space printing you cannot easily print multiple views of the same drawing at different scales.

Paper Space Layout Printing

The primary way to print in the AutoCAD software is to use Paper Space Layouts. Think of the layout as a sheet of paper on which you can place snapshots of your model in *viewports*. These snapshots can be any size and at any scale, as shown in Figure 10–3. You can arrange, enlarge or crop them, as required.

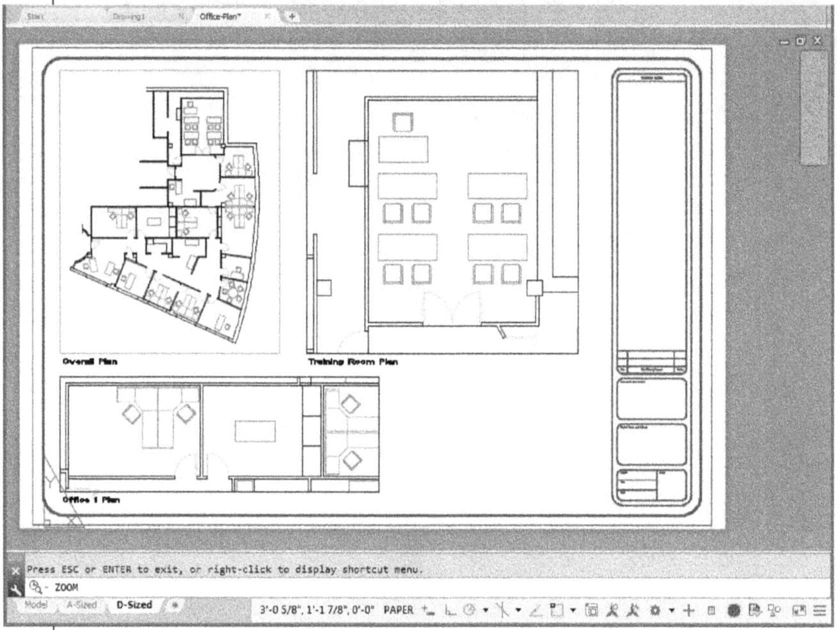

Figure 10–3

Using this method of printing separates the tasks of drawing into two stages:

1. In Model Space, all of the elements are drawn full scale (i.e., at their actual real-world size).
2. In Paper Space Layouts, all of the elements are drawn at the appropriate size for the sheet of paper and you add viewports to display the model.

- The border, titleblock, general notes, schedules, and titles are placed on the layout. They should be drawn at the actual size at which you want them to print on the sheet of paper. Most dimensions and text can be added through the viewport on the model. Their size is controlled by the scale of the viewport and the associated annotation scale.

Only one model can be displayed per drawing, but you can have multiple layouts. Each layout can have a different sheet size, scales, and plotter and these settings are stored in the layout.

10.2 Printing Layouts

When creating layouts in a drawing, each layout represents one sheet, as shown in Figure 10–4. By creating the layout, you define what should be printed. The layout is based on a paper size that is determined by the printer. If the layout is set up correctly, you can plot it without reviewing any additional information in the Plot dialog box.

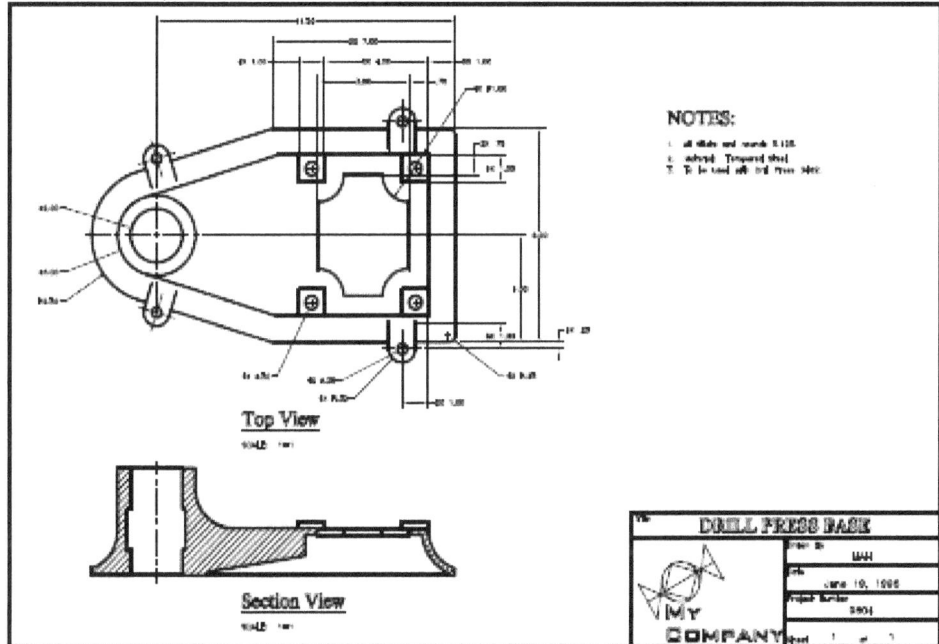

Figure 10–4

How To: Plot a Layout

1. Select the layout that you want to plot.

2. In the *Output* tab>Plot panel, click ▨ (Plot).
3. If everything is set up as required, in the Plot dialog box, click **OK**.

*You can also start the **Plot** command in the Application Menu by selecting **Print**.*

- If the drawing has multiple layouts, a Batch Plot notification dialog box opens where you can either use the **Try Batch Plot (Publish)** or select **Continue to plot a single sheet**, as shown in Figure 10–5.

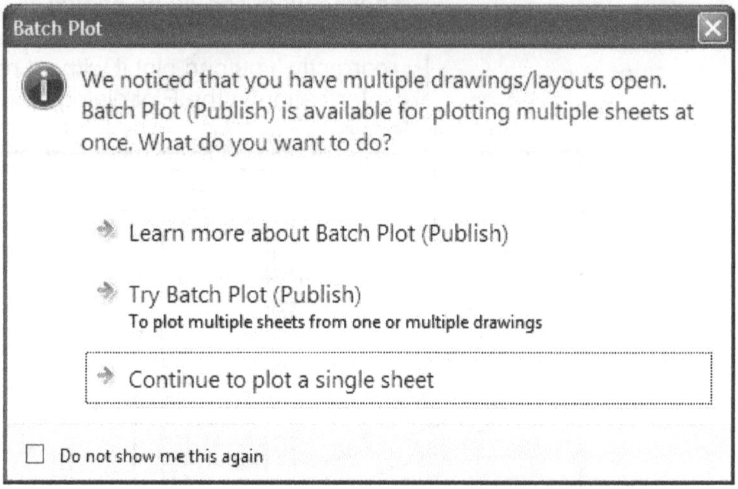

Figure 10–5

- If you are plotting to a DWF plotter or creating a PDF file (which creates a file rather than a paper plot), you are prompted for a name and location for the file in the Browse for Plot File or a Save PDF File As dialog boxes respectively.

- When the plot is finished, a balloon notification displays in the Status Bar, as shown in Figure 10–6. You can click on the link in the balloon to display details about the plot job.

Figure 10–6

Previewing the Plot

Previewing your plot can be helpful to ensure that you are plotting the correct objects before wasting paper and ink.

- You can access the preview in the *Output* tab>Plot panel by clicking , or in the Application Menu by selecting **Print>Plot Preview**.

- You can also click **Preview** in the Plot dialog box. This is useful when you are making changes in the dialog box and want to display the results before printing.

- In Preview mode, viewing tools, such as Pan and various Zoom options display instead of the ribbon. You can also right-click and select an option, as shown in Figure 10–7.

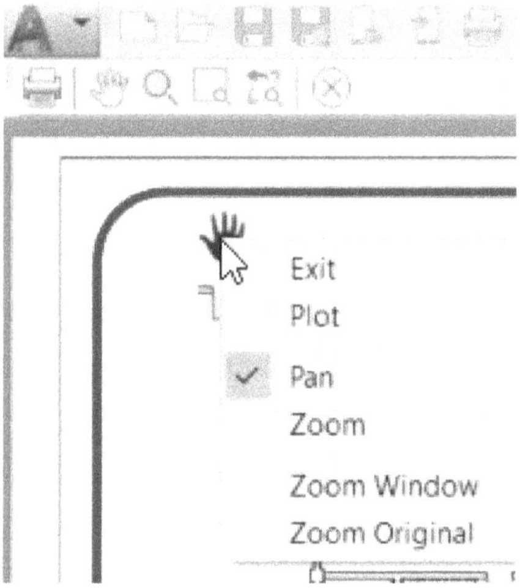

Figure 10–7

10.3 Print and Plot Settings

While most of the options are typically set in a layout, you can adjust some additional options when plotting. For example, you might want to make a half-sized plot or just plot part of a layout or model so that you can check the design, as shown in Figure 10–8. You can make changes in the Plot dialog box without impacting the layout.

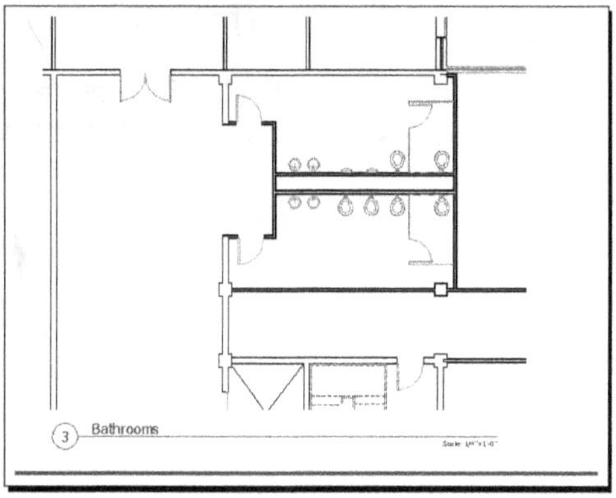

Figure 10–8

You can modify the plot settings in the Plot dialog box, as shown in Figure 10–9.

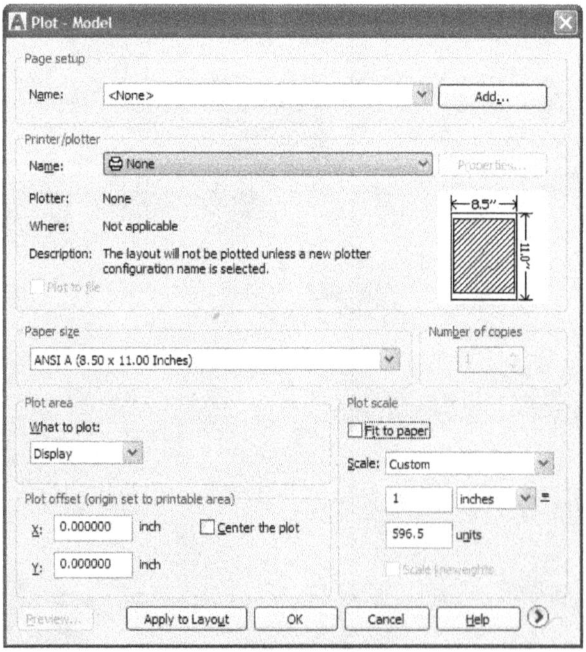

Figure 10–9

Printer/Plotter

- You need to select the plotter first because it determines the paper size.

- Depending on the type of plotter specified, the *Number of copies* area might be available, to set the number of copies to print, as shown in Figure 10–10. It is grayed out when you are using a DWF plotter and some options of PDF version because it plots to a file, rather than directly to paper.

Number of copies

1

Figure 10–10

What to Plot

The *Plot area* controls the part of the drawing that is plotted.

- The **Display** or **Window** options, as shown in Figure 10–11, can be used to plot part of a layout or model. While the **Display** option plots the objects that display on the screen, the **Window** option enables you to create a window around the area that you want to plot.

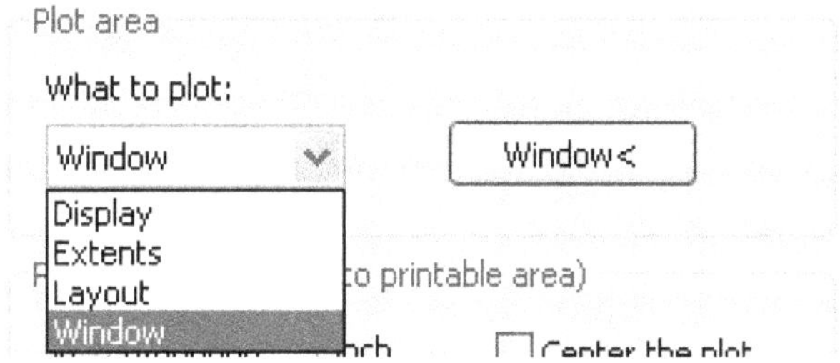

Plot area

What to plot:

| Window | Window< |

Display
Extents
Layout
Window

to printable area)

Center the plot

Figure 10–11

- The **Extents** option plots a view that includes every object in the drawing. It includes any objects that might be outside your main drawing. Note that with this option, the objects in the plot might be very small depending on how far apart they are in the drawing.

- The **Limits** option is only available in Model Space and plots an area that is defined by the limits that have been set in the drawing.

Setting the Plot Scale

- While you typically print layouts at a 1:1 scale, you can print half-sized plots by selecting a *Scale* of **0.5=1.0**.

- The **Fit to paper** option, as shown in Figure 10–12, can be used when printing a check plot to a letter-sized plotter. Note that the drawing is not to scale when this option is selected.

Plot scale

☑ Fit to paper

Scale: Custom

1   inches   =

1.19   units

☐ Scale lineweights

Figure 10–12

- You can also specify a *Scale* of **1/4"=1'-0"**. This is typically done if you are plotting from Model Space and want to have it to scale.

- The **Scale lineweights** option scales the lineweights in proportion to the plot scale. If not selected (the default), the lineweights plot at the line width size.

Plot Offset

- By default, the lower left corner of the plot area starts printing at the lower left corner of the page margin. You can move the plot area to the left or up from the lower left margin by specifying an X- or Y-offset, as shown in Figure 10–13.

*The **Center the plot** option is not available when the Plot area is set to **Layout** because the layout fills the printable area completely.*

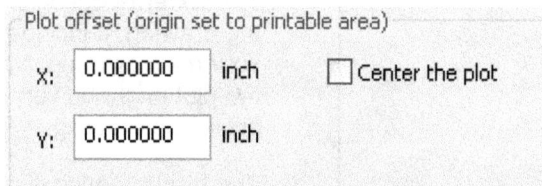

Plot offset (origin set to printable area)

X: 0.000000   inch   ☐ Center the plot

Y: 0.000000   inch

Figure 10–13

- The **Center the plot** option automatically calculates X- and Y-offsets so that the plot is centered on the paper.

More Options

If the dialog box displays in the compressed form, click ⊘ (More Options) in the lower right corner to display more options. Some of the options are shown in Figure 10–14.

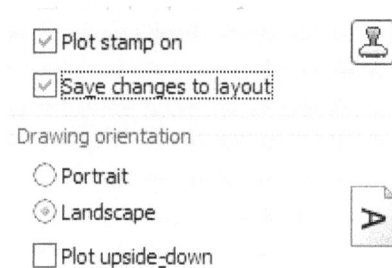

Most of the options relate to advanced features.

☑ Plot stamp on 　　　　　🔲

☑ Save changes to layout

Drawing orientation

○ Portrait

◉ Landscape 　　　　　🔲

☐ Plot upside-down

Figure 10–14

Plot stamp on	Adds a plot stamp with standard information, such as drawing name, date and time, etc. The 🔲 (Plot Stamp Settings) icon becomes available when the **Plot Stamp On** is selected.
Save changes to layout	Automatically saves any changes you make to the plot settings with the layout, which become the new defaults when you plot the layout.

- **Apply to Layout** is similar to the **Save changes to layout** option, except that it only saves changes to the layout when you click the button, rather than automatically, all the time.

- You can also select the *Drawing orientation* options such as printing with **Portrait** or **Landscape** orientation.

Practice 10a

Printing Layouts and Check Plots

Practice Objectives

- Plot a layout to a file.
- Print a check plot from Model Space.

In this practice, you will plot a layout to a file and create a check plot, as shown in Figure 10–15.

Figure 10–15

Task 1 - Print layouts.

In this task, you will plot a layout to a file, as shown in Figure 10–16.

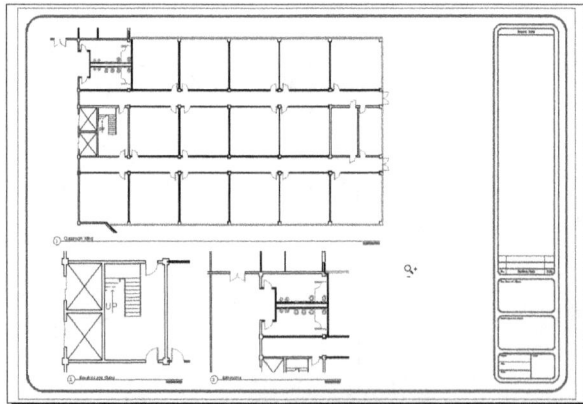

Figure 10–16

1. Open **College Building1-A.dwg** from your practice files folder.

2. Switch to the **Classroom Wing** layout tab and verify that you are in Paper Space.

3. In the *Output* tab>Plot panel, click (Plot). As there are multiple layouts in the drawing, the Batch Plot confirmation dialog box opens. Click **Continue to plot a single sheet**.

4. In the Plot dialog box, note that *Printer/plotter*, *Paper size*, and other options are all set according to the page setup for this layout. The layout is set to use the **DWF6 ePlot.pc3** plotter, which automatically plots to a file.

5. Click **Preview**. Note that your cursor has changed to a magnifying glass indicating that you are in **Zoom Realtime** mode. Zoom in a little, right-click, and select **Pan**.

6. After experimenting with panning and zooming, right-click and select **Zoom Original**. Right-click again and select **Exit** to return to the Plot dialog box.

7. Click **OK** to create the plot file. Accept the default file name for the dwf file and save it in your practice folder.

8. In the Status Bar, a balloon message displays when the plot is complete. Select **Click to view plot and publish details...** to display the plot details. Click **Close**.

Task 2 - Print check plots.

In this task, you will create a check plot, as shown in Figure 10–17.

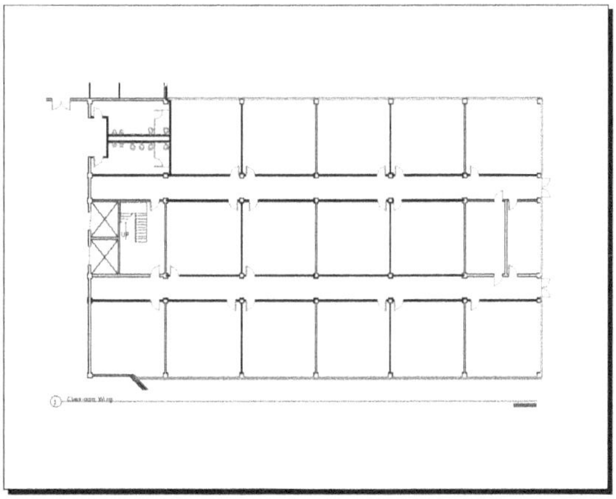

Figure 10–17

1. Start the **Plot** command again. In the Batch Plot confirmation dialog box, click **Continue to plot a single sheet**.

2. Set the *Paper size* to **ANSI A (8.50 x 11.00 Inches)** and click **Preview**. Only a small portion of the entire plot displays, as shown in Figure 10–18. Right-click and select **Exit**.

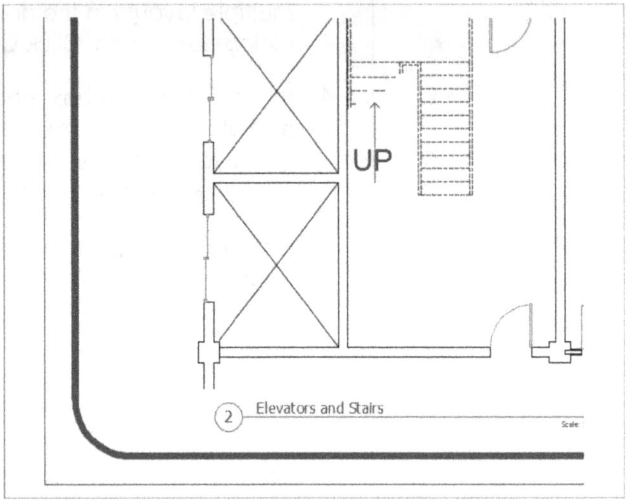

Figure 10–18

3. In the *Plot area*, expand the What to plot drop-down list and select **Window**. Draw a window around the Elevators and Stairs viewport, and preview again. The selected viewport displays as it fits on an 8.5 x 11 sheet of paper at a 1/4"=1'0" scale. Exit the preview.

4. Click **Window<**, draw a window around the Classroom Wing viewport at the top of the layout, and preview the plot. Only a portion of the selected viewport is displayed. Exit the preview.

5. Set the *Plot Scale* to **Fit to paper** and the *Plot Offset* to **Center the plot**. Preview again. The whole viewport displays but is not to scale. Exit the preview.

6. Click **OK** to plot the drawing and name the file **Check Plot.dwf** and click Save to save it in the practice files folder.

7. Ensure that you are in the **Classroom Wing** layout tab. In the *Output* tab>Plot panel, click **Preview**. The preview indicates that the entire layout is going to be plotted as was intended. The changes you just made to the **Plot** command did not change the layout information.

8. Exit the preview. Save and close the drawing.

10.4 Publishing Drawing Sets

The **Batch Plot/Publish** command provides an easy way to create either electronic or paper drawing sets using the interface shown in Figure 10–19. With **Batch Plot/Publish** you can create multi-sheet and multi-drawing DWFx or PDF files that can be viewed using the Autodesk Design Review software or Adobe Reader. The same list of drawing sheets can also be plotted directly to paper.

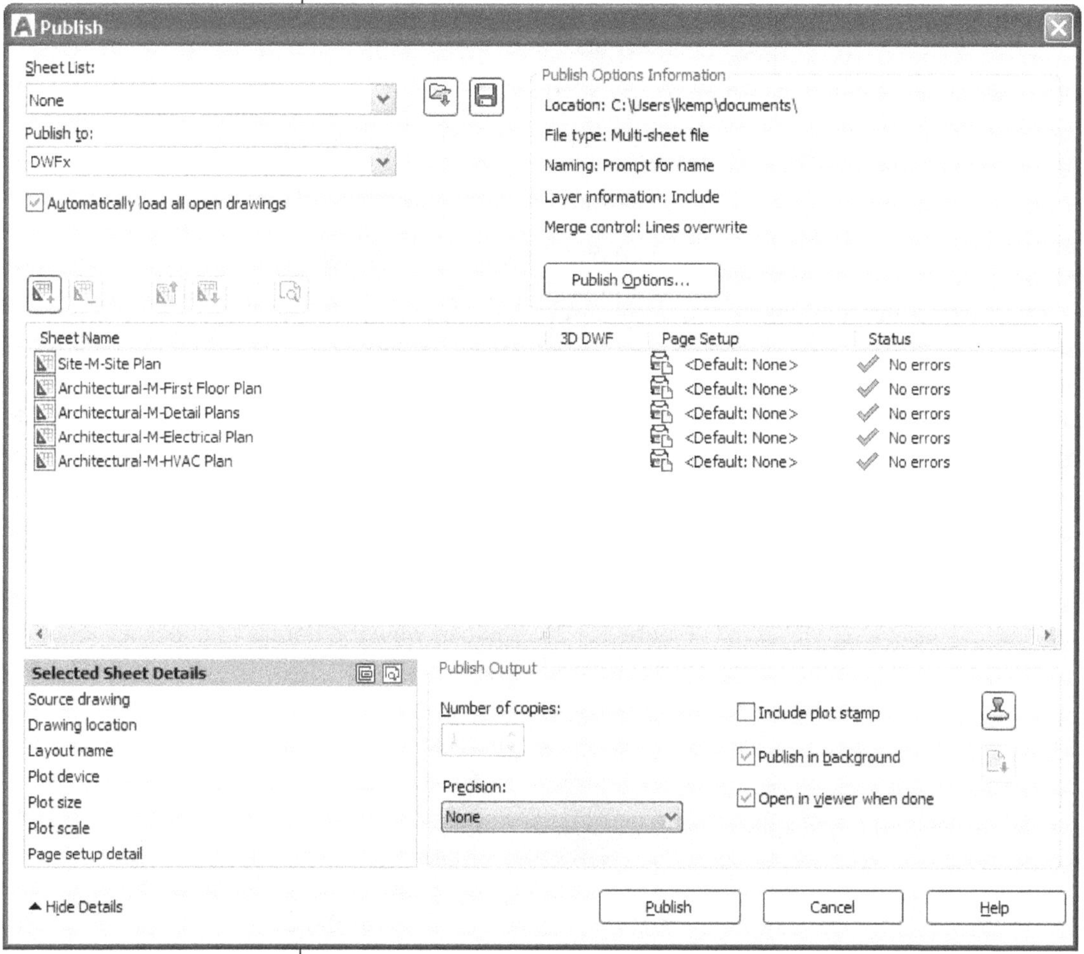

Figure 10–19

You can add layouts to the list for publishing from any drawing while controlling the order in which they are printed or presented. Once the list of sheets has been created, you can save it and easily reload it later to publish the same set of sheets again.

How To: Publish a Set of Drawings

1. Open a drawing containing multiple layouts that you want to publish.
2. In the ribbon, in the *Output* tab>Plot panel, click 🖨️➡️ (Batch Plot).
3. In the Publish dialog box, a list of drawing sheets that were automatically created from the existing layouts in the drawing displays.

   - Click 📇₊ (Add Sheets) to include other drawings. Selecting a drawing file automatically imports all of its layouts.

   - Click 📇₋ (Remove Sheets) to remove any sheets that you do not want to include in the list.

   - Reorder the sheets as required using 📇⬆️ (Move Sheet Up) and 📇⬇️ (Move Sheet Down).

4. In the Publish to drop-down list, specify whether you are publishing to the plotters named in the page setup for each layout: a DWF, DWFx, or PDF file.
5. Click **Publish**.
6. You might be prompted to save the current list of sheets. Do so if you are planning to print the same group of layouts again. A DSD file is created.

- The publishing process takes place in the background, enabling you to continue with other projects. When it is finished, an alert balloon opens in the Status Bar, as shown in Figure 10–20. You can view the details to check for any errors or warnings.

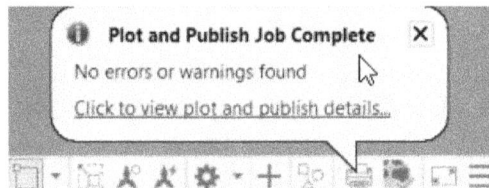

Figure 10–20

- Click 🔍 (Preview) to display the plot preview of the sheet that has been selected in the list.

- In the Publish Options dialog box you can specify the output, type of file (single or multi-sheet), prompt or default name for the multi-sheet file, security, and layer information, as shown in Figure 10–21.

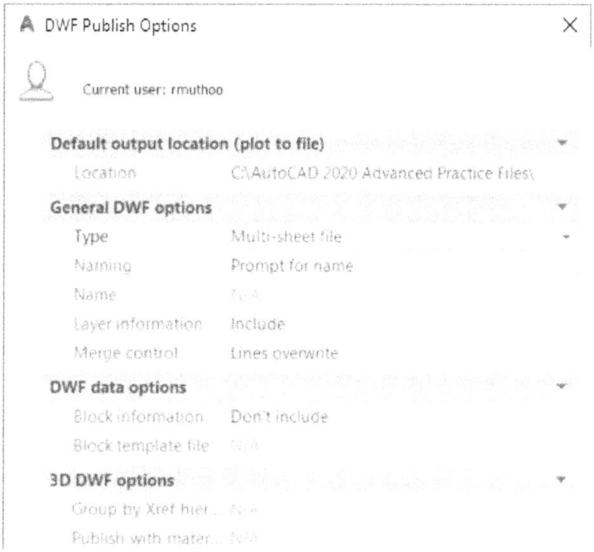

Figure 10–21

- **Show Details** displays additional information about the selected sheet details, number of copies, plot stamp, publish in background, and viewer options. Click **Hide Details** to close the additional options.

How To: Work with Sheet Lists Files

1. In the ribbon, in the *Output* tab>Plot panel, click (Batch Plot).

2. In the Publish dialog box, click (Load Sheet List).
3. Select the DSD file that you want to load.
4. In the Load Sheet List dialog box (shown in Figure 10–22), select to either replace or append sheets to the current list.

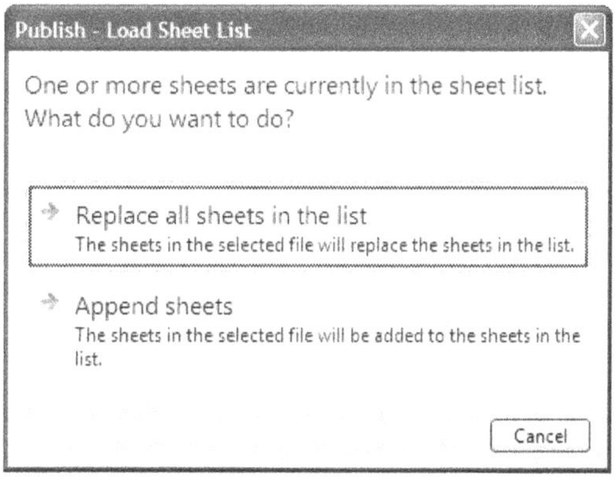

Figure 10–22

5. In the Publish dialog box, make any required changes and click **Publish**.

- You can change the default page setup in the list of page setups in the drawing. You can also import page setups from another drawing or template that contains named page setups. To change the page setup for a sheet, select its default setup in the list and then select from the drop-down list.

- The **Batch Plot** command automatically adds all of the open drawings to the Sheet list, including their Model tabs. This might create a problem when several drawings are open. An alert box opens and prompts you to change the names of the model sheets. To keep this from happening, clear the **Automatically load all open drawings** option.

10.5 Output for Electronic Review

You often need to share information in an AutoCAD drawing electronically with users who do not have the AutoCAD software or who only need to view (and not edit) the information. There are two main options for this: creating a DWF or DWFx file that can be viewed and marked up in the Autodesk Design Review software or creating a PDF file that can be viewed in Adobe Reader.

*   Autodesk Design Review is a free program from Autodesk. You can download the software from: *http://www.autodesk.com/products/design-review/*.

*   Adobe Reader is a free third-party program and can be downloaded from *http://get.adobe.com/reader/*.

*   You can create DWF, DWFx, and PDF files using the **Plot** command, **Batch Plot/Publish** command, or **Export DWF/DWFx/PDF** commands, as shown in Figure 10–23.

Figure 10–23

Hint: DWF vs DWFx

DWF (**Design Web Format**) is a compressed vector format that loads and displays faster than normal DWG files.

DWFx can create multiple page DWF files with the **Batch Plot/Publish** command. It enables you to open DWFx files in Internet Explorer without having any Autodesk products installed.

Plotting Electronic Files

Layouts can be set up to create DWF, DWFx, or PDF files, or you can specify the plotter type in the **Plot** command. Multiple PDF plotters are available. Each one sets the level of print quality.

How To: Plot to a DWF, DWFx, or PDF File

You can also access the
Plot *command in*
Application Menu>Print.

1. In the Quick Access Bar or in the *Output* tab>Plot panel, click

   🖨️ (Plot).

   • If the software detects multiple drawings or layouts open, a Batch Plot dialog box displays. You can either use **Batch Plot** or plot a single sheet.

2. Select the appropriate plotter from the list, as shown in Figure 10–24:

   • **DWF6 ePlot.pc3** for DWF files
   • **DWFx ePlot (XPS Compatible).pc3** for DWFx files
   • Any of the **AutoCAD PDF** printers for PDF files

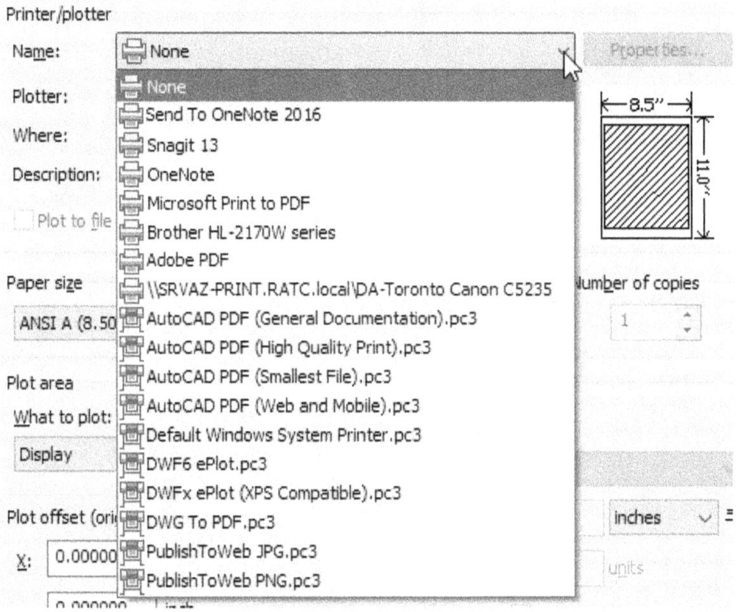

Figure 10–24

3. Click **OK** to plot the file.

• DWF, DWFx, and PDF files cannot be opened directly in the AutoCAD software, but can be accessed using DWF or PDF Overlays or the Markup Set Manager (for DWF).

• Normal DWF plots are in 2D. A separate command, **3DDWF**, enables you to create DWFs of 3D models, so that you can change the viewing angle in the DWF viewer.

Exporting DWF or PDF Files

Exporting to DWF, DWFx, or PDF is another way of creating electronic files to share with other companies or within your company.

How To: Export Layouts to DWF, DWFx, or PDF

- If you want to create a multi-sheet DWFx or PDF, use <Ctrl> or <Shift> to select multiple layout tabs before you start the **Export** command.

*You can also access the required **Export** command in Application Menu>Export.*

1. In the ribbon, in the *Output* tab>Export to DWF/PDF panel, click the required **Export** command, ⬤ (DWFx)/ ⬤ (DWF)/ 📄 (PDF).

2. Review the information in the Save As dialog box, as shown in Figure 10–25.

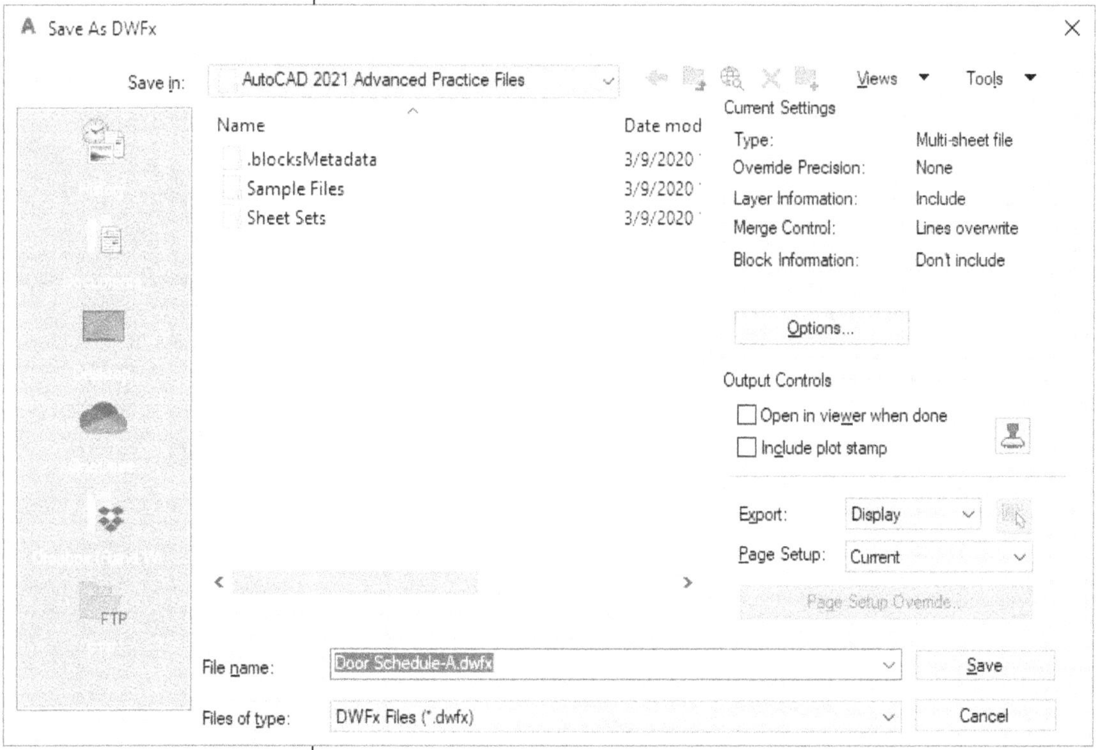

Figure 10–25

3. Click **Options** to modify any of the settings that need to be changed.
4. Select the required Output Controls.
   - If you selected the **Open in viewer when done** option, the associated viewer program opens, enabling you to view the exported file.
5. Specify whether you want to export the current layout or all of the layouts and the associated Page Setup.
6. Assign the correct filename and location and click **Save**.

In the ribbon, in the *Output* tab>Export to DWF/PDF panel. you can set the following options:

- For the *Model* tab, you can set up what to export (**Display**, **Extents**, and **Window**
- For the layout tabs, you can set up what to export, (**Current layout** or **All layouts**), and the Page Setup.

- Click ⌕ (Preview) to display the proposed export.

- Click (Export to DWF Options) or (Export to PDF Options) to modify any of the options.

Export to PDF Options

When exporting drawing files to PDF files, you can control the quality of vectors, rasters, and merge control (enables lines to merge or overwrite each other), as shown in Figure 10–26.

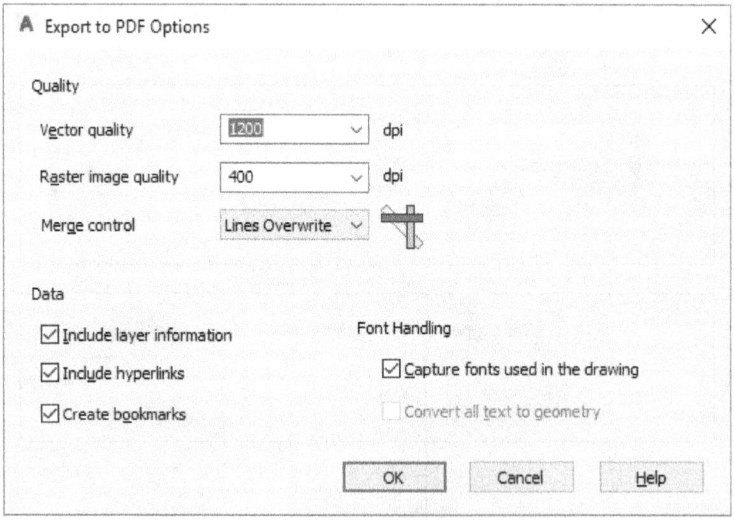

Figure 10–26

You can also include information about data, such as:

Layer information	Layer information can be included in PDF files.
Hyperlinks	Hyperlinks in the drawing file works inside the PDF file. This works for sheets that are linked and weblinks.
Bookmarks	Bookmarks are enabled. Each sheet and each sheet view becomes a bookmark in the PDF.
Fonts	TrueType fonts are embedded in the PDF file and do not have to be available in the PDF viewer. If this option is not selected, the PDF viewer uses substitute fonts. If you have a PDF file with shx fonts, they are converted to geometry and display as a comment in the PDF file. You can also convert all text to geometry during the export process.

The AutoCAD PDF printers provide various print qualities. The table below lists the output settings for each PDF printer.

Printer/Plotter	Vector Quality	Raster Image Quality	Merge Control	Include Layer Info.	Include Hyperlinks	Create Bookmarks	Capture fonts used in the drawing
General Documentation	1200	400	Lines Overwrite	X	X	X	X
High Quality	2400	600	Lines Overwrite	X	X	X	X
Small Files	200	400	Lines Overwrite				
Web and Mobile	200	400	Lines Overwrite	X	X	X	X

Practice 10b | Reviewing and Publishing Drawing Sets

Practice Objectives

- Plot and export a single layout and multi-sheets to DWF and DWFx files, and view and mark them up in the Autodesk Design Review software.
- View DWF markups to revise its associated DWG file in the AutoCAD software using the Markup Set Manager.
- Set up a list of multiple layouts from multiple drawings to batch plot them.

To complete this practice, you must have the Autodesk Design Review software. The software must be installed before you start the practice.

In this practice, you will plot a layout to a DWF file and open the file in the Autodesk Design Review software. You will also export a multi-sheet DWFx file, view it in the Autodesk Design Review software, and make several markups. Finally, you will import the DWFx file into the original drawing file using the Markup Set Manager and make a change based on the markup. You will then republish the DWFx and review the changes in the Autodesk Design Review software, as shown in Figure 10–27. Finally, you will Batch Plot multiple drawings.

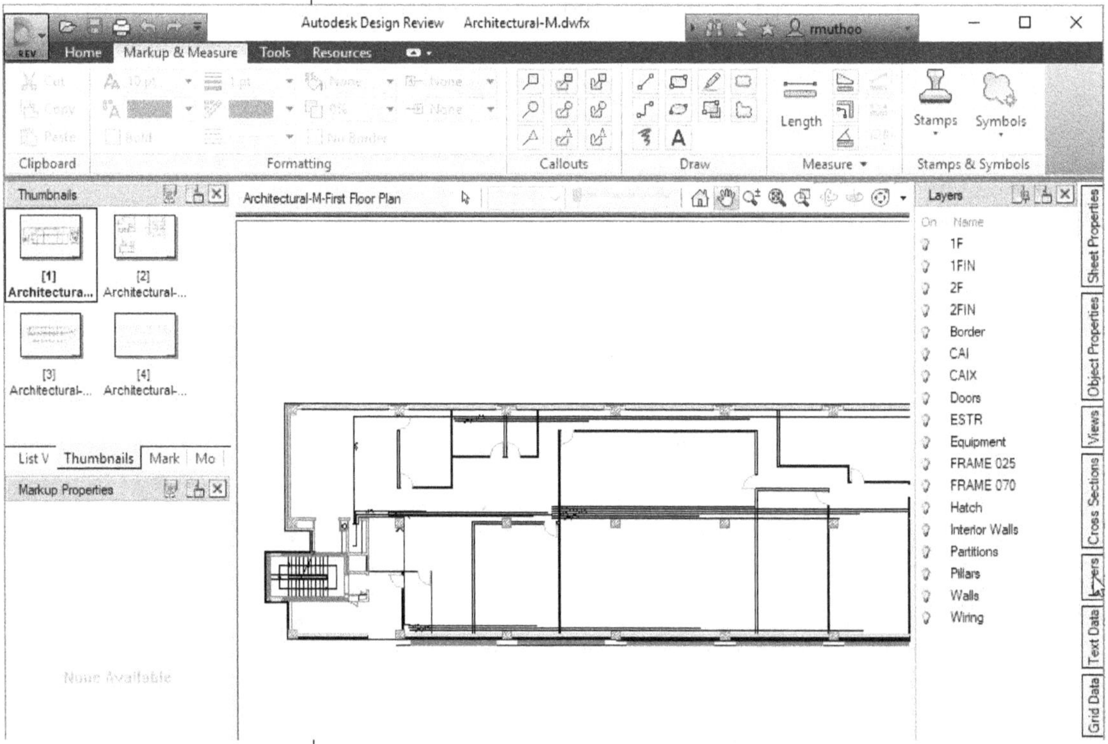

Figure 10–27

Task 1 - Plot a DWF file.

1. Open **Architectural-M.dwg** from the practice files folder.

2. Switch to the **First Floor Plan** layout.

3. Start the **Plot** command. In the Batch Plot warning dialog box, click **Continue to plot a single sheet**.

4. In the Plot dialog box, verify that the *Printer/plotter* is set to **DWF6 ePlot.pc3**. (It was set in the page setup for the layout.)

5. Click **Properties** to open the Plotter Configuration Editor.

6. Select **Custom Properties** in the list. In the *Access Custom Dialog* area, click **Custom Properties**.

7. In the DWF6 ePlot Properties dialog box, in the *Additional Output Settings* area, select **Include layer information**, as shown in Figure 10–28. Click **OK** twice.

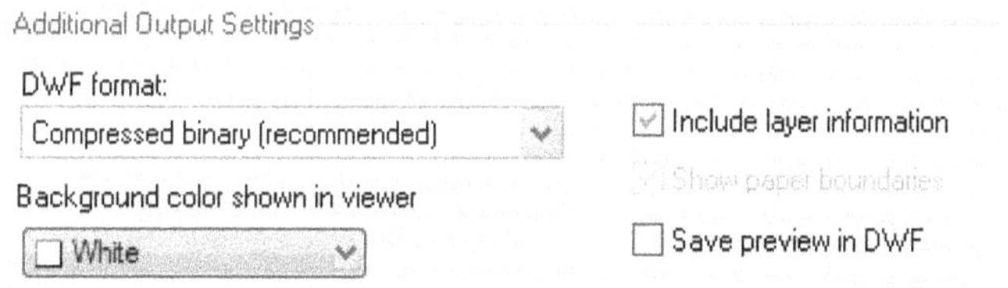

Figure 10–28

8. Click **OK** again to accept **Apply changes for the current plot only**.

9. The **Plot to file** option is on by default for this plotter. Set the *Plot Area* to **Layout**.

10. Click **OK** to create the plot. Save the DWF file in the practice files folder and name it **First Floor Plan.dwf**.

11. Close the *Plot and Publish Job Complete* balloon in the Status Bar.

12. In the Status Bar, right-click on ⎙ (Plot/Publish Details) and select **View Plotted File...** to open the **First Floor Plan.dwf** in the Autodesk Design Review software.

13. Pan and zoom to view the image.

14. Along the right side of the drawing window, expand the Layers palette. A list of layers are displayed.

15. Close the Autodesk Design Review software.

*The Autodesk Design Review software must already be installed. If Windows prompts you to select which application to use to open the file, select **Autodesk DWF Application.***

Task 2 - Export a multi-sheet DWFx file.

Note that the selected layouts are highlighted.

1. Select all four layout tabs by pressing <Ctrl> or <Shift> as you select each one.

2. Start the 🏷 (Export DWFx) command (*Output* tab>Export to DWF/PDF panel).

3. In the Save as DWFx dialog box, browse to the practice files and click **Options**, as shown in Figure 10–29.

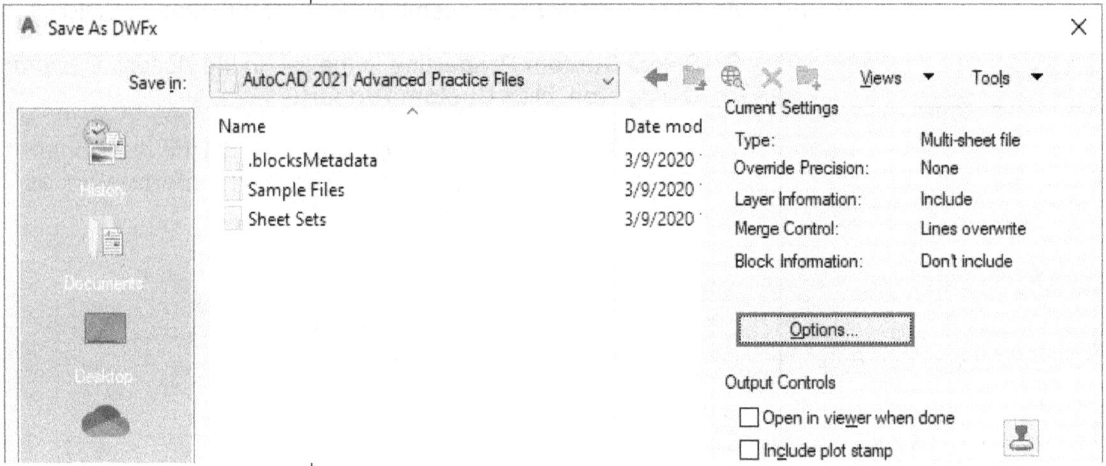

Figure 10–29

4. Verify that *Layer information* is set to **Include**, as shown in Figure 10–30. Click **OK**.

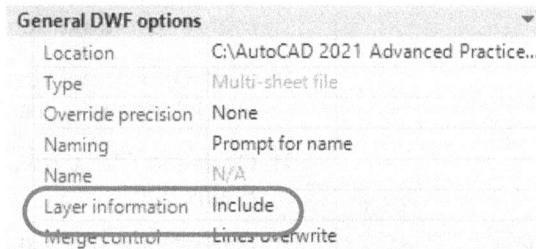

Figure 10–30

Export is automatically set to All layouts because you selected more than one layout before starting the command.

5. In the Save as DWFx dialog box, in the *Output Controls* area, select **Open in viewer when done**.

6. Verify that you are still in the practice files folder and use the drawing name as the filename. Click **Save**.

If the exported DWFx file opens in Internet Explorer, close it and open the file in the Autodesk Design Review software manually.

7. The Autodesk Design Review software opens after the file is exported. Click on the *Thumbnails* tab to display the four thumbnails, one for each layout. Select the *Layers* tab to display the list of layers, as shown in Figure 10–31.

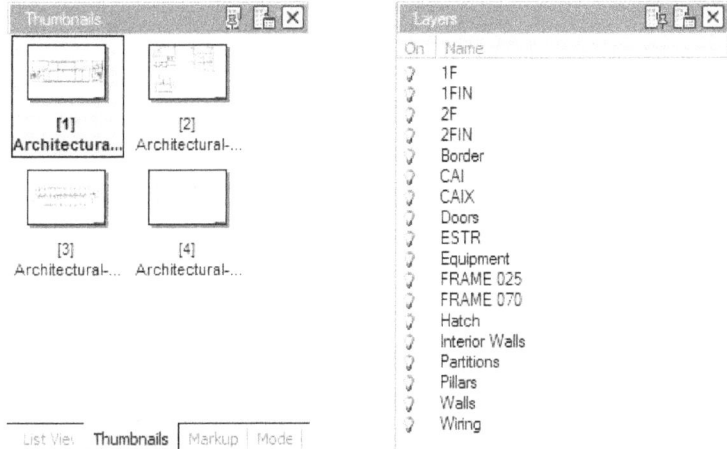

Figure 10–31

8. Open each of the thumbnails.

9. In the First Floor Plan layout, toggle off several layers to display the change. Toggle them back on.

Task 3 - Create a markup.

1. In the Autodesk Design Review software, ensure that you are in the First Floor Plan layout. In the ribbon, open the *Markup & Measure* tab.

2. In the Stamps & Symbols panel, expand (Stamps) and select **PRELIMINARY**. Place it near the top of the title block, as shown in Figure 10–32.

Figure 10–32

3. Zoom in to the middle of the First Floor Plan layout, where you see some long horizontal lines and small tick marks, as shown in Figure 10–33.

4. In the *Markup & Measure* tab>Draw panel, click

   (Polycloud) and add a revision cloud (click four points of the polygon) around some of the objects, as shown in Figure 10–33.

5. In the Draw panel, click **A** (Text Box), place a text box near the cloud, and type the words shown in Figure 10–33. Set the size of the text in the Formatting panel as required.

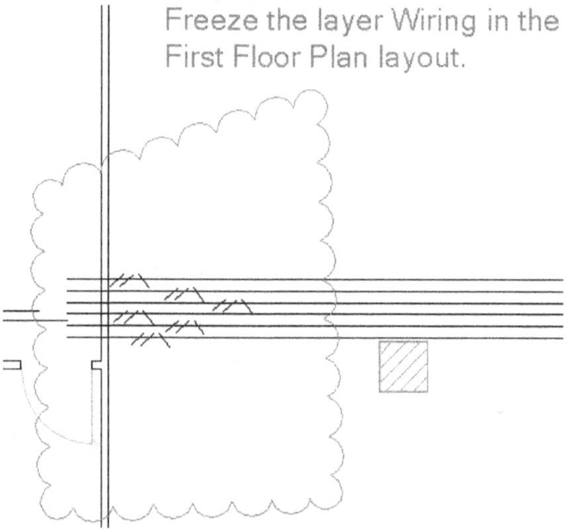

Figure 10–33

6. Save the DWFx file.

7. Close the Autodesk Design Review software.

Task 4 - Use the Markup Set Manager.

---

1. In the AutoCAD software, select the First Floor Plan layout if you are not already in it.

2. In the *View* tab>Palettes panel, click (Markup Set Manager), if it is not already open.

3. In the Markup Set Manager, click **Open...**, as shown in Figure 10–34.

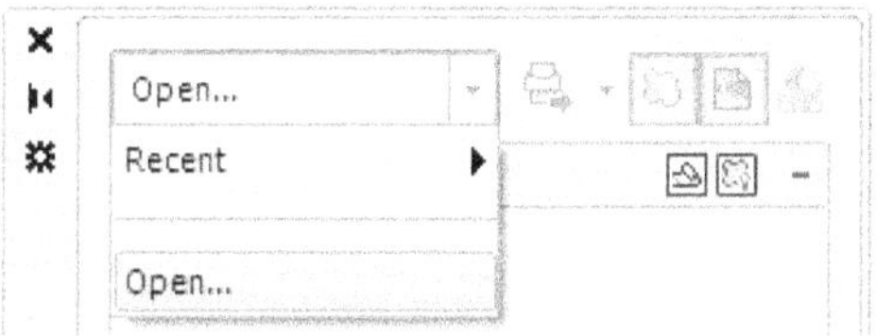

Figure 10–34

4. In the Open Markup DWF dialog box, select **Architectural-M.dwfx** from the practice files folder and click **Open**.

5. In the Markup Set Manager, expand the list of markups, as shown in Figure 10–35.

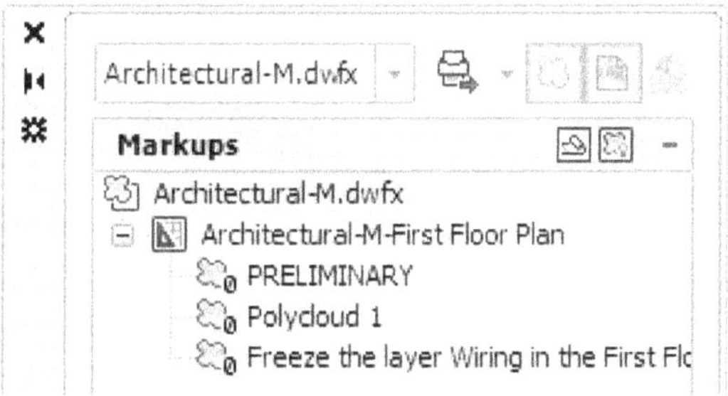

Figure 10–35

6. Double-click on one of the markups to display it in the drawing.

7. Double-click on **Polycloud 1** and zoom in on the revision cloud that is now displayed in the drawing.

8. Double-click inside the viewport to activate it.

9. In the *Home* tab>Layers panel, click (Freeze).

10. Select the horizontal lines or small tick marks to freeze the layer. Press <Enter> to end the command.

11. Zoom out to display the entire layout.

12. In the Markup Set Manager, select **Polycloud 1**.

13. In the *Details* area, change the *Markup status* to **Done**, as shown in Figure 10–36.

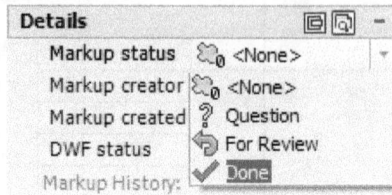

Figure 10–36

14. Repeat the process for the text **Freeze the layer Wiring...**.

15. Save the drawing.

16. In the Markup Set Manager, expand 🖳 ▾ (Republish Markup DWF) and select **Republish All Sheets**.

17. The Specify DWFx file dialog box should automatically list the associated DWFx file. Click **Select** and then click **Yes** to replace the existing file.

18. When the file has finished printing, open the Autodesk Design Review software. The changes are displayed and the markups are checked, as shown in Figure 10–37.

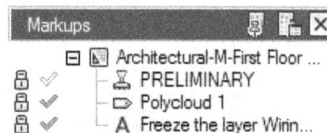

Figure 10–37

19. Close the Autodesk Design Review software.

20. Save the drawing.

Task 5 - Publish drawing sets.

In this task, you will use the **Batch Plot** command to set up a list of drawing layouts using two different drawings, as shown in Figure 10–38, and to create a multi-sheet DWF file. You will also view the file in the Autodesk Design Review software.

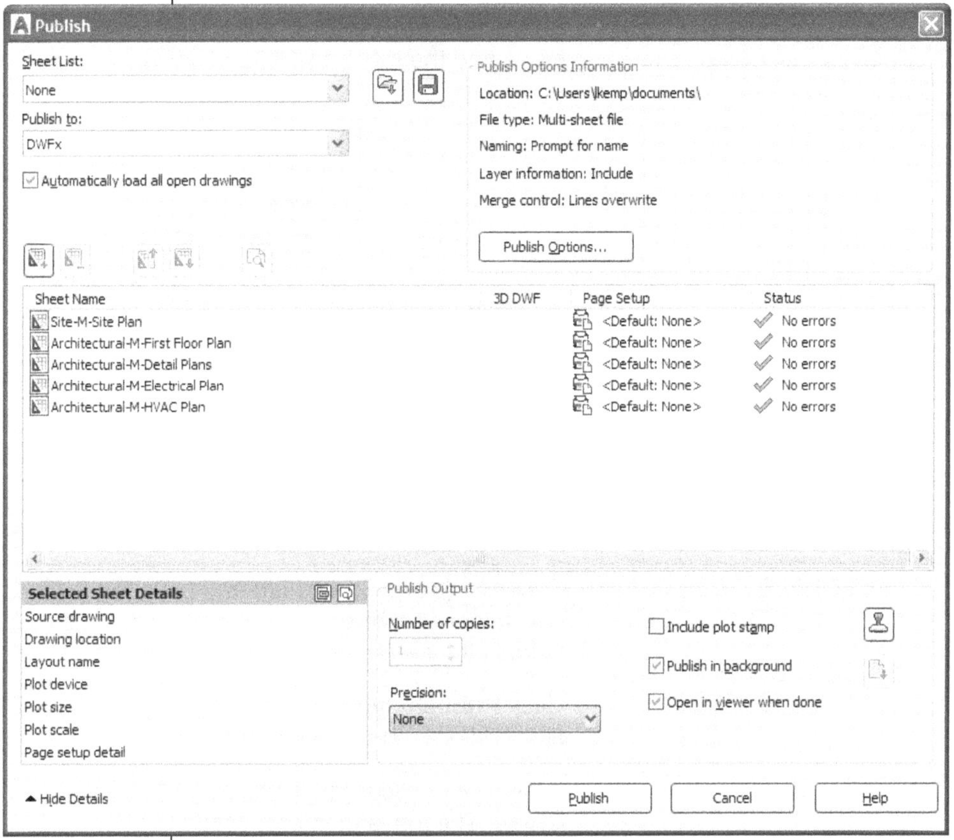

Figure 10–38

1. Verify that **Architectural-M.dwg** is open.

2. Save the drawing. Note that all of the sheets are must be saved before saving the sheet list in the **Batch Plot** command.

3. In the ribbon, in the *Output* tab>Plot panel, click (Batch Plot). In the Publish dialog box, the drawing file *Model* tab and the layouts are listed as sheets.

4. Select the **Architectural-M-Model** sheet and click (Remove Sheets) to remove it from the list.

5. To add a sheet, click ⬛₊ (Add Sheets) and select the file **Site-M.dwg** in the Practice Files folder. Two sheets from this drawing (the *Model* tab and one layout tab) are added to the list.

6. Remove the **Site-M-Model** sheet.

7. Select **Site-M-Site Plan**. Click ⬛↑ (Move Sheet Up) and move it to the top of the list, as shown in Figure 10–39.

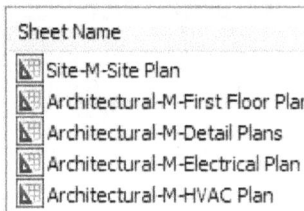

Sheet Name
Site-M-Site Plan
Architectural-M-First Floor Plan
Architectural-M-Detail Plans
Architectural-M-Electrical Plan
Architectural-M-HVAC Plan

Figure 10–39

8. In the Publish to drop-down list, select **DWFx**.

   • Publishing to DWFx creates individual files for each layout, even if you have set multi-sheet files using the **Publish Options**.

9. Click 💾 (Save Sheet List) and save the list in the practice files folder (**Architectural-M.dsd**). This makes it easy to publish the same set of sheets again.

10. Click **Publish**, type a new filename, and specify the practice files folder as the location of the file. Click **Select**.

11. If the Plot - Processing Background Job alert box opens, click **Close**. The job is then processed in the background and wait till the *Plot and Publish Job Complete* balloon displays indicating that the job is finished.

12. In the Status Bar, right-click on 🖨 (Publish Details) and select **View Plotted File...**.

13. In the Autodesk Design Review software, zoom and pan as required.

14. Close the Autodesk Design Review software.

15. Close the drawing file.

Plot Styles and eTransmit

Exam Objectives Covered in This Chapter

- 4.2.b Control how objects appear during output using plot styles
- 4.2.c Create a zipped transmittal package (eTransmit)

11.1 Plot Styles

Concepts

Plot styles enable you to plot objects with a different appearance (color, linetype, lineweight, etc.) from their appearance in the drawing. Plot styles also enable you to control the plotted properties of objects. For example, in one layout, you might want to plot the room walls in grayscale and the ductwork in a heavier lineweight to have it stand out. In another layout, you might want to have the reverse. One way this can be accomplished is to use plot styles, so you can plot the same drawing with different display settings to highlight specific features.

You can use plot styles to control the appearance of the plot including:

- Color, linetype, and lineweight

- End, join, and fill styles for wide lineweights

- Gray-scaling and dithering (combining color dots to give the impression of displaying more colors than are actually available)

- Pen assignments

Notes

- A drawing can use a *color-dependent plot style table*, a *named plot style table*, or *neither*. When a plot style table is used, the objects are plotted as defined by the plot style table.

- New drawings use either color-dependent or named plot styles depending on the template that is used to create them. There are two versions of each predefined template with the AutoCAD software: one that uses color plot styles and one that uses named plot styles.

- A plot style table can be used for any output device. Some output devices might not be able to plot exactly as the plot style table dictates. For example, even if you use a plot style table to plot all of the black lines in the drawing in green, a black-and-white laser printer is still only able to plot the lines in black.

- Plot style tables are stored in files with the extensions CTB (for color-dependent) or STB (for named). These files are stored in the *Plot Styles* folder.

- A drawing can only use one type of table (color-dependent or named) at a time. Only one plot style table can be used per layout.

- You can edit the tables to add new styles (for named plot style tables) and assign properties (for both types of plot styles).

Types of Plot Style Tables

Color-Dependent Plot Style Tables

A color-dependent plot style table contains 255 styles, one for each ACI color. You can specify the plotted effects that you want to use for each color. You cannot rename, add, or delete the color-dependent styles.

- Think of the styles in a color plot style table as a set of pens. A pen has specific characteristics, such as thickness and color. You can assign a pen to each color in the drawing file. For example, you could assign a wide black pen to the color green. Everything green in the drawing is then plotted in wide black lines.

- The plot style table for a drawing can be assigned in the Page Setup or Plot dialog box. The *Plot style table* area is located in the *Plot Device* tab.

Named Plot Style Tables

With named plot styles, you can define any combination of color, linetype, lineweight, dithering, etc. that you need and give it a name (for example, **New Construction** or **Demolition**). You can define as many named styles as required and apply them in the drawing.

- Using named plot styles can be more involved than using color plot styles, since named styles can be assigned by layer or by object.

- To assign a named plot style for a layer, open the Layer Properties Manager, and select the plot style icon of the layer that you want to set. This is the same way that you assign a layer's color or linetype.

- To assign a named plot style for an object, select the object and access Properties. You can also select the object (it displays grips) and select the plot style in the *Home* tab> Properties panel.

How To: Use a Plot Style Table in a Drawing

Color-Dependent Plot Style Table

1. Create a plot style table that specifies the effect of plot styles.
2. Assign the plot style table in the Page Setup of a layout.

Named Plot Style Table

1. Create a plot style table that specifies the effect of plot styles.
2. Assign the plot style table in the Page Setup in a layout.
3. Assign plot styles to layers or specific objects in the drawing.

Creating Plot Style Tables

You can define the visual effects for your plot styles in plot style tables using the Add Plot Style Table wizard, as shown in Figure 11–1.

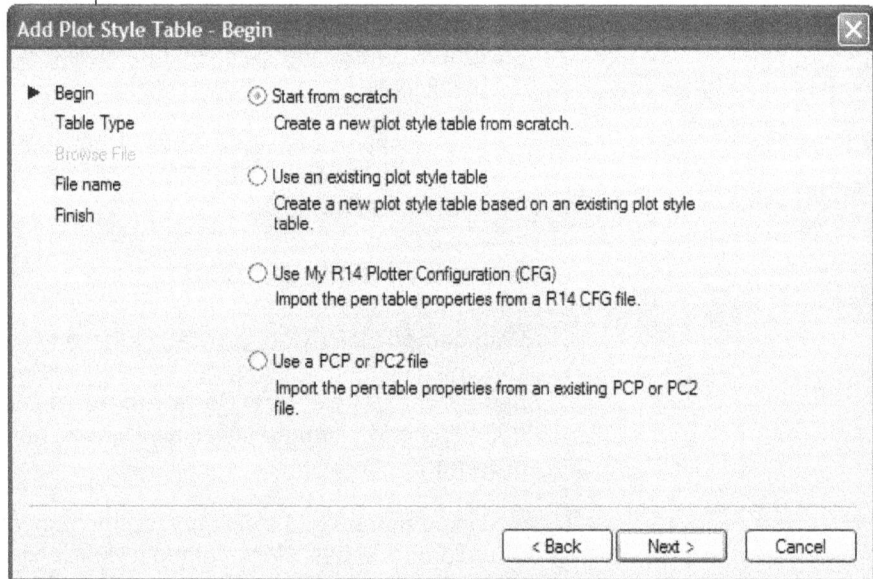

Add Plot Style Table - Begin

► Begin
Table Type
Browse File
File name
Finish

○ Start from scratch
   Create a new plot style table from scratch.

○ Use an existing plot style table
   Create a new plot style table based on an existing plot style table.

○ Use My R14 Plotter Configuration (CFG)
   Import the pen table properties from a R14 CFG file.

○ Use a PCP or PC2 file
   Import the pen table properties from an existing PCP or PC2 file.

[< Back] [Next >] [Cancel]

Figure 11–1

How To: Create a Plot Style Table

1. Open the Page Setup Manager in **Application Menu>Print** by clicking (Page Setup), or by right-clicking on a layout and selecting **Page Setup Manager**.
2. In the *Page setups* area, select a page setup and click **Modify**.
3. In the Page Setup dialog box, in the Plot style table (pen assignments) drop-down list, select **New**, as shown in Figure 11–2.

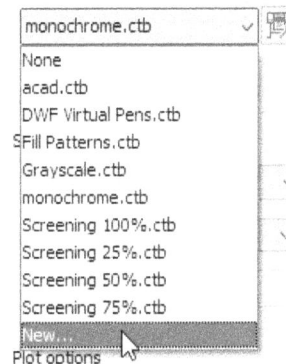

Figure 11–2

4. Select whether to start a new table from scratch or based on an existing table. You can import pen table properties from an R14 CFG file or PCP/PC2 files as the basis of your new table.
5. Select whether to create a **Color-Dependent Plot Style Table** or **Named Plot Style Table**.
6. In the *File name* field, type a name for the plot style table file.
7. Click **Plot Style Table Editor** to edit the table to suit your needs. For named plot style tables, you can add styles and for color plot style tables, you can edit the existing styles.
8. Click **Finish**.

Attaching Plot Style Tables to Layouts

Plot styles are assigned to a layout in the layout's Page Setup. You can also assign a plot style table in the Plot dialog box when you plot.

How To: Attach a Plot Style Table to a Layout

1. Open the Page Setup Manager (right-click on a layout and select **Page Setup Manager**).
2. In the *Page setups* area, select a page setup and click **Modify**.

3. In the Page Setup dialog box, in the Plot style table (pen assignments) drop-down list, select the plot style table that you want to use, as shown in Figure 11–3.

Plot style table (pen assignments)

| monochrome.ctb | ∨ | 🖳 |

☑ Display plot styles

Figure 11–3

4. To display the plot style effects in the drawing window, select **Display plot styles**. The effects display when you use **Regenall**.
5. Click **OK** and close the Plot Style Manager.
6. For named plot styles, after the table has been attached you must also assign plot styles to the layers or objects to which you want the effects to be applied.

Notes

- You can use a different plot style table for each layout, but a table attached to a layout applies to all of the viewports in that layout.

- Several predefined plot style tables are supplied with the software, such as **Grayscale** and **Monochrome**.

- You can edit the selected plot style table in Page Setup by clicking 🖳 (Edit) to the right of the drop-down list.

- If a plot style does not display in the drawing window, you might need to **Preview** the plot first. After you see the changes in the plot, try the **Regenall** command again.

- For plot styles to take effect in the plotted output, verify that the **Plot with plot styles** option is selected in the Plot dialog box.

Practice 11a | Color Plot Styles

Practice Objective

- Create a color plot style table and apply it to a layout.

In this practice, you will create a color plot style table and apply it to a layout, as shown in Figure 11–4.

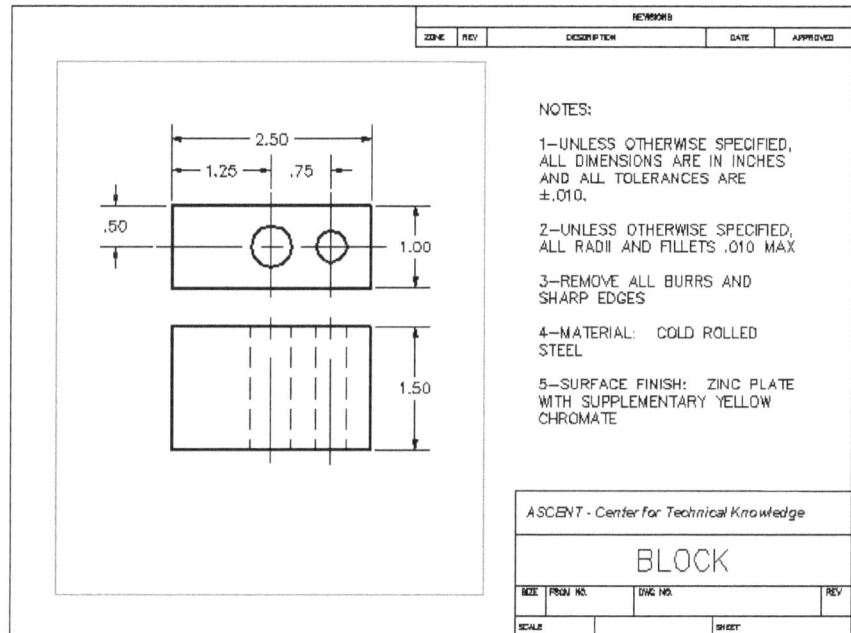

Figure 11–4

- If the effects of the plot styles do not display, use **Plot Preview** to view the effects. The layout view might not always display the effects correctly, especially if you have different plot style tables applied in different layouts.

1. Open **Block-I.dwg** from the practice files folder. It contains two identical layouts **A-Sized** and **A-Sized (2)**.

2. Select **Application Menu>Print>Page Setup** to open the Page Setup Manager.

3. In the *Page setups* area, select **A-Sized** and click **Modify**.

4. Set the *Plot style table (pen assignments)* to **Grayscale.ctb** (one of the tables supplied with the software). Select the **Display plot styles** option and click **OK**. Click **Close** in the Page Setup Manager. The layout should display in grayscale.

5. In the Status Bar, toggle on ▤ (Show/Hide Lineweight). Zoom in to examine the objects. They have the same lineweights.

6. Switch to the second layout (**A-Sized (2)**). A plot style table has not yet been assigned to this layout.

7. Open the Page Setup Manager by right-clicking on the **A-Sized (2)** layout and selecting **Page Setup Manager**.

8. In the *Page setups* area, select **A-Sized (2)** and click **Modify**.

9. In the Page Setup dialog box, in the Plot style table (pen assignments) drop-down list, select **New**.

10. On the Add Color - Dependant Plot Style Table - Begin page, select **Start from scratch** and click **Next >** to continue.

11. On the *File name* page, name the new table **Mechanical** and click **Next >**.

12. Click **Plot Style Table Editor** to edit the new table. Select the Color in the *Plot styles* area and then change the settings in the *Properties* area, as follows:

*If the lineweight is not in the list, click **Edit Lineweights**.*

Plot styles	Color 1	Color 2	Color 4	Color 5	Color 7
Color	Black	Black	Black	Black	Black
Lineweight	0.5000mm	0.3000mm	0.3000mm	0.5000mm	0.7000mm

13. Click **Save & Close** to close the Plot Style Table Editor.

14. Clear the **Use this plot style table for new and pre-AutoCAD <version-language> drawings** option. Click **Finish** to complete the process.

15. Modify the Page Setup for the **A-Sized (2)** layout. Select **Mechanical.ctb** as the *Plot style table (pen assignments)* and select **Display plot styles**. Click **OK** and **Close**.

16. Verify that ▤ (Show/Hide Lineweight) is toggled on.

17. Zoom in to examine the objects, which should all be black with different lineweights for the centerlines, dimension lines, and object lines.

18. Save and close the drawing.

Practice 11b | Named Plot Styles

Practice Objective

- Create a named plot style table and apply the styles to a drawing.

In this practice, you will create a named plot style table and apply the styles in a drawing, as shown in Figure 11–5.

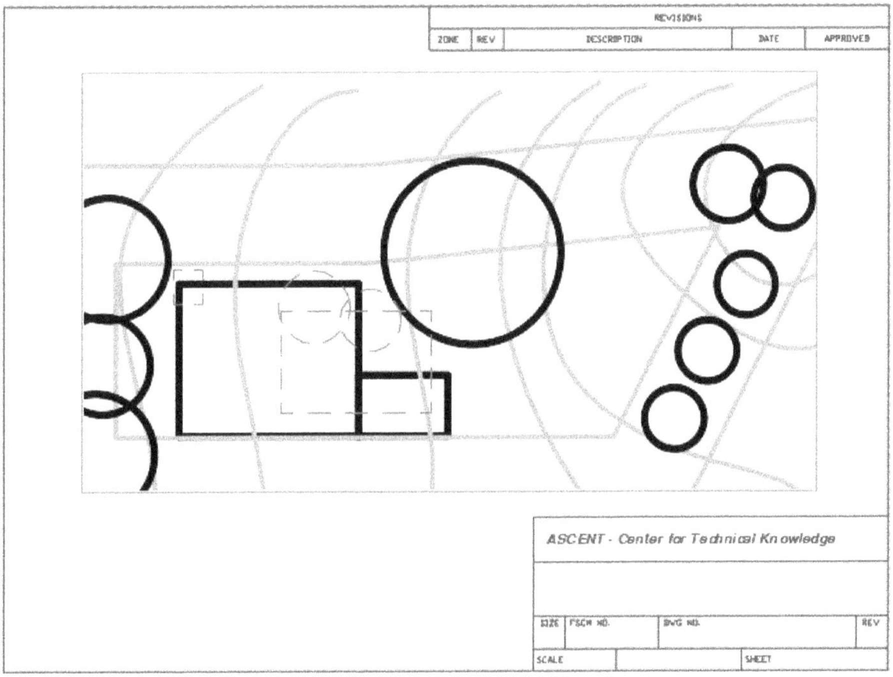

Figure 11–5

1. Open **Lot-F.dwg** from the practice files folder.

2. Open the Page Setup Manager by right-clicking on the *Layout1* tab and selecting **Page Setup Manager**.

3. In the *Page setups* area, select a page setup and click **Modify**.

4. In the Page Setup dialog box, in the Plot style table (pen assignments) drop-down list, select **New**.

5. Start the table from scratch. Click **Next>**.

6. Set the name to **Lot**. Click **Next>**.

7. Click **Plot Style Table Editor** and add the following styles, as shown in Figure 11–6:

*Click **Add Style** to create additional columns for each style and then edit the new style column.*

Name	Guide lines	Finished	Remove
Description	Contour and boundary lines	Final lines	Objects to be removed
Color	Green	Black	Magenta
Linetype	Solid	Solid	Dashed
Lineweight	1.0000mm	1.5800mm	0.0000mm

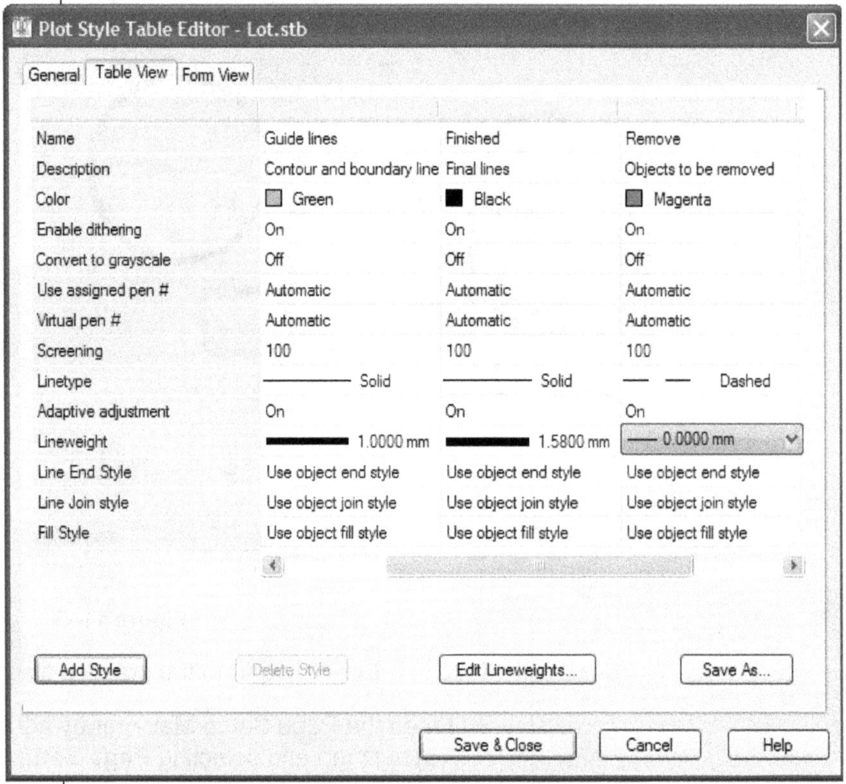

Figure 11–6

8. Click **Save & Close** and **Finish**.

9. In the Page Setup Manager, set the Plot style table to **Lot.stb**. Select **Display plot styles**. Click **OK** and **Close** the Page Setup Manager.

10. Switch to Model space, if required.

11. Open the Layer Properties Manager and apply plot styles to the layers as follows, as shown in Figure 11–7:

Plot Style	Layers
Guide lines	Boundary, Buildable Area, Contours
Finished	New, Road, Trees
Remove	Existing

Status	Name	On	Freeze	Lock	Plot	Color	Linetype	Lineweight	T...	Plot Style
	0					white	Continuous	Default	0	Normal
	Border					blue	Continuous	Default	0	Normal
✓	Boundary					white	PHANTOM	0.50...	0	Guide lines
	Buildable area					yellow	Continuous	Default	0	Guide lines
	Contours					cyan	Continuous	Default	0	Guide lines
	Dimensions					blue	Continuous	Default	0	Normal
	Existing					red	Continuous	Default	0	Remove
	New					white	Continuous	0.35...	0	Finished
	Road					magenta	Continuous	Default	0	Finished
	Text					cyan	Continuous	Default	0	Normal
	Trees					green	Continuous	Default	0	Finished
	Viewports					8	Continuous	Default	0	Normal
	Walls					white	Continuous	Default	0	Normal

Figure 11–7

12. Switch to **Layout1**. Note the colors and lineweights of the different objects in the viewport. Double-click in the viewport to switch to Model Space.

13. Type **regenall**. The plot styles are applied to the objects in the viewport.

14. In the Status Bar, toggle on (Show/Hide Lineweight) and note that the lineweights were applied by the plot styles.

15. Select the two trees (circles) that overlap the building and use Properties to change the plot style of the selected objects to **Remove**. They become magenta and dashed, as defined by this plot style.

16. Switch back to Paper Space.

17. Save and close the drawing.

11.2 eTransmit

The **eTransmit** utility (shown in Figure 11–8) packs an open drawing with all of its associated files (such as drawing reference files, images, fonts, etc.) into a single compressed file or transmittal set. This makes it easy to email all of the files associated with a project to clients, partners, members of a design team, etc.

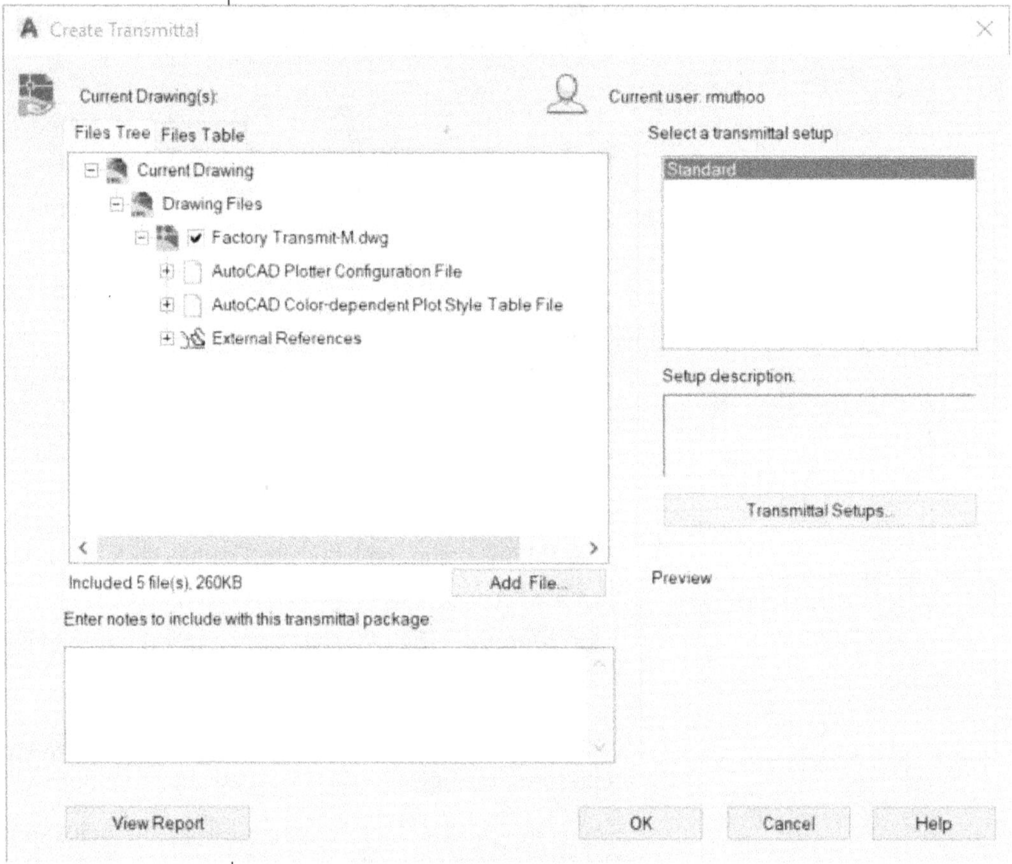

Figure 11–8

- It is recommended that you save all open files before using the **eTransmit** utility to pack them.

- The *Files Tree* tab lists the actual drawing files and other files that are going to be packaged. The files are listed hierarchically under the current drawing with font maps, image files, plotter configuration files, and drawing reference files listed in separate categories.

- The *Files Table* tab lists all of the files that are going to be packaged alphabetically, as shown in Figure 11–9. You can use **Add File** to include other files in the transmittal set.

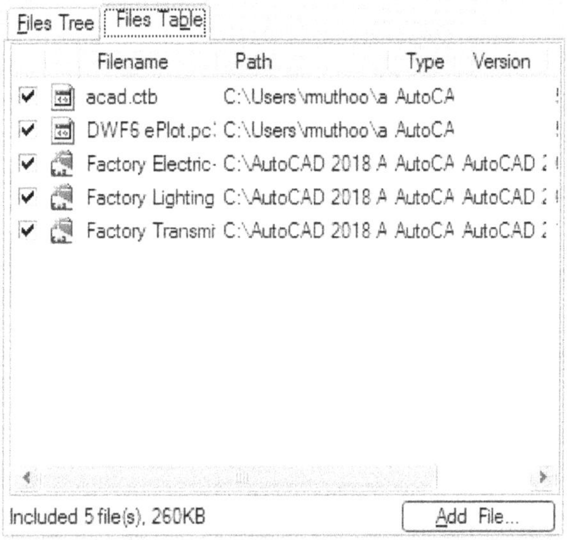

Figure 11–9

- **eTransmit** works well with Sheet Set Manager.

How To: Create a Transmittal Set

1. Open a drawing that you want to transmit. Save the file if any changes are made.
2. In **Application Menu>Publish**, click ▊ (**eTransmit**).
3. The Create Transmittal dialog box opens displaying a list of all of the associated files.
4. Add additional files as required.
5. Select a Transmittal Setup (you can create a new one as required).
6. Add notes in the *Notes* area as required.
7. Click **View Report** to see details of the transmittal. The text of the report is included in the transmittal set.
8. Click **OK** to create the transmittal set. The next steps depend on the options selected in the Transmittal Setup file. You might be prompted for a filename or to override another transmittal file.

Transmittal Setups

You can create *Transmittal Setups* with specific properties and save them to easily generate future transmittals using the same properties. If you often use eTransmit, this is a big time-saver.

How To: Create a Transmittal Setup

1. In the Create Transmittal dialog box, click **Transmittal Setups**.
2. In the Transmittal Setups dialog box (shown in Figure 11–10), click **New** to create a new setup.
   - Or select a setup you want to change and click **Modify**.

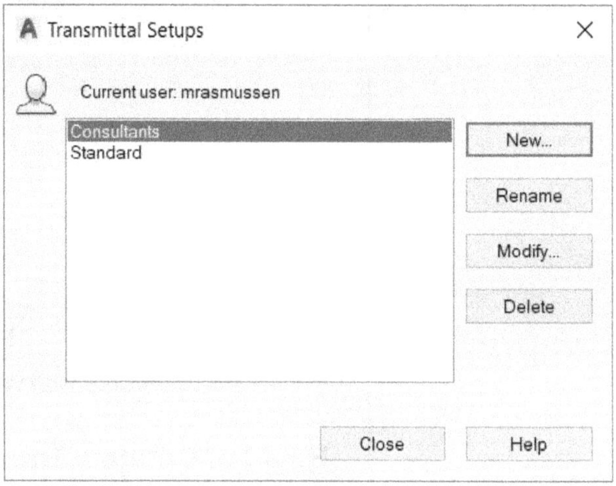

Figure 11–10

3. If creating a new setup, you are prompted for a new name, as shown in Figure 11–11. A Transmittal Setup uses an existing setup style as a starting point.

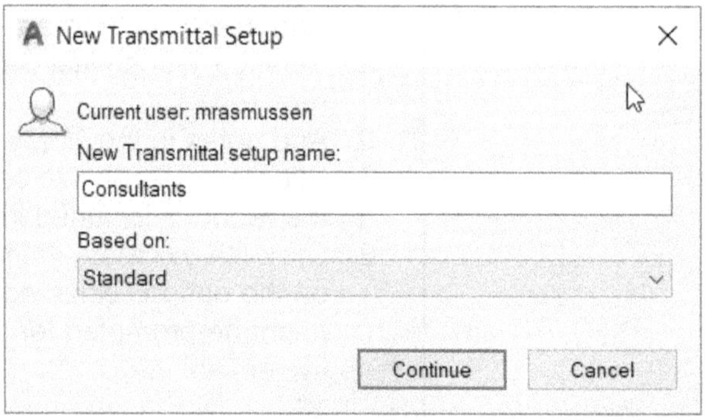

Figure 11–11

4. In the Modify Transmittal Setup dialog box, define the settings and options for the setup, as shown in Figure 11–12.

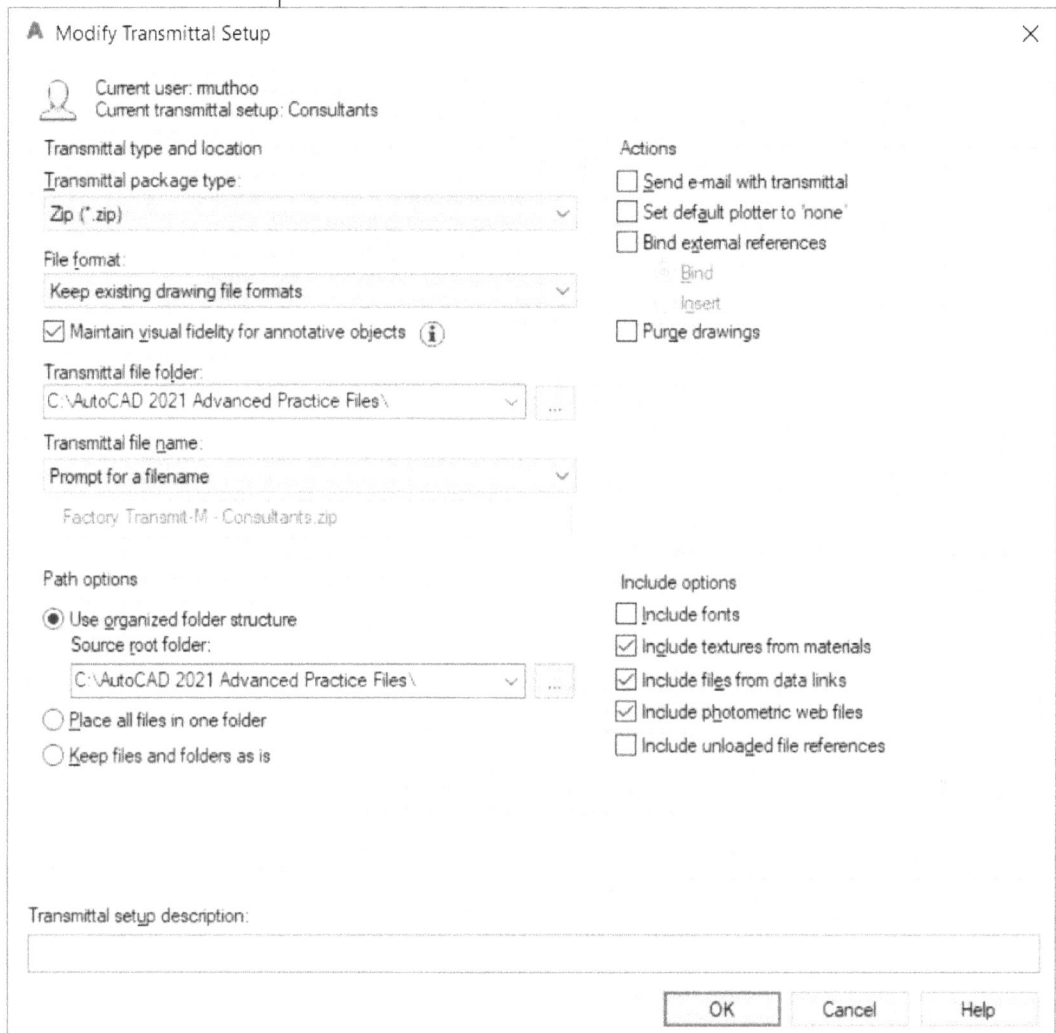

Figure 11–12

5. Click **OK** and then **Close** to create the setup. The new setup becomes the default setup for the current transmittal set.

Transmittal Setup Options

Transmittal package type	Select the type of file for the transmittal set: **Folder:** Creates a set of uncompressed files in a folder. **Self-extracting executable:** Creates a compressed .EXE file. **Zip:** Creates a compressed Zip file.
File format	Specifies the file format for the drawings. Select to keep the existing file format or to save in the AutoCAD® software (and the AutoCAD LT® software) 2018, 2013, 2010, 2007, 2004, or 2000 formats.
Maintain visual fidelity for annotative objects	Separates annotative objects and saves them as scaled representations in blocks into new separate layers (for software versions that are before 2010).
Transmittal file folder	The folder in which the file(s) are created. You can click ⬚ (Browse) and specify a folder.
Transmittal file name	You can have the transmittal set prompt you for a filename, overwrite the filename, or increment the filename as required. By default, the name is the <name of the drawing - name of the transmittal setup>.
Use organized folder structure	If selected, you can also specify the *Source* root folder.
Place all files in one folder	If selected, all of the files are placed in a single target folder when installed.
Keep files and folders as is	If selected, files from the transmittal are installed in the directory structure that is used on the source computer.
Send email with transmittal	Opens your email application when a transmittal is created.
Set default plotter to 'none'	Sets the default plotter to **none**.
Bind external references	Inserts all of the external references to the base drawing file and detaches the drawing reference files.
Prompt for password	Enables you to specify a password to be required to open the transmittal set.
Purge Drawings	Runs the **Purge** command on drawings before including them in the transmittal set.

Include fonts	Includes all of the font files. If you know that the company you are sending the file to uses the same fonts, you can save space in the set by not sending them.
Include textures from materials	Includes textures with materials that are attached to faces.
Include files from data links	Includes external files that are referenced by data links.
Include photometric web files	Includes photometric web files that are associated with web lights in the drawing.
Include unloaded file references	Includes all of the unloaded referenced files in the set and keeps them unloaded in the package.
Transmittal setup description	Type a description for this setup.

Practice 11c

eTransmit

Practice Objective

- Create a compressed transmittal set of all of the files related to a drawing, using the **eTransmit** command.

In this practice, you will use **eTransmit** to create a compressed transmittal set of all of the files related to a drawing, as shown in Figure 11–13.

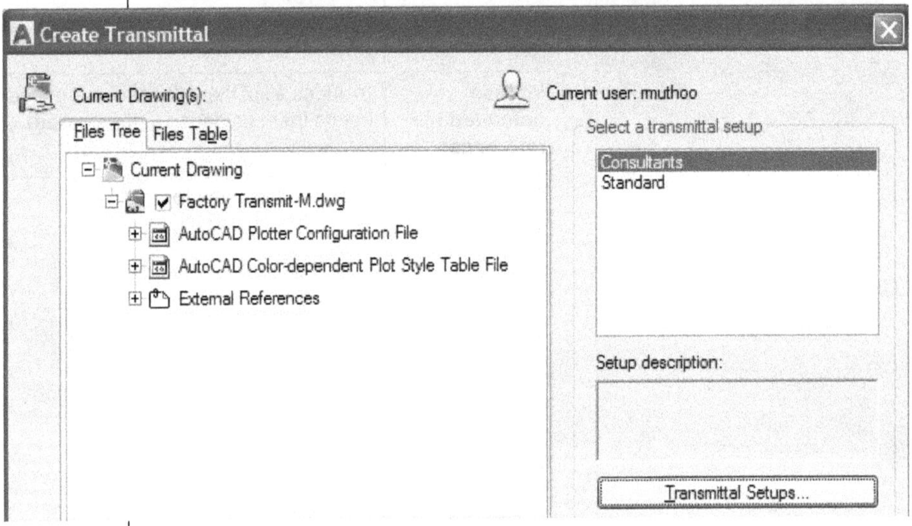

Figure 11–13

1. Open **Factory Transmit-M.dwg** from the practice files folder.

2. Open the External References palette. Verify that **Factory Electric-Adv-M.dwg** and **Factory Lighting-Adv-M.dwg** are attached, as shown in Figure 11–14.

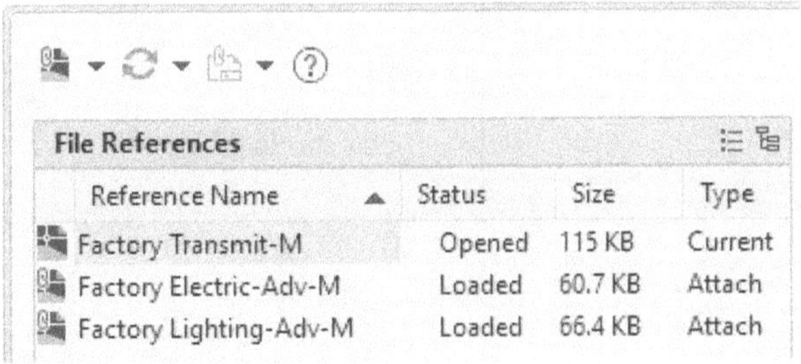

Figure 11–14

If prompted, save the drawing.

3. Start the **eTransmit** command (in the Application Menu, expand **Publish** and click 🖺 (eTransmit)).

4. In the Create Transmittal dialog box, click **Transmittal Setups**.

5. Click **New** to create a new transmittal setup (based on **Standard**) named **Consultants**. Click **Continue**.

6. In the Modify Transmittal Setup dialog box, for the *Transmittal package type*, verify that **Zip (*.zip)** is selected.

7. For the *Transmittal file folder*, select the practice files folder. Leave the default settings for the other options.

8. Click **OK** and then click **Close** to create the setup. Ensure that **Consultants** is current.

9. In the Create Transmittal dialog box, click **View Report** to preview the report that is going to be generated. Click **Close** to close the View Transmittal Report dialog box.

10. Click **OK** and save the transmittal set in the practice files folder.

11. Open Windows Explorer and, in the practice files folder, locate **Factory Transmit-M - Consultants.zip**. Double-click on this file to open the zip file. Extract the files to *C:\Factory Files*.

12. Navigate to the folder in which you extracted the files and note the files that were included. Double-click on **Factory Transmit-M.txt** to open the report.

SECTION 5

Annotation Techniques

Exam Objective	Chapter(s)
5.1 Apply markup tools	
5.1.a Create and modify revision clouds	Ch. 12
5.1.b Use wipeouts to mask underlying objects in specific areas of a drawing	Ch. 2
5.1.c Compare two drawings for differences	Ch. 12
5.2 Manage Hatch or Fill options	
5.2.a Specify Hatch and Fill options	Ch. 13
5.2.b Recreate the boundary around a selected Hatch or Fill pattern	Ch. 13
5.3 Format text and tables	
5.3.a Apply text and multiline text properties	Ch. 14
5.3.b Create, modify, and apply text styles	Ch. 17
5.3.c Create and adjust text columns	Ch. 14
5.3.d Insert tables and manipulate cell data	Ch. 15
5.3.e Use fields in text and tables	Ch. 15
5.3.f Insert symbols from the character map	Ch. 14
5.3.g Check the spelling of text and dimension annotation	Ch. 14

Exam Objective	Chapter(s)
5.4 Adjust multileaders	
5.4.a Create and modify multileaders	Ch. 14
5.4.b Add and remove leaders	Ch. 14
5.4.c Align and collect leaders	Ch. 14
5.5 Create and edit annotation with advanced dimensioning techniques	
5.5.a Create and modify dimension styles	Ch. 17
5.5.b Create multiple dimensions with a single command	Ch. 16
5.5.c Set the dimension layer	Ch. 16
5.5.d Associate or re-associate dimensions to objects	Ch. 16
5.5.e Break and restore dimension and extension lines	Ch. 16
5.5.f Adjust the spacing between dimensions	Ch. 16
5.6 Apply annotative properties and styles	
5.6.a Understand annotative properties and styles as they pertain to objects	Ch. 17
5.6.b Define and apply annotative object styles	Ch. 17
5.6.c Control the annotative scale of an object or viewport	Ch. 17
5.6.d Add annotative scales to an object	Ch. 17

Markup Tools

Exam Objectives Covered in This Chapter

- 5.1.a Create and modify revision clouds
- 5.1.c Compare two drawings for differences

Note: The objective *5.1.b Use wipeouts to mask underlying objects in specific areas of a drawing* is covered in *2.3 Controlling the Draw Order*.

12.1 Revision Clouds

Revision clouds are cloud-shaped objects that can be used to designate areas that you need to draw attention to in the drawing. The revision cloud creation options are located in the *Annotate* tab>Markup panel, as shown in Figure 12–1.

Figure 12–1

The creation options available include:

• Rectangular
• Polygonal
• Freehand

You can also turn an object into a revision cloud and any revision cloud option can be used for the purpose.

How To: Create a Rectangular Revision Cloud

1. In the *Annotate* tab>Markup panel, in the Revision Cloud flyout, click (Rectangular).
2. In the drawing, click the first corner of the rectangle to start the revision cloud.
3. In the drawing, click the opposite corner of the rectangle (as shown in Figure 12–2) to complete the revision cloud.

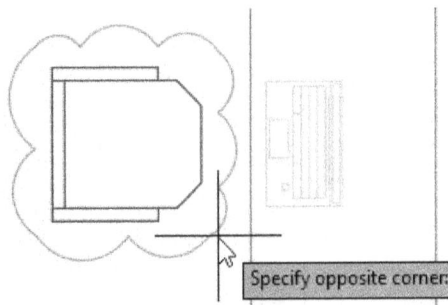

Figure 12–2

How To: Create a Polygonal Revision Cloud

1. In the Annotate tab>Markup panel, in the Revision Cloud flyout, click ⬡ (Polygonal).
2. In the drawing, click the first point of the polygon to start the revision cloud.
3. In the drawing, click the second point of the polygon.
4. Continue clicking points as required, as shown in Figure 12–3.

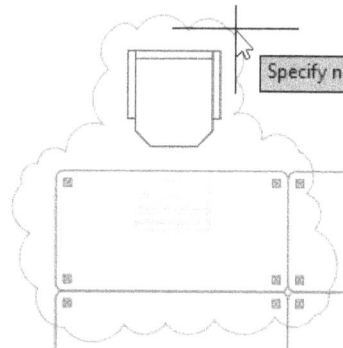

Figure 12–3

5. Press <Enter> to complete the revision cloud.

How To: Create a Freehand Revision Cloud

1. In the *Annotate* tab>Markup panel, in the Revision Cloud flyout, click ☁ (Freehand).
2. In the drawing, click to start the revision cloud.
3. Move the mouse freely to draw the revision cloud.
4. Move the mouse close to the beginning point to complete the revision cloud. It should automatically close itself.
    • Alternatively, if you prefer to have an open revision cloud, left-click the end point and press <Enter> to end the command without closing the revision cloud object.

How To: Create a Revision Cloud from an Object

1. In the *Annotate* tab>Markup panel, click 🔲 (Revision Cloud).
2. Select **Object** from the <Down Arrow> menu (as shown in Figure 12–4) or in the Command line.

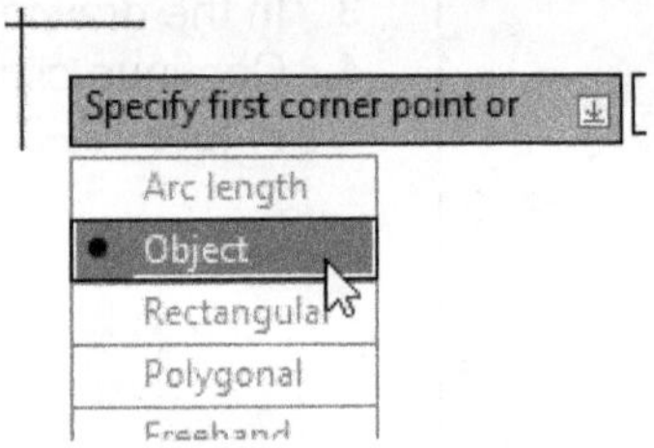

Specify first corner point or 🔽
Arc length
● Object
Rectangula▸
Polygonal
Freehand

Figure 12–4

3. In the drawing, select the object. A preview of the revision cloud is displayed.
4. Select **Yes** or **No** to the set direction of the revision cloud arcs and end the command. The revision cloud is created, as shown in Figure 12–5.

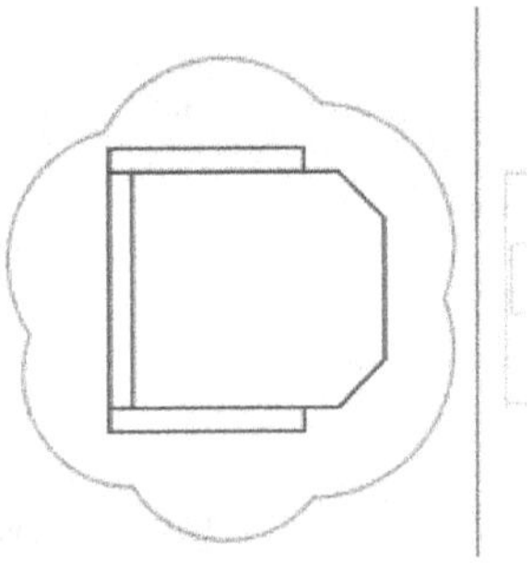

From Object (Circle)

Figure 12–5

Modifying Revision Clouds

You can edit revision clouds using their grips. When you select a revision cloud, its grips are displayed. You can click and drag the grip to change the shape of the revision cloud, as shown in Figure 12–6.

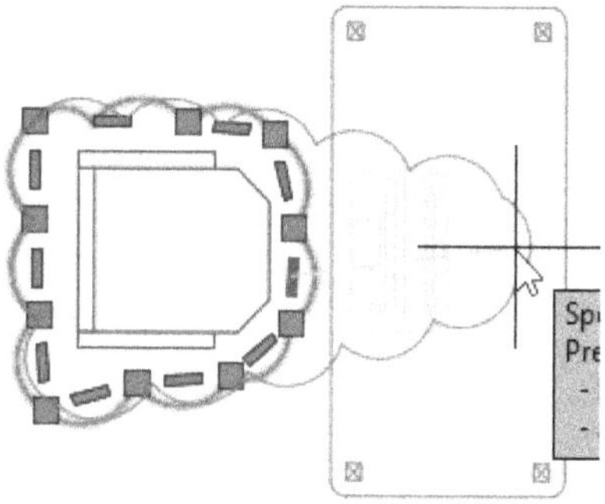

Figure 12–6

- If a revision cloud is created by converting an object, the grips for the original object display, as shown for the revision cloud created from a circle object in Figure 12–7.

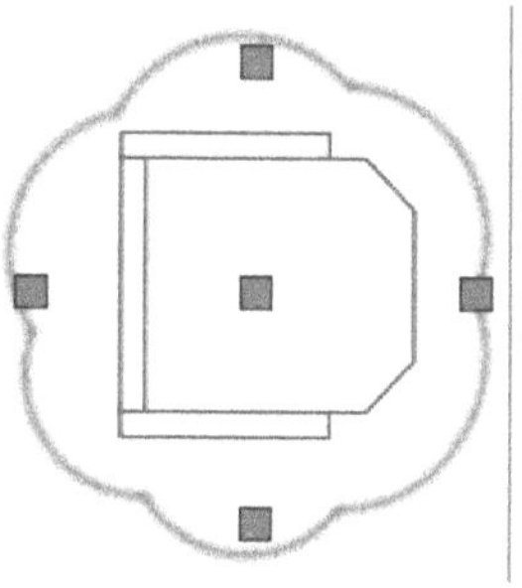

Figure 12–7

- If the revision cloud is created using the rectangular or polygonal methods, grips are displayed at multiple locations, as shown in Figure 12–8.

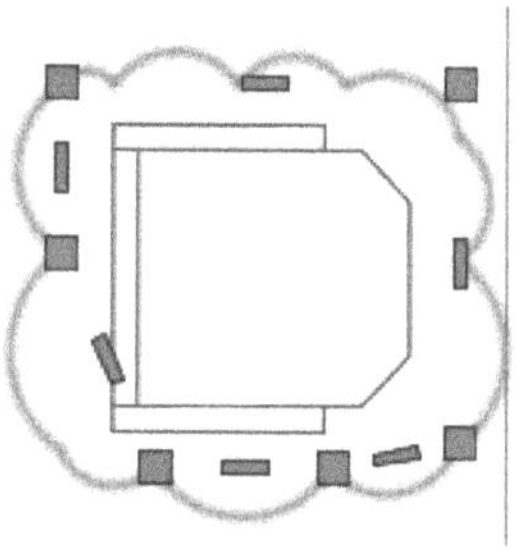

Figure 12–8

- You can change the arc length of the arcs in the revision cloud from the Properties palette. Select the revision cloud and in the *Misc* area, enter a new value for **Arc Length**, as shown in Figure 12–9.

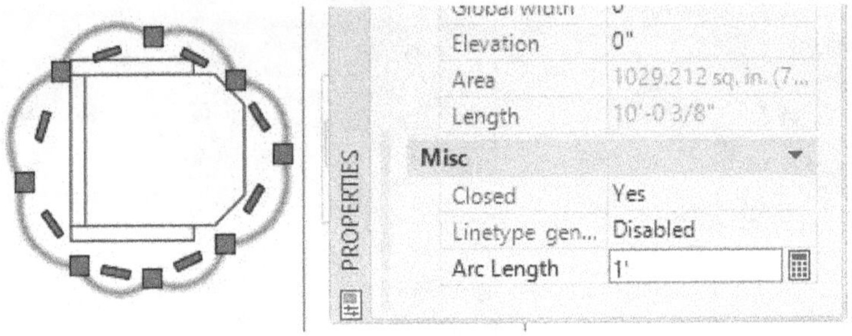

Figure 12–9

12.2 Compare Drawings

Shared files have a higher chance of edits made by one user being overwritten by another user who might be making edits at the same time. The **Drawing Compare** command provides a way to quickly highlight the differences between two versions of the same drawing file or two different drawing files.

You can also modify the drawing while in the compare state. While in compare state, the changes that you make are compared in real-time and the differences are dynamically highlighted.

The software compares documents by displaying the objects that are unique to the open drawing in one color, and the objects unique to the comparison drawing in another color. The objects that are common in both the drawings are displayed in gray. This enables you to easily visualize the differences and import the required changes. It also places a revision cloud around the changes, as shown in Figure 12–10.

Only drawing objects are supported during the compare process. If there are coordination models, underlays (PDF, DWF, and DGN), Map 3D GIS objects, images, OLE objects, or point clouds in the drawing, they are ignored during the comparison process.

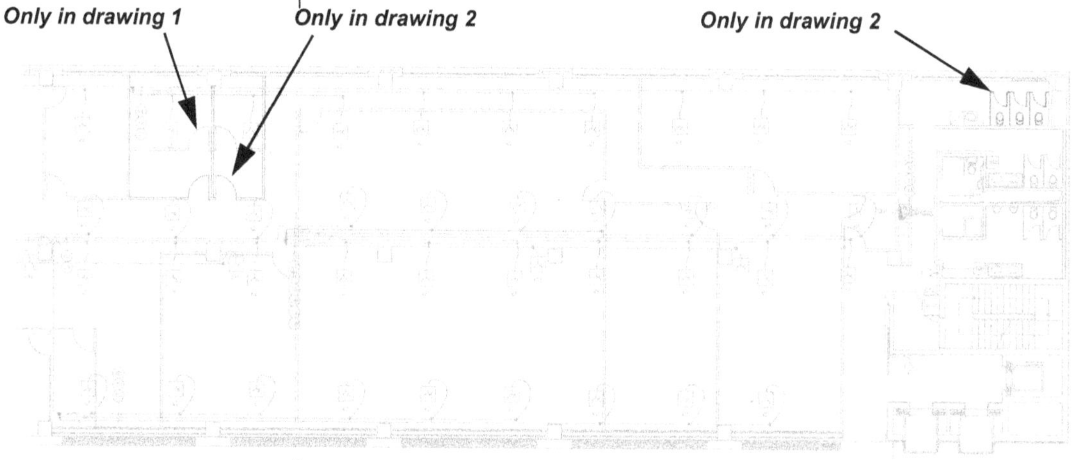

Only in drawing 1 *Only in drawing 2* *Only in drawing 2*

Figure 12–10

How To: Compare Two Drawings

1. Open one of the drawings that you want to compare.
2. In the *Collaborate* tab>Compare panel, click ⊞ (DWG Compare).
3. In the Select a drawing to compare dialog box, select the other drawing that you want to compare to the current drawing.
4. Review and edit the comparisons in the open drawing.

Compare Toolbar

The comparison is displayed in the Compare window, which is enclosed in a thick blue border. The Compare toolbar (shown in Figure 12–11) displays in the Compare window with the drawings displayed in the compare state.

Figure 12–11

- The ⚲ (On/Off) icon controls the visibility of the objects that are different and highlighted in either one of the comparison colors.

- To jump and zoom to the previous or next comparative difference, click on the ⇐/ ⇒ (Previous/Next) arrows.

- Click ⎘ (Import Objects) to import the changes from the compared drawing into the current drawing. Once the objects are imported, they are no longer highlighted in the compared drawing color, and are displayed in gray.

- ⎘ (Export Snapshot) creates a new drawing that contains all of the similarities and differences in both of the drawings, maintaining the colors of the differences.

- Select ⚙ (Settings) to display the detailed tools that can be used on the comparison objects, as shown in Figure 12–12.

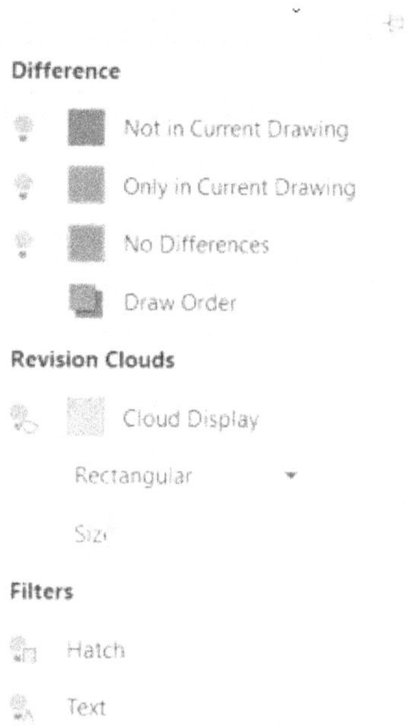

Difference

Not in Current Drawing

Only in Current Drawing

No Differences

Draw Order

Revision Clouds

Cloud Display

Rectangular

Size

Filters

Hatch

Text

Figure 12–12

- Using the color blocks, you can customize the color of the compared objects.

- You can toggle the display of a revision cloud around the different objects using (Revision Cloud). You can set these revision clouds to be either **Rectangular** or **Polygonal** using the Revision Cloud drop-down list, as shown in Figure 12–13.

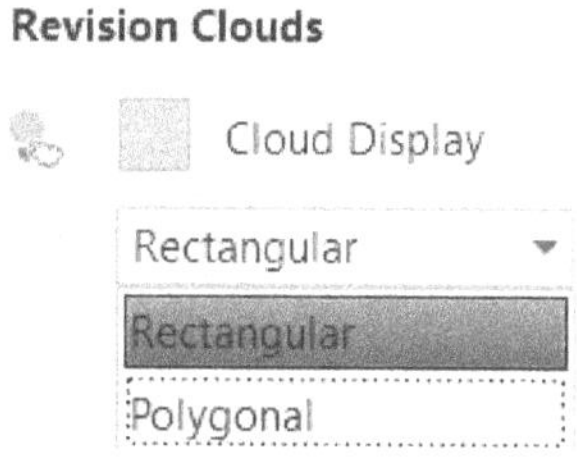

Revision Clouds

Cloud Display

Rectangular

Rectangular

Polygonal

Figure 12–13

Practice 12a | Compare Drawings

Practice Objectives

- Compare two versions of the same drawing file for differences.
- Use the various Compare options provided.

In this practice, you will compare two drawings to find the differences shown in Figure 12–14.

Only in drawing 1   *Only in drawing 2*   *Only in drawing 2*

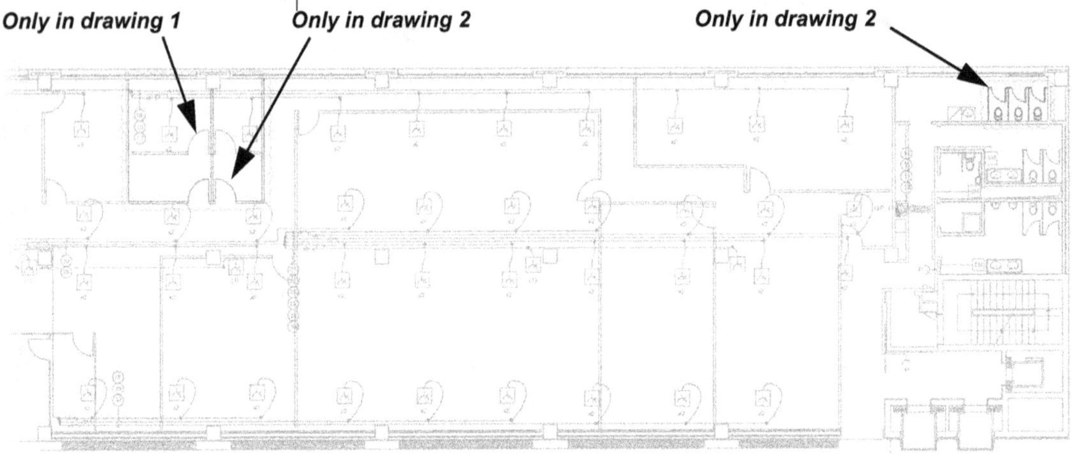

Figure 12–14

Task 1 - Compare two versions of the same drawing file.

1. In the practice files folder, open **Compare-1.dwg**. This is the DWG1 file. In the top right area, note that only the sink is displayed.

2. In the *Collaborate* tab>Compare panel, click [icon] (DWG Compare).

3. In the Select a drawing to compare dialog box, navigate to the practice files folder and open **Compare 2.dwg**.

4. Note that the comparison is displayed in the Compare window in the current drawing (**Compare-1.dwg**). Review the comparison and note the differences shown in Figure 12–14.
   - Green objects are specific to **Compare-1.dwg**, red objects are specific to **Compare-2.dwg**, and common objects are displayed in gray.

5. Draw a circle anywhere in the drawing and note that it is drawn in green (as shown in Figure 12–15) because it is being dynamically compared and is drawn in the current drawing (**Compare-1.dwg**).

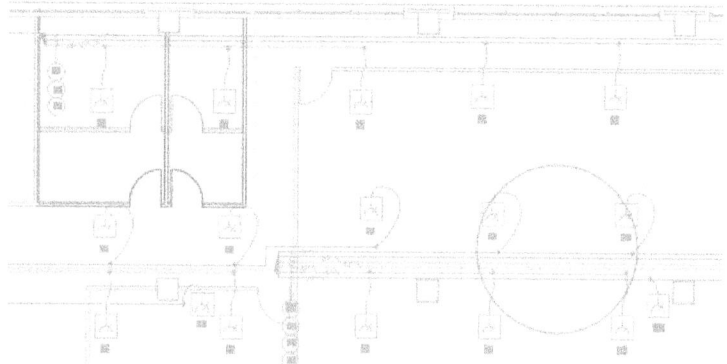

Figure 12–15

Task 2 - Use the Compare options.

1. In the DWG Compare toolbar, click ⚙ (Settings) to display the detailed tools and pin it for further use.

2. Click on the color block beside **Not in Current Drawing**. In the Select Color dialog box, select the color blue and click **OK**. Note that the red objects have changed to blue in the drawing.

3. In the Settings display of the DWG Compare toolbar, click ⚌ beside **Only in Current Drawing** and **No Differences** to toggle off their display. Note that only the objects that are specific to **Compare-2.dwg** are displayed in the drawing, as shown in Figure 12–16.

Figure 12–16

4. Click ⚌ beside **Only in Current Drawing** and **No Differences**, to toggle on their display.

5. In the Settings display of the DWG Compare toolbar, ensure that ![icon] (Revision Cloud) is set to **On**. In the drawing, note that the colored areas have a yellow rectangular revision cloud around them.

6. Zoom into the left revision cloud and note that the shape is a rectangle.

7. In the Revision Clouds drop-down list, select **Polygonal**. Note that a revision cloud changes its shape and displays around the colored objects. Select the revision cloud to highlight it, as shown in Figure 12–17.

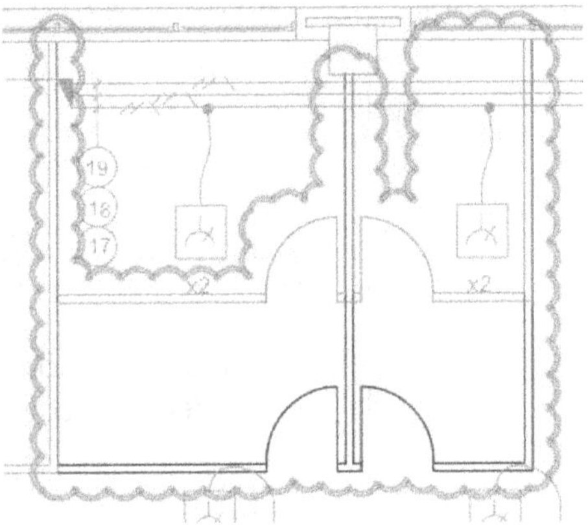

Figure 12–17

8. Press <Esc> to exit the selection of the revision cloud.

9. In the DWG Compare toolbar, click ![icon] (Import Objects).

10. Using a selection window, select the 3 toilet stalls (along the right side of the drawing). Press <Enter> to complete the selection. Note that the objects change from blue to gray indicating that they are now a part of both the drawings.

11. In the DWG Compare toolbar, click ![icon] (Exit Compare). The drawing ends compare mode with only those objects that were imported from the other drawing added to the current drawing. All other comparison changes are discarded.

12. Save and close **Compare-1.dwg**.

Hatching

Exam Objectives Covered in This Chapter

- 5.2.a Specify Hatch and Fill options
- 5.2.b Recreate the boundary around a selected Hatch or Fill pattern

13.1 Hatching

Hatching is a pattern of lines or shapes that is used to distinguish certain areas of a drawing from other areas. For example, hatching might be used to indicate which rooms on a floor plan are occupied by a specific department, as shown in Figure 13–1. In mechanical design, hatching is typically used to indicate section views. The AutoCAD® software contains many predefined hatch patterns.

*There are two ways to apply hatching: Tool Palettes and the **Hatch** command.*
Many patterns for specific applications can be purchased from commercial third-party developers.

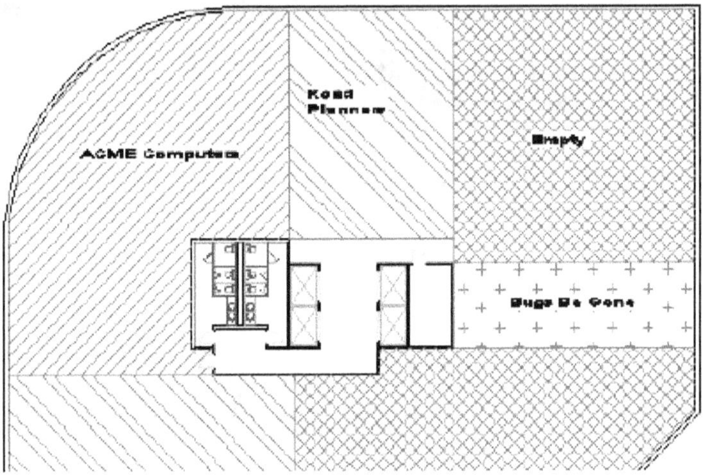

Figure 13–1

- Hatching should be placed on a separate hatch layer so that it can be easily toggled off or frozen.

- Hatching can be annotative, so you should apply it after a viewport has been prepared and scaled.

Applying a Hatch: Tool Palettes

Tool Palettes (*Hatches and Fills* tab) contains several hatch patterns that can be used for hatching a closed area in a drawing.

- Click on a pattern. It is attached to the cursor, as shown in Figure 13–2. Move the cursor inside the closed area that you want to hatch. A preview of the hatch in the area displays. Click to hatch the area.

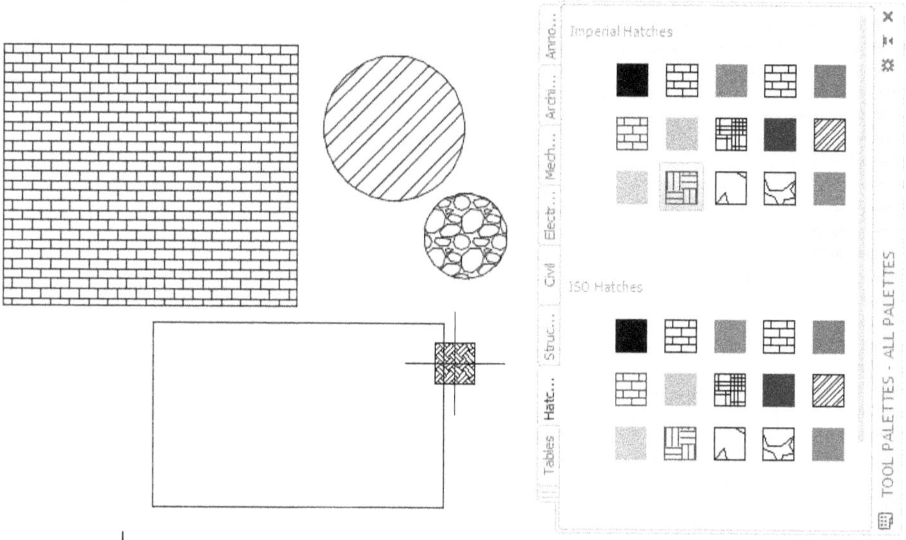

Figure 13–2

- The area for hatching should be completely bounded, with no gaps.

- Closed objects and text inside the bounded area (known as *islands*) are not normally hatched.

*In the Tool Palettes, if the tab is hidden, click on the area just below the bottom tab and select **Hatches and Fills**.*

- The default *Hatches and Fills* tab in Tool Palettes comes with hatches that are scaled for Imperial and ISO (Metric) drawings, and several gradient hatches, as shown in Figure 13–2.

- By default, the hatch patterns provided are not annotative. You can change that after the hatch has been applied to the object by opening its Properties palette, and changing *Annotative* to **Yes**, as shown in Figure 13–3.

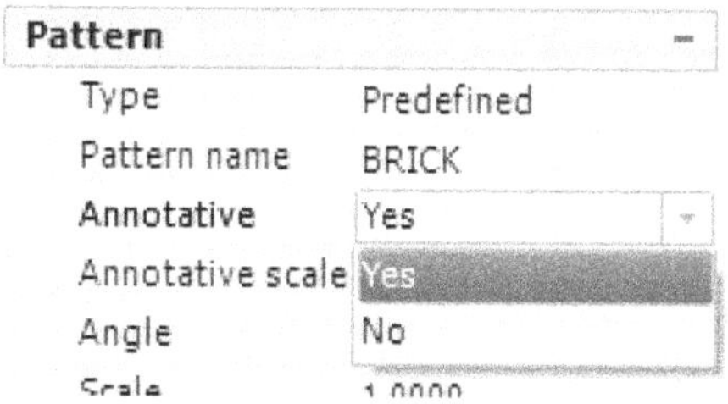

Figure 13–3

Applying a Hatch: Hatch Command

The **Hatch** command provides more control and options than hatching using Tool Palettes. Using this command, you can select from many different patterns and adjust the scale or angle of the hatch as you apply it, as shown in Figure 13–4.

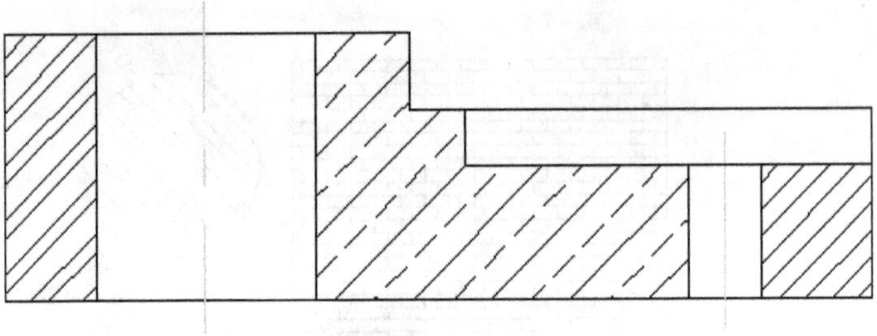

Figure 13–4

How To: Hatch Objects

1. In the *Home* tab>Draw panel, click (Hatch), located in the Hatch flyout.
2. In the *Hatch Creation* contextual tab, set the *Pattern*, *Scale*, *Angle*, and *Transparency*, as shown in Figure 13–5.

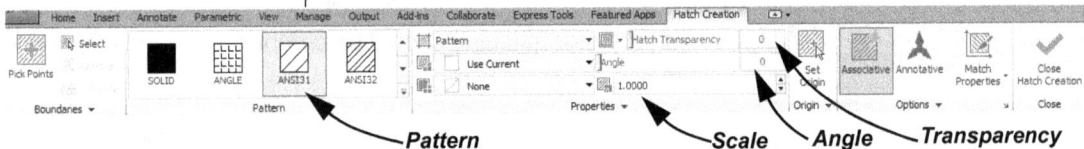

Figure 13–5

3. Click (Pick Points) and hover the cursor inside the bounded area to preview the hatch. Click to add the hatch or modify the settings until the correct results display in the preview.

    *   You can also click (Select Boundary Objects) and select a closed object or group of objects that form a closed boundary.
    *   If the hatch cannot be created due to invalid hatch boundaries, an alert box opens, as shown in Figure 13–6.

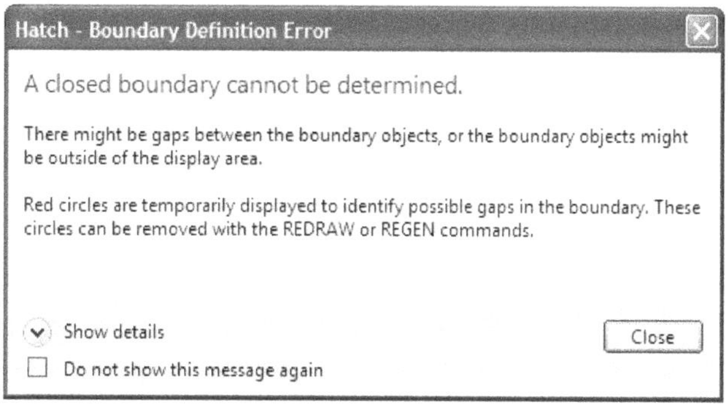

Figure 13–6

- Click ▨ (Remove Boundaries) to select objects in the drawing to remove them from the selection.

4. Press <Enter> or click ✓ (Close Hatch Editor) to end the command.

Hatch Pattern and Properties

If your ribbon is reduced in size due to the size of the interface, you might need to expand

▨ *(Hatch Pattern) in the Pattern panel first.*

In the *Hatch Creation* contextual tab, you can set the *Pattern*, *Scale*, *Angle*, and *Transparency* of the hatch.

Pattern Panel

In the Pattern panel, select a pattern from the list. You can expand the list by clicking ▾, as shown in Figure 13–7.

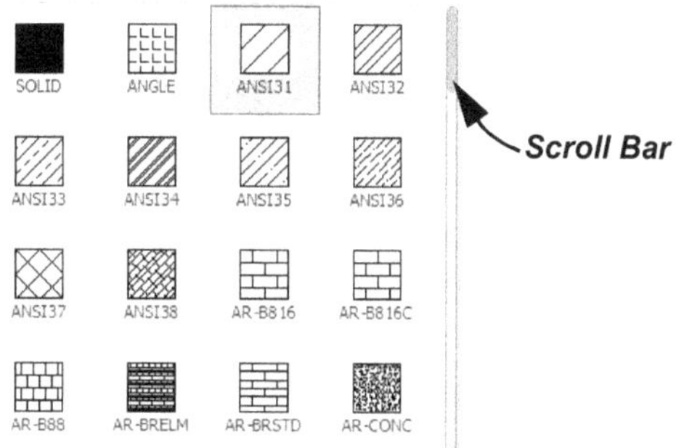

Figure 13–7

Properties Panel

In the Properties panel, you can set the *Hatch Type*, *Hatch Color*, *Background Color*, *Hatch Transparency*, *Hatch Angle*, *Hatch Pattern Scale*, and *Hatch Layer Override*. These enable you to customize how the hatch displays in the drawing.

Hatch Type

The type of hatch can be **Solid**, **Gradient**, **Pattern**, or **User defined**, as shown in Figure 13–8. Select the hatch type, and then select a pattern in the Pattern list.

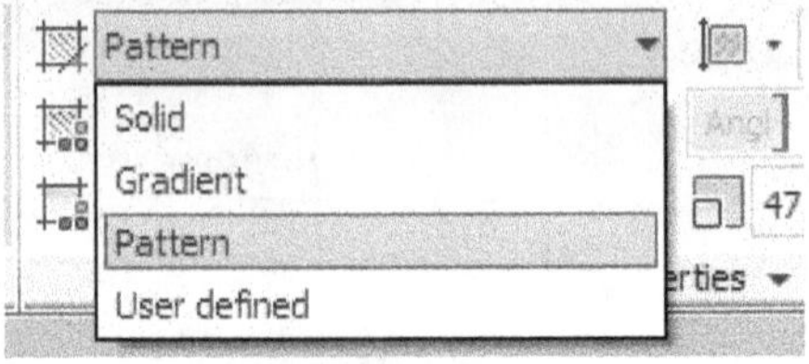

Figure 13–8

- User-defined patterns are parallel lines with a spacing and angle that you specify. You can create a cross-hatch by

  expanding the Properties panel and clicking ⊞ (Double).

- To create a solid fill, set the *Hatch Type* to **Solid** and the *Hatch Color* to **ByLayer** or a color.

- To create a gradient fill, set the *Hatch Type* to **Gradient** and set the colors for *Gradient Color 1* and *Gradient Color 2*.

Hatch Color

Use this option to set the color of the hatch. You can select a specific color, use the current color, or set the color to **ByLayer**, where the color of the hatch is controlled by the color of the layer.

Background Color

Use this option to add a background color to the hatch. For example, if you have two hatches of the same pattern, you can set a different background color for each one.

Hatch Transparency

Use this option to control the level of transparency for the hatch. This is useful for displaying objects below the hatch, such as furniture, walls, or annotations. You can use the slider or enter the value, as shown in Figure 13–9. You can also expand

▦ ▾ (Transparency Values) and set the transparency to **ByLayer Transparency** or **ByBlock Transparency**.

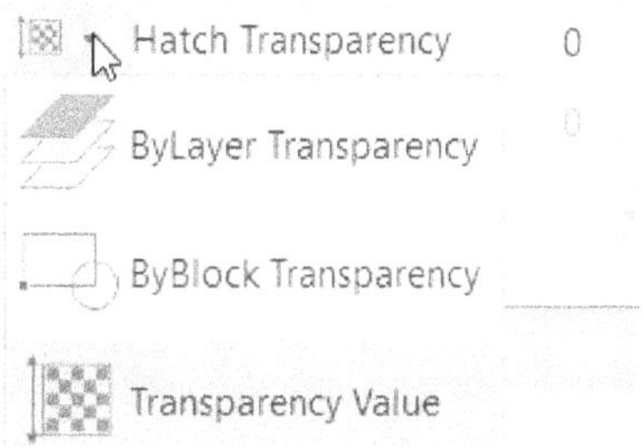

Figure 13–9

Hatch Angle

The *Hatch Angle* sets the rotation angle of the hatch pattern. An angle of **0** creates the pattern at its original angle. Increase the value to get an angled pattern, as shown in Figure 13–10.

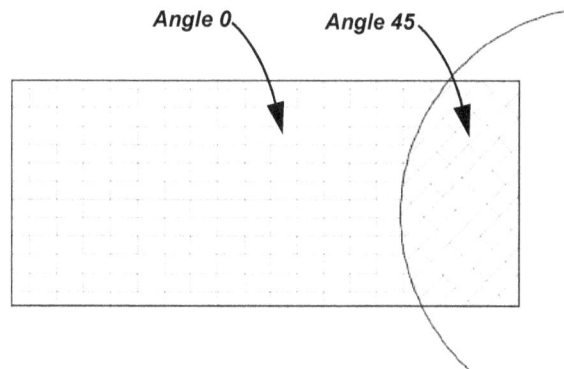

Figure 13–10

Hatch Pattern Scale

The *Hatch Pattern Scale* controls the space between the lines in the pattern (which are normally based on the drawing's plot scale factor). Enter the scale required to correctly display the hatch pattern so that its lines and spaces display clearly.

- If you are working in a viewport and using Annotative scaling, you should expand the Properties panel and click

  (Relative to Paper Space). It calculates the scale based on the viewport scale. **Annotative** maintains the hatch scale relative to Paper Space if the viewport scale is changed.

Hatch Layer Override

You can set the layer on which the hatch is placed, overriding the current layer.

- You can use the **HPLAYER** system variable to set the layer on which the hatch is placed, overriding the current layer.

- If the layer you want to use does not exist in the drawing, type the new layer name. The next time you start the **Hatch** command, the layer is created and the hatch is placed on it.

Hatch Origin

The hatch origin determines how the hatch fits into the selected area. If you are using a pattern (such as brick hatching), the hatch origin enables you to start and end the pattern appropriately inside the boundary.

- Click  (Set Origin), select the point at which the pattern is going to start, and then select an internal point to set the boundary. You can use the preset options to set the origin to the **Bottom Left**, **Bottom Right**, **Top Left**, **Top Right**, or **Center**, as shown in Figure 13–11.

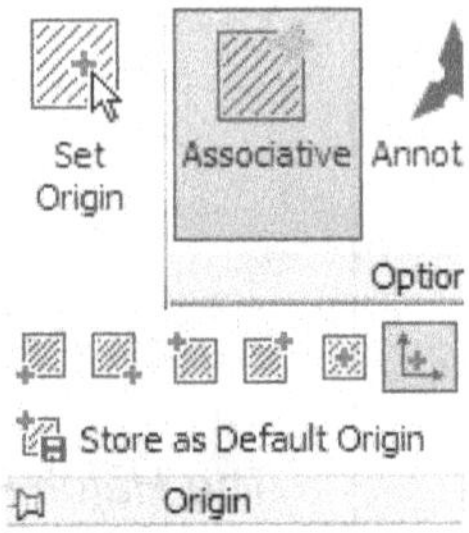

Figure 13–11

- You can select **Use Current Origin** to return to the default origin point.

- You can select **Store as Default Origin** to save the current location as the default origin.

Hatch Options

You can set the hatch to be **Annotative**, so that it uses the annotative scale of the viewport in which it displays, as shown in Figure 13–12.

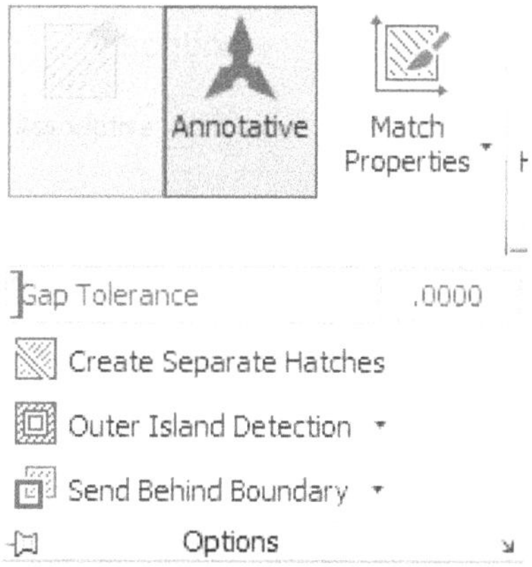

Figure 13–12

- Hatches are typically set to **Associative** (the default if **Annotative** is selected). This means that the hatch is associated with the boundary. If the boundary is changed (i.e., moved, stretched, etc.), the hatch pattern area changes to fill the new boundary.

- Click (Create Separate Hatches) if you want each boundary selected during one command to be created as individual hatches. Otherwise, they are all one hatch object no matter how many boundaries you select.

- (Send Behind Boundary) drop-down options, (as shown in Figure 13–13.) controls whether the hatch is behind or in front of overlapping objects or boundaries. You can specify the relationship for any overlapping objects or just the boundary.

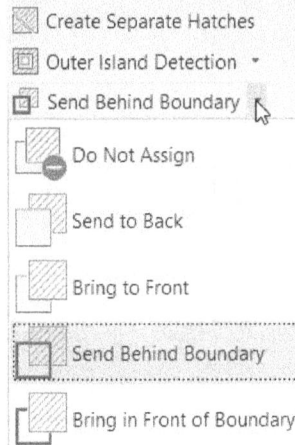

Figure 13–13

- Click (Match Properties) to select an existing hatch object in the drawing and use it to hatch other areas.

- **Island Detection** sets whether or not the areas in overlapping or complex objects are hatched. Expand the drop-down list and select the required type of detection, as shown in Figure 13–14.

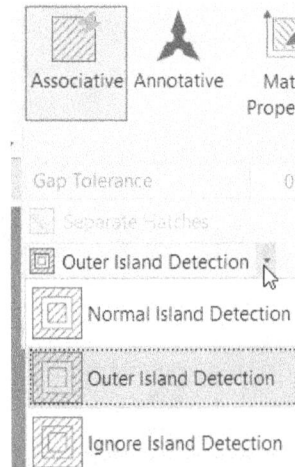

Figure 13–14

- **Gap Tolerance** sets the largest gap permitted in the boundary of an area to be hatched. If set to **0** (the default), no gaps are permitted.

Hint: Finding the Area of a Hatch

The *Area* of a hatch displays in the Properties palette, as shown in Figure 13–15. It can be used as a quick way to find the area of an object with holes.

Figure 13–15

If more than one hatch is selected, it provides the cumulative area. For example, you might want to know the area of several rooms in a building. Hatch the rooms, select the hatches, and note the *Cumulative Area* in the Properties palette, as shown in Figure 13–16.

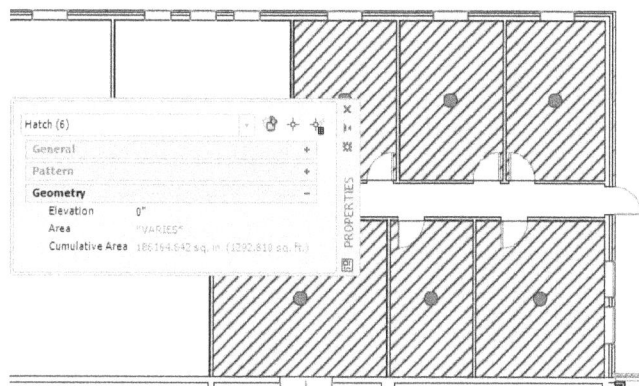

Figure 13–16

13.2 Editing Hatches

Instead of erasing and reapplying hatching to change the pattern or scale, you can adjust the hatch using:

- The *Hatch Editor* contextual tab in the ribbon.

- The **Edit Hatch** command.

- Grips.

You can change the hatch pattern, scale, or angle, and add or remove areas from the existing hatch boundary.

When you modify the boundaries of associative hatches, the hatch automatically updates, as shown in Figure 13–17.

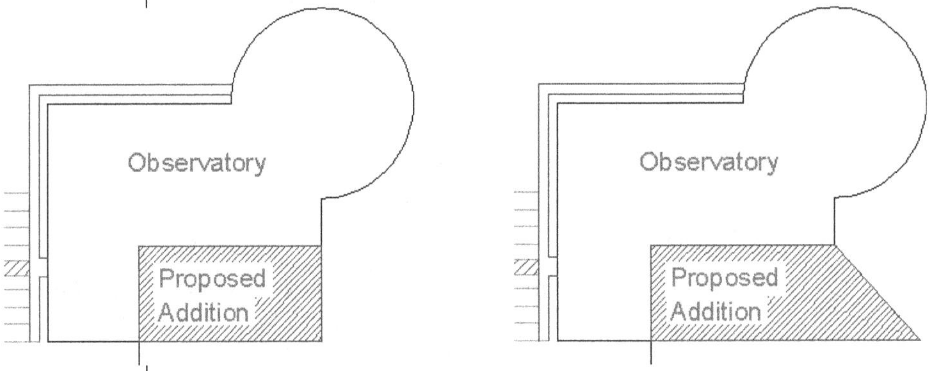

Figure 13–17

Hatch Editor Tab

To edit an existing hatch, select a hatch by clicking on it to display the *Hatch Editor* contextual tab.

How To: Edit a Hatch Using the *Hatch Editor* Tab

1. Select the hatch to be modified.
2. In the *Hatch Editor* contextual tab, change the properties as required.
   - The options in this contextual tab are the same as those available for placing the hatch.

3. If required, modify the boundaries using ⌸ (Recreate Boundary) or ▨ (Display Boundary Objects).

Recreate Boundary: Creates a new object around the hatch area, and associates the hatch with the new object separate from the original boundary.

Display Boundary Objects: Displays the selected objects and their boundary with grips. Modifying the grips changes both the boundary and the hatch if the hatch is associative. If the hatch is not associative, different grips display and you can modify the hatch separately from the original boundary.

4. Press <Enter> to apply the changes.

Edit Hatch Command

To open the Hatch Edit dialog box (shown in Figure 13–18), in the *Home* tab>expanded Modify panel, click 🖉 (Edit Hatch). The dialog box contains tools that are similar to the Hatch Editor.

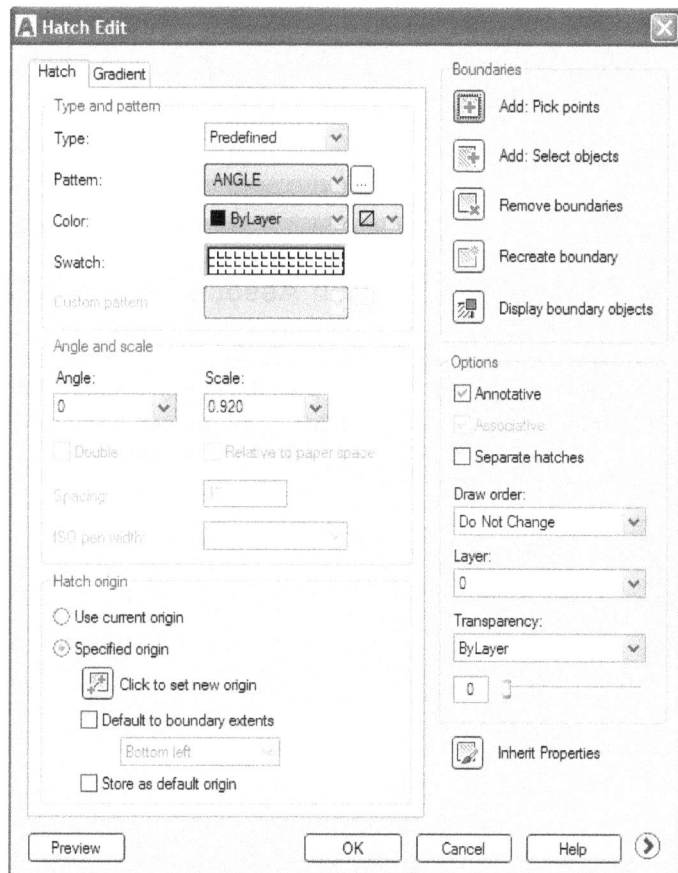

Figure 13–18

Grip Editing Hatch Boundaries

When associative hatches are selected, a single grip displays at the centroid of the hatch, as shown on the left in Figure 13–19. However, non-associative hatch boundaries display grips at each of their corners and at the midpoint of the edges, as shown on the right in Figure 13–19.

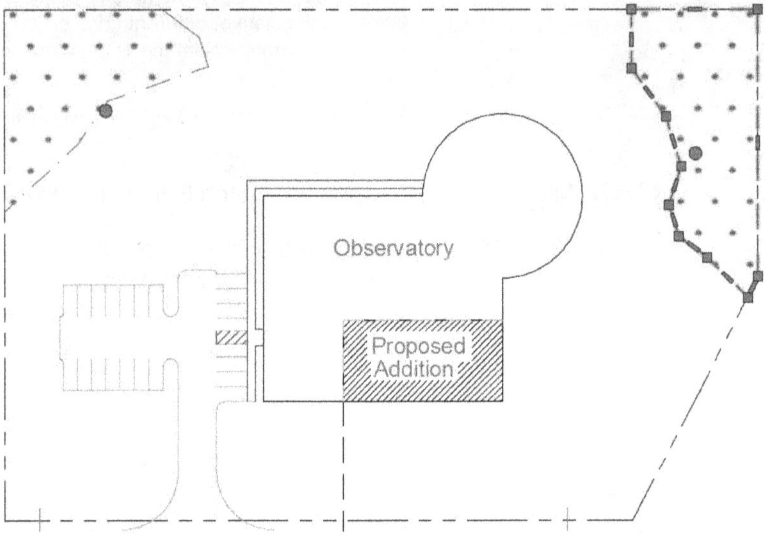

Figure 13–19

Non-Associative Hatch Boundaries

Add Vertex: To add a vertex to the boundary, hover over a multifunctional edge grip at the required location and select **Add Vertex** in the dynamic list, as shown in Figure 13–20. Drag and place the new vertex point.

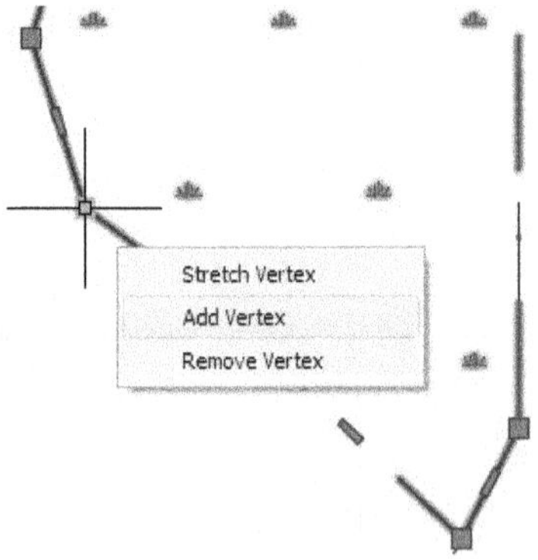

Figure 13–20

Convert to Arc: To change an edge to an arc, hover over the multifunctional edge grip and select the **Convert to Arc** option, as shown in Figure 13–21. Drag and place the midpoint of the arc.

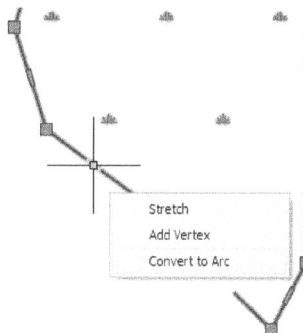

Figure 13–21

Arc Grip Options: When you hover over a multifunctional arc grip, the options enable you to stretch it, add a vertex, or convert the arc to a line.

Remove Vertex: To delete a vertex, hover over the multifunctional vertex grip, and select the **Remove Vertex** option.

Associative Hatch Boundaries

When you are editing associative hatches, you can use one multifunctional grip to access several options (**Stretch**, **Origin Point**, **Hatch Angle**, and **Hatch Scale**) using the dynamic list, as shown in Figure 13–22.

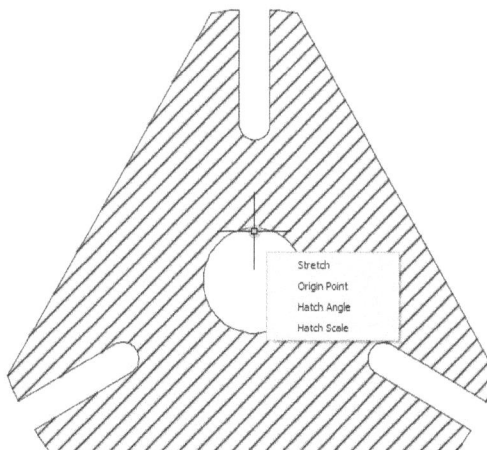

Figure 13–22

Hover the cursor over the grip and select one of the following options:

Stretch	Moves the entire hatch and makes it non-associative. This is the default when you select the grip.
Origin Point	Enables you to select a new point for the origin of the hatch.
Hatch Angle	Enables you to specify an angle at the Command Line or select a point to define the angle.
Hatch Scale	Enables you to specify a scale at the Command Line or select a point to define the scale.

Practice 13a | Hatching Using the Tool Palettes

Practice Objective

- Add hatching to a floor plan.

In this practice, you will add hatches to a floor plan using the Tool Palettes, as shown in Figure 13–23.

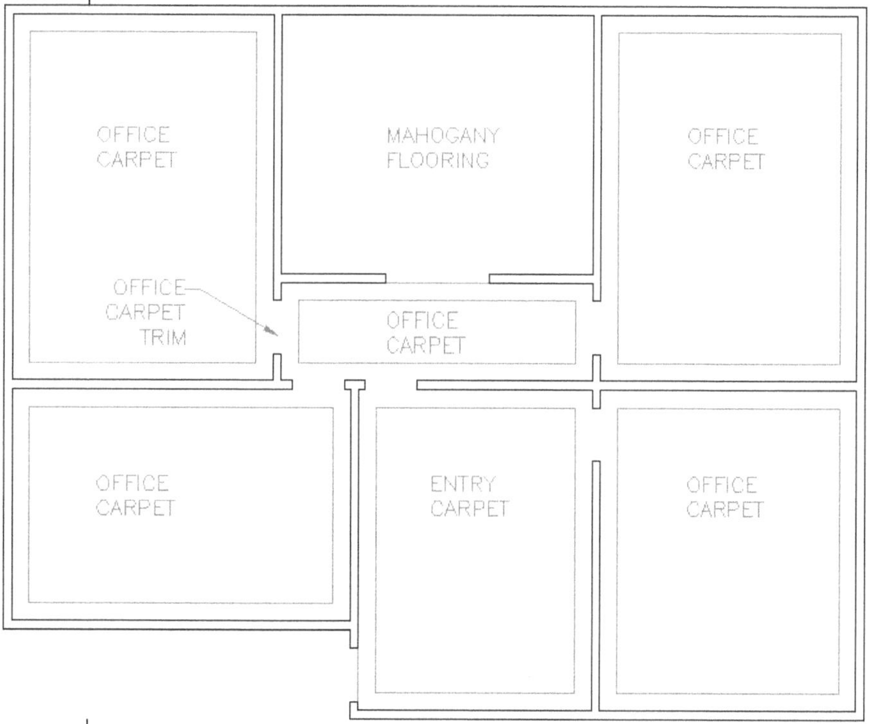

Figure 13–23

1. Open **Law Office-A.dwg** from your practice files folder.

2. Toggle off the layer **A-Door**. Toggle on the layer **A-Flor**, and make it active.

3. Open Tool Palettes (*View* tab>Palettes panel) if it is not already open.

4. In Tool Palettes, in the *Hatches and Fills* tab, click on any of the solid colors. Click inside one of the *Office Carpet* areas.

5. Similarly, use the same solid color to fill all of the Office Carpet areas.

*In the Tool Palettes, if the tab is hidden, click on the area just below the bottom tab and select **Hatches and Fills**.*

6. Use different solid colors for the Office Carpet Trim, Entry Carpet, and Mahogany Flooring.

7. Use the Properties palette to find the areas of the Office Carpet Trim and the Mahogany Flooring. Select the hatch, and open the Properties palette. The Area displays in the Geometry section, as shown for Mahogany Flooring in Figure 13–24.

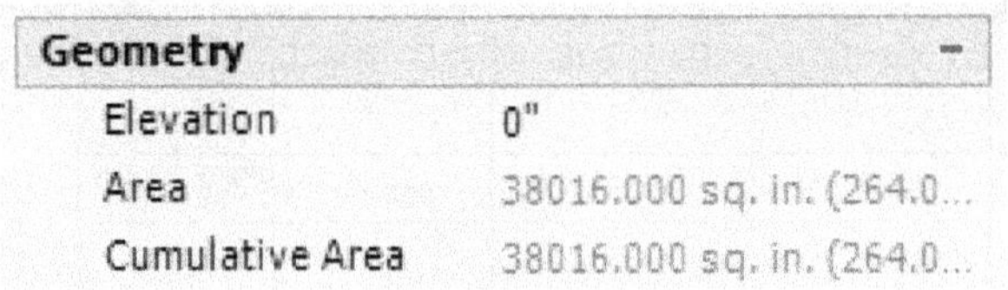

Geometry		−
Elevation	0"	
Area	38016.000 sq. in. (264.0...	
Cumulative Area	38016.000 sq. in. (264.0...	

Figure 13–24

8. Save and close the drawing.

Practice 13b | Hatching (Mechanical)

Practice Objectives

- Apply hatching to a section and modify it.
- Create a hatch with an annotative scale.

In this practice, you will apply hatching to a section and then modify it using the *Hatch Creation* contextual tab. You will also create a hatch with an annotative scale, as shown in Figure 13–25.

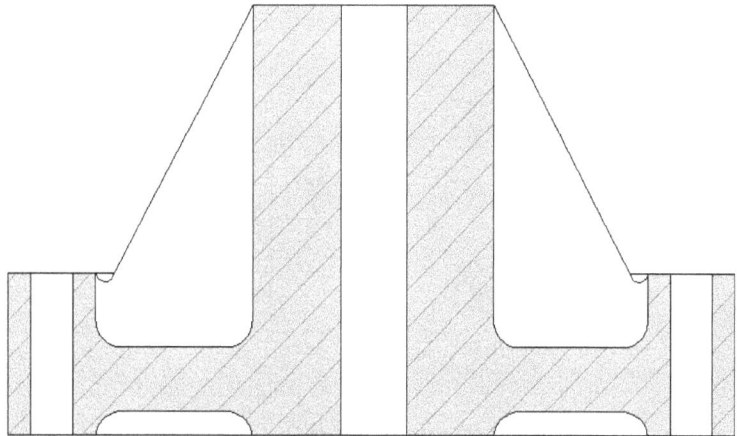

Figure 13–25

Task 1 - Apply a hatch.

1. Open **Wheel-Section-I.dwg** from your practice files folder.

2. Set the current layer to **Hatching**.

3. In the *Home* tab>Draw panel, click (Hatch).

4. In the *Hatch Creation* contextual tab>Properties panel, verify the following:
    - *Hatch Type* is set to **Pattern**.
    - *Scale* is set to **1.0000**.
    - *Angle* is set to **0**.

5. In the Pattern panel, verify that *Hatch Pattern* is set to **ANSI31**.

6. In the Options panel, select **Annotative**. In the expanded Options panel, verify that ▨ (Create Separate Hatches) is NOT selected.

7. In the Boundaries panel, click ⊞ (Pick Points). Select points inside the areas of the section view that display hatching. as shown in Figure 13–26.

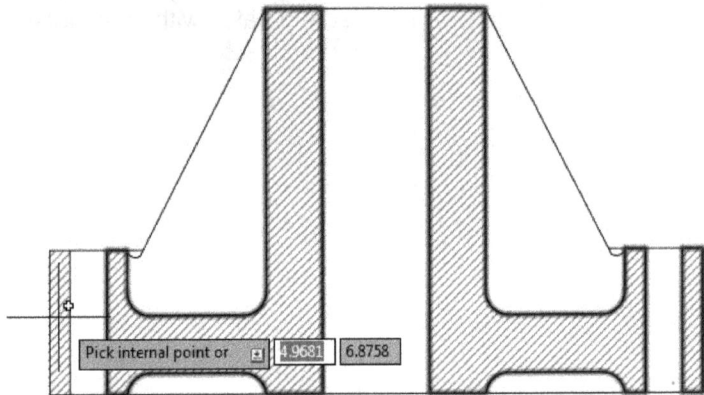

Figure 13–26

8. The hatch pattern lines are very close together. Change the *Scale* to **2.0**. Press <Enter> to apply the new scale to hatching. The hatch updates in the drawing.

9. Press <Esc> to exit the hatching selection.

10. Hover the cursor over the hatching. Note that it is a single object.

Task 2 - Edit a hatch pattern.

---

1. Select the hatching. The *Hatch Editor* contextual tab opens.

2. Set the *Scale* to **4.0** and click ✔ (Close Hatch Editor).

3. Use the **Move** command to move each of the two vertical lines near the center of the part, **0.5** units closer to the center. The hatch pattern automatically adjusts, as shown in Figure 13–27.

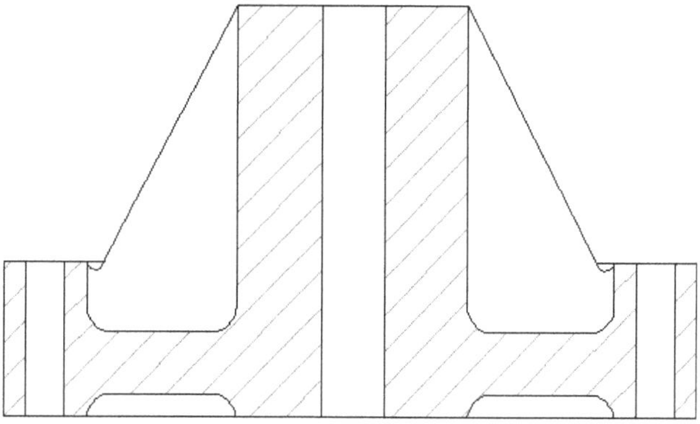

Figure 13–27

4. Save the drawing.

Task 3 - Change the background color, origin, and transparency of the hatch.

---

1. While not in a command, select the hatch object. The grip and the *Hatch Editor* contextual tab display.

2. Change the *Background Color* to **Cyan,** as shown in Figure 13–28.

3. Set the *Hatch Angle* value to **15,** as shown in Figure 13–28.

4. Set the *Hatch Transparency* value to **6,** as shown in Figure 13–28.

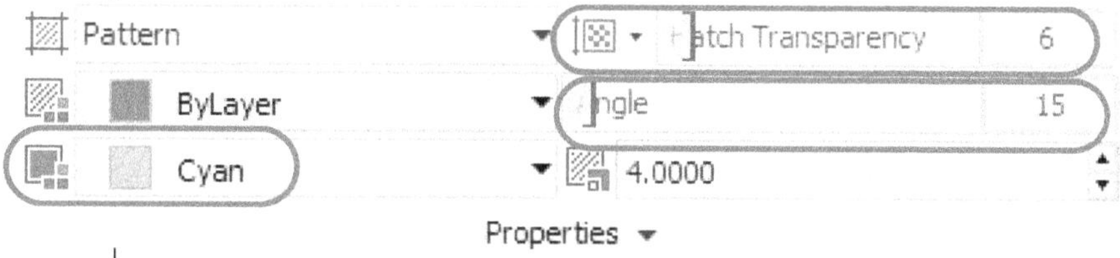

Figure 13–28

5. Click ✓ (Close Hatch Editor).

Task 4 - Hatch with the Annotative Scale (optional).

---

1. Switch to the **B-sized** layout. It contains two viewports that have been set to different scales. Hatching is not displayed in either viewport because **Annotative** was selected while applying the hatch and in Model Space the hatch was set to 1:1.

---

2. Make the bottom viewport active by double-clicking in it.

3. Start the **Hatch** command.

4. Use the **ANSI31** pattern and set the *Scale* to **1.**

5. In the expanded Properties panel, select **Relative to Paper Space**. In the Options panel, verify that **Annotative** is selected.

6. Select the points for hatching the appropriate areas and accept the hatch. Click ✔ (Close Hatch Editor). The hatch displays in the bottom viewport but does not display in the top viewport.

7. With the bottom viewport still active, in the Status Bar, note that the scale is **1:2**.

8. Click inside the top viewport to make it active. In the Status Bar, note that the scale is **1:4**.

9. Activate the bottom viewport. Select the hatch, right-click and then select **Properties**.

10. With the hatch still selected, in the Properties palette>*Pattern* area, click the button to the right of *Annotative scale*, as shown in Figure 13–29.

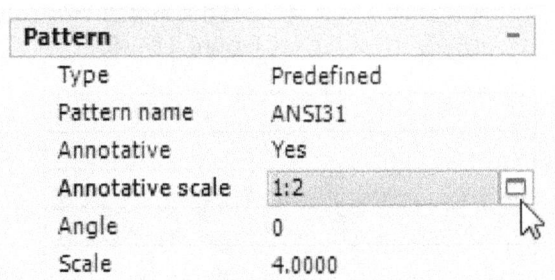

Pattern		
Type	Predefined	
Pattern name	ANSI31	
Annotative	Yes	
Annotative scale	1:2	☐
Angle	0	
Scale	4.0000	

Figure 13–29

11. In the Annotation Object Scale dialog box, click **Add**.

12. In the Add Scales to Object dialog box, select the **1:4** scale from the list.

13. Click **OK** in both the dialog boxes. The hatch displays in the top viewport automatically, as shown in Figure 13–30.

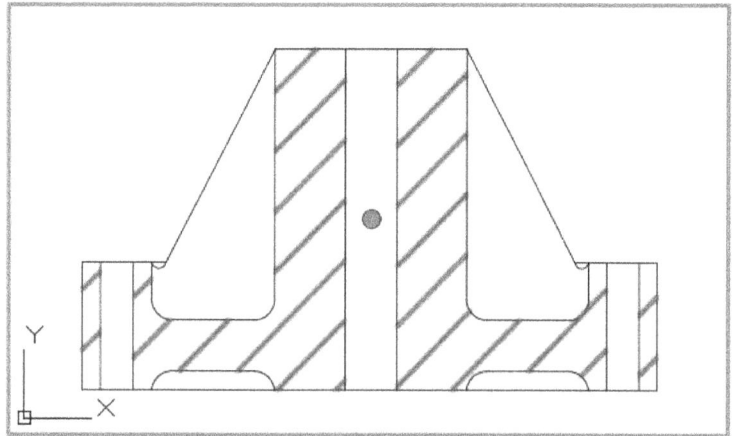

Figure 13–30

14. Press <Esc> to clear the hatch selection.

15. Save and close the drawing.

Practice 13c | Hatching (Architectural)

Practice Objective

- Apply hatching to a floor plan.

In this practice, you will apply hatching to a floor plan using the **Hatch** command, as shown in Figure 13–31.

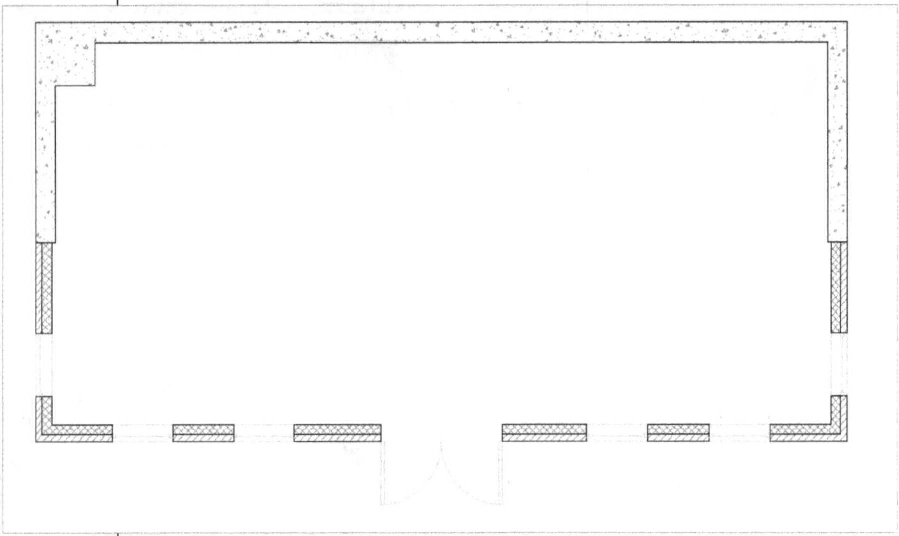

Figure 13–31

1. Open **Basement-A.dwg** from your practice files folder.

2. Set the layer to **Hatching**.

3. Switch to the **D-sized** layout tab. This layout has two viewports at different scales.

4. Double-click in the larger viewport to make it active.

5. Start the **Hatch** command. Set the *Hatch type* to **Pattern** and the *Pattern* to **AR-CONC** (used to show poured concrete). Leave the *Scale* at **1.000** and the *Angle* at **0**.

6. Click (Pick Points). At the *Pick internal point:* prompt, select a point inside the back wall.

7. Click  (Close Hatch Creation) to close the *Hatch Creation* contextual tab.

8. Start the **Hatch** command again. Set the *Hatch Pattern* to **ANSI37** (a crosshatch that symbolizes a concrete block). Set the *Scale* to **1.000**. In the expanded Properties panel, select **Relative to Paper Space.** In the Options panel, select **Annotative**. Use ⊞ (Pick Points) to select internal points on the inside portions of the other walls, as shown in Figure 13–32. Zoom in as required to accurately select the areas to hatch. Ensure that the *Scale* is still at 1.000. If it is not, reset it to 1.000.

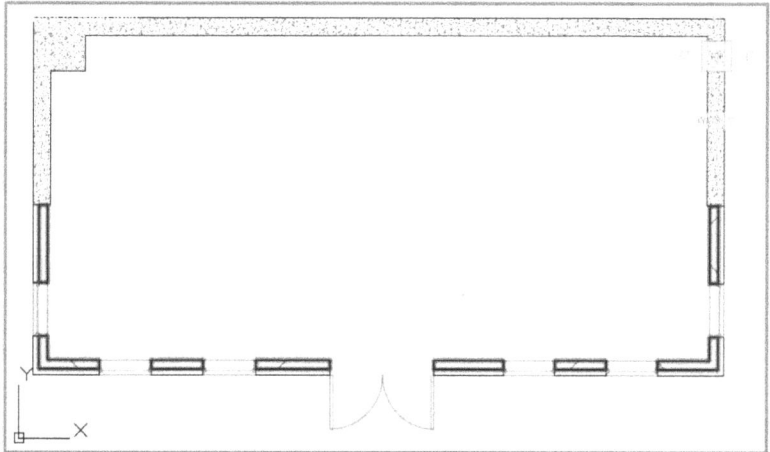

Figure 13–32

9. Press <Enter> to apply the hatch. If the hatch does not display correctly (i.e., as a cross hatch), you might have to select it and reset the *Scale* to **1.000** in the *Hatch Editor* contextual tab. You might also need to click on **Relative to Paper Space** again and reset the scale to **1** until you get the correct crosshatch pattern, as shown in Figure 13–33. Press <Esc> to clear the hatch selection.

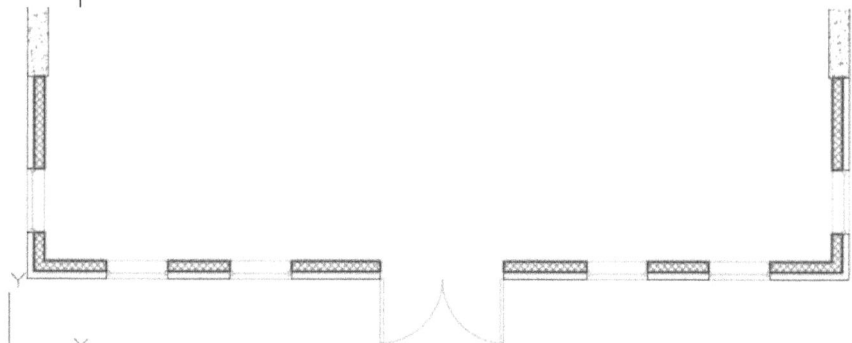

Figure 13–33

*If the hatch displays at the wrong scale, select the hatch and reset the Scale to **1.000** in the Hatch Editor contextual tab.*

10. Hatch the outside portions of the walls, as shown in Figure 13–31, using the *Hatch pattern* **ANSI31** (a hatch that symbolizes brick). Use a *Scale* of **1.000**, and select **Relative to Paper Space** and **Annotative**.

11. Click ✓ (Close Hatch Creation) to close the *Hatch Creation* contextual tab.

12. Zoom out to display both viewports. The first hatch pattern that you applied displays in both viewports, while the other two hatch patterns only display in the larger viewport. This is because they are annotative and only display in a viewport matching the scale 1/2"=1'0".

13. Hover the cursor over the **ANSI37** hatch. ⌂ (Annotative) displays next to the cursor, indicating that it is annotative. Hover the cursor over the **AR-CONC** hatch. An icon is not displayed because it is not annotative.

14. Select the **AR-CONC** hatch pattern.

15. The *Hatch Editor* contextual tab opens. Change the *Scale* to **0.25** and select **Annotative**. The **AR-CONC** hatch does not display in the smaller viewport as it is now annotative.

16. Click ✓ (Close Hatch Editor) to close the *Hatch Editor* contextual tab.

17. Save and close the drawing.

Text

Exam Objectives Covered in This Chapter

- 5.3.a Apply text and multiline text properties
- 5.3.c Create and adjust text columns
- 5.3.f Insert symbols from the character map
- 5.3.g Check the spelling of text and dimension annotation
- 5.4.a Create and modify multileaders
- 5.4.b Add and remove leaders
- 5.4.c Align and collect leaders

Note: The objective *5.3.b Create, modify, and apply text styles* is covered in *Chapter 17: Annotation Features and Styles*.

14.1 Adding Text in a Drawing

Many drawings include notes about the objects and about the project, as shown in Figure 14–1. This might be a set of general notes in the titleblock or notes specific to a particular view.

Multiline Text

You can use the **Multiline Text** command to create, edit, and format paragraphs of text.

Text should be placed on its own layer.

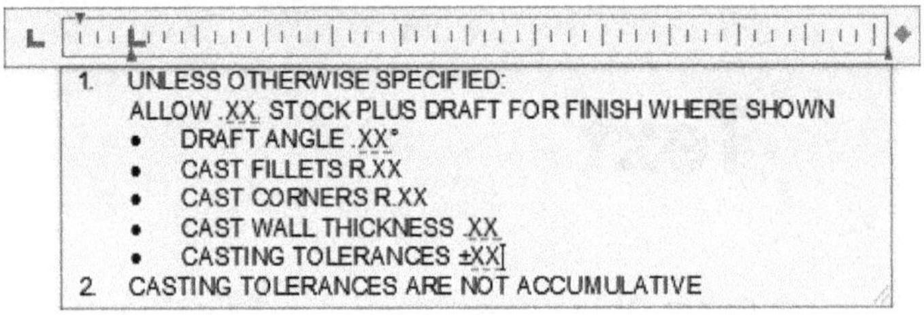

Figure 14–1

- Any text created in the Text Editor becomes one object, no matter how many lines it contains. Because you type it in a Text Editor, the text automatically wraps at the end of the line.

- Set the layer and the text style before you start the **Multiline Text** command. The text style sets the default font of the text.

How To: Add Multiline Text

If you are creating an annotative object, you might be prompted to set the annotation scale.

1. In the *Annotate* tab>Text panel or in the *Home* tab>
   Annotation panel, click A (Multiline Text).
   - An example text string (abc) displays near the cursor as shown in Figure 14–2. This preview indicates the current text height and font.

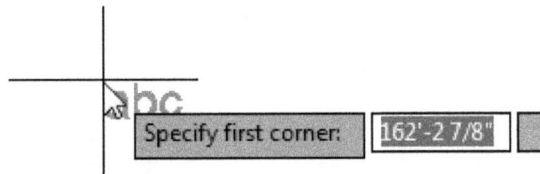

Figure 14–2

2. Select two points in the drawing to define a boundary box for the text. The Text Editor opens, as shown in Figure 14–3.

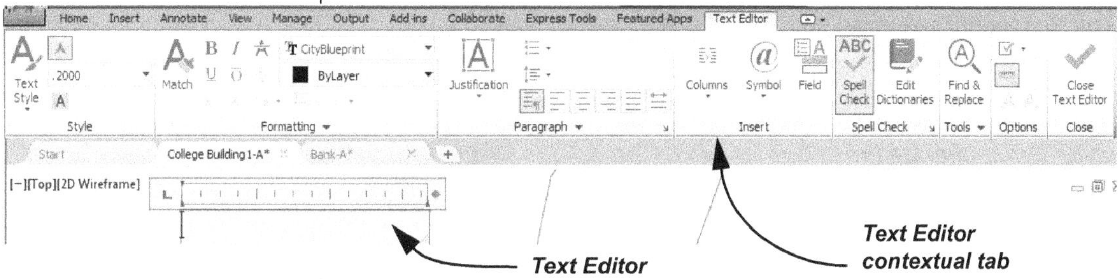

Text Editor

Text Editor contextual tab

Figure 14–3

- When creating the boundary box for the text, an arrow displays indicating the direction in which the text is going to flow, based on the current vertical justification. The boundary determines the position of the text and its width (i.e., the length of a line before words wrap to the next line), but does not limit the number of lines you can type.

3. Type the text in the Text Editor and apply formatting options from the contextual tab.

4. Click ✓ (Close Text Editor) or click in the drawing window to finish creating the text. The text is inserted in the drawing as one object.

- The background of the text editor is transparent. This enables any drawing objects that are covered by the text box to be displayed.

How To: Set the Text Height

1. In the *Annotate* tab>Text panel or in the *Home* tab> Annotation panel, click A (Multiline Text).
2. Select the first point of the boundary box.

3. Select **Height** from the Command Line or shortcut menu (<Down Arrow>), as shown in Figure 14–4.

Figure 14–4

4. Enter the text height and press <Enter>.
5. Select the other point of the boundary box.

• Text can be placed in Paper Space or Model Space. In most cases, and especially if you are using an annotative text style, you should specify the height of the text to be the final plotted size.

Copying and Importing Text

You can copy text from a word processing software or other text editor and paste it directly into the Text Editor, as shown in Figure 14–5. You can also import text files that are saved in the ASCII or RTF format.

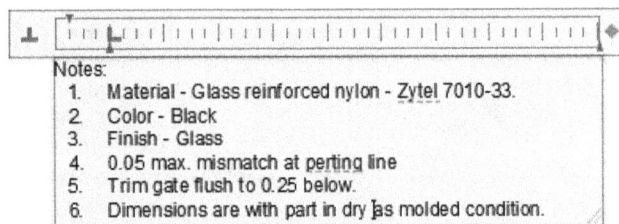

Notes:
1. Material - Glass reinforced nylon - Zytel 7010-33.
2. Color - Black
3. Finish - Glass
4. 0.05 max. mismatch at perting line
5. Trim gate flush to 0.25 below.
6. Dimensions are with part in dry as molded condition.

Figure 14–5

How To: Copy and Paste Text into the Text Editor

1. In a document file, copy the text to the Windows Clipboard.
2. In the AutoCAD software, in the *Annotate* tab>Text panel or in the *Home* tab>Annotation panel, click A (Multiline Text).
3. Select points for the boundary box.
4. In the Text Editor, right-click and select **Paste**. The text you copied is pasted into the Text Editor.

- If you use **Paste Special**, you can set the copied text to be pasted without character or paragraph formatting, as shown in Figure 14–6.

Paste	Ctrl+V	
Paste Special	▶	Paste without Character Formatting
Insert Field...	Ctrl+F	Paste without Paragraph Formatting
Symbol	▶	Paste without Any Formatting

Figure 14–6

When you copy and paste text created with Microsoft Word, it keeps the formatting from the document, including numbering or bullets and specific headings.

How To: Import Text

1. In the *Annotate* tab>Text panel or in the *Home* tab> Annotation panel, click A (Multiline Text).
2. Select points for the boundary box.
3. In the *Text Editor* contextual tab>expanded Tools panel, click **Import Text**. You can also right-click in the Text Editor and select **Import Text**.
4. In the Select File dialog box, select the file that you want to use and click **Open** to import the text.

- Imported text does not include formatting.

Hint: Insert Symbols

You can add symbols to your text. In the *Text Editor* contextual tab>Insert panel, expand @ (Symbol) and select a symbol in the list. You can select **Other...** at the end of the list to open the Character Map dialog box to access specialty symbols in different fonts, as shown in Figure 14–7.

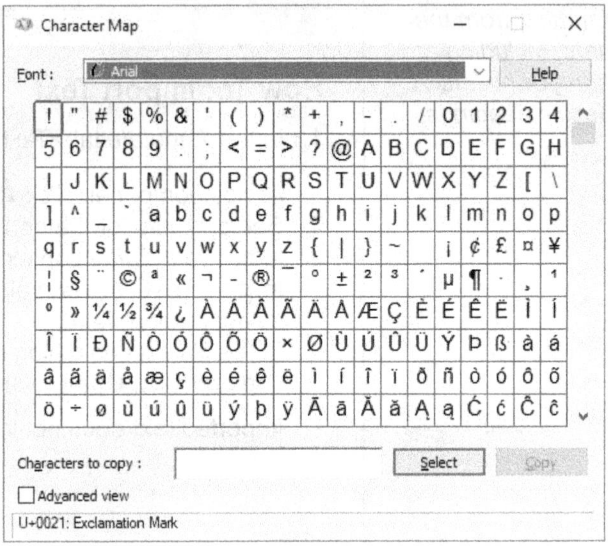

Figure 14–7

In the *Text Editor* contextual tab>Insert panel, click (Field) to add text objects that gather their information from objects or system variables, such as the date or drawing name in the AutoCAD software.

Spell Checking

The spellings are checked by default when you are in the Text Editor. It can be toggled on and off in the *Text Editor* contextual tab>Spell Check panel, as shown in Figure 14–8.

Figure 14–8

- Any misspellings are underlined with a dashed red line, but only in the Text Editor. Right-click on the word to display a list of suggestions, as shown in Figure 14–9. You can also add words to the dictionary or ignore the misspelled words.

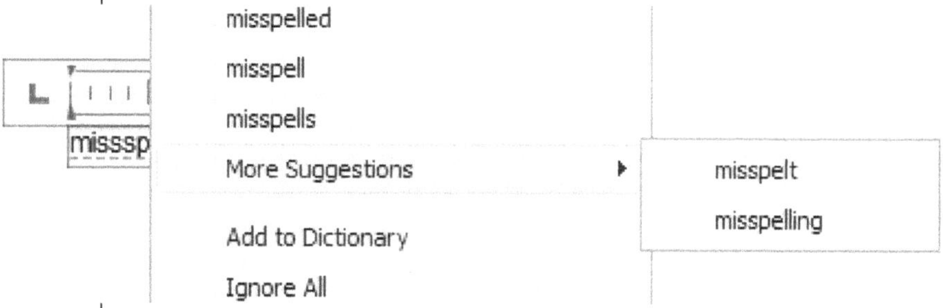

Figure 14–9

- Click ⌄ in the Spell Check panel title to open the Check Spelling Settings dialog box.

Practice 14a | **Adding Text in a Drawing**

Practice Objectives

*   Add text to a cover sheet with different text styles and sizes.
*   Import text into the Text Editor.

In this practice, you will use the **Multiline Text** command to place text on a cover sheet using two different text styles and sizes, as shown in Figure 14–10. You will also import text into the Text Editor.

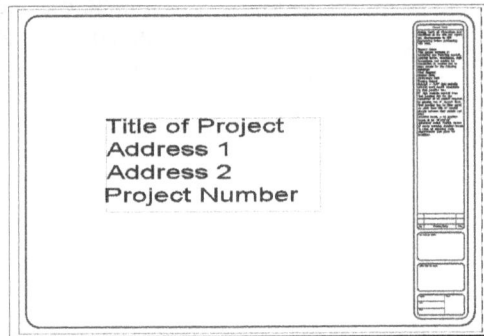

Figure 14–10

Task 1 - Add General Notes to the Cover Sheet.

1. Open **Cover Sheet-A.dwg** from your practice files folder.

2. Ensure that you are in the **Cover Sheet** layout tab.

3. Set the current layer to **Notes**.

The text style can also be set in the Annotate tab>Text panel.

4. In the *Home* tab>expanded Annotation panel, set the current text style to **Standard**, as shown in Figure 14–11.

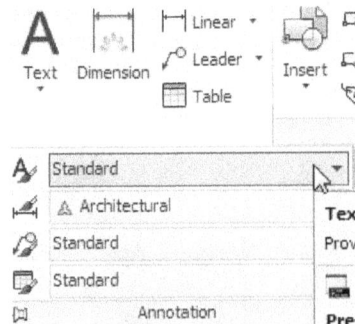

Figure 14–11

The **Multiline Text** command can also be accessed in the Annotate tab>Text panel.

5. Zoom in on the top right corner of the layout, where it says General Notes.

6. In the *Home* tab>Annotation panel, click A (Text), which is the **Multiline Text** command. The alphabet is attached to the cursor indicating the height of the text.

7. To avoid snapping to the lines in the titleblock, toggle off **Object Snap** if required.

8. In the *General Notes* area of the titleblock, select near the upper left corner under the General Notes line as the first point of the boundary box. Right-click, select **Height**, enter **1/8"**, and press <Enter>. For the second point, click approximately in a diagonally opposite corner in the *General Notes* area, as shown in Figure 14–12. The Text Editor displays and the *Text Editor* contextual tab opens.

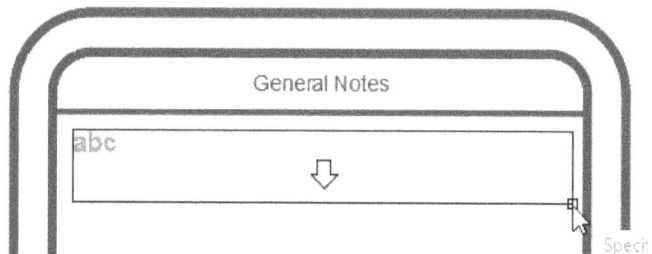

Figure 14–12

9. Type the text shown in Figure 14–13 and remain in the Text Editor.

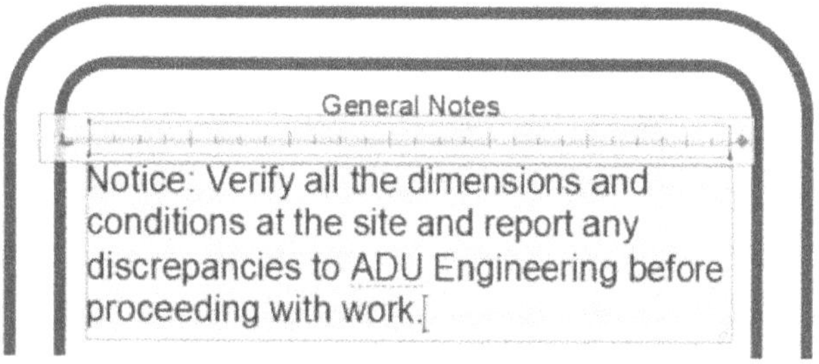

Figure 14–13

For the words to be underlined, in the Text Editor tab, in the Spell Check panel, **Spell Check** must be toggled on.

10. Note that **ADU** is underlined in red because the word is not recognized by the spell checker. Highlight it, right-click, and select **Add to Dictionary**.

11. Ensure that the cursor is at the end of the text, and press <Enter> twice to go to the next line and add a new empty line.

12. Right-click in the Text Editor and select **Import Text**.

13. In the Select File dialog box, select the **General Notes.txt** file from your practice files folder and click **Open**. The text from the file is added.

Your word wrap might be different because the size of your text boundary box might be different.

14. Select a point anywhere on the screen, outside of the Text Editor, to close it. The text displays as shown in Figure 14–14.

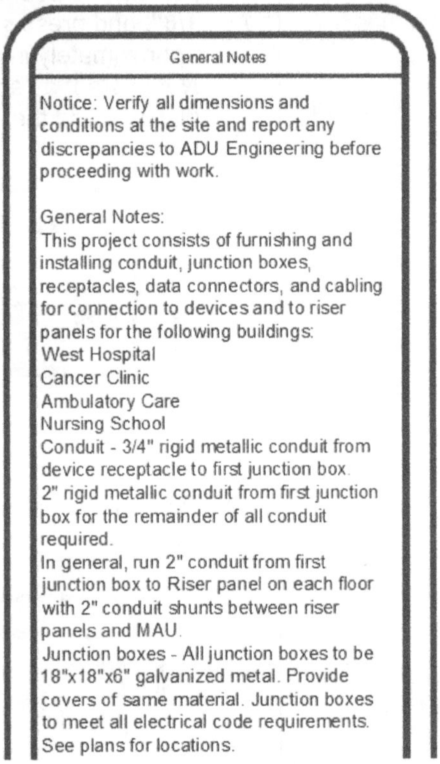

General Notes

Notice: Verify all dimensions and conditions at the site and report any discrepancies to ADU Engineering before proceeding with work.

General Notes:
This project consists of furnishing and installing conduit, junction boxes, receptacles, data connectors, and cabling for connection to devices and to riser panels for the following buildings:
West Hospital
Cancer Clinic
Ambulatory Care
Nursing School
Conduit - 3/4" rigid metallic conduit from device receptacle to first junction box.
2" rigid metallic conduit from first junction box for the remainder of all conduit required.
In general, run 2" conduit from first junction box to Riser panel on each floor with 2" conduit shunts between riser panels and MAU.
Junction boxes - All junction boxes to be 18"x18"x6" galvanized metal. Provide covers of same material. Junction boxes to meet all electrical code requirements. See plans for locations.

Figure 14–14

Task 2 - Add Project Information to the Cover Sheet.

1. Zoom out to display the entire cover sheet.

2. In the *Annotate* tab>Text panel, select the **Title** text style. Then, click A (Multiline Text).

The text style can also be set in the Home tab> expanded Annotation panel.

3. For the first corner, select the top left corner of the green rectangle at the center of the layout. (Use **Object Snap**.) Right-click, select **Height**, enter **1"**, and press <Enter>. Then, select the bottom right corner of the green rectangle.

4. Type the text shown in Figure 14–15, pressing <Enter> at the end of each line to go to the next one.

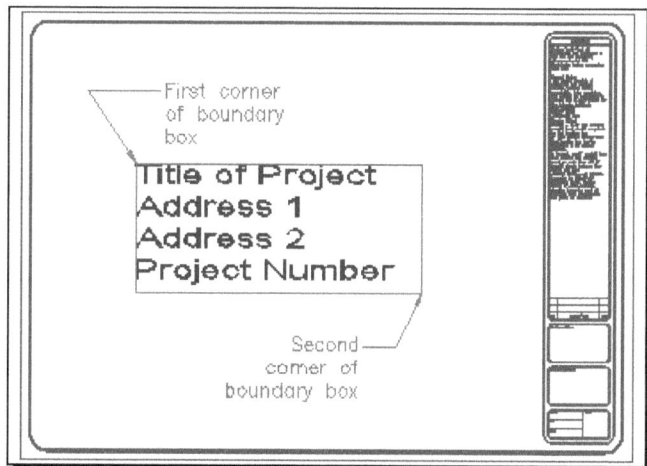

Figure 14–15

5. After entering the last line of text, in the *Text Editor* contextual tab, click ✔ (Close Text Editor) to end the command and close the Text Editor.

6. Save and close the drawing.

14.2 Modifying Multiline Text

You can manipulate Multiline text with grips and adjust its various settings in the Properties palette. However, changing the text's layer, and copying, moving, and rotating the text can be achieved by using standard AutoCAD commands and processes.

Editing Multiline Text

*You can also right-click on the selected text and select **Mtext Edit**.*

You can edit the already existing multiline text in the Text Editor.

How To: Edit Multiline Text

1. Double-click on a text object to open the Text Editor. The *Text Editor* contextual tab also opens.
2. Edit the text, as shown in Figure 14–16.

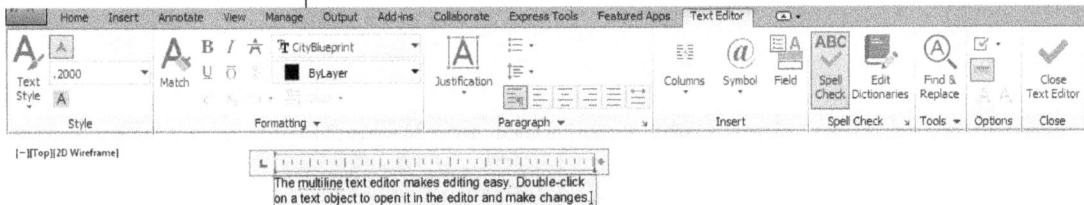

Figure 14–16

3. In the *Text Editor* contextual tab, click ✓ (Close Text Editor) or click in the drawing window to finish editing the text.

• If you press <Esc> to close the Text Editor, you are prompted to save your text changes.

Changing Text Width and Length

After you have placed Multiline text in your drawing, you can control the text boundary box width and length using grips or the Text Editor.

• Select some Multiline text without any commands running. Grips display at the location point and at the column width and height, as shown in Figure 14–17. Click on a grip to select it (it turns red), and then move the cursor and select another point to stretch the column width or height to a different size. To clear the grips, press <Esc>.

Figure 14–17

- The location grip (square grip box) moves the entire Multiline text. It also designates the justification of the object.

- You can modify the text width and length in the Text Editor by hovering the cursor over the edges or the corner of the Text Editor and then dragging the double-arrows. You can also use the horizontal diamond on the right end of the ruler to modify the text box *Width*, as shown in Figure 14–18.

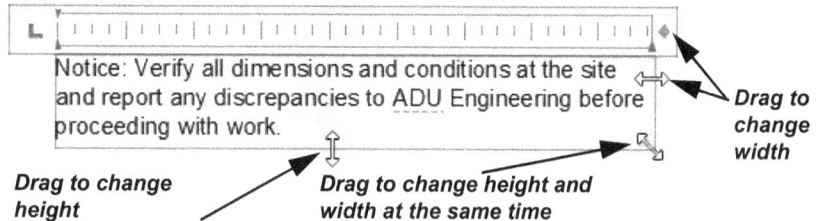

Notice: Verify all dimensions and conditions at the site and report any discrepancies to ADU Engineering before proceeding with work.

Drag to change width

Drag to change height

Drag to change height and width at the same time

Figure 14–18

Changing Text Properties

The Properties palette is useful for changing multiple instances of text. You can change general properties (such as the layer) or specific properties (such as style, height, or justification).

- You can also add a Text Frame around multi-line text, as shown in Figure 14–19.

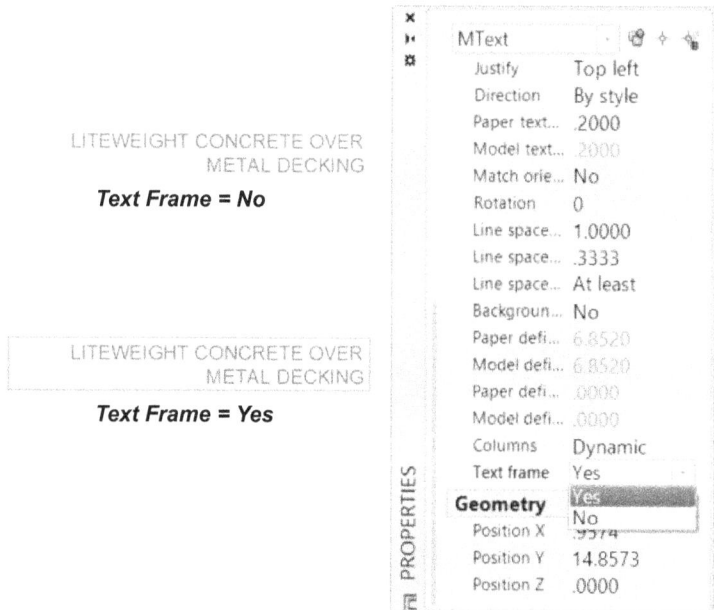

LITEWEIGHT CONCRETE OVER
METAL DECKING

Text Frame = No

LITEWEIGHT CONCRETE OVER
METAL DECKING

Text Frame = Yes

MText	
Justify	Top left
Direction	By style
Paper text...	.2000
Model text...	.2000
Match orie...	No
Rotation	0
Line space...	1.0000
Line space...	.3333
Line space...	At least
Backgroun...	No
Paper defi...	6.8520
Model defi...	6.8520
Paper defi...	.0000
Model defi...	.0000
Columns	Dynamic
Text frame	Yes
Geometry	Yes / No
Position X	.9574
Position Y	14.8573
Position Z	.0000

PROPERTIES

Figure 14–19

How To: Add a Text Frame

1. Select the multi-line text.
2. Right-click and select **Properties**.
3. In the Properties palette, change the *Text Frame* field to **Yes**.

Hint: Frame Offset Value

The Text Frame is offset from the text by the value of **Border offset factor** in the Background Mask dialog box, as shown in Figure 14–20.

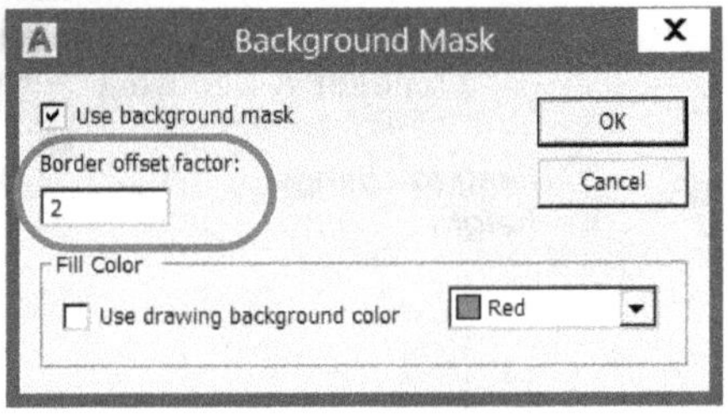

Figure 14–20

Spell Checking

While you are in the Text Editor you can have spell checking on and fix spelling errors on the fly. You can also check the spelling in an entire drawing or part of a drawing.

How To: Check the Spelling in a Drawing

1. In the Annotate tab>Text panel, click ABC ✓ (Check Spelling).
2. In the Check Spelling dialog box (shown in Figure 14–21), expand the Where to check drop-down list and select **Entire drawing**, **Current space/layout**, or **Selected objects**.

You can also click

(Select Objects) to specify which objects to check.

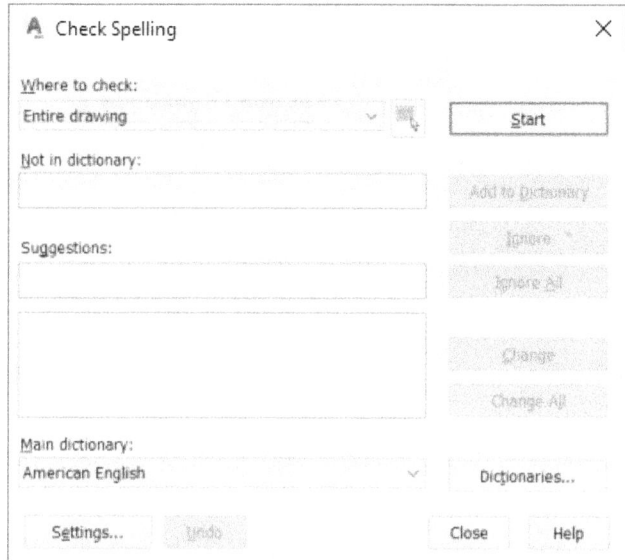

Figure 14–21

3. Click **Start**.
4. The AutoCAD software zooms to the text being checked and highlights any misspelled words. As with other spell checkers, you can:
   - Click **Change** or **Change All** to change the word to the selected suggestion.
   - Click **Ignore** or **Ignore All** to maintain the spellings.
   - Click **Add to Dictionary** to add a word to your custom dictionary.
   - Click **Undo** if you modify a spelling error by mistake.
5. When the spelling check is complete, a message box opens. Click **OK** and then **Close** in the Check Spelling dialog box.

- Click **Dictionaries...** to specify the Main and Custom dictionaries, and add words to your custom dictionary.

- Click **Settings...** to specify the types of items you want to check and how you want the checker to deal with specific variations of words.

Practice 14b | Modifying Multiline Text

Practice Objectives

- Modify Multiline text objects.
- Check the spelling in the drawing.

In this practice, you will modify text using grips, the Text Editor, and the Properties palette to clean up a redlined detail, as shown in Figure 14–22. You will also check the spelling in the drawing file.

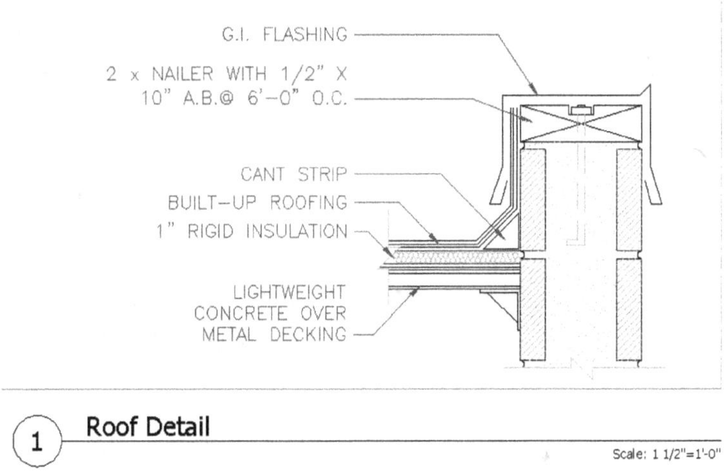

G.I. FLASHING

2 x NAILER WITH 1/2" X
10" A.B.@ 6'-0" O.C.

CANT STRIP
BUILT-UP ROOFING
1" RIGID INSULATION

LIGHTWEIGHT
CONCRETE OVER
METAL DECKING

1) Roof Detail

Scale: 1 1/2"=1'-0"

Figure 14–22

Task 1 - Edit multiline text in a drawing.

1. Open **Detail Sheet-A.dwg** from your practice files folder.

2. Ensure that you are in the **Detail Sheet** layout.

3. Zoom in on the Roof Detail viewport in the upper left corner of the layout.

4. Double-click inside the viewport to make it active.

5. Click once on the text that ends with **O.C.** Select the top left grip and select a point farther to the left to make the text fit in two lines, as shown in Figure 14–23. Press <Esc> to clear the grips.

The red text and markings are for reference only.

Pressing <Esc> in the Text Editor requires you to save the changes whereas clicking outside the Text Editor automatically saves the changes.

6. Double-click on the same piece of text. In the Text Editor, change **8"** to **10"**, as shown in Figure 14–24. Verify that the complete text is still in two lines, and use the left double-arrows to adjust the width as required. Press <Esc>.

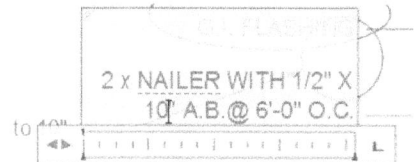

Figure 14–23

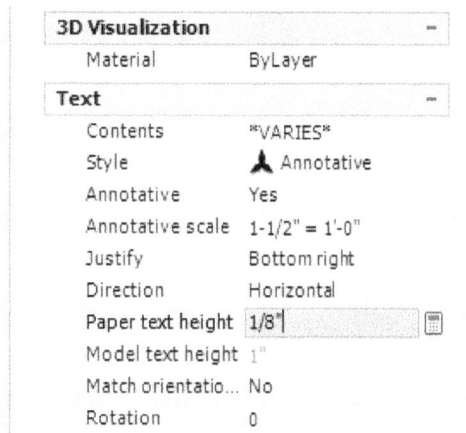

Figure 14–24

7. Click **Yes** to save the text changes.

8. Select the two pieces of text for the lower two leaders (starting with **1"** and Liteweight), right-click and select **Properties**.

9. In the Properties palette, in the *Text* area, the *Paper text height* is **1/16"**. Click on it, change it to **1/8"** (as shown in Figure 14–25), and press <Enter>.

3D Visualization		−
Material	ByLayer	
Text		−
Contents	*VARIES*	
Style	Annotative	
Annotative	Yes	
Annotative scale	1-1/2" = 1'-0"	
Justify	Bottom right	
Direction	Horizontal	
Paper text height	1/8"	
Model text height	1"	
Match orientatio...	No	
Rotation	0	

Figure 14–25

10. Close the Properties palette. Note that the selected text has become larger. Press <Esc> to clear the text.

You will correct the spelling in the next task.

11. Select the text **1" RIGID INSSULATION**. Use grips to stretch the text to the left so that it fits on one line. Press <Esc> to clear the text.

Task 2 - Check the spelling.

1. Remain in the Roof Detail viewport.

2. In the *Annotate* tab>Text panel, click ^{ABC} ✓ (Check Spelling).

3. In the Check Spelling dialog box, in the *Where to check* drop-down list, select **Current space/layout**. Click **Start**.

4. Work through each of the spelling errors, correcting them as required and ignoring proper names. Note that the word **NAILER** is highlighted although it is spelled correctly. It is a technical term that is not found in the standard dictionary. Click **Ignore**.

5. Next, **INSSULATION** is highlighted. Correct it by clicking **Change** to use the spelling in the *Suggestions* area, as shown in Figure 14–26.

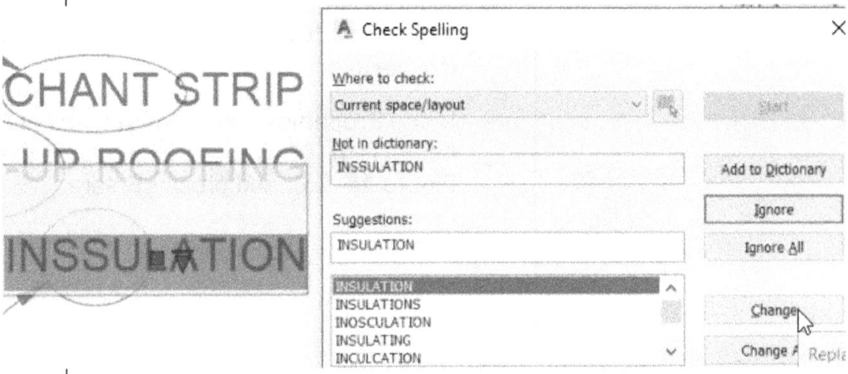

Figure 14–26

6. Similarly, the word **liteweight** should be corrected.

7. In the message box, click **OK** to finish checking the spelling.

8. Click **Close** to close the Check Spelling dialog box.

9. Two of the misspelled words are not modified by the Spell Checker because they are actual words. You need to modify these directly.

10. Double-click on the text *CHANT* and in the Text Editor, correct the spelling to **CANT** and then save the change.

11. Similarly, change the text *BUILD-UP* to **BUILT-UP**.

12. Toggle the layer **redline** off.

13. Double-click outside the viewport to return to Paper Space.

14. Save the drawing.

14.3 Formatting Multiline Text

Multiline text offers formatting features similar to those found in word processing software. For example, you can bold, underline, or strikeout specific text, use bullets or numbered lists, and create columns of information, as shown in Figure 14–27.

Construction Notice:
1. Remove *existing steps and walks*; provide new access ramp from sidewalk up to grade of existing garden walk. Provide handrail.
2. Remove *existing porch*; replace with porch at finished floor elevation. Provide new steps and wheelchair lift.

Figure 14–27

- Some options affect the entire Multiline text object, some modify specific paragraphs in the text, and some only change selected text.

Formatting the Multiline Text Object

Changing the *Text Style* and *Justification* affects the entire Multiline text object. If you need to change these features, do so before you make any other modifications to the formatting.

Changing the Text Style

You can change the *Text Style* of the overall text object once you are in the Text Editor.

- Changing the style overrides any other formatting you have done. A warning box opens if you select a different style, as shown in Figure 14–28.

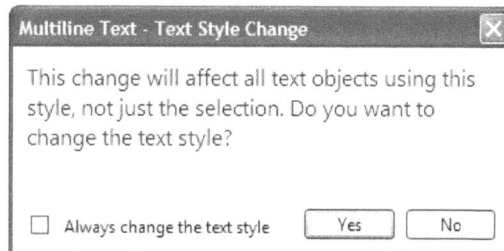

Multiline Text - Text Style Change

This change will affect all text objects using this style, not just the selection. Do you want to change the text style?

☐ Always change the text style   Yes   No

Figure 14–28

- If you are not using an annotative text style, you can click

  (Annotative) in the *Text Editor* contextual tab to make that instance of the text annotative without changing the text style.

Changing the Justification

The *Justification* sets the overall justification for the entire text object. In this case, the width and height of the boundary box are considered. For example, if you set the *Justification* to **Middle Center**, the text is centered in the middle of the boundary box, as shown in Figure 14–29. To change the Multiline text object, use the Justification tools located in the *Text Editor* contextual tab>Paragraph panel in the ribbon.

Figure 14–29

- (Background Mask) in the Style panel places a masking element behind the text so that other objects do not show through. You can use the drawing background color or a specific color, as shown in Figure 14–30.

Setting a background mask applies it to the entire Multiline text object.

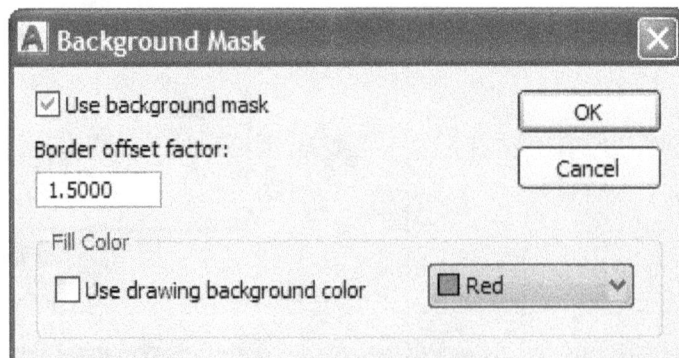

Figure 14–30

Formatting Selected Text

In hand drafting, most text was placed on a drawing using all uppercase letters. However, as computers have taken over much of the text work, many people are using the sentence case format.

The Formatting panel in the *Text Editor* contextual tab enables you to change the font of individual text that you have selected, as well as bold, italicize, underline, overline, strikethrough, and change the case of the text, as shown in Figure 14–31.

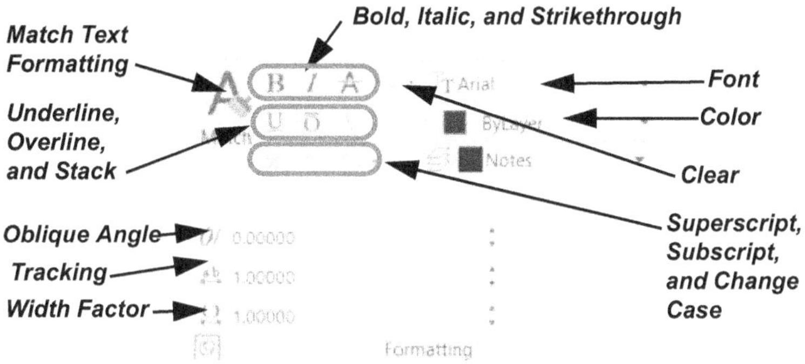

Figure 14–31

- Buttons are grayed out if the text is not selected or if the font does not support an option, such as **Bold** or *Italic*.

- In many cases, setting the color impacts the printed weight of the text, because colors are often used to control plotted line width.

- Three other text modification tools in the expanded area in the Formatting panel enable you to modify the text angle or spacing: **Oblique Angle**, **Tracking**, and **Width Factor**.

- You can use **Match Text Formatting** to copy the formatting from one set of text to another while using the Text Editor. You can also use this option to modify dimensions and tables.

- To remove the formatting from an mtext object, expand (Clear) and select the required option, You can remove the formatting from selected characters, from selected paragraphs, or from all of the text in a text object, as shown in Figure 14–32.

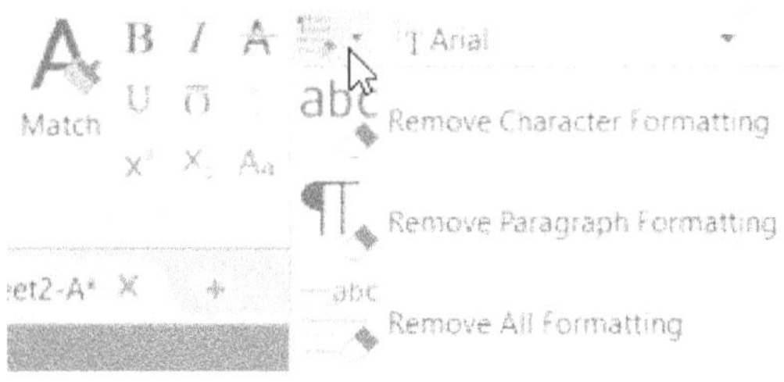

Figure 14–32

Hint: Fractions in Multiline Text

To display a fraction as stacked, use [icon] (Stack) when you enter a fraction in the Text Editor. Click on the stacked number to display [icon]. Click [icon] to display the basic **Stack** options, as shown inFigure 14–33.

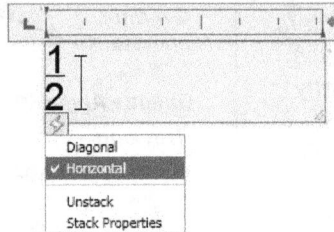

Figure 14–33

Double-click on the stacked number to open the Stack Properties dialog box where you can modify the more advanced settings, as shown in Figure 14–34.

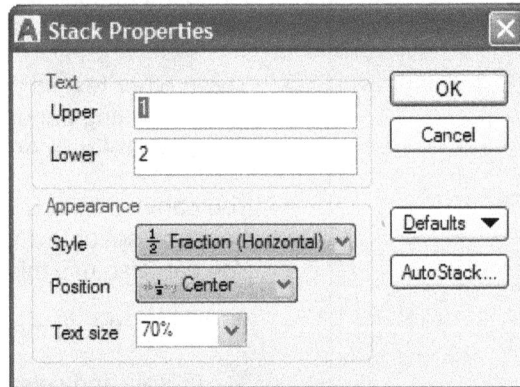

Figure 14–34

Formatting Paragraph Text

Paragraph settings also affect the next paragraph typed.

You can modify entire paragraphs of text including changing paragraph level justifications, line spacing, indents, bullets, and numbering, as shown in Figure 14–35.

This project consists of furnishing and installing conduit, junction boxes, receptacles, data connectors, and cabling for connection to devices and to riser panels for the following buildings:

Verify all dimensions and conditions at the site and report any discrepancies to ADU Engineering before proceeding with the work.

Figure 14–35

- The paragraph formatting tools are located in the *Text Editor* contextual tab>Paragraph panel, as shown in Figure 14–36.

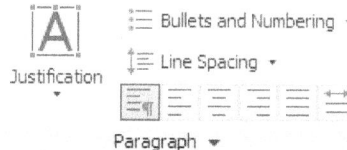

Figure 14–36

- A paragraph is any text that is typed before you press <Enter> to create a new line.

- To modify paragraphs, you can either select the entire paragraph or place the cursor somewhere in the paragraph.

Justifications

You can set justifications for individual paragraphs in a Multiline text object. The options are as follows:

- ☰ (Default)

- ☰ (Left)

- ☰ (Center)

- ☰ (Right)

- ☰ (Justify (Fit))

- ☰ (Distribute)

An example of some of the justifications is shown in Figure 14–37.

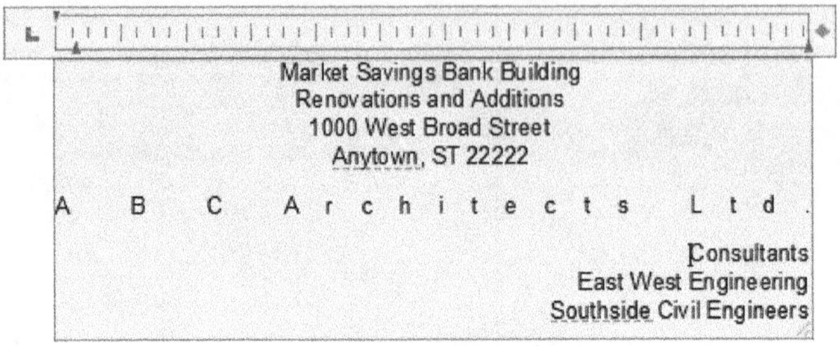

Figure 14–37

- **Justify (Fit)** spreads out the text so that the sentences are left- and right-justified. **Distribute** justifies to the left and right sides and spreads out whole words and individual letters across the space.

Line Spacing

You can set the line spacing using the supplied multiples of the text height, as shown in Figure 14–38, or select **More...** to create custom line spacing in the Paragraph dialog box. **Clear Line Spacing** returns the distance to the default setting.

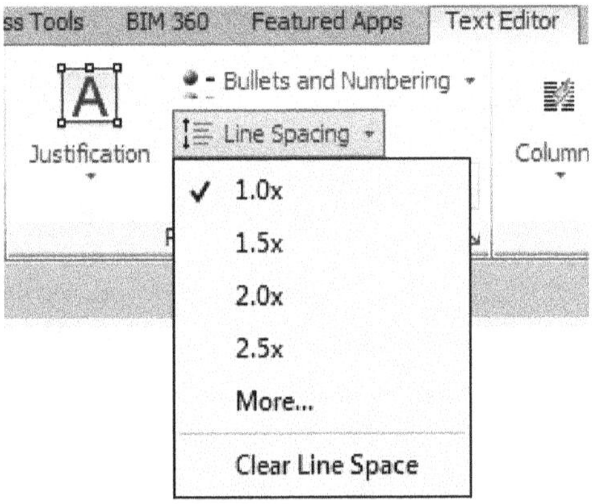

Figure 14–38

Bullets and Numbers

You can add bullets, numbers, or letters to text as you are typing, or add them to paragraphs that are already in the text object.

Select the type of list from the **Bullets and Numbering** list in the *Text Editor* contextual tab, as shown in Figure 14–39.

To create a sub-list of a list, press <Tab> at the beginning of the line. Press <Shift>+<Tab> to back up.

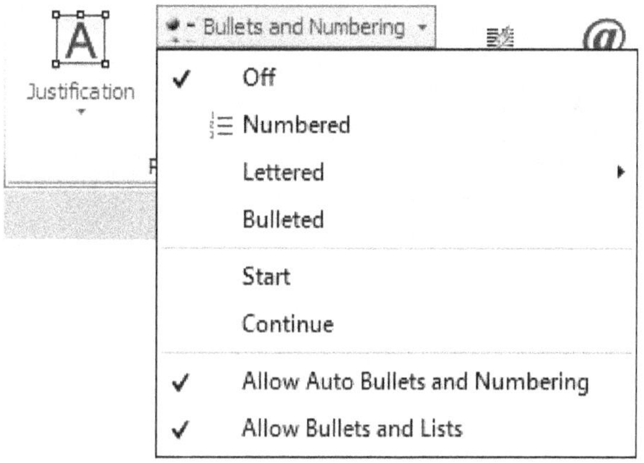

Figure 14–39

- The list can be in upper or lowercase letters, numbers, or bullets. Each time you press <Enter>, a new paragraph is created and numbered appropriately.

- You can **Restart** or **Continue** a numbered list and modify the default methods of using lists in the menu.

- Modify the indent and tab settings to set the locations of the numbers and text.

- Bullets and numbering are automatically applied to the text as you type if the line begins with a symbol or number followed by a space or <Tab>.

Setting Indents and Tabs

You can set the indents and tabs by using the ruler at the top of the Text Editor.

- Select the text that you want to indent and slide the markers to locate the indent. The top marker controls the first line of a paragraph and the bottom marker controls subsequent lines in the paragraph, as shown in Figure 14–40.

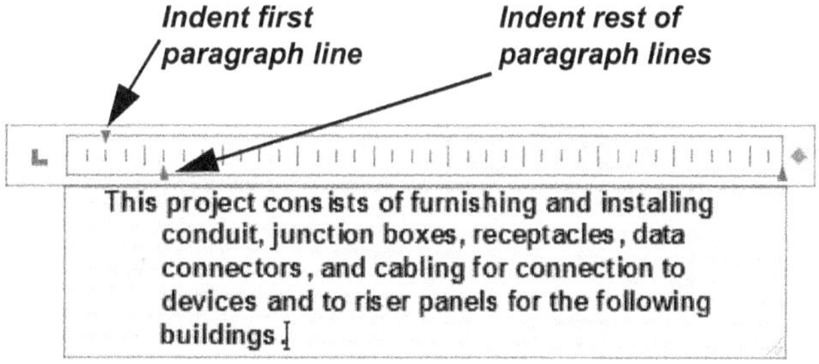

Figure 14–40

- The heavy **L** in the ruler marks preset tab stops, as shown in Figure 14–41. To add a manual tab, click on the ruler at the required location. You can drag the tab marker along the ruler to move it, or drag it off the ruler to delete it.

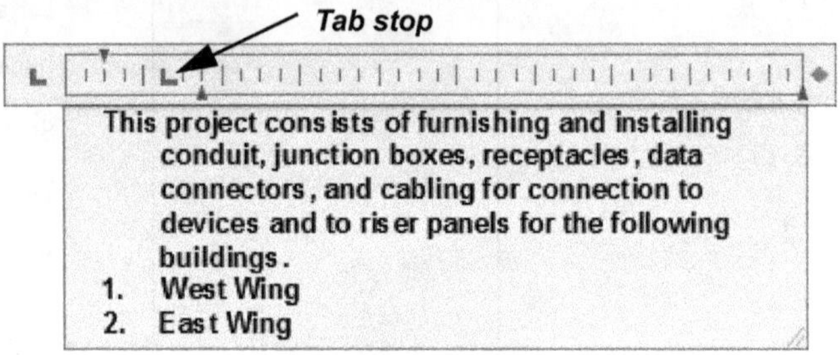

Figure 14–41

- There are tabs for ⌐ (Left), ⊥ (Center), ¬ (Right), and ⊥ (Decimal). Click the tab box on the left side of the ruler to switch between the different types of tabs.

- You can also modify the tab settings in the Paragraph dialog box.

Creating Paragraph Formats

To modify the Paragraph settings, click ⌐ in the Paragraph panel title. You can set the paragraph format options at any time using the Paragraph dialog box, as shown in Figure 14–42.

- You can only set the *Paragraph Spacing* in the Paragraph dialog box. It controls the distance before or after any paragraph.

If you do not select items in the dialog box, they do not affect the selected paragraph.

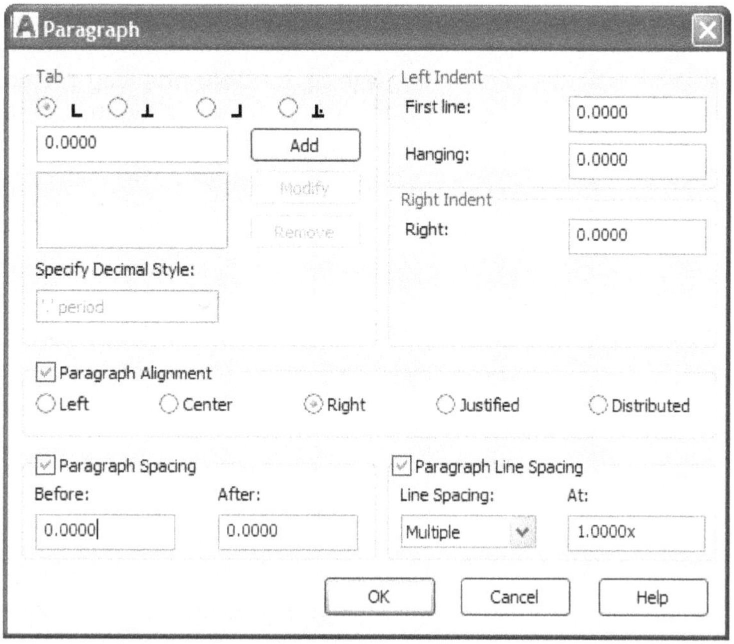

Figure 14–42

Creating Columns

You can place the text in a column format, as shown in Figure 14–43, using the column options in the Text Editor. There are two methods of column creation: **Dynamic** and **Static**.

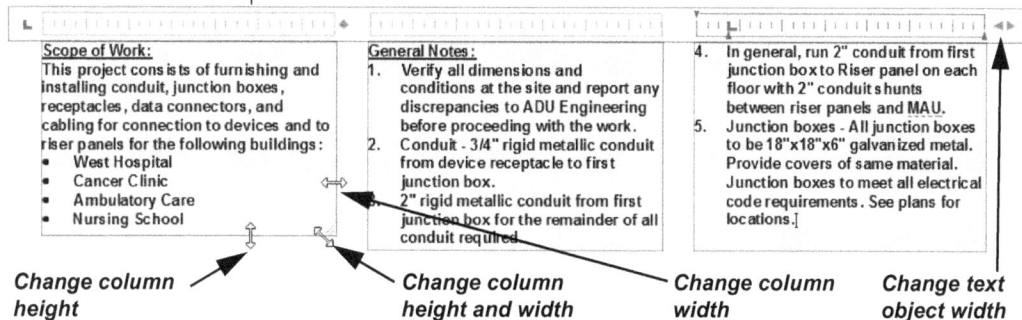

Change column height

Change column height and width

Change column width

Change text object width

Figure 14–43

Column settings affect the entire Multiline text object.

• By default, all of the Multiline text is set up to display dynamic columns with a manual height. This can be adjusted with grips or by dragging the edges of the first column to adjust the height and width separately, or both at the same time, as shown in Figure 14–43.

Static Columns

With **Static Columns**, you can specify the number of columns in the list, as shown in Figure 14–44. The columns are evenly divided in the text box.

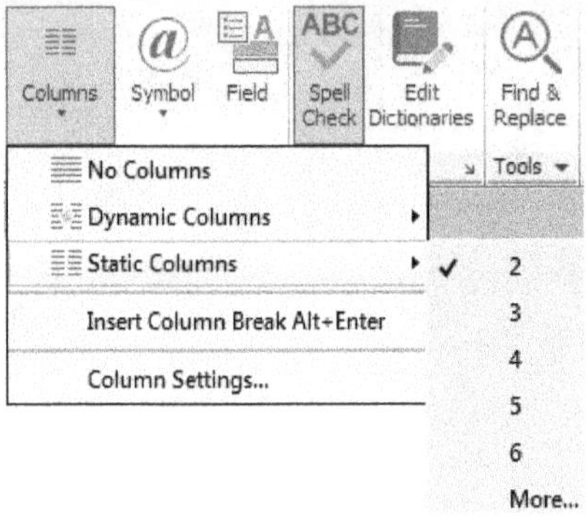

Figure 14–44

- If you need more than six columns, select **More...** or **Column Settings...** In the Column Settings dialog box, you can set the number of Static Columns, their height and width, and the gutter width.

Dynamic Columns

With **Dynamic Columns**, you can specify an automatic or manual height, as shown in Figure 14–45. The number of columns varies depending on the amount of text.

Figure 14–45

You can also set the height and width of columns in the Column Settings dialog box and modify them with grips.

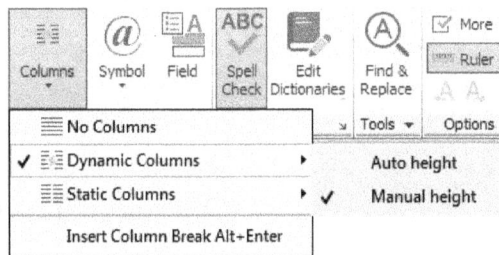

- After you start typing column information in the Mtext boundary, you can select **Insert Column Break** or type <Alt>+<Enter> to add a break before the end of the column. This enables you to control the flow of text in the Mtext object.

- When you have columns in your drawing, you can control the spacing with grips, depending on the type of columns and their settings.

Practice 14c

Formatting Multiline Text in a Drawing

Practice Objectives

- Change the formatting options of text objects.
- Add text and create columns.

In this practice, you will use formatting options in the Text Editor to set the style, modify individual objects, add numbering and indents, and set the justification of the text, as shown in Figure 14–46. If you have time, you can also add text and create columns.

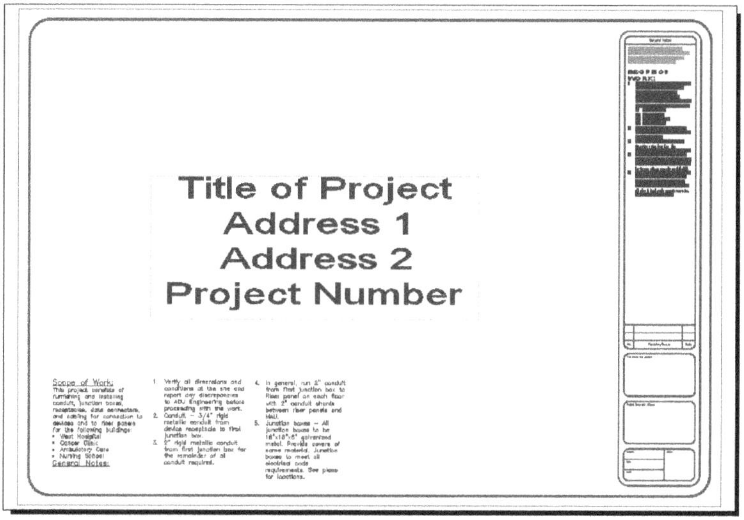

Figure 14–46

Task 1 - Format multiline text in a drawing.

1. Open **Cover Sheet2-A.dwg** from your practice files folder.

2. Zoom in on the *General Notes* area in the upper right corner of the titleblock.

3. Double-click on the text below the General Notes to open it in the Text Editor.

4. In the *Text Editor* contextual tab>Style panel, click and select the style **Hand**. In the alert dialog box, click **Yes**. The entire text object updates to the new style.

5. Highlight the first sentence (four lines), which starts with **Notice**. In the *Text Editor* contextual tab>Formatting panel, click U to make the sentence underlined and in the Color list, select **Red**, as shown in Figure 14–47.

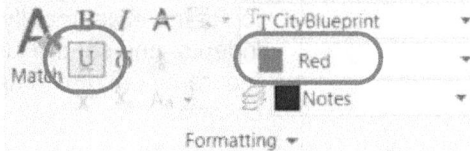

Figure 14–47

6. In the next paragraph of the text, highlight the text **General Notes** and change it to read **Scope of Work**. Change its *Font* to **Arial**, *Text Height* to **3/16"**, and make all of the words **Uppercase,** as shown in Figure 14–48.

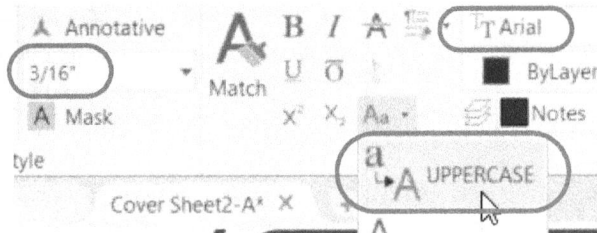

Figure 14–48

7. Select all of the text below SCOPE OF WORK. In the *Text Editor* contextual tab>Paragraph panel, expand **Bullets and Numbering** and select **Numbered** to apply autonumbering. Each paragraph becomes numbered.

8. Items 2-5 in the list should be sub-items under the first note. Select the insertion point in front of the text *West Hospital* and press <Tab>. The line becomes a sub-item as 1.1. Repeat for the next three lines.

9. To adjust the indent for the sub-items, highlight those four lines. In the ruler, drag the first line indent marker to the **3/8"** mark, as shown in Figure 14–49.

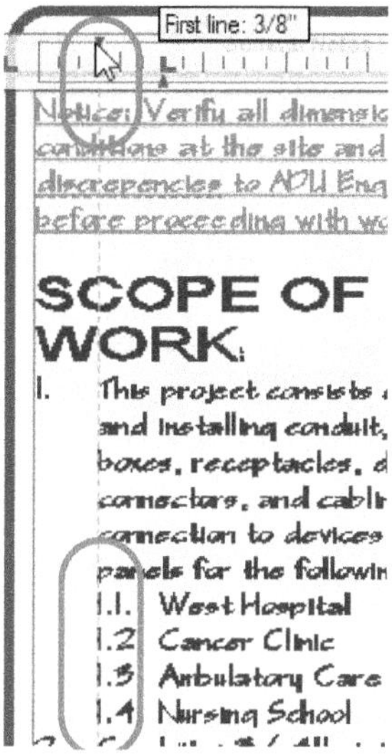

Figure 14–49

10. Click ✓ (Close Text Editor) to close the Text Editor.

11. Zoom out to display the entire layout.

12. Double-click anywhere on the four lines of Title text in the center of the cover sheet.

13. In the *Text Editor* contextual tab>Paragraph panel, change the *Justification* to **Middle Center MC**, as shown in Figure 14–50.

Figure 14–50

14. Close the Text Editor.

15. Save the drawing.

Task 2 - (Optional) Create columns.

In this task, you will import a text file, apply formatting, and divide the text into columns, as shown in Figure 14–51.

Scope of Work:

This project consists of furnishing and installing conduit, junction boxes, receptacles, data connectors, and cabling for connection to devices and to riser panels for the following buildings:

- West Hospital
- Cancer Clinic
- Ambulatory Care
- Nursing School

General Notes:

1. Verify all dimensions and conditions at the site and report any discrepancies to ADU Engineering before proceeding with the work.

2. Conduit - 3/4" rigid metallic conduit from device receptacle to first junction box.

3. 2" rigid metallic conduit from first junction box for the remainder of all conduit required.

4. In general, run 2" conduit from first junction box to Riser panel on each floor with 2" conduit shunts between riser panels and MAU.

5. Junction boxes - All junction boxes to be 18"x18"x6" galvanized metal. Provide covers of same material. Junction boxes to meet all electrical code requirements. See plans for locations.

Figure 14–51

1. In the lower left corner of the cover sheet, create a new Multiline Text object. Set the current text style to **Standard** with a *Height* of **3/16"**.

2. In the Text Editor, right-click and select **Import Text.** From the practice files folder, import the text file **Scope of Work.txt**. (This is similar to the text you placed under General Notes.)

3. Modify the formatting so that the items are bulleted and numbered (as shown in Figure 14–51). Use numbered for the text under *General Notes* and use bullets for the buildings under *Scope of Work*. Use **1/4"** height and underline for the titles (Scope of Work and General Notes).

4. In the *Text Editor* contextual tab>Insert panel, expand the (Columns flyout) and select **Static Columns>2**. The text is divided into two columns.

5. Click (Columns flyout)) and select **Column Settings**. The Column Settings dialog box opens.

6. In the *Width* area, set the *Column* to **3"** and *Gutter* to **1/2"**, as shown in Figure 14–52.

Figure 14–52

7. Click **OK** to close the Column Settings dialog box. The columns adjust to match the new values.

8. Close the Text Editor. The text is not completely on the sheet.

9. Double-click on the text to open the Text Editor again.Expand

   ![] (Columns flyout)), and select **Dynamic Columns>Manual height**. Close the Text Editor.

10. The text is a single column flowing below the sheet. Click on the text to display the grips. Use the top right pointing arrow grip to widen the column width slightly (the text **furnishing** to display at the end of first line), then move the upward facing arrow at the bottom of the column to just above the General Notes section. This creates two columns.

11. In the second column, drag and drop the upward facing arrow just below the point 3, creating the third column. Use the arrows to adjust the columns, as shown in Figure 14–53.

The right pointing arrow increases the width. Drag and drop the bottom arrow to create columns and modify the column height.

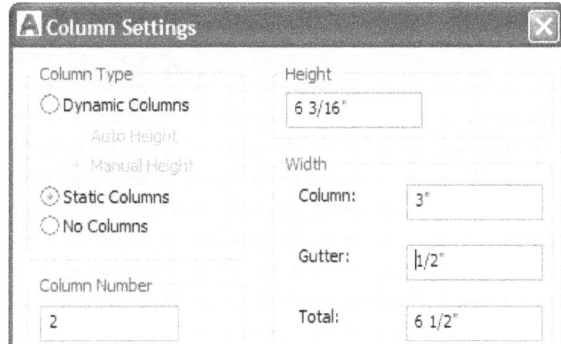

Scope of Work:
This project consists of furnishing and installing conduit, junction boxes, receptacles, data connectors, and cabling for connection to devices and to riser panels for the following buildings:
- West Hospital
- Cancer Clinic
- Ambulatory Care
- Nursing School

General Notes:
1. Verify all dimensions and conditions at the site and report any discrepancies to ADU Engineering before proceeding with the work.
2. Conduit - 3/4" rigid metallic conduit from device receptacle to first junction box.
3. 2" rigid metallic conduit from first junction box for the remainder of all conduit required.

4. In general, run 2" conduit from first junction box to Riser panel on each floor with 2" conduit shunts between riser panels and MAU.
5. Junction boxes - All junction boxes to be 18"x18"x6" galvanized metal. Provide covers of same material. Junction boxes to meet all electrical code requirements. See plans for locations.

Figure 14–53

12. Save and close the drawing.

14.4 Adding Notes with Leaders to Your Drawing

In a drawing, you often need to use an arrow to point to objects in the drawing and add either text or keynotes. This can be done using the **Multileader** command. Multileaders consist of straight lines or splines and can contain multiple leaders. You can use Multiline text or blocks for content, as shown in Figure 14–54.

The style of a multileader determines whether it uses text for the note or a block, such as a circle.

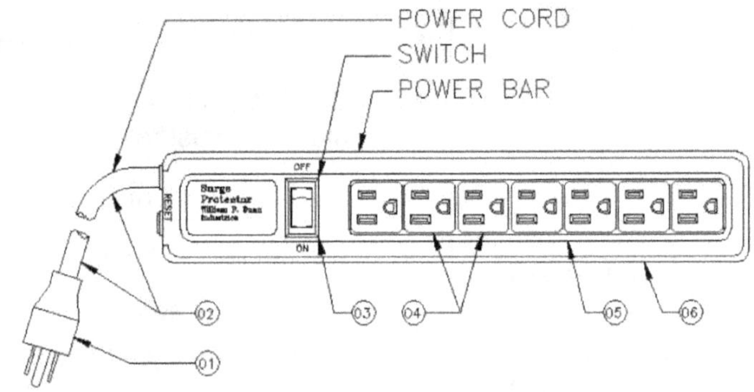

Figure 14–54

- As with other text and dimension objects, multileaders use a style and can be annotative.

How To: Add a Text Note

1. Select a Multileader style that uses text. Both the Standard and Annotative styles provided with the AutoCAD templates are designed this way.
2. In the *Annotate* tab>Leaders panel or in the *Home* tab>Annotation panel, click   (Multileader).
3. Select a point for the leader arrowhead location.
4. Select a point for the leader landing. By default, a horizontal tag is attached to the end.
5. Type the text. To specify the text width so that it word-wraps, you can use the Text Width arrows in the Text Formatting ruler.

6. Click ✓ (Close Text Editor) in the *Text Editor* contextual tab or click away from the text in the drawing. The multileader displays as shown in Figure 14–55.

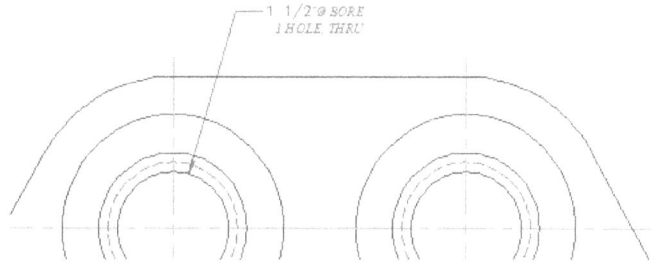

Figure 14–55

- The *Text Editor* contextual tab displays when you place multiline text using the **Multileader** command.

- You can change the order in which you place the leader using the **Leader Landing first** or **Content first** options, as shown in Figure 14–56. If you change the method of placing the leader, it becomes the default and is used the next time you start the command.

*You can use **Options** to modify the appearance of the leader, but creating Multileader Styles is recommended.*

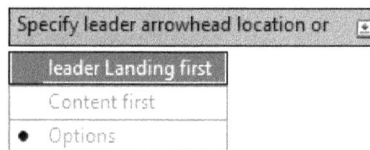

Figure 14–56

Drawing Keynotes

You can draw Multileaders with numbers in a block that are related to a list of keynotes located elsewhere in the drawing, as shown in Figure 14–57. You need to use a multileader style that uses blocks.

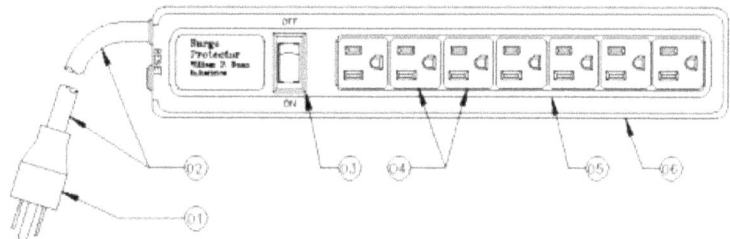

Figure 14–57

Modifying Multileaders

The leader and text (or block) of a multileader are one object. Multileaders can be modified using grips and text editing tools.

Grip Editing

You can use grips to modify the landing length (as shown in Figure 14–58), leader length and angle, and to move the multileader.

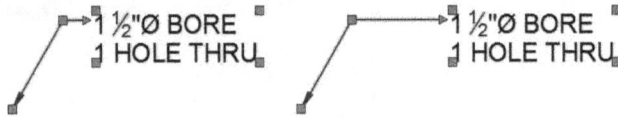

Figure 14–58

- The square grip at the end of the leader line changes the location at which the leader line is pointing.

- The square grip at the top left of the text moves the multileader.

- The arrow grip on the landing changes its length.

- If you hover over the square multi-functional grips on the leader line as shown in Figure 14–59, additional options display, such as **Add Vertex** and **Add/Remove Leader**.

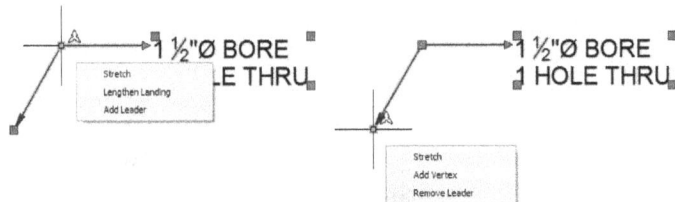

Figure 14–59

- If you are working with text leaders that have a specific text length, you can modify the text boundary using grips, as shown in Figure 14–60.

Figure 14–60

- If the text does not have a specified boundary, you can create one by clicking on the text again and modifying the boundary box using the Text Width ruler, as shown in Figure 14–61.

1 ½"Ø BORE
1 HOLE THRU

1 ½"Ø BORE
1 HOLE THRU

Figure 14–61

Adding and Removing Leaders

You can add or remove leader lines to create a single leader object, which points to multiple locations in the drawing, as shown in Figure 14–62.

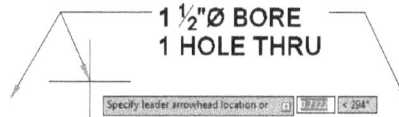

1 ½"Ø BORE
1 HOLE THRU

Specify leader arrowhead location or

Figure 14–62

How To: Add Leaders

1. In the *Annotate* tab>Leaders panel, click (Add Leader).
2. Select an existing Multileader.
3. Select the location at which you want to add the new leader.
4. Continue adding leaders as required.
5. Press <Enter> to complete the command.

How To: Remove Leaders

1. In the *Annotate* tab>Leaders panel, click (Remove Leader).
2. Select an existing Multileader.
3. Select the leaders that you want to remove.
4. Press <Enter> to complete the command.

Select Individual Leaders to Edit

You can select individual leaders and modify them. For example, in Figure 14–63, several leaders were modified to distinguish new plants from existing plants of the same type.

Figure 14–63

How To: Select and Edit Individual Leaders

1. Select an existing Multileader.
2. Hold <Ctrl> and click to select one or more leaders in a Multileader. The leaders display with red grips.
3. Once selected, right-click and select Properties. Use the Properties palette to change the properties of the selected leaders, such as their color, leader, or arrowhead size, as shown in Figure 14–64.

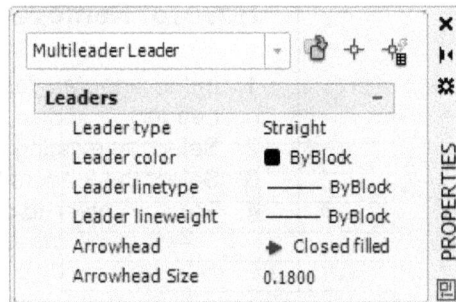

Figure 14–64

Aligning Multileaders

You can use the **Multileader Align** command to arrange multileaders so that they are evenly spaced and aligned, as shown in Figure 14–65.

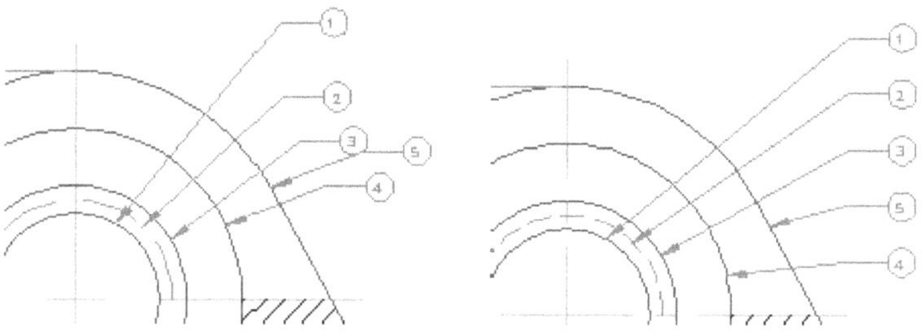

Figure 14–65

How To: Align Multileaders

1. In the *Annotate* tab>Leaders panel, click (Align, Multileader).
2. Select the multileaders that you want to align and press <Enter>.

The last option used becomes the default when you use the command again.

3. You can change the current mode of aligning by pressing <Down Arrow>, selecting **Options**, and selecting an option.
4. Select the multileader or points to which you want to align.

Distribute	Select two points. The multileaders are evenly spaced between them.
Make leader segments Parallel	Select a multileader to which to make the other leader segments parallel. The content remains in place and the leaders' angles are made parallel to the selected leader.
Specify Spacing	Select to type a distance for the spacing and then select a multileader to which to align and direction for alignment.
Use current spacing	Select to use the current spacing settings. The content is aligned and the spacing between the multileaders does not change.

Collecting Multileaders

You can collect several multileaders together using one leader, as shown in Figure 14–66. This only works with multileaders that have block content, not those with text content. This enables you to combine multiple blocks into a string. The blocks can be displayed vertically, horizontally, or wrapped to fit into a selected space.

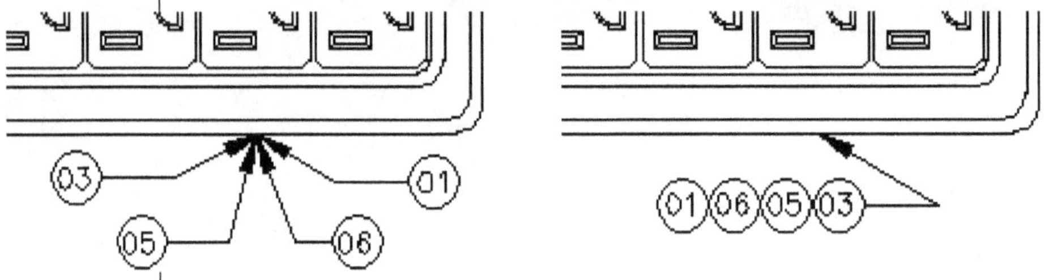

Figure 14–66

How To: Collect Multileader Blocks

1. In the *Annotate* tab>Leaders panel, click ⟋○ (Collect).
2. Select the leaders that you want to group together and press <Enter>
3. Select a location for the newly collected leaders.

- The default layout is **Horizontal**, but you can change it to **Vertical** using the shortcut menu. If there is a long line of bubbles, select the **Wrap** option and specify the wrap distance.

Practice 14d | Adding Notes to Your Drawing

Practice Objectives

- Add text and block-based multileaders to a drawing.
- Add leaders to multileaders, align and modify multileaders.

In this practice, you will add text and block-based multileaders. You will add leaders to multileaders and then align and modify leaders with grips as required, as shown in Figure 14–67.

- The multileader style **Keynotes** was created for this drawing.

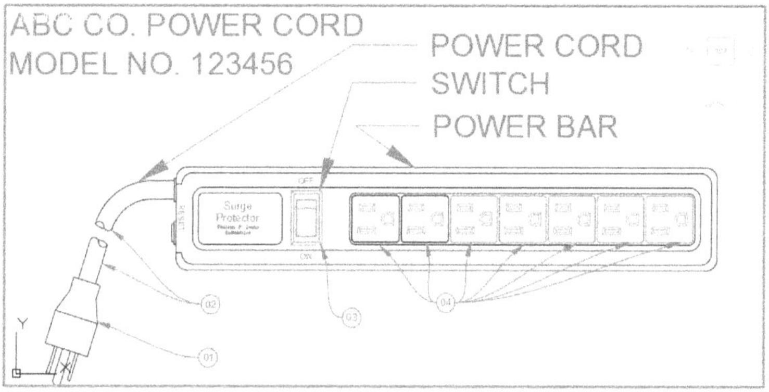

Figure 14–67

Task 1 - Draw multileaders.

1. Open **Power Protector-I.dwg** from your practice files folder.

2. Switch to the **A-Sized** layout and activate the viewport. Use **Zoom Extents** to display the drawing in the viewport. Pan the model down so that more empty space is left at the top. You can also use the viewport grips to add space around the surge protector. Once done, lock the viewport.

3. Set the *current layer* to **Text.**

4. In the *Annotate* tab>Leaders panel, in the *Multileader style* list, click **Annotative**.

5. In the *Annotate* tab>Leaders panel, click ⌐ (Multileader).

6. Add multileaders as shown in Figure 14–68, and label them as **POWER CORD**, **POWER BAR**, and **SWITCH**. Place the multileaders so they are not aligned.

Figure 14–68

7. Set the current *Multileader style* to **Keynotes**.

8. Start the **Multileader** command. Add several multileaders and with each multileader, in the Edit Attributes dialog box, enter tag numbers to label the components as **01**, **02**, **03**, and **04**, as shown in Figure 14–69.

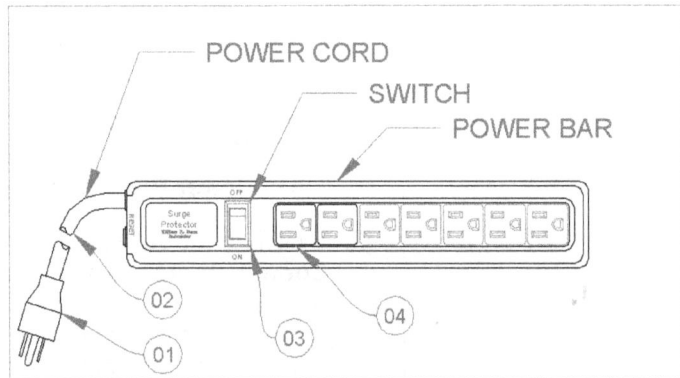

Figure 14–69

Task 2 - Modify multileaders.

1. Select the multileader with the label **02** and then in the

   Annotate tab>Leaders panel, click ⁺ᵀ (Add Leader). A leader is attached to the cursor and to the label. Click to place a leader to the other half of the power cord (as shown in Figure 14–70) and press <Enter>.

2. Similarly, add leaders to the multileader labeled **04** to point to each of the remaining sockets.

3. In the *Annotate* tab>Leaders panel, click (Align, Multileader).

4. Select the multileaders **POWER BAR**, **POWER CORD**, and **SWITCH** and then press <Enter>. Align the multileaders to **SWITCH** by selecting it. To set the direction, move the cursor perpendicularly above the **SWITCH** multileader. Click to place the multileaders.

5. Use grips to modify the exact locations of the leaders and text, as required .

Task 3 - Add text.

---

1. Set the current *Text style* to **Annotative** (*Annotate* tab>Text panel).

2. Start the **Multiline Text** command.

3. Use a height of **0.125** and then add a note above and to the left of the power bar, as shown in Figure 14–70. Use the grips to place the note in two lines.

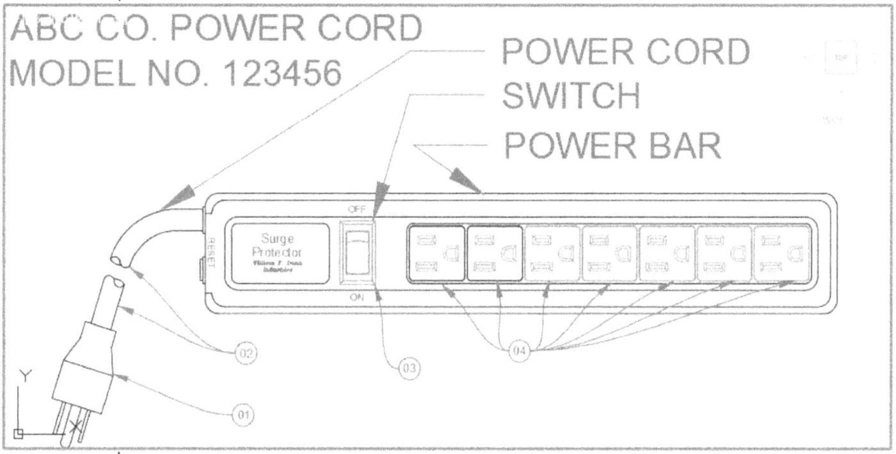

Figure 14–70

4. Save the drawing.

Chapter 15

Working with Tables

Exam Objectives Covered in This Chapter

- 5.3.d Insert tables and manipulate cell data
- 5.3.e Use fields in text and tables

15.1 Creating Tables

The **Table** command creates a unified table typically containing title and column headers with any number of rows/columns of data, as shown in Figure 15–1.

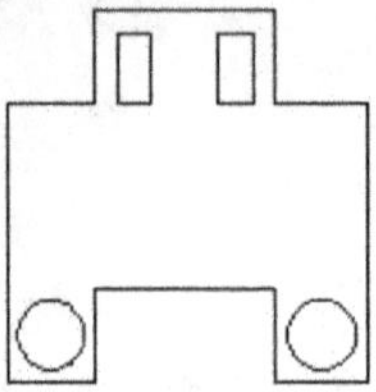

DESCRIPTION OF HOLES

SIZE	DESCRIPTION	QTY
A	Ø.375 THRU	2
B	.187X.375 RECT	2

Figure 15–1

- You can create table styles that define custom standard properties. When you insert a table object, you add the values for each of the cells.

- You can also create tables to which you can add custom information by linking external Excel spreadsheet files, or by extracting AutoCAD object data and creating a table from the information.

- Tables can include calculations.

How To: Create an Empty Table

The **Table** command is used to create tables from scratch, and from links and data extractions.

1. In the *Annotate* tab>Tables panel or in the *Home* tab>Annotation panel, click ⊞ (Table).

2. The Insert Table dialog box opens, as shown in Figure 15–2. In the Table style drop-down list, select the table style.

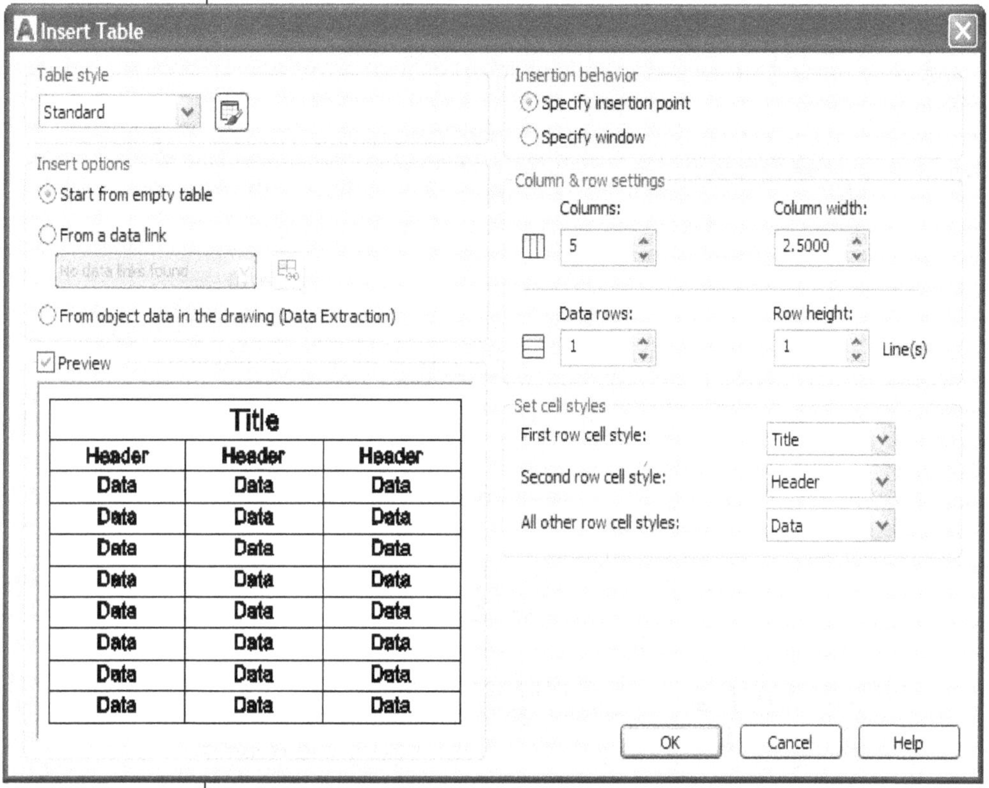

Figure 15–2

3. In the *Insert options* area, select **Start from empty table**.
4. In the *Insertion behavior* and *Column & row settings* areas, select the required options.
   - If you select the **Specify insertion point** option, you can set the number of columns and rows and their sizes.
   - If you select the **Specify window** option, you can set either the number of columns or the column width, and the number of rows or the row height (where the information not specified is automatically calculated by the size of the window).
5. In the *Set cell styles* area, select the required styles.
6. Click **OK** to place the table in the drawing.
7. Select a point in the drawing window to place the table or select two points to draw a window, depending on the option that you selected in the *Insertion behavior* area.

8. The *Text Editor* contextual tab opens and the title bar of the table is highlighted, as shown in Figure 15–3. Type the title.

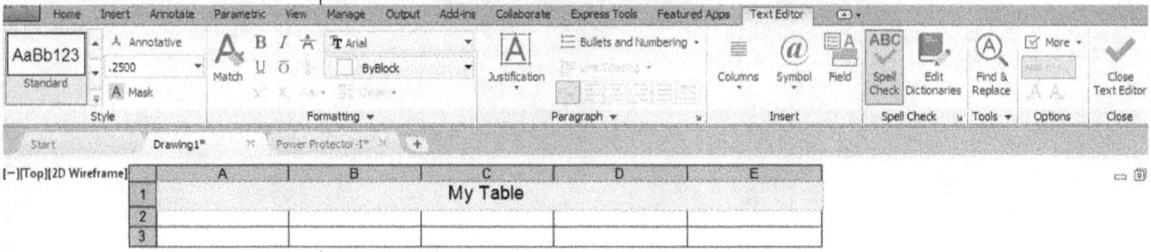

Figure 15–3

9. Press <Tab>. The first column and row highlight. Type the column heading or other information.
10. Continue to press <Tab> to move through the cells. You can also use the arrow keys on the keyboard to move from cell to cell. Press <Enter> to move down a row.
11. Click ✓ (Close Text Editor) to end the command.

• In the Insert Table dialog box, click 🖉 (Launch the Table Style dialog) in the *Table style* area to create a table style.

Populating Table Cells

Table cells can contain plain text, blocks, and fields (which can contain mathematical equations). The example shown in Figure 15–4 has blocks in the *Room #* column, fields that are linked to the area of polyline objects in the *Area* column, and the total area of the building using a formula next to the *Total Area* cell.

Occupancy Table			
Room #	Department	Area	Use
101	Marketing	452.0 SQ. FT.	Office
102	Marketing	463.2 SQ. FT.	Office
103	Sales ▫	452.0 SQ. FT.	Office
104	Engineering	2712.8 SQ. FT.	Drafting Room
105	Engineering	463.9 SQ. FT.	Office
106	Engineering	466.9 SQ. FT.	Office
107	Engineering	463.9 SQ. FT.	Office
	Total Area:	5474.6876 SQ. FT.	

Figure 15–4

- Click once in a cell to open the *Table Cell* contextual tab. It contains a variety of tools for adding and modifying cells. The current cell is highlighted with a gold edge, as shown in Figure 15–5.

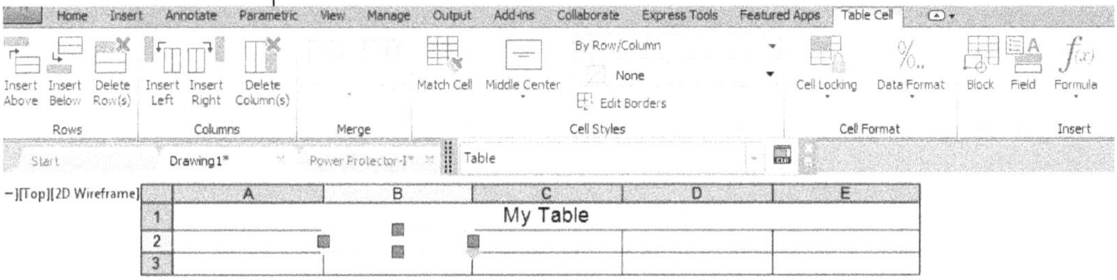

Figure 15–5

- Double-click in a cell to place the text and open the *Text Editor* contextual tab.

Inserting Blocks, Fields, and Formulas

Table cells can include text, blocks, fields, and formulas. Tools for inserting them are located in the *Table Cell* contextual tab> Insert panel and in the shortcut menus.

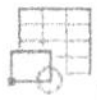

Insert Block: Opens the Insert a Block in a Table Cell dialog box. Select the name of the block or browse for a file. Then set the properties and cell alignment. The **AutoFit** option scales the size of the block to fit the cell size.

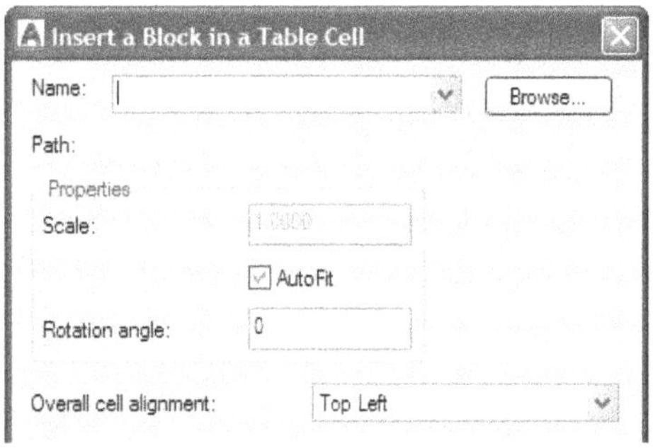

Insert Field: Adds a field selected in the Field dialog box into the cell. Hyperlinks are added using fields.

Insert Formula: Select **Sum**, **Average**, **Count**, **Cell**, or **Equation** to add a formula to the cell.

- To remove cell content, select the cell(s) and press <Delete>. You can also right-click and select **Delete All Contents**. This only deletes the selected cell(s).

- Tables are typically created in Paper Space. However, you sometimes need to access information in Model Space, such as the area of a hatch or polyline. When you are working with Object fields in a text object or table, you can select an object in a viewport even if the table is in Paper Space.

Calculations in Tables

You can make calculations directly in an AutoCAD table and the basic mathematical calculations are available, such as addition, subtraction, multiplication, division, and exponents, as well as **Sum** (as shown in Figure 15–6), **Average**, and **Count**. You can combine arithmetic functions, including parentheses, to create formulas.

	A	B	C	D
1		Replacement Costs		
2	Item #	Cost	Count	Total
3	AZ–408	255.45	12	3065.40
4	DG–411	18.29	22	402.38
5	DA–862	35.30	8	282.40
6			Grand Total:	=Sum(D3:D5)

Figure 15–6

- When the table is in edit mode, it displays letters for the columns and numbers for the rows. As in a standard spreadsheet, you specify a cell by its location, such as D3 (Column D, Row 3). When you finish editing, the table displays without this information.

- Cells used for calculations must only contain numeric information. The numeric information can be text or fields that have a numeric value (i.e., the area of a hatch or polyline).

Types of Calculations

Sum	Adds up numbers in the selected table cells.
Average	Computes the average of the numbers in the selected table cells. It adds up all of the numbers and divides the sum by the number of cells selected.
Count	Adds the number of selected cells, not the information in the cells. The cells must only contain numerical information.
Cell	Repeats the information from a selected cell in the current cell. The selected cell can be in another table. The selected cell must have numerical information; otherwise, #### displays in the field.
Equation	Computes the entered equation. You can add (+), subtract (-), multiply (*), divide (/), and set exponents (^). You can also group items together in parentheses, such as =(B3 / B7) * 2. The calculation in parentheses is computed first.

How To: Add Calculations to a Table

1. Create a table containing the numeric information that you want to calculate.
2. Click once in the cell in which you want the calculated value to be placed.
3. In the *Table Cell* contextual tab>Insert panel, expand

   $f_{(x)}$ (Formula) and select the type of formula that you want to calculate, as shown on the left in Figure 15–7. Alternatively, right-click and select **Insert>Formula** and select the type of formula, as shown on the right in Figure 15–7.

Figure 15–7

- **For Sum, Average, and Count:** Select two points for the corners of the table cell range. Click in the cells to be calculated when you select the points.

- **For Cell:** Click in another cell to place its value in the current cell. This can be a cell in another table.

- **For Equation:** Enter an equation using the cell coordinates, such as = B4 * C4.

- You can modify the equations created by any of the formulas. For example, you might select a cell range and want to add a cell or group of cells that are not in that range. In such a case, separate the new cell or range of cells by a comma, as follows.

=SUM (B3:E3)	Original formula
=SUM (B3:E3,C4)	Adding an additional cell
=SUM (B3:E3,C4:E4)	Adding a range of cells

- The calculated value in the cell is a formula field. It displays with a shaded background. You can edit the field to display the formula or change the formatting by double-clicking on the text.

Practice 15a	Creating Tables

Practice Objective

- Create a table and add a formula.

In this practice, you will create a table that includes text, blocks, fields, and a hyperlink using the **Table** command. You will also add a formula summing up the values in one column using the **Formula** command.

1. Open **Occupancy-A.dwg** from your practice files folder.

2. Switch to the **Occupancy** layout.

3. Make the layer **0** current, and freeze all of the layers except **0**, **A-Area**, **A-Room-Symb**, and **Viewports**.

4. In the *Annotate* tab>Tables panel, start the **Table** command.

5. In the Insert Table dialog box, verify that the **Standard** table style and the **Specify insertion point** option are selected.

6. In the *Column & row settings* area, set the *Columns* to **4**, set the *Column width* to **2 1/2"**, and set the *Data rows* to **8**. Click **OK** and place the table in the drawing below the Floor Plan viewport.

7. Double-click inside the top row and type **Occupancy Table** for the title, as shown in Figure 15–8. Type the remaining titles for each of the column headings shown, using <Tab> to move to the next column.

	A	B	C	D
1		Occupancy Table		
2	Room #	Department	Area	Use

Figure 15–8

Click once on a cell (until the individual cell is highlighted and grips displayed) to open the Table Cell contextual tab. The tools required are located in the Insert panel.

8. For the cells in each column, add the following information, as shown in Figure 15–9. (**Hint:** Use the Auto-Fill cells grip for similar content.)

Room #	Use ⊞ (Block) to open the Insert a Block in a Table Cell dialog box. Select Room Number as the block name. Set the *Overall cell alignment* to **Middle Center**. Toggle on **Auto-Fit**. Click **OK**. Change the attribute to be the correct room number. Click **OK**.
Department	Type the text shown in Figure 15–9 for the departments.
Area	Use ⊞ (Field) to insert a field in each cell in the column (for the 7 rooms). In the Field dialog box, set the *Field category* to **Objects** and the *Field names* to **Object**. In the *Object type* area, click ⊕ (Select object) and then select the magenta polyline around the corresponding room in the floor plan. In the *Property* area, select the **Area** property. Set the *Format* to **Architectural** and the *Precision* to **0.0**.
Use	Type the text shown in Figure 15–9 into each cell in the column.

9. In the bottom cell of the *Area* column, add a formula using **Sum** (select the cell, right-click, and select **Insert>Formula> Sum**). Using a window, select the room areas in that column as the range and then press <Enter>. The calculated sum displays in the last Area column, as shown in Figure 15–9.

Occupancy Table			
Room #	Department	Area	Use
101	Marketing	452.0 SQ. FT.	Office
102	Marketing	463.2 SQ. FT.	Office
103	Sales □	452.0 SQ. FT.	Office
104	Engineering	2712.8 SQ. FT.	Drafting Room
105	Engineering	463.9 SQ. FT.	Office
106	Engineering	466.9 SQ. FT.	Office
107	Engineering	463.9 SQ. FT.	Office
	Total Area:	5474.6876 SQ. FT.	

Figure 15–9

10. Select the cell with the sum, right-click, and select **Insert> Edit Field**. Set the *Precision* to **0.0**.

11. Thaw all of the layers that you had previously frozen.

12. Save the drawing.

15.2 Modifying Tables

You can modify tables and table data in a variety of ways. Modifications can be made to individual cells, rows, columns, or to the entire table.

Modifying Cells, Rows, and Columns

When you select multiple cells, rows, or columns you can add and remove rows and columns, merge and unmerge cells, and modify cell properties. You can also modify an individual cell using grips.

- To select more than one cell, hold <Shift> or click and drag across the cells that you want to select.

- To select an entire row or column, select the corresponding letter or number that displays (gold) when a cell is selected with grips.

- You can also **Cut**, **Copy**, and **Paste** cell contents using the shortcut menu.

Cell Grips

The square grips around a cell change its height and width. If you modify the grips of a selected cell, it impacts all of the rows or columns in which it is located. The diamond shaped grip is used to click and drag to automatically fill the selected cells with the contents of the current cell. First select, and then right-click on the diamond grip to change the options, as shown in Figure 15–10.

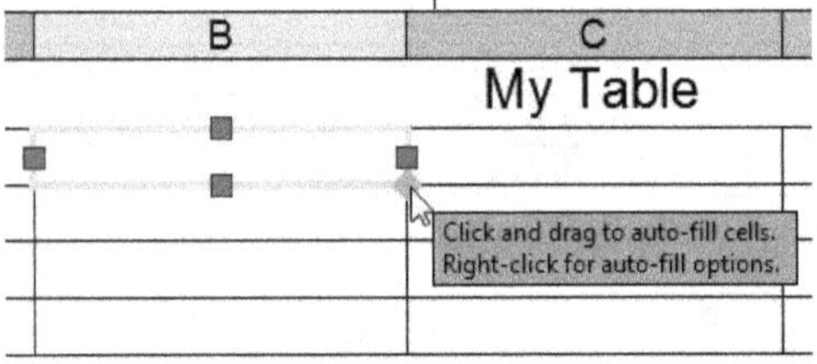

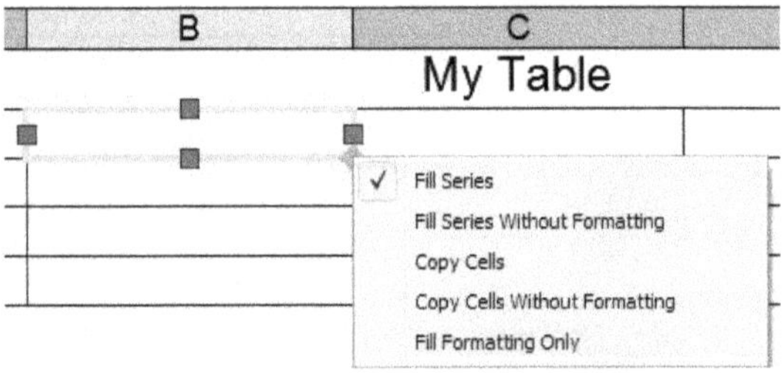

Figure 15–10

Modification Tools

With a cell selected, use the various tools available in the *Table Cell* contextual tab (as shown in Figure 15–11) to modify the tables.

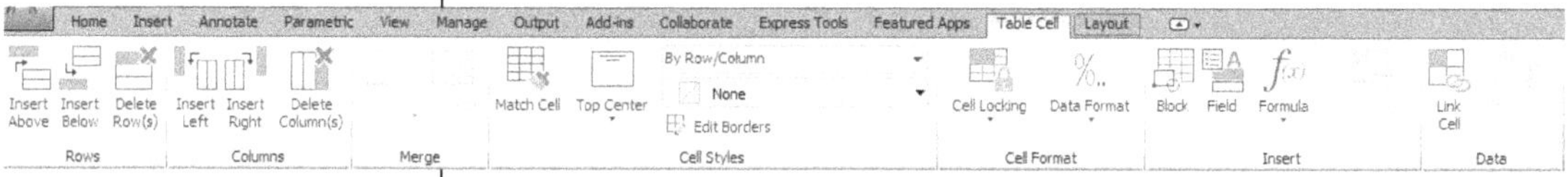

Figure 15–11

Adding and Removing Rows and Columns

	Insert Above: Inserts a row above the selected cell or row.
	Insert Below: Inserts a row below the selected cell or row.
	Delete Row(s): Deletes the selected row(s).
	Insert Left: Inserts a column to the left of the selected cell or column.
	Insert Right: Inserts a column to the right of the selected cell or column.
	Delete Column(s): Deletes the selected column(s).

Merging and Unmerging Cells

	Merge Cells: Merges selected cells depending on the selected option (**All**, **By Row**, or **By Column**). Multiple cells must be selected for this to be available.
	Unmerge Cells: Returns merged cells to an unmerged state. Merged cells must be selected for this option to be available.

Modifying Cell Properties

	Match Cell: Applies the properties of a selected cell to other cells, similar to the **Match Properties** command.
	Alignment: Applies the alignment selected from a list to the objects in the cell. You can align multiple cells at the same time. The current cell alignment icon might be displayed.
N/A	**Cell Styles:** Changes the style of the cell to the one selected from the list.
N/A	**Background Fill:** Changes the background color of the cell to the color selected from the list.
	Cell Locking: Sets cells to be **Unlocked**, **Content Locked**, **Format Locked**, or **Content and Format Locked**.
%..	**Data Format:** Sets the data format of items in a cell. It is set to **General** by default. However, you can change the numerical data to **Angle**, **Currency**, **Data**, **Decimal Number**, **General**, **Percentage**, **Point**, **Text**, and **Whole Number**. If you need to customize the data format, right-click in the cell and select **Custom Table Cell Format** to open the Table Cell Format dialog box.
	Manage Cell Contents: Controls the location and flow of objects if there is more than one type of content in a cell, such as a block and text. This opens the Manage Cell Content dialog box.

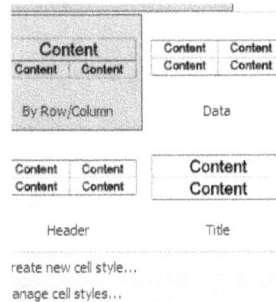

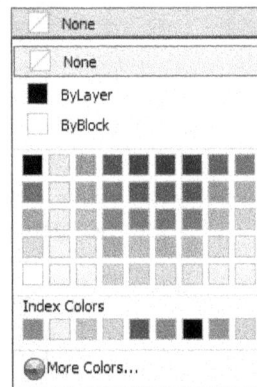

Edit Borders: Opens the Cell Border Properties dialog box, in which you can specify lineweights, linetypes, color, and border types for individual cells, rows, or columns. Toggle on **Lineweight** in the Status Bar, expanded Customization list to display the lineweights.

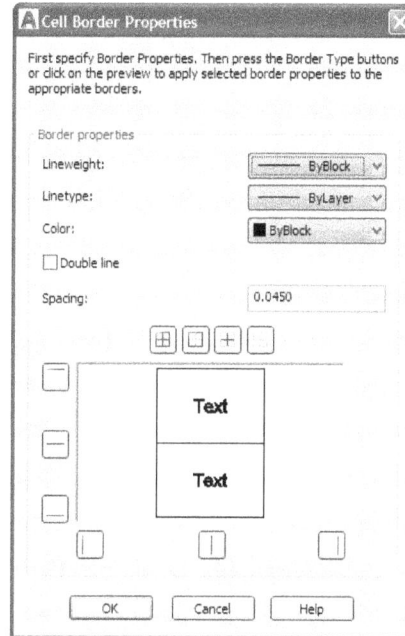

Modifying the Entire Table

When you select the entire table (click the edge of the table), as shown in Figure 15–12, you can use grips to modify its overall size, the width of columns, the height of rows, and to break the table into columns. You can also modify some of these options in the Properties palette or through the shortcut menu.

Figure 15–12

- Table-specific shortcut options include **Table Style**, **Size Columns Equally**, **Size Rows Equally**, **Remove All Property Overrides**, **Export**, and **Table Indicator Color**.

- **Table Indicator Color** is the color of the row numbers and column letters that display when the table is selected.

Table Grips

Tables can be extensively modified with grips, as shown in Figure 15–13. You can use them to adjust the width, height, and columns to fit the available space as required.

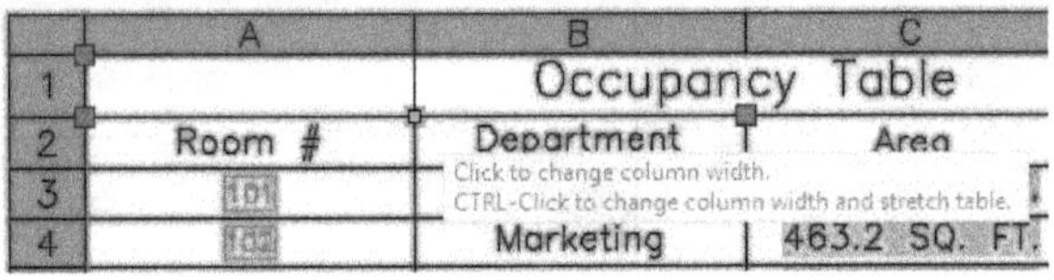

Figure 15–13

▪	**Column Width:** Controls the column width. Click the grip to change the width without changing the overall table width. The adjacent columns resize accordingly. Hold <Ctrl> to modify the overall width of the table. The upper left square grip moves the entire table.
▼	**Table Height:** Uniformly stretches the table height. The height of each row changes, including the title and headers. Rows are not added.
▶	**Table Width:** Uniformly stretches the table width. The width of each column changes. Columns are not added.
◀	**Table Height and Width:** Uniformly stretches both table height and width.
▽	**Table Breaking:** Activates table breaking, enabling you to control where the table is broken when it is in columns.

Breaking a Table

When a table is too long to fit on a sheet, you can break it and change its overall height. Click the grip ▽ (Table breaking) and drag it upwards until it reaches the required location in the table, as shown in Figure 15–14. The rest of the table is placed next to it in as many columns as required to contain all of the rows.

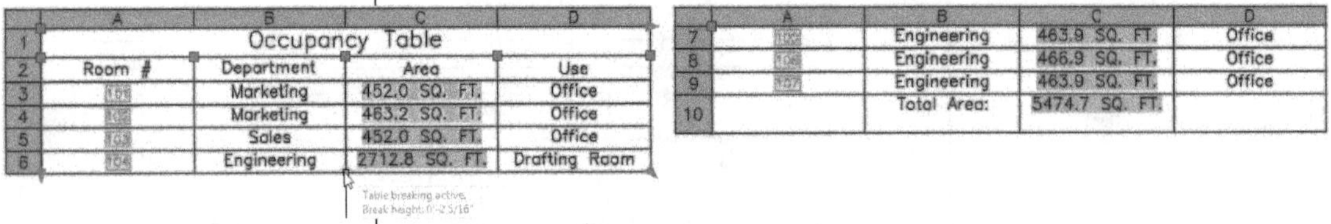

Figure 15–14

Practice 15b

Modifying Tables

Practice Objective

- Modify the table using various modification tools.

In this practice, you will use grips to modify the width and height of rows and columns, add and merge rows to create a new header, insert rows, copy and paste information, use Auto-fill to add information to cells, and break the table into columns. The completed table is shown in Figure 15–15.

Occupancy Table			
First Floor			
Room #	Department	Area	Use
101	Marketing	452.0 SQ. FT.	Office
102	Marketing	463.2 SQ. FT.	Office
103	Sales	452.0 SQ. FT.	Office
104	Engineering	2712.8 SQ. FT.	Drafting Room
105	Engineering	463.9 SQ. FT.	Office
106	Engineering	466.9 SQ. FT.	Office
107	Engineering	463.9 SQ. FT.	Office
	Total Area:	5474.6876 SQ. FT.	

Occupancy Table			
Second Floor			
Room #	Department	Area	Use
201	Marketing		Office
202	Marketing		Office
203	Sales		Office
204	Engineering		Drafting Room
205	Engineering		Office
206	Engineering		Office
207	Engineering		Office

Figure 15–15

1. Open **Occupancy1-A.dwg** from your practice files folder.

2. Zoom into the **Occupancy Table** area of the drawing.

3. Select the table to display the grips. Hold <Ctrl>, click and drag the right side square grip of the *Area* column to the right to increase the *Area* column width while also stretching the table, as shown in Figure 15–16. Click again to accept the stretch.

Figure 15–16

4. Click on the last row and use the bottom middle grip to decrease its height such that it is similar to the height of other rows.

5. Select the Row 2 of the table. In the *Table Cell* contextual tab>Rows panel, click ⊟ (Insert Above) to place a new row above Row 2. Fill in the first cell of the new row with the text **First Floor**.

6. Select the newly created Row 2. Right-click and select **Merge>By Row**.

7. With the row still selected, in the *Table Cell* contextual tab>Cell Styles panel, expand the Table Cell Styles list, and set the *style* to **Title**, as shown in Figure 15–17.

	A	B	C	D
1		Occupancy Table		
2		First Floor		
3	Room #	Department	Area	Use
4	101	Marketing	452.0 SQ. FT.	Office
5	102	Marketing	463.2 SQ. FT.	Office
6	103	Sales	452.0 SQ. FT.	Office
7	104	Engineering	2712.8 SQ. FT.	Drafting Room
8	105	Engineering	463.9 SQ. FT.	Office
9	106	Engineering	466.9 SQ. FT.	Office
10	107	Engineering	463.9 SQ. FT.	Office
11		Total Area:	5474.7 SQ. FT.	

Figure 15–17

8. Select the bottom row. In the *Table Cell* contextual tab>Rows panel, click ⊟ (Insert Below) until the last row number displays as 22.

9. Select one of the cells containing a room number block. Right-click and select **Copy** to copy the cell to the clipboard.

10. Leave three open rows after the *Total Area* row and paste the block into the cell in the *Room #* column (Row 15).

11. Select the copied cell and click on the Auto-fill grip (cyan diamond) of the cell. Drag it to the Room # cell of Row 21, as shown in Figure 15–18. Click to copy the block to the next six cells below.

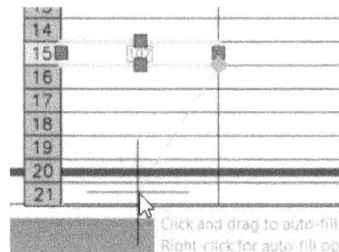

Figure 15–18

12. Double-click on the first new block to open the Edit Block in a Table Cell dialog box. Click **OK**. In the Enter Attributes dialog box, change the *Room Number* to **201** and click **OK**.

13. Modify the rest of the room numbers with subsequent numbers.

14. Enter **Engineering**, in *Department* column for row 201. Use **Auto-fill** to fill the rest of the *Department* cells (leave the last.

15. Repeat the **Copy** and **Auto-fill** process for the *Use* columns. Do not fill in the *Area* column.

16. Select the entire table and break it under the *Total Area* row. Select ▼ (Table breaking) and then drag it near the right side of the existing table. Move the cursor down until all eleven rows display and click to break the table, as shown in Figure 15–19.

	A	B	C	D
1		Occupancy Table		
2		First Floor		
3	Room #	Department	Area	Use
4		Marketing	452.0 SQ. FT.	Office
5		Marketing	463.2 SQ. FT.	Office
6		Sales	452.0 SQ. FT.	Office
7		Engineering	2712.8 SQ. FT.	Drafting Room
8		Engineering	463.9 SQ. FT.	Office
9		Engineering	466.9 SQ. FT.	Office
10		Engineering	483.9 SQ. FT.	Office
11		Total Area:	5474.7 SQ. FT.	

	A	B	C	D
12				
13				
14				
15		Marketing		Office
16		Marketing		Office
17		Sales		Office
18		Engineering		Drafting Room
19		Engineering		Office
20		Engineering		Office
21		Engineering		Office

Figure 15–19

17. You can add and merge rows to specify an additional Title and Headers for the Second Floor, as shown in Figure 15–20. Set the Cell Styles, as required.

Occupancy Table			
Second Floor			
Room #	Department	Area	Use
201	Engineering		Office
202	Engineering		Office
203	Engineering		Office
204	Engineering		Office
205	Engineering		Office
206	Engineering		Office
207	Engineering		Office
	Total Area:		

Figure 15–20

18. Save the drawing.

15.3 Working with Linked Tables

Many companies store information in spreadsheets that can be used in a drawing set. Instead of creating a table in the AutoCAD software and filling it in from scratch, you can create a table linked to an Excel spreadsheet. This can be done using the **Copy** and **Paste Special** from clipboard method or by linking to the table using the **Table** command. Figure 15–21 shows an Excel table that has been copied into the AutoCAD software.

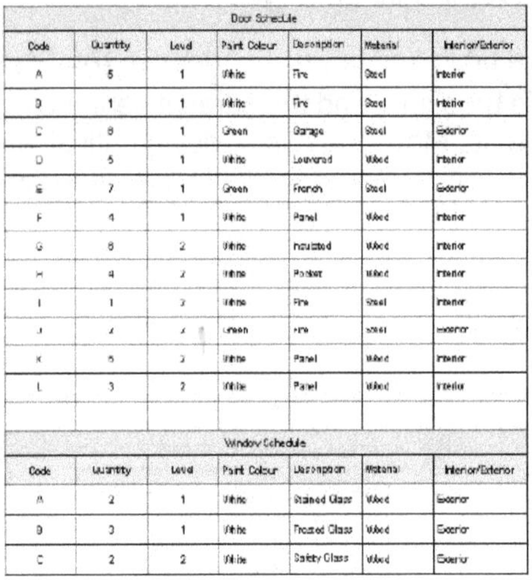

Door Schedule						
Code	Quantity	Level	Paint Colour	Description	Material	Interior/Exterior
A	5	1	White	Fire	Steel	Interior
B	1	1	White	Fire	Steel	Interior
C	8	1	Green	Garage	Steel	Exterior
D	5	1	White	Louvered	Wood	Interior
E	7	1	Green	French	Steel	Exterior
F	4	1	White	Panel	Wood	Interior
G	6	2	White	Insulated	Wood	Interior
H	4	2	White	Pocket	Wood	Interior
I	1	2	White	Fire	Steel	Interior
J	2	2	Green	Fire	Steel	Exterior
K	6	2	White	Panel	Wood	Interior
L	3	2	White	Panel	Wood	Interior
Window Schedule						
Code	Quantity	Level	Paint Colour	Description	Material	Interior/Exterior
A	2	1	White	Stained Glass	Wood	Exterior
B	3	1	White	Frosted Glass	Wood	Exterior
C	2	2	White	Safety Glass	Wood	Exterior

AutoCAD table

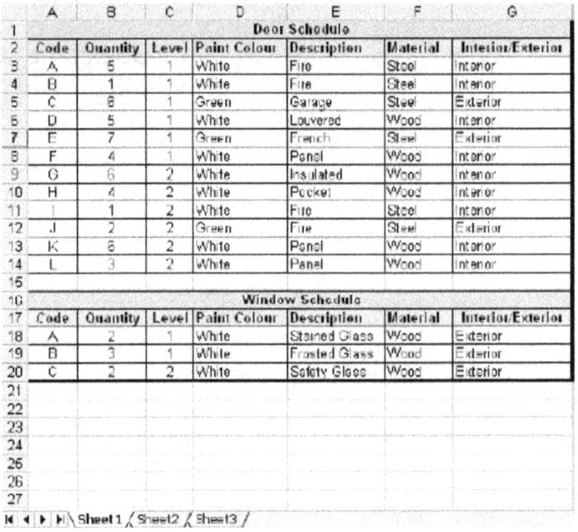

	A	B	C	D	E	F	G
1	Door Schedule						
2	Code	Quantity	Level	Paint Colour	Description	Material	Interior/Exterior
3	A	5	1	White	Fire	Steel	Interior
4	B	1	1	White	Fire	Steel	Interior
5	C	8	1	Green	Garage	Steel	Exterior
6	D	5	1	White	Louvered	Wood	Interior
7	E	7	1	Green	French	Steel	Exterior
8	F	4	1	White	Panel	Wood	Interior
9	G	6	2	White	Insulated	Wood	Interior
10	H	4	2	White	Pocket	Wood	Interior
11	I	1	2	White	Fire	Steel	Interior
12	J	2	2	Green	Fire	Steel	Exterior
13	K	6	2	White	Panel	Wood	Interior
14	L	3	2	White	Panel	Wood	Interior
15							
16	Window Schedule						
17	Code	Quantity	Level	Paint Colour	Description	Material	Interior/Exterior
18	A	2	1	White	Stained Glass	Wood	Exterior
19	B	3	1	White	Frosted Glass	Wood	Exterior
20	C	2	2	White	Safety Glass	Wood	Exterior
21							
22							
23							
24							
25							
26							
27							

Excel table

Figure 15–21

- The imported table uses the formatting from the Excel file.
- Any changes that you make to the linked Excel file can be updated in the AutoCAD table. You can also make changes in the AutoCAD table and save them back to the Excel file.

How To: Copy and Link a Spreadsheet to a Table

1. In Excel, select the cells that you want to include in the AutoCAD drawing and copy them to the clipboard.
2. In the AutoCAD software, in the *Home* tab>Clipboard panel, expand (Paste) and click (Paste Special).
3. In the Paste Special dialog box, select **Paste Link** and **AutoCAD Entities** as shown in Figure 15–22.

Figure 15–22

4. Click **OK**.
5. In the AutoCAD drawing, pick an insertion point for the table.

- If you use the **Paste** command rather than **Paste Special**, the table can still be updated in Excel but is not linked to the original file.

Table from a Data Link

The simplest way to link a table to an external file is to use **Cut** and **Paste**. Alternatively, you can use the **Table** command. The table can be linked to an entire Excel spreadsheet, a single cell, or a range of cells.

- You can have multiple data links in a drawing, all of which can be modified using the Data Link Manager.

How To: Create a Table from a Data Link

1. In the *Home* tab>Annotation panel or *Annotate* tab>Tables panel, click ⊞ (Table) to start the **Table** command.
2. In the Insert Table dialog box, select the **From a data link** option, as shown in Figure 15–23.

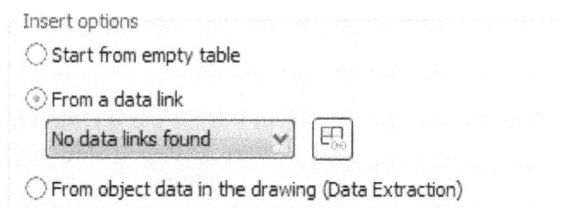

Figure 15–23

3. If you have an existing link, select it in the list and skip to Step 12.

4. If you want to create a new link, click ⬚ (Launch the Data Link Manager dialog) to open the Select a Data Link dialog box.

5. In the Select a Data Link dialog box shown in Figure 15–24, select **Create a new Excel Data Link**.

Figure 15–24

6. In the Enter Data Link Name dialog box, type a name for the link and click **OK**.

7. In the New Excel Data Link dialog box, you can select a file in the list or click ⬚ (Browse) to browse for a file.

8. In the Save As dialog box, select a file and click **Open**.

9. In the New Excel Data Link dialog box, specify the Link options, as shown in Figure 15–25.

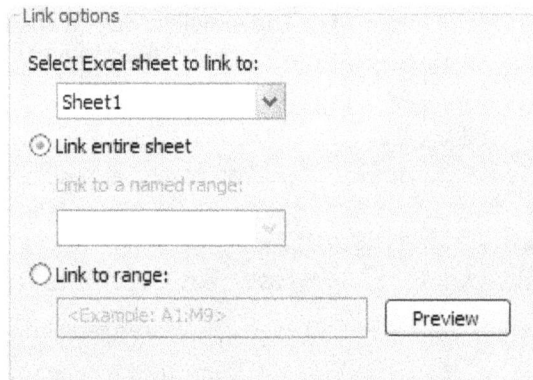

Figure 15–25

10. You can select a sheet (if there are several in the spreadsheet) and then link the entire sheet, a named range, or specify a range of cells.

11. When you have finished adding information to the table, click **OK**.

12. In the Select a Data Link dialog box, verify that the link you want to use is selected and click **OK**.

13. In the Insert Table dialog box, click **OK**.

14. Pick an insertion point on the sheet.

- If you are specifying a range of cells and do not use the correct form, the Invalid Range alert box opens, as shown in Figure 15–26.

Figure 15–26

- Numbered ranges are functions in Excel that enable you to select a cell or range of cells and assign them a name. This name can be used in formulas and anywhere you would type a cell identifier or range of cells. It is a labeled shortcut to a set of data. By labeling a range of cells with a descriptive name, you can quickly identify the function or origin of the data contained in them.

Link Cell: Displayed in the *Table Cell* contextual tab>Data panel when at least one cell is selected. Can be used to link individual cells or groups of cells to a cell(s) in a spreadsheet.

Using the Data Link Manager

If you know that you are going to link several files in your drawing, you can set them up in the Data Link Manager before you start the **Table** command. You can then select the link from a list in the Insert Table dialog box, as shown in Figure 15–27. You can open the Data Link Manager using (Link Data), which is located in:

- The *Annotate* tab>Tables panel, and
- The *Insert* tab>Linking & Extraction panel.

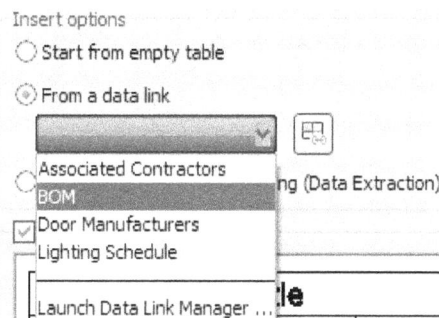

Figure 15–27

- To create a new Excel data link, in the Data Link Manager dialog box, select **Create a new Excel Data Link**, as shown in Figure 15–28.

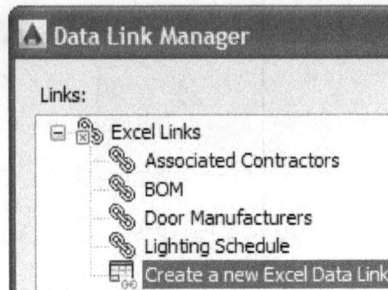

Figure 15–28

- Clear the **Preview** option to save time when working in the Data Link Manager.

- Expand the New or Modify Excel Data Link dialog box to display the extra options for modifying and creating data links, including cell content and formatting, as shown in Figure 15–29.

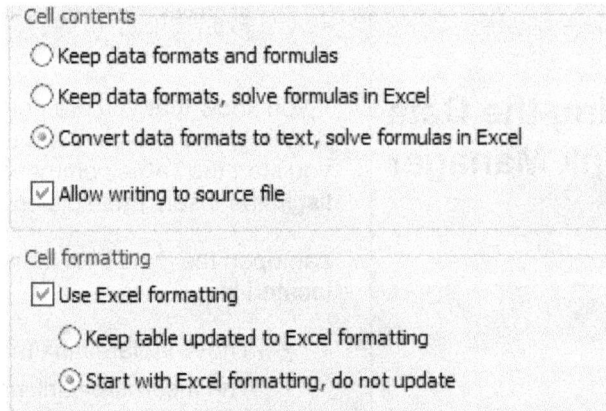

Figure 15–29

- Select **Allow writing to source file** to write modified data from the AutoCAD file to the source file.

Updating Table Links

You can update table data in two directions in a linked table, in the current drawing.

*   In the shortcut menu, use the **Update Table Data Links** option (shown in Figure 15–30) to update the AutoCAD table from the source. Use **Write Data Links to External Source** to write the AutoCAD data to the source (this only works if **Allow writing to source file** is selected in the *Cell contents* area, in the New or Modify Excel Data Link dialog box).

*   In the *Annotate* tab>Tables panel or *Insert* tab>Linking & Extraction panel, you can also use 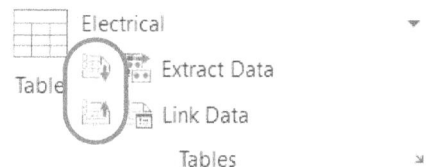 (Download from Source) to update the linked table data from the external source file and (Upload to Source) to update the linked data in the external source file from the current AutoCAD table, as shown in Figure 15–31.

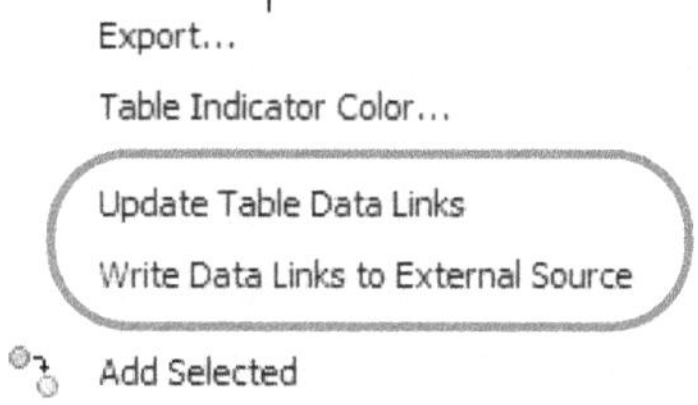

Export...

Table Indicator Color...

Update Table Data Links

Write Data Links to External Source

Add Selected

Figure 15–30

Electrical

Table   Extract Data

Link Data

Tables

Figure 15–31

*   The **Data Link Has Changed** bubble displays when the AutoCAD software detects that a linked file has been modified, as shown in Figure 15–32.

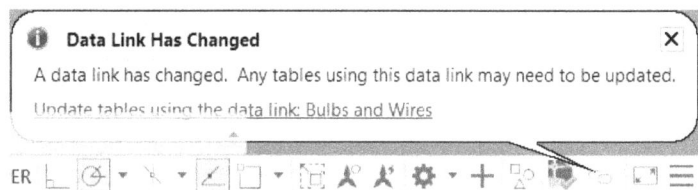

Data Link Has Changed   ✕

A data link has changed. Any tables using this data link may need to be updated.
Update tables using the data link: Bulbs and Wires

Figure 15–32

- In the Status Bar, right-click on ⌖ (Data Link) as shown in Figure 15–33, and either open the Data Links dialog box or update all data links.

Figure 15–33

- Linked and locked tables display icons when they are selected and you move the cursor over them. If you hover the cursor, it displays information about the data link, as shown in Figure 15–34.

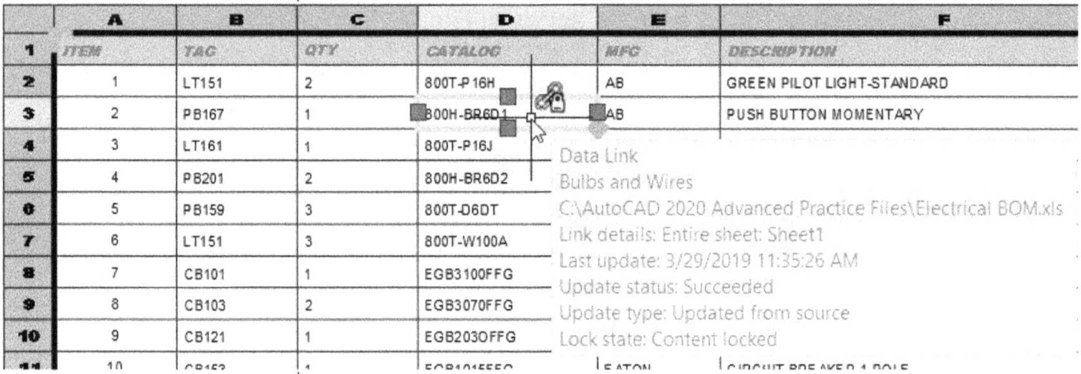

Figure 15–34

- Linked cells are locked by default to protect them from accidental modification. Green corner brackets display when the table is selected, indicating their status. To edit a cell, select it, right-click, expand Locking and select **Unlocked**. When a cell is unlocked, it can be modified.

- You can add columns and rows to a linked AutoCAD table. They are not removed when the data is updated from the source file.

> **Download from source:** Available in the *Table Cell* contextual tab>Data panel when at least one cell is selected. Can be used to update the information in a linked file.

Practice 15c | Working with Tables

Practice Objectives

- Add a table whose data is linked to an external spreadsheet file.
- Modify a table and update the data in the linked file.
- Create a new table style and apply it to an existing table.

In this practice, you will create and update a table from an external link. You will also create and apply a table style and apply a cell style to individual cells. In the first two tasks you will create a table from an external link and then update it from the source and to the source. The completed drawing is shown in Figure 15–35.

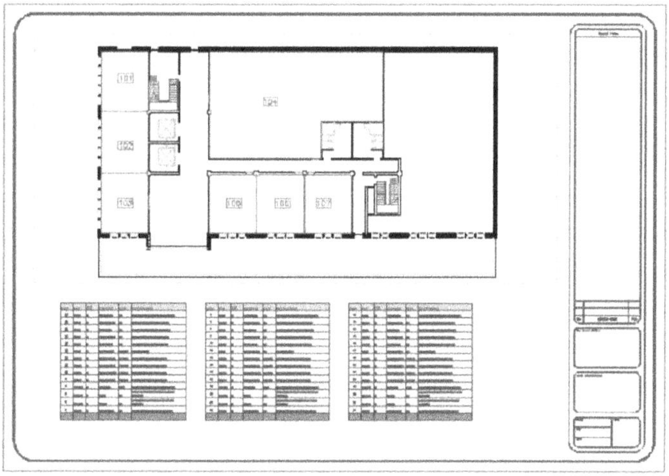

Figure 15–35

Task 1 - Create an externally linked table.

1. Open **Occupancy-Ad-A.dwg** from the practice files folder.

2. Switch to the **Electrical** layout.

3. In the *Home* tab>Annotation panel, click ⊞ (Table) and set the *Table style* to **Electrical** in the Insert Table dialog box.

4. In the *Insert options* area, select **From a data link** to create a table from an external source.

5. Click 🔗 (Launch the Data Link Manager dialog) to open the Select a Data Link dialog box.

6. Select **Create a new Excel Data Link**. The Enter Data Link Name dialog box opens.

7. Type **Bulbs and Wires** and click **OK**. The New Excel Data Link dialog box opens.

8. Click ⋯ (Browse) to browse for a source file. The Save As dialog box opens.

9. Select **Electrical BOM.xls** in the practice files folder and click **Open**. The New Excel Data Link dialog box now displays additional options.

10. In the *Link options* area, ensure that **Link entire sheet** is selected, and then click **OK**.

11. In the Select a Data Link dialog box, click **OK**.

12. In the Insert Table dialog box, click **OK** and pick an insertion point below the viewport to locate the table in the drawing.

13. The table is too long to fit on the page. Use grips to break it into three columns, as shown in Figure 15–35.

14. Save the drawing.

Task 2 - Update the table and write data to the source.

To complete this part of the practice, you need to have a copy of Microsoft Excel on the workstation.

1. Open **Electrical BOM.xls** in Excel from the practice files folder.

2. Change several of the *QTY* (quantity) numbers.

3. Save and close the Excel file.

4. Switch back to the AutoCAD software. An information bubble opens (as shown in Figure 15–36) indicating that the external source has been modified.

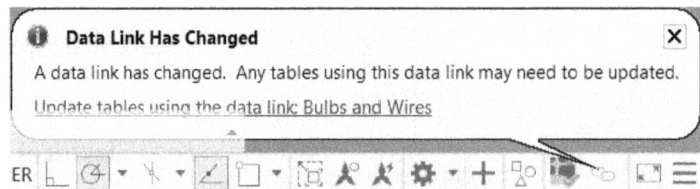

Figure 15–36

5. In the information bubble, select **Update tables using the data link** to update the data in the table with the modified data from the Excel file. The changes that you have made display in the updated table.

6. Zoom in on the top of the AutoCAD table and select the cells E2 through E7. Right-click and select **Locking>Unlocked** (as shown in Figure 15–37) to unlock the cells.

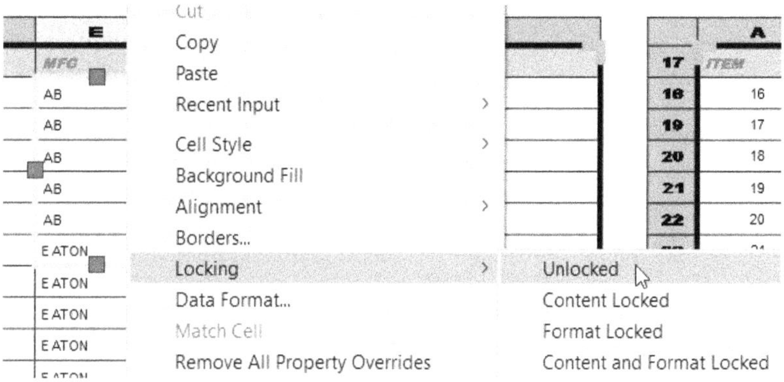

Figure 15–37

7. Change the *MFG name* in each of the cells to **SQD**.

8. In the *Insert* tab>Linking & Extraction panel, click (Upload to Source). Select the table and press <Enter>. All of the modifications in the AutoCAD table are written to the source file.

9. Open **Electrical BOM.xls** and note the changes to the cells.

10. Close the Excel file and save the drawing.

15.4 Using Fields

Fields are text objects that are designed to hold information that updates in a drawing when the base information changes, as shown in Figure 15–38. Fields can contain information, such as Date, Filename, Sheet Number, or Login name. They can be used in standard multiline text objects and in attributes and tables.

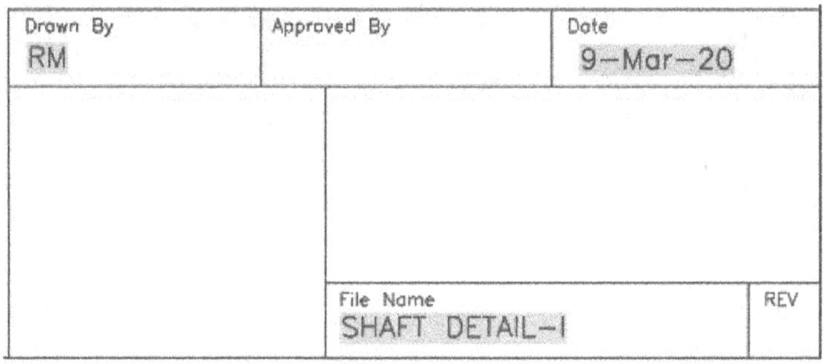

Figure 15–38

- Fields can be based on standard data or any property of an AutoCAD object, any AutoCAD system variable, and various other data information.

The Field dialog box can be opened in the following ways:

- In the ribbon, *Insert* tab>Data panel, click  (Field)

- *Text Editor* contextual tab>Insert panel in the Multiline Text Editor

- The shortcut menu in a Table cell

- The Attribute Definition dialog box

- The Enhanced Attribute Editor

How To: Insert Fields

1. In the ribbon, *Insert* tab>Data panel, click ![icon] (Field).
2. In the Field dialog box, select the field that you want to include, as shown in Figure 15–39.

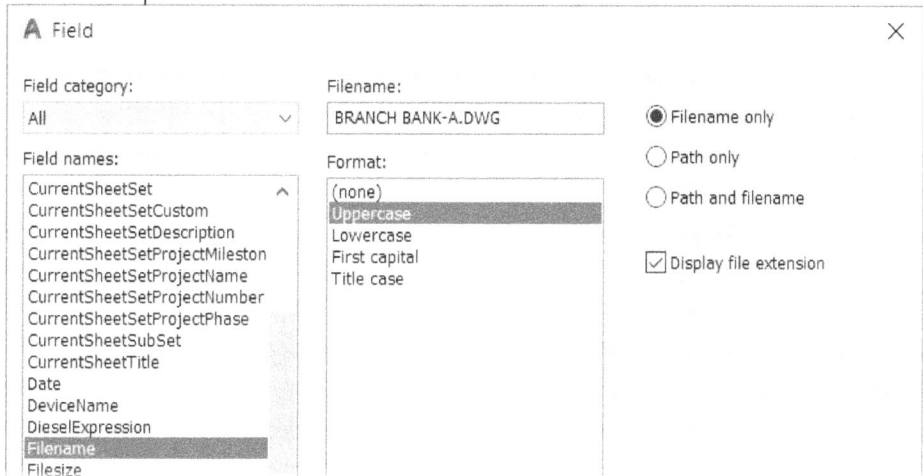

Figure 15–39

3. Select the required format and other options for the field.
4. Click **OK** to place the field in the drawing.

- When you select a field in the *Field names* area, the list of options changes in the *Format* area. For example, for the *Filename* field, you can specify the case for the text and whether or not to include the path; for the *Date* field, you can specify the date format, such as **9 March 2020** or **09/03/2020**, as shown in Figure 15–40.

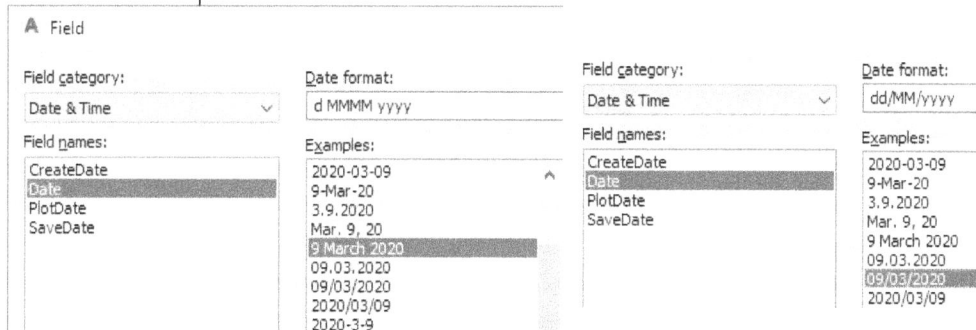

Figure 15–40

- You can select a *Field category* in the Field dialog box to filter the list of fields and narrow the options.

- The field displays with the current value highlighted in gray (the gray background does not plot). You can toggle it off in the Options dialog box in the *User Preferences* tab>*Fields* area by clearing the **Display background of fields** option.

- When you are working with *Object* fields in a text object or table, you can select an object even if it is in Model Space and you are working in Paper Space.

Updating and Modifying Fields

To manually update or modify a field, double-click on the text to open it in the text editor. Then right-click in the field and select the appropriate option from the shortcut menu, as shown in Figure 15–41.

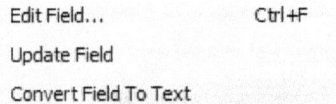

If the text editor is not active, the options are not available.

Edit Field...	Ctrl+F
Update Field	
Convert Field To Text	

Figure 15–41

Edit Field...	Opens the Field dialog box in which you can change the format, etc.
Update Field	Forces an update of the field, regardless of the automatic update settings.
Convert Field to Text	The field background is removed and the object becomes plain text.

- Fields that do not have a current value assigned, display as four dashes (----).

Field Settings

By default, the current values for fields update automatically in a drawing when you do any of the following: **Open**, **Save**, **Plot**, **eTransmit**, or **Regen** the drawing.

- To control which actions cause an update, use the Field Update Settings dialog box, as shown in Figure 15–42. Put a check in the options to automatically update fields.

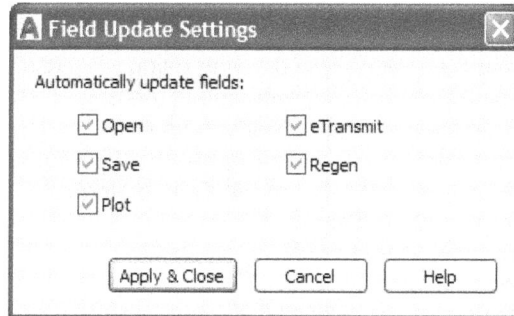

Figure 15–42

- To access the Field Update Settings dialog box, in the Options dialog box>*User Preferences* tab, click **Field Update Settings**, as shown in Figure 15–43.

Figure 15–43

Object Fields

Any property of an AutoCAD object can be used as a field. In the example shown in Figure 15–44, the fields display the area of several boundary polylines. When the boundaries are changed, the fields update to display the new area values of the polylines.

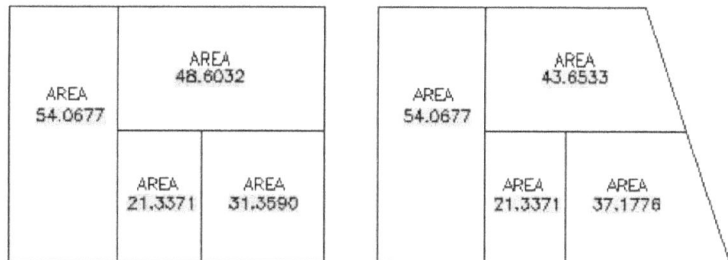

Figure 15–44

The *Object* field requires you to select a specific object in the drawing using ▧ (Select Objects) in the Field dialog box. After you select the object, its properties are listed. Select the property that you want to use (such as *Length* in the case of a line shown in Figure 15–45). Its current value displays in the top right corner of the Field dialog box.

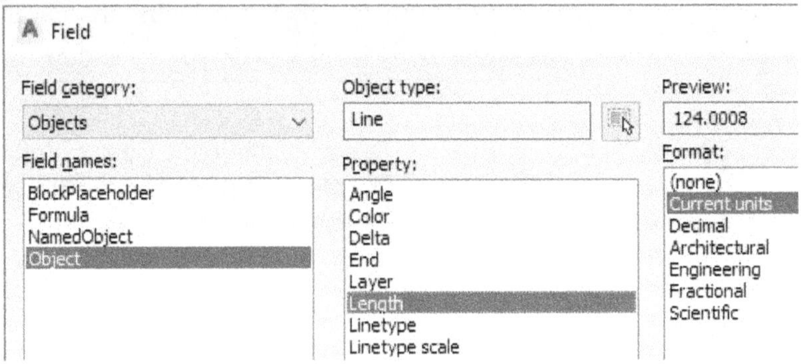

Figure 15–45

Fields in Blocks

Most fields can be included in a block definition and update within the block. For instance, the *Filename* field in a block updates with the name of the drawing file in which the block is inserted.

- Fields that do not update in blocks include those in the *Plot* category (*PaperSize*, *PlotScale*, etc.) and in the *Sheet Set* category. The value of these fields depends on the layout in which they have been placed or their location in Model/Paper Space.

- Similar to block insertions, fields in Xrefs use values from the host file (such as the filename).

Fields in Attributes

Fields can also be added to blocks by using a field to define the value of an attribute. For example, data in a title block, such as Filename or Title, would typically be created as attributes. If you use fields, these attributes automatically obtain their values from the drawing's properties. Having the field as an attribute value makes it easier to edit the value in the block as required.

- You can set the attribute value of a field in the Attribute Definition dialog box when you create the attribute or by editing it later.

- In the Attribute Definition dialog box, click ⬚ (Insert Field) next to the *Default* field, as shown in Figure 15–46.

Attribute	
Tag:	Date
Prompt:	
Default:	10-Jul-14

Figure 15–46

- For an existing attribute, double-click on the block to open it in the Block Editor and then double-click on the attribute to open the Enhanced Attribute Editor. You can assign a field to an attribute by right-clicking in the value field and selecting **Insert Field**.

- Alternatively, in the *Home* tab>Block panel or in the *Insert* tab>Block panel, expand

  the Edit Attribute flyout and click ⬚ (Single). Select the block to open the Enhanced Attribute Editor.

Practice 15d | Fields

Practice Objective

- Automate information in a title block by adding fields.

In this practice, you will add fields to automate some of the information in a title block, as shown in Figure 15–47.

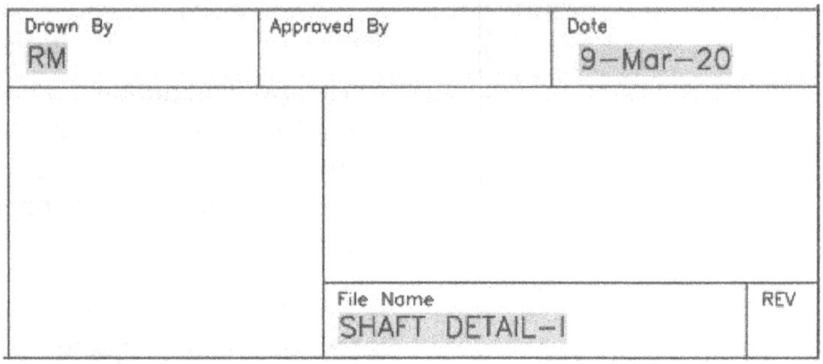

| Drawn By | Approved By | Date |
| RM | | 9–Mar–20 |

| | File Name | REV |
| | SHAFT DETAIL–I | |

Figure 15–47

1. Open **TBLK-A Landscape.dwg** from the practice files folder.

2. Zoom in on the title block information in the lower right corner.

3. In the *Insert* tab>Data panel, click ▤A (Field).

4. In the Field dialog box, set the *Field category* to **Date & Time**. For *Field names,* select **SaveDate**, and in *Examples,* select the format that displays the current date in the form **d-MMM-yy** (For example, **9-Mar-20**). Click **OK** to close the dialog box.

5. In the *Date* area, pick a point to place the date in the title block. Note that the date when this file was last saved is displayed.

6. In the *Drawn By* area, double-click on **xxx** to edit this text. In the Text Editor, delete **xxx**. In the *Text Editor* contextual tab> Insert panel, click ▤A (Field).

7. In the Field dialog box, change the *Field category* to **Document**. For *Field names,* select **Author**, leave the *Format* as **(none)**, and click **OK** to close the dialog box.

8. Close the Text Editor. The field displays as **----** because a drawing author has not been specified in the file.

9. Repeat the process and edit the **xxx** in the *File Name* area. In the Text Editor, delete **xxx**. In the *Text Editor* contextual tab> Insert panel, click (Field).

10. In the Field dialog box, change the *Field category* to **Document**, if required. For *Field names*, select **Filename** and set the *Format* to **Uppercase**. Select **Filename only** and clear the **Display file extension** option. Click **OK** to close the Field dialog box and then close the Text Editor.

11. Save the drawing. Note that your date updates to the current date as the **Save** command automatically updates the values for fields. Close the drawing.

12. Open **Shaft Detail-I.dwg** from the practice files folder.

13. In the **A-Sized** layout, insert the file **Titleblock-Shaft.dwg** as a block, with its insertion point as **0,0,0** in addition to the default scale and rotation. Close the Blocks palette.

14. Zoom in on the title block information.

15. In the Application Menu, expand Drawing Utilities, and select **Drawing Properties**. In the Properties dialog box, select the *Summary* tab. Enter your initials as the *Author* and click **OK**.

16. Save the drawing. The information in the fields updates with your initials in the *Drawn By* field, and the current date in the *Date* field.

17. Close the drawing.

Practice 15e | Object Fields

Practice Objective

- Display numerical values of closed polylines by adding text with fields.

In this practice, you will add text with fields that display the area of a polyline, as shown in Figure 15–48.

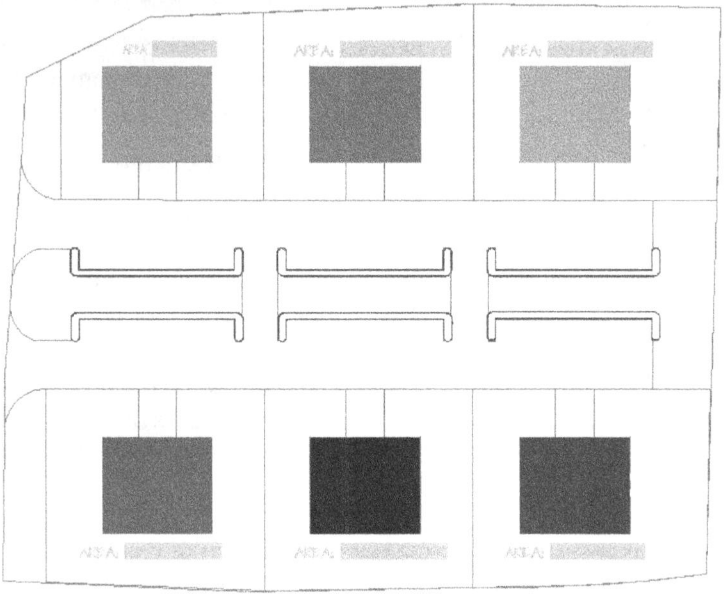

Figure 15–48

1. Open **Industrial Park-A.dwg** from the practice files folder.

2. Set the current layer to **Text**.

3. Start the **Multiline Text** command. Near the top of the top left lot, pick a point to place the text. Using the <Down Arrow>, select the **Height** option and set the *Height* to **5'**. Select the other corner for the text.

4. In the Text Editor, type **AREA:**. In the *Text Editor* contextual tab>Insert panel, click 　 (Field).

5. Set the *Field* category to **Objects** and for *Field names*, select **Object**.

6. In the *Object type* area, click 　 (Select object) and select the magenta polyline around the lot in which you are placing the text.

7. In the Field dialog box, set the following, as shown in Figure 15–49:
   - *Property*: **Area**
   - *Format*: **Architectural**
   - *Precision:* **0**

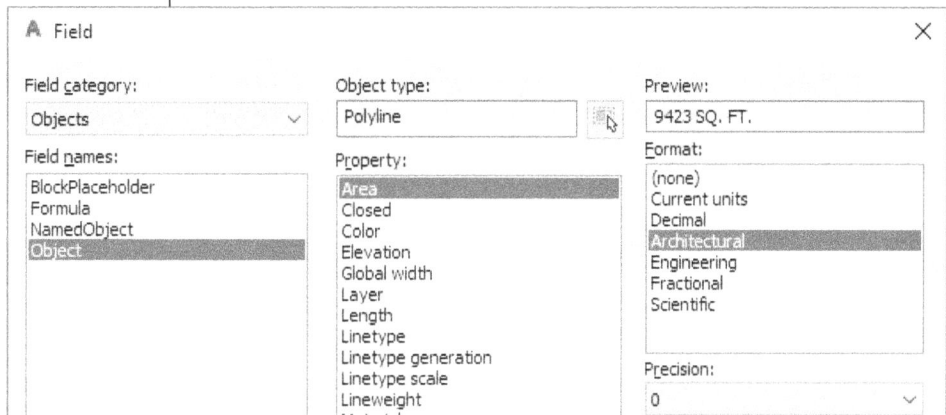

Figure 15–49

8. Click **OK** to close the Field dialog box.

Your font might be different than the font shown in Figure 15–48.

9. In the Text Editor, use the arrow to increase the width to display the information in a single line. Click ✔ (Close Text Editor) to end the **Multiline Text** command.

10. Repeat Steps 3 to 8 in several of the lots. (You cannot copy the text because you have to select a different polyline object corresponding to each plot.)

11. Use grips to stretch one of the boundary polylines to make it larger.

12. **Regen** the drawing to update the field. The area value changes based on the changes made to the polyline.

13. Save and close the drawing.

Practice 15f | Fields and Tables

Practice Objective

- Create fields in a table to display the floorplan areas of each space.

In this project, you will use fields to display the areas of the spaces in a floorplan and create a table for calculating the quantity of paint required to paint several rooms. The completed drawing is shown in Figure 15–50.

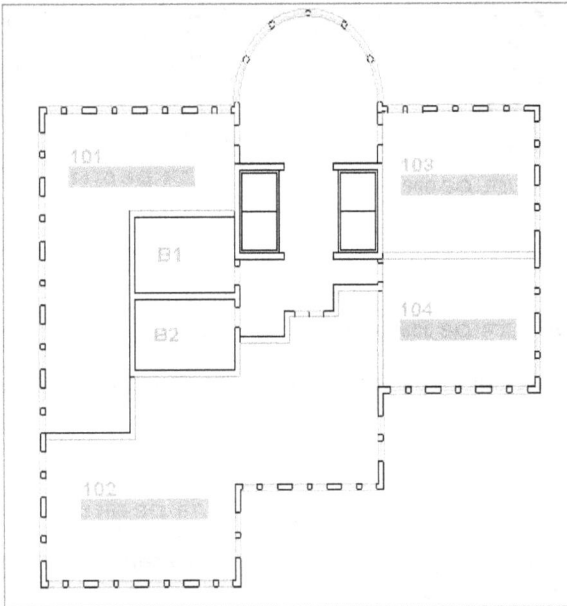

PAINT ESTIMATE—WALLS

Room	Perimeter	Height	Wall Area	Doors	Windows
101	176	9	1584	1	18
102	224	9	2016	2	22
103	104	9	936	1	10
104	100	8	800	1	10
TOTALS:			5336	5	60

Door Area	100	
Window Area	900	
Wall Area:	4336	
Wall Paint (Gallons):	12.4	
Trim Paint (Gallons):	1.6	

Figure 15–50

1. Open **Tenants-A.dwg** from the practice files folder.

2. Toggle off the layer **Doors** and set the layer **Space** to be current.

3. Use the **Boundary** command, with *Island detection off*, to create a polyline (*Object type - **Polyline***) in each numbered room. (Hint: The full boundary area must be visible on screen.)

4. Edit the room number text to include an *Object* field that displays the area of the room (**Architectural** with *Precision **0***). Select the boundary polylines (green) as the object for the field (it can help to toggle off the layer **Walls**). Modify the text format and line length as required. The areas are shown in Figure 15–51.

(Boundary) is available in the Home tab>Draw panel>Hatch flyout.

The color of the layer
Text *has been changed*
for printing clarity.

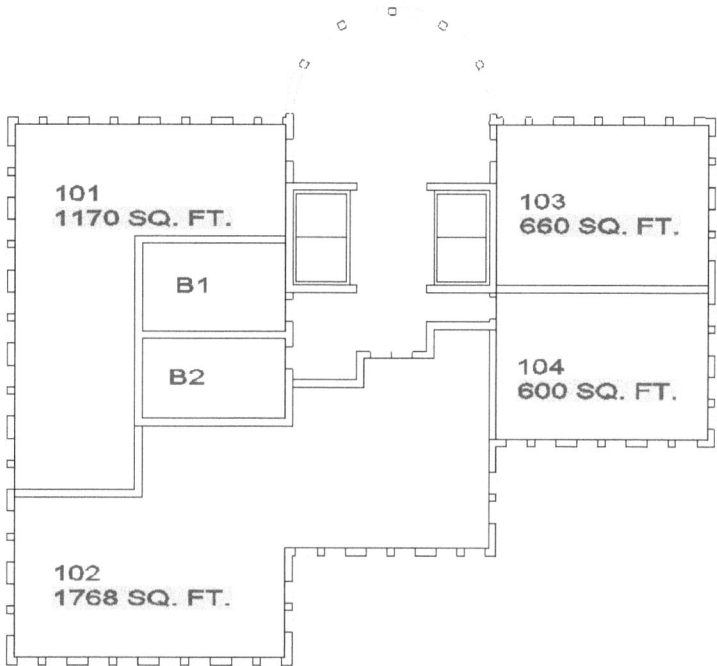

Figure 15–51

5. Switch to the **D-Sized** layout and make the layer **Text** the current layer.

6. Create a table that looks like the one shown in Figure 15–52. Use the **Standard** table style.

PAINT ESTIMATE—WALLS					
Room	Perimeter	Height	Wall Area	Doors	Windows
101	176	9		1	18
102	224	9		2	22
103	104	9		1	10
104	100	8		1	10
TOTALS:					
Door Area:					
Window Area:					
Wall Area:					
Wall Paint (Gallons):					
Trim Paint (Gallons):					

Figure 15–52

7. Add formulas in the appropriate cells for the following calculations. The required calculations are outlined for you and you need to decide how to create the formulas in the cells. Complete as many of the calculations as time permits.

Wall Areas:	Perimeter multiplied by the Height.
Total Wall Area:	Sum of all Wall Areas.
Total # Doors:	Sum of all Doors.
Total # Windows:	Sum of all Windows.
Door Area:	Number of Doors multiplied by 20.
Window Area:	Number of Windows multiplied by 15.
Paintable Wall Area:	Total Wall Area minus Door and Window Areas.
Wall Paint (Gallons):	Paint-able Wall Area divided by 350.
Trim Paint (Gallons):	Number of Doors multiplied by 20 plus Number of Windows multiplied by 7.5, all divided by 350.

Adding Dimensions

Exam Objectives Covered in This Chapter

- 5.5.b Create multiple dimensions with a single command
- 5.5.c Set the dimension layer
- 5.5.d Associate or re-associate dimensions to objects
- 5.5.e Break and restore dimension and extension lines
- 5.5.f Adjust the spacing between dimensions

Note: The objective *5.5.a Create and modify dimension styles* is covered in *Chapter 17: Annotation Features and Styles*.

16.1 Dimensioning Concepts

The AutoCAD® dimensioning commands create dimensions based on points that you specify or by selecting the object for dimensioning. The AutoCAD software automatically draws the dimension with the appropriate extension lines, arrowheads, dimension lines, and text, as shown in Figure 16–1.

Figure 16–1

- Dimensions recalculate automatically when the objects that they refer to are modified. For example, when you stretch a wall 2'-0" to the right, the associated dimensions update.

As you prepare to dimension, you should:

- Set up a viewport in a layout that displays the part of the model that you want to dimension. You should set the Viewport Scale before you start dimensioning.

- Select the layer for dimensioning.

- Select a Dimension Style to be used for dimensioning.

- Use the *Annotate* tab>Dimensions panel, as shown in Figure 16–2, to access the dimensioning commands and set up the layer and dimension style.

Figure 16–2

Lock the viewport to make it easier to zoom around the drawing without changing the scale by mistake.

Dimension styles can be annotative.

Some dimensioning commands can also be accessed in the Home tab>Annotation panel.

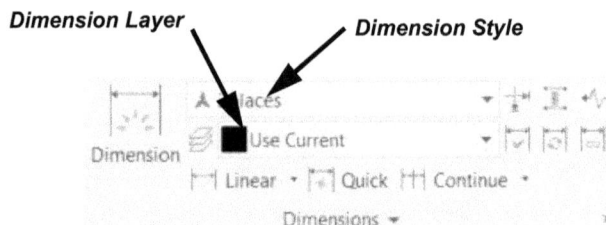

General Dimensioning

Dimensions can be added using a general dimension command or using commands specific to the type of dimension being added. The general dimension command automatically determines the type of dimension required based on the object or point selected.

- You can use a single **Dimension** command to add various dimensions, such as linear (horizontal, vertical), aligned, angular, radial etc. After placing a required dimension, the **Dimension** command remains active, enabling you to add other dimensions as required, without re-launching the command. The real-time [ ] Dimension command is located in the *Annotate* tab>Dimensions panel or in the *Home* tab>Annotation panel, as shown in Figure 16–3.

- You can also use the explicit dimensioning commands such as Linear, Angular, Aligned and so on. These are available in the *Annotate* tab>Dimensions panel>Linear flyout or in the *Home* tab>Annotation panel Linear flyout, as shown in Figure 16–3.

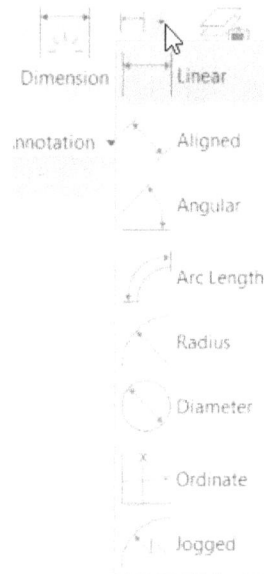

Figure 16–3

How To: Add Dimensions

Instead of selecting an object for dimension, you can use object snaps to snap to points to be dimensioned.

1. In the *Annotate* tab>Dimensions panel, click 🔲 (Dimension) or in the *Home* tab>Annotation panel, click 🔲 (Dimension).
2. Hover the cursor on the object that you want to dimension. Depending on the object that touches the cursor, a preview of a relevant dimension displays, as shown in Figure 16–4.

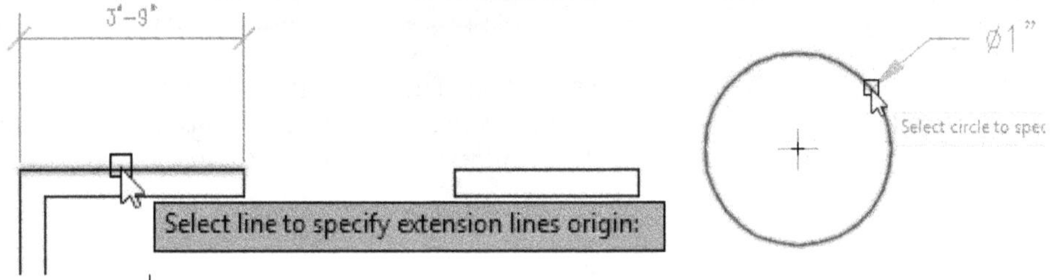

Figure 16–4

3. If the preview dimension is the correct one, click to save the dimension.
4. Drag the cursor to the location where you want the dimension to be located. Click to place the dimension or select an option from the Command Line (or use the <Down Arrow> menu).
5. Dimension another object in the drawing or press <Esc> to exit the command.

16.2 Adding Linear Dimensions

Linear dimensions measure a distance from one point to another, as shown in Figure 16–5.

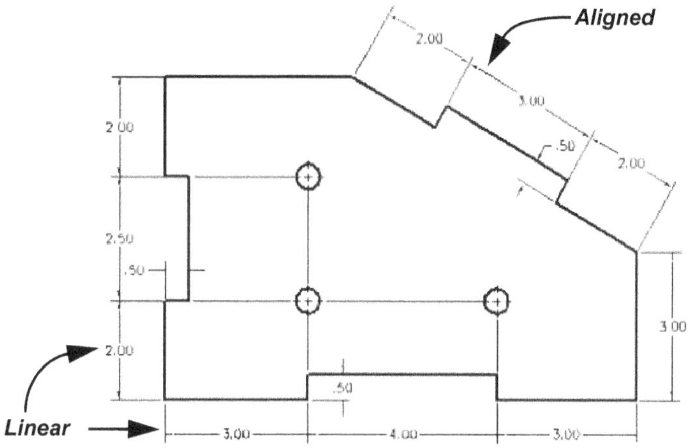

Figure 16–5

Individual Linear Dimensions

Linear dimensions can be horizontal or vertical, as shown in Figure 16–5. Aligned dimensions are also linear dimensions, however, they measure the linear distance parallel to the selected line or the selected points. The dimension line is placed parallel to the line between the points, as shown in Figure 16–5.

• The AutoCAD software determines the linear orientation (horizontal, vertical, or aligned) based on the selected object or where you select the point for the dimension line location.

How To: Add Linear and Aligned Dimensions

1. In the *Annotate* tab>Dimensions panel or the *Home* tab> Annotation panel, click [ ] (Dimension).
2. Select a line in the drawing.
3. Select a point to place the dimension line.

or

1. In the *Annotate* tab>Dimensions panel, click [ ] (Linear).
2. Select a point for the first extension line origin.
3. Select a point for the second extension line origin.
4. Select a point to place the dimension line.

Use Object Snaps to select the exact points for the extension line origins.

Hint: Oblique Extension Lines

If you want the extension lines of a linear dimension to be at an angle, you can click ⊢⌁ (Oblique) in the *Annotate* tab> expanded Dimensions panel, to angle the lines.

Adding a Break in a Linear or Aligned Dimension

In some cases, you need to have a dimension with a break because the length of the dimension is too long to display on a sheet, as shown in Figure 16–6.

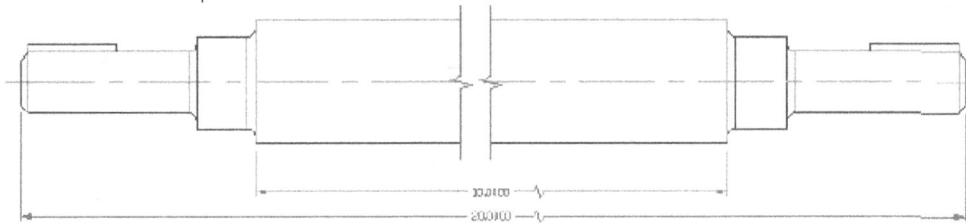

Figure 16–6

How To: Create a Jogged Linear Dimension

1. In the *Annotate* tab>Dimensions panel, click ⁺⋁ (Dimjogline).
2. Select the dimension to which you want to add the jog.
3. Specify the jog location along the dimension or press <Enter> to accept the default location.

• To remove a jog line, use the command's **Remove** option.

Multiple Linear Dimensions

These commands can be used with Linear, Aligned, or Angular dimensions.

After you have placed a linear, aligned, or angular dimension, you can use that dimension as the beginning of a series of related dimensions by clicking ⊢⊤⊣ (Continue) or ⊢⊣ (Baseline), as shown in Figure 16–7.

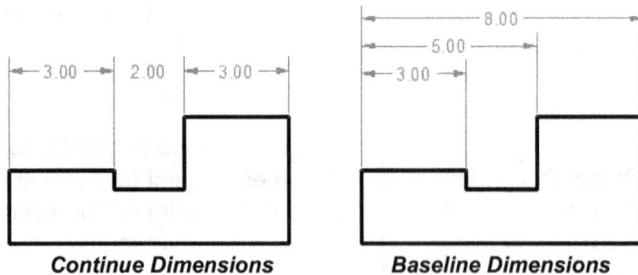

Continue Dimensions   **Baseline Dimensions**

Figure 16–7

Continue dimensions use the last extension line placed as the first extension line for the next dimension. The dimension line remains at the same distance from the object.

Baseline dimensions use the first extension line as the base for all other dimensions. As you select additional extension line points, the new dimension is placed over the previous one. The distance between the dimension lines is set by the dimension style.

How To: Add Continue and Baseline Dimensions

1. Place a linear or aligned dimension.

2. In the *Annotate* tab>Dimensions panel, click ⊢┼┤ (Continue) or ⊢⊣ (Baseline).

3. Select a point for the second extension line origin. The first extension line origin is automatically assumed to be from the last dimension you placed.

4. Continue selecting points for additional extension line origins.

5. Press <Enter> twice to finish the command.

- By default, the AutoCAD software uses the last dimension placed as the starting dimension. Use the **Select** option to select a different dimension to be referenced.

Quick Dimensioning

In some cases, you can place all of your dimensions along one edge of an object using one command, regardless of whether it is **Linear**, **Aligned**, **Baseline**, or **Continue**. As shown in Figure 16–8, the outside lines of the walls were selected using the **Quick Dimension** command and dimensioned at the same time.

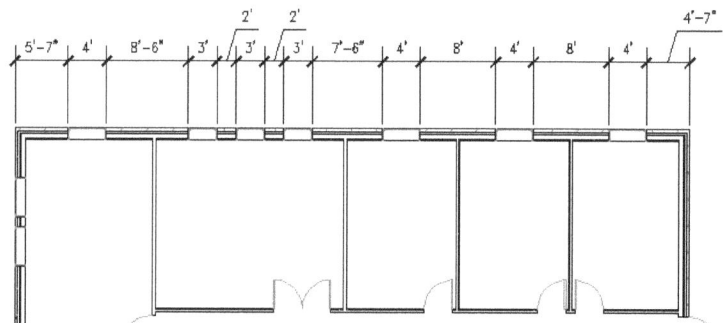

Figure 16–8

Quick Dimension does not enable you to place a type of dimension that is not appropriate for the selection. For example, if you select a line, you cannot place a Radius or Diameter dimension on that line.

How To: Add Quick Dimensions

1. In the *Annotate* tab>Dimensions panel, click ⊢⚡⊣ (Quick Dimension).
2. Select the objects that you want to dimension. When you have finished selecting objects, press <Enter>.
3. Specify the dimension line position.

• By default, the AutoCAD software creates continuous dimensions if you select linear objects or more than one object.

• You can switch between a number of other types of dimensions, including **Staggered**, **Baseline**, and **Ordinate**, in the Command Prompt, shortcut menu, or dynamic input drop-down list.

• Dimensions created using ⊢⚡⊣ (Quick Dimension) are placed on the current layer.

• Baseline and Ordinate dimensions start from a common point. You can set that point using the **datumPoint** option.

• There is also an **Edit** option that enables you to add or remove points. However, it is easier to do this using other commands.

Practice 16a | Adding Linear Dimensions (Architectural)

Practice Objective

- Add dimensions using various dimensioning techniques.

In this practice, you will start to add dimensions using the general **Linear** dimension command. You will then dimension different portions of the architectural drawing using **Quick**, **Baseline**, and **Continue** dimensions, as shown in Figure 16–9.

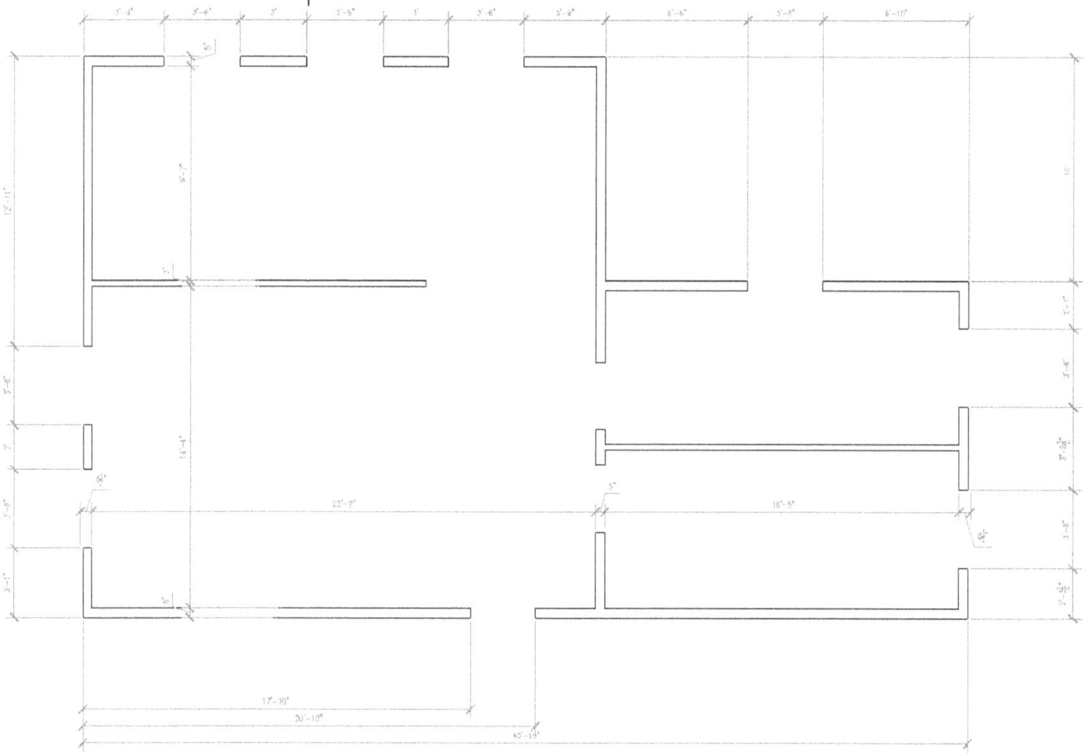

Figure 16–9

1. Open **Dimensioned Plan-A.dwg** from your practice files folder.

2. Switch to the **D-sized** layout. Make the existing viewport active and zoom to the extents.

3. In the Status Bar, set the *Viewport Scale* to **1/2"=1'-0"**. Pan the drawing to center it in the viewport. Ensure that the *Viewport Scale* is still set at **1/2"=1'-0"** and lock the viewport.

*You can also set the **Dimensions** layer current in the Home tab>Layers panel.*

4. In the Quick Access Toolbar, in the Layer Control bar, set the layer to **Dimensions**, as shown in Figure 16–10. The dimensions are drawn on this layer because the dimension layer is set to **Use Current**. Also, *ensure* that the active Dimension Style is set as **Architectural**. This is an annotative style.

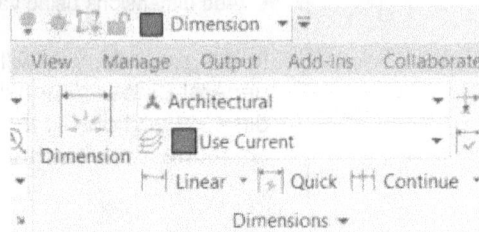

Figure 16–10

5. Freeze the layers **Doors** and **Windows** to make it easier to only select the walls to be dimensioned.

6. In the Status Bar, verify that **Object Snap** is toggled on and the **Endpoint** object snap is selected.

You can also use the

⊢⊣ *(Linear) dimension command, where you need to select the two endpoints of the wall.*

7. While still active in the viewport, in the *Annotate* tab> Dimensions panel, click ⊡ (Dimension). Hover the cursor on the top left wall (outer line), as shown in Figure 16–11.

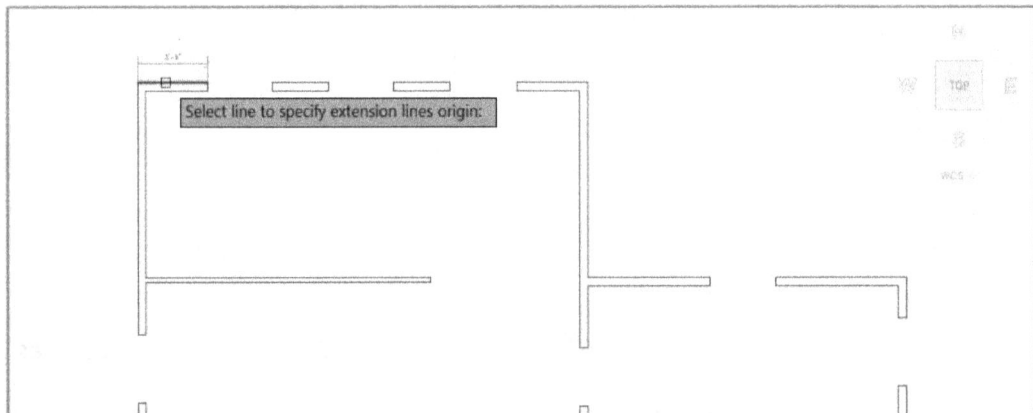

Figure 16–11

8. Select the object, drag the cursor up and click to place the dimension outside the building.

9. Start the ⊢⊤⊣ (Continue) dimension command. Note that the cursor is attached with the last dimension you placed. Select the left endpoint of the second wall, as shown in Figure 16–12.

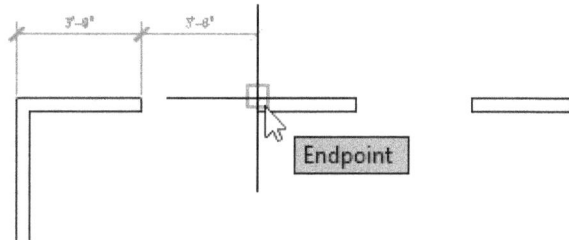

Figure 16–12

10. Select the rest of the dimension points (endpoints) along the same wall (as shown in Figure 16–9). Press <Enter> twice to complete the command.

The order of selection of points determines the start point of the baseline.

11. Start the **Dimension** command. Select the two endpoints (first left and then right) of the bottom left wall. Place the dimension along the bottom side of the building.

12. Start the ⊢⊣ (Baseline) dimension command and note that the cursor dimension is attached to the left extension line of the dimension.

13. Select the left endpoint of the right side bottom wall to place the dimension.

14. Select the right endpoint of the right side bottom wall to place the third dimension. Press <Enter> twice to complete the command.

15. Start the ⊢⊣ (Quick) dimension command.

16. Add dimensions to the left side of the building (as shown in Figure 16–9) by selecting three outside wall objects, pressing <Enter>, and then clicking to place the dimensions.

17. Add dimensions to the right exterior and the interior of the building, as shown in Figure 16–9.

18. Save and close the drawing.

Practice 16b

Adding Linear Dimensions (Mechanical)

Practice Objective

- Add linear dimensions to a mechanical drawing.

In this practice, you will add Linear and Aligned dimensions to a mechanical drawing.

Task 1 - Add Linear dimensions.

1. Open **Bearing Dimensions-I.dwg** from the practice files folder.

2. Switch to the **C-Sized** layout. Set the current active layer to **Viewports**.

3. Using grips, resize the existing viewport around the objects and move the viewport to the left side of the sheet to make room for a second viewport, as shown in Figure 16–13. Ensure that you leave space on the left and bottom of the objects such that you can enter the dimensions. Set the *Scale* to **1:1**, if it got changed.

4. In the *Layout* tab>Layout Viewports panel, use ⬚ (Insert View) to create a view of the right half of the model. Place this viewport to the right side of the original viewport at a scale of **2:1**. Resize it so that there is space along the right, top, and bottom of the model, as shown in Figure 16–13.

5. Lock both the viewports.

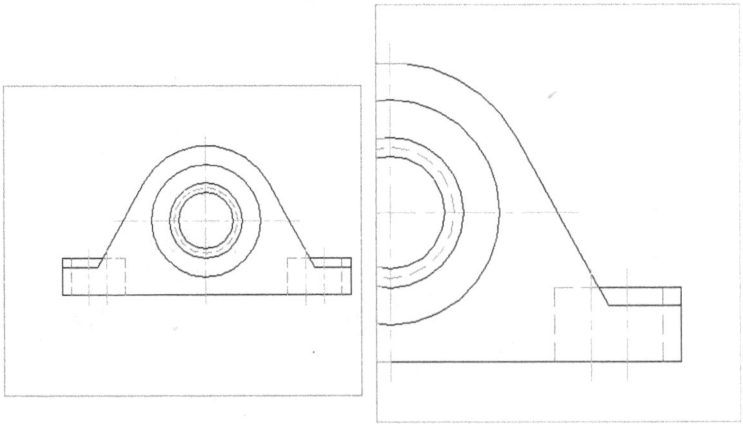

Figure 16–13

6. Make the left **1:1** viewport active.

7. Change the active dimension layer to **Dimensions** (*Annotate* tab>Dimensions panel, layer **Dimensions**), as shown in Figure 16–14.

8. Set the active *Dimension Style* to **2places**. This is an annotative style, as shown in Figure 16–14.

Figure 16–14

When you drag the cursor to the left, an aligned dimension might display, as shown on the left in Figure 16–15. Drag the cursor downwards to force the display of a vertical dimension instead.

9. Start the ⬜ (Dimension) command. Select the bottom left endpoint and then select the left endpoint of the green horizontal center line. Drag the cursor left and down until a vertical dimension displays, as shown on the right in Figure 16–15. Click to place the dimension.

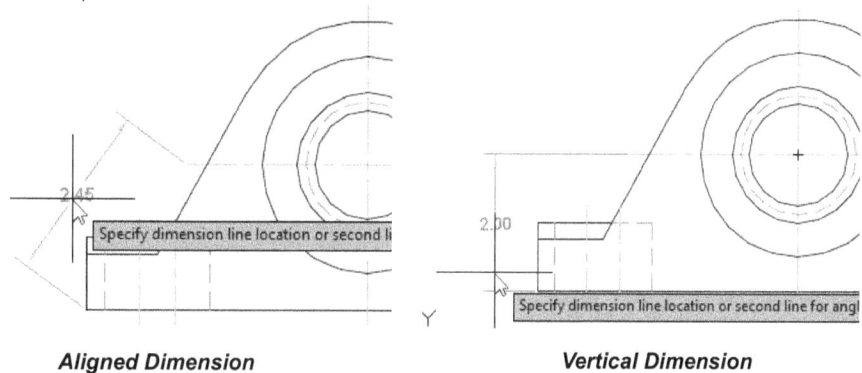

Aligned Dimension   *Vertical Dimension*

Figure 16–15

10. While remaining in the **Dimension** command, add the remaining vertical and horizontal dimensions shown in Figure 16–16. After placing all of the dimensions, exit the command.

*Start the **Dimension** command once, select the relevant endpoints and place the dimension for each vertical and horizontal dimension using the same command. You do not have to exit or relaunch the **Dimension** command after placing each dimension.*

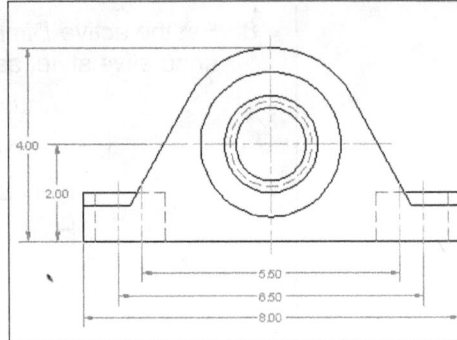

Figure 16–16

11. If required, use grips to resize the viewport to fit the dimensions into the available space.

Task 2 - Add aligned dimensions.

1. Make the **2:1** viewport active.

2. Start the **Dimension** command and add the vertical dimension shown in Figure 16–17.

You can also use the (Linear) dimension the (Aligned) dimension commands instead.

3. While remaining in the **Dimension** command, select the two endpoints of the aligned line on the right side and add the aligned dimension as shown in Figure 16–17. Exit the command.

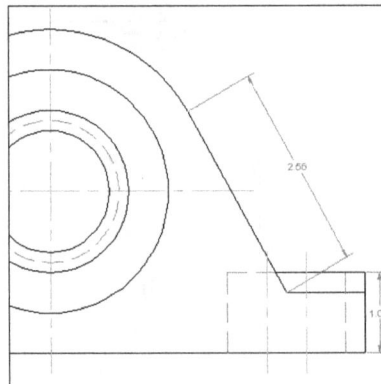

Figure 16–17

4. Save and close the drawing.

16.3 Adding Radial and Angular Dimensions

Other types of dimensions include Radius, Diameter, and Angular dimensions. Radius/Diameter dimensions for arcs and circles are placed with a leader from the object. You can also create a Jogged Radial dimension for arcs whose center point would be outside the drawing and for dimensioning the length around the curve of an arc. Angular dimensions measure the angle of an arc or the angle between two objects.

Radius and Diameter Dimensions

Radius is typically used on arcs, while **Diameter** is normally used on full circles, as shown in Figure 16–18. You can also add a radius dimension for a circle.

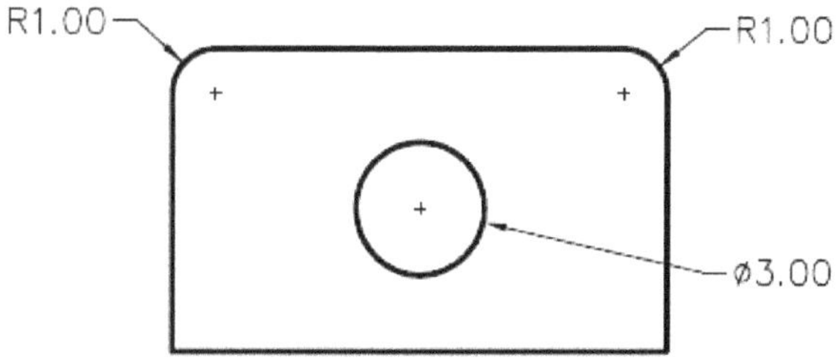

R1.00 R1.00 Ø3.00

Figure 16–18

How To: Add Radius or Diameter Dimensions

1. In the *Annotate* tab>Dimensions panel, click ⬚ (Dimension). You can also use ⟍ (Radius) or ⊘ (Diameter) individually.
2. Select a point on the rim of an arc or circle. (You do not need to use Object Snaps for this.)
3. Select a location along the arc or circle for the dimension line text.

- When you are dimensioning a radius, you can place the dimension beyond the arc. The AutoCAD software creates an additional arc extension line as required.

- **Quick Dimension** creates a radial dimension by default if you select an arc or circular object. However, you can select **Diameter** in the options.

Associative Center Marks and Centerlines

There are two new tools which indicate the center of a arc or circle regardless of the objects' perspective. Both tools are on the *Annotate* tab>Centerlines panel.

- The ⊕ Center Mark tool adds an associate center mark at the center of selected circles, arcs, or polygonal arcs, as shown in Figure 16–19.

- The ⚌ Centerline tool creates centerline geometry that is associated with selected lines and polylines, as shown in Figure 16–20.

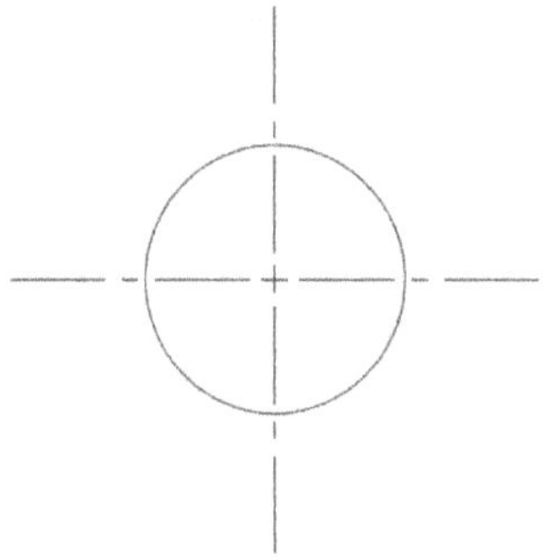

Figure 16–19    **Figure 16–20**

- If the associated objects move, the centerlines and center marks also update.

When a center mark or centerline is selected, grips display that enable you to control the extension line lengths, as shown in Figure 16–21. The appearance of center marks and centerlines is controlled by multiple system variables. Figure 16–21 and the table below lists the controlling variables and describes their effects.

CENTEREXE	• Sets the length of the extension line overshoots for centerlines and center marks.
CENTERMARKEXE	• Determines whether extension lines are created for center marks.
CENTERLAYER	• Sets the layer on which the centerlines and center marks are created.
CENTERLTYPE	• Sets the linetype used by centerlines and center marks.
CENTERLTSCALE	• Sets the linetype scale used by centerlines and center marks.
CENTERCROSSSIZE	• Sets the size of the central cross for center marks.
CENTERCROSSGAP	• Sets the extension line gap between the central cross and the extension lines in center marks.

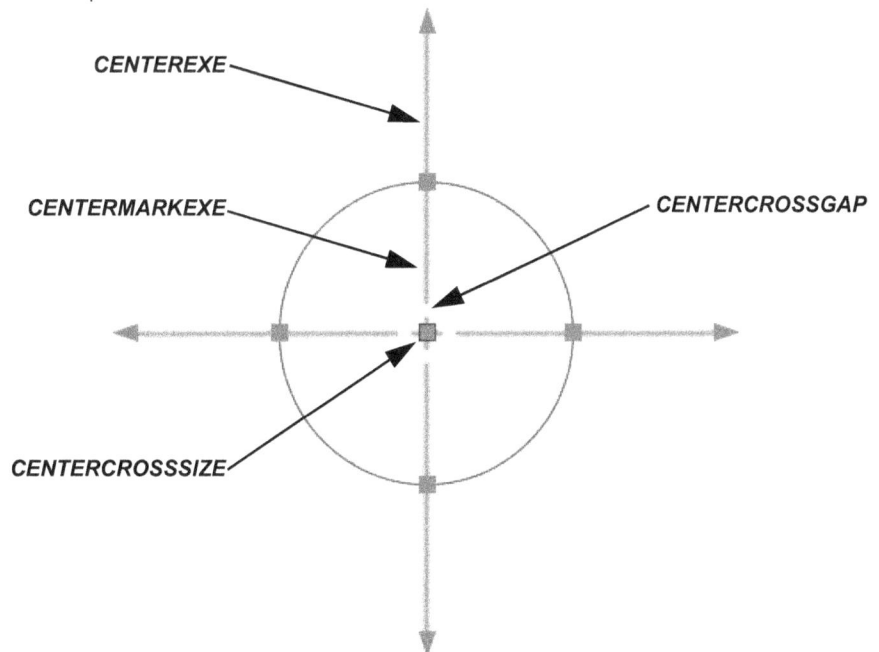

Figure 16–21

- The system variables must be set prior to creating the center mark or centerline for the variable to take effect.

- The Properties palette can be used to modify select attributes, as shown in Figure 16–22.

- A multi-functional grip menu offers additional controls, as shown in Figure 16–23.

Figure 16–22

Figure 16–23

Jogged Radial Dimension

If the center mark of the circle or arc you are dimensioning does not display in the view, you can use the **Jogged** command to create an override for the center, as shown in Figure 16–24.

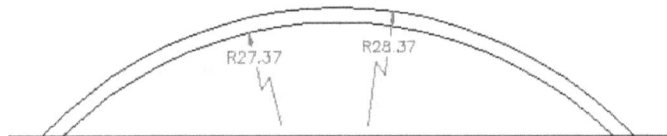

Figure 16–24

How To: Create a Jogged Radial Dimension

You can also find the **Jogged** *option (<Down Arrow>) in the* **Dimension** *command.*

1. In the *Annotate* tab>Dimensions panel, click ⟋ (Jogged).
2. Select the arc or circle that you want to dimension.
3. Specify a point for the center location override.
4. Specify the dimension line location. This also sets the location of the text.
5. Specify the jog location.

Arc Length Dimension

The arc length describes the distance from one end point of an arc to the other end point along the curve of the arc, as shown in Figure 16–25. This command can be used to dimension individual arcs or arcs that are parts of polylines.

Figure 16–25

How To: Dimension the Arc Length

1. In the *Annotate* tab>Dimensions panel, click ⬚ (Dimension) or click 🖉 (Arc Length) in the Linear drop-down list.
2. Hover the cursor over the arc that you want to dimension.
3. Press <Down Arrow> and select **arc Length** from the list.
4. Specify the dimension location.

The current set option is dependent on the previous DIM option used.

Angular Dimensions

You can add angular dimensions to lines, circles, and arcs and from a vertex, as shown in Figure 16–26.

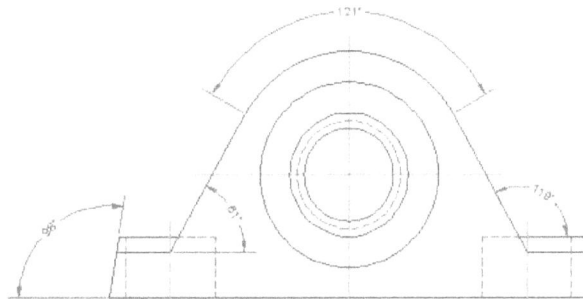

Figure 16–26

• When you are placing the Angular dimension, you can place it at any of the four quadrants of the angle.

How To: Add Angular Dimensions

1. In the *Annotate* tab>Dimensions panel, click ⊡ (Dimension) or click △ (Angular) in the Linear drop-down list.
2. Select a line, arc, or circle.
3. If you select a **line**, you are prompted to place a linear dimension. As you hover the cursor over another line, the preview changes to an angle dimension, as shown in Figure 16–27. Select the second line and specify the location of the dimension line.

First line selected

118°

Select line to s

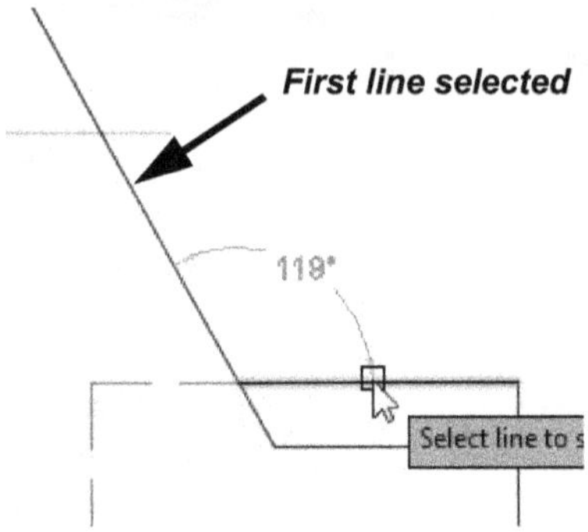

Figure 16–27

4. If you hover over an **arc**, by default you can place a radial dimension. Press <Down Arrow> and select **Angular**. Then, click the arc to select it. Click again to set the location of the dimension line.
5. If you hover over a **circle**, by default you can place a diameter dimension. Press <Down Arrow> and select **Angular**. Then click the circle to select it. Click to specify the first side of the angle. Click again to set the second side of the angle. Click one more time to set the location of the dimension line.

• You can also dimension an angle from a vertex. Before selecting an object, press <Enter> and use Object Snaps to select an angle vertex. Specify the first and second angle end points and place the dimension line.

Practice 16c | Adding Radial and Angular Dimensions (Architectural)

Practice Objective

- Add dimensions including radial and angular to a drawing.

In this practice, you will add Angular, Radial, Diameter, Aligned, and Arc Length dimensions, as shown in Figure 16–28.

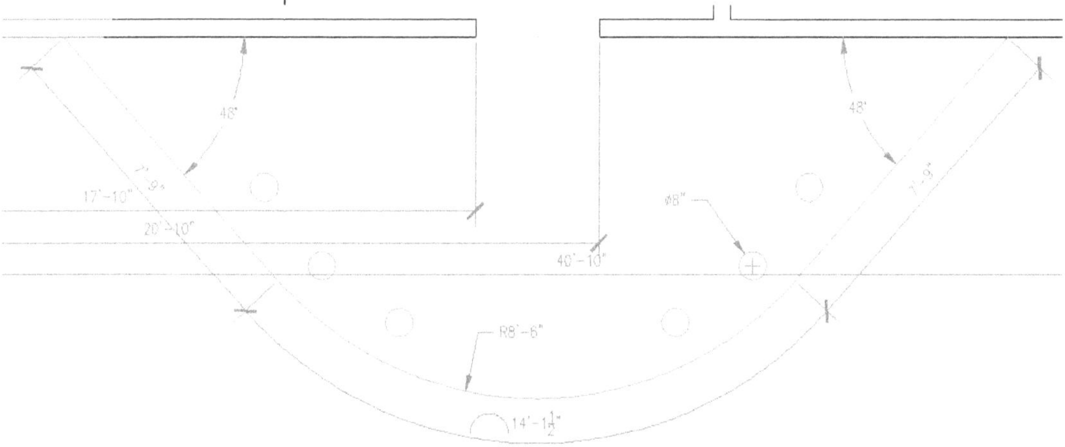

Figure 16–28

1. Open **Dimensioned Plan1-A.dwg** from your practice files folder.

2. In the Layer Control, toggle on the layer **Misc** to display the green entrance portico.

3. If required, use viewport grips to modify the viewport to display the entire entrance portico. Ensure that the *Viewport Scale* is set at **1/2"=1'-0"**.

4. Activate the viewport. In the Layer Control, ensure that the layer **Dimensions** is the current active layer.

5. In the *Annotate* tab>Dimensions panel, ensure that the dimension layer is set to **Use Current** which is the **Dimensions** layer.

If the cursor does not
display the diameter
dimension (while
hovering over the
circle), toggle off **Object
Snap** in the Status Bar.

Note that the prompt is
displaying as "Select arc
to specify radius"
indicating that the
radius option is the
current one.

6. In the *Annotate* tab>Dimensions panel, click ⬚ (Dimension).

7. Hover the cursor over one of the six circled columns. Select the circle to accept the diameter dimension and click again to place it at the required location, as shown in Figure 16–29.

8. While remaining in the **Dimension** command, hover the cursor over the arc of the portico. The dimension that is displayed is dependent on the previously used option.

9. If the selection prompt displays an option other than arc Length, press <Down Arrow> and select **arc Length**, as shown in Figure 16–29.

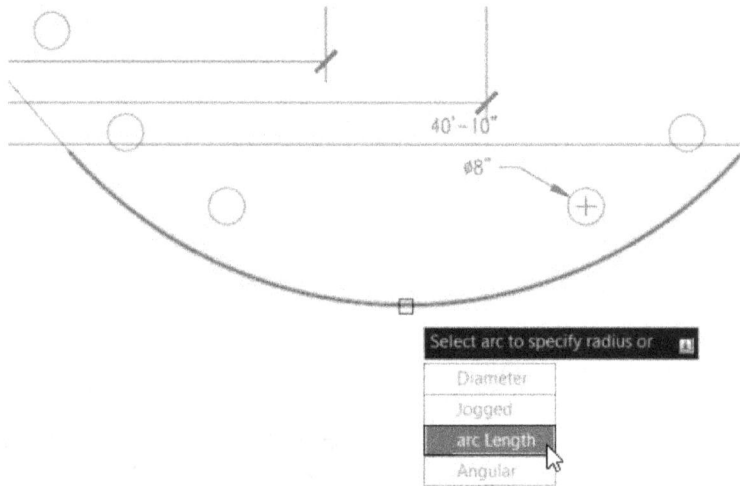

Figure 16–29

10. Select the arc and click again to place the dimension outside the arc, as shown in Figure 16–28.

11. While remaining in the **Dimension** command, hover the cursor over the arc of the portico again. Note that it displays the arc length option in the prompt, as shown in Figure 16–30. Press <Down Arrow> and select **Radius**. Select the arc and click again to place the radius dimension on the inside of the portico arc, as shown in Figure 16–28.

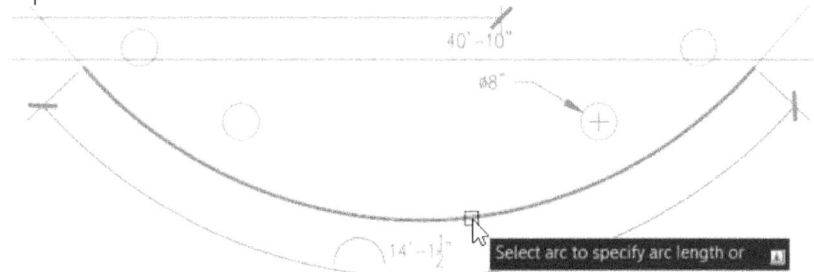

Figure 16–30

12. Toggle on **Object Snap** in the Status Bar, if you had toggled it off.

You can also use the

(Aligned) dimension command.

13. While remaining in the **Dimension** command, hover your cursor over the angled line that joins the portico arc with the building wall. Add Aligned dimension to both the angled lines, as shown in Figure 16–31. (Use the end of the arc length dimension line to keep the connected dimensions in line, as shown in Figure 16–31.)

Figure 16–31

You can also use the

△ *(Angular)*
dimension command.

14. While remaining in the **Dimension** command, select one of the angled line again. Hover the cursor over the wall line that touches the selected angled line to display the angled dimension, as shown in Figure 16–32.

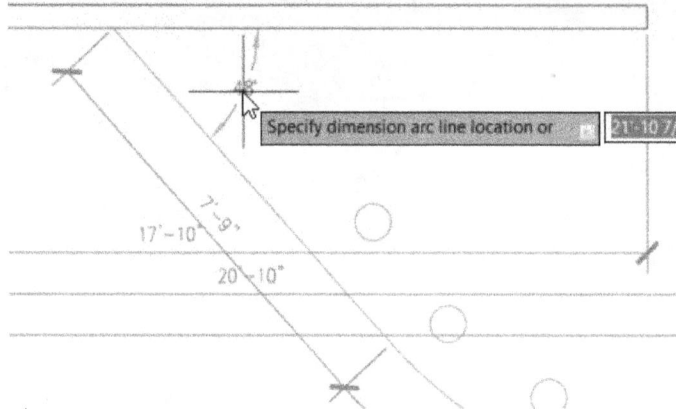

Figure 16–32

15. Select the line to accept the angled dimension and click again to place it, as shown in Figure 16–28.

16. Add **Angular** dimensions on the other side as well.

17. Save and close the drawing.

Practice 16d | Adding Center Marks and Dimensions (Mechanical)

Practice Objective

*   Add a center mark, radius, diameter, and angular dimensions to a drawing.

In this practice, you will add a center mark, radius, diameter, and angular dimensions to a mechanical drawing, as shown in Figure 16–33.

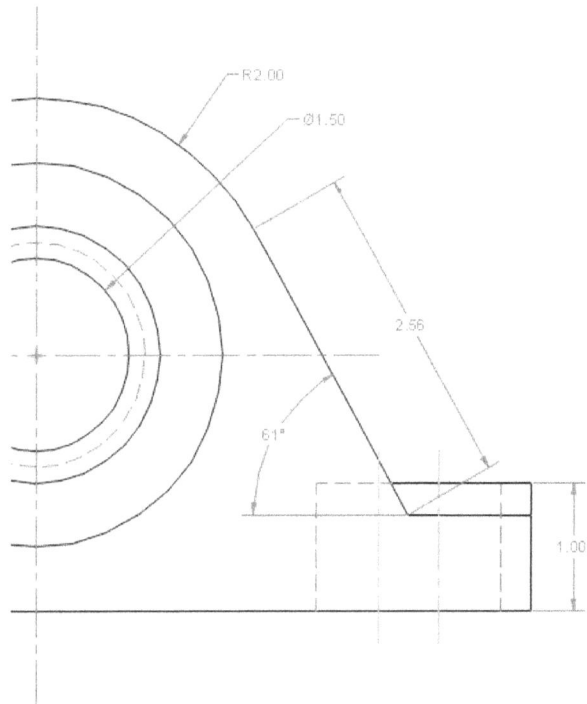

Figure 16–33

1. Open **Bearing Dimensions1-I.dwg** from your practice files folder. The drawing opens in the *C-Sized* layout tab.

2. Activate the **2:1** (right side) viewport.

3. In the Layer Control, ensure that the dimension layer is set to **Dimensions**.

4. In the *Annotate* tab>Dimensions panel, ensure that the dimension layer is set to **Use Current**.

5. In the *Annotate* tab>Centerlines panel, click ⊕ (Center Mark). Select the innermost circle to add a center mark. Note that the extension lines of the center mark are just touching the dashed circle. Exit the command.

6. In the Command Line, type **CENTEREXE**. Enter **2** for the value and then press <Enter>.

7. In the Command Line, type **CENTERRESET**.

8. In the viewport, select the center mark and press <Enter>. The center mark extension lines extend beyond the outermost circle, as shown in Figure 16–33.

9. Add a **Radius** dimension to the arc at the top of the bearing.

10. Add a **Diameter** dimension to the innermost circle.

11. Add an **Angular** dimension to the inner angle of the sloped line, as shown in Figure 16–33. (Select the horizontal line first and then hover on the sloped line.)

12. Save and close the drawing.

16.4 Editing Dimensions

If the dimensions are interfering with other parts in a drawing, as shown in Figure 16–34, you can edit and modify them using grips and special tools in the shortcut menu. You can also edit the dimension text. Additional tools available to clean up dimensions include: aligning dimensions and breaking extension lines.

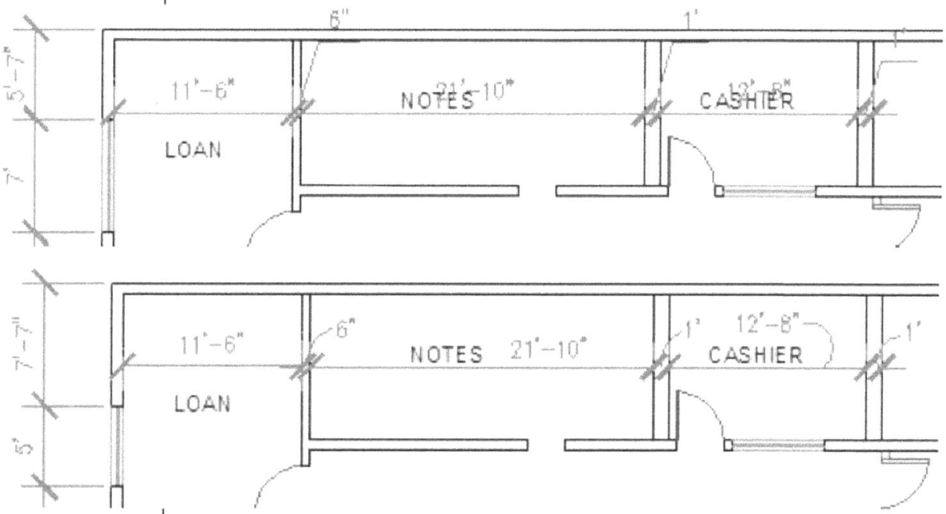

Figure 16–34

- The AutoCAD dimensions are associative. Therefore, when you change a dimensioned object, the dimensions update to reflect the change. If you move an object, the dimensions move as well. If you change the size of an object, the dimensions display the change.

- To change the dimension style of an existing dimension, select it and then set the appropriate dimension style in the Dimension Style drop-down list, in the *Annotate* tab> Dimensions panel.

Dimension Shortcut Menu

You can select a dimension or multiple dimensions, and then right-click to access additional options in the shortcut menu, as shown in Figure 16–35.

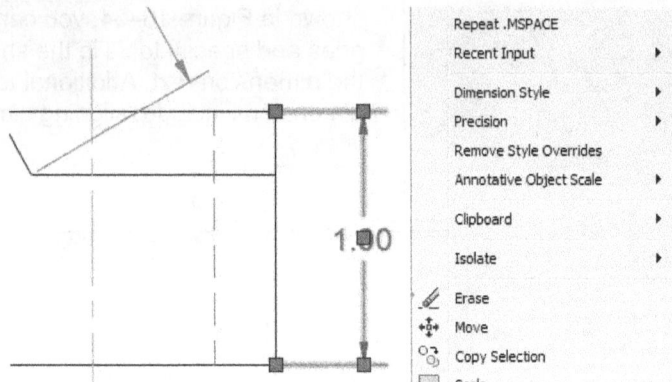

Figure 16–35

- You can change the Dimension Style of selected dimensions using the **Dimension Style** option. The dimension style controls the basic features of a dimension, such as the text location and number of decimal places.

- You can change the precision of selected dimensions using the **Precision** option. Precision helps you to display dimensions to a specific number of decimal places.

Editing Dimensions Using Grips

Grips can be used to relocate dimension elements. Without starting a command, select the following to display its grips at various parts of the dimension, as shown in Figure 16–36.

- Where extension lines touch the dimensioned object

- Where the extension line and dimension line meet

- On the dimension text

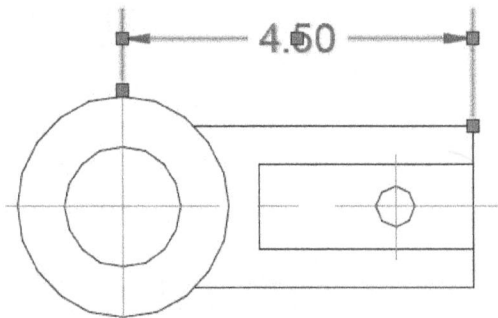

Figure 16–36

Once the dimension grips display, you can edit the dimension as follows:

- Select the grip at the dimension line and move it to change the distance from the object.

- Select the grip on the text and move it to change the location of the text (and sometimes the dimension line).

- Select the grip at the extension line origin to change the length of the dimension. (This option might disconnect the associativity to the object it is dimensioning.)

- Press <Esc> to clear the grips.

Dimension Grips Shortcut Options

Additional options are available for editing dimensions using the multifunctional grips. Hover the cursor over a grip, and select an option in the dynamic input list. Depending on the specific grip you hover over, a different list of options displays, as shown in Figure 16–37.

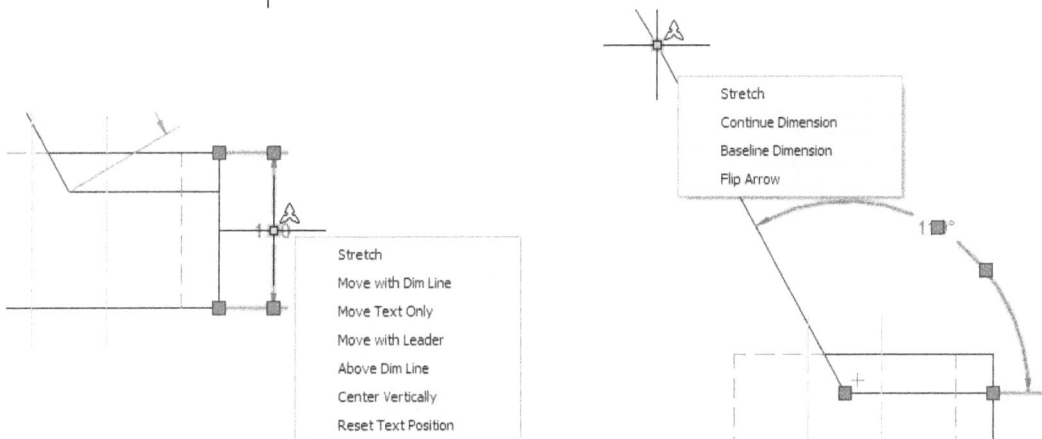

Stretch
Continue Dimension
Baseline Dimension
Flip Arrow

Stretch
Move with Dim Line
Move Text Only
Move with Leader
Above Dim Line
Center Vertically
Reset Text Position

Figure 16–37

- Use the various text options, such as **Move Text Only** and **Above Dim Line** to move the text to a different position.

- **Reset Text Position** returns the moved text to its original location.

- You can use an existing dimension as the beginning of a series of related dimensions in either **Continue** or **Baseline**.

- Use **Flip Arrow** if the arrowheads on a dimension were pushed out and you want them to be inside the extension lines or on the opposite side.

- You can also access these options by selecting a grip (making it hot), and then using <Ctrl> to cycle through the options, or right-clicking and selecting one in the shortcut menu, as shown in Figure 16–38.

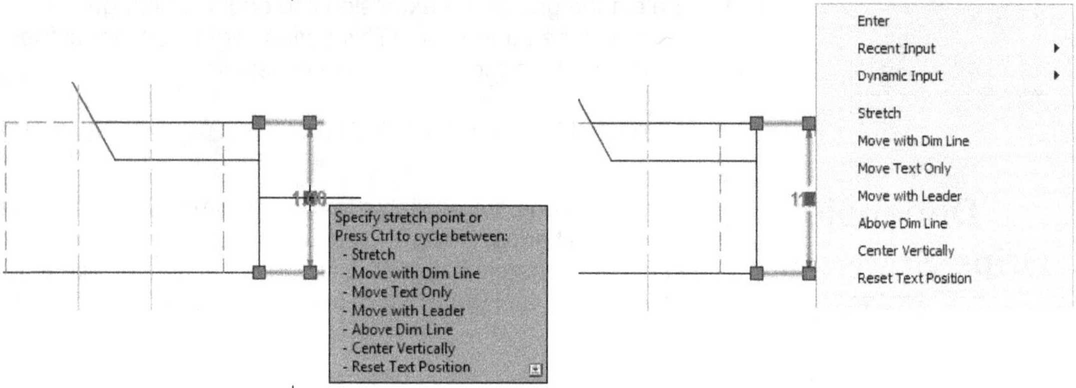

Figure 16–38

Editing the Dimension Text

Dimensions are associated with the objects they reference. However, sometimes you might need to add text to a dimension (such as +/- in renovation work), as shown in Figure 16–39.

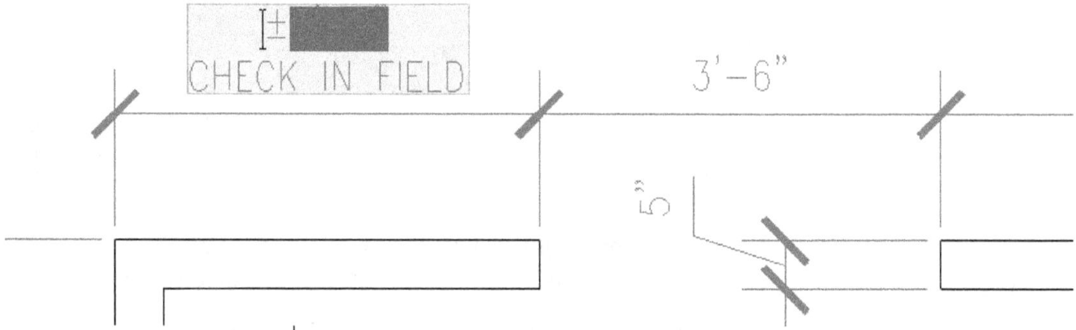

Figure 16–39

- To change the dimension text, double-click on the dimension text or type **textedit**. The default dimension text or value is inserted as a special field in the Text Editor. You can add text before or after the field, or delete the field to completely replace the default text When editing dimension text, a width sizing control displays above the text. This enables you to adjust the text width for text wrapping, as shown in Figure 16–40.

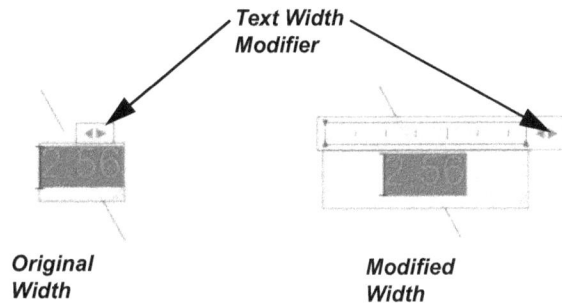

Text Width Modifier

Original Width   *Modified Width*

Figure 16–40

- If you remove the text associated with the dimension by mistake and want to get it back, type **<>** in the Text Editor.

Adjusting Dimension Spacing

When you create stacked angular or linear dimensions of any type, they might be too close together or unevenly spaced, as shown in Figure 16–41. Instead of moving each dimension, you can modify the space between sets of dimensions using the **Adjust Space** command.

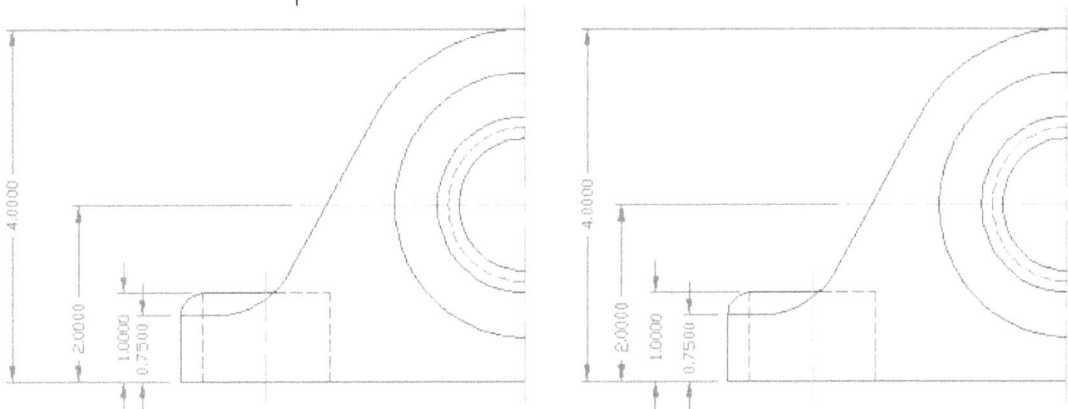

Figure 16–41

How To: Modify the Space Between Dimensions

1. In the *Annotate* tab>Dimensions panel, click ⊥ (Adjust Space).
2. Select the base dimension (the one closest to the object) of the group you want to modify.
3. Select the rest of the dimensions in the group.
4. Enter the distance that you want to have between dimensions or press <Enter> to accept the automatic distance.

Dimension Breaks

When there are many dimensions in a drawing, the various extension lines and dimension lines can start to overlap. In that case, you can create dimension breaks without changing the associativity of the dimension object, as shown in Figure 16–42.

- When the object is stretched, the dimensions change and the breaks remain in place. This makes revising a drawing easier, as you no longer need to re-dimension a modified part.

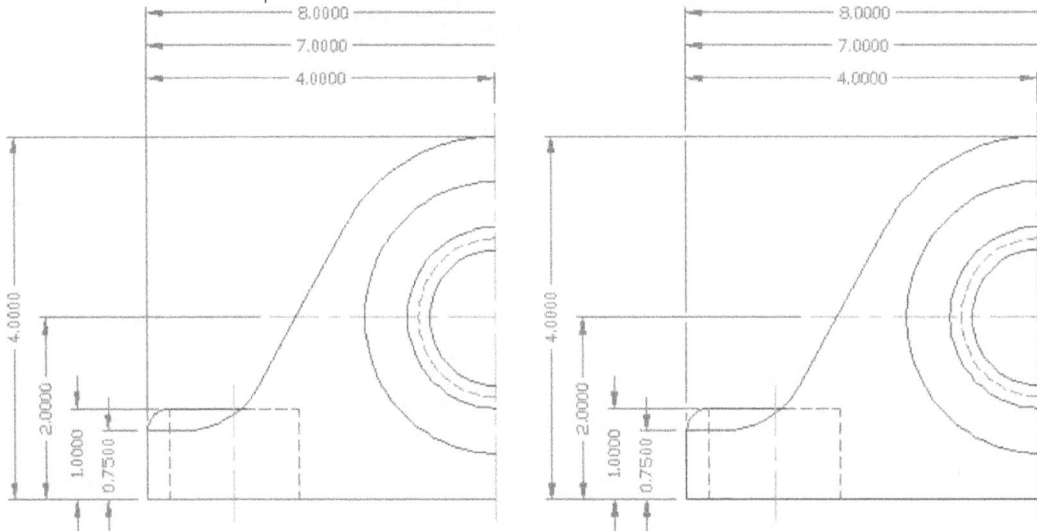

Figure 16–42

How To: Break One Dimension

1. In the *Annotate* tab>Dimensions panel, click $\perp$ (Dimension Break).
2. Select a dimension to break.
3. Select an object to break the dimension or select one of the options.
4. Continue to select other objects to break their dimensions as required.
5. Press <Enter> to complete the command.

- The **Multiple** option enables you to select more than one dimension to break. The selected dimensions are broken where they overlap other dimensions.

- To remove breaks from a dimension, start the **Break** command, select the dimension, and select the **Remove** option.

Practice 16e | Editing Dimensions (Architectural)

Practice Objective

- Modify dimensions, edit dimension text, and break dimensions in a drawing.

In this practice, you will modify dimensions using grips, edit the dimension text, and break dimensions using the **Dim, Break** command, as shown in Figure 16–43.

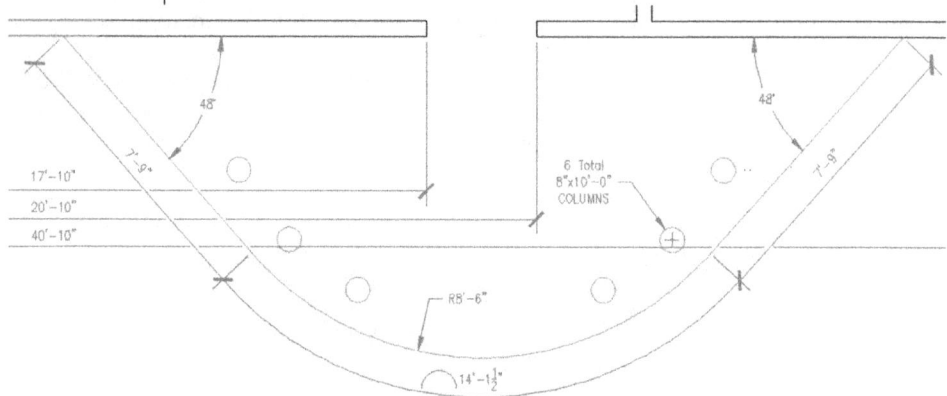

Figure 16–43

1. Open **Dimensioned Plan2-A.dwg** from your practice files folder.

2. Make the viewport active and verify that it is locked, so that you can zoom and pan as required to modify the dimensions.

*If required, you might need to toggle off **Object Snap** to move the dimensions freely.*

3. Focusing on the portico area, use grips (as shown in Figure 16–44 to move the three horizontal dimension text to the left hand side, outside of the portico area.

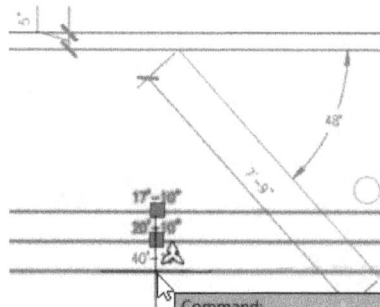

Figure 16–44

4. In the *Annotate* tab>Dimensions panel, click ⊥ (Break) and press <Down Arrow> to open the options menu. Select **Multiple**.

5. Select the three horizontal dimension lines and press <Enter>.

6. Select the green portico line. Note that the three horizontal dimension lines break where they are passing through the portico arc object.

7. Select the aligned dimension line (red) on both sides to create a break with them as well.

8. Press <Enter> to exit the command.

You can also use the **textedit** *command.*

9. Double-click on the diameter **Ø8"** dimension for the green circle and enter **6 Total 8"x10'-0" COLUMNS,** as shown on the left in Figure 16–45.

10. Use ◄► to change the width for text wrapping, as shown on the right in Figure 16–45.

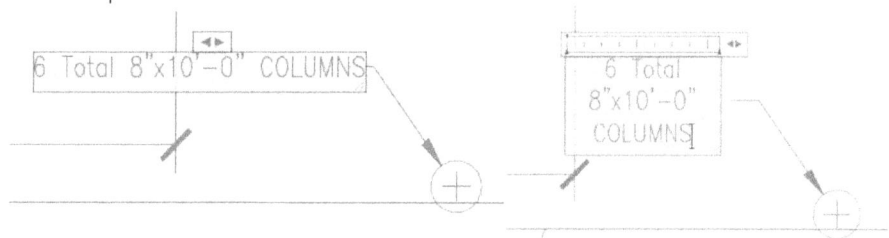

Figure 16–45

11. Exit the command.

12. Save and close the drawing.

Practice 16f | Editing Dimensions (Mechanical)

Practice Objective

- Modify the text and move dimensions.

In this practice, you will modify the text of several dimensions and move the dimensions as required using grips, as shown in Figure 16–46.

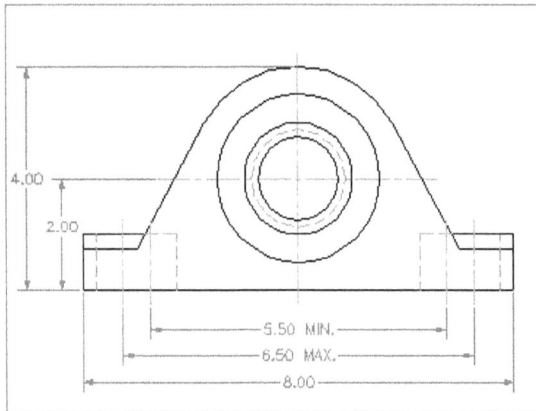

VIEWPORT SCALE: 1:1   VIEWPORT SCALE: 2:1

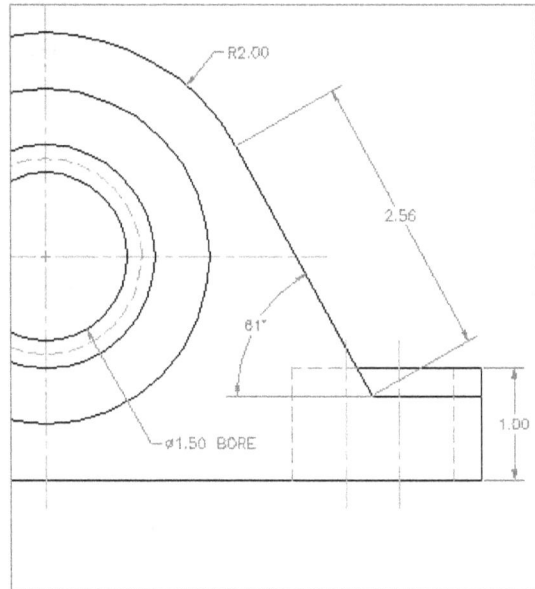

Figure 16–46

1. Open **Bearing Dimensions2-I.dwg** from your practice files folder.

2. Activate the **2:1** viewport (right side) and modify the text of the diameter dimension (of the innermost circle) so that it reads **Ø1.50 BORE**. Then change the width for text wrapping to display it in single line.

3. Using the grip, move the diameter dimension outside of the circles, as shown in Figure 16–47.

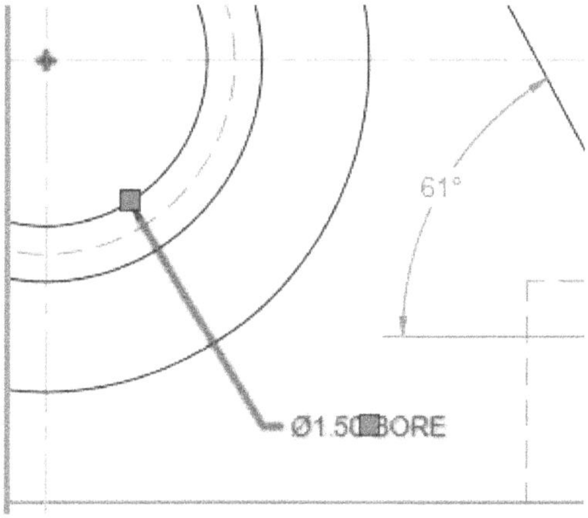

Figure 16–47

4. Activate the **1:1** viewport, modify the text of the two horizontal dimensions (by adding **MIN.** and **MAX.**), as shown in Figure 16–48.

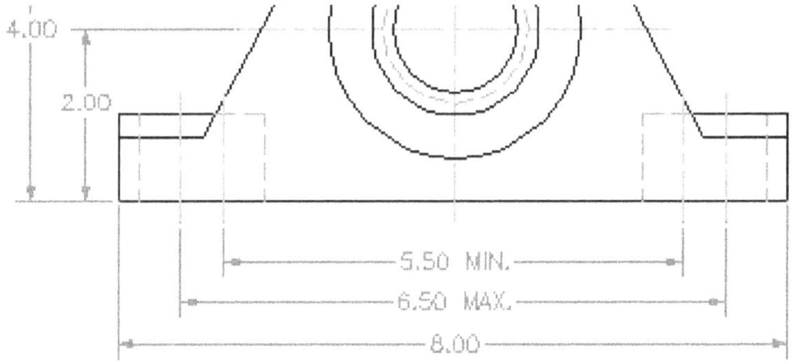

Figure 16–48

5. Use grips to move any of the other dimensions as required to a location where they are easier to read. You can also use the **Adjust Space** command to even out the bottom dimensions as required.

6. Save and close the drawing.

Annotation Features and Styles

Exam Objectives Covered in This Chapter

- 5.3.b Create, modify, and apply text styles
- 5.5.a Create and modify dimension styles
- 5.6.a Understand annotative properties and styles as they pertain to objects
- 5.6.b Define and apply annotative object styles
- 5.6.c Control the annotative scale of an object or viewport
- 5.6.d Add annotative scales to an object

17.1 Working with Annotations

When you set up layouts with viewports at various scales, the parts of the model display at different sizes. However, the final printed sheet should have text and dimensions that are all of the same size when they are plotted, as shown in Figure 17–1. The Annotation Scale feature enables you to add text and dimensions to a drawing with views at many different scales. These annotation objects are scaled to suit and do not display in viewports with other annotation scales.

- Annotation objects include text, dimensions, hatches, and multileaders.

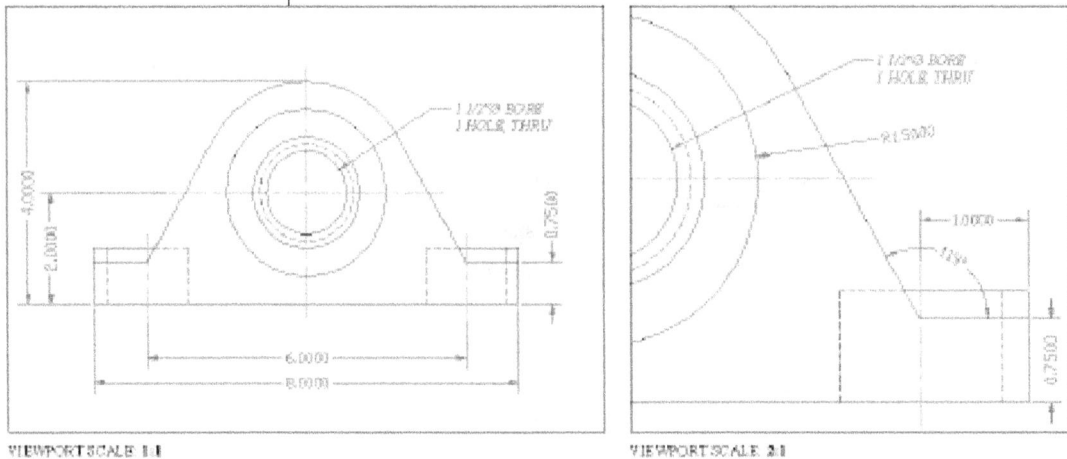

Figure 17–1

- When you create each viewport, set the viewport scale by using the ▽ (Middle arrow grip) of the selected viewport boundary or 🗔 1:2 ▾ (Viewport Scale) in the Status Bar, as shown in Figure 17–2. The Annotation Scale is automatically matched to the viewport scale.

Figure 17–2

Click 🔒 (Lock/Viewport) to lock the viewport so that the scale and location are not changed by mistake.

- To add annotation objects, double-click inside the viewport to make it active and select the annotation tool. It is automatically scaled to match the viewport/annotation scale.

- To understand the differences between annotations placed in Model Space and Paper Space, open the Properties palette and note the two parameters: **Paper text height** and **Model text height**. For example, in the room shown in Figure 17–3, the text **Service Area** is placed in a viewport at a scale of **1/4"=1'-0"**, while the text for the title and scale is placed in Paper Space at a scale of 1:1. Note that the two text objects look the same size.

Figure 17–3

- If you select the text in Paper Space and then note the values of the parameters in the Properties palette, the **Paper text height** and **Model text height** are the same, as shown on the left in Figure 17–4. If you select the text inside the viewport and then note the values of the parameters in the Properties palette, the **Paper text height** and the **Model text height** are different, as shown on the right in Figure 17–4.

  The AutoCAD® software automatically scales the text inside the viewport so that it is **1/4"**.

Text	▲
Contents	\A1;{\W1;\LStairs\P\H0.7x\...
Style	△ Title
Annotative	Yes
Annotative scale	1:1
Justify	Top left
Direction	By style
Paper text height	1/4"
Model text height	1/4"

Paper Space

Text	▲
Contents	Service Area
Style	△ Title
Annotative	Yes
Annotative scale	1/4" = 1'-0"
Justify	Top left
Direction	By style
Paper text height	1/4"
Model text height	9 5/8"

Model Space

Figure 17–4

17.2 Creating Text Styles

When you add text to your drawing, it uses the properties (e.g., height, font, etc.) of the current *text style,* as shown in Figure 17–5. Text styles should be created in the template file so that everyone on the same project uses the same styles. You can create a new style by assigning the height, width, and slant to a text font, or to a typeface design.

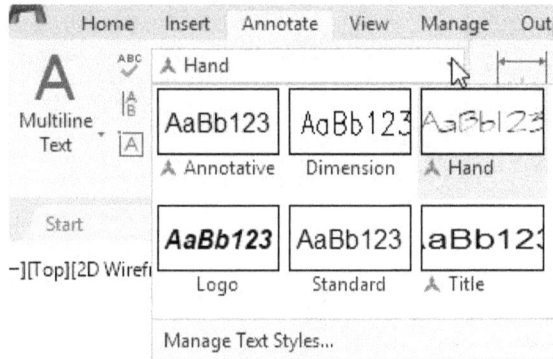

Figure 17–5

- There are two default styles: **Standard** and **Annotative**. You can create other styles as required.

- A variety of font files are available for creating different styles of text. There are two different types of fonts: Truetype fonts (used by most Microsoft Windows software) and AutoCAD® shape fonts. You can use the fonts that the AutoCAD software installs or the other Truetype fonts that were installed with Windows.

How To: Create a Text Style

You can also open the dialog box by clicking ⌐ (Panel Arrow) in the *Annotate tab>Text panel.*

1. In the *Annotate* tab>Text panel>Text Style list, select **Manage Text Styles...**.
2. In the Text Style dialog box (shown in Figure 17–6), click **New...**. The new style takes on the attributes of the current text style.

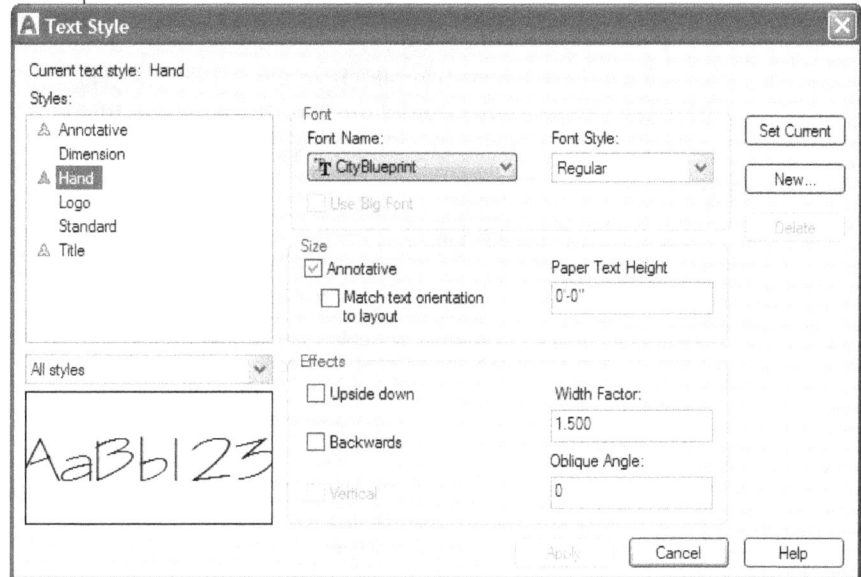

Figure 17–6

3. In the New Text Style dialog box, type a new name and click **OK**.
4. Expand the Font Name drop-down list, select a font (a preview of the font displays in the *Preview* area). For some fonts, you can also specify a Font Style (such as bold or italic).
5. Select the **Annotative** option if you want the text style to scale per viewport. You can also set a default height for the style, but this is typically left at **0** so that you can use one style for different sizes of text.
6. In the *Effects* area, set up the required properties.
7. Click **Apply** to continue working in the dialog box or **Close** to close the dialog box. The style that was created is now the current style.

- You can change the current style in the Text Style Control in the *Home* tab>expanded Annotation panel, the *Annotate* tab>Text panel, or the *Text Editor* contextual tab>Style panel when you have started the **Multiline Text** command.

- You can change the style of existing text by selecting the text object and then selecting a style in the *Home* tab>Annotation panel or *Annotate* tab>Text panel.

- If you modify an annotative style, you need to use **annoupdate** to update any existing objects to match the revised annotative style.

Style Effects

The style effects make a text style different from a standard font. You can define several text styles that use the same font but differ in width, oblique angle, etc.

Width Factor	Defines the character width relative to the height. A width factor of **1** is the default. Numbers greater than one increase the width and numbers less than one decrease the width. Typical width factors are in the range of 0.8 to 1.5.
Oblique Angle	Enables you to slant the lettering. Positive values incline the top of the text to the right and negative values slant it to the left. Typical obliquing angles range from +10 to -10. Angles of +30 and -30 are commonly used to label isometric drawings.

- Text is normally placed horizontally in a drawing. Vertical, upside-down, or backward text orientation can also be defined when creating text styles.

Notes on Text Styles

- The *Preview* displays an image of how your text style is going to be displayed when used in the drawing. All of the effects of a text style are previewed except the height.

- To rename a text style, double-click on the style name. In the Edit box, type the new name.

- To delete a text style, highlight it in the list and click **Delete**. It is only deleted if it is not in use.

- Some TrueType fonts can be filled or outlined. To have them filled in your drawing, you need to set the **textfill** system variable to **ON** (textfill = 1).

- **Match Properties** (in the *Home* tab>Properties panel) enables you to copy the style from one text object to another in your drawing. It is also available in the *Text Editor* contextual tab.

Practice 17a

Creating and Using Text Styles

Practice Objective

- Create several new text styles.

In this practice, you will define several new text styles using the **Text Style** command, as shown in Figure 17–7.

The color has been changed to black for printing clarity.

The Standard Style | Hand lettering Style
Title Text Style | Dimensions Style

Figure 17–7

1. Open **AEC-Facilities1-A.dwg** from your practice files folder. It is an empty file.

2. Make the layer **Notes** active.In the *Annotate* tab>Text panel, note that the active text style is **Standard**.

3. Switch to one of the layouts. Start the **Multiline Text** command. Note that the preview text (abc) is not currently visible with the cursor. Zoom in until it displays. Place the text **The Standard Style** anywhere in the drawing.

4. In the Text Style list, select **Manage Text Styles** or click ☑ (Panel Arrow) in the *Annotate tab>Text panel*. Modify the Standard Style by changing the *Font Name* to **romans**. Click **Apply** and **Close**. Note how the text you just entered has updated.

5. Open the Text Style dialog box again and click **New**.

6. Create a new style named **Title**. Set the *Font Name* to **Arial**, the *Font Style* to **Bold** and the *Width Factor* to **1.5**. Click **Apply** to save the changes.

7. Create another new text style named **Hand2**. For the *Font Name*, select **CityBlueprint**. Set the *Width Factor* to **1.5**. Click **Apply** to save the changes.

8. Create another new text style named **Dimensions**. For the *Font Name*, select **romans**. Set the *Width Factor* to **0.8**. Click **Apply** to save the changes and click **Close**.

9. Make each style current and then add text to the drawing using a text string to test the styles.

10. Set the current style to **Hand**. Erase all of the text and save the drawing.

17.3 Creating Dimension Styles

The dimension style controls all aspects of how your dimensions display (type and size of arrows, type of units displayed, text specifications, text placement, etc.). You might need to have several styles in a drawing to display different information, as shown in Figure 17–8. For example, in mechanical drawings you might have one style with decimal units that displays two decimal places of precision, another that displays three decimal places, and a third that displays both English and Metric units at the same time.

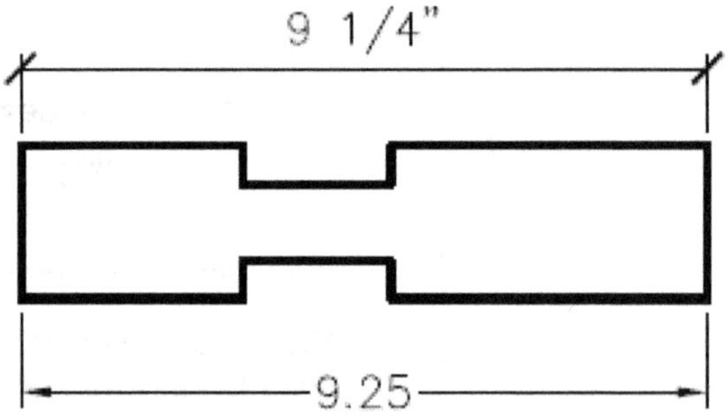

Figure 17–8

- You can set the current dimension style in the Dimension Style Control in the *Home* tab>Annotation panel or *Annotate* tab>Dimensions panel.

- There are two default styles: **Standard** and **Annotative**. You can create other styles as required.

How To: Create a Dimension Style

You can also open the dialog box by clicking ⬡ (Panel Arrow) in the *Annotate tab> Dimensions panel.*

1. In the *Annotate* tab>Dimensions panel>Dimension Style list, select **Manage Dimension Styles...**.
2. Click **New...** in the Dimension Style Manager, as shown in Figure 17–9.

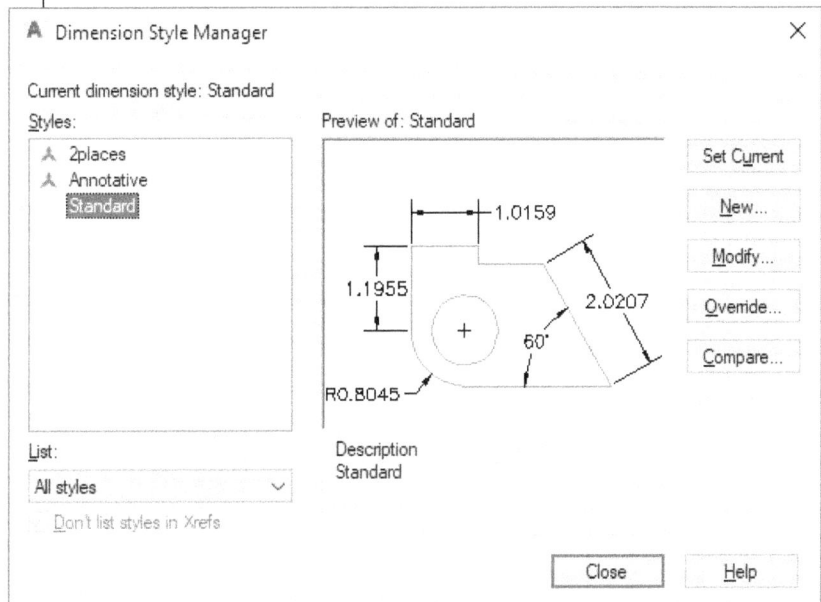

Figure 17–9

3. The Create New Dimension Style dialog box opens, as shown in Figure 17–10. In the Start With drop-down list, select a style to use as a template. In the *New Style Name* field, type a new style name and then select the **Annotative** option as required. Click **Continue**.

Figure 17–10

4. Modify the tabs as required and click **OK**.
5. If you want to make the new style current, double-click on its name in the *Styles* area or select it and click **Set Current**.
6. Click **Close**.

• All of the distances and sizes specified for the dimension style should be at their final plotted distance or size.

Modifying Dimension Styles

In the Dimension Sytle Manager, click **Modify** to open the Modify Dimension Style dialog box.

Dimension Style Lines Tab

The *Lines* tab controls the appearance of the dimension lines and extension lines, as shown in Figure 17–11.

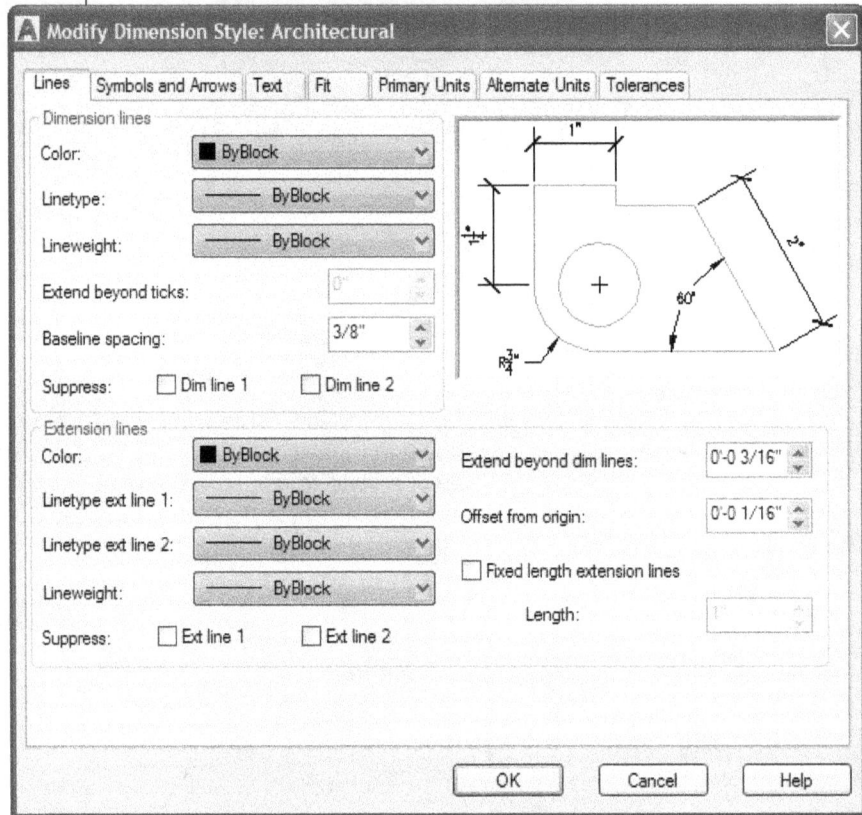

Figure 17–11

- *Color* and *Lineweight* are set to **ByBlock** by default. This is essentially the same as **ByLayer**. The dimension elements use the color and linetype of the current layer.

- *Extend beyond ticks* only applies if ticks are used rather than arrowheads.

- *Baseline spacing* is used for baseline dimensions that are applied with the **Baseline** or **Quick Dimension** commands.

- *Offset from origin* controls the size of the gap between the object and the start of the extension line.

- *Fixed length extension lines* controls how far the line reaches from the dimension line toward the dimensioned object.

Dimension Style Symbols and Arrows Tab

The *Symbols and Arrows* tab controls the size and style of the arrowheads on the dimension lines and leaders, and other symbols, such as Center marks (for circles and arcs) or the Arc length symbol, as shown in Figure 17–12.

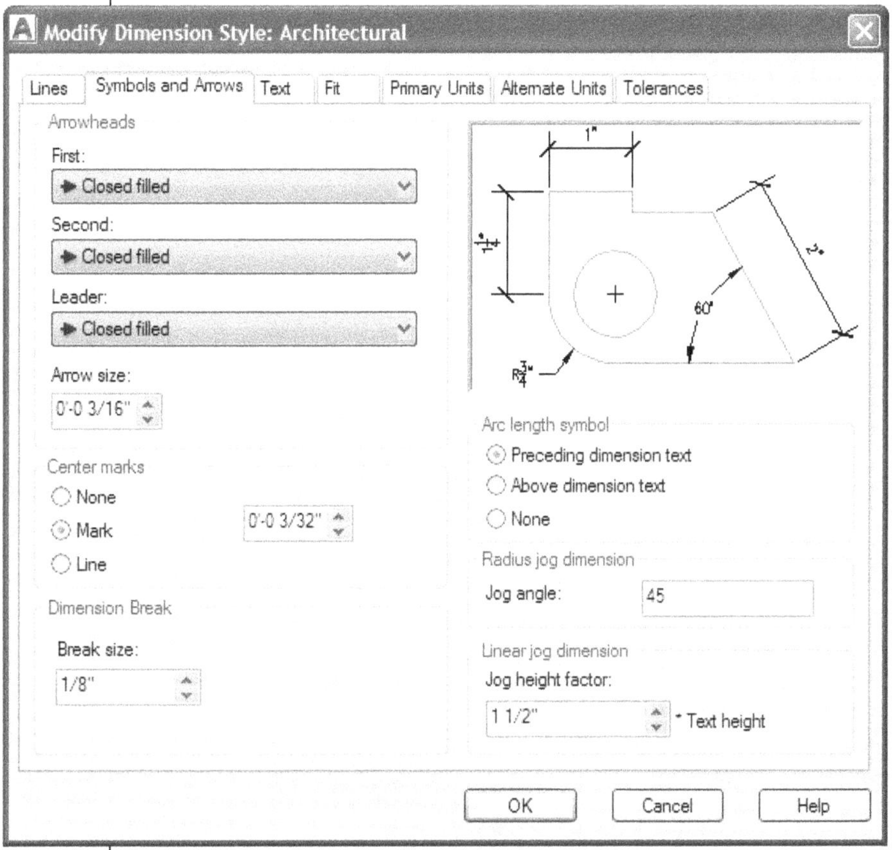

Figure 17–12

- The *Leader* (used for Radius, Diameter, and Angular dimensions) can have a different arrow style from the dimension lines.

- *Center marks* are used with Radius and Diameter dimensions and the **Center Mark** command.

Dimension Style Text Tab

The *Text* tab controls the placement and appearance of the dimension text, as shown in Figure 17–13.

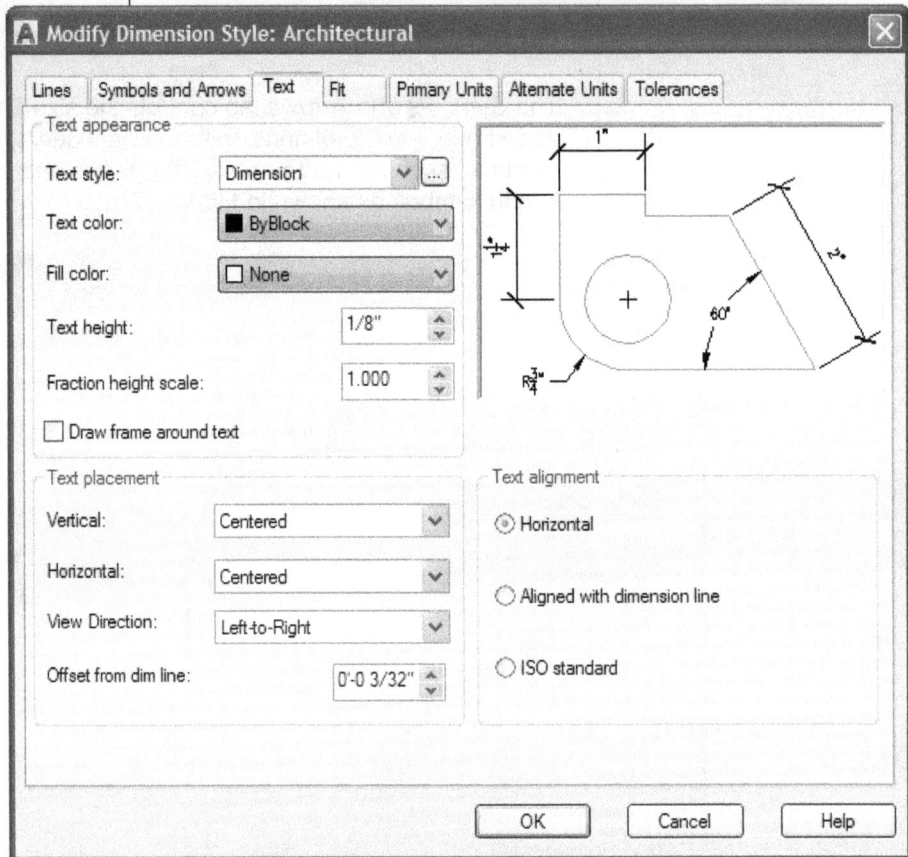

Figure 17–13

Do not set a height in text styles to be used for dimensioning. Use the dimension style to control the height.

- You can specify a text style in the Text style drop-down list. If you have not defined one, you can click ⌷ (Browse) to open the Text Style dialog box to create a new style. The text height should be set to the required plotted height.

- If you want the text to plot at a heavier weight than the rest of the dimensions (a standard drafting technique), set the text color to be a color that plots to a medium weight and leave the rest of the dimension elements with the *Text color* set to **ByBlock**. You can set the layer **Dimensions** to be a lightweight color.

- The *Fill* color can be set to **Background** or another color so that the text masks any objects behind it.

- In the *Text placement* area, you can set the text placement to **Vertical** and **Horizontal** dimensions.

- *Offset from dim line* controls the size of the gap between the text and dimension lines. This applies when the text is centered on the line and above the line.

- *View Direction* displays the dimension text **Left-to-Right** or **Right-to-Left**.

Dimension Style Fit Tab

The *Fit* tab controls the positions of arrows, text, leader lines, and the dimension line, as shown in Figure 17–14. It also controls the scale for dimension features.

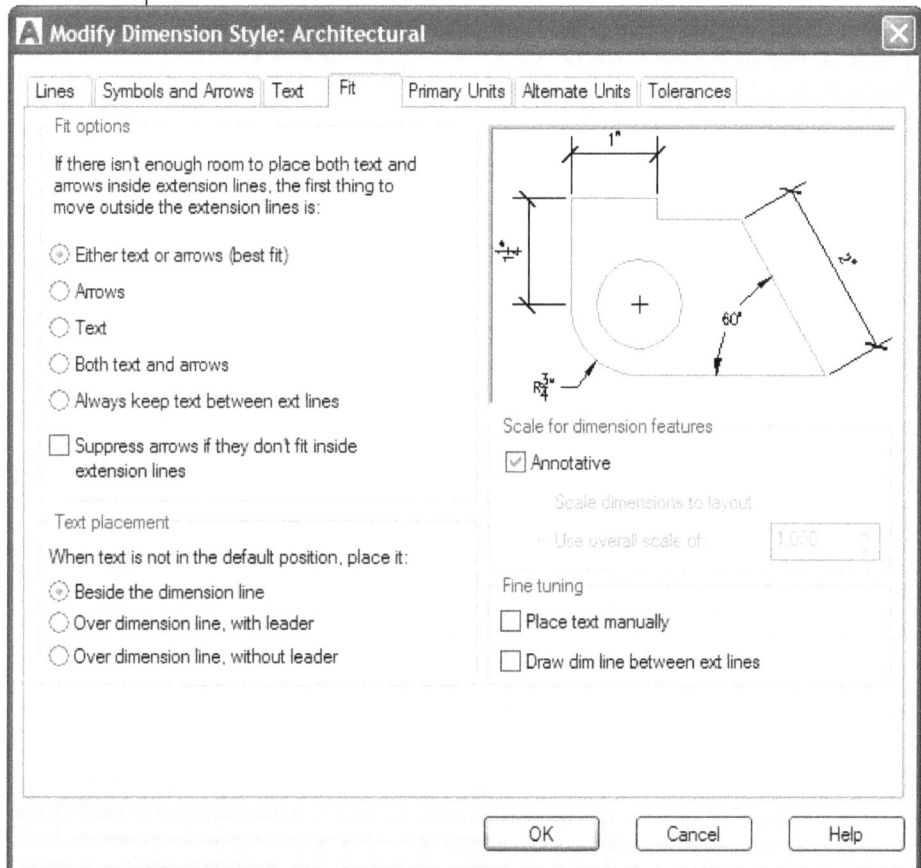

Figure 17–14

- When you set the *Scale for dimension features* to **Annotative**, the other options are grayed out. The dimensions are scaled according to the scale of the viewport through which they are inserted.

- If you are not using Annotative dimensions, you can use **Scale dimensions to layout** to display the objects in all viewports. You can also select **Use overall scale of** to dimension directly on the model when you are plotting from Model Space.

Dimension Style Primary Units Tab

The *Primary Units* tab controls the format of the primary units in the dimension text, as shown in Figure 17–15. This is independent of the type of units that are used in the drawing.

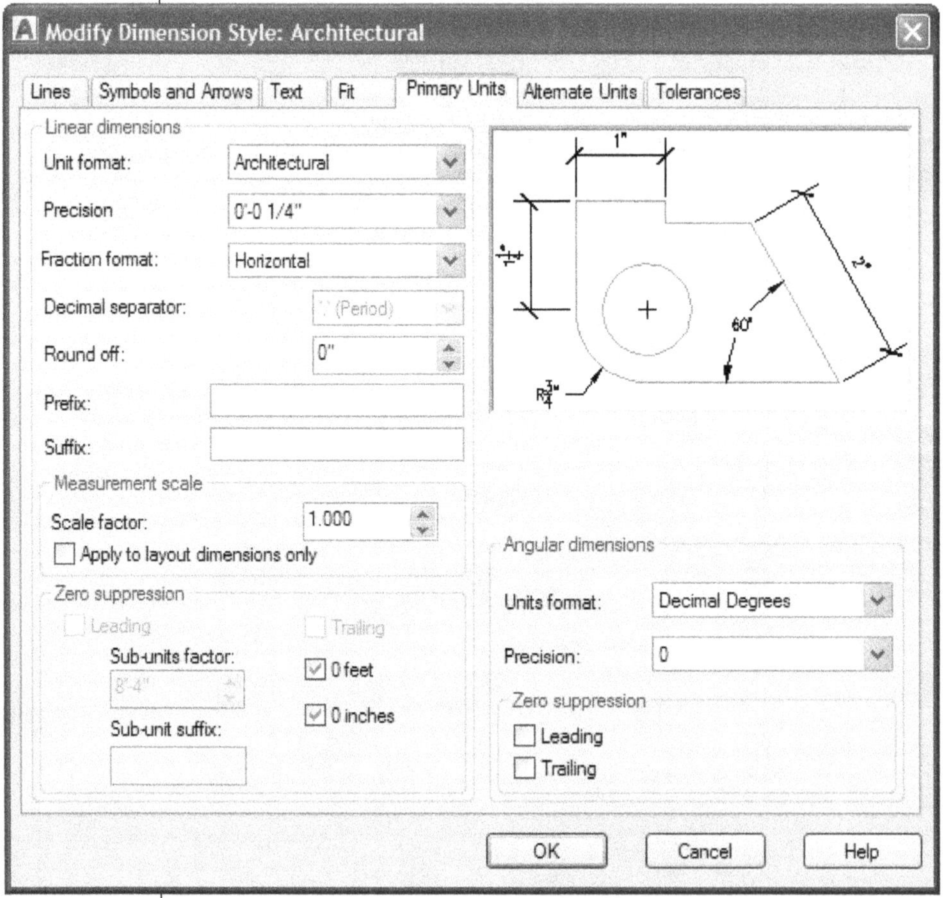

Figure 17–15

- You can set the required type of units for dimensioning, the number of decimal places, and other information to define the appearance of the text.

- A default *Prefix* and *Suffix* can be added in front or after all of the dimension values (for example, a suffix of mm for millimeters).

- The *Scale factor* multiplies the actual dimension value. For example, if the actual distance is 5 and the scale factor is 2, the value that displays in the dimension text is 10. If objects are drawn at full size, the scale should normally be set to 1.

- The *Sub-units factor* eliminates the leading zeros in dimension values by specifying that any measurement less than one primary unit be dimensioned in a smaller unit of measure. The *Sub-unit suffix* automatically appends a different dimension suffix to such dimensions.

Dimension Style Alternate Units Tab

The *Alternate Units* tab is very similar to the *Primary Units* tab.

- *Multiplier for alt units* is the conversion factor between the units in which your drawing was created and the units you want to use for alternative dimensions. For example, if the Primary Units are decimal inches and the Alternate Units are millimeters, *Multiplier for alt units* should be **25.4** (1 inch = 25.4mm).

Dimension Style Tolerances Tab

The *Tolerances* tab is usually used in mechanical design to indicate the degree of precision required in manufacturing.

- *Method* determines how the tolerance is calculated and displayed. The options are **None**, **Symmetrical** (equal bilateral), **Deviation** (unequal bilateral), **Limits**, and **Basic** (places a box around the dimension and is used with Geometric Dimensioning & Tolerancing).

Creating Dimension Sub-Styles

You might need to use a slightly different style for a specific type of dimension. For example, you might want linear dimensions to use tick marks instead of arrows and to always be forced above the dimension line. You can create a style that uses arrows, and then create a sub-style that is only used for linear dimensions, as shown in Figure 17–16. When using that style, all of the dimensions that you place have arrows, except for the linear dimensions.

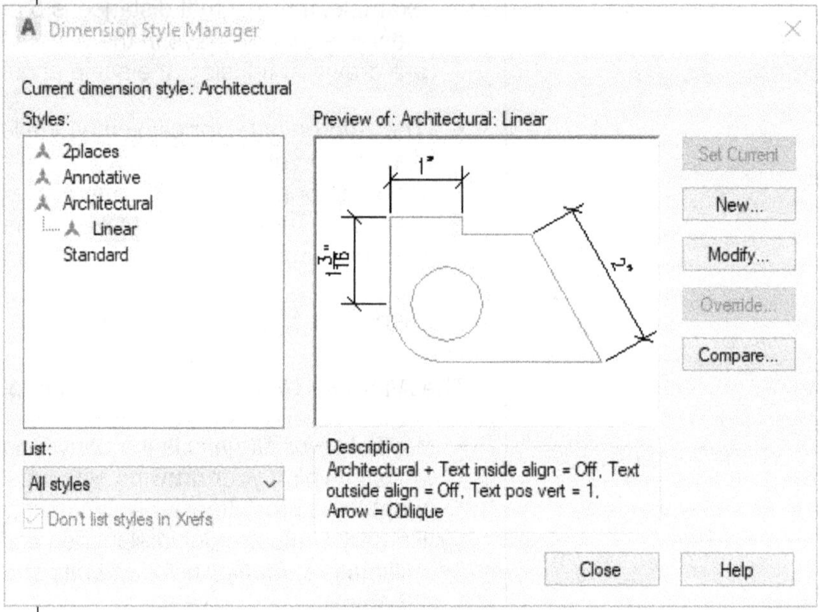

Figure 17–16

How To: Set Up a Dimension Sub-Style

1. Open the Dimension Style Manager.
2. Click **New...**.
3. In the Create New Dimension Style dialog box, in the Start With drop-down list select the style to use as a template.
4. In the Use for drop-down list, select a dimension type for the sub-style (linear, angular, etc.) that you are creating, as shown in Figure 17–17.

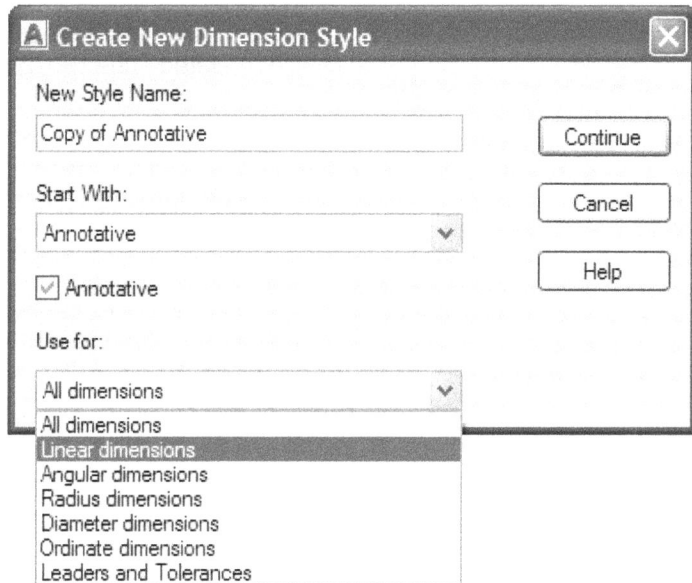

Figure 17–17

5. Click **Continue**.
6. In the New Dimension Style dialog box, define the sub-style as required with settings for lines, arrows, text, fit, etc.
7. When all of the settings have been adjusted, click **OK**. The new sub-style is listed in the Dimension Style Manager under the main style.

Hint: Modifying a Single Dimension

Select a dimension and use the Properties palette to modify the style of a single dimension without changing the style definition. In the Properties palette, all of the dimension style settings are listed. Each setting can be changed for the selected dimension.

Practice 17b | Creating Dimension Styles (Architectural)

Practice Objectives

- Change the dimension style of various dimensions.
- Create a new dimension style and a related sub-style.

In this practice, you will test existing dimension styles and change them as required. You will also create a new dimension style with a related sub-style, as shown in Figure 17–18.

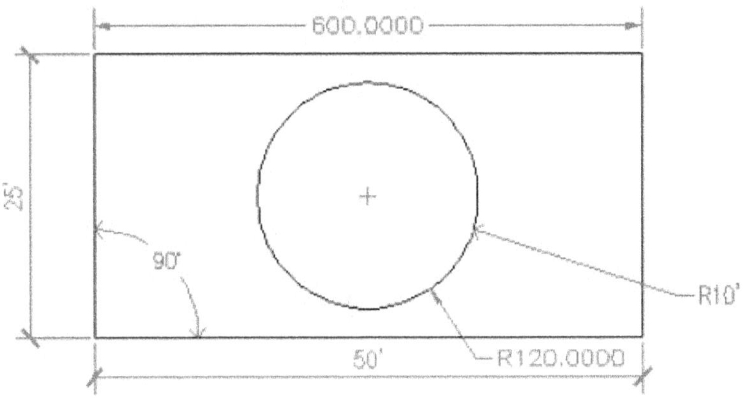

Figure 17–18

Task 1 - Test the existing dimension styles.

1. Open **AEC-Facilities2-A.dwg** from your practice files folder. It is an empty drawing.

2. Switch to the Model layout.

3. Change the current layer to **Walls** and draw a **50'-0" x 25'-0"** rectangle with a **10' radius** circle at its center.

4. Switch to the **A-Sized Landscape** layout.

5. Double-click in the viewport to activate it. Pan in the viewport to display the rectangle and the circle. Return the *Viewport Scale* to **1/8"=1'-0",** if it changed.

Use grips to move the dimensions to the required location.

6. Set the current layer to **Dimensions**. Using the **Standard** dimension style, add a linear dimension for the top length line and a radius dimension to the circle. The dimension text and arrows are not displayed because this dimension style is not annotative.

7. Using the Properties panel for each of the dimensions, change the *Dim style* to **Annotative**. The dimension information is now available, but it is not designed to work with architectural dimensions.

Task 2 - Create a new dimension style.
---

1. In the Dimension Styles list, select **Manage Dimension Styles** or click ◪ (Panel Arrow) in the *Annotate* tab>Dimensions panel to open the Dimension Style Manager and click **New...**.

2. In the Create New Dimension Style dialog box, set the *New Style Name* to **Architectural**. In the Start With drop-down list, select the **Standard** style to use as a template. Select **Annotative** (as shown in Figure 17–19) and click **Continue**.

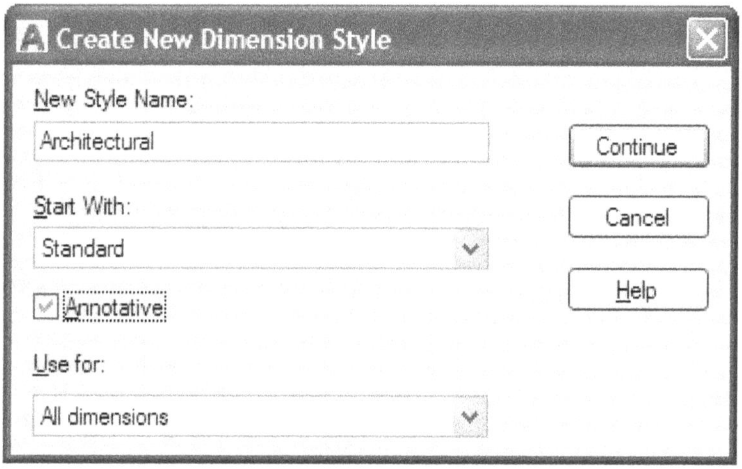

Figure 17–19

3. In the New Dimension Style dialog box, set the following options and click **OK**:

Symbols & Arrows tab	Arrowheads area	First, Second, and Leader: **Right angle**
Text tab	Text appearance area	Text style: **Dimensions**
Fit tab	Scale for dimension features area	Annotative
Primary Units tab	Linear dimensions area	Unit format: **Architectural**

4. Select **Architectural** and click **Set Current** in the Dimension Style Manager. Click **Close**.

5. Using the new style, add linear dimensions for the left and bottom edges of the rectangle. Add radial dimensions to the circle and angular dimensions to the left corner of the rectangle. Note the differences from the dimensions in the previous style.

Task 3 - Create a dimension sub-style.

1. In the Dimension Styles list, select **Manage Dimension Styles...**.

2. In Dimension Style Manager., select the new **Architectural** style and click **New...**.

3. Delete **Copy of Architectural** and leave the *New Style Name* blank.

4. In the Use for drop-down list, select **Linear dimensions** and click **Continue**.

5. Modify the options as follows:

Symbols & Arrows tab	*Arrowheads* area	First and Second: **Oblique**
Text tab	*Text alignment* area	Aligned with dimension line
Text tab	*Text placement* area	Vertical: Above

6. Click **OK** and **Close** to exit the Dimension Style Manager. Note that the linear dimensions update to display the new format, as shown in Figure 17–18.

7. Erase all of the dimensions.

8. Double-click outside the viewport to return to Paper Space.

9. Save the drawing.

Practice 17c | Dimension Styles (Mechanical)

Practice Objective

- Create dimension styles and apply them to dimensions.

In this practice, you will create two dimension styles and then apply dimensions with those styles, as shown in Figure 17–20 and Figure 17–21.

1. Open **Dim-I.dwg** from your practice files folder.

2. Create the two dimension styles (Tolerance and English_Metric) listed in the tables. *Start With* the **Standard** style, make each style **Annotative**, and use the default settings for options that are not specified.

	Tolerance	English_Metric
Lines tab		
Baseline spacing	0.38	0.5
Symbols and Arrows tab		
Arrowheads	Right angle	Closed filled
Center marks	Mark	Line
Text tab		
Text style	Standard	Standard
Text color	ByBlock	Magenta
Text height	0.18	0.125
Vertical Placement	Centered	Above
Horizontal Placement	Centered	Centered
Text Alignment	Horizontal	Aligned with dimension line
Primary Units tab		
Unit format	Decimal	Architectural (horizontal fractions)
Precision	0.00	0-0 1/16"
Alternate Units tab		
Alternate Units	None	Decimal, precision 0
		multiplier 25.4, suffix mm

Tolerances tab

Method	Limits	None
Upper Value	0.02	
Lower Value	0.03	
Scaling for height	0.75	

3. For English_Metric, create the following sub-styles.

   • To create a sub-style, in the Dimension Style Manager, select English_Metric, and click **New**. In the Use for drop-down list, select **Angular,** and then set the options below. Repeat this for **Diameter**.

	Angular	**Diameter**
Text tab		
Vertical text placement	Centered	Centered
Text alignment	Horizontal	Horizontal

4. Use the new dimension styles to dimension the objects shown in Figure 17–20 and Figure 17–21.

   • Set the layer **Dimensions** to be current.
   • A layout is prepared for each style. The scale of the viewport in the **B-Sized Eng-Met** layout is 1:1 and the scale of the one in the **C-Sized Tol** layout is 2:1.

Tolerance

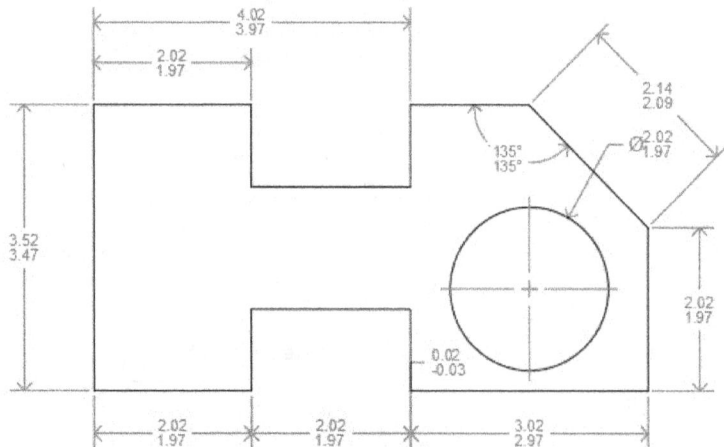

Figure 17–20

English_Metric

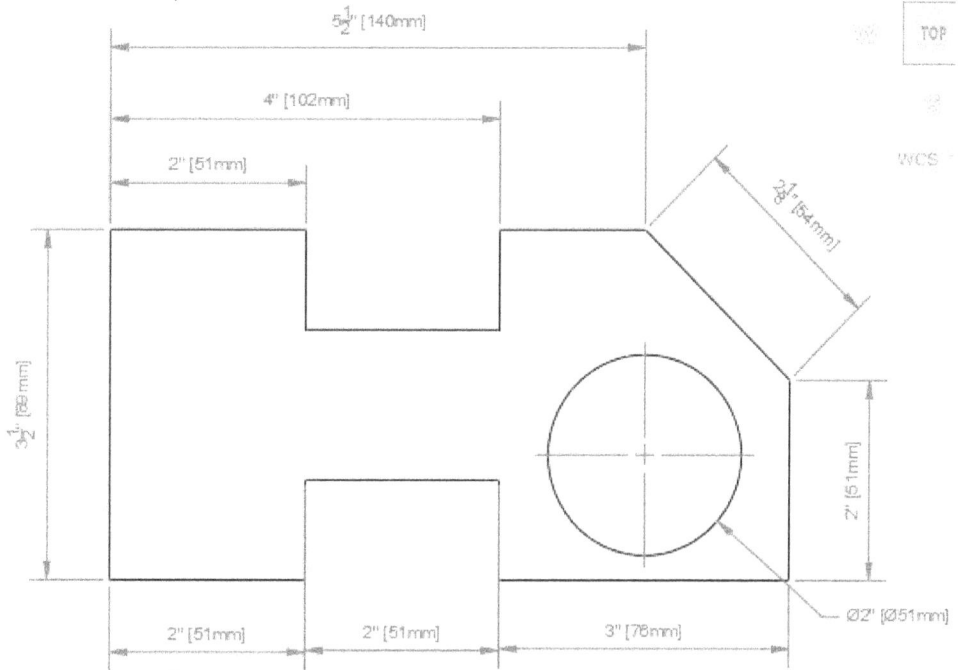

Figure 17–21

17.4 Creating Multileader Styles

Multileaders are used to point to objects in your drawing with text or symbols. Use the Multileader Style Manager to create styles that control the display options for different multileaders. The styles can be annotative or a specified scale, and have different arrowheads, text styles, colors, linetypes, etc., as shown in Figure 17–22. You can create styles for specific uses and then use the Multileader Style Manager to update them as required. This ensures accuracy throughout the drawing and makes it easy to modify multileaders.

Figure 17–22

How To: Create a Multileader Style

You can also open the dialog box by clicking ⬐ (Panel Arrow) in the *Annotate tab>Leaders panel.*

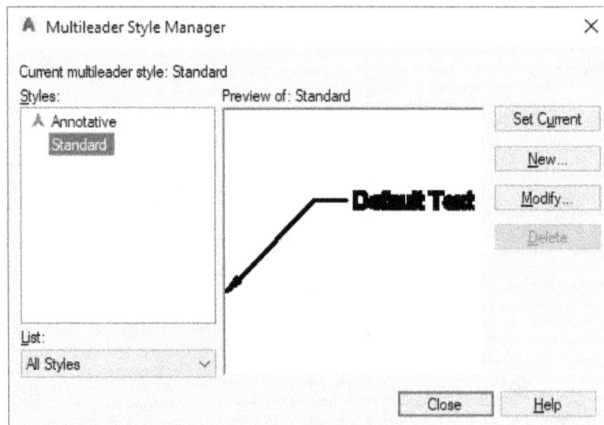

1. In the *Annotate* tab>Leaders panel>Leader Style list, select **Manage Multileader Styles...**. The Multileader Style Manager opens, as shown in Figure 17–23.

Figure 17–23

2. Click **New...**
3. In the Create New Multileader Style dialog box, type a *New style name*, expand the Start with drop-down list and select a style, and select or clear the **Annotative** option, as shown in Figure 17–24.

Figure 17–24

4. Click **Continue**. The Modify Multileader Style dialog box opens.
5. In the *Leader Format* tab, specify the leader's *Type* (**Straight**, **Spline**, or **None**), its formatting, the style and size of the Arrowhead, and the distance for the Leader break, as shown in Figure 17–25.

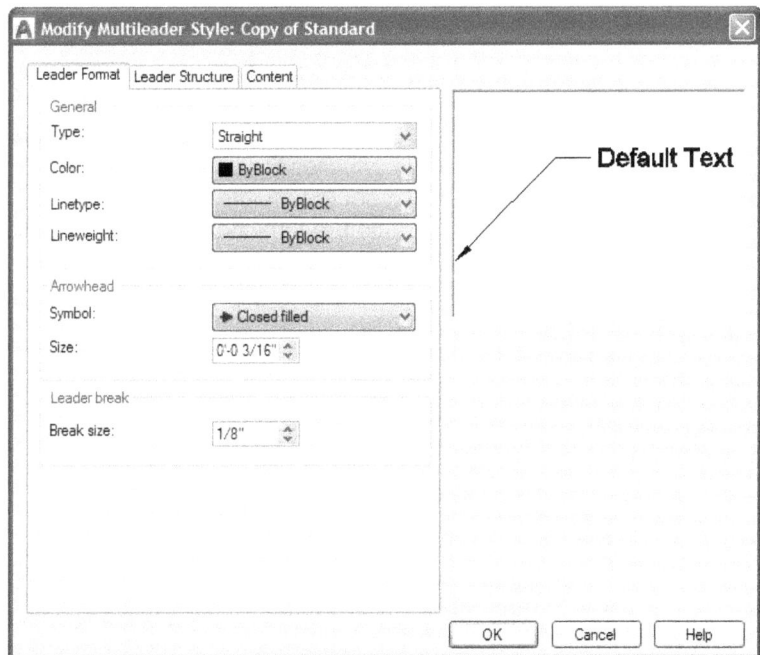

Figure 17–25

6. In the *Leader Structure* tab, specify how you want the leader to work, as shown in Figure 17–26. For example, the default leader style has the *Maximum leader points* set to **2** and *Landing Settings* toggled on. Select **Annotative** if you are using the annotative scaling tools.

If you are creating a spline leader style, you might need to clear the **Constraints** *and* **Landing Settings** *options.*

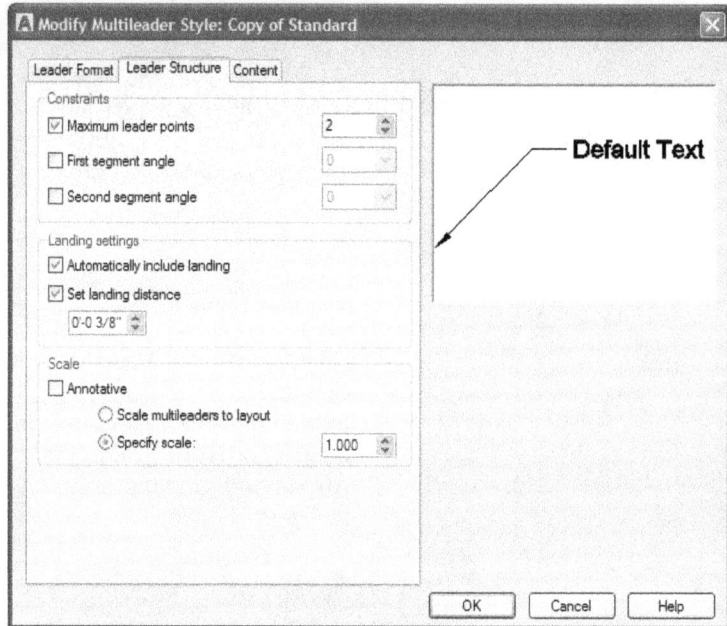

Figure 17–26

7. In the *Content* tab, you can specify whether you want the multileader content to be **Mtext**, **Block**, or **None**. Once you set the *Multileader type*, the rest of the options vary according to the selection. The **Mtext** option is shown in Figure 17–27.

When you have selected text, you can set the attachment to be **Horizontal** *or* **Vertical**.

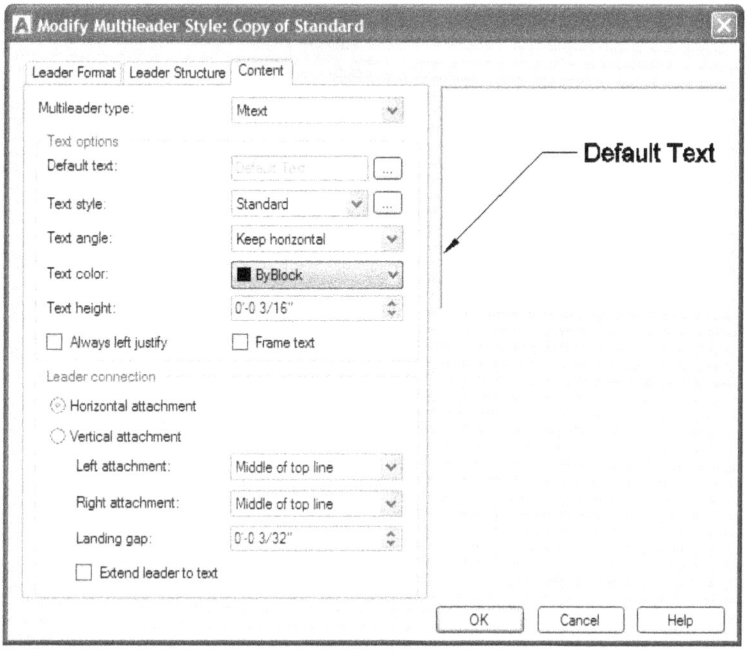

Figure 17–27

8. When you use the **Block** *Multileader type*, you can select from a variety of preset blocks with attributes or use your own blocks, as shown in Figure 17–28.

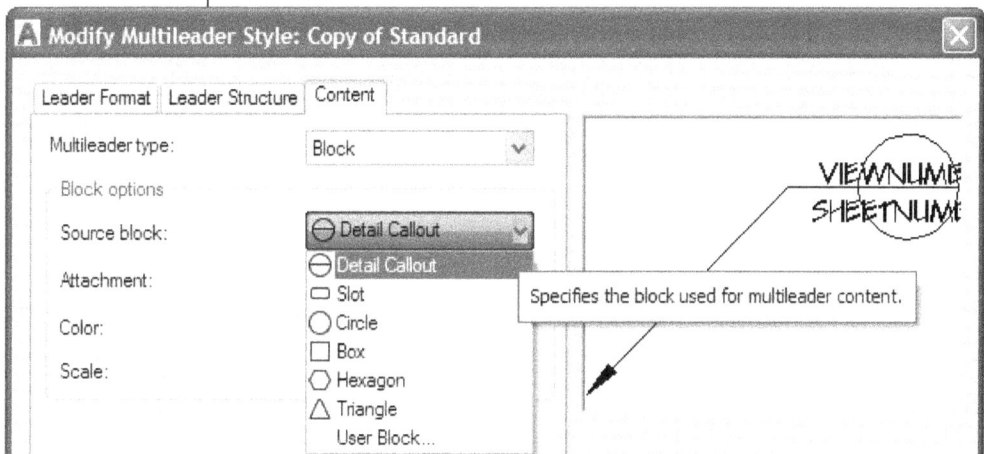

Figure 17–28

9. When you are satisfied with the style, click **OK**. In the Multileader Style Manager, select the new style and click **Set Current**.
10. Click **Close**.

- If you need to make a change to a style, open the Multileader Style Manager, select the style that you want to change, and click **Modify**.

- If you need to delete a style, open the Multileader Style Manager, select a style, and click **Delete**.

- You can also create style overrides for the Leader, Content, and Workflow by selecting **Options** in the **Multileader** command.

Practice 17d | Creating Multileader Styles

Practice Objective

- Create a multileader style.

In this practice, you will create a multileader style using a spline and a block, as shown in Figure 17–29.

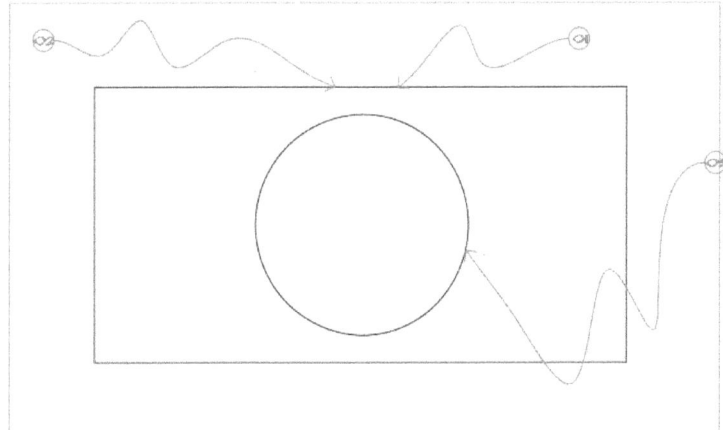

Figure 17–29

1. Open **AEC-Facilities3-A.dwg** from your practice files folder.

2. In the *Annotate* tab>Leaders panel, click ⬣.

3. In the Multileader Style Manager, click **New...**.

4. In the Create New Multileader Style dialog box, name the new multileader **Keynote**. Start with the **Standard** style and make it **Annotative**. Click **Continue**.

5. In the *Leader Format* tab, in the *General* area, set the *Type* to **Spline**. In the *Arrowhead* area, set the *Symbol* to **Right angle**.

6. In the *Leader Structure* tab, clear **Maximum leader points** (this enables you to make as many points on the spline as required).

7. In the *Content* tab, change the *Multileader type* to **Block**. In the *Block options* area, set the *Source block* to **Circle** and click **OK**.

8. In the Multileader Style Manager, select Keynote and click **Set Current**. Click **Close**.

9. Start the **Multileader** command to test the new multileader style by clicking several points to create a zig zag leader. Press <Enter> to stop selecting points along the spline.

10. In the Edit Attributes dialog box, enter a tag number (01,02,03 etc.) for the keynote. Click **OK**.

11. Erase the leaders, switch to Model Space, and save the drawing template.

17.5 Annotation Scale Overview

The Annotation Scale features enable you to avoid creating multiple copies of the same annotation objects at different scales. This makes it easier to quickly dimension drawings that contain views at different scales. Using Annotation Scale, you can control which dimensions, text, etc., display in each scaled detail viewport, as shown in Figure 17–30.

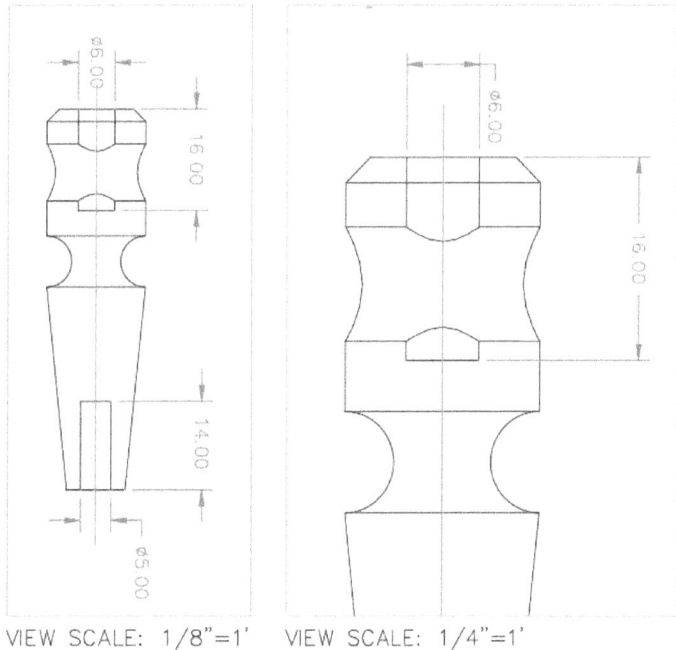

VIEW SCALE: 1/8"=1'   VIEW SCALE: 1/4"=1'

Figure 17–30

- Annotation objects include Single Line Text, Multiline Text, Text Styles, Dimensions, Dimension Styles, Multileaders, Multileader Styles, Geometric Tolerances, Blocks, Attributes, and Hatches.

Hint: Linetypes and Annotation Scale

Linetype spacing is controlled by the Annotation Scale through the **msltscale** system variable. This variable is set per drawing using templates.

- When set to **1** (the default in the template files supplied with the AutoCAD® software), linetypes are automatically scaled to the annotation scale.

- When set to **0**, they are not scaled to the annotation scale.

Working with Annotative Styles

Annotative styles are set by selecting the **Annotative** option in the Dimension Style, Multileader Style, Block Definition, Attribute Definition, and Text Style dialog boxes, as shown in Figure 17–31.

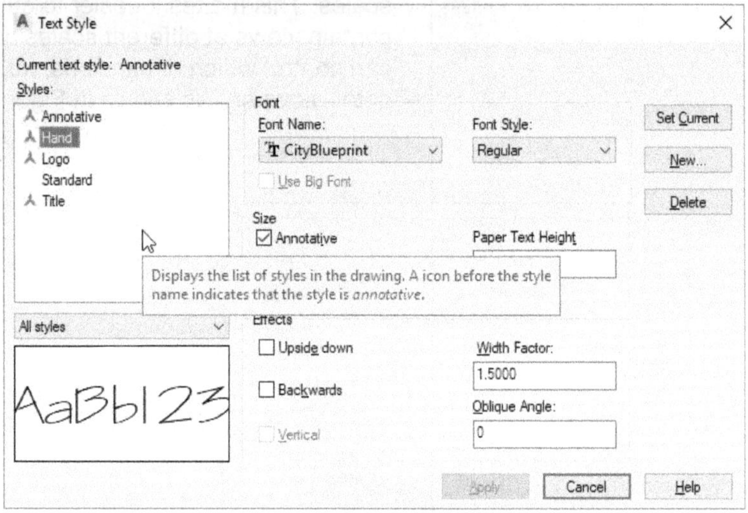

Figure 17–31

When set, you can identify an annotative style in one of the following ways:

- 𝄑 (Annotation) displays next to the style name in the Text Style dialog box and in the list of style names in the *Home* tab>Annotation panel, as shown in Figure 17–32.

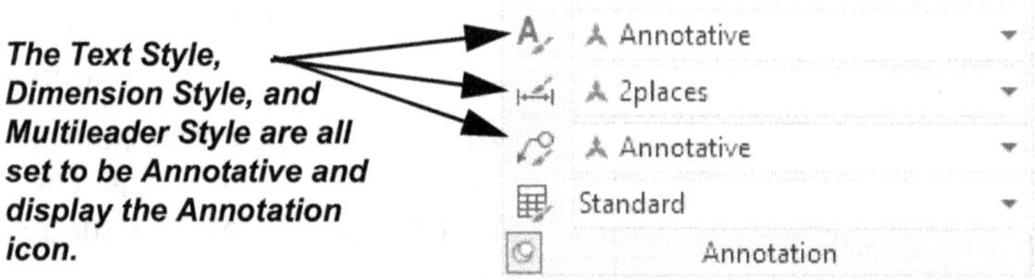

The Text Style, Dimension Style, and Multileader Style are all set to be Annotative and display the Annotation icon.

Figure 17–32

- 𝄑 (Annotation) also displays when you hover the cursor over an annotative object in the drawing window, as shown in Figure 17–33.

Annotation icon

NEW ACCOUNTS

Figure 17–33

How To: Add Annotative Objects

1. In a layout, switch to Paper Space and set up the viewports as required.
2. Select a viewport by selecting its border.
3. In the Status Bar, click **Viewport Scale** and select a scale in the list, as shown in Figure 17–34. The Annotation Scale automatically updates to match. Changing the Annotation Scale also changes the Viewport Scale.

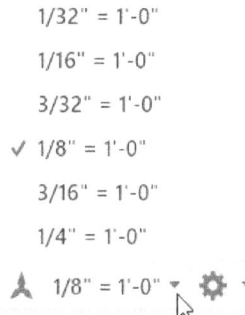

1/32" = 1'-0"

1/16" = 1'-0"

3/32" = 1'-0"

✓ 1/8" = 1'-0"

3/16" = 1'-0"

1/4" = 1'-0"

1/8" = 1'-0"

Figure 17–34

4. (Optional) Click (Lock/Unlock Viewport) to lock the viewport so that the scale and location cannot change.

- You can quickly lock or unlock viewports using (Lock/Unlock Viewport) in the Status Bar, as shown in Figure 17–35.

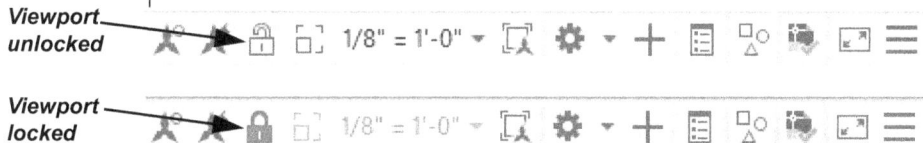

Viewport unlocked   1/8" = 1'-0"

Viewport locked   1/8" = 1'-0"

Figure 17–35

5. When you are ready to start adding annotative objects, activate one of the viewports.

6. Use annotative styles when creating the various annotation objects. They can be scaled to suit each viewport and do not display in viewports to which other annotation scales have been assigned.

- The annotative scale can also be set in the Properties of specific objects, such as text or dimensions, as shown in Figure 17–36.

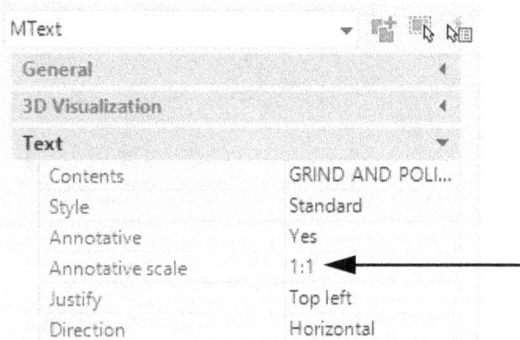

Figure 17–36

Hint: Changing Scale of Annotative Objects

In a viewport, when **Zoom** commands are used or the scale changes in the Viewports toolbar, the scale of the annotative objects is not modified. You must modify the Viewport Scale in the Status Bar for the annotative objects to change scale.

Viewing Annotative Objects at Different Scales

Annotation Scale is linked to the Viewport Scale, therefore, annotative objects (such as dimensions and text) display in layout viewports that have the same scale. If the Viewport Scale is changed, the annotative objects are not displayed. To ensure they remain displayed, add annotation scales to objects enabling them to be displayed in viewports of different scales. For example, you might want the room names to display in each view while the dimensions display in specific viewports, as shown in Figure 17–37.

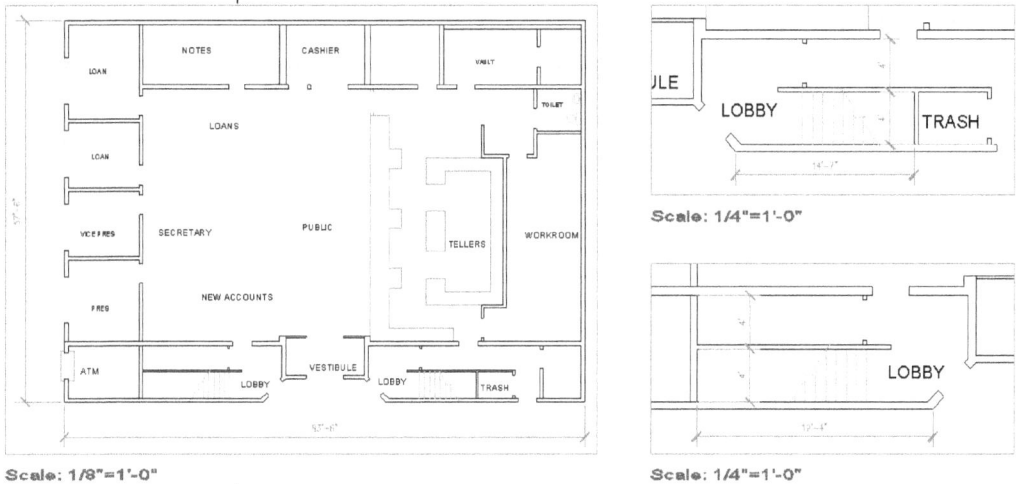

Scale: 1/8"=1'-0"

Scale: 1/4"=1'-0"

Scale: 1/4"=1'-0"

Figure 17–37

When a viewport's Viewport Scale is changed, the annotation objects displayed within it change as well. How the objects behave depends on how you set the annotation visibility and whether or not the scale is automatically added to the object.

	Annotation Visibility (Show annotation objects - At current scale): When toggled **Off**, only annotative objects with the current scale display. It is recommended that you use this option by default. It displays objects that are to be plotted.
	Annotation Visibility (Show annotation objects - Always): When toggled **On**, annotative objects for all of the scales display. Use when you need to add or remove an annotative object to the current scale.
	Add scales to annotative objects when the annotation scale changes: When toggled **Off**, annotation scales are not automatically added to objects in the viewport.
	Add scales to annotative objects when the annotation scale changes: When toggled **On**, any annotation objects in the drawing are updated to match the new annotation scale.

• When you add a scale to an object, a scale representation of that object is created.

- When you select an annotative object that has more than one scale, all of its scale representations display, as shown on the right in Figure 17–38. There is no limit to the number of scales that can be added to an object. However, too many scales can be confusing when you use grips to edit the object.

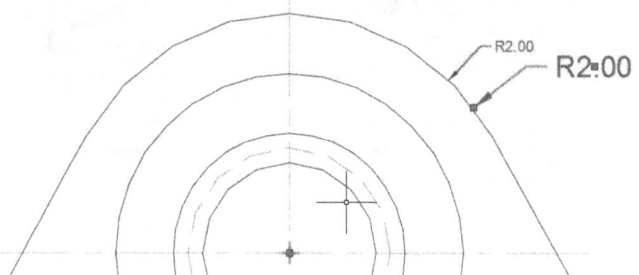

Figure 17–38

- If you modify the information contained in the annotation, all of the scale representations are updated.

- You can use grips to edit each scale representation separately in its associated viewport to suit the location.

Annotation Scale and Model Space

You can annotate objects in Model Space by setting the Annotation Scale in the Status Bar. It is linked to the Viewport Scale and displays in viewports that use the same Annotation Scale, as shown in Figure 17–39.

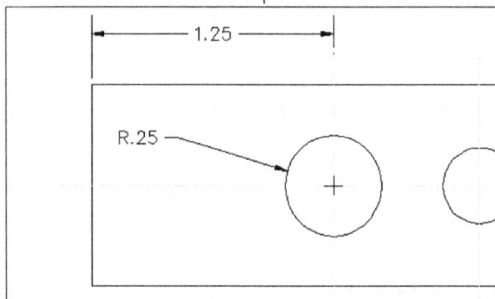

Figure 17–39

Modifying Annotative Object Scales

When you add annotative objects to a viewport, they automatically use the scale of the viewport. If you need to change the scale or move annotative objects out of a viewport, you can modify the scales associated with the objects or with the viewport.

- These tools are available in the *Annotate* tab>Annotation Scaling panel, or when you right-click on an annotative object, as shown in Figure 17–40.

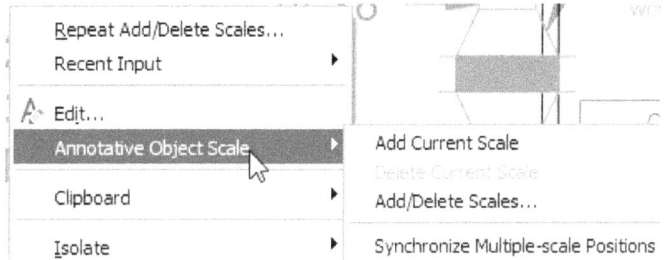

Add
Current Scale

Scale List

Add/Delete Scales

Sync Scale Positions

Annotation Scaling

Repeat Add/Delete Scales...
Recent Input
Edit...
Annotative Object Scale
Clipboard
Isolate

Add Current Scale
Delete Current Scale
Add/Delete Scales...
Synchronize Multiple-scale Positions

Figure 17–40

- If you want to display an annotative object that is not displayed in the current viewport scale, toggle on (Show annotation objects - Always) in the Status Bar to display all of the scale representations of the objects. Right-click on the object that you want to include in your scale, expand **Annotative Object Scale** and select **Add Current Scale**.

- To display an annotative object in several viewports that use different scales, right-click on an annotative object, select **Add/Delete Scales** or click ![icon] (Add/Delete Scale), and then select an annotative object. This opens the Annotation Object Scale dialog box (shown in Figure 17–41), where you can click **Add** to set the annotative scales that are used in each viewport.

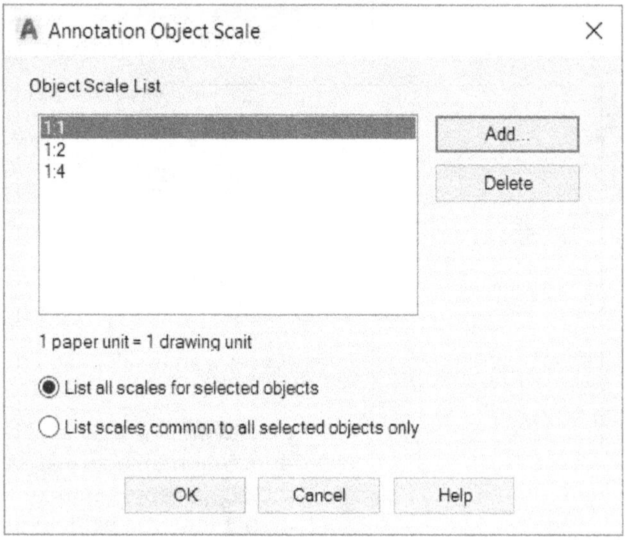

Figure 17–41

- You can change the locations of individual scale representations. If you need to return them to one position, right-click, expand **Annotative Object Scale**, and select **Synchronize Multiple-scale Positions** or in the Annotation Scaling panel, click ![icon] (Sync Scale Positions) to move all of the related representations to the same location as the selected object.

- If you do not want an annotative object to display in the current viewport, but want it to be visible in another viewport at a different scale, click ![icon] (Delete) to delete the current scale.

Hint: Editing the Scale List

The Scale List is stored in each drawing file and is accessed using the Edit Drawing Scales dialog box, as shown in Figure 17–42. The list can vary from drawing to drawing. Therefore, if you want to use a standard scale list in each drawing you should create it in a template drawing.

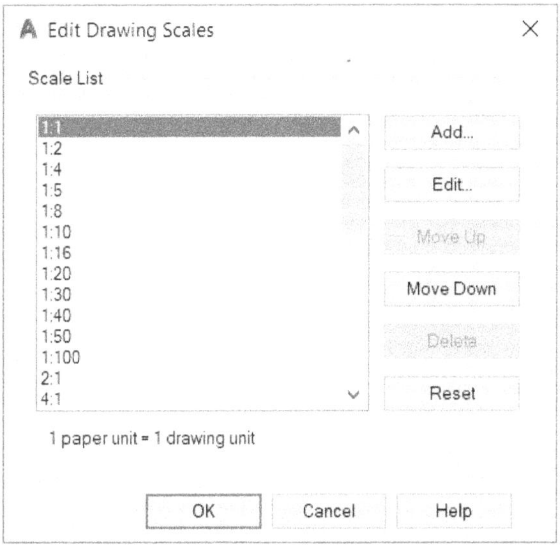

Figure 17–42

- To edit the Scale List, click **Viewport Scale** in the Status Bar and select **Custom...** at the bottom of the list.

- You can also click ⚘ (Scale List) in the *Annotate* tab> Annotation Scaling panel, as shown in Figure 17–43.

Figure 17–43

Practice 17e | Annotation Scale

Practice Objective

- Add annotative objects that are to be displayed in viewports that are set at a specific scale.

In this practice, you will specify the annotative styles for text, dimensions, multileaders, and hatches. You will then add annotative objects at different scales to only be displayed in viewports with the same scale setting, as shown in Figure 17–44.

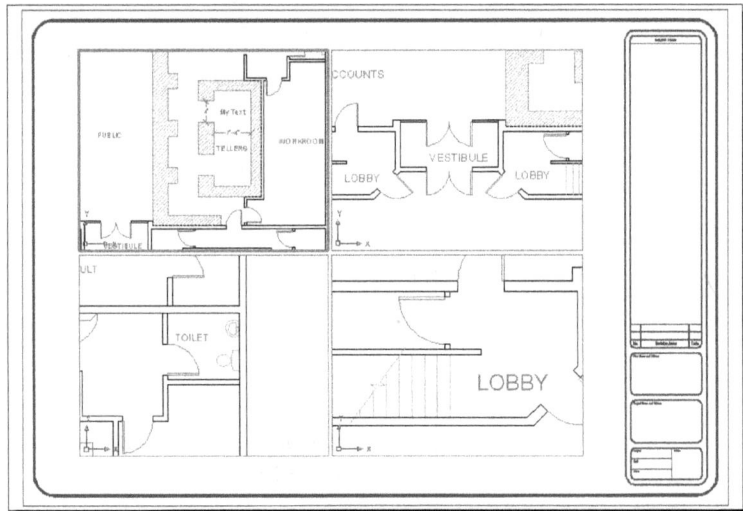

Figure 17–44

Task 1 - Annotative text and dimensions.

1. Open **Branch Bank-A.dwg** from the practice files folder.

2. In the *Home* tab>expanded Annotation panel, set the *Text, Dimension*, and *Multileader Style(s)* to **Annotative**, as shown in Figure 17–45.

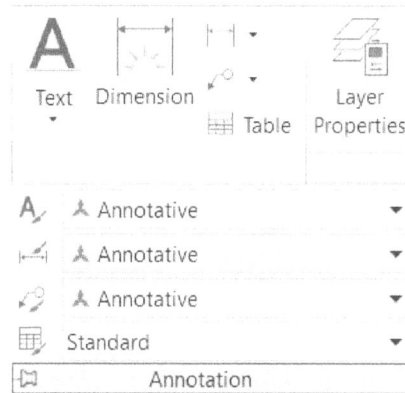

Figure 17–45

3. Switch to the **D-Sized** layout.

4. In Paper Space, select the border of the *Tellers* (top left viewport that displays the *Tellers* area) viewport. In the Status Bar, the Viewport Scale displays **1/4" = 1'-0"**. Press <Esc> to release the selected viewport.

5. Repeat the last step to verify that each viewport is displaying the correct Viewport Scale. The scales should be:

   • *Vestibule viewport:* **3/8"=1'-0"**

   • *Restroom viewport:* **1/2"=1'-0"**

   • *Lobby viewport:* **3/4"=1'-0"**

6. Select all four viewports. In the Status Bar, click

   (Lock/Unlock Viewport) to lock the viewports. Press <Esc> to release all selected viewports.

You can display the Layer Control in the Quick Access Toolbar for easy access.

7. Set the layer **Dimensions** to be current. Double-click inside the *Tellers* viewport to make it active. Add the text and dimensions, as shown in Figure 17–46. They only display in the current viewport.

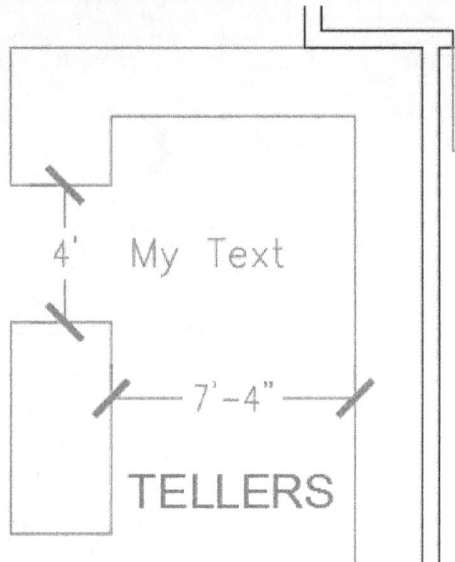

Figure 17–46

Task 2 - Set the annotative hatching.

---

1. Verify that the *Tellers* viewport is still active (or activate it) and set the layer **Hatching** to be current.

2. Verify that both Annotative options (and) are toggled off in the Status Bar.

3. Start the **Hatch** command.

4. In the *Hatch Creation* contextual tab>Options panel, click (Annotative) (highlighted).

5. In the Pattern panel, select **ANSI31**.

6. In the Properties panel, set the *Scale* to **1**.

7. Add hatching to the three counter areas inside the Tellers viewport.

8. In the Close panel, click (Close Hatch Creation).

9. In the *Vestibule* viewport, note that the counter area (top right corner) does not display the hatching. Since the hatching is annotative, it is only displayed in the *Tellers* viewport.

Task 3 - Add/delete scales.

1. Select the hatch object that you just created.

2. Right-click on the selected hatching, expand Annotative Object Scale and select **Add/Delete Scales**. The Annotation Object Scale dialog box opens. Note that only the **1/4"=1'-0"** annotation scale displays.

3. Click **Add** to add a scale. The Add Scales to Object dialog box opens.

4. Select **3/8"=1'-0"**, which is the scale of the *Vestibule* viewport.

5. Click **OK**. The scale is listed in the Annotation Object Scale dialog box.

6. Click **OK**. The hatching, which is an annotative object, now displays in the *Vestibule* viewport because it matches the scale of the vestibule.

Task 4 - Set the annotation object display.

1. Switch to the *Model* tab and note how the annotative objects (i.e., the hatch, text, and dimensions) display.

2. In the Status Bar, note that (Show annotation objects - Always) is toggled on. Click on it to toggle it to display

   (Show annotation objects - At current scale). Note how the annotation objects disappear.

3. Save and close the drawing.

Reusable Content and Drawing Management

6.3.b Create and manage saved sets of objects using groups is not covered in this learning guide. Refer to the AutoCAD Help documentation for "Group command" to review this objective.

Blocks

Exam Objectives Covered in This Chapter

- 6.1.b Create and modify block definitions
- 6.3.a Use the Blocks palette, Tool palettes, and the Design Center

18.1 What Are Blocks?

A group of objects can be converted into a single symbol or block. Blocks can be anything from furniture (as shown in Figure 18–1) to schematic symbols, to entire drawings, such as a roof detail. Different types of drawings use different blocks. For example, architects need blocks, such as doors, windows, and roof sections. Mechanical designers would have a stock of nuts, bolts, and reusable parts.

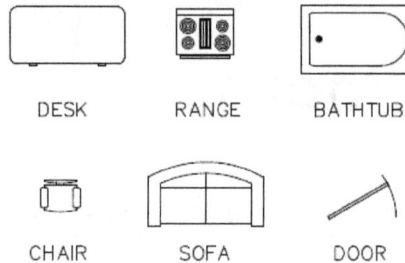

DESK   RANGE   BATHTUB

CHAIR   SOFA   DOOR

Figure 18–1

The benefits of using blocks in the AutoCAD software:

- Ease of manipulating the blocks in a drawing, since they are unified objects. Some blocks, called *dynamic blocks*, are designed so that you can adjust their size or other features after inserting them.

- Consistency of standard details or parts.

- Reduced file size, since each instance of the block in a drawing refers to a single block definition.

- Once you create a block, it is saved in the drawing and can be reused multiple times in the same drawing.

- The block can also be saved as a file to be used in other drawings.

- There are several ways to insert a block, such as the **Insert** gallery and Blocks Palette, Tool Palettes, and DesignCenter.

Hint: Blocks and Layers

When you insert a block, the insertion point is always placed on the current layer. The way the block was created determines whether the block objects use the properties of the current layer, or have a layer or layers that are already associated with objects in the block. Block objects created on layer **0** use the properties of the current layer. Block objects created on other layers use the properties of those layers, no matter which layer is current when the block is inserted.

While there is no absolute standard for how blocks are created, you are most likely to use multilayer compound blocks. For example, you might create a detail that includes hatching, text and the objects, as shown in Figure 18–2. These blocks should be inserted on layer **0**.

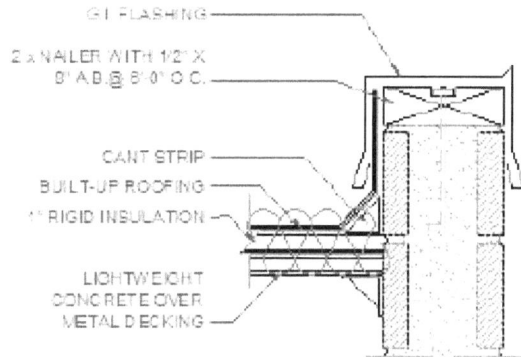

Figure 18–2

Simple blocks, such as a symbol or screw (as shown in Figure 18–3), are more likely to be created on layer **0** and inserted on the required layer.

Figure 18–3

18.2 Inserting Blocks Using the Blocks Palette

Once the block has been created, it can be reused in the drawing. A defined block is saved in the Insert gallery and the Blocks Palette. All the other blocks in the current drawing are also listed in the Insert gallery and in the Blocks Palette and can be quickly inserted into the current drawing. While inserting a block, you are required to specify the insertion point, scale, and rotation.

Insert Gallery

In the *Insert* tab>Block panel, when you expand the Insert gallery, the list of blocks present in the current drawing are displayed, as shown in Figure 18–4.

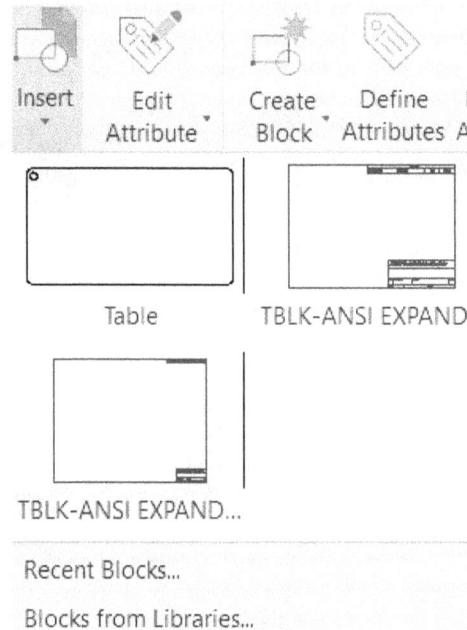

Figure 18–4

How To: Insert a Block from the Gallery

1. In the *Home* tab>Block panel or *Insert* tab>Block panel, expand (Insert Block) and select a block from the list.
2. In the drawing, either click to place the block at the required location or select the **Basepoint**, **Scale**, **X**, **Y**, **Z**, or **Rotate** options and set their values.

- In the Insert gallery, both the **Recent Blocks** and **Blocks from Libraries** open the Blocks Palette in their respective tabs.

- The Insert gallery and the Blocks Palette>*Current Drawing* tab displays the same list of blocks.

Blocks Palette

The Blocks Palette (as shown in Figure 18–5) provides you with an convenient and efficient way of inserting blocks and drawings into the current drawing.

- In the Insert gallery, select the **Recent Blocks** or **Blocks from Libraries** to open the Blocks Palette.

- In the *View* tab>Palettes panel>, click ⬚ (Blocks) to open the Blocks Palette.

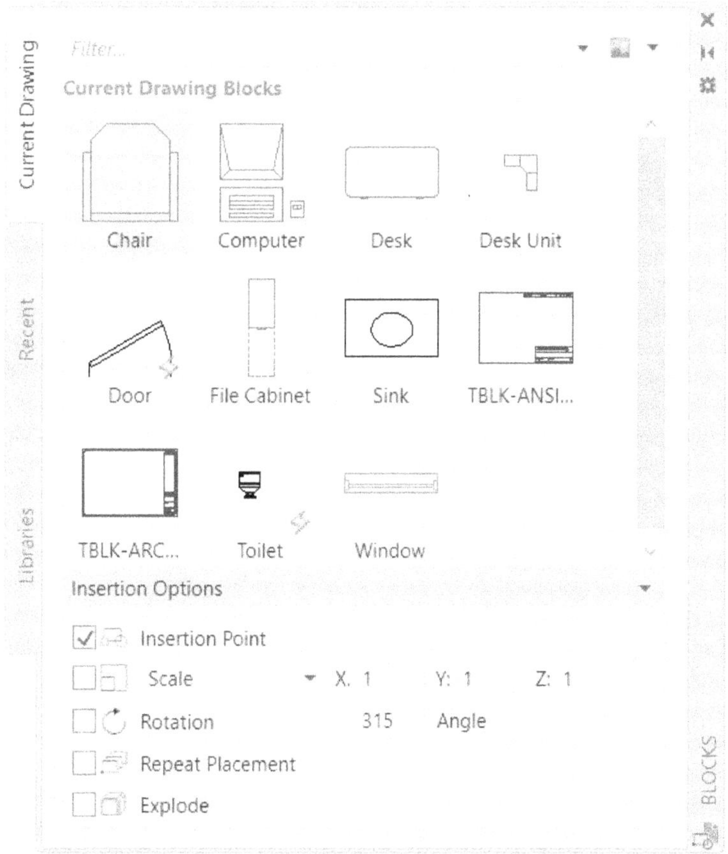

Figure 18–5

The Blocks Palette contains three tabs:

***Current Drawing* tab:** All the blocks in the current drawing are displayed in this tab. It is a replica of the Insert gallery.

***Recent* tab:** All the blocks that were inserted recently in the current drawing are displayed in this tab. It includes all the inserted blocks whether they are from the current drawing or inserted from other drawings. The blocks displayed in this tab also include the blocks that were inserted while working in other drawing sessions. To remove a block from this tab, right-click on the block and select **Remove from Recent List**.

***Libraries* tab:** You can insert any AutoCAD drawing as a block or insert blocks from other drawings. The file becomes a block in the current drawing and is then listed in the *Libraries* tab. The tab also displays the drawings that were inserted while working in

other drawing sessions. You can use the (navigation tool) near the top right corner of the palette to navigate to the drawing that you want to insert. In addition to a drawing file, you can also insert a folder or any other block definition stored in the drawing in the current drawing and these blocks are listed in the *Libraries* tab.

How To: Insert a Block from the Blocks Palette

1. In the *View* tab>Palettes panel> (Blocks), or *Insert* tab>Block panel, (Insert Block), select **Recent Blocks** or **Blocks from Libraries** to open the Blocks Palette.
2. In the Blocks Palette, open the required tab and select the block or the drawing for insertion.
3. Specify the *Insertion Point*, *Scale*, and *Rotation*. You can set these in the Blocks Palette or on-screen.
4. Click **OK**.

Insertion Options:

In each tab, various Insertion Options have been provided that can be used while inserting the blocks.

- The drag and drop method inserts the block without any options. The block is placed where you drop it. If you click on the block image in the palette instead, the block image gets attached to the cursor along with the *Specify insertion point:* prompt. You can either click to place the block at the required location or select one of the command options (<Down Arrow>), as shown in Figure 18–6.

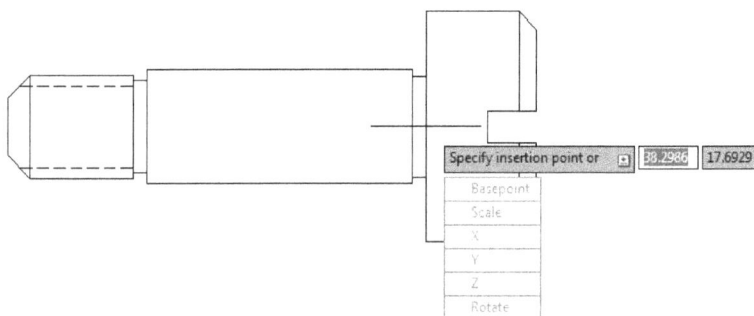

Figure 18–6

- Since you do not usually know the precise X,Y coordinates of the *Insertion Point*, you can specify them in the drawing rather than by entering them in the Blocks Palette.

- If you want to rotate the object before you insert it, select the **Rotate** option and enter the rotation angle. Click and drop the rotated block.

- Most blocks are correctly scaled for the drawing in which you are inserting them. However, the **Scale**, **X**, **Y**, and **Z** options enable you to change the scale.

- Blocks are normally created at the appropriate size for the drawing and the insertion scale should generally be set to **1**.

- The **Repeat Placement** option enables you to insert multiple blocks in a single step.

- The **Explode** option converts the block into its component parts when it is inserted into the drawing. If you use this option, the block is hidden while you specify its insertion point, scale, and rotation on-screen (you can also explode a block after it has been inserted using the **Explode** command).

- If a block is inserted into a drawing that uses different units, the block is scaled automatically.

Hint: Blocks and Object Snaps

You can snap to Object Snap points (**Endpoint**, **Midpoint**, etc.) on the objects in a block, as shown in Figure 18–7. Additionally, the **Insert** Object Snap snaps to the insertion base point of a block.

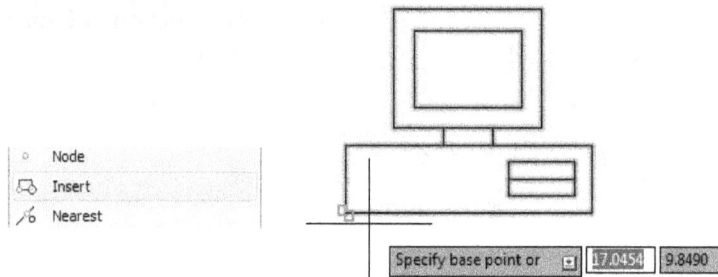

Figure 18–7

18.3 Creating Blocks

The objects that are reused frequently can be saved as a blocks. The blocks you need to use might already exist in your drawings, or you can buy block libraries for almost any type of drawing. You can also easily create your own blocks. A block can be locally defined in a drawing or saved as a file for use in other drawings.

Creating Single Named Objects

The **Create Block** command converts a group of selected objects into a single named object or *local block definition* that only belongs to the current drawing.

How To: Create a Block

1. Draw the objects that you want to include in a block.
2. In the *Insert* tab>Block Definition panel or *Home* tab>Block panel, click [icon] (Create Block).
3. In the Block Definition dialog box (as shown in Figure 18–8), specify the *Name*, *Base point*, *Objects*, *Behavior*, *Settings*, and *Description*.

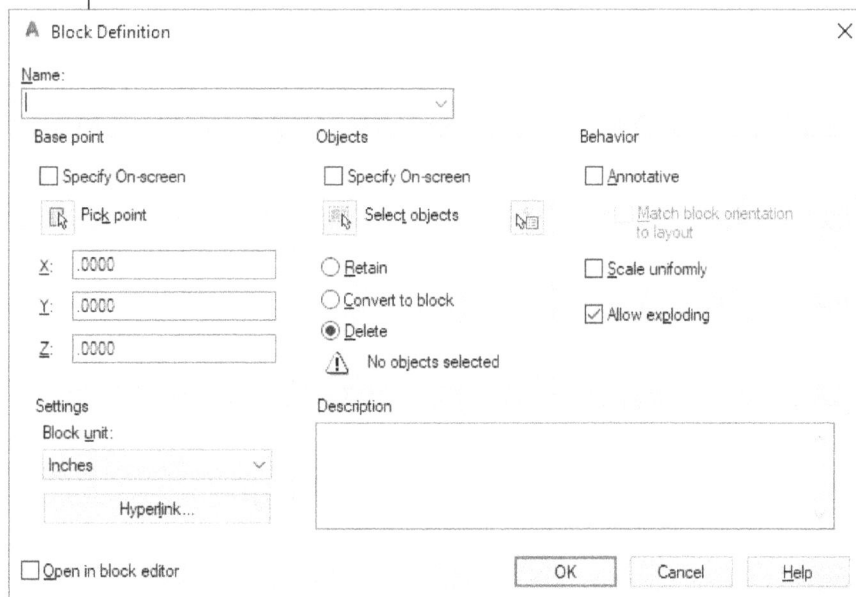

Figure 18–8

4. Click **OK**.

Block Settings

When you create a block, you need to specify various parameters in the Block Definition dialog box, as shown in Figure 18–9.

Figure 18–9

Base Point Area

The *Base point* is a critical setting, which controls the handle of the block when it is inserted. In the example shown in Figure 18–10, the block for a door has its base point at the hinge corner, where it attaches to the end of the wall and the block for the manhole cover has its base point at the center of the cover.

A good base point makes a block much easier to insert.

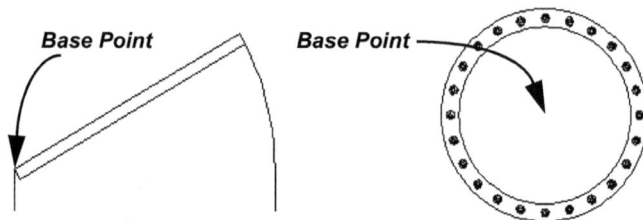

Figure 18–10

In the *Base point* area, you can specify the base point by doing one of the following:

- Select **Specify On-screen** to select the base point after you close the dialog box.

- Click [] (Pick point) to select a point on the screen and then return to the dialog box.

- Type an exact X,Y,Z coordinate.

Objects Area

- Select **Specify On-screen** to select the objects after you close the dialog box.

- Click ⬚ (Select objects) to select objects on the screen and then return to the dialog box.

- Define what you want to do with the objects after you select them. You can retain them, convert them to a block, or delete them.

- Click ⬚ (Quick Select) to start the **Quick Select** command, which can be used to filter out objects in your selection as required.

Behavior Area

- Blocks can be annotative, which means they scale appropriately to the sheet of paper when they are plotted. This is used when you are creating annotation blocks, which often include text (such as a section callout bubble or room tags), as shown in Figure 18–11. Use **Annotative** to make the new block annotative.

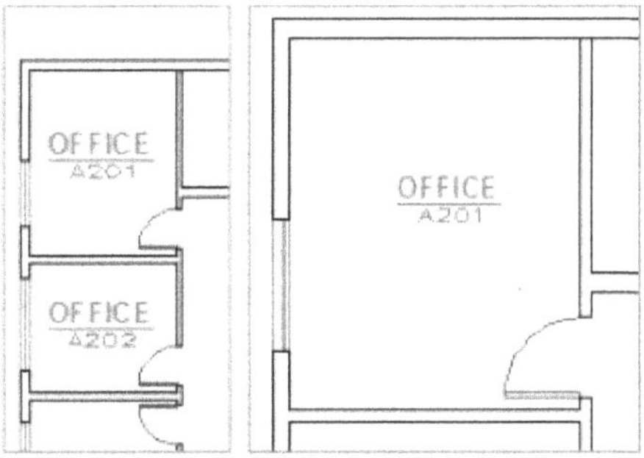

Create annotative blocks at the correct size for plotting. The Annotation Scale factor of a viewport scales them when they are inserted through the viewport.

Figure 18–11

- When you insert an annotative block, an annotative icon displays in the preview in the Insert dialog box, as shown in Figure 18–12.

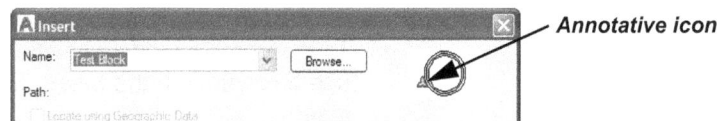

Figure 18–12

- You can also use **Scale uniformly** to force the X- and Y-scaling of the block to be the same when the block is inserted into the drawing.

- Use **Allow exploding** to explode the block into its components when it is inserted into the drawing.

Settings Area

- Select a type of measurement in the Block unit drop-down list. This controls the scaling of the block when it is inserted into another drawing that uses a different type of unit. For example, if the unit in the block and the units in the drawing are different, the block is automatically scaled when it is inserted.

- Click **Hyperlink...** to add a link to another file or to a web address.

- Select **Open in block editor** to add dynamic features to the block.

- In the *Description* area, you can type a description of the block or any notes as required.

Creating Drawing Files from Objects (WBlock)

Blocks created with the **Create (Block)** command are stored in the drawing file in which they were created and are only available through that drawing. If you want to select objects and save them as a separate drawing file that can be used in other drawings, use the **Write Block (Wblock)** command.

- The **Write Block** command saves a copy of a block definition on your computer as a drawing file. Each use of **Write Block** creates a separate drawing file (.DWG).

- As with any .DWG file, the drawing files created with the **Write Block** command can be inserted into other drawings. Drawings to be used as blocks are often stored in a *block library*, which is a shared network folder containing drawings that are available to everyone in an office.

- You can use **Write Block** to break a large drawing into smaller components.

- To insert a file made with **Write Block** into another drawing, use **Browse...** in the Insert dialog box and select a file to insert.

- Once you have inserted the file, it creates a local block definition in the drawing. The local block definition is not linked to the DWG file that was made with **Write Block**.

How To: Create a Wblock

1. In the *Insert* tab>Block Definition panel, expand Create Block and click (Write Block). The Write Block dialog box opens, as shown in Figure 18–13.

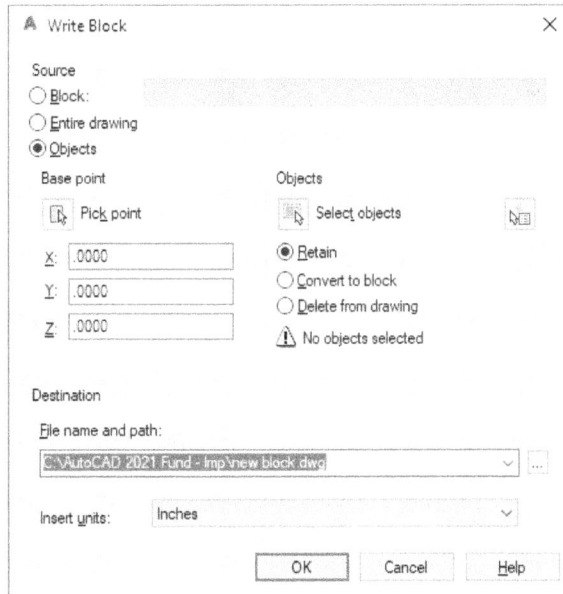

Figure 18–13

2. Select an option in the *Source* area:
   - **Block:** Select a block name from the drop-down list to create a Wblock from an existing block in the drawing.
   - **Entire Drawing:** Selects all of the objects in the drawing including any named objects (such as layers and dimension styles that are associated with the objects), and the current layer. Any unused named objects (such as empty layers) are not included. This is a quick way to clean up a file before it is stored.
   - **Objects:** Select the objects using the options in the *Base point* and *Objects* areas.
3. In the *Destination* area, specify the destination filename and path.
4. Also, specify the *Insert units* if they are to be different than the default units.
5. Click **OK**.

18.4 Editing Blocks

You might have a library of standard details, but need to change one of them for your current project. You can change a local block definition in a drawing using the **Block Editor**, as shown in Figure 18–14.

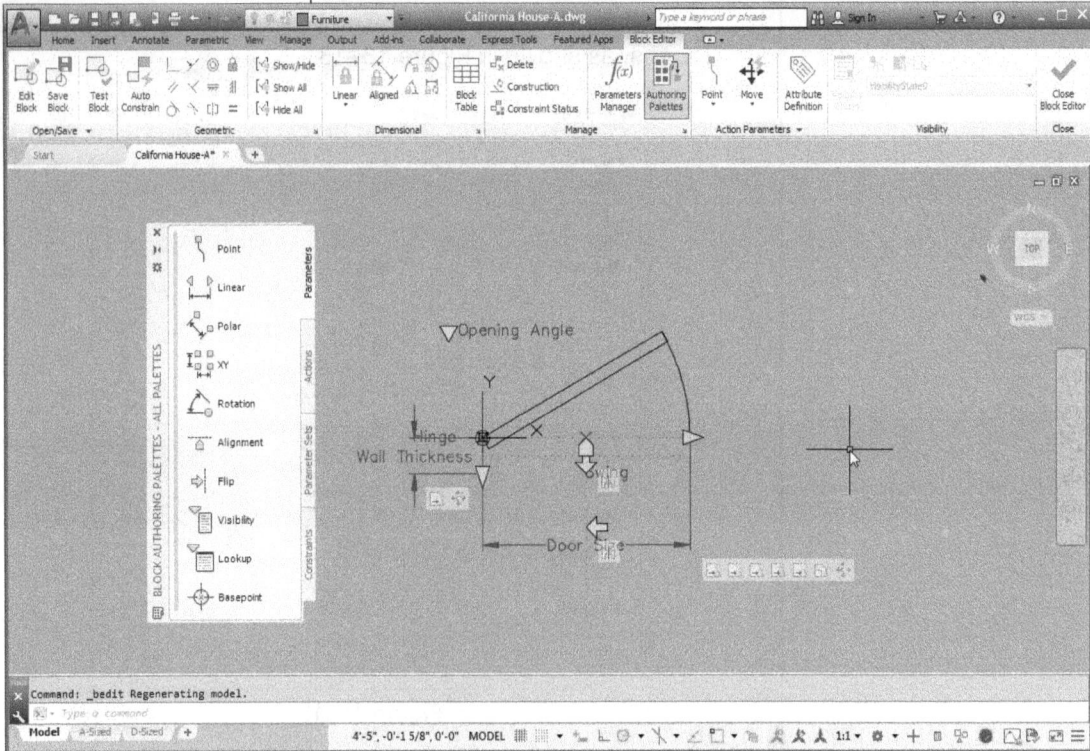

Figure 18–14

- When you open the Block Editor, the *Block Editor* contextual tab opens containing the tools that are required to create complex dynamic blocks, including constraints and special parameters. You can use the tools on any of the other tabs as well to create or modify block objects.

- Changing the block definition modifies all of the instances of the block in the drawing.

- The fastest way to start the Block Editor is to double-click on the block that you want to edit.

How To: Edit a Block in the Block Editor

1. Double-click on the block that you want to edit. Alternatively, in the *Insert* tab>Block Definition panel, click ⬚ (Block Editor).

2. In the Edit Block Definition dialog box (as shown in Figure 18–15), select the block that you want to edit and click **OK**.

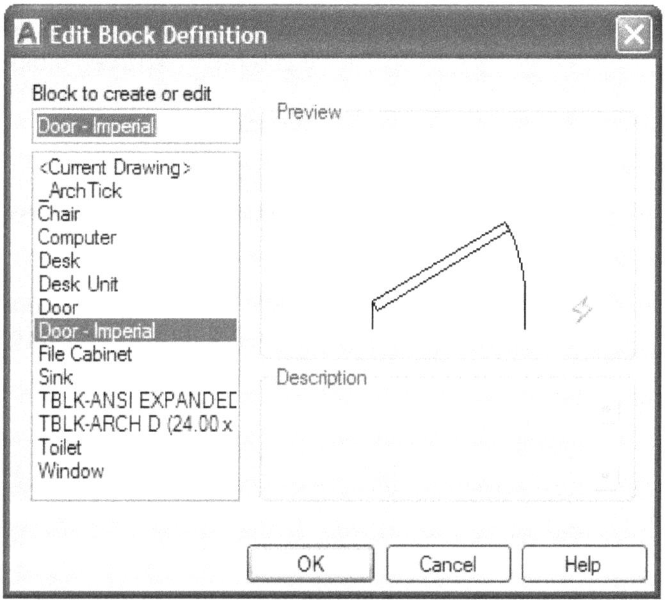

Figure 18–15

3. The *Block Editor* contextual tab opens, the drawing window background changes to gray, the Block Authoring Palette displays, and many of the constraint tools display with the selected block.

4. Modify the block.

5. When you are finished, click ✓ (Close Block Editor).

• The selected block displays in the Block Editor in its original position, even if you selected an instance that was rotated.

Remaking Blocks

- To modify a single instance of a block (rather than the block definition), you can **Explode** the block into its original raw components, provided that the **Allow Exploding** option was toggled on when the block was created. This command also converts polylines into lines and arcs.

- If the block objects were originally created on layer **0**, they revert to this layer when the block is exploded.

- If you have exploded a block and modified its components, you can use the **Create (Block)** command to make the components into a block again.

- If other instances of the block are in the drawing, select the insertion point that was used for the previous block.

- If you use the same name as the original block when you redefine it, all of the instances of that block in the drawing update to match the new block definition.

Practice 18a | Create and Edit Blocks

Practice Objectives

- Define a block.
- Create a new drawing file from a local block.
- Create a new file and then redefine the block.

In this practice, you will define a block for a couch, first drawing the objects and then using the **Create Block** command. You will then use **Write Block** to create a new drawing file from your local block. You will also use **Write Block** to select part of a drawing and create a new file, and then use **Block Editor** to redefine a block.

Task 1 - Creating a local block.

In this task, you will define a block for a couch, first drawing the objects and then using the **Create Block** command, as shown in Figure 18–16.

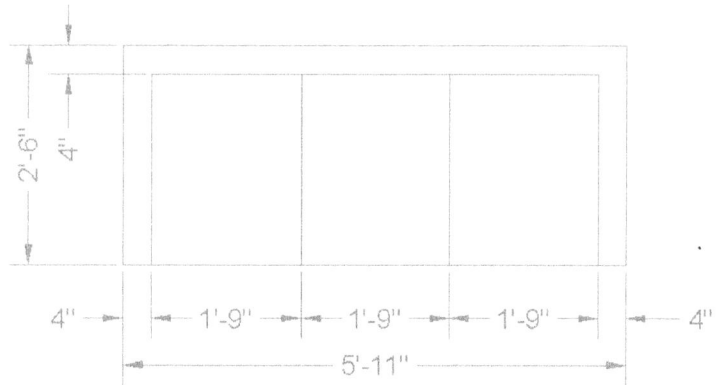

Figure 18–16

1. Open **California House-A.dwg** from your practice files folder.

For quick access, you can display the Layer Control in the Quick Access Toolbar.

2. Set the current layer to **Furniture**. (Hint: You will draw the block on this layer so that it retains the properties of the layer **Furniture** no matter what layer you insert it on.)

3. Zoom in on any one of the rooms and draw a couch (without the dimensions), as shown in Figure 18–16.

4. In the *Insert* tab>Block Definition panel, click (Create Block). In the Block Definition dialog box, name the block **Couch**.

5. In the *Base point* area, click (Pick point) and select the midpoint at the back of the couch as the base point.

6. In the *Objects* area, click (Select objects), select the couch objects, and press <Enter>. Select the **Delete** option.

7. Verify that the *Block unit* is set to **Inches**.

8. Verify that **Open in block editor** is NOT selected.

9. Click **OK**. The block is created and the couch is deleted from the active drawing.

10. Set the current layer to **0**.

11. Open the Blocks Palette in the *Current Drawing* tab. Using the **Repeat Placement** option, insert a couch in several rooms (note that it is still the color of the layer **Furniture**).

12. Save the drawing with a few couches inserted.

Task 2 - Creating a drawing file from a block.

---

1. In the *Insert* tab>Block Definition panel, expand the Block flyout and click (Write Block).

2. In the Write Block dialog box, for the *Source*, select **Block**, expand the drop-down list of local blocks in the drawing, and select **Couch**. You do not need to select the *Base point* or *Objects* because you are using an existing block definition.

3. In the *Destination* area, set the path to your practice folder and the filename to **Couch,** as shown in Figure 18–17. The *Insert units* should be set to **Inches**. Click **OK** to create the new drawing file.

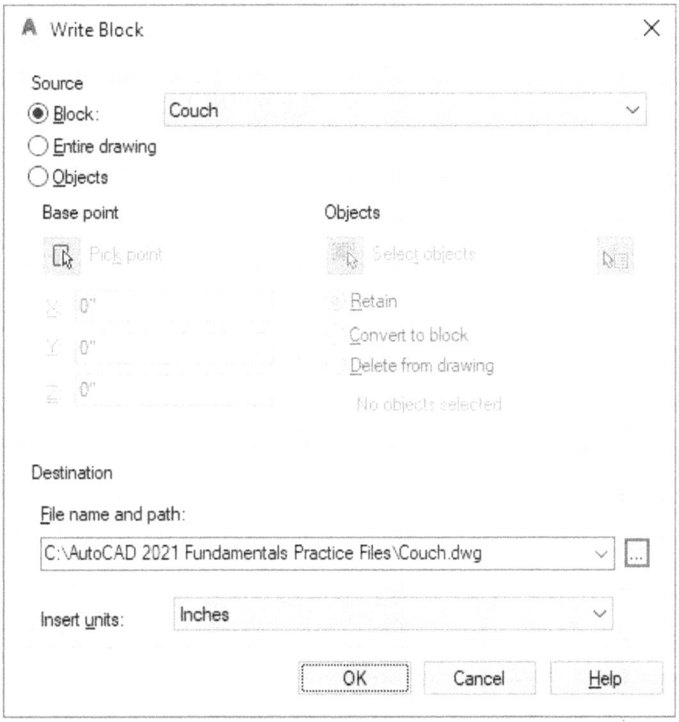

Figure 18–17

4. Open the new drawing **Couch.dwg** from the practice files folder.

5. Use the **Zoom Extents** command to display the couch. Save and close the drawing.

6. Open **Plan1-A.dwg** from your practice files folder.

7. In the Blocks Palette>*Current Drawing* tab, note the list of blocks displayed. The **Couch** block is not in the graphics list.

    Open the *Libraries* tab. Click (navigation tool) near the top right corner of the palette to open the Select a folder or file for Block Library dialog box. Navigate to your practice files folder and select the **Couch.dwg** file. Click **Open**. Note that it is listed in the *Libraries* tab of the Blocks Palette, as shown in Figure 18–18.

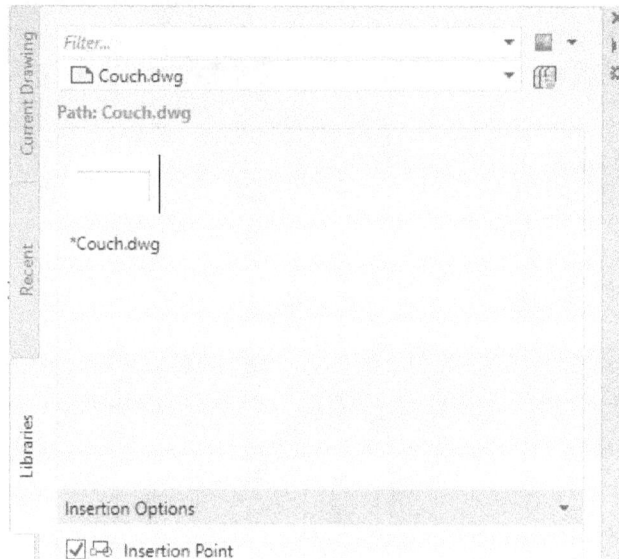

Figure 18–18

8. Insert a couch into one of the rooms. Open the *Current Drawing* tab of the Blocks Palette and note that it is listed there, which indicates that it is now a local block in the drawing **Plan1-A.dwg**.

9. Save and close all of the drawings.

Task 3 - Create a new drawing from part of a drawing.

In this task, you will toggle off most of the layers in a drawing and use **Write Block** to copy the remaining objects to a new file, as shown in Figure 18–19.

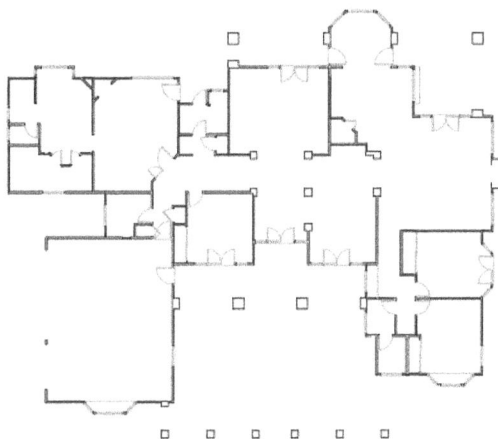

Figure 18–19

1. Open **California House-A.dwg** from your practice files folder.

2. Use the **Zoom Extents** command to display the entire plan.

3. Freeze all of the layers except **0**, **Doors**, **Walls**, and **Windows** (many layers are already frozen).

4. Start the **Write Block** command. In the Write Block dialog box, in the *Source* area, select **Objects**.

5. In the *Objects* area, click [icon] (Select objects) and select all of the visible objects. Right-click or press <Enter> to return to the dialog box.

6. Leave the *Base point* at **0,0,0**. Set the path to your practice folder and name the file **Floorplan.dwg**.

7. Click **OK** to close the dialog box.

8. Close **California House-A.dwg**. Do not save changes.

9. Open **Floorplan.dwg**. Only the objects that you selected display along with the layers **0**, **Doors**, **Walls**, and **Windows** (Layer Control).

10. Close the drawing. Do not save changes.

Task 4 - Edit a block.

In this task, you will use the Block Editor to redefine a block with a new design, as shown in Figure 18–20.

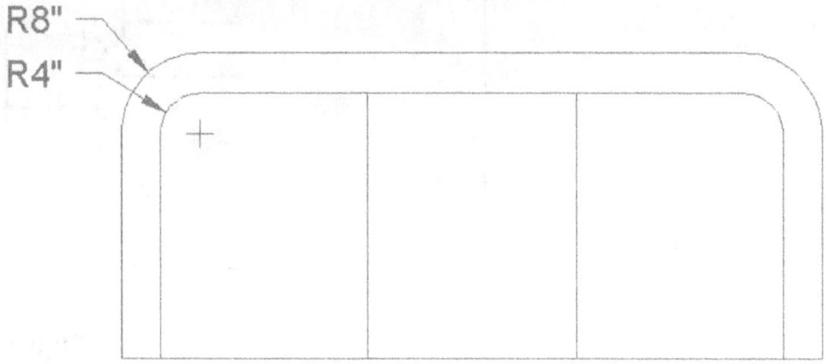

Figure 18–20

1. Open **California House-A.dwg** from your practice files folder.

2. Toggle on the layer **Furniture** if the Couch is not displayed. Double-click on one of the **Couch** blocks.

3. In the Edit Block Definition dialog box, **Couch** is highlighted with its preview displayed. Click **OK** to continue.

4. The Block Editor opens with the block filling the drawing area. Also the background is changed to gray and the Block Authoring Palettes displays. Close or hide the Block Authoring Palettes.

5. Fillet the back corners of the couch, as shown in Figure 18–20.

6. In the *Block Editor* contextual tab, click ✔ (Close Block Editor) and click **Save the changes to Couch**.

7. Note that all of the instances of the **Couch** block in this drawing are automatically updated to the new style. Insert another **Couch** and note that it has also changed.

8. Save and close the drawing.

18.5 Inserting Blocks Using the Tool Palettes

The AutoCAD software comes with many blocks, which are stored in the Tool Palettes window (*View* tab>Palettes panel>

▦ (Tool Palettes)). After you locate the required block in one of the Tool Palette tabs, you can drag and drop it from the palette into the drawing.

- The AutoCAD software comes with example blocks that are located on several tabs of the palette, as shown in Figure 18–21. You can also create custom palettes.

- In the Tool Palettes, dynamic blocks are indicated by a lightning bolt symbol, as shown in Figure 18–21.

Press <Ctrl>+<3> to toggle the Tool Palettes open or closed.

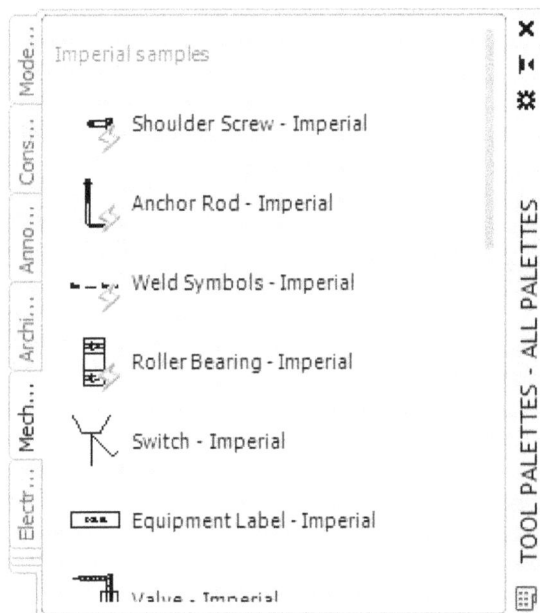

Figure 18–21

- If there are more objects than can fit in the window, a scroll bar displays next to the title bar, enabling you to scroll through the list.

Controlling the Tool Palettes Window

It is useful to display the Tool Palettes as you are working. For efficient use of screen space, you can dock and hide the palette to one side of the drawing window with either the icon or text displayed. When you need to display the full palette, move the cursor over the icon (or text depending on your setting), as shown in Figure 18–22.

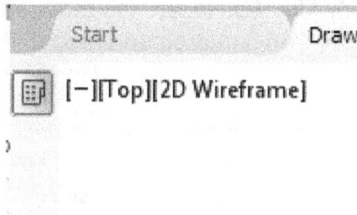

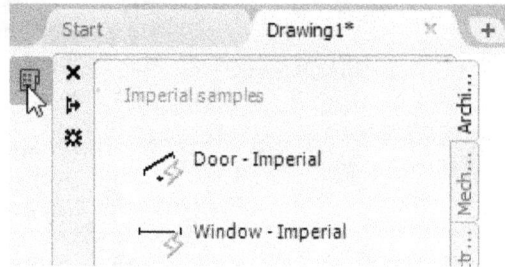

Figure 18–22

This process also applies to other palettes, such as Properties.

*Right-click on the title bar of an undocked palette, and select **Anchor Left** or **Anchor Right** to dock and auto-hide the palette. (**Allow Docking** must be selected first for anchoring to work.)*

How To: Dock and Hide a Palette

1. Open the Tool Palettes.
2. Place the cursor over the title bar of the palette and drag it to one side of the screen. It should dock. If it does not, right-click on the title bar, select **Allow Docking**, and try again.
3. Minimize the palette by clicking ▐◀ (Auto-hide). The palettes stack if more than one is docked.
4. Move the cursor over the title bar or icon to display the full-size palette.

- When a palette is hidden, right-click on the palette title bar and set the docked view to **Icons only** or **Text only**, as shown in Figure 18–23.

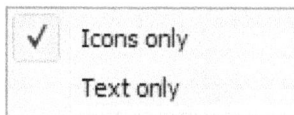

Figure 18–23

18.6 Inserting Blocks Using the DesignCenter

DesignCenter is available to manage your standards. It enables you to access named objects in any drawing to copy them into the current drawing and is also used for inserting blocks. You can have a library of drawings that include typical blocks grouped in a useful order, as shown in Figure 18–24. From the DesignCenter, you can open the drawing and then drag and drop the blocks into your current drawing.

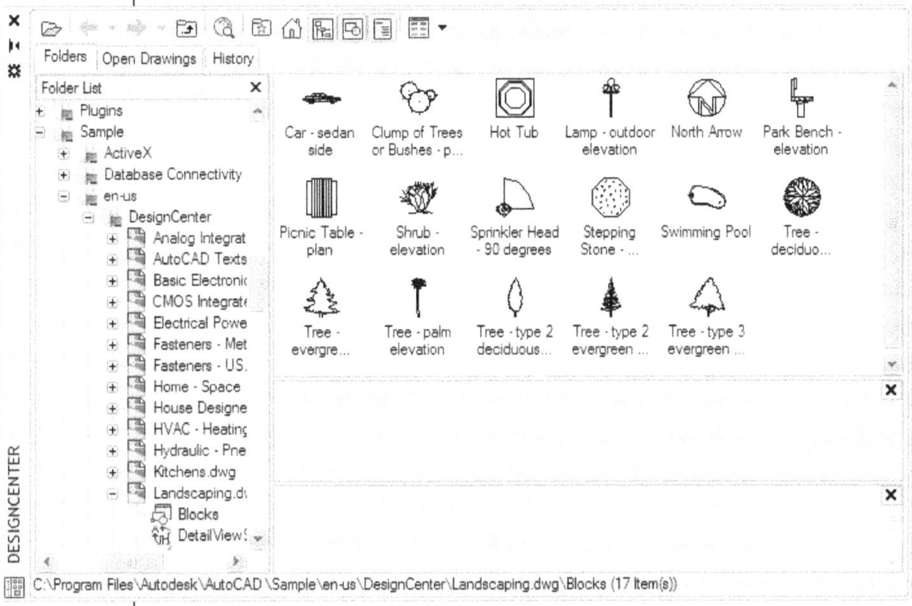

Figure 18–24

- In addition to blocks, you can copy other named objects using the DesignCenter, including layers, linetypes, layouts, reference files (xrefs), and text, table, or dimension styles. Open DesignCenter, locate the drawing containing the objects you want to use, and drag them into your current drawing.

- You can open the DesignCenter by clicking

  (DesignCenter) in the *View* tab>Palettes panel.

- Press <Ctrl>+<2> to toggle DesignCenter open or closed. DesignCenter is a palette and can be docked and hidden in the same way as the Tool Palettes and Properties palette.

DesignCenter Content

Three tabs across the top of DesignCenter provide access to different parts of its content. These tabs are:

Folders	Enables you to use the *Folder List* to navigate to drawings on your computer or network drives.
Open Drawings	Provides access to drawing(s) that are open in the AutoCAD software. You can copy components from any of the open drawings into your current drawing window.
History	Lists several of the last drawings used in DesignCenter. Double-click on the filename to load the drawing in the *Folders* tab.

Navigation and Display Options

The DesignCenter palette contains tools for navigating to drawings and changing the display, as shown in Figure 18–25.

Figure 18–25

	Load: Opens the Load dialog box. When you select a drawing, it opens in DesignCenter without opening in the AutoCAD software.
	Back/Forward: Returns to the previous drawing selected. Click ▼ to expand the list of the available drawings.
	Up: Backs up one folder level each time the button is clicked. Use this if you have toggled off the tree view.
	Search: Opens the Search dialog box in which you can search for drawings, blocks, layers, etc., by name.
	Favorites: Similar to other Windows programs, you can specify favorite places from which to get drawings or web sites. Right-click in DesignCenter to add items to your favorites list.
	Home: Switches to the *DesignCenter* folder.
	Tree View Toggle: Toggles the left side of DesignCenter off and on. If it is off, only the level to which you have expanded displays.
	Preview: Displays a preview of the selected block.

	Description: Displays a description of the selected block if one is available.
▼	**Views:** Toggles through the various types of views. Use the **Large Icons** option to display a thumbnail image of the blocks.

- Set the drawings or folders that you need to access most often as **Favorites**. Right-click on the file or folder in DesignCenter and select **Add to Favorites**. Click (Favorites) in the toolbar for quick access.

18.7 Working with Dynamic Blocks

Dynamic blocks are special kinds of blocks that can be changed dynamically. Once they are in your drawing, they can be manipulated in a variety of ways, including lengthening a side, flipping the direction, aligning to other objects, rotating, or selecting from a list of options, as shown in Figure 18–26. Dynamic blocks are powerful tools and in many cases, several standard blocks can be replaced by one dynamic block.

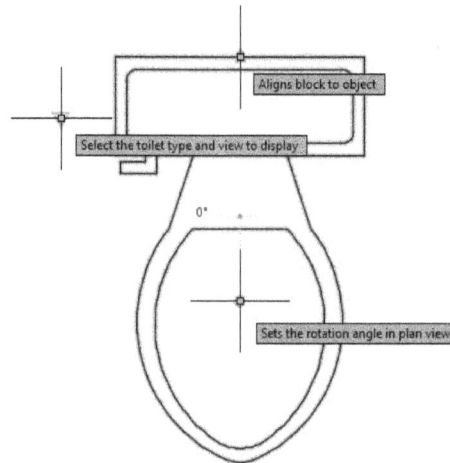

Figure 18–26

Manipulating Dynamic Blocks

When you select a dynamic block, special grips display the types of modifications that are available. Hover the cursor over one of the grips to display its tooltip. Click on the required grip to change the block, as shown in Figure 18–27.

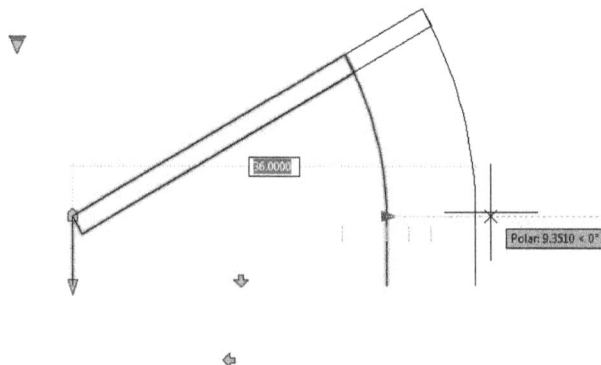

Figure 18–27

- The modification features in dynamic blocks can differ from one block to another. For example, one block might only have the Lengthen/Shorten grip, while another might have the Flip, List, and Rotate grips.

Dynamic Block Grips

The available block grips are described as follows.

▷	**Lengthen/ Shorten**	Enables you to scale, stretch, or array a block. The action depends on how the block was defined.
▽	**List**	Opens a list of options from which to select, such as size, number of items, view displayed, etc.
▣	**Insert/Move**	Indicates the insertion point of the block and other points that might have been assigned in the block. It can move the entire block or just one entity in the block.
⇩	**Flip**	Flips the entire block in the direction of the arrow.
⌂	**Align**	Aligns the entire block at the angle of an object when you move the block near that object. Use <TAB> to cycle through placement of dynamic blocks to orient it in the required direction.
◉	**Rotate**	Enables you to rotate the block or specific objects in the block. The objects that rotate are preset in the block definition.

- Blocks that are not dynamic only have an Insert/Move grip, which you can use to drag the block to a new location.

- After you have finished modifying the dynamic block, press <Esc> to clear it and its grips from modification.

Practice 18b | Working with Blocks

Practice Objective

- Add blocks and dynamic blocks using the Blocks Palette, Tool Palettes, and DesignCenter.

In this practice, you will add blocks and dynamic blocks using the Blocks Palette and the Tool Palette. You will also add landscaping blocks using the Design Center, as shown in Figure 18–28.

Figure 18–28

Task 1 - Insert blocks.

In this task, you will insert blocks in a floor plan, as shown in Figure 18–29. You will use the various tabs and options in the Blocks Palette. The blocks in this drawing were created on their own layers. You will insert them all on layer **0**.

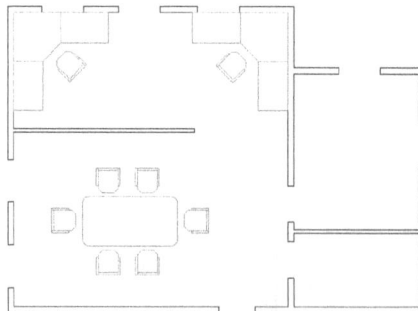

Figure 18–29

1. Open **Plan-A.dwg** from your practice files folder.

2. Select layer **0** in the Layer drop-down list.

3. Ensure that 🔲 (Object Snap) is toggled on and **Endpoint** is selected.

4. In the *Insert* tab>Block panel, expand 📥 (Insert) and select the block named **Desk Unit,** as shown in Figure 18–30.

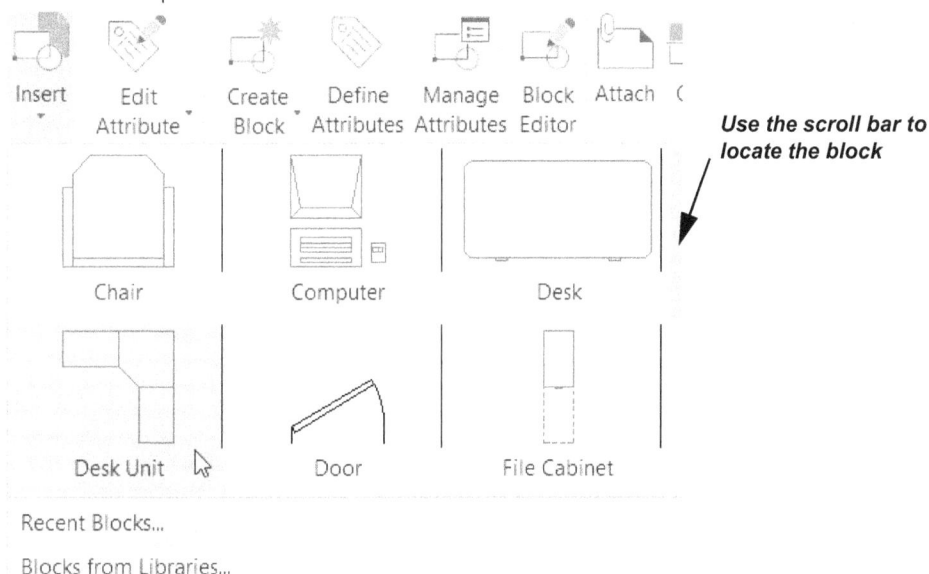

Insert   Edit   Create   Define   Manage   Block   Attach   (
         Attribute   Block   Attributes Attributes Editor

Use the scroll bar to locate the block

Chair   Computer   Desk

Desk Unit ⌖   Door   File Cabinet

Recent Blocks...

Blocks from Libraries...

Figure 18–30

5. The desk is attached to the cursor. Type **R** and press <Enter> to select the **Rotate** option. Ensure that **0** is set for rotation angle, and press <Enter>.

6. Type **X** and press <Enter>. Ensure that **1** is set as the X scale factor, and press <Enter>.

7. Similarly, ensure that both for the Y and Z scale factors are set as **1**.

8. Place the desk in the top right corner of the office, as shown in Figure 18–29.

Using Blocks Palette is an efficient way of inserting blocks.

9. Expand 📥 (Insert) and select **Recent Blocks** in the gallery. Note that the Blocks Palette opens in the *Recent* tab with the Desk Unit displayed.

*If a Redefine Block dialog box opens, select **Don't redefine "Desk Unit"**.*

10. In the *Insertion Options* area, Set the *Rotation Angle* to **90**, as shown in Figure 18–31. Click on the Desk Unit. It is attached with the cursor and is rotated at 90 degrees. Move it to the top left corner (as shown in Figure 18–31) and click to place it.

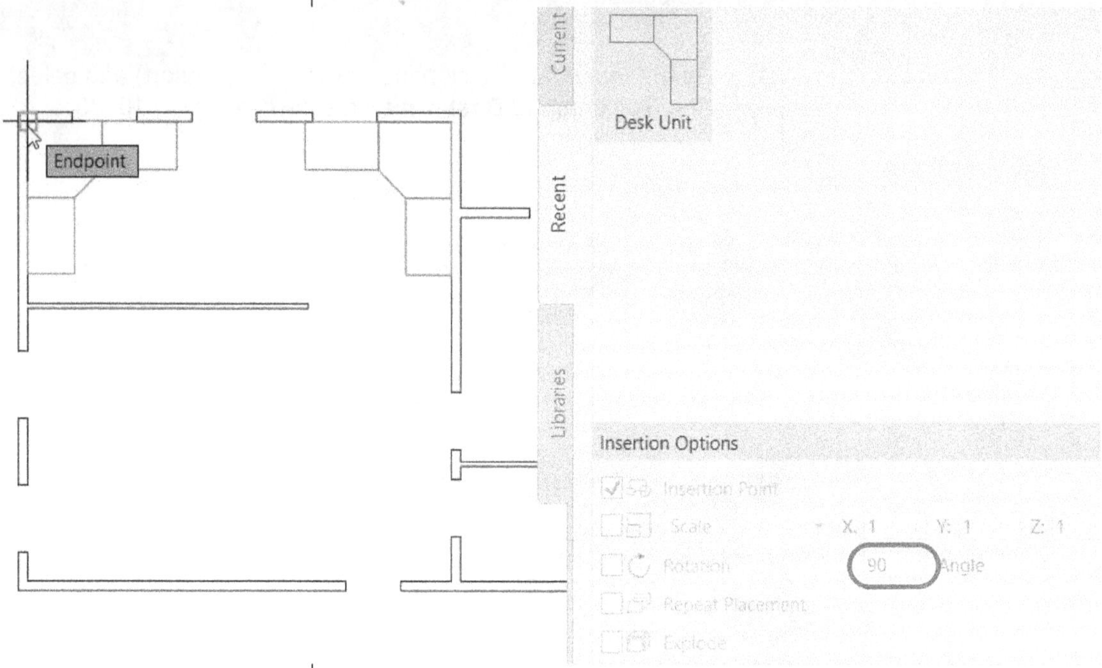

Figure 18–31

11. Click on the *Current Drawing* tab of the Blocks Palette.

12. Locate the **Chair** block and select it. Set the *Rotation Angle* to **45**. Click and place it facing the top left corner Desk Unit.

13. Change the *Rotation Angle* to **-45**. Click and place it facing the top right corner Desk Unit.

14. Set the *Rotation Angle* back to **0** for the next insertion. Click on the *Libraries* tab of the Blocks Palette.

15. Click the ▦ (navigation tool) which opens the Select a folder or a file for Block Library dialog box. Select **Table-A.dwg** (in your practice files folder) and click **Open**. Press <Enter>. It is listed in the *Libraries* tab.

16. Select **Table-A** block and place it in the largest room.

17. Switch to the *Recent* tab.

18. Click to set the **Repeat Placement** option.

19. Select the block **Chair** and place two chairs facing the lower horizontal edge of the table.

20. With the block still attached with the cursor, click <Down arrow> and select **Rotate** in the menu. Enter **90** at the *Specify rotation angle* prompt. Place a chair facing the right vertical edge of the table.

21. Similarly, using the **Rotate** option in the <Down arrow> menu, insert chairs around the table. Use the rotation angles of **-90** and **180**. Press <Esc> to exit the Block Insertion command.

22. Leave the Blocks Palette open.

Task 2 - Work with dynamic blocks.

In this task, you will add dynamic blocks from the Tool Palettes to the floor plan and then manipulate them, as shown in Figure 18–32.

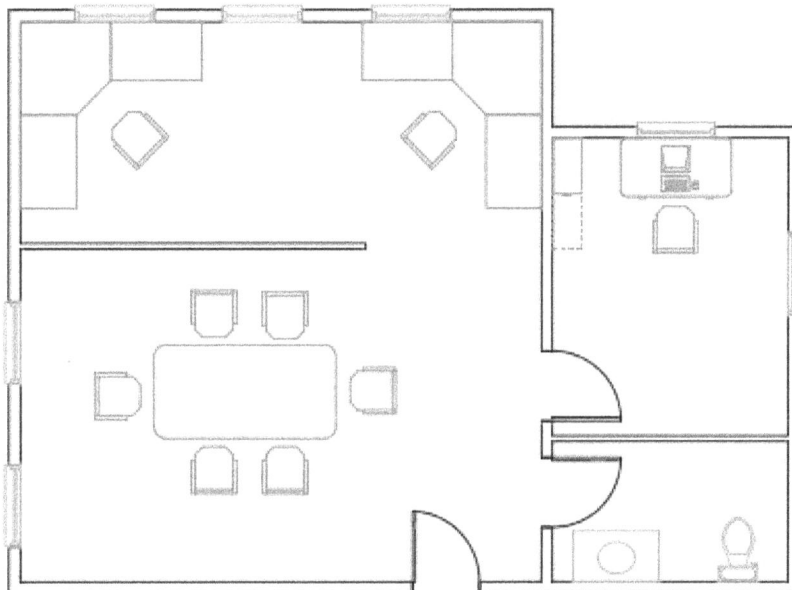

Figure 18–32

1. Zoom in on the opening along the bottom wall of the plan.

View tab>Palettes

panel, ▦ (Tool
Palettes).

2. Open Tool Palettes. Note the types of blocks that are available in the different tabs.

3. In the Tool Palettes, select the *Architectural* tab and select **Door-Imperial**. Note that it is attached to the cursor. Hover the cursor so that the door snaps to the upper endpoint of the left wall. If the door snaps vertically, press <Tab> until it aligns horizontally along the wall (as shown in Figure 18–33), and then click to place it. Note that the door does not fit in the opening.

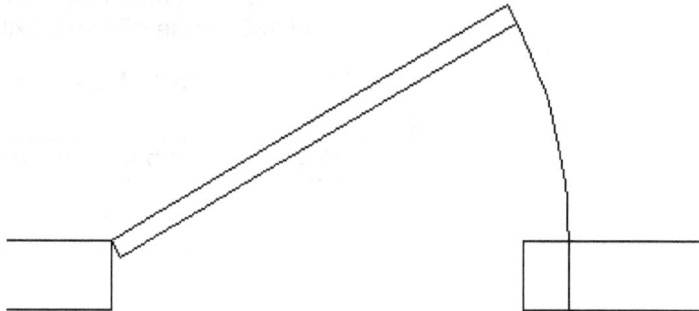

Figure 18–33

4. Select the inserted door to display the grips. Click
   ▷ (Lengthen) at the right end of the door and note the current length (**3'-4"**). Drag the cursor to the left to make the length **3'** (as shown in Figure 18–34), and click to place it at that location.

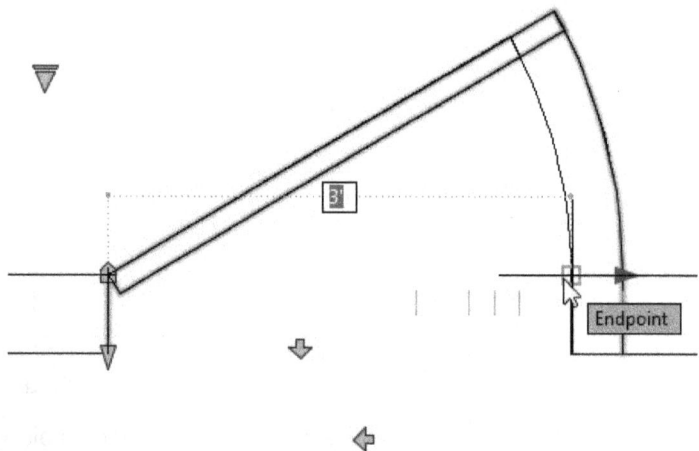

Figure 18–34

5. Click ▽ (List) and select **Open 90°**. The door swing changes to this angle. Press <Esc> to clear the door selection.

6. Pan to the smallest room, and then click and drop a **Toilet-Imperial** into it. The toilet displays as a front view.

7. Select the **Toilet** to display the grips. Click ▽ (List) and select **Elongated (Plan)**. A plan (top) view of the toilet displays.

Move the toilet from inside the room and then toward the inside wall.

8. Click ⬠ (Align) and move the cursor to place the toilet along the bottom wall. It aligns with the wall. Press <Esc> once it is at the correct location.

9. In the Blocks Palette> *Current Drawing* tab, add a **Sink** along the bottom wall on the left side of the toilet.

10. Move the sink and toilet to the layer **Plumbing**.

11. Add doors (**Door-Imperial** in Tools Palette) to the bathroom and the small office as shown in Figure 18–32. (Place one door, rotate it, and adjust it with grips, as required. Then, copy it to create the other door and flip it using grips.)

12. Add windows using the **Window** block in the *Current Drawing* tab of the Blocks Palette.Use the **Repeat Placement** option and then use the **Rotate** option in the <Down arrow> menu with rotation angles of **90** and **-90**.

13. You can also add a desk, chair, and a file cabinet to the office from the Blocks Palette.

14. Close the Tools palette and the Blocks palette.

Task 3 - Insert blocks using DesignCenter.

In this task, you will insert landscaping blocks using DesignCenter, as shown in Figure 18–35.

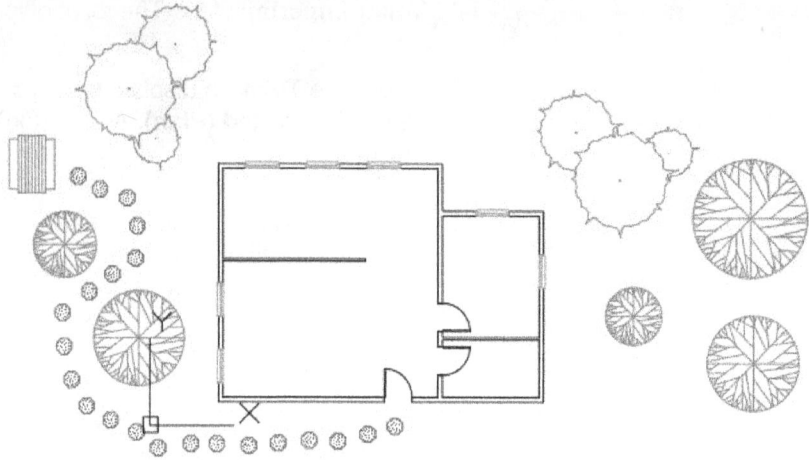

Figure 18–35

1. Toggle off the layers **Furniture** and **Plumbing**.

2. In the Layer Control, make the layer **Planting** as the current layer.

3. Zoom out so that there is room around the outside of the building.

4. Open DesignCenter.

5. In the *DesignCenter* folder supplied with the AutoCAD software (generally in *Sample>en-us* folder), find the file **Landscaping.dwg**. Expand it and select **Blocks** to open it.

6. Drag and drop several trees (in plan view) into the drawing. **Move**, **Rotate**, and **Scale** them similar to that shown in Figure 18–35.

7. Set the current layer to **Furniture-Outdoor**. Place a **Picnic Table** similar to that shown in Figure 18–35.

8. Set the current layer to **Hardscape**.

9. Create a path of **Stepping Stone-Hexagonal** blocks around the trees, similar to that shown in Figure 18–35.

10. Save and close the drawing.

*The blocks in DesignCenter are created on layer **0**. Therefore, you need to select the layer on which you want to place them.*

You can open the DesignCenter in the View tab>Palettes panel, and click

(DesignCenter).

Dynamic Blocks

Exam Objective Covered in This Chapter

- 6.1.a Insert and modify blocks

19.1 Working with Dynamic Blocks

With conventional AutoCAD blocks, an individual block cannot easily be modified. You need to redefine or explode the block. Dynamic blocks are designed to be easily resized or modified in a variety of other ways. For example, you can define a bolt block that stretches to fit any of the standard bolt lengths that you use, as shown in Figure 19–1. In an electrical diagram, one block of a switch can display its open or closed state, as shown in Figure 19–1.

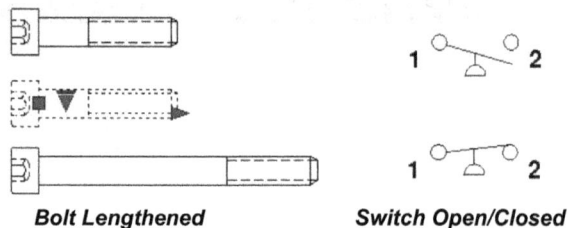

Bolt Lengthened   **Switch Open/Closed**

Figure 19–1

Using dynamic blocks can reduce the number of blocks in your block library.

- Not all dynamic blocks have the same modification features. The features depend on the modifications that are built into the block when it is defined.

- When a dynamic block is selected, special grips on it display the available types of modification. The arrow grip on the end of the bolt (shown in Figure 19–1) enables you to stretch the object. You can use grips to modify a block after it has been inserted.

- The AutoCAD software contains several sample dynamic blocks that display in the Tool Palettes. You can identify dynamic blocks by the lightning bolt that displays on the block icon, as shown in Figure 19–2.

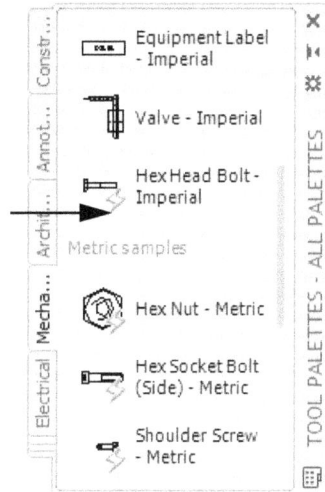

Figure 19–2

Inserting Dynamic Blocks

Inserting dynamic blocks follows the procedures that are used when inserting standard blocks. However, dynamic blocks can include special insertion options: insertion point cycling and automatic alignment.

*   Only blocks that are created with these features have this functionality.

*   Some dynamic blocks are annotative and are automatically scaled according to the Annotation Scale that is set in the Status Bar.

How To: Insert a Block with Multiple Insertion Points

You cannot drag-and-drop the block for insertion point cycling to work.

1. Click on the block in the tool palette.
2. Press <Ctrl> to step to the next insertion point.
3. Continue pressing <Ctrl> until you reach the insertion point that you want to use. You can press <Ctrl>+<Shift> to cycle back through the insertion points. A block with multiple insertion points is shown in Figure 19–3.

Figure 19–3

4. Pick a location in the drawing at which to place the block.

How To: Insert a Block Using Automatic Alignment

You cannot drag-and-drop the block for automatic alignment to work.

1. Click on the block in the tool palette. Move the cursor toward the object to which you want to align the block.
2. When the block is aligned correctly (as shown in Figure 19–4), click to place it.

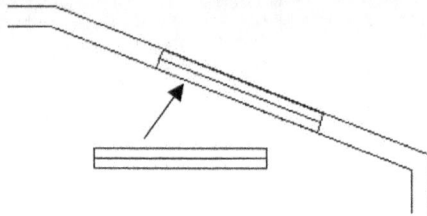

Figure 19–4

- Object snaps work with the **Alignment** option. To place the block anywhere along the line, you might need to toggle off the default object snaps or use the **Nearest** osnap.

Modifying Dynamic Blocks

Depending on the features built into the dynamic block, you can use a variety of methods or *actions* to modify it. All of the actions are rarely available in one block, but blocks can have more than one action. The special grips displayed on a selected block indicate the available actions, as shown in Figure 19–5.

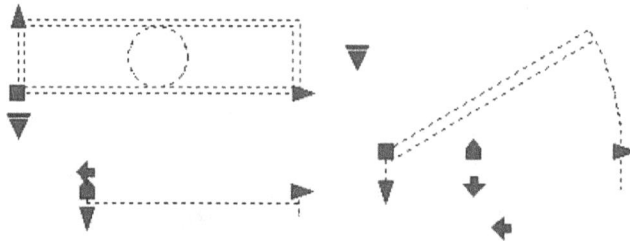

Figure 19–5

- Some of the special grips display a tooltip when you hover over them. The tooltip explains its use and indicates the action required, as shown in Figure 19–6.

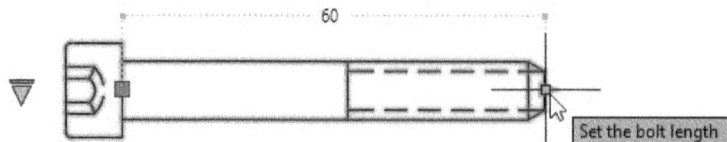

Figure 19–6

Typical Dynamic Block Grips

▶ Stretching, Arraying, and Scaling

The Lengthen/Shorten grip ▶ can scale, stretch, and in some cases array objects. In the example shown in Figure 19–7, you can add many different sized bolts by using the ▶ grip on the right side. The grip stretches the length to the various lengths.

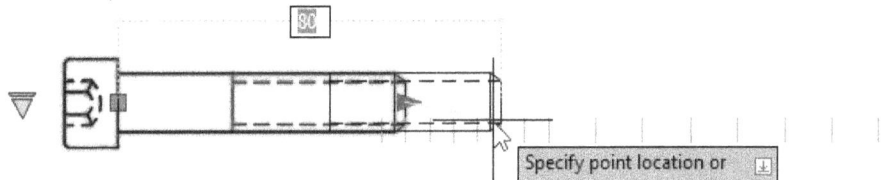

Figure 19–7

The line marks display preset increments for scaling/stretching. These can be set in the block definition for the required standard sizes (for example, standard bolt lengths or window lengths).

● ◀ Rotating and Flipping Objects

Use the Rotate grip ● to rotate the block or objects in the block. In the callout block shown in Figure 19–8, only the arrow rotates. The circle and text stay in place. As with the Stretch/Scale/Array grip, tick marks display any preset increments for rotating, if they have been defined in the block.

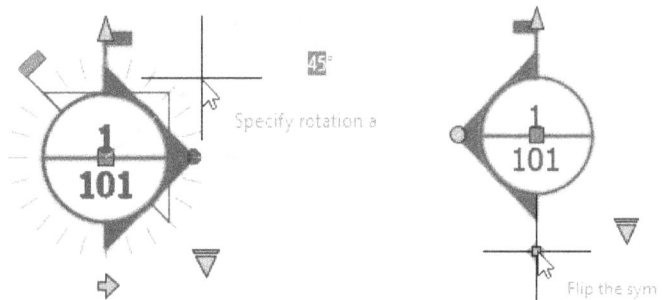

Figure 19–8

Click once on the Flip grip ◀ to flip the block or the objects in it. In the example shown in Figure 19–8, only the arrow flips, not the text.

⬟ Aligning Objects

Blocks using the Align feature can be aligned during insertion or you can use the Align grip ⬟ at any time. Select the grip and drag the block close to an object. The block automatically uses the rotation angle of that object, as shown in Figure 19–9. Therefore you do not need to determine the rotation angles.

Window inserted on wall   *Window aligned with wall*

Figure 19–9

▼ Selecting from Lists

The List ▼ grip opens a list of options that are defined in the block. The options can be size parameters, the number of blocks arrayed, or even different views of a block to be displayed. In the example of the bolt block in Figure 19–10, it contains a list where you can select the standard sizes for the bolt.

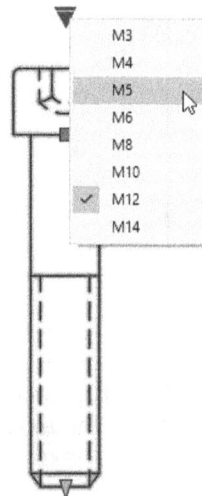

M3
M4
M5
M6
M8
M10
✓ M12
M14

Figure 19–10

■ Inserting and Moving Objects

The Base point ■ grip indicates the insertion point of the block, and other points that might have been assigned in the block. It can move the entire block or just one entity within it. A block with multiple insertion points is shown in Figure 19–11.

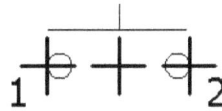

Figure 19–11

Practice 19a | Inserting and Modifying Dynamic Blocks

Practice Objective

- Add various dynamic blocks from the Tool Palette and adjust them dynamically using their grips.

Mechanical Practice

In this practice, you will insert a dynamic bolt and use grips to adjust its size, as shown in Figure 19–12.

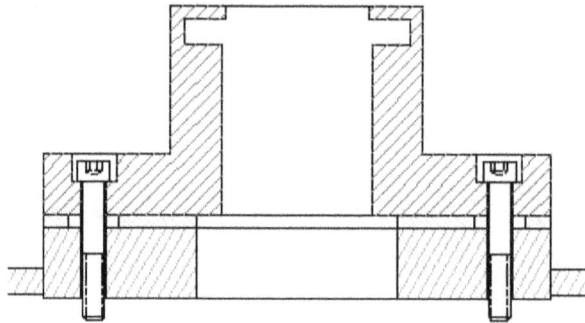

Figure 19–12

1. Open **Assembly-M.dwg** from the practice files folder.

2. Open the Tool Palettes if it is not already open.

3. In the *Mechanical* tab, drag and drop the block **Hex Socket Bolt (Side) - Metric** anywhere in the drawing. Using the **Rotate** command, rotate it **–90** degrees and place it to one side of the objects.

4. Zoom in on the block and select it to display the grips.

5. Select the ▼ grip to open the list of sizes. Try several different sizes and then select **M12**.

6. Use the square grip to move the bolt into one of the holes, as shown in Figure 19–12.

7. Verify that ⊞ (Dynamic Input) is toggled on and select the arrow grip on the bottom end of the bolt shaft. Note the current length of the shaft (60mm) and the marks below the bottom end that display the preset increments. Stretch the shaft to the *length* of **75mm**.

8. Copy the bolt to the other hole.

9. Save and close the drawing.

Architectural Practice

In this practice, you will add titles, a section callout, a graphic scale, and a north arrow to a layout, as shown in Figure 19–13. In another layout you will insert and manipulate a detail layout grid.

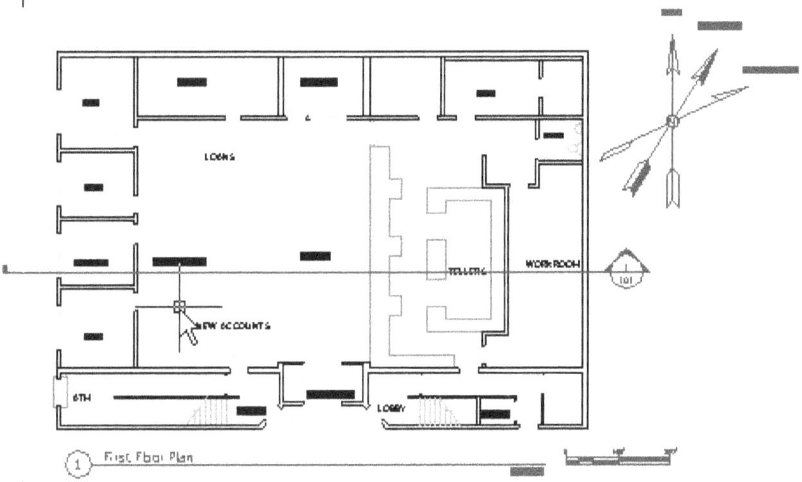

Figure 19–13

1. Open **Bank Layouts-A.dwg** from the practice files folder.

2. Switch to the **Plans and Sections** layout.

3. Open the Tool Palettes if it is not already open.

4. In the Tool Palettes>*Annotation* tab, add the block **Drawing Title - Imperial** under each of the viewports. Use the ▶ grip to stretch the title lines so that they extend to the full length of the viewports.

5. Add the block **Section Callout - Imperial** at the right side of the floor plan view. Use the grips to ● rotate and ▶ stretch it so that it cuts through the building, as shown in Figure 19–13.

6. Add the block **Graphic Scale - Imperial** to the floor plan view near the right side of the drawing title block, as shown in Figure 19–13. Click the ▼ list grip to display the list and select one of the scales.

7. Add the block **North Arrow - Imperial** near top right side of the floor plan and modify the angle of the Geometrical arrow. Modify the angles of the other arrows and move their labeling along with them.

8. Switch to the **Details** layout.

9. Insert the block **Detail Layout Grid - Imperial** in the lower left corner.

10. Using the AutoCAD **Scale** command, scale the block by a *scale factor* of **8**.

11. Modify the block using the ■ grip in the upper right corner, which enables you to create an array of six detail grids, as shown in Figure 19–14.

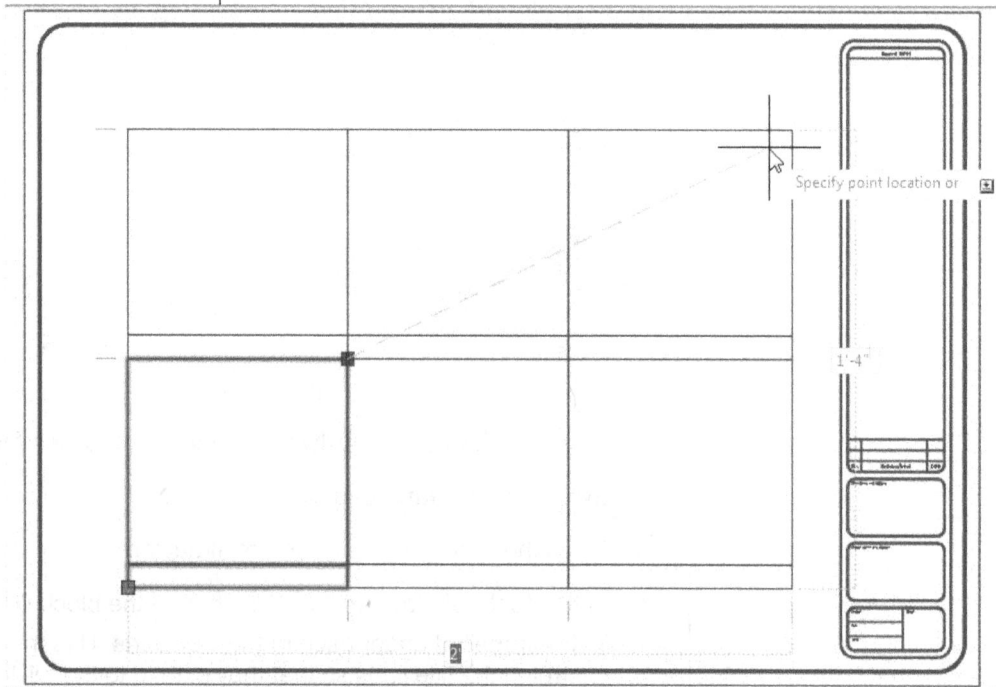

Figure 19–14

12. Move the array as required to center it in the sheet.

13. Save and close the drawing.

19.2 Creating Dynamic Block Definitions

The Block Editor enables you to create new dynamic block definitions from scratch or modify an existing block to make it a dynamic block. Additionally, you can add actions and parameters that turn a conventional block into a dynamic block.

- When you start the **Block Editor** command, the Edit Block Definition dialog box opens, as shown in Figure 19–15. Once you select a block or enter a new name and click **OK**, the Block Editor environment opens with a *Block Editor* contextual tab. If you right-click on an existing dynamic block in the drawing window and select **Block Editor** from the shortcut menu, it opens the block directly in the Block Editor environment with the *Block Editor* contextual tab.

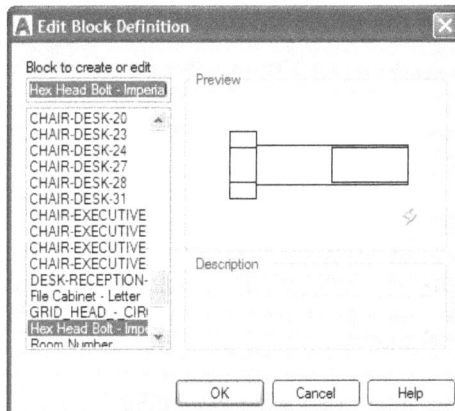

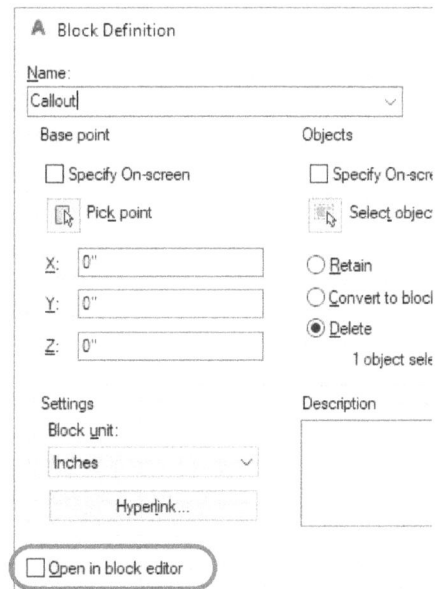

Figure 19–15   Figure 19–16

- Alternatively, if the objects have already been drawn, you can use the Block Definition dialog box (*Home* tab>Block panel or

  Insert tab>Block Definition panel, click (Create Block)) to create a block and use the **Open in block editor** option, as shown above in Figure 19–16. This option opens the newly created block in the Block Editor environment, where you can add actions and parameters which converts the conventional block into a dynamic block.

How To: Create a Dynamic Block from Scratch

1. In the *Home* tab>Block panel or in the *Insert* tab>Block Definition panel, click ⬚ (Block Editor).
2. In the Edit Block Definition dialog box, type a name for the new block.
3. Click **OK**. The *Block Editor* contextual tab opens without any objects.
4. Draw objects for the block using the regular drawing and editing tools.
5. Add parameters and actions as required.
6. Click ✔ (Close Block Editor) to create the block.

How To: Turning a Conventional Block into a Dynamic Block

1. Double-click on an existing block to open the Edit Block Definition dialog box.
2. Select the block that you want to edit from the list and click **OK**.
3. In the *Block Editor* contextual tab, add dynamic parameters and actions.

Hint: Locking the Block Editor

Double-clicking on a block opens the Edit Block Definition dialog box. However, if you do not have experience creating dynamic blocks, or are not authorized to modify them, you might want to change the default.

- Setting the system variable *blockeditlock* to **1** causes the Properties palette to open when double-clicking on a block rather than the Block Editor. You cannot open the Block Editor using any other methods, such as the ribbon or Command Line.

- Setting the system variable *blockeditlock* back to **0** enables you to open the Block Editor again.

19.3 Dynamic Block Authoring Tools

In the Block Editor, you can add *parameters* and *actions* to objects in the block to make it dynamic. Figure 19–17 shows the Block Editor environment, where the drawing window changes into a Block Editor window with a *Block Editor* contextual tab displayed in the ribbon and the opened Block Authoring Palettes.

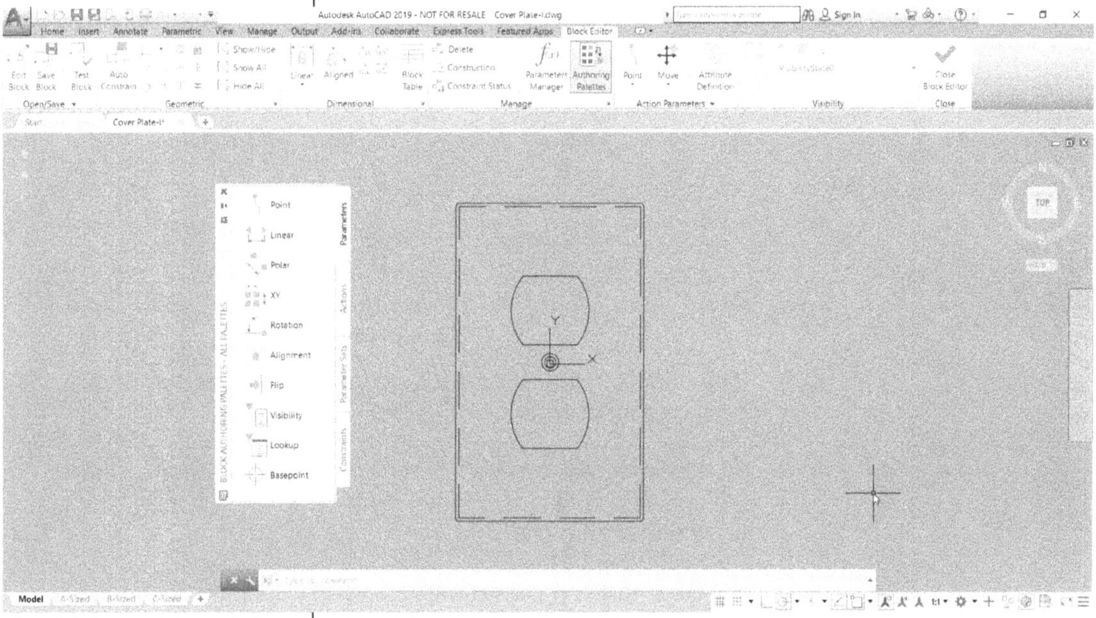

Figure 19–17

- By default, the Block Authoring Palettes for adding parameters and actions is open in the Block Editor.

- *Parameters* are similar to dimensions but they control the block geometry. For example, in a bolt block, you would add a linear parameter to define the length to be able to adjust the length of the bolt.

- *Actions* are added to parameters so that you can modify the parameter in the completed block. In the bolt example, the linear parameter specifies the dimension that you want to control. You can add a stretch action to that parameter so that you are able to stretch the bolt to the required length.

- At least one parameter must be specified in a dynamic block. In most cases it has both a parameter and an action associated with the parameter.

- You can also use regular drawing and editing tools in the Block Editor to modify the block geometry as required, including geometrical and dimensional constraints.

- Only one block can be open in the Block Editor at a time.

Block Editor Contextual Tab

The *Block Editor* contextual tab (shown in Figure 19–18) contains tools for creating and saving blocks, adding constraints, and adding various parameters and actions.

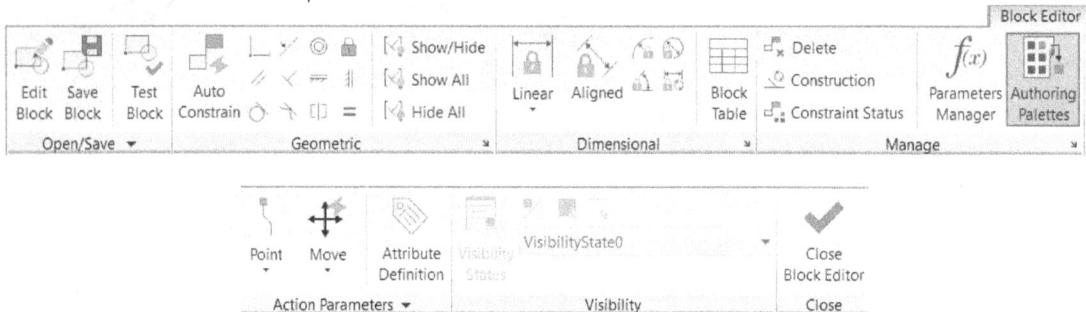

Figure 19–18

The panels in the *Block Editor* contextual tab perform the following functions:

- **Open/Save panel:** Includes commands to open a new or existing block, save the current block, or test the actions of the current block.

- **Geometric & Dimensional panels:** Include commands to apply geometrical or dimensional constraints to the current block (the same methods used in a standard drawing).

- **Manage panel:** Includes visibility commands for constraints, construction geometry, parameters in the Properties palette, and the Authoring Palette.

- **Action Parameters panel:** Enables you to add parameters and actions to the dynamic block.

- Other tools in the *Block Editor* contextual tab control the Visibility Parameters.

- Clicking the arrow in the bottom right corner of the Manage panel in the *Block Editor* contextual tab opens the Block Editor Settings dialog box shown in Figure 19–19. This enables to control all of the settings (including application of colors to objects) for the Block Editor environment.

Figure 19–19

Parameters

Parameters are the first item that is added to dynamic blocks. They define any aspects of the geometry that you want to control with actions. The Parameters palette is shown in Figure 19–20.

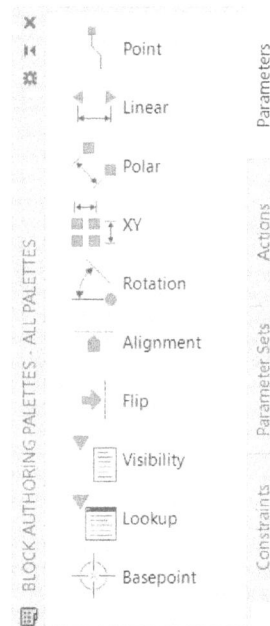

Figure 19–20

(Point)	Displays an X,Y coordinate position in the drawing.
(Linear parameter)	Displays the distance between two points. Only the distance, not the angle, can be changed.
(Polar parameter)	Displays the distance between two points and an angle value. Both the distance and angle can be changed.
(XY parameter)	Displays a pair of horizontal and vertical dimensions from a specified base point.
(Rotation parameter)	Defines an **Angle** option.
(Alignment parameter)	Forces the entire block to rotate at an angle that is defined by another object in the drawing. This parameter does not need to have a specified action specified as well.
(Flip parameter)	Describes a line across which the block or selected objects can be mirrored. You need to associate a flip action with this parameter.
(Visibility parameter)	Controls the visibility of objects in the block. Automatically creates a list of the visibility states that you define for the block. This parameter does not need to have a specified action.
(Lookup parameter)	Creates a list of options that are stored in a table from which you can select. Typically this can hold various sizes that are related to other parameters and actions.
(Basepoint parameter)	Creates a base point that is relative to the block geometry. It can be included in an action selection set but cannot be associated with an action.

Actions

To use actions, you must associate them with a parameter. Typically, you select a key point of the parameter and the geometry that you want to include in the action. For example, if you want to stretch a dynamic block in one direction, you are required to associate the **Stretch** action with either a **Linear**, **Polar**, or **XY** parameter. The Actions palette is shown in Figure 19–21.

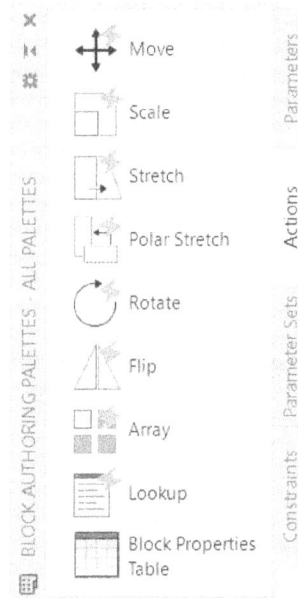

Figure 19–21

 (Move Action)	Similar to the standard **Move** command. Works with **Point**, **Linear**, **Polar**, and **XY** parameters. Action is related to a specific grip in the dynamic block. Can be linked to the entire block contents or to individual objects in block.
 (Scale Action)	Similar to the standard **Scale** command. Works with **Linear**, **Polar**, and **XY** parameters and can be linked to the entire block or individual objects in the block.
 (Stretch Action)	Similar to the standard **Stretch** command. Works with **Linear**, **Polar**, and **XY** parameters. Can be linked to specific objects in block. Apply a stretch action to both ends of the parameters if action needs to work in both directions. **Stretch** only works in the direction of the parameter's arrow.
 (Polar Stretch Action)	Similar to the standard **Stretch** command but includes an **Angle** option. Only works with **Polar** parameters.

(Rotate Action)	Similar to the standard **Rotate** command. Works with **Rotation** parameters and can be linked to entire block or to individual objects in block.
(Flip Action)	Mirrors objects around a reflection line. Works with **Flip** parameters.
(Array Action)	Similar to the standard rectangular **Array** command. Works with **Linear**, **Polar**, and **XY** parameters.
(Lookup Action)	Works with **Lookup** parameters. Creates a table in which you can assign data to the block based on the parameter information.
(Block Properties)	Defines the property sets for the block definition.

Parameter Sets

Parameter Sets create related parameters and associated actions at the same time. For example, if you want to flip objects in a block, you can apply a **Flip Set** and specify the reflection line. The Parameter Sets palette is shown in Figure 19–22.

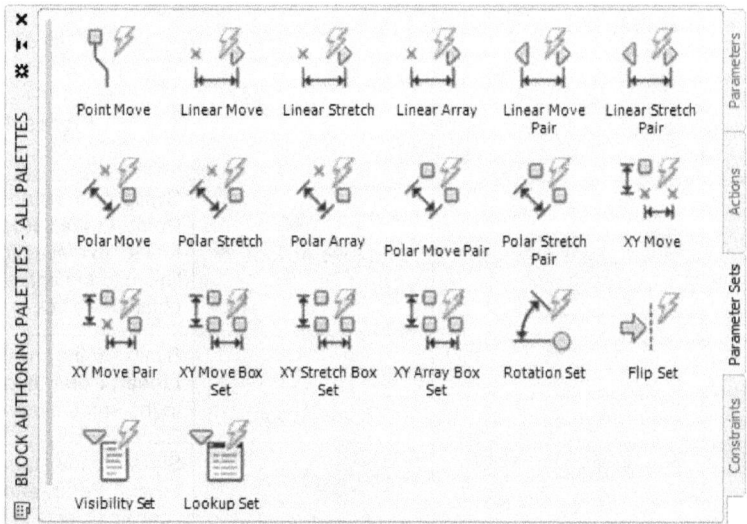

Figure 19–22

How To: Place a Parameter from a Parameter Set

1. Select the Parameter Set that you want to use and follow the prompts to place the parameter.

2. ⬚ (Action) displays an exclamation point in the icon, indicating that objects are not yet associated with the action.

3. Right-click on ⬚ (Action) and select **Action Selection Set>New Selection Set**. Follow the prompts to select the objects.

- *Pair Sets* include two actions with the parameter (such as the Linear Stretch Pair Set, which includes a Stretch action at each end of the **Linear** parameter so that you can stretch either end).

- *Box Sets* include four actions with the parameter. With Pair and Box sets, you need to select the objects for each action separately.

Constraints

Constraints in a Dynamic Block help to retain the correct shape and geometry of the objects in the block, while the parameters and actions are applied to the objects. Constraints can be geometric or dimensional, and can be found in the *Block Editor* contextual tab, and in the Block Authoring Palettes, as shown in Figure 19–23.

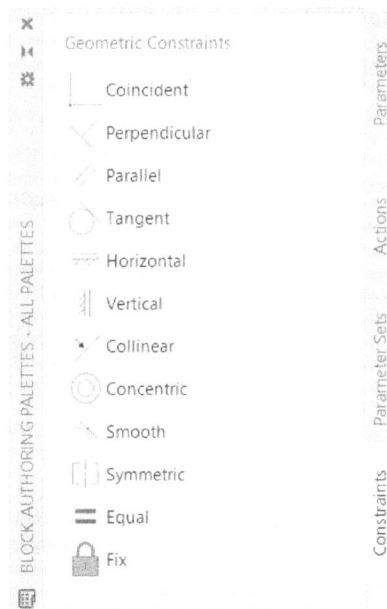

Figure 19–23

Figure 19–24 shows an example of a Dynamic Block with constraints.

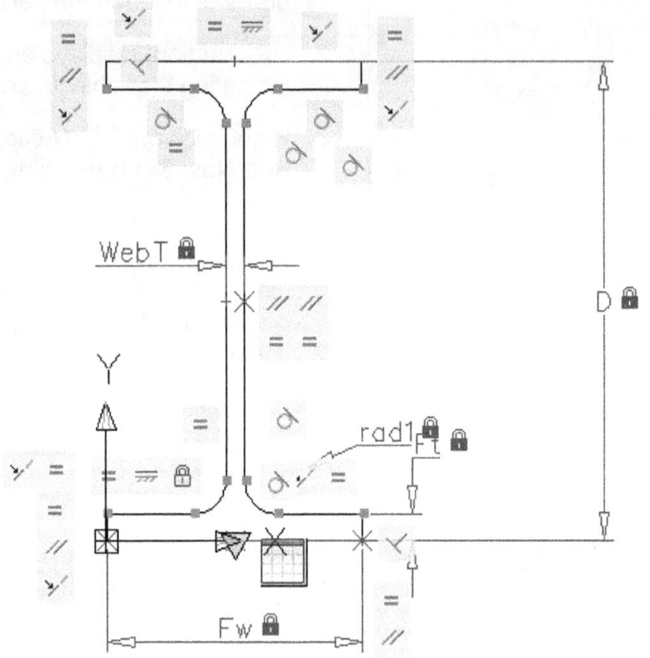

Figure 19–24

Labeling Parameters

If you want to label the grips in dynamic blocks you can select the related parameter and add a description in the *Property Labels* area in Properties, as shown in Figure 19–25.

- The *Distance name* contains the text that displays in the Dynamic Block Editor.

- *Parameter type* is the type of parameter that is being used.

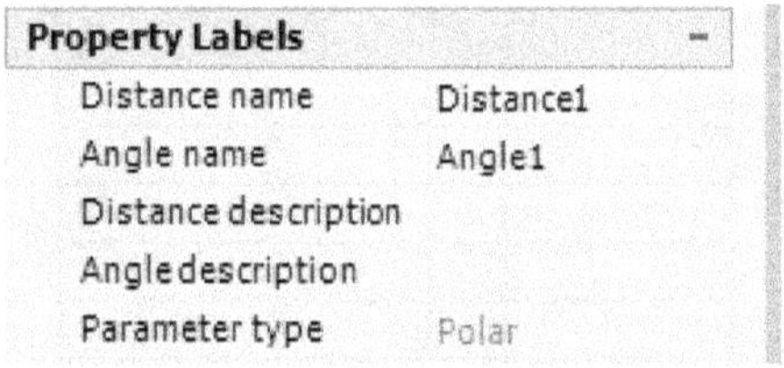

Figure 19–25

- The full name of the label and description varies according to the type of parameter selected.

Testing the Block

When you are working with a dynamic block that has constraints, testing the block helps to ensure that it works correctly. You can test the block without having to save it and without closing the Block Editor.

- In the *Block Editor* contextual tab>Open/Save panel, click

  (Test Block). It opens the block in a new test drawing named Test Block Window - [Block name].

- When you have finished testing the block, you can close the Text Block Window in the *File Name* tabs bar to return to the Block Editor Window.

Construction Geometry

When working with constraints, you might need to dimension an object (such as to the center line of a shelf), as shown in Figure 19–26. However, you might not want the center line to display when the block is in use. The center line can be changed to construction geometry, which does not display in the final block.

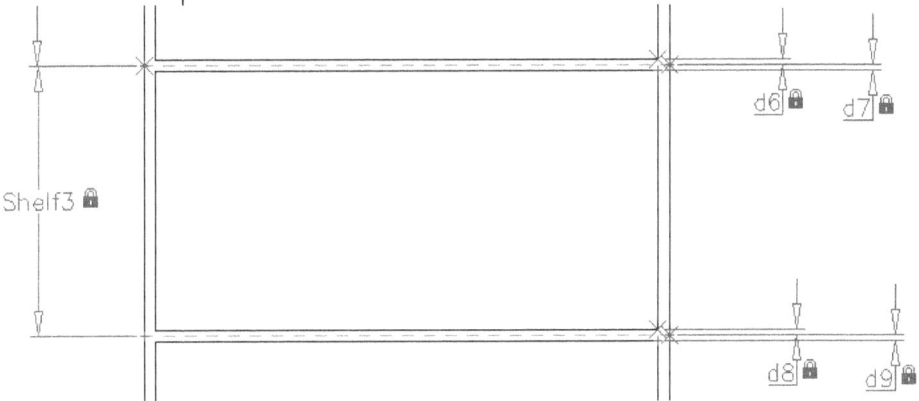

Figure 19–26

How To: Change Objects to Construction Geometry

1. In the *Block Editor* contextual tab>Manage panel, click

   (Construction).
2. Select the objects that you want to modify and press <Enter>.
3. Press <Enter> again to accept the default **Convert** option.

- You can use this command to show or hide all of the construction geometry, or to revert the geometry back to standard objects.

Applying Constraints in Dynamic Blocks

The methods of applying constraints in dynamic blocks are the same as when you use them in a standard drawing. First, use

(Auto Constrain) to automatically place as many geometric constraints as possible and then add the dimensional constraints or additional geometric constraints. You can modify the parameters and add user parameters in the Parameters Manager.

All of these tools are located in the *Block Editor* contextual tab as shown in Figure 19–27.

Figure 19–27

Working with Parameters

The dimensional tools create constraint parameters that can be modified in the Parameters Manager. User parameters can also be added here. If attributes are added to the block, they also display in the Parameters Manager, as shown in Figure 19–28.

Do not use the tools in the Parametric tab when you are working in the Block Editor contextual tab. They do not display correctly in blocks.

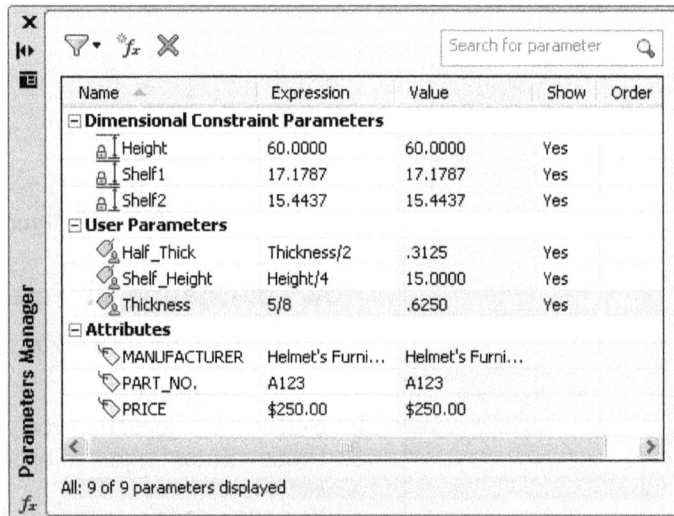

Figure 19–28

- When the block is inserted, the parameters displayed in the Parameters Manager are also displayed in the *Custom* area in Properties, as shown in Figure 19–29.

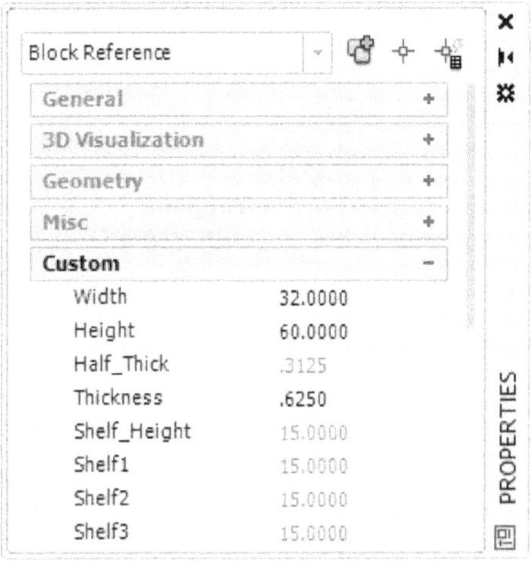

Figure 19–29

- If you do not want a constraint parameter to display, select it in the Block Editor. Then in Properties, change *Show Properties* to **No**, as shown in Figure 19–30.

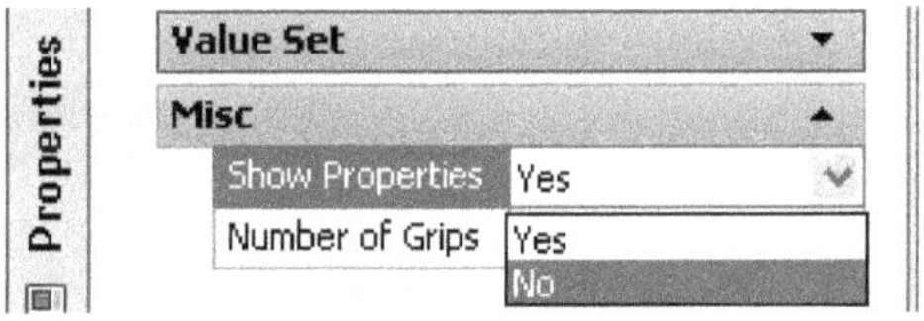

Figure 19–30

Fully Constrain a Dynamic Block

When constraints are created in a dynamic block, the block must be fully constrained to work correctly. Being fully constrained means that all relevant geometric and dimensional constraints have been applied. If this step is not done, the block might not work correctly.

- The block must have at least one fixed constraint. Click

  (Fix) in the Geometric panel and select a location for the constraint. This can be the same location as the base point.

If you save the block before doing this step, an alert box opens. You can return to the block to finish constraining it, or save it and modify it later.

- To determine whether objects have been constrained, click ⬚ (Constraint Status) in the Manage panel. When it is toggled on, all of the objects that have constraints display in blue, as shown in Figure 19–31.

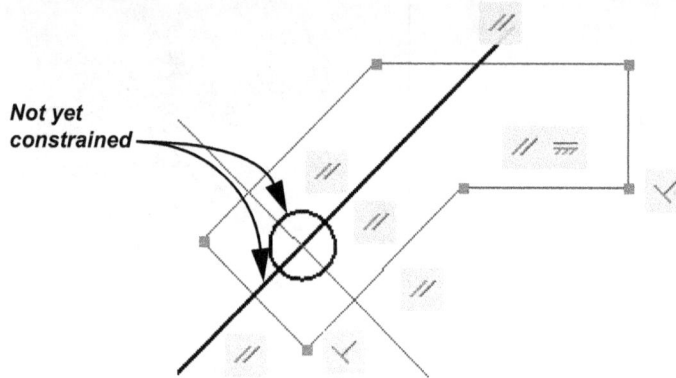

Figure 19–31

Creating a Block Table

In many cases, you want users of a dynamic block to select from a list of sizes rather than using grips to adjust the block. To do so, set up a Block Table using specific parameters that were created using constraints, as shown in Figure 19–32.

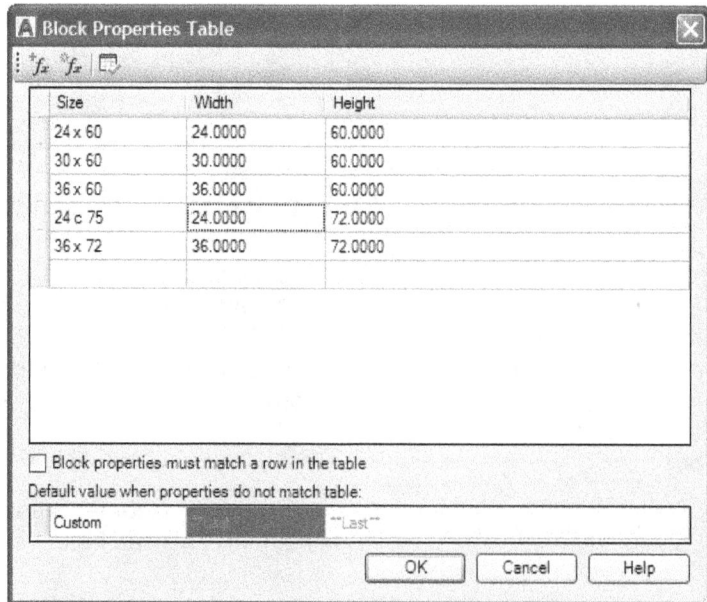

Size	Width	Height
24 x 60	24.0000	60.0000
30 x 60	30.0000	60.0000
36 x 60	36.0000	60.0000
24 c 75	24.0000	72.0000
36 x 72	36.0000	72.0000

☐ Block properties must match a row in the table
Default value when properties do not match table:
Custom   ""Last""

Figure 19–32

- A dynamic block can only have one block table.

How To: Create a Block Table

1. Create the required parameters and name them in the Parameters Manager.
2. In the Dimensional panel, click ⊞ (Block Table).
3. Specify a location for the block table in the drawing. At the prompt, accept one grip. The Block Properties Table dialog box opens.

This is where the List grip ▽ displays in the final block.

4. In the Block Properties Table dialog box, click ^+f_x (Add properties...) to add an existing parameter to the table.
5. In the Add Parameter Properties dialog box, select one or more parameters to add to the table, as shown in Figure 19–33. Click **OK**.

The available parameters can include attributes, parameters created with dimensional constraints, and user parameters.

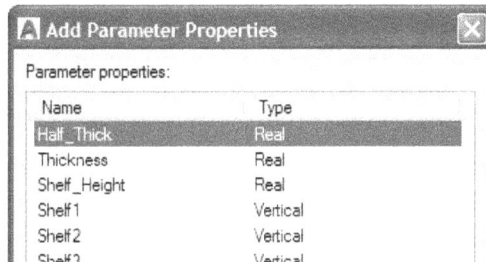

Figure 19–33

6. The table displays the selected parameters, as shown in Figure 19–34.

You can reorder the table columns by dragging and dropping the column name to a new location.

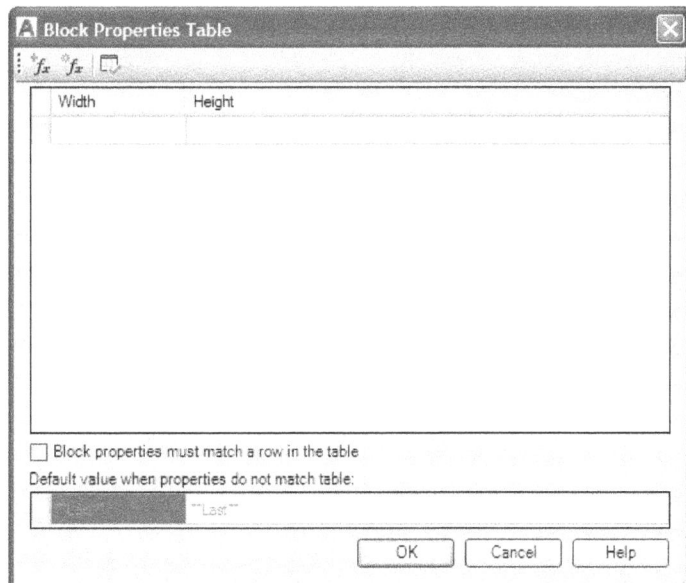

Figure 19–34

7. To add a parameter that does not exist in the drawing, click

   f_x (Add parameters...). The New Parameter dialog box opens as shown in Figure 19–35. Specify a name, a default value, and the type of parameter (**Real**, **Distance**, **Area**, **Volume**, **Angle**, or **String**).

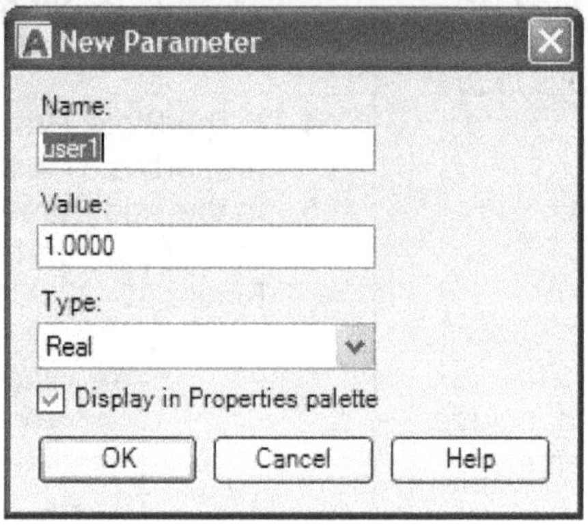

*If you want this parameter to display in Properties when the finished block is selected, select **Display in the Properties palette**.*

Figure 19–35

8. Click **OK**.
9. Fill out the table with the required information, as shown in the example in Figure 19–36.

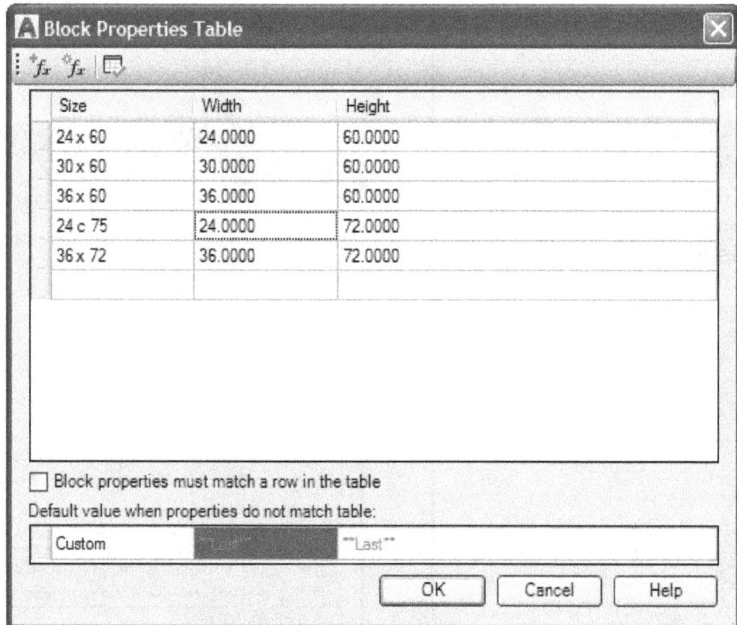

Figure 19–36

- If you select **Block properties must match a row in the table**, you can only select one of the sizes available in the table when using the block. If the option is not selected (as shown in Figure 19–37), you can create a custom size using the grips on the block.

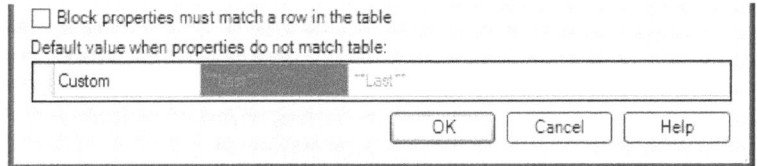

☐ Block properties must match a row in the table
Default value when properties do not match table:

| Custom | | "Last" |

| OK | Cancel | Help |

Figure 19–37

10. Click **OK** to close the Block Properties Table dialog box.

Auditing the Block Table

Before you try to close the Block Properties Table dialog box, verify that the parameters are working correctly. Click

(Audit) to audit the Block Properties Table. If there are any errors, an alert box opens explaining the problem as shown in Figure 19–38.

Follow the prompts in the alert box to correct the problem.

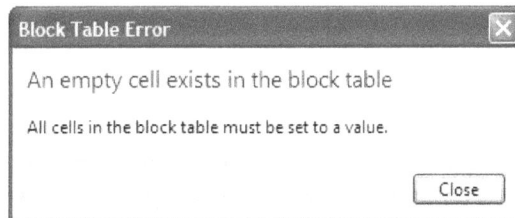

Block Table Error ☒

An empty cell exists in the block table

All cells in the block table must be set to a value.

Close

Figure 19–38

Practice 19b

Creating Dynamic Block Definitions

Practice Objectives

- Create a dynamic block with parameters and actions in it.
- Test its new dynamic properties.

This series of practices teaches you how to use a combination of parameters and actions in dynamic block definitions.

In this practice, you will create a dynamic block for a receptacle plate that can stretch to display one, two, or three sets of holes, as shown in Figure 19–39. You will apply a **Linear** parameter and Stretch and Array actions, and set an increment on the parameter.

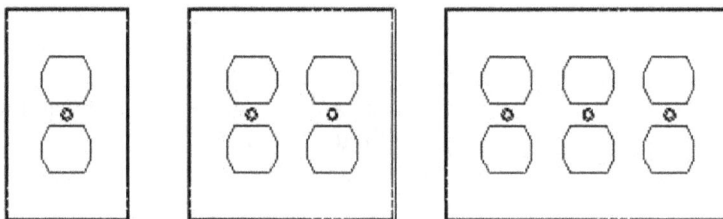

Figure 19–39

Task 1 - Create the block.

1. Open **Cover Plate-I.dwg** from the practice files folder.

2. In the *Home* tab>Block panel or *Insert* tab>Block Definition panel, click ⬚ (Create Block).

3. In the Block Definition dialog box, name the block **Receptacle Cover**.

4. For the *Base point*, select the center of the screw hole. For *Objects*, select all of the objects.

5. Select **Open in block editor** and click **OK**.
   - The newly created block opens in the Block Editor environment with the *Block Editor* contextual tab and the Block Authoring Palettes displayed.

Task 2 - Add a linear parameter.

1. In the Block Authoring Palettes, in the *Parameters* tab, click ⊢⊣ (Linear).

2. Select the two outer end points to display the full width across the top of the plate and place the dimension, as shown in Figure 19–40. The exclamation point indicates that an action has not yet been associated with the parameter.

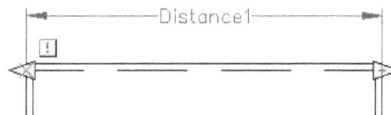

Figure 19–40

Task 3 - Add stretch actions.

1. In the Block Authoring Palettes, in the *Actions* tab, click (Stretch).

2. Select the **Distance** parameter that you just created.

3. Select the right endpoint of the parameter to associate with the action.

4. Create a Crossing Window around the right vertical edge of the plate for the stretch frame, as shown in Figure 19–41.

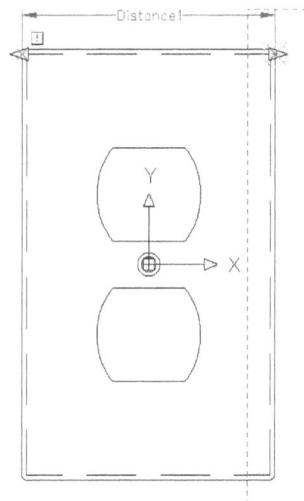

Figure 19–41

5. Create another crossing window around the same right vertical edge of the plate to select the objects. Do not select the holes, only the edge of the plate. Press <Enter> to complete the command.

6. Repeat the process to add another ⬚ (Stretch) action to the other end of the **Linear** parameter.

Task 4 - Set up the increment values.

1. Select the **Distance** parameter and open the Properties palette.

2. In the Properties palette, set the *Value Set*, as shown in Figure 19–42 (*Dist type:* **Increment**; *Dist increment:* **1.8**; *Dist minimum:* **2.8**; *Dist maximum:* **6.4**).

Value Set	
Dist type	Increment
Dist increment	1.8000
Dist minimum	2.8000
Dist maximum	6.4000

Figure 19–42

3. Close the Block Editor and select **Save the changes to Receptacle Cover**.

4. In the drawing window, insert the block **Receptacle Cover** and test the Stretch Actions. The edge of the plate should stretch to two additional positions on either side, as shown for the right side in Figure 19–43.

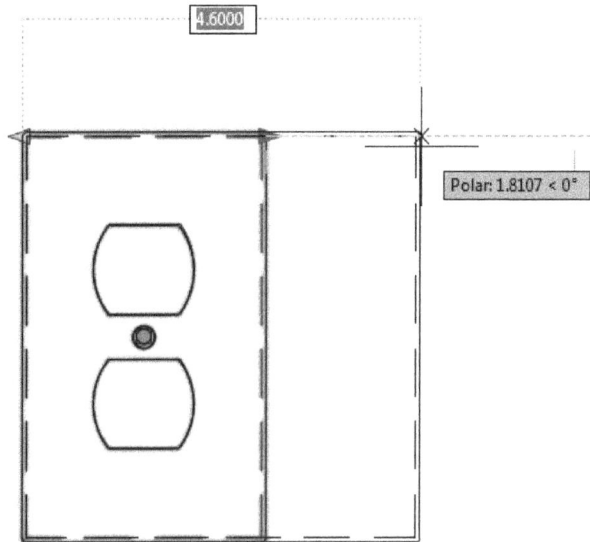

Figure 19–43

5. Right-click on the block **Receptacle Cover** and select **Reset Block** to restore it to its original size.

Task 5 - Create an array action.

1. Double-click on the block to open the Edit Block Definition dialog box and click **OK** to edit the block. You are in the *Block Editor* environment.

2. In the Block Authoring Palettes>*Actions* tab, click

   (Array).

3. Select the **Distance** parameter that you created earlier.

4. At the *Select objects:* prompt, select the interior hole objects and press <Enter>.

5. For the distance between the columns, type **1.8** and press <Enter>.

6. Close the Block Editor and save the changes.

7. In the drawing window, test the block. You should be able to use the stretch grips to display 1, 2, and 3 sets of holes.

8. Save and close the drawing.

Practice 19c	# Creating Dynamic Blocks with Constraints

Practice Objectives

- Add geometric and dimensional constraints to objects in a dynamic block to maintain its shape.
- Create user parameters to assign values and formulas to a dynamic block.
- Create a block table within a dynamic block to enable the block to be modified using a list.

In this practice, you will add geometric and dimensional constraints to objects in the Block Editor. You will modify dimension parameters and create user parameters, assigning values and formulas. You will test the block and flex the parameters to test how it works. Finally, you will create a Block Table with sizes so that the block can only be modified by size, as shown in Figure 19–44.

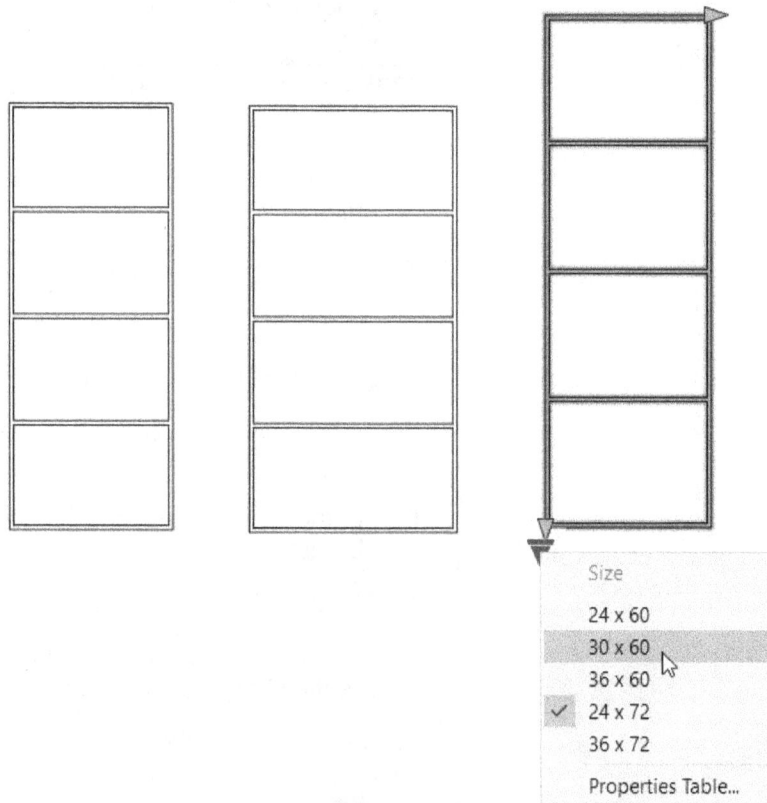

Figure 19–44

Task 1 - Create geometric constraints.

1. Open **Bookcase.dwg** from the practice files folder.

2. Double-click on the bookcase geometry to open the Edit Block Definition dialog box, which indicates that it is a block named **Bookcase-Elevation**.

3. In the Edit Block Definition dialog box, click **OK**. The **Bookcase-Elevation** block objects open in the Block Editor environment, with the *Block Editor* contextual tab and the Block Authoring Palettes displayed.

4. Open the Constraint Settings dialog box. In the *Auto Constrain* tab of the dialog box, verify that all of the constraint types, except **Equal**, are set to **Apply**. Close the dialog box.

5. In the *Block Editor* contextual tab>Geometric panel, click ⬚ (Auto Constrain).

6. Select all of the objects in the drawing and press <Enter>. The parameters display as shown in Figure 19–45.

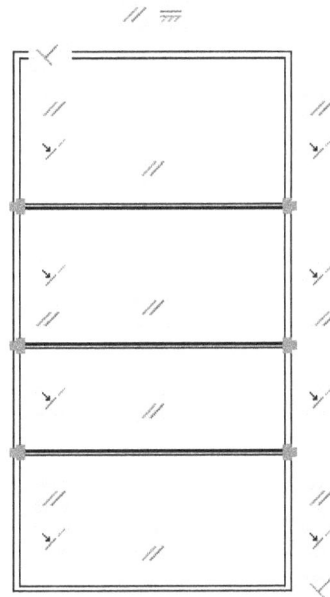

Figure 19–45

7. Review the parameters that were placed. They include **Horizontal**, **Perpendicular**, **Parallel**, and **Colinear** constraints.

8. In the *Block Editor* contextual tab>Geometric panel, click 🔒 (Fix). Place the point in the lower left corner of the bookcase elevation.

9. In the *Block Editor* contextual tab>Geometric panel, click ⊠ (Hide All) to toggle off the geometric constraints.

Task 2 - Add dimensional constraints.

1. In the *Block Editor* contextual tab>Dimensional panel, click 🔒 (Linear) and add two linear dimensions to the overall top and side, as shown in Figure 19–46. When adding the dimensions, select the top left outer corner first and then either the bottom left outer corner (for the side) or the top right outer corner (for the top). Press <Enter> to accept all of the defaults.

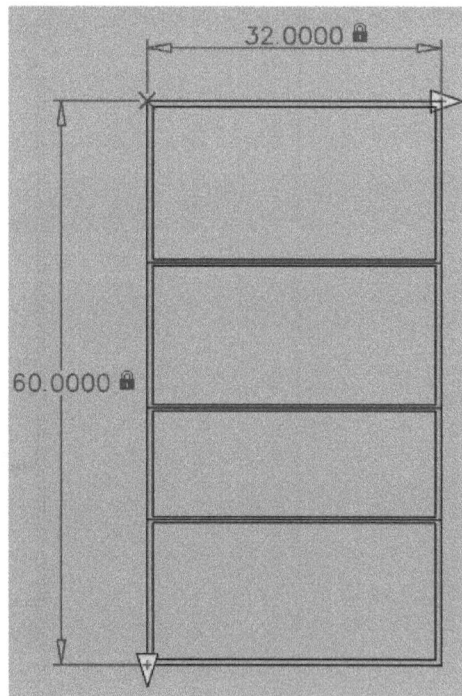

Figure 19–46

2. In the Open/Save panel, click 🖫 (Test Block).

3. Use grips to resize the block. Only the outside rectangle moves. The inside objects are not yet connected.

4. Undo any changes.

5. Close the Test Block Window drawing by clicking **X** in the *File Tabs* bar. This returns you to the drawing in the Block Editor.

Task 3 - Create user parameters.

1. In the Manage panel, click $f_{(x)}$ (Parameters Manager) to open the Parameters Manager.

2. Change the name of the horizontal parameter to **width** and the vertical parameter to **height**.

3. In the Parameters Manager, click $^*\!f_x$ (Create a new user parameter) three times to add three user parameters with expressions.

   • After adding the three new user parameters, modify them by double-clicking in the three *Name* columns. Enter the names first and then edit the values in the *Expression* column, as shown in Figure 19–47.

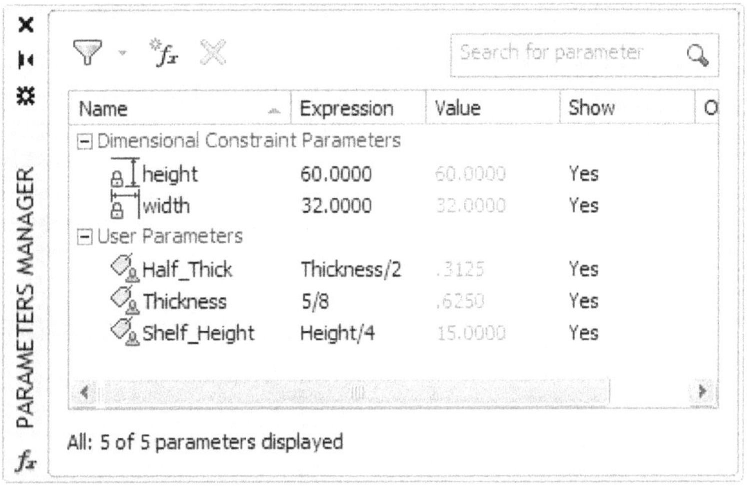

Name	Expression	Value	Show	O
⊟ Dimensional Constraint Parameters				
height	60.0000	60.0000	Yes	
width	32.0000	32.0000	Yes	
⊟ User Parameters				
Half_Thick	Thickness/2	.3125	Yes	
Thickness	5/8	.6250	Yes	
Shelf_Height	Height/4	15.0000	Yes	

All: 5 of 5 parameters displayed

Figure 19–47

Task 4 - Continue constraining geometry.

1. In the Block Editor, zoom in to the top of the bookcase and the three shelves.

2. Add a Linear constraint between the top of the bookcase and the centerline of the first shelf, as shown in Figure 19–48. Accept the default name and distance.

*In the Constraints Settings dialog box> Dimensional tab, use the **Name and Expression** format to display the name and the value of the constraint.*

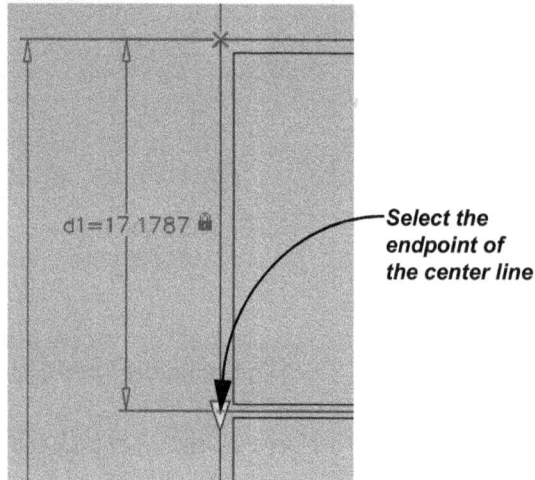

d1=17.1787

-Select the endpoint of the center line

Figure 19–48

3. Add two more Linear constraints (d2 and d3) between the centerlines of the three bookshelves. Accept the default name and distance.

Select the endpoints of the center lines of the shelves. Ensure that you do not select the shelf geometry by mistake.

4. Add a Linear constraint between the centerline of the bottom shelf and the bottom end of the bookcase. Once you click to place the constraint, an alert box opens, as shown in Figure 19–49, prompting you that adding this constraint parameter would over-constrain the geometry. Click **Close**. The constraint is not placed.

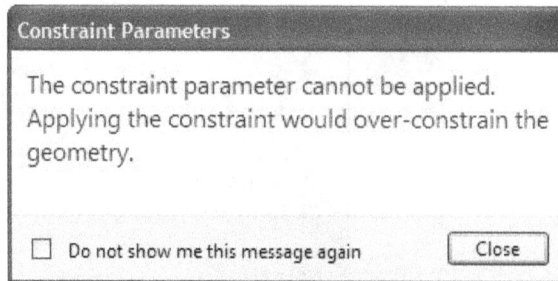

Constraint Parameters

The constraint parameter cannot be applied. Applying the constraint would over-constrain the geometry.

☐ Do not show me this message again   Close

Figure 19–49

If the constraint does not display vertically,

click 🔒 *(Vertical) in the*

🔒 *(Linear) drop-down list.*

5. Zoom in to a shelf intersection along the right side of the bookcase. Add two linear constraints using the default name and distance, as shown in Figure 19–50. This constrains the shelf geometry to the center line of the shelf.

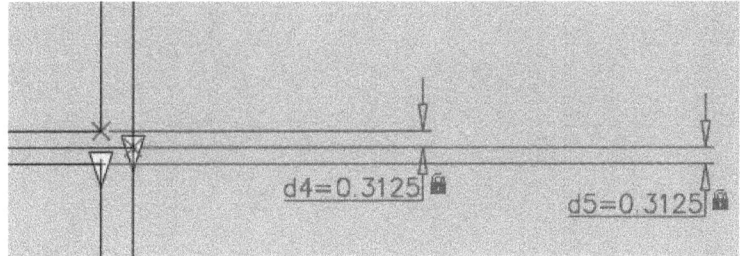

Figure 19–50

6. Repeat with the other two shelves.

7. In the Parameters Manager, change the name of the three shelf center line location parameters (d1,d2,d3) to Shelf1, Shelf2, and Shelf3. For each of them, set the *Expression* to **Shelf_Height**, as shown in Figure 19–51.

   - As you do this, the shelves value changes and they move into place. The shelf thicknesses also move, because they are constrained to the shelf center line.

Name	Expression	Value	Show
⊟ Dimensional Constraint Parameters			
Shelf1	Shelf_Height	15.0000	Yes
Shelf2	Shelf_Height	15.0000	Yes
Shelf3	Shelf_Height	15.0000	Yes
d4	.3125	.3125	Yes
d5	.3125	.3125	Yes
d6	.3125	.3125	Yes

Figure 19–51

8. In the Open/Save panel, click 🔲 (Test Block).

9. Use grips to modify the height and width of the bookcase. The shelves move correctly, but some constraints are missing, as shown in Figure 19–52.

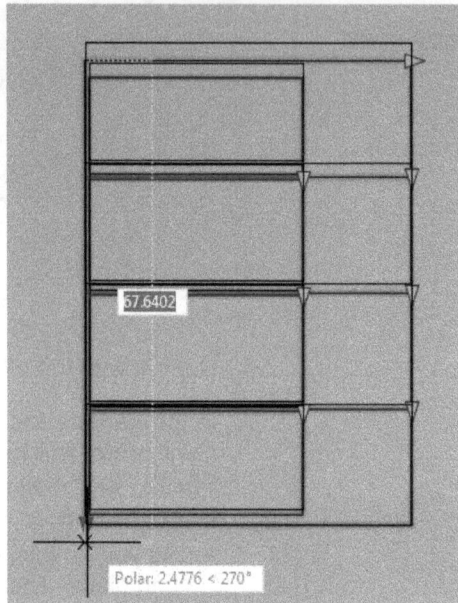

Figure 19–52

10. Undo any changes and close the Test Block Window.

*In the Constraints Settings dialog box> Dimensional tab, use the **Name** format to display only the name of the constraint.*

11. Linear constraints are missing for the thickness of the wood around the outer edge of the bookshelf. Add three constraints near the bottom (left side wall thickness, right side wall thickness, and one bottom wall thickness), as shown in Figure 19–53. Add one more constraint to the top horizontal wall thickness of the bookshelf.

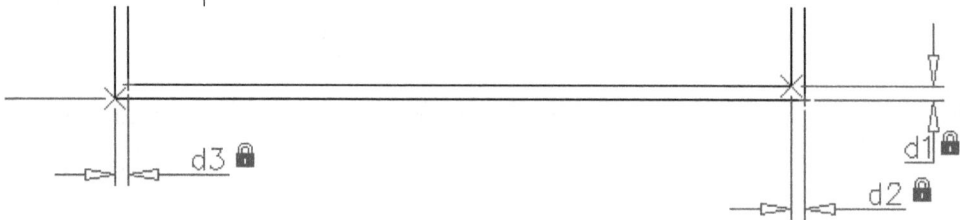

Figure 19–53

12. Test the block again. This time, everything should move correctly.

13. Undo any changes and close the test window to return to the *Block Editor* contextual tab.

Task 5 - Clean up parameters.

You do not need to change the names of these parameters, because no one outside the Block Editor needs to use them.

1. In the Parameters Manager, change all of the *main* bookshelf wall *Expressions* to **Thickness** and all of the shelf *Expressions* to **Half_Thick**, as shown in Figure 19–54. Also, for the top and bottom wall edge thickness, change the *Expressions* to **Thickness**. This enables you to change the thickness of the wood that is used in the bookcase and have all of the related items update.

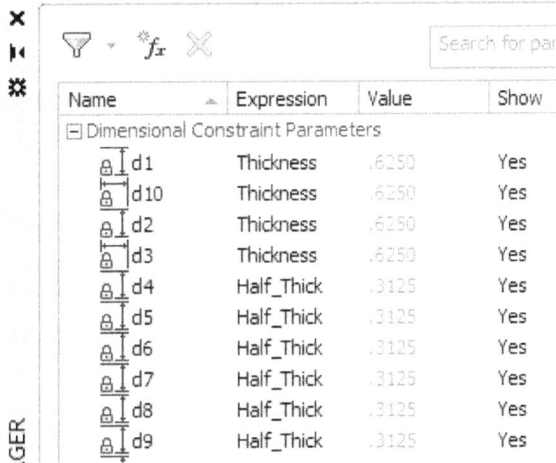

Name		Expression	Value	Show
□ Dimensional Constraint Parameters				
	d1	Thickness	.6250	Yes
	d10	Thickness	.6250	Yes
	d2	Thickness	.6250	Yes
	d3	Thickness	.6250	Yes
	d4	Half_Thick	.3125	Yes
	d5	Half_Thick	.3125	Yes
	d6	Half_Thick	.3125	Yes
	d7	Half_Thick	.3125	Yes
	d8	Half_Thick	.3125	Yes
	d9	Half_Thick	.3125	Yes

Figure 19–54

2. Test the parameters in the User Parameters list by changing the *Expression* of the **Thickness** parameter to **1/2**. Verify that everything moves correctly.

3. Change it back to **5/8** and check it again.

4. Test the **Height** and **Width** parameters using several different sizes. End with a *Height* of **60** and a *Width* of **30**.

Construction geometry does not plot or display outside the Block Editor contextual tab.

5. In the *Block Editor* contextual tab>Manage panel, click

   (Construction Geometry). Select each of the three shelf center lines. Press <Enter> to end the selection set and <Enter> again to convert them to construction geometry.

Task 6 - Create a block table.

In most cases, an object (such as a bookcase) is available in specific sizes. Creating a Block Table creates a list of sizes that can be used when inserting and manipulating the block.

1. In the Dimensional panel, click ▦ (Block Table).

2. Select a parameter location near the lower left corner of the bookcase and set it to display **1** grip.

3. In the Block Properties Table dialog box, click *fx* (Add properties...) to add an existing parameter to the table. Select both **Width** and **Height**. (Hold <Ctrl> to select both.) Click **OK**.

   • The dialog box updates as shown in Figure 19–55.

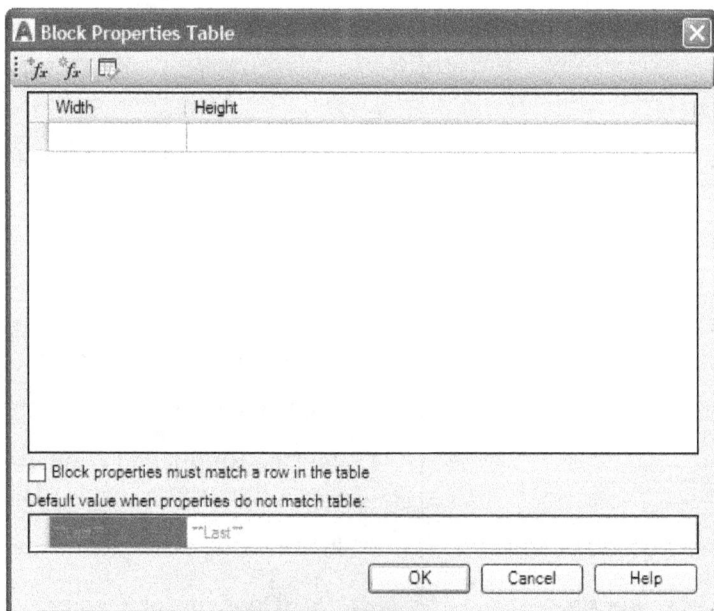

Figure 19–55

4. To add a new parameter, click *fx* (Add parameters). In the New Parameter dialog box, set the following, as shown in Figure 19–56:
   • *Name*: **Size**
   • *Value*: **30 x 60**
   • *Type*: **String**

Figure 19–56

5. Click **OK**.

6. In the Block Properties Table dialog box, drag the *Size* column to the beginning before *Width* and *Height* as shown in Figure 19–57.

7. Fill out the table as shown in Figure 19–57.

*Select **Block properties must match a row in the table** to restrict the block to only being resized using the sizes available in the table.*

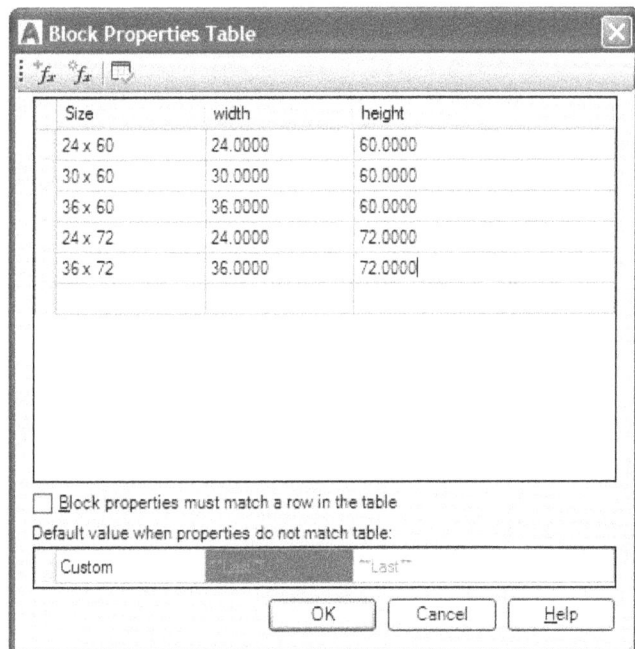

Size	width	height
24 x 60	24.0000	60.0000
30 x 60	30.0000	60.0000
36 x 60	36.0000	60.0000
24 x 72	24.0000	72.0000
36 x 72	36.0000	72.0000

Figure 19–57

8. Click (Audit) to audit the Block Properties Table.

9. If the table contains any errors, the audit can fix them. If the table does not contain any errors, click **Close** and **OK**.

10. Save the block and close the Block Editor.

11. Test the block in the drawing.

12. Insert several copies of the block and set them at different sizes.

13. Save the drawing.

Attributes

Exam Objective Covered in This Chapter

- 6.1.c Modify attribute definitions with the Block Attribute Manager

20.1 Inserting Blocks with Attributes

What Are Attributes?

Attributes are data elements that are associated with blocks. Each time a block with attributes is inserted into a drawing, a new data record is inserted into the master database of the drawing.

From these records in the drawing database, the AutoCAD® software can extract information for creating parts lists and bills of materials, estimating takeoffs, doing inventory counts, and creating schedules. Attributes also enable you to create graphic standards for tasks, such as reference and location numbering. Attributes are also used to assign tag labels on blocks and store information, such as part numbers in a drawing.

How Attribute Values Are Entered

A block that contains attributes inserts them into the drawing database each time the block is inserted. The AutoCAD software prompts you to provide values for each of the attributes that are associated with the block. Figure 20–1 shows an example of attribute tags in a block definition and populated attribute values in a block reference.

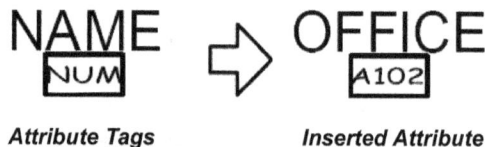

NAME ⇨ OFFICE
NUM   A102

Attribute Tags   *Inserted Attribute*

Figure 20–1

The **attdia** system variable controls how attribute values are entered.

- **attdia** = **0** causes attributes to be entered at the Command Prompt, as shown in Figure 20–2.

- **attdia** = **1** (the default value) causes attributes to be entered in a dialog box, as shown in Figure 20–3.

- Entering the values using a dialog box enables all of the categories of information to be displayed at the same time and enables you to edit a value before closing the dialog box.

- Some blocks with attributes are set to enter the information automatically. You can modify them when they are in the drawing.

Attdia set to 0

```
Command: _insert
Specify insertion point or [Basepoint/Scale/Rotate]:
Enter attribute values
Voltage <120>: 120/240
KVA <75>:
# of Taps: 4
Coil: Auto
```

Figure 20–2

Attdia set to 1

Figure 20–3

Retain Attribute Display

When inserted as part of a block, some attributes can be visible and some not. The visibility of an attribute is determined when the attribute is created, before it is associated with a block. If you want to display the invisible attributes, you can make them visible temporarily, as shown in Figure 20–4.

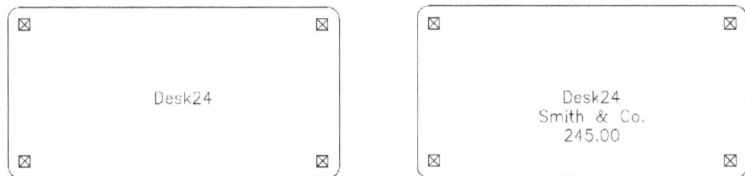

Attribute Display set to Normal   *Attribute Display set to On*

Figure 20–4

- The **Retain Attribute Display** command enables you to toggle the visibility of attributes on or off.

- In the ribbon, in the *Home* tab>expanded Block panel, or in the *Insert* tab>expanded Block panel, expand the Attribute Display drop-down list.

Command Options

Retain Attribute Display: Displays attributes according to their defined modes. Invisible attributes do not display, while visible attributes display.

Display All Attributes: Displays all of the attributes, regardless of their defined visibility modes, making them all temporarily visible.

Hide All Attributes: Hides all of the attributes, regardless of their defined visibility modes, making them all temporarily invisible.

20.2 Editing Attribute Values

When attributes have been inserted into a drawing, you might need to change their values. For example, the cost of a part might change, or one with a different model number might replace the part number that you originally specified. Attribute values in multiple blocks can be replaced using **Find and Replace**.

Editing Attributes One at a Time

The Enhanced Attribute Editor dialog box (shown in Figure 20–5) enables you to change the attribute values in individual blocks. It also enables you to change the text appearance and properties (layer, color, etc.) for each attribute in a block. The quickest way to start this command is to double-click on the block containing the attributes you want to edit.

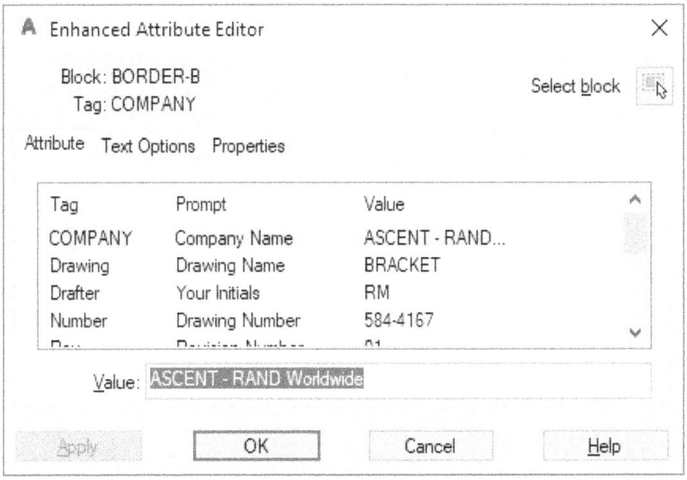

Figure 20–5

How To: Edit an Individual Attribute

You can also double-click on the attribute that you want to modify.

1. In the *Home* tab>Block panel or *Insert* tab>Block panel, click (Edit Attribute) and select the block.
2. In the Enhanced Attribute Editor dialog box, in the *Attribute* tab, select the tag you want to modify from the list, if it is not already selected.

3. In the *Value* field, change the information as required, as shown in Figure 20–6.

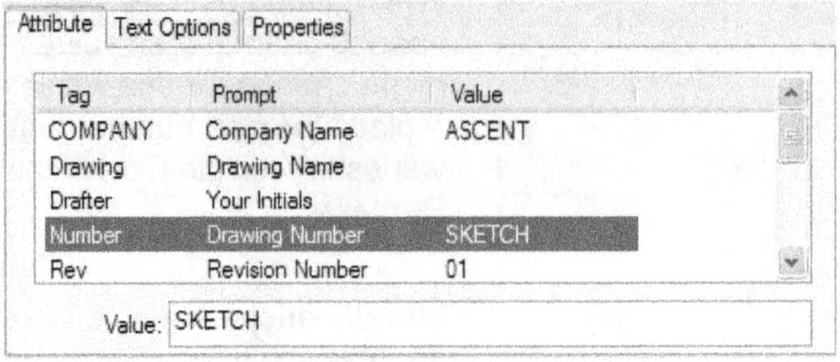

Attribute	Text Options	Properties

Tag	Prompt	Value
COMPANY	Company Name	ASCENT
Drawing	Drawing Name	
Drafter	Your Initials	
Number	Drawing Number	SKETCH
Rev	Revision Number	01

Value: SKETCH

Figure 20–6

4. In the *Text Options* tab (shown in Figure 20–7), you can modify the *Text Style*, *Justification*, *Height*, and other text options that are typically set in the text style.

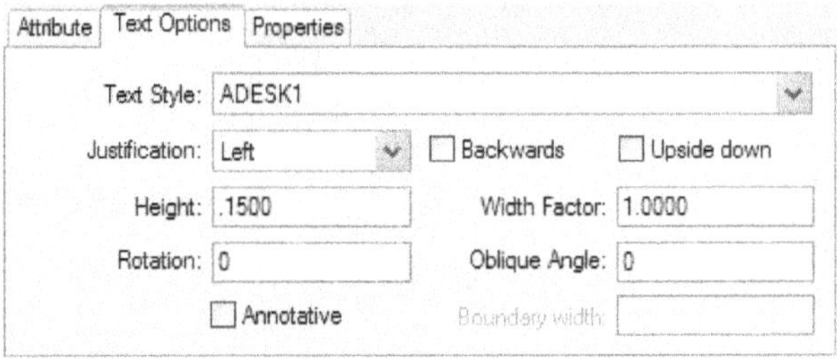

Attribute	Text Options	Properties

Text Style: ADESK1

Justification: Left ☐ Backwards ☐ Upside down

Height: .1500 Width Factor: 1.0000

Rotation: 0 Oblique Angle: 0

☐ Annotative Boundary width:

Figure 20–7

5. In the *Properties* tab (shown in Figure 20–8), you can modify the *Layer*, *Linetype*, *Color, Lineweight*, and *Plot style* of the attribute.

Attribute	Text Options	Properties

Layer: Border

Linetype: ByLayer

Color: ByLayer Lineweight: ByLayer

Plot style: ByLayer

Figure 20–8

*Note that it is recommended that you leave these as **ByLayer** in most cases.*

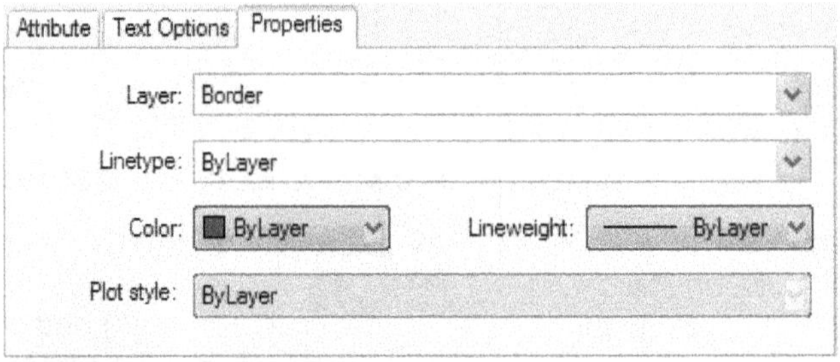

• You can only edit the attributes one block at a time, but you can switch to another block in the Enhanced Attribute Editor using ⬚ (Select block). It displays the drawing window and enables you to select another block with attributes to edit. If you changed the previous attribute, a warning box opens prompting you to save the changes.

- When you edit a multiline attribute, the *Value* field is grayed out. Click ⬚ (Browse) to open a simplified version of the Text Formatting toolbar in which you can modify the attribute content, as shown in Figure 20–9.

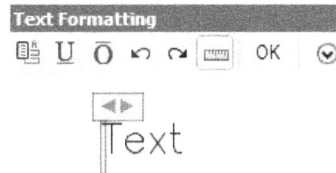

Figure 20–9

- Tag names and prompts cannot be changed in the Enhanced Attribute Editor dialog box, you must edit the block that contains the attributes to update this information.

- The *Text Options* and *Properties* tabs apply to the attribute that is selected in the list in the *Attribute* tab.

Editing Multiple Attribute Values

To change multiple attribute values, the easiest tool to use is **Find and Replace**, as shown in Figure 20–10. It works on attributes and regular text.

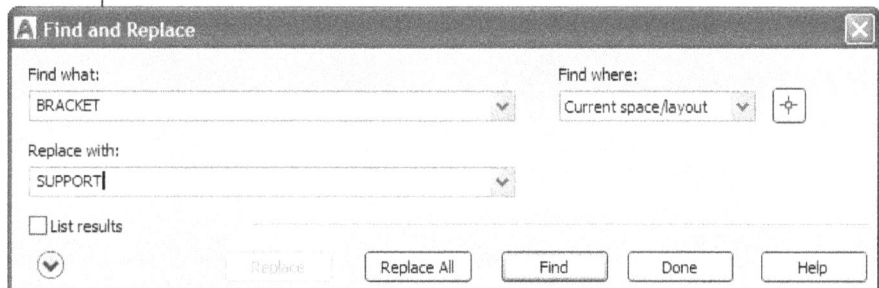

Figure 20–10

For example, you might want to change a department name in all of the related attributes in a drawing or you might want to change a part number. If you know the original information, it is easy for the AutoCAD software to find and replace it for you.

How To: Edit Multiple Attribute Values

*You can also right-click in the drawing window and select **Find** in the shortcut menu.*

1. In the *Annotate* tab>Text panel, type the string you want to find in the *Find text* field and click ⊿ (Find). The Find and Replace dialog box opens.
2. In the *Replace with:* field, type the string you want to use to replace the existing text.

3. Specify how you want to select the objects to be modified in the Find where: drop-down list. This can be **Entire drawing**, **Current space/layout**, or **Selected objects**.

4. Click ▣ (Select objects) to specify a selection set.

5. Click **Find** to find the first instance of the text in the drawing and display it in the context box on the left. The button changes to **Find Next**.

6. Click **Replace** to replace the instance of the word highlighted in the drawing window or click **Replace All** to replace all of the instances of the word in the drawing.

7. When you are finished, click **Done**.

• Click ⊗ to expand the Find and Replace dialog box and modify the type of objects to be included in the search, as shown in Figure 20–11. You can also set the command to match the case of the letters or to only find whole words.

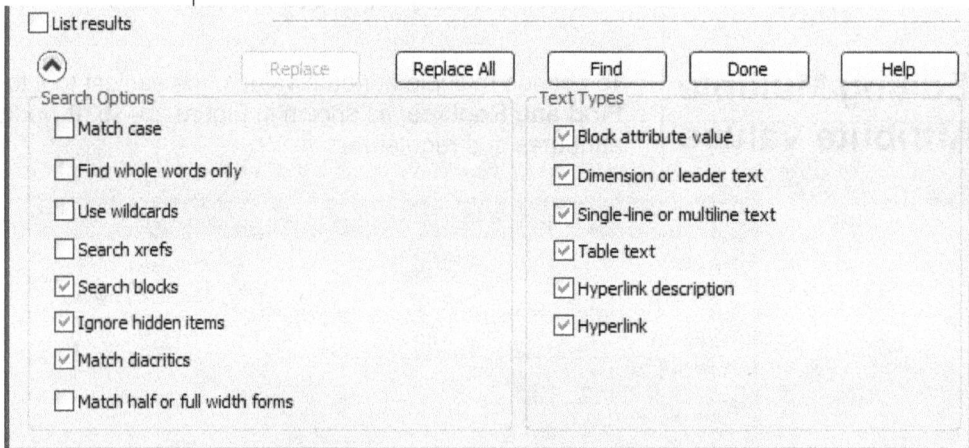

Figure 20–11

Practice 20a | Inserting and Editing Attribute Values

Practice Objectives

- Insert blocks with attributes.
- Modify both the value and properties of attributes in a title block.

In this practice, you will insert several blocks with attributes. You will also use **Find and Replace** and the Enhanced Attribute Editor to change the value and properties of attributes in a title block.

Task 1 - Insert attributes.

In this task, you will insert several blocks with attributes. The completed drawing is shown in Figure 20–12.

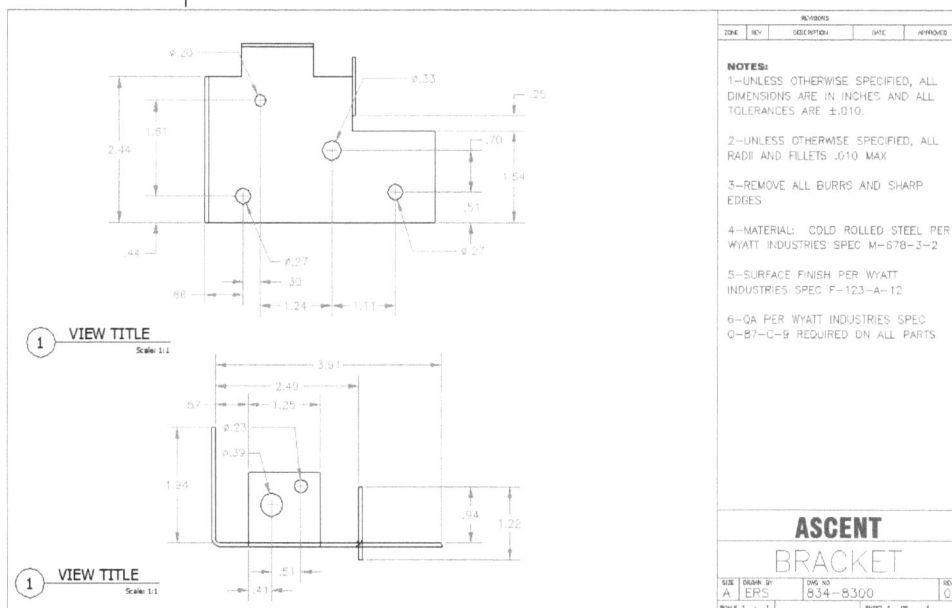

Figure 20–12

1. Open **Bracket-Ad-I.dwg** from the practice files folder.

2. Insert the block **BORDER-B** at **0,0**. The Edit Attributes dialog box opens automatically.

If the Edit Attribute dialog box does not open, set attdia to 1.

3. In the Edit Attributes dialog box, fill out the fields as shown in Figure 20–13, and click **OK**. Note that the information is added to the title block.

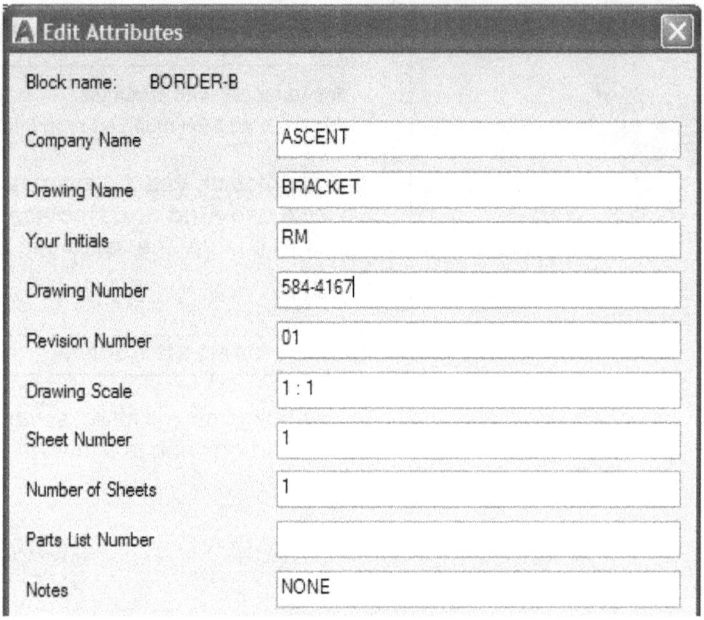

A Edit Attributes	☒
Block name: BORDER-B	
Company Name	ASCENT
Drawing Name	BRACKET
Your Initials	RM
Drawing Number	584-4167|
Revision Number	01
Drawing Scale	1 : 1
Sheet Number	1
Number of Sheets	1
Parts List Number	
Notes	NONE

Figure 20–13

4. Open the Tools Palette and select the *Annotation* tab, if required.

5. Insert a copy of **Drawing Title-Imperial** under top and bottom model views. It is inserted without prompting for the values. All of the attribute values in this block have been preset, as shown in Figure 20–14.

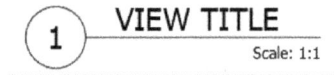

$$\underbrace{1}\; \text{VIEW TITLE} \atop \text{Scale: 1:1}$$

Figure 20–14

6. Insert an additional copy of the **Drawing Title-Imperial** block anywhere to one side.

7. Explode it. The information is lost and the attribute tag information displays instead, as shown in Figure 20–15.

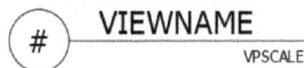

$$\underbrace{\#}\; \text{VIEWNAME} \atop \text{VPSCALE}$$

Figure 20–15

8. Erase all the components of the exploded block.

9. Zoom in to the lower right corner of the title block.

10. In the *Insert* tab>expanded Block panel, expand the Attribute Display drop-down list and click (Hide All Attributes). All of the attributes become invisible.

11. In the *Insert* tab>Block panel, expand the Attribute Display drop-down list and click (Retain Attribute Display). All of the attributes return to their normal visibility status.

12. Save the drawing.

Task 2 - Edit attributes.

In this task, you will use **Find and Replace** and the Enhanced Attribute Editor to change the value and properties of attributes in a title block, as shown in Figure 20–16.

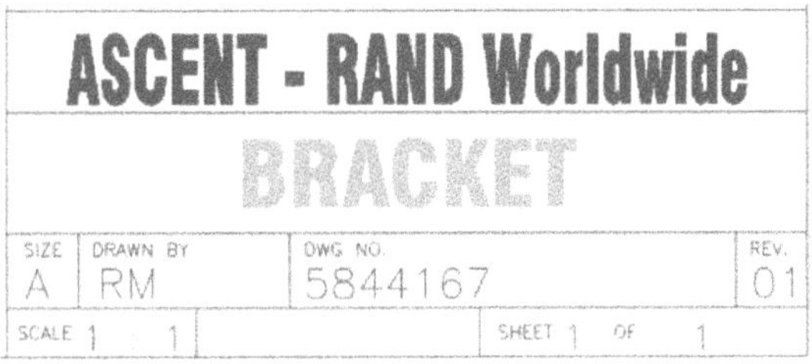

Figure 20–16

1. In the *Annotate* tab>Text panel, type **ASCENT** in the *Find text* field and click (Find).

2. In the Find and Replace dialog box, click to expand it and verify that **Block attribute value** is selected to be included in the search. Ensure the *Find what* string is set to **ASCENT** and in the *Replace with* string, enter **ASCENT - RAND Worldwide**. Click **Replace All** to replace all of the strings.

3. A smaller Find and Replace dialog box opens indicating the number of matches that were found and changed. Click **OK**, and then click **Done** to close the Find and Replace dialog box.

4. In the title block, note that the new company name is bigger than the space provided and extends beyond it. Double-click anywhere on the title block to start the **Edit Attribute** command that opens the Enhanced Attribute Editor dialog box.

5. In the *Attribute* tab, in the list of attributes, select **Company**. In the *Text Options* tab, change the *Width Factor* to **0.7**, as shown in Figure 20–17.

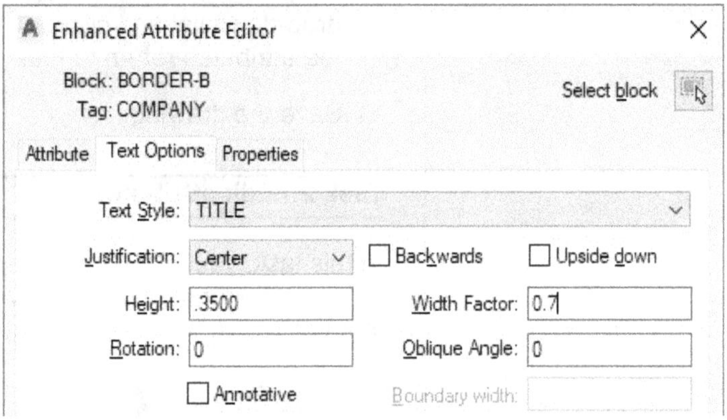

Figure 20–17

6. In the *Attribute* tab, select the **Drawing** attribute. In the *Text Options* tab, change the *Text Style* to **TITLE**. In the *Properties* tab, change the *Color* to **Green**.

If the drawing attribute Bracket is not at the correct location, use grips to move it.

7. Click **OK** to close the Enhanced Attribute Editor dialog box. Note the affected changes in the title block, as shown previously in Figure 20–16.

8. Save and close the drawing.

20.3 Defining Attributes

Attribute definitions are special objects that you include with a block when the block is defined. The **Define Attribute** command creates an attribute definition using a dialog box.

How To: Create a Block with Attributes

1. Draw the objects that you want to include in the block.
2. In the *Home* tab>expanded Block panel or *Insert* tab>Block Definition panel, click (Define Attributes) to create the attributes.
3. Using the **Block** command, select the attributes and other objects that make up the block.
4. Insert the block and fill in the attribute information.

- Attributes can be annotative.

- A block can contain other objects in addition to the attributes, or just attributes without other objects.

- You can also add attributes using (Attribute Definition) in the *Block Editor* contextual tab>Action Parameters panel.

- Block attribute information can contain multiple lines of text while remaining a single attribute. This is very useful for title block information, such as addresses or information that varies in length, but needs to remain in one area in a block.

Attribute Definition

The Attribute Definition dialog box (shown in Figure 20–18) is used to configure attributes before they are associated with a block.

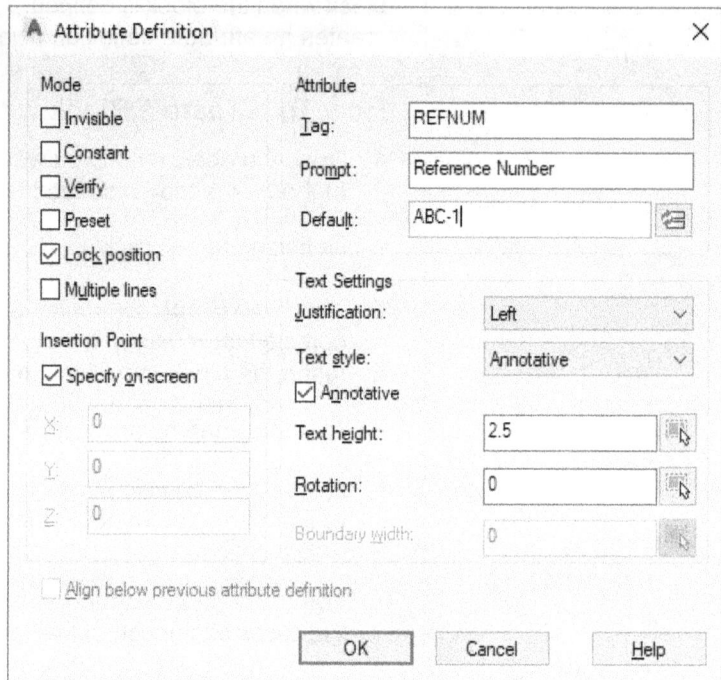

Figure 20–18

Attribute Components

Tag	A label for the category of information that is stored in a particular attribute. Attribute tags in the software are similar to the *field names* or *column labels* in other data systems. Some common tags are *type*, *cost*, *rating*, *manufacturer*, *reference_number*, and *material*. This label cannot be blank or have spaces.
Prompt	The prompt that displays in the Command Line or dialog box when a block with this attribute is inserted. If empty, the Tags name is used for the prompt. Phrase your prompt to help users to enter the correct information. For example, you could write a question for the prompt.
Default	The initial contents or actual data value of a specific block instance. This value is used as a default value and can be blank in the dialog box. You can click (Insert field) to insert a field as the value.

Attribute Modes

The Attribute Mode controls how an attribute value displays in a drawing and how much control you have over the value.

Invisible	Controls whether an attribute value normally displays in the drawing, or is just stored in the database. For example, reference numbers and part locations WOULD NOT typically be invisible, while costs, remarks, and manufacturers would be invisible.
Constant	Controls whether the attribute is defined ahead of time or is entered by the operator when the block is inserted. The part number of a specific part can be constant, while a reference number or detail sheet number would not be constant. Constant attributes CANNOT be edited.
Verify	Use for some non-constant attributes, such as serial numbers and costs, which are so important that they need to be confirmed by the operator. The Verify mode causes the software to prompt for the value twice when the block is inserted. If dialog boxes are used, verify does not have an effect.
Preset	Similar to **Constant**, except that values can be edited after insertion. Preset values are not requested at the Command Line when the block is inserted. However, the value displays in the dialog box for editing.
Lock position	Select if you do not want the attributes to move separately from the rest of the block.
Multiple lines	Select if you want to create a multiline attribute. When selected, the *Default* field is grayed out. Click ⌐…⌐ (Browse) to specify the location and default text.

Insertion Point and Text Settings

Use these options to determine the attribute text placement and properties. You can specify the *Justification*, *Text style*, *Text height*, and *Rotation* of the text, or make the text *Annotative*. The **Specify On-screen** option is the most common method that is used to place the attribute definition text.

- Once you have placed one attribute, you might want to speed up the process by using the same text options. To do so, select **Align below previous attribute definition**.

- The *Boundary width* setting is only available for multiline attributes.

Associating Attributes with Blocks

Once the attributes have been defined, they must be associated with a block. This is done by including attributes as part of the block while in the **Block** or **Wblock** command or in the Block Editor authoring mode.

Select the attributes individually, rather than with a window or crossing box. The order in which the attribute information displays during block insertion depends on the order in which the attributes were selected for inclusion in the block.

- To edit an attribute before it is associated with a block, double-click on the attribute. This opens the Edit Attribute Definition dialog box (shown in Figure 20–19), which enables you to change the *Tag*, *Prompt*, or *Default* value.

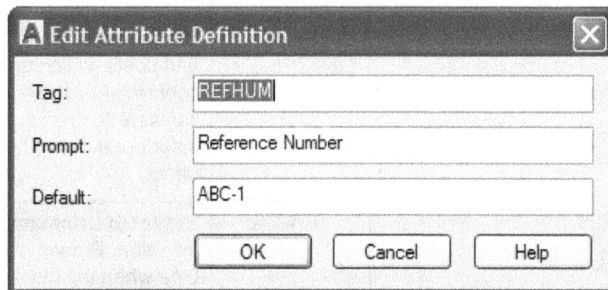

Figure 20–19

Practice 20b

Defining Attributes

Practice Objective

- Define multiple attributes using given values and use them to create a block for use in a drawing.

In this practice, you will create attributes in a block that you will then use in another drawing. The block with attribute definitions is shown in Figure 20–20.

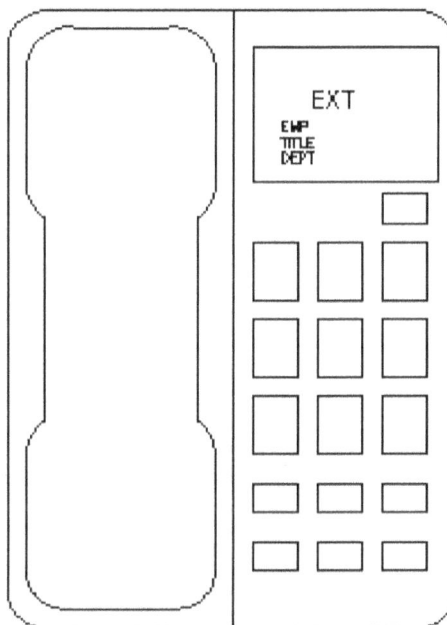

Figure 20–20

1. Open **Attributes-A.dwg** from the practice files folder.

*You need to create each of the attributes separately. Enter the settings for each attribute and click **OK** to place it in the drawing.*

Start (Define Attributes) again to create other remaining attributes.

2. In the *Insert* tab>Block Definition panel, click (Define Attributes) to create four attributes using the values given in the table below. In the Attribute Definition dialog box, select the specified *Mode* option and enter the values in the appropriate fields, as shown for the EXT tag in Figure 20–21.

Tag:	EXT	EMP	TITLE	DEPT
Prompt:	Extension	Employee Name	Title	Department
Default:	(blank)	(blank)	(blank)	Design
Mode:	none (all checkboxes cleared)	Invisible and Multiple lines	Invisible	Invisible and Preset
Justification:	Center	Middle left	Click **Align below previous attribute definition** near the bottom of the dialog box.	Click **Align below previous attribute definition** near the bottom of the dialog box.
Text style:	BLOCK	Standard	---	---
Annotative	Yes (Select checkbox)	No (none)	---	---
Text height:	1/4"	1/8"	---	---
Insertion Point: X, Y, Z	6,7,0	5.25,6.75,0	---	---

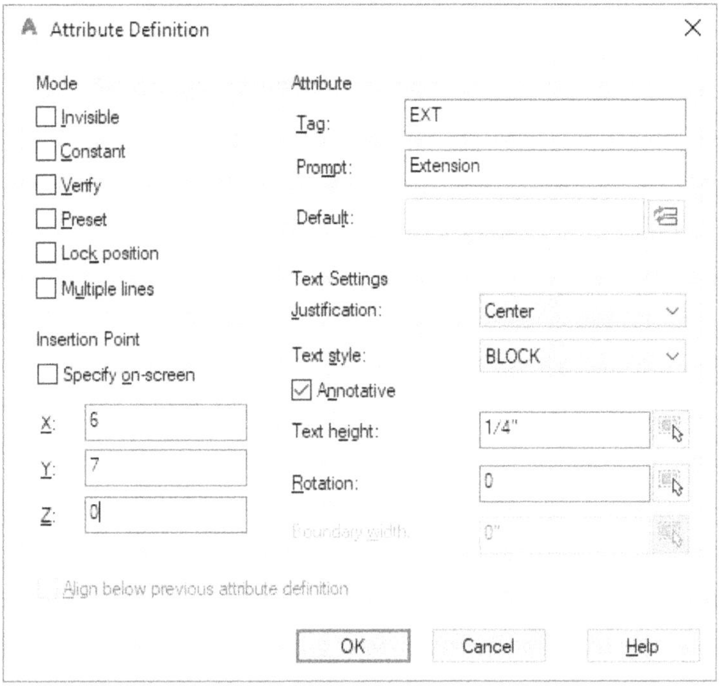

Figure 20–21

3. Use **Wblock** to create a new drawing called **Phone.dwg** containing the drawing of the phone and the attributes. Set the *Source* to **Objects**. Set the *Base point* to the middle of the top of the phone (using the *Pick point*). Set the file path to the practice files folder and *Insert units* to **Inches**.

4. Save and close the drawing.

5. Open **Office-A.dwg** from the practice files folder.

6. Use the *Libraries* tab of the Blocks palette and locate the **Phone.dwg**. Insert the block **Phone** and place it on one of the desks.

7. Double-click on the block **Phone** to open the Enhanced Attribute Editor. Select **Extension** and enter any *Value* for extension. Click **OK**. Note that the extension number is displayed at the place where you had placed the **EXT** attribute in the block Phone.

8. Insert the block **Phone** on each of the remaining three desks and test the attributes by entering the value.

9. Save and close the drawing.

20.4 Redefining Blocks with Attributes

The Block Attribute Manager (shown in Figure 20–22) simplifies the process of modifying attributes in blocks and updating the blocks.

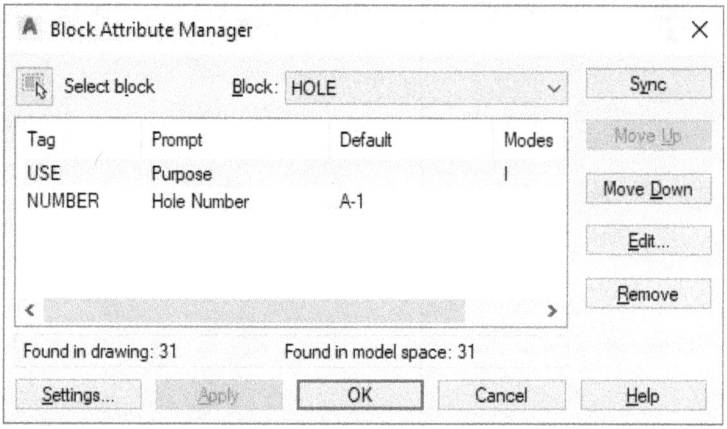

Figure 20–22

- The Block Attribute Manager does not affect (or enable you to modify) the attribute values in blocks. To modify those values, use the **Edit Attribute** command.

- You cannot add attributes to a block using the Block Attribute Manager. You need to explode the block, add the new attribute, and redefine the block. Then use the **Synchronize Attributes** command to update the blocks and their attributes.

How To: Use the Block Attribute Manager

1. In the *Home* tab>expanded Block panel, or in the *Insert* tab>Block Definition panel, click (Manage Attributes) to open the Block Attribute Manager dialog box.
2. Expand the Block drop-down list and select a block.

   - You can also use (Select block) to select a block in the drawing window.

3. The block's attributes display. To modify an attribute, select it in the list and click **Edit**.
4. In the Edit Attribute dialog box, make the required changes.

Only blocks with attributes are listed

5. In the Block Attribute Manager, click **Apply** to apply the changes and stay in the dialog box, or click **OK** to apply the changes and close the dialog box.

- Use **Move Up** and **Move Down** to change the position of an attribute in the list. The location in the list determines the order in which the prompts display when you insert the block and fill in the attribute values. It does not change the physical order of the attributes.

- **Sync** updates existing blocks that were not updated automatically when you made a change using the Block Attribute Manager.

- You can remove an attribute from a block definition by selecting it in the list and clicking **Remove**.

Editing Options

When an attribute is edited, the Edit Attribute dialog box is used as it was when the attribute was defined, as shown in Figure 20–23.

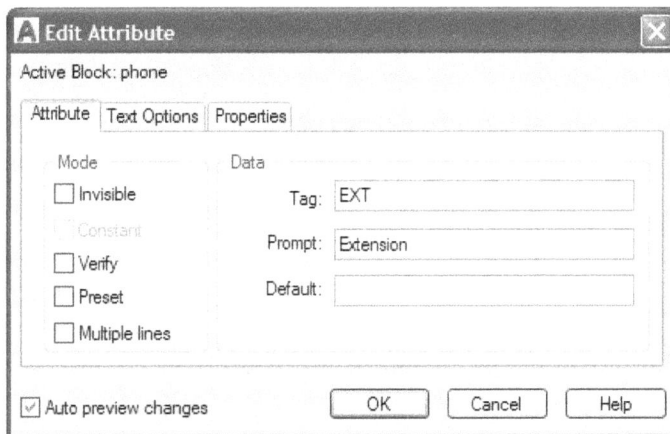

Figure 20–23

- The *Text Options* and *Properties* tabs apply to the attribute selected in the list in the *Attribute* tab.

- **Auto preview changes** makes the changes visible in the drawing immediately. Toggling this off provides a slightly faster performance.

Settings

The Settings control the properties that display in the Block Attribute Manager. By default, only the **Tag**, **Prompt**, **Default**, **Modes**, and **Annotative** properties display, as shown in Figure 20–24.

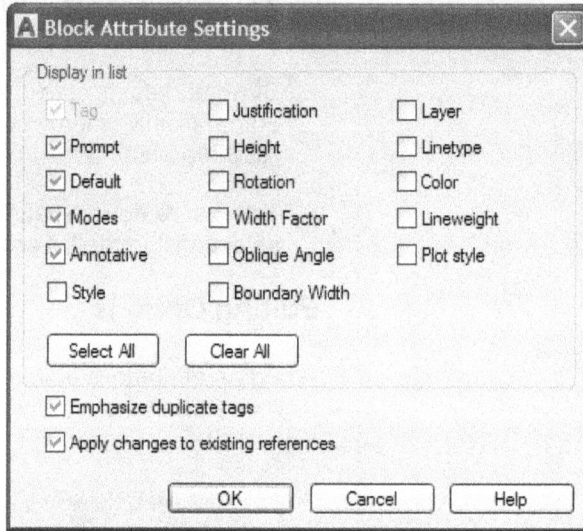

Figure 20–24

Emphasize duplicate tags	If selected, duplicate tag names display in red in the Block Attribute Manager.
Apply changes to existing references	If selected, all of the existing and new instances of the block reference are updated with the changes specified in the Block Attribute Manager. If not selected, only new instances of the block display the changes. You can use the **Synchronize Attributes** command if this option has been toggled off.

Updating Blocks with New Attributes

To add an attribute to a block, open the block definition in the Block Editor authoring environment and add the attribute. Alternatively, you can explode a copy of the block, add the attribute, and redefine the block. New instances of the redefined block include the new attribute, but existing instances of the block do not. You can use **Synchronize Attributes** to update all of the blocks and their attributes.

How To: Synchronize Attributes

1. Open the block in the Block Editor authoring environment, add the required attribute(s), and save the block.
2. In the *Home* tab>expanded Block panel, or in the *Insert* tab>expanded Block Definition panel, click (Synchronize Attributes).
3. Press <Enter> to select a block (type **?** to display a list or **N** to type a name).
4. Select the block.
5. At the *Resync Process* prompt, enter **yes** or **no**.

- This command also works on existing blocks that were not automatically updated when you made a change using the Block Attribute Manager.

- At least one attribute must already be in the block that you are trying to update with other attributes.

Practice 20c

Redefining Blocks with Attributes

Practice Objectives

- Modify block attribute values and block attribute settings using the Block Attribute Manager.
- Redefine a block and then synchronize all of the existing instances of that block in the drawing to be updated.

In this practice, you will use **Edit Attribute**, make changes to existing attributes in the Block Attribute Manager, and use **Synchronize Attributes**. The completed drawing is shown in Figure 20–25.

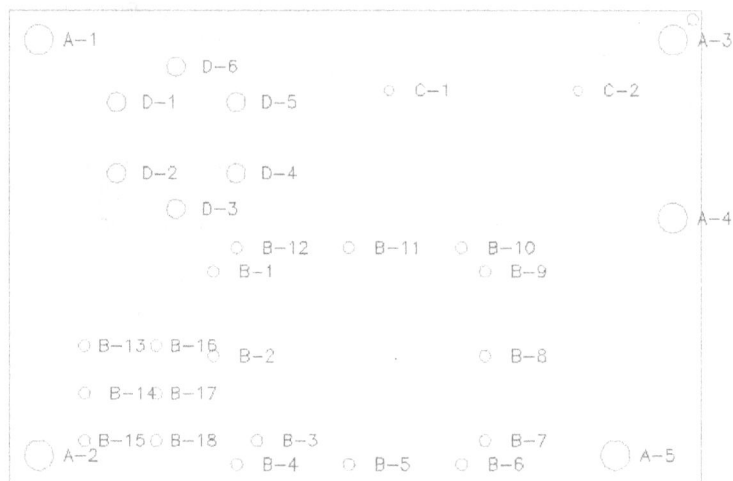

Figure 20–25

1. Open **PCB-I.dwg** from the practice files folder.

2. Double-click on the **A-3** attribute in the bottom right corner of the part to open the Enhanced Attribute Editor.

3. In the *Value* edit box, change the *NUMBER* value to **A-5**, and note that *USE* is listed above *NUMBER*, as shown in Figure 20–26. Click **OK** to close the Enhanced Attribute Editor dialog box. In the drawing, note that the attribute changes to **A-5**.

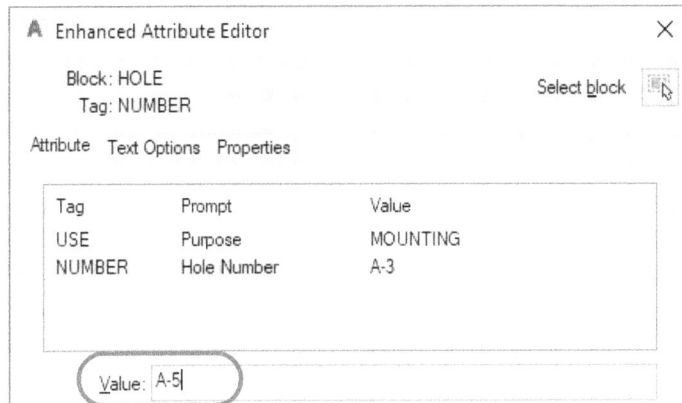

Figure 20–26

4. In the *Insert* tab>Block Definition panel, click ⬚ (Manage Attributes) to open the Block Attribute Manager. **HOLE** is the selected block, and its attributes are listed. The *USE* attribute has the **I** (Invisible) mode set.

5. Select the *NUMBER* attribute in the list and click **Move Up** to move it above *USE*.

6. With *NUMBER* selected, click **Edit**. In the *Properties* tab, change the *Color* to **Cyan**. Click **OK** to close the Edit Attribute dialog box.

7. If any of the blocks have not updated automatically, click **Sync** to update all of the instances of the block. Click **OK** to close the Block Attribute Manager. The *NUMBER* attribute now displays in cyan.

8. Double-click on any attribute to edit it. Note that *NUMBER* is now at the top of the list, above *USE*. Click **Cancel** to close the Enhanced Attribute Editor.

9. Insert the block **Hole Plus** to one side of the part, using the default values for the attributes, and explode it. It contains three attributes: *NUMBER*, *LOCATION*, and *USE*.

10. In the *Insert* tab>Block Definition Panel, click **Create Block** to start the **Create Block** command. Set the following:
    - In the Block Definition dialog box, name the block **HOLE**.
    - In the *Objects* area, use **Select objects** to select the three attributes (from the Hole Plus block that was exploded) to be used for the block object.
    - In the *Base Point* area, select **Specify On-screen**.
    - In the *Objects* area, select **Delete**, and then clear the **Open in block editor** option.

You might need to select a different Block first and then reselect the original Block before you click **Sync**.

11. Click **OK** to close the Block Definition dialog box.

12. When prompted, select **Redefine block** to redefine the block **HOLE**.

13. Select a point just to the left of *NUMBER* to specify the insertion base point.

14. Insert a copy of the redefined block **HOLE** to one side, using the default values for the attributes. It includes the *LOCATION* attribute with the default value of **Unknown**. The attributes for the existing blocks named **HOLE** in the part have not changed.

15. In the *Insert* tab>expanded Block Definition panel, click

    (Synchronize Attributes). Press <Enter> and select the new block **HOLE**.

16. At the *ATTSYNC block HOLE?* prompt, select **Yes**. Note that the existing blocks update to include the new attribute with the default value **Unknown**.

17. In the *Insert* tab>Block Definition panel, click (Manage Attributes) to open the Block Attribute Manager dialog box.

18. For the block **HOLE**, select the *Tag* named **LOCATION** in the list, and click **Edit**. The Edit Attribute dialog box opens.

*If the **Auto preview changes** option is toggled on, the drawing changes immediately. If this option is off, the change displays after you exit the Block Attribute Manager.*

19. In the *Attribute* tab, in the *Mode* area, toggle on **Invisible** and then click **OK** to return to the Block Attribute Manager dialog box.

20. Click **OK** to apply the changes and exit the Block Attribute Manager dialog box. The *LOCATION* attribute with the default value **Unknown**, to which all of the other blocks were updated, is now invisible.

21. Save the drawing.

20.5 Extracting Attributes

Attributes can be used in a drawing for labels, tags, etc. They can also be used to extract information into a database or in an AutoCAD table format, as shown in Figure 20–27. The extracted information can then be used for parts lists, inventories, etc.

1084X
Steelcase
Fabric
Red

Furniture Schedule					
QUANITY	TYPE	STYLE	MANUFACTURER	MATERIAL	COLOR
2	CHAIR	1084X	Steelcase	Fabric	Blue
6	CHAIR	1084X	Steelcase	Fabric	Red
2	CHAIR	1084X	Steelcase	Fabric	Green
4	CHAIR	1084X	Steelcase	Fabric	Cherry

Figure 20–27

- In the *Annotate* tab>Tables panel, or in the *Insert* tab>Linking & Extraction panel, click (Extract Data) to start data extraction.

- The **Extract Data** command uses a wizard that automates the process. The major steps in the process are to select the drawing(s) from which to extract the attributes that you want in a table, and select the format to use for the extracted data.

- You can also extract attributes and other data using the **Table** command.

- You can extract information from multiple drawings at the same time.

- Once you have set up the extraction information, you can save it to a *template* so that you do not have to go through the entire wizard again. The template is a text file (Block Template File, .BLK) that specifies the parameters for extraction.

- Data can be exported to a file or made into an AutoCAD table object.

You can create a table by extracting data from objects in the current drawing or from other drawings. In the **Table** command, in the Insert Table dialog box, select **From object data in the drawing (Data Extraction)**, as shown in Figure 20–28. The Data Extraction Wizard opens. It guides you through the selection of objects, whether you want to extract data from the current drawing or another one, and how the data displays in the table.

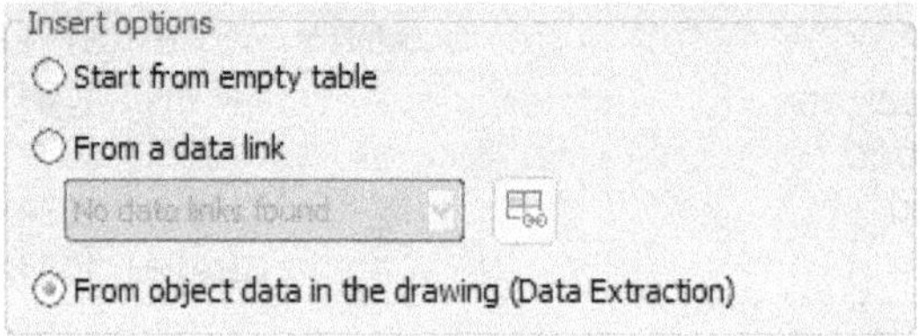

Figure 20–28

How To: Extract Attributes to a Table or File

1. In the *Annotate* tab>Tables panel, or in the *Insert* tab>Linking & Extraction panel, click (Extract Data). Alternatively, you can use the **Table** command.

   • If you are using the **Table** command, select **From object data in the drawing (Data Extraction)** and click **OK**. The Data Extraction Wizard opens.

2. On the *Begin* page, select **Create a new data extraction**, as shown in Figure 20–29.

   • If you have an existing template that was made from another data extraction file (.DXE) or a block template file (.BLK), select the box and then select the template file.

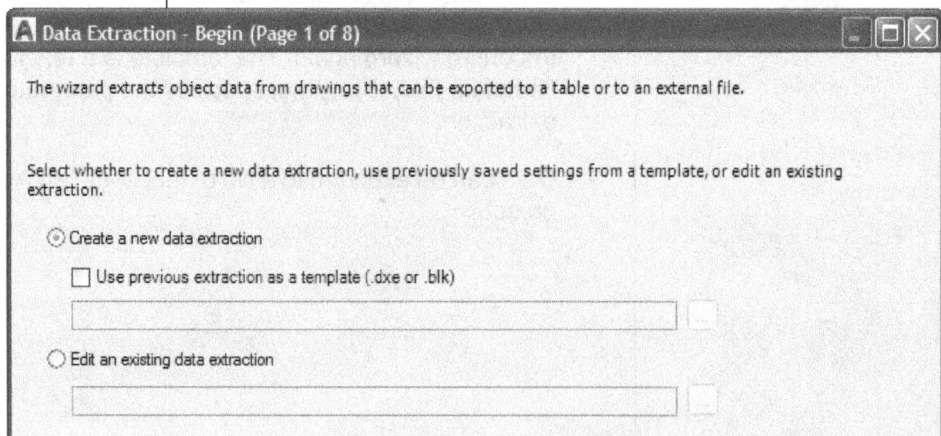

Figure 20–29

3. Click **Next >**.
4. Select a location. In the Save Data Extraction As dialog box, shown in Figure 20–30, type a name for the new data extraction files (.DXE) and click **Save**.

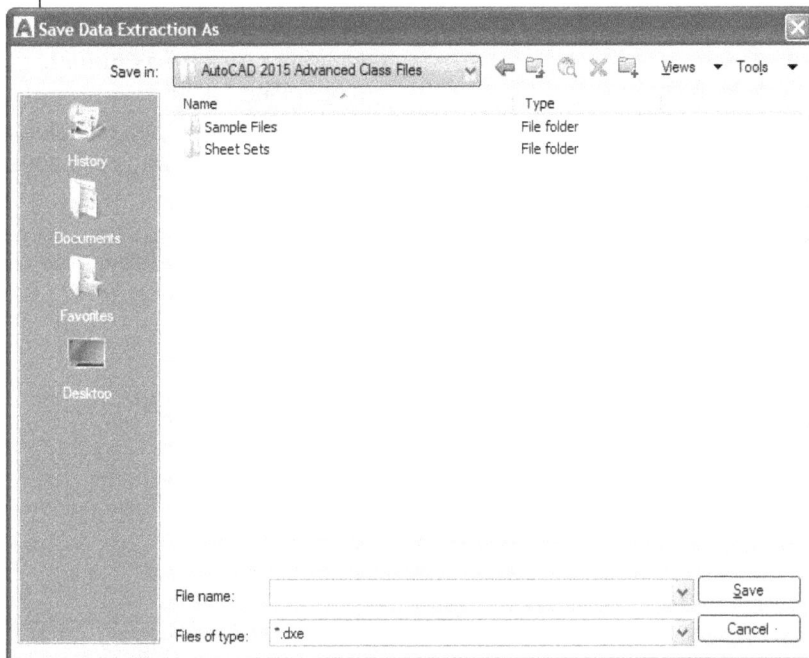

Figure 20–30

5. On the *Define Data Source* page, you can select the file(s) or objects in a drawing from which you want to extract information, as shown in Figure 20–31.

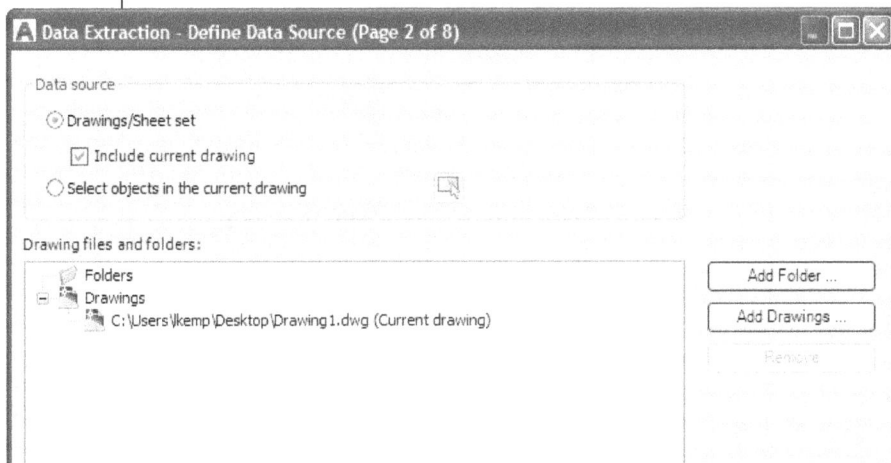

Figure 20–31

- If you select **Select object in the current drawing**, click
  (Select Objects) and select the required objects.
- If you select **Drawings/Sheet set**, you can select **Include current drawing** and add other folders or drawings. Click **Add Drawings** to add one or more drawings to the selection or click **Add Folder** to include all of the drawings in a specified folder.
- In the Add Folder Options dialog box, you can specify the folder and how drawings are added to the list, as shown in Figure 20–32.

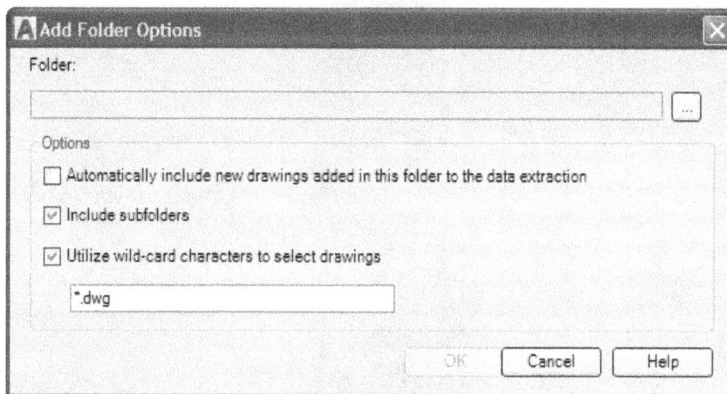

Figure 20–32

6. In the Define Data Source dialog box, you should also click **Settings** to verify that you are extracting the correct information, as shown in Figure 20–33.

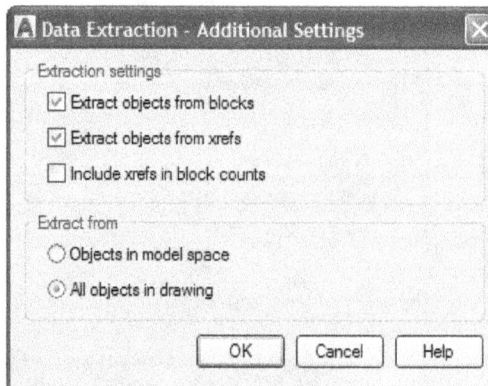

Figure 20–33

7. Click **Next >** when you have finished adding drawings or objects.

8. On the *Select Objects* page, select the objects that you want to include in the data extraction, as shown in Figure 20–34.

   - These include attributes and other objects, such as blocks, lines, and polylines.
   - Use the **Display** options as selection aids.
   - You can also right-click in the *Objects* area and select **Check All**, **Uncheck All**, **Invert Selection**, and **Edit Display Name**.

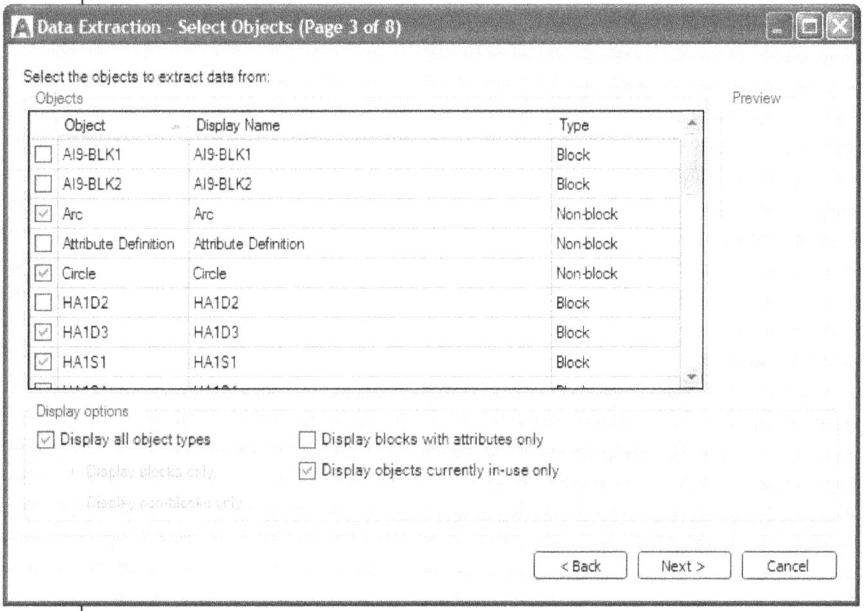

Figure 20–34

9. Click **Next >**.

10. On the *Select Properties* page, all of the properties are selected by default. Select or clear them as required (as shown in Figure 20–35), to select the options you want to use.

- Right-click to clear everything to more easily select only the objects you want to use.
- You can also modify the *Display Name*, which controls the name that displays in the table.

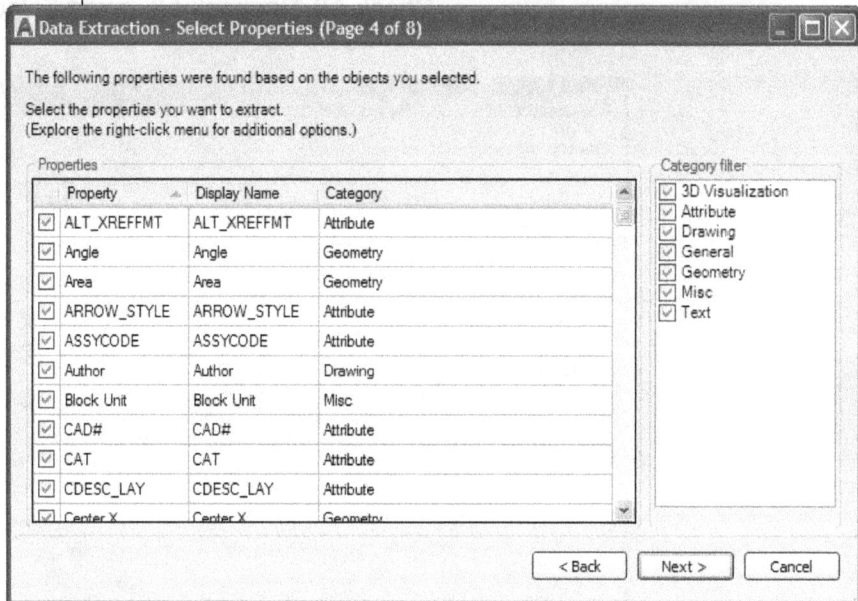

Figure 20–35

11. Click **Next >**.
12. The data is extracted from the drawings and the results display on the *Refine Data* page, as shown in Figure 20–36.

- You can modify the appearance of the columns. Select the options that you want to display. Reorder the column locations by dragging the headers to new locations.
- To reorder the column information alphabetically, click once on the column name.
- To rename a column, right-click on the header.
- If you have additional information stored in a spreadsheet, click **Link External Data** to select the data link.
- Click **Sort Columns Options** to open the Sort Columns dialog box, in which you can also modify the column information.

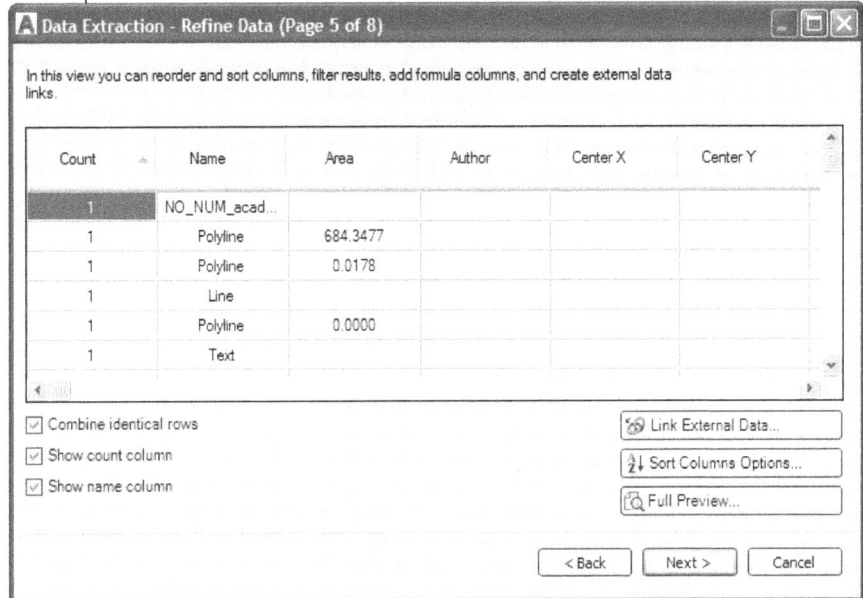

Figure 20–36

13. Click **Full Preview** to display the results.
14. Click **Next >**.
15. On the *Choose Output* page, in the *Output options* area (shown in Figure 20–37), select **Insert data extraction table into drawing** and/or **Output data to external file**.
    - The external files that you can create include XLS, CSV, MDB, and TXT.

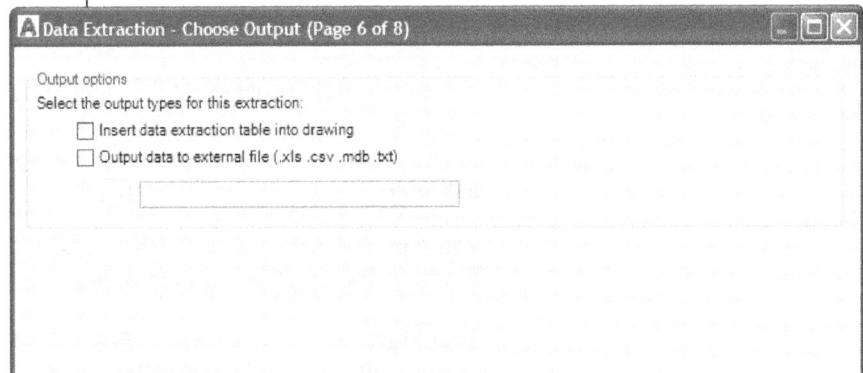

Figure 20–37

16. Click **Next >**.

17. If you select the AutoCAD table option, the *Table Style* page opens, in which you can set up the Table Style information and add a title for the table, as shown in Figure 20–38.

- By default, the Headers are the attribute tag names, unless you modified them in the previous step.

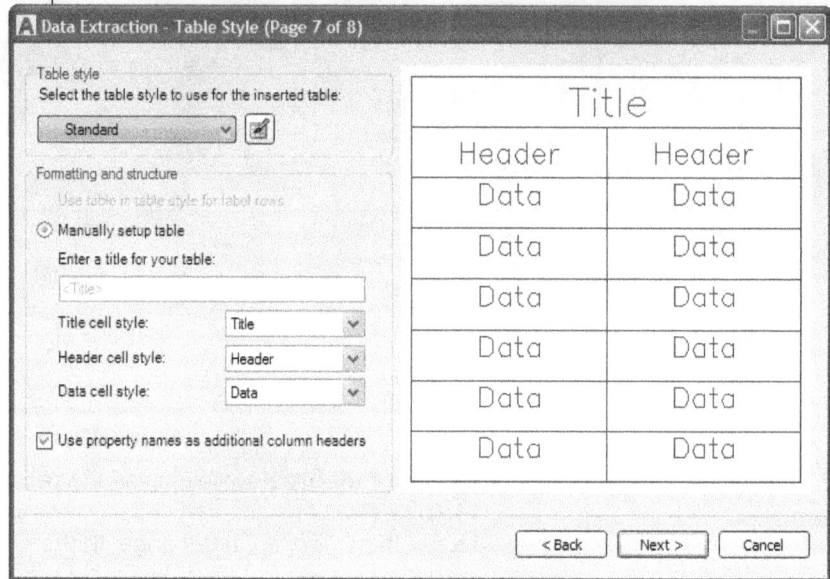

Figure 20–38

18. Click **Next >**.
19. Click **Finish** to close the Data Extraction Wizard. Pick a point in the drawing to insert the table.
20. Use grips to adjust the table to fit in the available space.

- The text in the resulting table is linked to the attribute data. Any manual changes that you make in the table are lost if you refresh the table data. A warning box opens when you place the table.

- You can add data columns from external sources next to those containing the data extracted from the objects.

- To update the table to include any modifications you have made to the data in the drawing, either:

  - right-click on the table and select **Update Table Data Links**, or

  - in the Status Bar, right-click on ⌨ (Data Link) and select **Update All Data Links**.

Practice 20d

Extracting Object Data to a Table

Practice Objective

- Extract attribute information from blocks and insert that information into a table.

In this practice, you will extract attribute information from blocks in a drawing and insert the information into a table, as shown in Figure 20–39.

Bill of Materials			
Count	Name	Catalog	Manufacturer
1	HTS12	9025-GXW2	SQD
1	HPS12		
1	HLS12	CR115B201	GE
1	HA1S1		
1	HA1D3		
1	PLCIO_9EE	1771-OA	AB
1	PLCIO_7E9	1771-IA	AB
1	AI9-BLK2		
1	AI9-BLK1		
2	HA1S4		
2	HCR1	700-R220A1	AB
2	HPB12	800H-BR6D2	AB
3	HMS1	AN16DN0AB	EATON
3	HLT1G	800T-P16H	AB
3	HCR1	700-P400A1	AB
3	HPB11	800H-BR6D1	AB
4	HA1D2		
5	HCR21		
6	HCR22		

Figure 20–39

1. Open **Control-l.dwg** from the practice files folder.

2. In the *Annotate* tab>Tables panel, click (Extract Data). The Data Extraction Wizard opens.

3. Select **Create a new data extraction** (if required) and click **Next >**.

4. In the Save Data Extraction As dialog box, navigate to the practice files folder, enter **BOM** as the *File name*, and click **Save**.

5. In the Data Extraction Wizard, in the *Data source* area, ensure that **Drawings/Sheet Set** and **Include current drawing** are selected, and then click **Next >**.

*You can also start the Table command, select From object data in the drawing (Data Extraction), and then click OK. Note that the Files of type is *.dxe.*

6. In the *Select Objects* page, clear the **Display all object types** option and select **Display blocks only**, as shown in Figure 20–40.

7. Scroll through the list of blocks and clear **LOGO**, **NO_NUM_acade_title**, and the five blocks starting with **WD**, as shown in Figure 20–40.

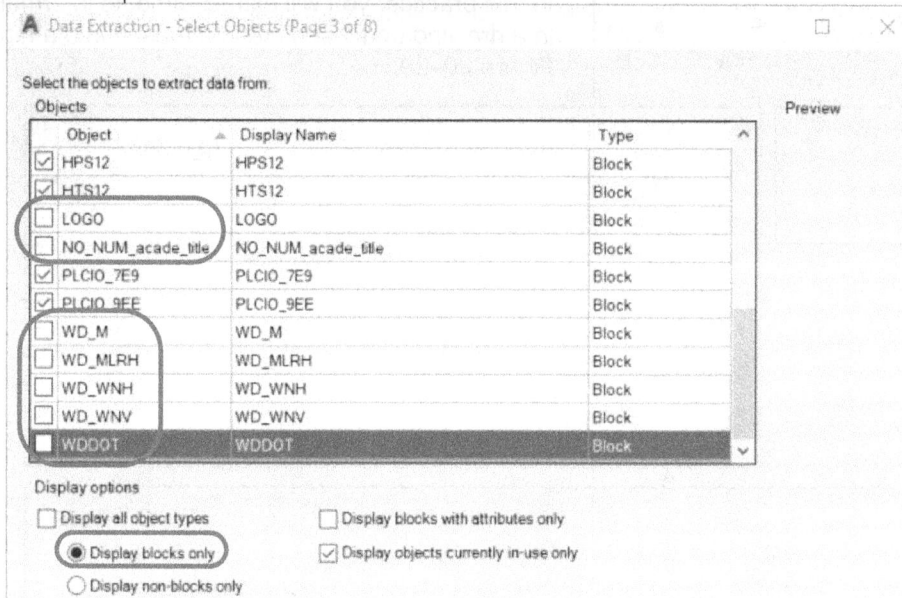

Figure 20–40

8. Click **Next >**.

9. In the *Select Properties* page>*Category filter* area, clear all of the options except **Attribute**, as shown in Figure 20–41.

10. In the *Properties* area, all of the properties are selected by default. Right-click and select **Uncheck all**. Then select **CAT** and **MFG**.

11. Change the display name of CAT to **Catalog** (as shown in Figure 20–41) and display name of MFG to **Manufacturer**.

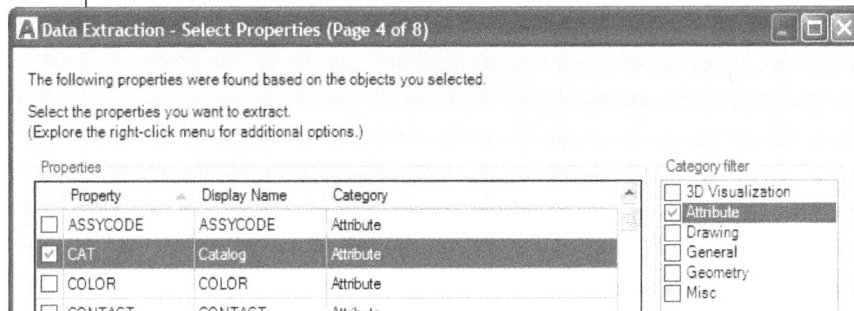

Figure 20–41

12. Click **Next >**.

13. The data is extracted from the drawings and the results display on the *Refine Data* page. Click **Next >**.

14. In the *Choose Output* page, in the *Output options* area, select **Insert data extraction table into drawing**.

15. Click **Next >**.

16. In the *Table Style* page, in the *Formatting and structure* area, type **Bill of Materials** for the title of the table, as shown in Figure 20–42.

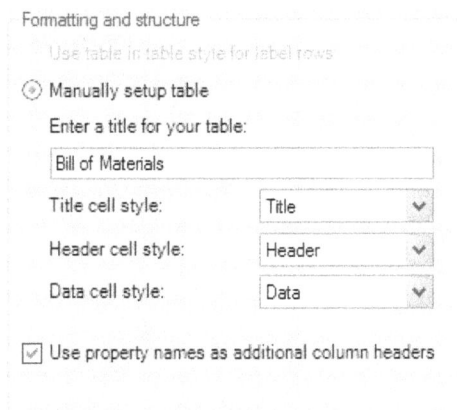

Figure 20–42

17. Click **Next >**.

18. Click **Finish** to close the Data Extraction Wizard.

19. Pick a point in the drawing inside the title block at which to insert the table. Note that the table contains only the Catalog and Manufacturer information, as shown previously in Figure 20–39.

20. Save and close the drawing.

External References

Exam Objectives Covered in This Chapter

- 6.2.a Attach external reference and underlay files
- 6.2.b Clip and control the visibility of referenced and underlay files
- 6.2.c Understand layer naming conventions when you bind a referenced drawing
- 6.2.d Adjust the settings of an underlay file or image
- 6.2.e Create a hyperlink to another file
- 6.2.f Snap to objects in external reference and underlay files

21.1 Attaching External References

When you insert one drawing into another as a block, the graphics are merged and no link remains between the two files. External References enable you to combine files and retain the link, as shown in Figure 21–1. This serves two main purposes: it controls the file size because objects in the referenced drawing do not become part of the host drawing, and objects modified in the reference file are automatically updated in the host drawing because the files are linked.

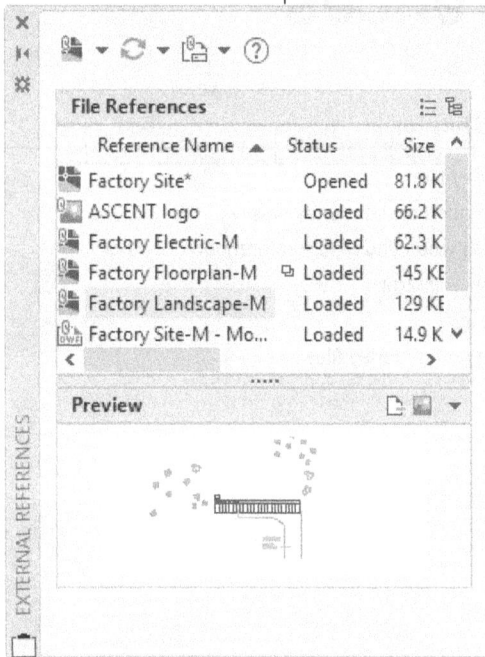

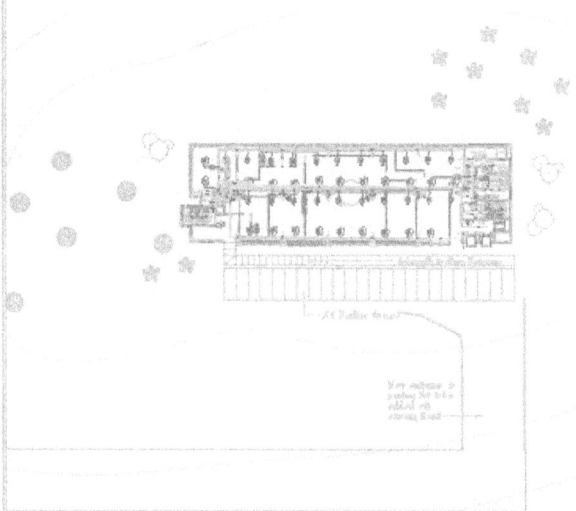

Figure 21–1

- Reference files enable members of a design team to share common source files and still have the most current information.

- External reference files can be managed through the External References palette.

- When you open a drawing that contains an external reference file that cannot be found, a References - Not Found Files warning box opens, as shown in Figure 21–2. Here you can directly open the External Files palette, which enables you to check for the missing file and resolve the issue, or ignore the unresolved reference file.

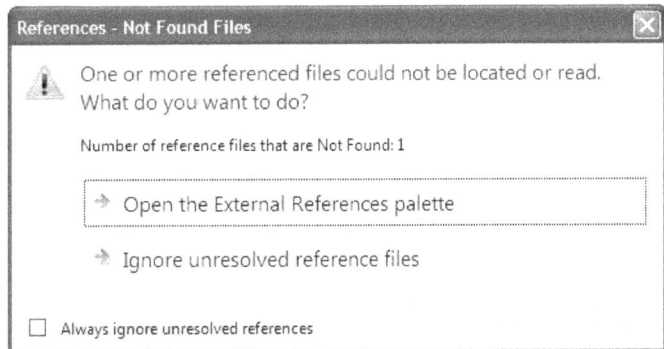

Figure 21–2

- When you open the External Reference palette, unresolved files display the ![icon] warning symbol file icon, and the ![icon] warning symbol displays beside the file with **Not Found** in the *Status* column.

Several file formats can be used as external references:

AutoCAD® drawing files	Also known as Xrefs, they are connections to other drawings that you can edit in-place or externally, while retaining the link. You can turn layers on and off in the host drawing.
Raster image files	Various types of graphic files, such as GIF, JPG, and PNG. They can be renderings or scanned images that can be used as a reference as you trace over existing drawings.
DWF underlays	Non-editable files that include vector information that can be displayed in the DWF viewer and incorporated as an underlay in any drawing file.
DGN underlays	Files that come from the MicroStation platform. You can also import and export to DGN files.
PDF Underlays	Attach PDF files as underlays one page at a time.

External References Palette

You can use the External References palette (shown in Figure 21–3) to attach, unload, reload, and detach reference files. You can open a reference file in an appropriate software to make modifications to the original file and can also change the location in which the original file is saved if it is moved.

- You can open the External References palette by clicking ⬒ in the *Insert* tab>Reference panel or by typing **Xref** in the Command Line.

- You can also open the External References palette by clicking ⬜ in the *View* tab>Palettes panel.

- If you have a reference file in the drawing, you can right-click on it and select **External References** to open the palette.

- When you have external references in a drawing, ⬒ (Manage Xrefs) displays near the right end of the Status Bar. Click it to open the External References palette.

⬒ *(Manage Xrefs) does not display in the Status Bar until the drawing contains at least one xref.*

The External References palette is similar to other palettes in that it can be either floating or docked and hidden.

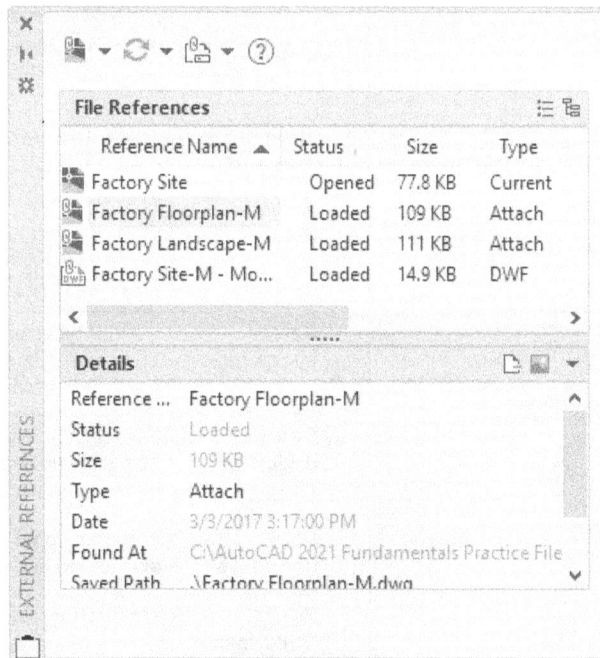

Figure 21–3

The External References palette is divided into two panes.

Top Pane

In the top pane, a list of file references displays as shown in Figure 21–4.

- By selecting the appropriate column heading, you can sort the files in the list according to name, status, size, date, and saved path.

List View *Tree View*

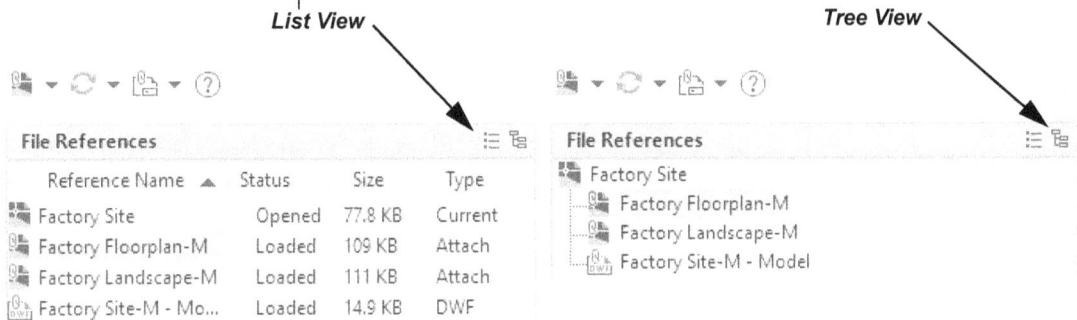

Figure 21–4

- ☰ (List View) displays all of the attached external references and detailed information including: size, date, and saved path.

- ⊞ (Tree View) switches to an hierarchical view that displays nested reference files (i.e., drawings that are attached to referenced drawings). Double-click on a reference filename in Tree View to display or hide the nested reference files below it.

Bottom Pane

In the bottom pane, a list of details about a selected file or a preview of the file displays as shown in Figure 21–5.

Details *Preview*

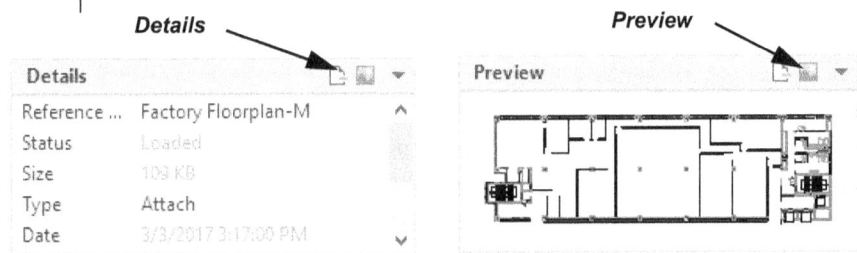

Figure 21–5

- ⊟ (Details) displays information about a selected file and enables you to modify the name of the reference. If the file is a drawing file, it enables you to modify the type of attachment.

- ▨ (Preview) displays a small image of the selected file.

How To: Attach a Reference File

You can also open the External References Palette by clicking the Reference panel arrow in the Insert tab.

1. In the *View* tab>Palettes panel, ▭ click (External References Palette).
2. In the External References palette, click on the arrow with

   ▨ ▾ (Attach DWG) to open the file list, as shown in Figure 21–6, and select a file format to attach.

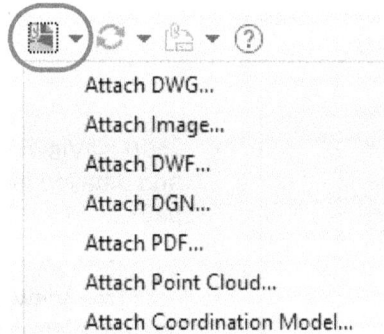

Attach DWG...
Attach Image...
Attach DWF...
Attach DGN...
Attach PDF...
Attach Point Cloud...
Attach Coordination Model...

Figure 21–6

3. In the Select Reference File dialog box, select the file that you want to attach and click **Open**.
4. In the Attach External Reference dialog box, set the options as required, as shown in Figure 21–7.

The options and title of the dialog box (External Reference, Image, or Attach DWF Underlay) vary depending on the type of file selected. Several options are used in every situation.

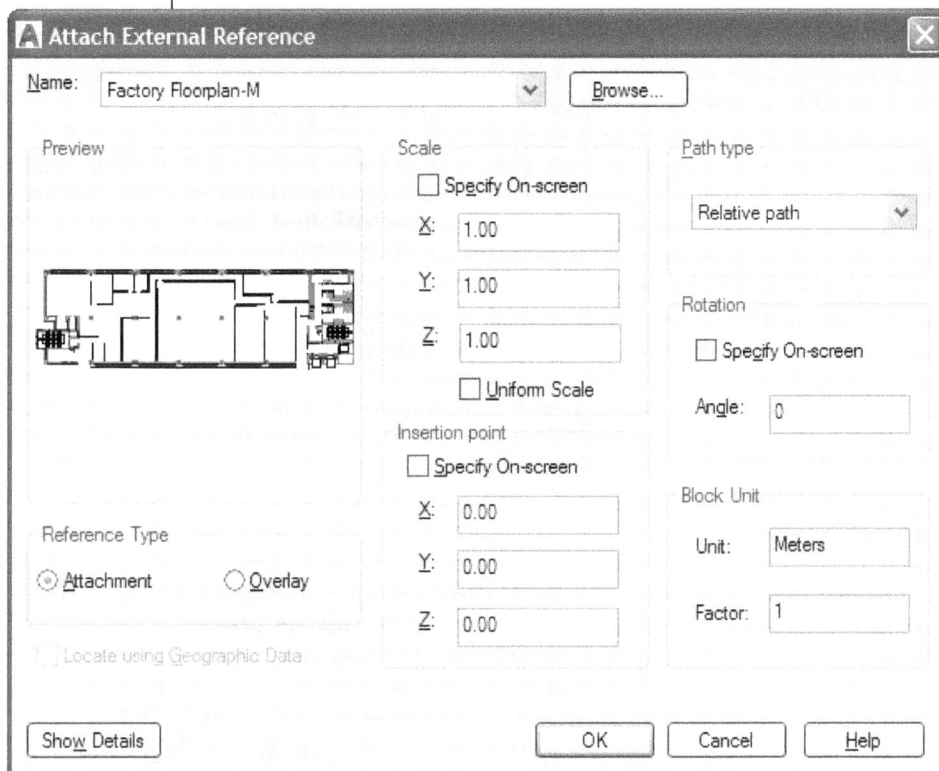

Figure 21–7

5. Click **OK**.
6. If you used the **Specify On-screen** option for *Insertion Point*, *Scale*, and *Rotation* in the dialog box, then specify them in the drawing window.

• You can use the Reference tools in the *Insert* tab> Reference panel to attach or modify various types of externally referenced files, as shown in Figure 21–8.

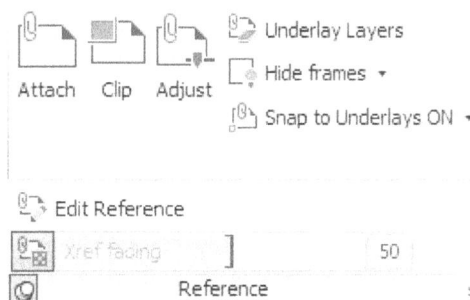

Figure 21–8

General Attachment Options

Name	Select a name from the list or click **Browse...** and select a different file to attach.
Path type	Controls how the AutoCAD software searches for the reference file to load it. By default, the Path type is set to **Relative Path**. It starts from the folder of the host drawing. **Full path** uses the entire path. With **No path**, the AutoCAD software searches in the current folder of the host drawing, and in the project paths, support paths, and *Start-in* folder. The default **Relative path** type can be changed using the REFPATHTYPE system variable.
Insertion Point, Scale, and Rotation Angle	These options are similar to the selections for block insertions. The values can be entered in the Attach External Reference dialog box or in the Command Line.

- When a drawing has an external reference that has been moved and cannot be found, the shortcut menu offers you options to find the file, as shown in Figure 21–9. The **Select New Path** option enables you to fix the missing path by selecting the file from the new location. Once the reference file's new location has been selected, the software prompts you to use the new path for the other missing references or leave the rest of the paths as is. The **Find and Replace** option opens the Find and Replace dialog box, which enables you to find the current path and replace all of its instances with the new path, all at once.

- The shortcut menu also provides you with the option of changing the path type by selecting **Change Path Type**. If the path type option of the selected reference file is grayed out and cannot be selected, it indicates that it is the current path type. Figure 21–10 shows an example of the referenced file using the **Relative Path** type, which is grayed out to indicate that the path type is currently used.

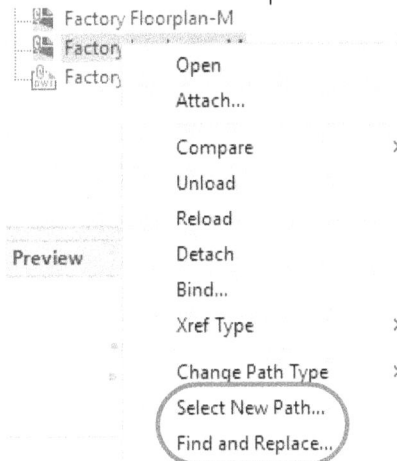

Figure 21–9

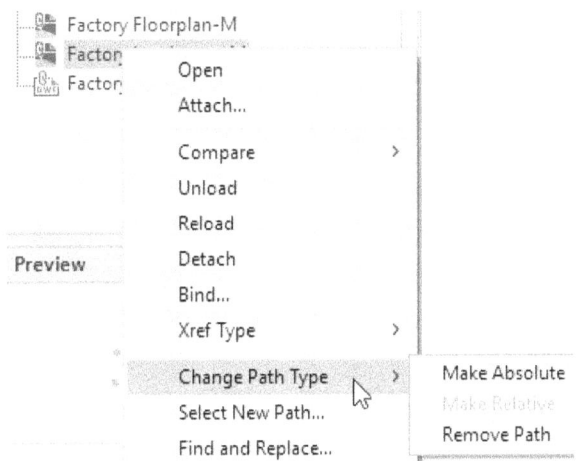

Figure 21–10

Xref Specific Attachment Options

Reference Type	Two types of references are available when one AutoCAD drawing is inserted into another: **Attachment** and **Overlay**.
Block Unit	The Insertion Scale units of the reference file and host drawings (expand Application Menu, expand Drawing Utilities, click 0.0 (Units)) control the automatic scale factor that displays in the *Block Units* area.

Image Specific Attachment Options

You can attach an image as many times as required in the same drawing file. If a raster image by that name already exists in the drawing (even if the extension type is different) a Substitute Image Name dialog box opens in which you can type a new name. This name displays in the External References palette.

DWF Specific Attachment Options

Select one or more sheets	If you are using a multi-sheet DWF file you can select any of the sheets to insert into the host drawing.

- If you set the *scale factor* to **Specify on Screen** then, at the *Specify Scale Factor or [Unit]:* prompt, you have the option to select the units of the existing drawing and have the software automatically scale the DWF file to those units. For example, if you are working in a drawing whose insertion scale units are set to **Meters** and the DWF file is in Architectural units, it automatically scales the DWF file by 0.0254. The default insertion scale unit is set to the current drawing units.

- You can insert multiple copies of a DWF file using the same sheet or different sheets in a multiple sheet file.

DGN Specific Attachment Options

MicroStation DGN file units are set up in *Master units* and *Sub units*. When you insert a DGN as an underlay, you need to specify the units that you want to convert. For example, if you attach a mechanical drawing that is created with *Master units* of millimeters and *Sub units* of thousandths of millimeters you would convert the *Master units*. However, if you are working with a file that has *Master units* of feet and *Sub units* of inches and you want to insert it into an AutoCAD Architectural unit file (which uses inches as its default units) you would convert the *Sub units*.

PDF Specific Attachment Options

Select one or more pages	If you are using a multi-sheet PDF file, you can select any sheet(s) to insert into the host drawing.

- All the supported objects in the PDF file are converted into 2D geometry, raster images, and TrueType text.

- Once you have attached the PDF file as an overlay, you can modify how the PDF objects are converted using ⬚ (Import as Objects). In the External References palette, select the attached PDF file. It opens the *PDF Underlay* contextual tab.

  In the PDF Import panel, click ⬚ (Import as Objects) and then click **Settings** in the Command Line. The PDF Import Settings dialog box opens and you can set the import options for the PDF file, as shown in Figure 21–11.

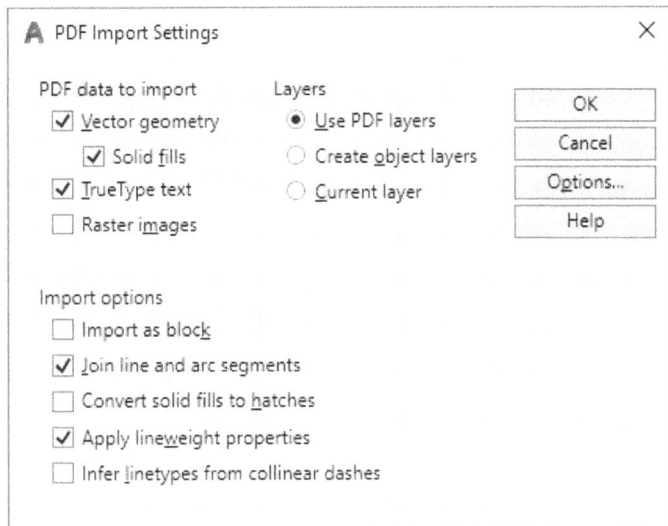

Figure 21–11

- In the *PDF data to import* area, select the types of data to import, as follows:

  - **Vector geometry:** Lines that touch become connected polylines.
  - **Solid Fills:** Joins 2D solids with coincident edges to create hatch objects.
  - **TrueType text:** Converts TrueType fonts to text objects. If the PDF file contains SHX fonts, these are converted to separate geometric representations, which can be converted to multiline text objects using the **Recognize SHX Text** tool in the *Insert* tab>Import panel (**PDFSHXTEXT** command).
  - **Raster images:** Extracts images to PNG files, which are then attached to the drawing as reference files.

- In the *Layers* area, set which layers the attached objects are added to.

- In the *Import options* area, set options that are used as geometry is imported:

  - **Import as block:** Creates a single block rather than separate lines.
  - **Join line and arc segments:** Creates polylines from connected objects.
  - **Convert solid fills to hatches:** Joins 2D solids with coincident edges to create hatch objects.
  - **Apply lineweight properties:** Assigns a lineweight to the imported geometry according to its thickness in the PDF.
  - **Infer linetypes from collinear dashes:** Creates a single polyline from collinear dash and dot segments.

21.2 Modifying External References

When you have attached external references to your drawing, you can modify the way they function in the drawing.

- You can **Open**, **Unload**, **Reload**, and **Detach** individual references, as shown in Figure 21–12.

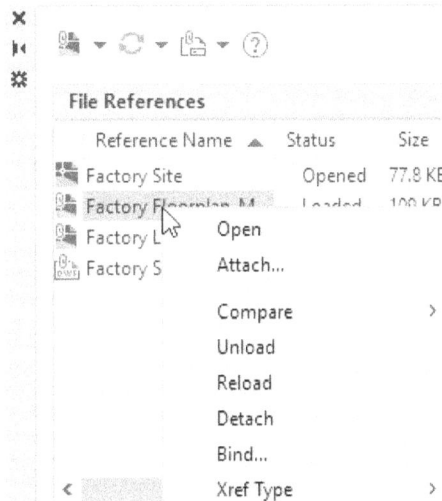

Figure 21–12

- All of the reference file formats can be clipped to display part of the reference. You can make changes to a selected reference in the Properties palette.

- You can use standard AutoCAD® commands, such as **Move**, **Rotate**, and **Scale** on references. Raster images can also be used to trim or extend to another object.

Opening Reference Files

You can modify a reference file in the software in which it was created and then reload it into the drawing. You can open a reference file from within the host drawing. Select the file in the External References palette, right-click, and select **Open**.

- A drawing reference file opens the drawing in the AutoCAD software.

- Image files open the image in the software with which the file format is associated.

- Autodesk® Viewer (https://viewer.autodesk.com/) is a free online file viewer that enables you to view DWF files.

- DWF files also open in the Autodesk® Design Review software, if it is installed. DGN files cannot be opened with the AutoCAD software.

- You can also open drawing reference files by picking the reference in the drawing window, right-clicking and selecting **Open Xref**, as shown in Figure 21–13.

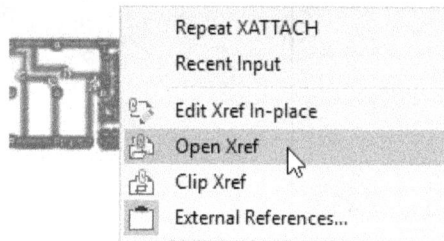

Figure 21–13

Detaching and Unloading Reference Files

There are two ways of removing a reference file from your drawing: **Unload** and **Detach** (as shown in Figure 21–14).

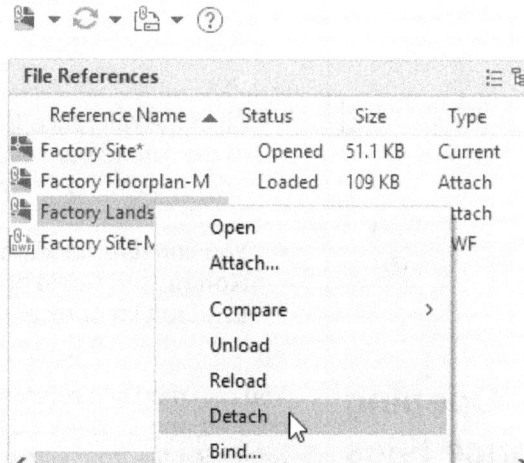

Figure 21–14

Detaching Files

Use **Detach** to permanently remove a reference file from your drawing.

- It severs the link between the current drawing and the external reference drawing.

- To get the reference back after detaching it, you need to re-attach it.

- If you have attached multiple copies of a DWF file, **Detach** removes all of them.

Unloading and Reloading Files

Use **Unload** to temporarily remove a reference file.

- When you unload a reference file, the AutoCAD software hides the reference geometry. However, it keeps the file in the External References palette list and remembers its insertion point, scale, and other attachment information.

- Unloading references that are not currently required causes a drawing to open and perform faster.

- To display an unloaded reference again, it must be reloaded using the **Reload** option.

- You can use the **Open** option in the shortcut menu to quickly open the unloaded reference file.

- Reloading loads the most recently saved version of the reference.

- All of the references reload automatically when you open the host drawing.

- Renaming the unloaded reference file in the External Reference palette does not automatically reload the renamed file. You have to explicitly reload it, as it remains unloaded till then.

- **Refresh** synchronizes information stored in memory when used with the Autodesk® Vault software.

- **Reload All References** (shown in Figure 21–15) updates all of the references in a drawing so that you are using the most up-to-date versions that have been saved.

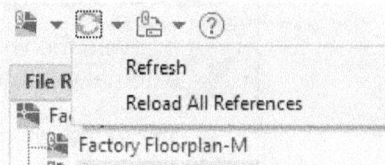

Figure 21–15

Comparing Xrefs

Once you have made changes to an Xref, you can now compare the original and the modified Xref. By comparing the two xrefs, you can now identify the modifications that were made to the drawing file that is attached as an external reference in the current drawing. The differences in the changed xref are highlighted by a revision cloud. The comparison can be started by selecting Compare in right-click menu as shown in Figure 21–16.

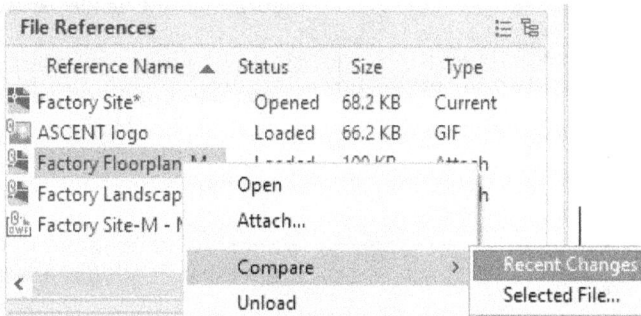

Figure 21–16

- When a drawing which is referenced in a drawing is changed, a alert balloon is displayed in the Status Bar, as shown in Figure 21–17. Select the link in the balloon to reload the reference and also to compare the changes. This message also displays when someone else changes a reference while you have the host file open.

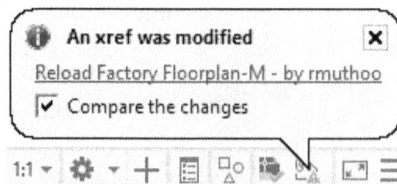

Figure 21–17

- When you start the **Xref Compare** command, the drawing opens in a Compare window which is indicated by drawing being enclosed in a blue border and the Xref Compare toolbar displayed along the top of the Drawing Window, as shown in Figure 21–18. The changes are highlighted in a revision cloud as shown in Figure 21–18.

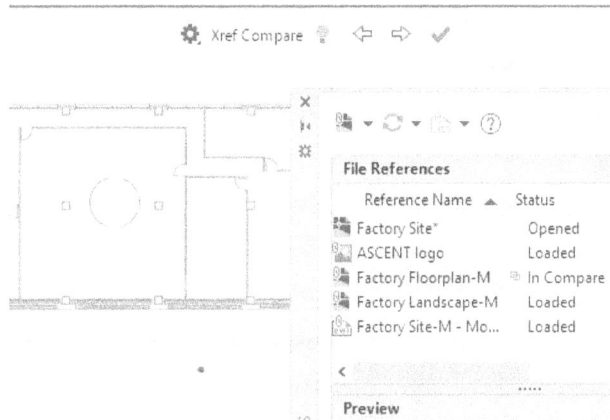

Figure 21–18

- You can expand the Compare toolbar to toggle the various display options, change the color and shape of the revision clouds, and zoom to the previous and next comparison in the drawing, as shown in Figure 21–19. Use ✓ to end the comparison.

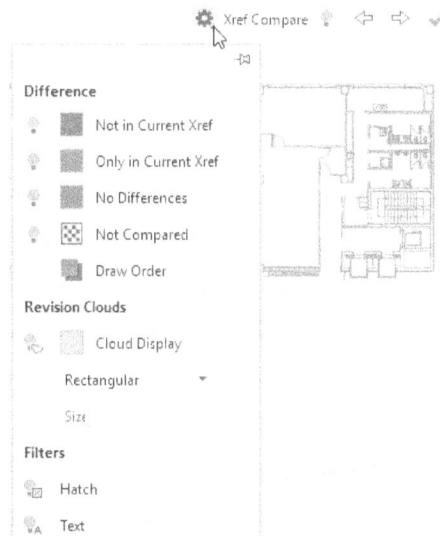

Figure 21–19

Clipping Reference Files

When you attach an external reference to your drawing, the entire reference file displays. However, you might not want the entire file to display, even in Model Space. You can control which part of the referenced file is visible by clipping it, as shown in Figure 21–20.

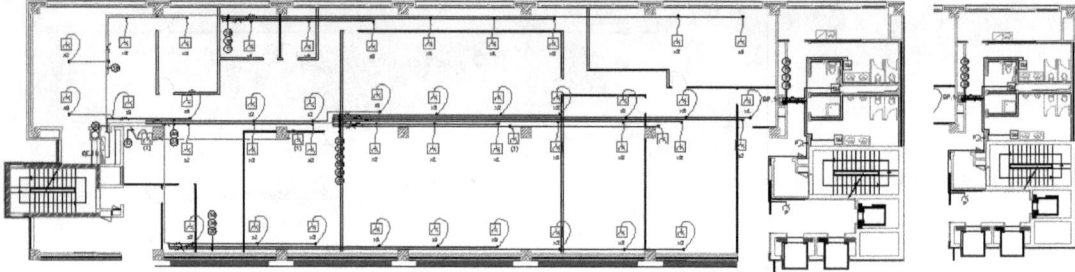

Figure 21–20

How To: Clip a Reference File

1. In the drawing, select the reference that you want to clip, right-click and select the appropriate **Clip** command for the type of reference selected. (Drawings: **Clip Xref**; Images: **Image>Clip**; DWF files: **DWF Clip**; DGN files: **DGN Clip**.)
2. Enter a **Clipping** option. Press <Enter> to accept the default **New boundary** option.
3. Select the **Rectangular** or **Polygonal** boundary option and draw a boundary.
4. Specify the points or existing polyline. The reference is clipped so the reference information outside the boundary is invisible.

If you have selected a drawing file, you have the additional option of selecting an existing polyline as the boundary.

- You can only clip one image (.DWF or .DGN file) at a time, but you can clip multiple drawing files.

- Drawing reference files have an additional clip option: **Invert Clip**. Instead of masking everything outside the boundary it covers everything within the boundary. This can be very useful if you are working on a renovation project in which you are moving interior walls but not changing other parts of the building.

Other Clip Options

On/Off	Turns the clip boundary on or off without removing it from the reference. If the boundary is off the entire reference displays.
Clipdepth	Controls the front and back clipping planes in the Z-direction of the clip. Drawing reference files only.

Delete	Removes the clipping boundary from the reference files. You cannot use the **Erase** command to remove the clipping boundary.
Generate Polyline	Creates a polyline at the location of an existing clip boundary. This is a separate entity from the boundary. Drawing reference files only.

- If you run the command on a file that already has a boundary, the AutoCAD software prompts you to delete the current boundary first.

- To modify the clip boundary, start the associated **Clip** command. You can toggle the **Clip Boundary** on or off or delete it.

Clip Frames

The lines around clipped references are called *Clip Frames*. They can be toggled on or off for all of the references in a drawing using system variables that are related to each reference type: **xclipframe** for drawing references, **imageframe**, **dwfframe**, **pdfframe**, and **dgnframe**, as shown in Figure 21–21.

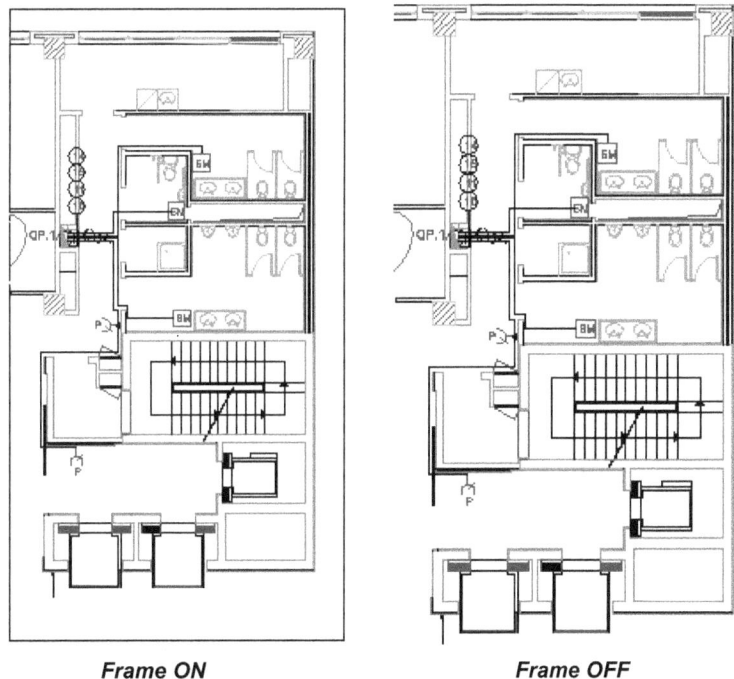

Frame ON   *Frame OFF*

Figure 21–21

- **Frame Boundaries** have three options. When set to **0**, the boundary is invisible. When set to **1**, the boundary is visible. When set to **2**, the boundary is visible but does not plot.

- When the boundary is visible, you can select the external reference by selecting the boundary or any visible part of the reference file.

Modifying References

When you select the border of a reference file, a contextual tab displays according to the type of reference file that was selected.

- A DWF underlay has panels for Adjust, Clipping, Options, and DWF Layers, as shown in Figure 21–22. PDF and DGN underlays are the same.

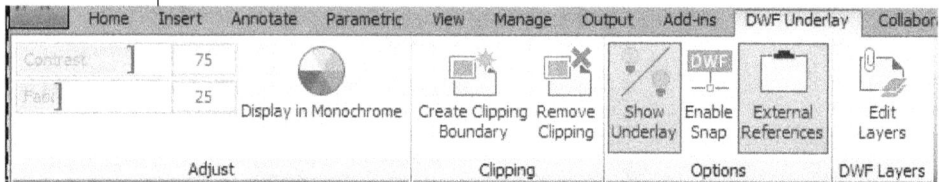

Figure 21–22

- Modification options for drawing reference files include editing the reference, clipping, and access to the External References palette, as shown in Figure 21–23.

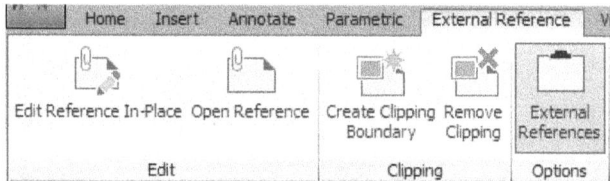

Figure 21–23

- Image panels include Adjust and Clipping, and an additional **Transparency** option, as shown in Figure 21–24.

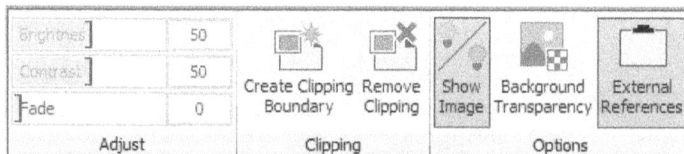

Figure 21–24

- Underlays and image references can only be selected when the frame surrounding them is on. You can change the state of the frames in the *Insert* tab>Reference panel, as shown in Figure 21–25.

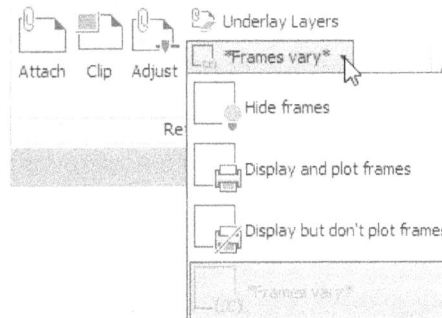

Figure 21–25

Reference File Properties

DWF, DGN, and Image references have several properties that can be modified, including how and what they display in the drawing.

These options can be modified in the Properties palette.

Miscellaneous Options

In the *Misc* area in the Properties palette, you can toggle off DWF or DGN underlays or Images without unloading the files. Set *Show image* to **No**, as shown in Figure 21–26.

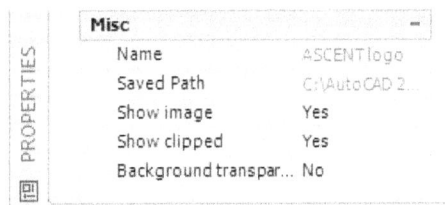

Figure 21–26

- The **Show clipped** option changes the status of displaying whether the object is clipped or not clipped. This is different than displaying the clipping frame.

- Images have the additional **Background Transparency** option. This permits the background of the image to become transparent, so that it matches the general background. However, not all of the file formats enable transparency. You can also access this option in the ribbon and in the shortcut menu under **Image**.

Adjusting Underlays and Images

DWF and DGN underlays and image reference properties can be adjusted.

- With a reference file selected, in the Properties palette, in the *Underlay Adjust* or *Image Adjust* areas, you can specify the amount of *Contrast* and *Fade*, as shown in Figure 21–27. DWF and DGN files can be set to **Monochrome** and Image files have an additional **Brightness** adjustment.

Underlay Adjust	
Contrast	75
Fade	25
Monochrome	No
Adjust colors for bac..	Yes

Figure 21–27

- DWF underlays have an option to adjust the colors for the background.

- Click ⬚ (Adjust) in the *Insert* tab>Reference panel to adjust the *Fade*, *Contrast*, or *Monochrome* settings for underlay and image files.

- Image references can also be adjusted in the *Image* contextual tab as shown in Figure 21–28. A preview of the changes displays in the drawing window as the modifications are made. The contextual tab is opened by selecting the underlay or image.

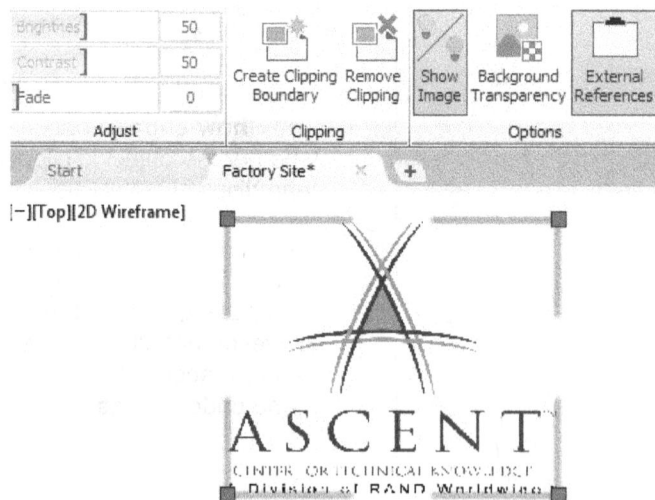

Figure 21–28

- The quality of an image can be set to **High** or **Draft** by typing **imagequality** at the Command Line.

Hint: Creating an Image File

In the AutoCAD software, there are several ways of creating a raster file, which can then be used as an image:

- You can copy the contents of the current viewport using **saveimg** at the Command Line. The image can be saved in the .BMP, .PCX, .TGA, .TIF, .JPEG, or .PNG file formats.

- You can render the display to a file (usually done with 3D objects). Rendering can create several different raster formats.

DWF Specific Adjustments

DWF reference files have two additional options because they are created from drawing files: toggling layers on and off and snapping to objects in the DWF underlay.

- Layer visibility can be controlled in DWF underlays (as shown in Figure 21–29), if the DWF file was created with the layers toggled on. When you have selected a DWF underlay, right-click and select **DWF Layers**. Select the layers you want to toggle on or off and click **OK**.

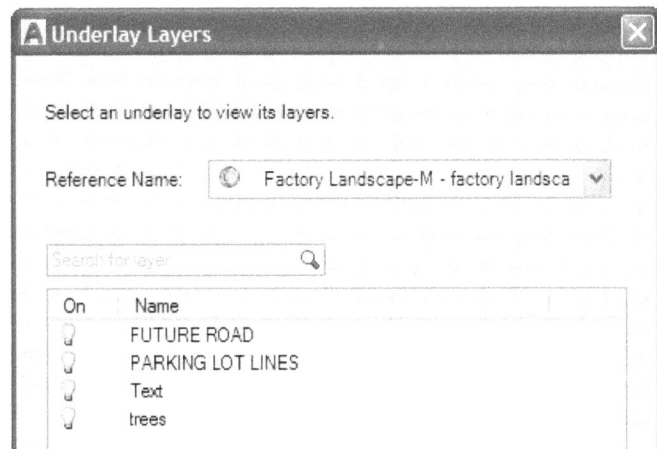

Figure 21–29

- To adjust another reference file's layers, select it in the Reference Name drop-down list.

- If a reference file does not contain layers, this is indicated in the Underlay Layers dialog box. By default, layers are not saved in the **DWF6ePlot.pc3** file supplied with the software.

• You can snap to objects in a DWF underlay. If you do not want object snaps to work with DWF files, select the DWF underlay, right-click and clear **DWF Object Snap**, as shown in Figure 21–30. This impacts all of the DWF underlays in a drawing.

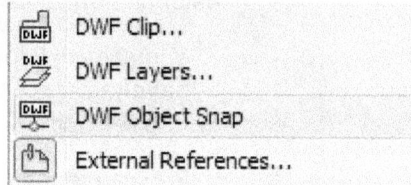

Figure 21–30

21.3 Xref Specific Information

The reference file tools works slightly differently with drawing references (also known as Xrefs). Because drawing reference files contain the same components as the host files, you can manipulate them using methods that cannot be applied to raster images, .DWF, and .DGN files. You can set drawing reference files to be attachments or overlays and can modify Xref layer states in the host drawing without impacting the original file. You can also import (bind) layers and block components of the drawing reference file into your drawing.

Attachments vs. Overlays

You can specify whether a drawing reference file should be an attachment or an overlay when it is originally referenced. Attachments and overlays work in the same way in the host file. You only notice the difference if you reference that host file in another file, as shown in Figure 21–31.

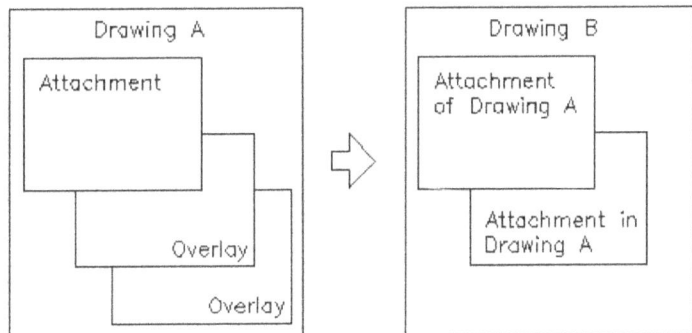

Figure 21–31

Attachment	When a file is referenced as an attachment, it displays with the host file if the host file itself is then referenced in another drawing. Using attachments enables a file to travel along the path with its host. A typical use for this option would be if there were a part referenced inside a subassembly, which is then referenced into a larger assembly.
Overlay	When a file is referenced as an overlay, it does not display in the host file if the host file itself is referenced in another drawing. Using overlays helps to avoid problems of circular references. (Circular references occur when a file references itself, usually indirectly. For example, drawing A references drawing B, which references drawing C, which references drawing A.)

- To change a drawing reference file from an attachment to an overlay, select the reference in the External References palette and modify it in the **Details** pane, as shown in Figure 21–32.

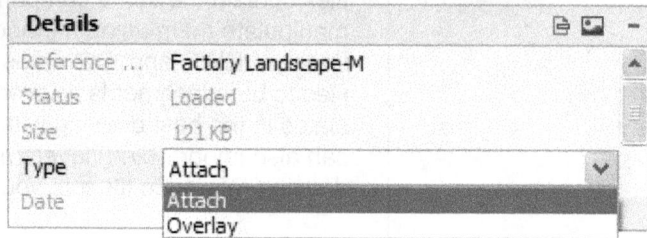

Figure 21–32

- You can also right-click on a filename(s) in the External References palette, expand Xref Type, and select **Overlay**.

Binding Drawing Reference Files

The **Bind** option in a drawing reference file copies all of the referenced drawing's data into the current drawing and then detaches the reference. The referenced drawing becomes an inserted block.

How To: Bind a Drawing Reference File

1. Open the External References palette.
2. Right-click on the drawing reference file that you want to bind in the list and select **Bind**.
3. In the *Bind Type* area, select **Bind** or **Insert** (as shown in Figure 21–33) and click **OK**.

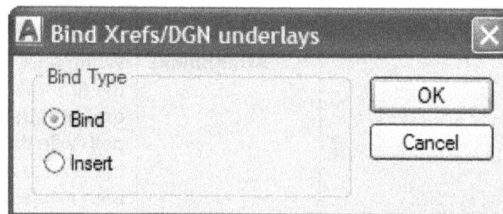

Figure 21–33

When a drawing reference file is bound, it brings all of its layers, blocks, and other named objects into the host drawing. The **Bind Type** controls how these named objects are named in the host drawing.

- When you use the *Bind Type* **Bind**, the object names are prefixed with the name of the reference file (filename0layername). For example, if the layer **Ref¦Floor** (from the drawing **Ref.dwg**) was bound to the current drawing, its name would become **Ref0Floor**. This can result in long names, but keeps the layers that were originally in the drawing reference file separate from the layers that were originally in the host file.

- When a drawing reference file is bound as an **Insert**, the block and layer names are added to the current file without change. For example, the Xref layer **Ref¦Floor** would become **Floor**. If the current file contains a block or layer with the same name, the drawing reference file object is updated to match the definition already in the current drawing.

- Binding a drawing reference file as an **Insert** is equivalent to detaching the reference file and inserting it as a block.

Binding Drawing Reference File Components

Instead of binding the entire drawing reference file, you can bind one or more blocks, layers, linetypes, text styles, and dimension styles. Binding any of these named objects adds their definition to the host drawing so that you can use them in the drawing.

- The **Xbind** command, accessed in the Command Line, enables you to bind specific named objects from a drawing reference file (such as layers or blocks).

- **Xbind** opens the Xbind dialog box (shown in Figure 21–34), in which you can select the drawing reference file from which to bind, the type of object (layer, block, etc.), and the specific named object to bind. Click the **+** sign to display the listings under each category. Select the object and click **Add** to add it for binding.

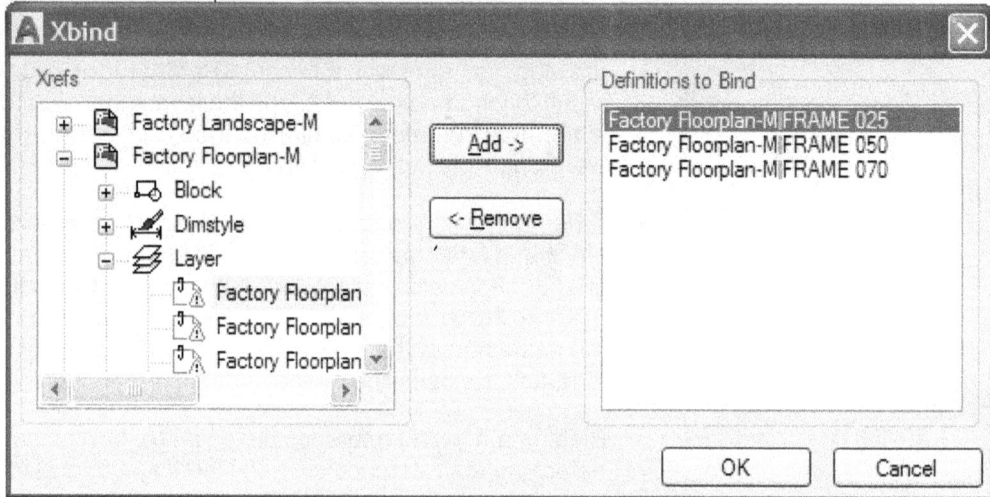

Figure 21–34

- When named objects are bound with **Xbind**, the "¦" in the name is replaced with "0". For example, the block **Office3¦Lamp** becomes **Office3$0$Lamp**. There is no option, such as **Insert**, to add the name without a change. However, you can rename the resulting objects using **Rename**.

- You can use DesignCenter to copy these components into your current drawing without using the long names.

Demand Loading

Demand Loading controls how much of a drawing reference file is loaded. With **Demand Loading** enabled, only the visible parts of the drawing reference file (that are not clipped or on layers that are off or frozen) are loaded. Since it does not have to load the entire drawing reference file, the AutoCAD software responds more quickly.

- **Demand Loading** can be set in the Options dialog box, in the *Open and Save* tab, by selecting the **Demand load Xrefs** options, as shown in Figure 21–35.

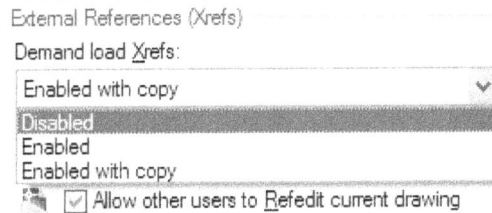

External References (Xrefs)

Demand load Xrefs:

Enabled with copy

Disabled
Enabled
Enabled with copy

☑ Allow other users to Refedit current drawing

Figure 21–35

- When **Demand Loading** is enabled, others cannot edit the file that is being referenced. To enable others to use the file that is being referenced and take advantage of the improved performance, set *Demand Loading* to **Enabled with copy**. A copy of the file is used in place of the drawing reference file, so that others can use the file.

Practice 21a | Attaching External References

Practice Objectives

- Attach and modify external references and overlay drawing references.
- Adjust the layers in a referenced file.
- Bind a reference to a file.

In this practice, you will attach and modify external references using the External References palette. You will also attach and overlay drawing references and note how they function in another file. You will then adjust layers in a referenced file and bind a reference to a file, as shown in Figure 21–36.

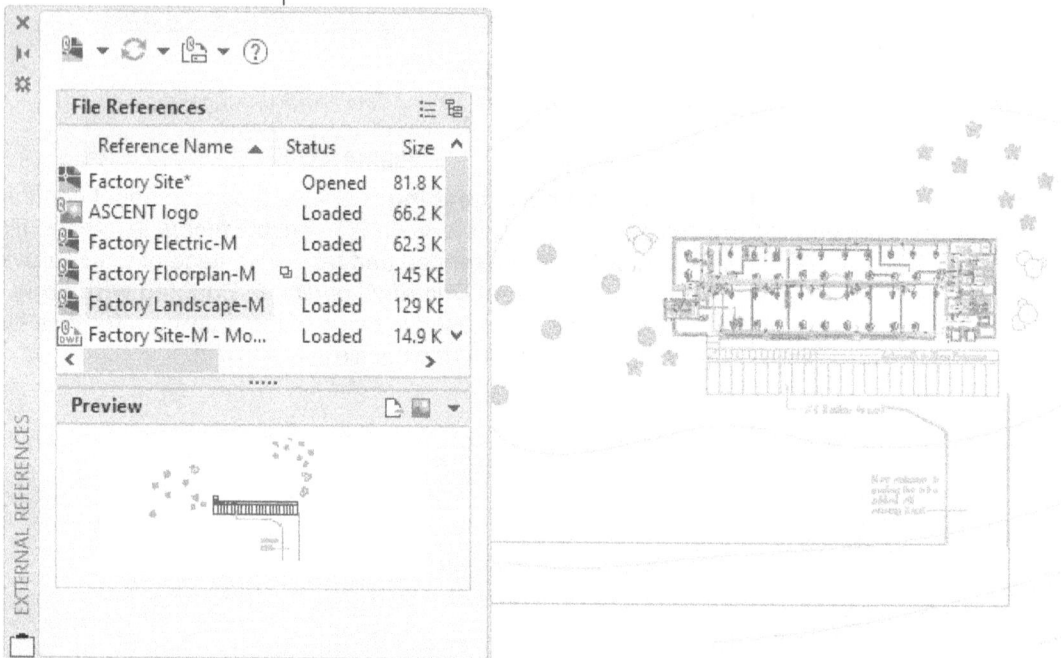

Figure 21–36

Task 1 - Attach external references.

In this task, you will explore the features of the External References palette. You will attach a Reference File DWG, Raster Image, and DWF Underlay.

1. Start a new drawing based on **Civil-Meters.dwt**, which is located in your practice files folder and save the drawing as **Factory Site.dwg**.

2. In the *View* tab>Palettes panel, click ⬚ (External References Palette) to open the External References palette.

3. Near the top of the External References palette, click on the arrow with ▦ ▼ (Attach DWG) and select **Attach DWF...**.

4. In the Select Reference File dialog box, open **Factory Site-M.dwf** from your practice files folder.

5. In the Attach DWF Underlay dialog box, for *Insertion point*, clear Specify on-screen and verify X,Y,Z values are set as **0,0,0**. Select **Specify on-screen** for the *Scale*. Click **OK** to continue.

6. Right-click and select **Unit**. Verify that **Meter** is selected and press <Enter> to accept the default selection.

7. Press <Enter> to finish placing the DWF underlay.

8. Using the above steps, and using **Attach DWG**, attach **Factory Floorplan-M.dwg** from your practice files folder at **0,0,0** *Insertion point* with the default scale and rotation. Verify that the *Reference Type* is set to **Attachment**.

9. **Zoom Extents** to display **Factory Site-M.dwf** and **Factory Floorplan-M.dwg**.

10. Attach **Factory Landscape-M.dwg** from your practice files folder at any location (*Insertion point*: **Specify On-screen**) towards left side of the drawing (you will move it later).

11. Close the External References palette.

12. In the Status Bar, click ▦ (Manage Xrefs) to open the External References palette again.

13. Select **Factory Landscape-M.dwg**. In the Details pane, click ▦ (Preview) to display an image of the landscape reference file in the Palette.

14. Switch to the **ISO A0** layout. Activate the viewport by double-clicking inside it and **Zoom Extents**.

15. Activate the Paper Space (double-click outside the viewport).

16. In the External References palette, using **Attach Image**, attach **ASCENT logo.gif** from your practice files folder at a scale of **50**. Place it near the left of the title block.

17. Save the file.

Task 2 - Modify external references.

In this task, you will move a reference file to a new location, clip a DWF file, open a reference file and make a change to that drawing, close and reload it, and detach and unload it. The completed drawing is shown in Figure 21–37.

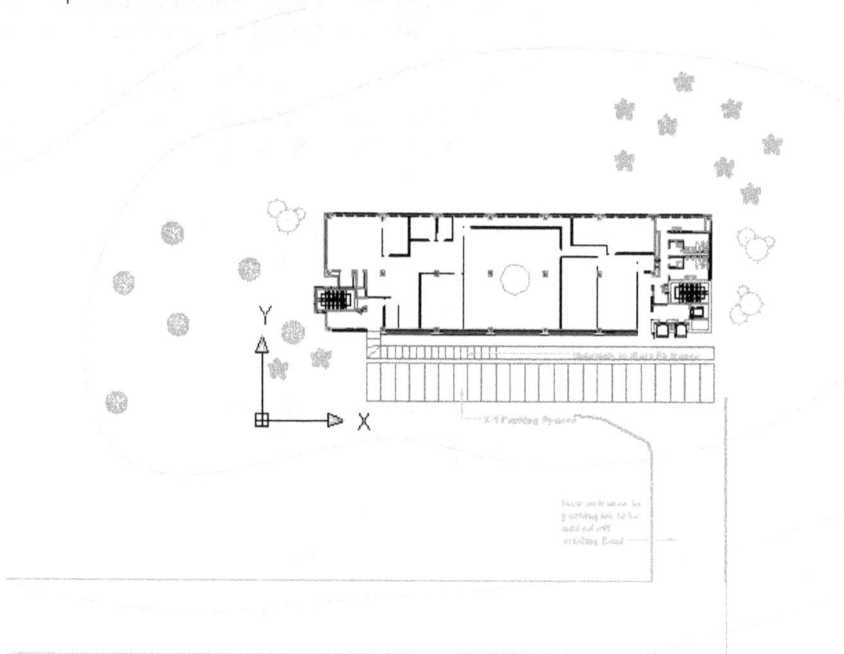

Figure 21–37

You can also use
Enable Snap*, found in the DWF Underlay contextual tab.*

1. Switch to the *Model* tab. In the drawing window, select **Factory Site-M.dwf** (the outer rectangle). Right-click and verify that **DWF Object Snap** is enabled (higlighted), as shown in Figure 21–38. Press <ESC> to exit selection.

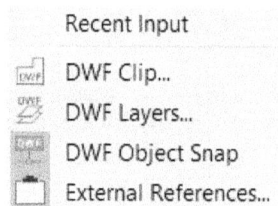

Figure 21–38

2. Move **Factory Landscape-M.dwg** (file with trees which was placed along the left side of the drawing) so that the existing road in the DWF file is at the end of the entrance to the parking lot, as shown in Figure 21–39.

Hint: In the landscape drawing, use the bottom left endpoint of the vertical portion of the road as your base point and move it to the right endpoint of the top horizontal line of the road in the site dwf.

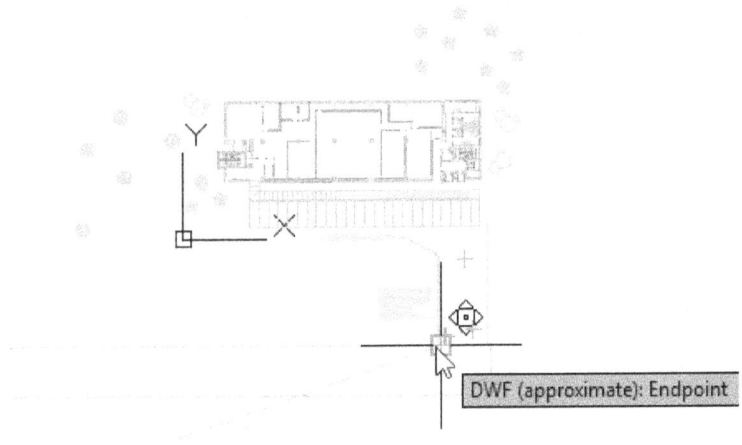

DWF (approximate): Endpoint

Figure 21–39

3. Select **Factory Site-M.dwf** (outer rectangle), right-click and select **DWF Clip...**. Press <Enter> to accept the **New boundary** option and create a new rectangular boundary close to the landscape elements, building, and road, similar to the area shown in Figure 21–37.

4. In the *Insert* tab>Reference panel, expand **Frames vary** flyout, and select **Hide frames** to hide the boundary frame.

*You can also type **dwfframe** and set the system variable to **0.***

5. Check the Layer Control, and note that the layers associated with **Factory Floorplan-M.dwg** are listed but they are grayed out.

6. In the External References palette, right-click on **Factory Floorplan-M.dwg** and select **Detach**. The building is removed from the drawing window and the file is removed from the External References palette.

7. Save the drawing.

8. Attach **Factory Floorplan-M.dwg** from your practice files folder to your file at an *Insertion point* of **0,0,0** and a *Rotation* of **0**.

9. In the External References palette, unload **Factory Floorplan-M.dwg** (right-click and select **Unload**). Note that the building is removed from the drawing window but the file is still listed in the palette with a red arrow displayed along with it, as shown in Figure 21–40.

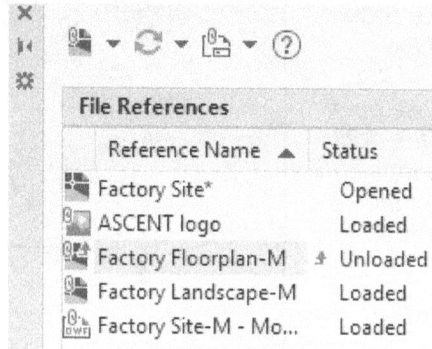

Figure 21–40

10. Reload **Factory Floorplan-M.dwg**. (Right-click and select **Reload**).

11. In the External References palette, select **Factory Floorplan-M.dwg**. Right-click and select **Open**.

12. Set the layer **Equipment** to be current and draw a circle with a *radius* of **2** near the middle of the floorplan.

13. Save and close **Factory Floorplan-M.dwg**.

14. In **Factory Site.dwg**, note that the new circle is not displayed. In the External References palette, reload **Factory Floorplan-M.dwg**.

15. Note that the new circle displays.

16. In the External References palette, right-click on **Factory Floorplan-M.dwg** and select **Compare>Recent Changes**. Note that the drawing is in the Compare mode, enclosed in a blue border and the Xref Compare toolbar displayed along the top of the Drawing Window, as shown in Figure 21–41. Also note that the circle that you added to **Factory Floorplan-M.dwg** is surrounded by a yellow rectangular revision cloud, as shown in Figure 21–41.

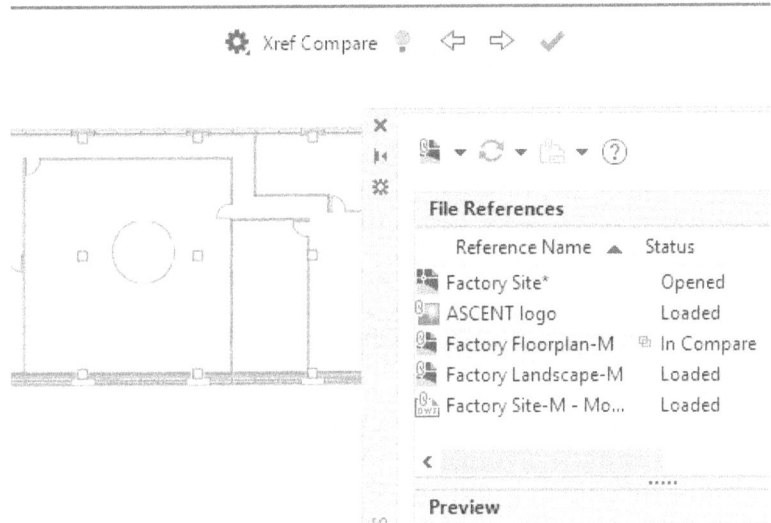

Figure 21–41

17. Click ✔ in the Compare toolbar to end the comparison.

18. Save and close the drawing.

Task 3 - Attach and overlay drawing references in another file.

In this task, you will attach and overlay drawing references and note how they function in another file. You will then adjust layers in a referenced file and finally bind a reference to a file. The completed drawing is shown in Figure 21–42.

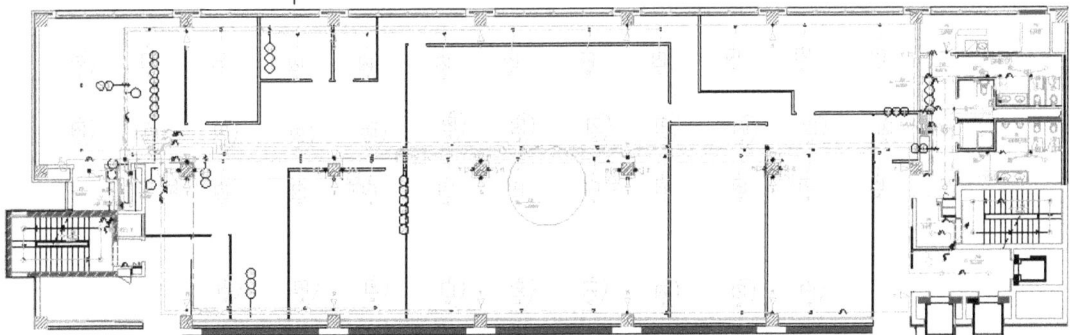

Figure 21–42

1. Open **Factory Floorplan-M.dwg** from your practice files folder.

2. Set layer **0** to be current and attach **Factory Electric-M.dwg** from your practice files folder to the current drawing at **0,0,0** as an attachment. Accept the defaults for the *Scale, Rotation,* and other options. Note that there might be some **Unreconciled New Layers**.

3. Attach **Factory Lighting-M.dwg** from your practice files folder to the current drawing at **0,0,0**. Accept the defaults for the other options.

You can also change it in the Details pane.

4. In the External References palette, right-click on **Factory Lighting-M.dwg**, expand **Xref Type**, and select **Overlay**. Close the palette. The overlay file remains visible in the drawing.

5. Save and close the drawing.

6. Open **Factory Site.dwg** if it is not already open. Note that the attached reference **Factory Electric-M.dwg** displays but the overlaid lighting reference is not displayed. Note that the Xref comparison bubble is also displayed.

7. Click on the link to compare and note that the **Factory Electric-M.dwg** has a revision cloud around it. Click ✔ in the Compare toolbar to end the comparison.

8. Save and close the drawing.

Task 4 - Work with drawing reference file layers.

---

1. Open **Factory Floorplan-M.dwg** from your practice files folder.

2. Expand the Layer Control and note the layers that begin with **Factory Electric-M** and **Factory Lighting-M** are all gray. All of these layers belong to the drawing reference files.

3. Open the Layer Properties Manager.

4. In the left pane, note that **Xref** is added, which is an xref filter group that is added when an xref is attached.

5. Expand the **Xref** group and select **Factory Electric-M**. All of the layers in the drawing reference file display in the right pane.

6. In the right pane, right-click and select **Select All**.

7. Select one of the color blocks and change the *color* to **light gray**. The selected layers display in that color in the current drawing.

8. In the left hand pane, note that the **Xref Overrides** filter is added and that the listed layers have a blue background with their icons changed to ⬍. Hover the cursor over the icon to display the xref override details, as shown in Figure 21–43.

Filters	«	S..	Name	▲ O.	Fre...	Lo...	Color	Linetype
⊟ All			Factory Electric-M|B...	🔆	☀	🔓	☐ 9	Continuous
└ All non-Xref Layers			Factory Electric-M|C...	🔆	☀	🔓	☐ 9	Continuous
└ All Used Layers			Factory Electric-M|...	🔆	☀	🔓	☐ 9	Continuous
└ Unreconciled New			Factory Electric-M|...	🔆	☀	🔓	☐ 9	Continuous
⊟ Xref			Factory Electric-M|...	🔆	☀	🔓	☐ 9	Continuous
└ Factory Electric			Factory Electric-M|E...	🔆	☀	🔓	☐ 9	Continuous
└ Factory Lightin						🔓	☐ 9	Continuous
└ Xref Overrides			Layer: Factory Electric-M|Doors			🔓	☐ 9	Continuous
			Xref Color override: 9			🔓	☐ 9	Continuous
			Factory Electric-M|...	🔆		🔓	☐ 9	Continuous

Figure 21–43

9. Open **Factory Electric-M.dwg**In your practice files folder and verify that the layers retain their original colors. Close the file.

10. In the **Factory Floorplan-M.dwg**, note that the layers from the **Factory Electric-M** referenced drawing are still gray.

11. In the left pane, right-click on **Xref Overrides**. Expand **Reset Xref Layer Properties** and select **All Properties**. Note that all of the layers retain their original color and that the **Xref Override** filter option is no longer displayed.

Task 5 - Bind drawing reference files.

1. Continue working in **Factory Floorplan-M.dwg**.

2. In the External References palette, right-click on **Factory Lighting-M.dwg** and select **Bind...** to bind it to the host file. In the dialog box, ensure that **Bind** is selected and click **OK**.

3. In the Layer Properties Manager, note that all of the Factory Lighting-M layers contain **0** and are no longer gray, as shown in Figure 21–44. Note that all of the Factory Electric-M layers are still displayed in light gray, indicating that they are xref layers.

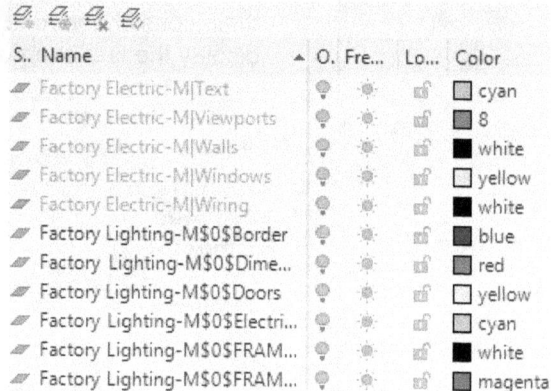

S..	Name		O.	Fre...	Lo...	Color	
	Factory Electric-M|Text		☀	☀	🔓	⬜	cyan
	Factory Electric-M|Viewports		☀	☀	🔓	⬛	8
	Factory Electric-M|Walls		☀	☀	🔓	⬛	white
	Factory Electric-M|Windows		☀	☀	🔓	⬜	yellow
	Factory Electric-M|Wiring		☀	☀	🔓	⬛	white
	Factory Lighting-M0Border		☀	☀	🔓	⬛	blue
	Factory Lighting-M0Dime...		☀	☀	🔓	⬛	red
	Factory Lighting-M0Doors		☀	☀	🔓	⬜	yellow
	Factory Lighting-M0Electri...		☀	☀	🔓	⬜	cyan
	Factory Lighting-M0FRAM...		☀	☀	🔓	⬛	white
	Factory Lighting-M0FRAM...		☀	☀	🔓	⬛	magenta

Figure 21–44

4. Undo the **Bind** process.

5. **Bind** the same file (**Factory Lighting-M.dwg**) again, but this time as an **Insert**.

6. Look at the layers. They are now integrated into the main layer names.

7. Save and close the drawing.

8. Open **Factory Site.dwg**. In the External Reference palette, note that the **Factory Lighting-M.dwg** is no longer displayed, as it is now a part of the **Factory Site** drawing file and not an overlay in the referenced file.

9. Save and close the drawing.

21.4 Hyperlinks

A hyperlink is a pointer to a file that opens when the link is activated. The file can be on the Internet or a local drive.

You can add hyperlinks to specific objects in a drawing, as shown in Figure 21–45. They can be used for easy access to any information you want to associate with the drawing, such as technical information in a document file, an inventory in a spreadsheet, a project proposal, or other AutoCAD drawings. You can also have a hyperlink point to a named view or layout in a drawing, or send a message to an email address.

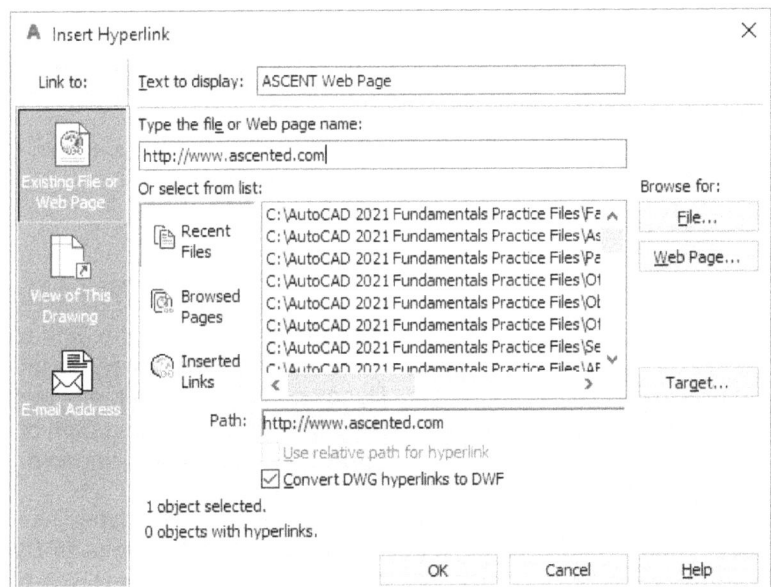

Figure 21–45

How To: Insert a Hyperlink

1. In the *Insert* tab>Data panel, click (Hyperlink).
2. Select the object(s) to which you want to attach the link and press <Enter>. The Insert Hyperlink dialog box opens.
3. In the *Link to:* area on the left side of the dialog box, select the type of link you want to use:
    - To a file or web address,
    - To a named view in the drawing, or
    - To an email address (send a message to that address).

4. In the *Text to display:* area, type the text you want to display in the drawing as the hyperlink's tag or description.
5. Depending on the type of link that you selected in Step 3, specify one of the following:
   - A URL for a web address or a filename with a path,
   - A named view or layout in the drawing, or
   - An email address.
6. Click **OK** to end the command.

- When linking to an existing file or Web page, **Target** enables you to specify a location in the file, as shown in Figure 21–46. For example, this could be a named view or layout in an AutoCAD drawing.

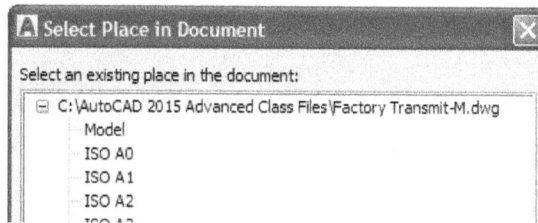

Figure 21–46

- When linking to a file, the path can be relative or absolute. If **Use Relative Path for Hyperlink** is selected, only the filename is stored with the hyperlink. The AutoCAD software uses the current drawing path or the path stored in the **hyperlinkbase** system variable.

- When linking to a file, hyperlinks can be converted. With **Convert DWG hyperlinks to DWF** selected, and when publishing to a DWF, the DWG hyperlink is converted to a DWF hyperlink.

- If you link to an email address, activating the link opens a new email message in your default email software to that address.

- Hyperlinks can be added to blocks using the **Create Block** command or using **Hyperlink** in the *Insert* tab>Data panel.

- You can add a hyperlink to text by inserting a hyperlink **Field**.

Using a Hyperlink

When you move the cursor near an object with an attached hyperlink, a small hyperlink icon displays, and the tip box containing the hyperlink description or path, as shown in Figure 21–47.

ASCENT   Center for

ASCENT Web Page
CTRL + click to follow link

Figure 21–47

- To activate the hyperlink, hold <Ctrl> and select the object. Alternatively, you can select the object with the hyperlink, right-click, expand Hyperlink and select **Open "<name of hyperlink>"**. The associated file opens.

- To edit the hyperlink information, select the object, right-click in the drawing window, expand Hyperlink and select **Edit Hyperlink**.

- To remove a hyperlink, open the Edit Hyperlink dialog box, and click **Remove Link**.

Hint: Sharing Drawings on a Network Using the WhoHas Command

Only one person at a time can access a drawing for editing. If you share drawings with others on a network and discover that a drawing you need is currently open by another user, you can use the **WhoHas** command to determine who has the file.

- Type **WhoHas** at the Command Line and select the drawing that you want to query.

- The software reports the user name and computer name in which the drawing is open, and the time it was opened.

Practice 21b | Hyperlinks

Practice Objective

- Attach hyperlinks to objects in a drawing, which are used to open another drawing and access a site on the internet.

In this practice, you will attach hyperlinks to objects in a drawing and use them to open a drawing and access a site on the Internet. One of the hyperlinks is shown in Figure 21–48.

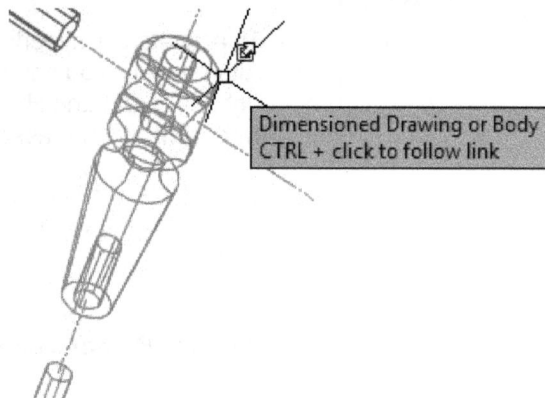

Figure 21–48

1. Open **Trammel-M.dwg** from the practice files folder.

2. In the *Insert* tab>Data panel, click 🌐 (Hyperlink). In the title block, select the text **ASCENT – Center for Technical Knowledge** and press <Enter>.

3. In the Insert Hyperlink dialog box, set the following:
   - *Link to:* Ensure that **Existing File or Web Page** is selected.
   - *Text to display*: **ASCENT Web Page**
   - *Web page name*: **http://www.ascented.com**

4. Click **OK** to set the hyperlink.

5. Hover the cursor near the text **ASCENT – Center for Technical Knowledge**. The hyperlink icon and its description display as shown in Figure 21–49.

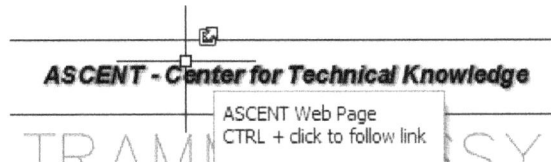

ASCENT - Center for Technical Knowledge

ASCENT Web Page
CTRL + click to follow link

Figure 21–49

6. Double-click on the assembly to enter Model Space.

7. Start the Hyperlink command and do the following:
    - Select the magenta part of the assembly and press <Enter> to open the Insert Hyperlink dialog box.
    - *Text to display*: **Dimensioned Drawing of Body**.
    - In the *Browse for:* area, click **File**.
    - Navigate to the practice files folder and open **Body-M.dwg**.
    - Click **OK** in the Insert Hyperlink dialog box.

8. Hover the cursor over the magenta part to display the hyperlink icon.

9. Select the magenta part. With the object highlighted, right-click, expand Hyperlink, and select **Open "Dimensioned Drawing of Body"**, as shown in Figure 21–50. **Body-M.dwg** opens in a separate window. Close the file and return to **Trammel-M.dwg**.

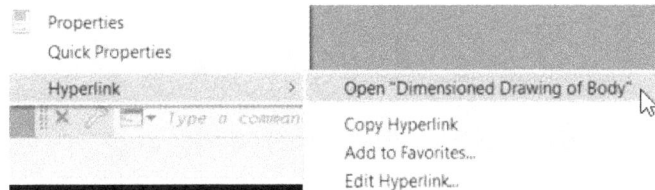

Properties
Quick Properties
Hyperlink   Open "Dimensioned Drawing of Body"
Type a command   Copy Hyperlink
                            Add to Favorites...
                            Edit Hyperlink...

Figure 21–50

10. Return to Paper Space.

11. Hold <Ctrl> and select the ASCENT text to which you applied the hyperlink. The web page opens in your web browser if you have Internet access on your computer.

12. Close the browser.

13. Save and close the drawing.

Chapter

22

Content Resources and File Maintenance

Exam Objectives Covered in This Chapter

- 6.3.c Transfer information between drawing files
- 6.4 Perform file maintenance with drawing utilities

22.1 Copying and Pasting Between Drawings

*The AutoCAD **Copy** command does not work between drawings.*

You can place information on the clipboard by copying or cutting it from a document. You can then paste the information from the clipboard into the same document or into a different one, even in a different application. To copy, move and paste information between drawings you must use the Windows **Copy** command.

- **Cut**, **Copy**, and **Paste** are available in the *Home* tab> Clipboard panel and in the shortcut menu.

Cut to the Clipboard

As with other Windows applications, (Cut Clip) removes the selected objects from their file and places them on the clipboard.

Copy to the Clipboard

When using the Windows **Copy** command, you have the following options:

	Copy Clip	Copies the selected objects to the clipboard, using the lower left corner of the bounding box of all of the objects as the base point. <Ctrl>+<C> starts the command.
	Copy with Base Point	In the shortcut menu, expand **Clipboard** and select **Copy with Base Point**. It enables you to select the base point after the objects have been selected. This option provides more control over the location of the objects when they are placed. The base point is only significant when the objects are pasted into the AutoCAD software.
NA	**Copy Link**	Type **copylink** at the Command Line. It copies the contents of the current view to the clipboard.

Paste from the Clipboard

When using the Windows **Paste** command, you have the following options:

	Paste	Prompts you to select a location for the base point at which it then places the objects. <Ctrl>+<V> starts the command.
	Paste as Block	The copied objects are placed as a block. The AutoCAD software gives the block an arbitrary name. This option is only available if the objects on the clipboard are AutoCAD objects.
XY	**Paste to Original Coordinates**	Places the objects at the same coordinates as in the drawing from which they were taken. This option is only available if the objects on the clipboard are AutoCAD objects.
	Paste as Hyperlink	Creates a hyperlink of an object, text or file already copied to clipboard, and then associates it with another object.
	Paste Special	Enables you to control the format of an already copied data while pasting it into the active drawing.

Drag-and-Drop Copying

When two drawing windows are open, you can also *drag-and-drop* objects to copy them from one drawing into another.

How To: Copy Using Drag-and-Drop

1. Without a command running, select the objects that you want to copy.
2. Hold the mouse button with the cursor on the objects (do not select a grip).
3. Drag the objects into the other drawing window and release the mouse button.

22.2 Removing Unused Elements

A drawing might contain elements that were defined once but are no longer used. Common examples of this include:

- Blocks that are defined but not inserted anywhere.

- Layers that do not contain any objects.

- Named components that are no longer used.

These unused (or unreferenced) definitions use disk space and can significantly increase the size of your drawing. Use the **Purge** command to remove these items.

Use the **Overkill** command to remove duplicate and overlapping geometric objects such as lines, arcs, and polylines. Examples of the changes made by the **Overkill** command include:

- Deleting duplicate line or arc segments.

- Deleting arcs that overlap portions of circles.

- Combining partially overlapping lines drawn at the same angle.

- Deleting zero-length and overlapping polylines.

The various Cleanup tools are available in the *Manage* tab>Cleanup panel, as shown in the Figure 22–1.

Figure 22–1

How To: Purge All Unreferenced Items

1. In the *Manage* tab>Cleanup panel, click ⬚ (Purge) or in the Application Menu, select **Drawing Utilities>Purge**. The Purge dialog box opens.Click **Purge All** and click **Close** to end the command.

How To: Purge Specific Types of Items or Individual Items

1. In the *Manage* tab>Cleanup panel, click ⬚ (Purge) or in the Application Menu, select Drawing Utilities> **Purge**.
2. In the Purge dialog box, in the *Named Items Not Used area*, select the category of the item that you want to purge (such as *Blocks*, *Layers*, etc.). You can also expand the list for any category and select individual items to purge, as shown in Figure 22–2. The *Preview* area displays the image of the item to be purged.

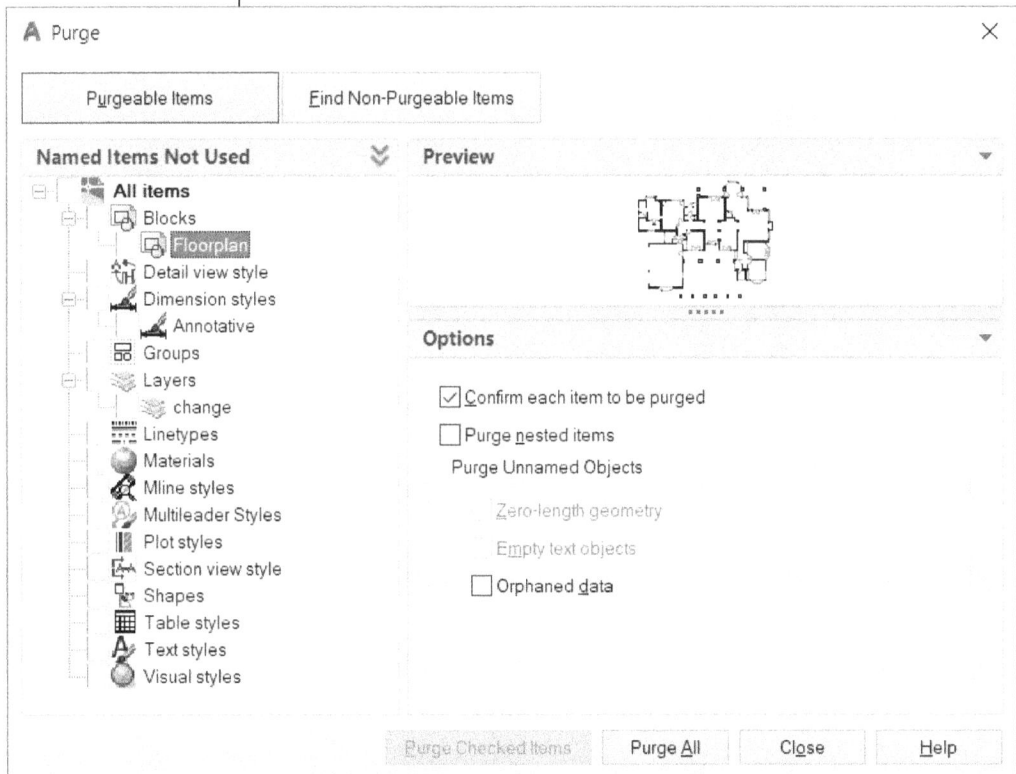

Figure 22–2

3. Click the check boxes of the items to be purged. Click **Purge Checked Items**.

4. Click **Close** when you are finished.

- If the **Confirm each item to be purged** option is selected, you are prompted to verify each item before it is purged.

- To completely purge all of the unreferenced elements in the drawing, select the **Purge nested items** option. For example, this enables you to purge any unreferenced layers that are part of (or *nested in*) an unreferenced block definition.

- The *Purge Unnamed Objects* area provides you with the options of purging **Zero-length geometry** and **Empty text objects** separately.

You can also use

⚐ *(Find Non-Purgeable Items) in the Manage tab>Cleanup panel.*

- Selecting the *Find Non-Purgeable Items* tab in the dialog box, displays a list of items that are in use and cannot be purged. Select an item to display the information about why it cannot be purged. A detailed information such as the number of items on each layer and their effect on the size of the file is also provided, as shown in Figure 22–3. You can also click the **Select Objects** button to zoom into the specific non-purgeable object.

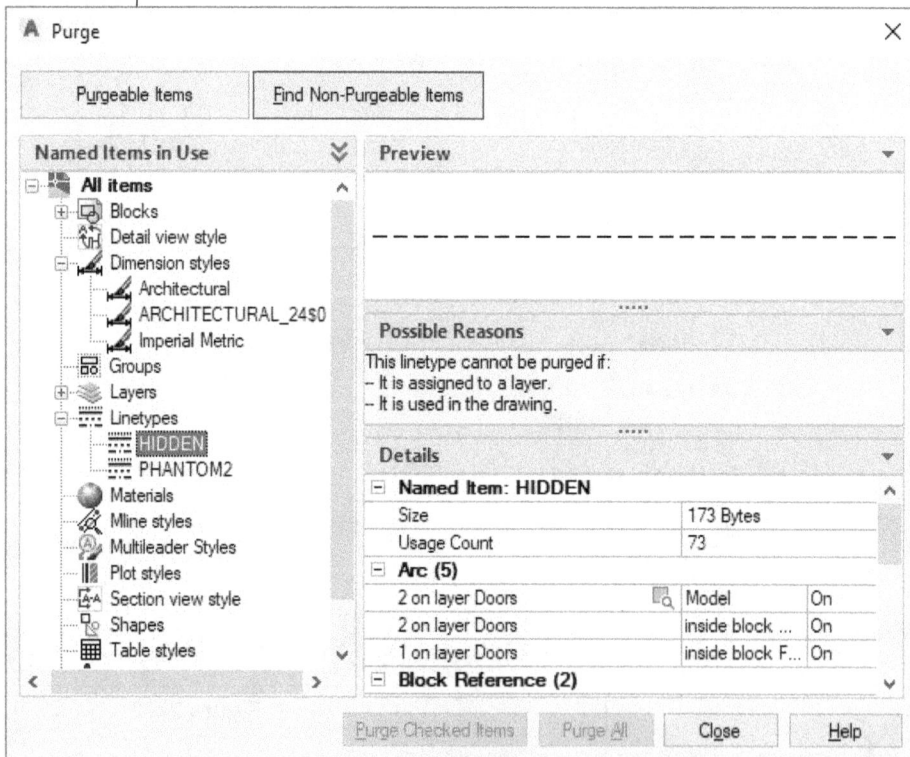

Figure 22–3

Practice 22a | # Purging

Practice Objective

- Remove unused block definitions and empty layers.

In this practice, you will remove unused block definitions and empty layers from a drawing using the **Purge** command.

1. Open **Purge-A.dwg** from your practice files folder.

2. Open the Layer Control and review the list of layers.

There are around 25 layers in the list.

3. Expand the **Insert Block** gallery and note that several blocks are defined in this drawing, but are not used.

4. In the *Manage* tab>Cleanup panel, click ⬜ (Purge), or in the Application Menu, expand Drawing Utilities and select **Purge**.

5. In the Purge dialog box, expand the **Blocks** category to display the list blocks that can be purged, as shown in Figure 22–4.

6. Expand the **Layers** category to display the layers that can be purged.

7. Click **Purge All**. In the Purge - Confirm Purge dialog box, select **Purge all checked items**.

8. Most of the unused items are purged, but some still remain. These items were nested in blocks, as shown in Figure 22–4.

9. Click **Purge All** again and select **Purge all checked items**. All of the unused items are purged, as shown in Figure 22–4.

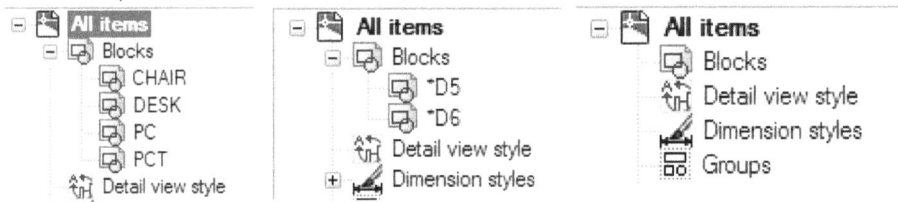

Figure 22–4

10. Click **Find Non-Purgeable Items** and expand **Blocks**. Select **_Arch Tick** and note the information about why it cannot be purged. Also note the additional information such as the number of items and their effect on the size of the file, as shown in Figure 22–5.

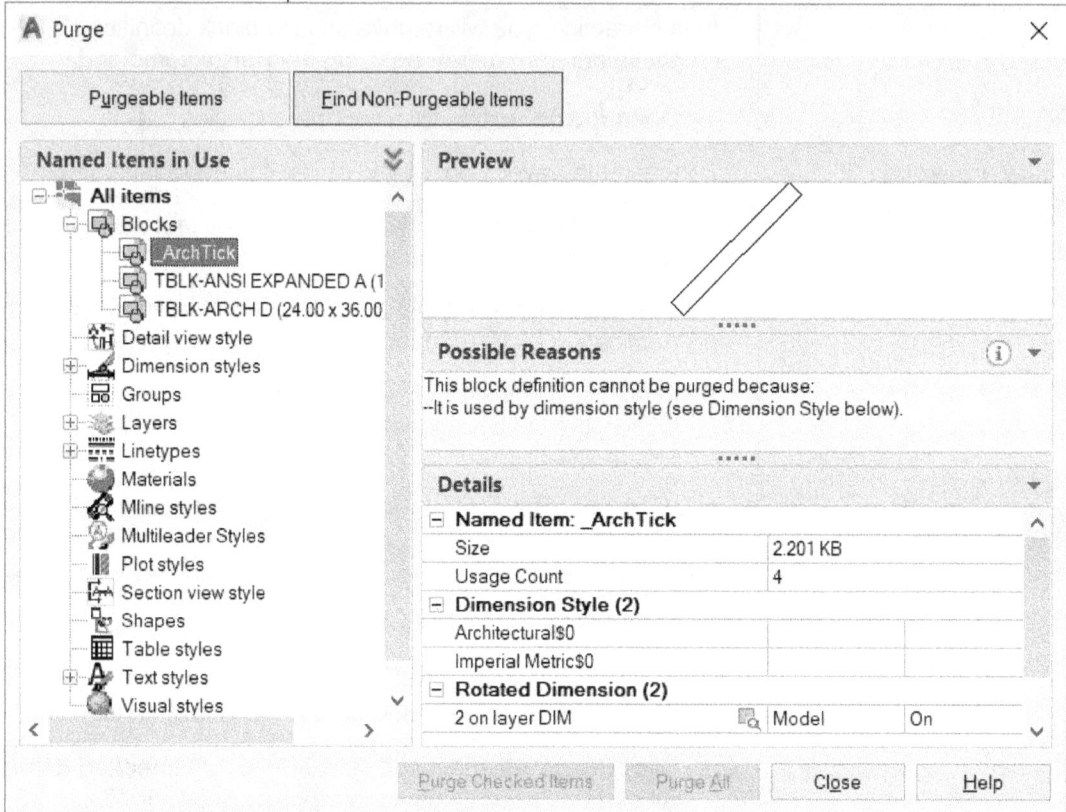

Figure 22–5

11. Close the Purge dialog box.

12. Open the Layer Control again. Only six layers are listed and the unreferenced layers have been removed.

13. Expand the **Insert Block** gallery. The unused blocks have been removed.

14. Save and close the drawing.

22.3 Drawing Utilities

The AutoCAD software includes several utilities to help you manage and maintain your drawing data.

Renaming Named Objects

Occasionally, you need to rename a named object that you or someone else has defined, such as a layer or block. The **Rename** command enables you to change the name of any named objects in the drawing, including blocks, layers, dimension styles, etc., as shown in Figure 22–6.

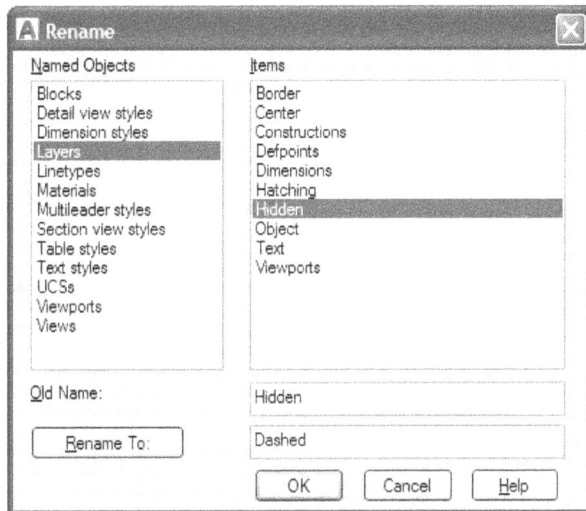

Figure 22–6

How To: Rename an Object

1. At the Command prompt, type **Rename** to open the Rename dialog box.
2. In the *Named Objects* pane, select the category.
3. In the *Items* pane, select the name to change.
4. In the *Rename To:* field, type the new name and click **Rename To:** to rename the object and remain in the Rename dialog box. Click **OK** to rename the object and close the dialog box.

- Names can be up to 255 characters long, including spaces.

- You cannot rename certain standard AutoCAD objects, such as the layer **0** or the linetype **Continuous**.

- Layers can also be renamed directly in the Layer Properties Manager.

Drawing Recovery and Repair

If your computer crashes you might need to determine which file is the latest version of a drawing. Is it the DWG file that you have been working on or the most recent BAK (backup file) or the SV$ file created when the automatic save feature is on? The Drawing Recovery Manager helps you make this decision.

To open the Drawing Recovery Manager (shown in Figure 22–7), expand the Application Menu, expand **Drawing Utilities**, and click ▦ (Open the Drawing Recovery Manager). The Drawing Recovery Manager opens automatically when you restart the software after a crash.

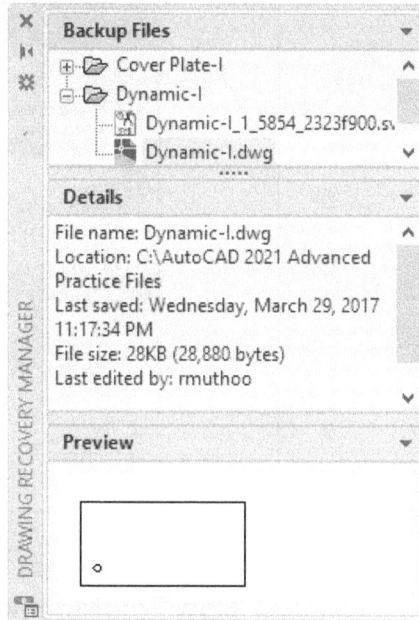

Backup Files
- ⊞ 🗁 Cover Plate-I
- ⊟ 🗁 Dynamic-I
  - 📄 Dynamic-I_1_5854_2323f900.s\
  - 📄 Dynamic-I.dwg

Details
File name: Dynamic-I.dwg
Location: C:\AutoCAD 2021 Advanced Practice Files
Last saved: Wednesday, March 29, 2017 11:17:34 PM
File size: 28KB (28,880 bytes)
Last edited by: rmuthoo

Preview

Figure 22–7

In the *Backup Files* area in the Drawing Recovery Manager, a list of the drawing files affected by the crash displays. The available versions of the file display under each drawing name. Select the name of the file to display its details, such as when the drawing was last saved and to display a preview of the file.

You can use the Drawing Recovery Manager to open the files. Double-click on a filename in the list to open it. You can open DWG, BAK, DWS, and SV$ files using this method. You can then decide which file holds the most current information and use **Save As** to rename it as the primary drawing filename and set the location.

If the data in a drawing file has been corrupted because of a system crash, two additional commands can help to restore the data.

- **Audit:** Scans and fixes problems in an open drawing.

- **Recover:** Audits and opens (if possible) any drawing file.

In the Application Menu, expand **Drawing Utilities**, and click

(Audit) to start the **Audit** command. The *Fix any errors detected?* prompt displays at the cursor. Select **Yes** to automatically fix any errors. The results of the audit display at the Command Line, as shown in Figure 22–8.

```
Command: audit
Fix any errors detected? [Yes/No] <N>: Y
Auditing Header
Auditing Tables
Auditing Entities Pass 1
Pass 1 700      objects audited
Auditing Entities Pass 2
Pass 2 700      objects audited
Auditing Blocks
 12        Blocks audited
Total errors found 0 fixed 0
Erased 0 objects
```

Figure 22–8

In the Application Menu, select **Drawing Utilities**, and then click

(Recover) to start the **Recover** command, which prompts you to select a drawing file. It then analyzes the data in the file, recovers as much of it as possible and audits it for errors, and (if possible) opens the recovered file.

- Click (Recover with Xrefs) to include all of the attached XREFs.

Checking a Drawing's Status

The **Status** command reports a variety of useful information about the current drawing and your system as shown in Figure 22–9. Drawing information includes the number of objects, drawing limits, and current settings for **Snap**, **Grid**, layer, color, etc. System information includes free disk space and memory. In the Application Menu, expand **Drawing Utilities** and click ⬜ (Status) to start the **Status** command

```
Command: _STATUS 707 objects in C:\AutoCAD Advanced 2011 Exercise Files\
Model Home 1-A-11.dwg
Model space limits are X: 16'-5 1/2"    Y: 19'-10 5/8"  (Off)
                       X: 65'-2 3/4"    Y: 55'-4 1/8"
Model space uses       X: 19'-3 9/16"   Y: 23'-3 1/8"
                       X: 65'-3 5/8"    Y: 56'-5 1/8" **Over
Display shows          X: 20'-11 5/16"  Y: 24'-11 1/16"
                       X: 63'-7 15/16"  Y: 54'-9 1/8"
Insertion base is      X:     0'-0"  Y:     0'-0"  Z:     0'-0"
Snap resolution is     X:     0'-1"  Y:     0'-1"
Grid spacing is        X:     0'-0"  Y:     0'-0"

Current space:         Model space
Current layout:        Model
Current layer:         "Walls"
Current color:         BYLAYER -- 7 (white)
Current linetype:      BYLAYER -- "CONTINUOUS"
Current material:      BYLAYER -- "Global"
Current lineweight:    BYLAYER
Current elevation:     0'-0"  thickness:    0'-0"
Fill on  Grid off  Ortho off  Qtext off  Snap off  Tablet off
Object snap modes:    Center, Endpoint, Midpoint
Free dwg disk (C:) space: 7034.6 MBytes
Free temp disk (C:) space: 7034.6 MBytes
Free physical memory: 2475.8 Mbytes (out of 3679.4M).
Free swap file space: 5346.8 Mbytes (out of 6591.6M).
```

Figure 22–9

Practice 22b | Drawing Utilities

Practice Objective

- Use various drawing utilities to rename a dimension style, check for errors, and review drawing information.

In this practice, you will use several of the drawing utilities. The results of the **Audit** command are shown in Figure 22–10.

```
Pass 1 400      objects audited
Auditing Entities Pass 2

Pass 2 400      objects audited
Auditing Blocks

 15       Blocks audited

Total errors found 0 fixed 0

Erased 0 objects
```

Figure 22–10

1. Open **Body2-M.dwg** from the practice files folder.

2. In the *Annotate* tab>Dimensions panel, note the current dimension style name, **20TO1**.

3. At the Command prompt, type **Rename**.

4. In the Rename dialog box, in the *Named Objects* pane, select **Dimension styles**. Then in the *Items* pane, select **20TO1**.

5. In the *Rename To:* field, type **Mechanical 20**, as shown in Figure 22–11.

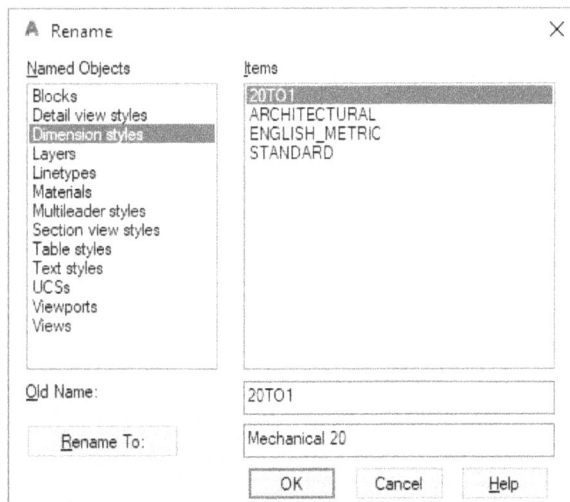

Figure 22–11

6. Click **Rename To:** to rename the dimension style *20TO1* as **Mechanical 20**. In the *Items* pane, note that **Mechanical 20** replaces **20TO1**. Click **OK** to close the Rename dialog box and note that the dimension style name in the ribbon has changed.

   - You might need to expand the Dimension Style control to refresh the list.

7. In the Application Menu, expand **Drawing Utilities**, and click

   (Audit). Select **Yes** to fix any errors. Press <F2> to open the Text Window to display the Audit information. Did the software find any errors in this file? Close the Text window.

8. In the Application Menu, expand **Drawing Utilities**, click

   (Recover) and select **Recover**. Open the drawing **2403-HVAC-M.dwg** from the practice files folder. The software scans the drawing and opens it. Were any invalid objects found?

9. In the Application Menu, expand **Drawing Utilities**, and then

   click (Status) and review the information. How many objects are in this drawing? How much free physical memory is available on your system?

10. Close both drawings. Do not save changes.

Index